Emotion

SECOND EDITION

MICHELLE N. SHIOTA
Arizona State University

JAMES W. KALAT
North Carolina State University

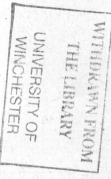
Australia • Brazil   United States

Emotion, Second Edition, International Edition

Michelle N. Shiota and James W. Kalat

Publisher/Executive Editor: Linda Schreiber-Ganster

Acquisitions Editor: Jon-David Hague

Development Editor: Kelly Miller

Editorial Assistant: Kelly Miller

Marketing Manager: Jessica Egbert

Marketing Coordinator: Anna Anderson

Marketing Communications Manager: Talia Wise

Content Project Management: PreMediaGlobal

Art Director: Pamela Galbreath

Print Buyer: Mary Beth Hennebury

RAS, Text: Dean Dauphinais

RAS, Image: Dean Dauphinais

Production House/Compositor: PreMediaGlobal

Cover Image: © alias/Shutterstock.com

Cover Design: Natalie Hill

Library of Congress Control Number: 2010932315

International Edition:

ISBN-13: 978-1-111-34613-3

ISBN-10: 1-111-34613-5

Cengage Learning International Offices

Asia
www.cengageasia.com
tel: (65) 6410 1200

Australia/New Zealand
www.cengage.com.au
tel: (61) 3 9685 4111

Brazil
www.cengage.com.br
tel: (55) 11 3665 9900

India
www.cengage.co.in
tel: (91) 11 4364 1111

Latin America
www.cengage.com.mx
tel: (52) 55 1500 6000

UK/Europe/Middle East/Africa
www.cengage.co.uk
tel: (44) 0 1264 332 424

Represented in Canada by Nelson Education, Ltd.
tel: (416) 752 9100 / (800) 668 0671
www.nelson.com

Cengage Learning is a leading provider of customized learning solutions with office locations around the globe, including Singapore, the United Kingdom, Australia, Mexico, Brazil, and Japan. Locate your local office at: **www.cengage.com/global**.

For product information: **www.cengage.com/international**
Visit your local office: **www.cengage.com/global**
Visit our corporate website: **www.cengage.com**

AVAILABILITY OF RESOURCES MAY DIFFER BY REGION. Check with your local Cengage Learning representative for details.

Printed in the United States of America
2 3 4 5 6 7 14 13 12 11

To our families

Brief Contents

Contents

Preface

For a student beginning the study of psychology, some of the most pressing questions about the human mind relate to emotion. For clinical psychologists, emotional problems are among the most striking and disabling symptoms of disorder. Nevertheless, psychological research was slow to address issues of emotion. During the middle of the twentieth century, when behaviorism completely dominated American experimental psychology, research on emotions was sparse. When laboratory research did occur, it was mostly limited to the "conditioned emotional response," which researchers used as a way to study classical conditioning, not emotion itself. Behaviorists considered emotion private, unobservable, and therefore barely fit for serious conversation. Introductory psychology texts included an obligatory section on emotion, but if we compare the textbooks of one decade after another, progress in understanding emotion was unimpressive ... until recently.

Since the 1970s, research on emotion has increased dramatically in both quantity and quality. Researchers in fields ranging from social psychology to developmental psychology to neuroscience have "discovered" emotion, and now have interesting stories to tell. This is not to say that the behaviorists were wrong. To a large extent, they were right: Emotion *is* fundamentally internal and difficult to measure—you will find us making that point repeatedly throughout this text. We hope that students start with a healthy skepticism that a scientific study of emotion is even possible. Despite these challenges, researchers have devised new and clever ways to evoke and measure emotion in the laboratory and in the real world. Their results say a great deal about when we have emotions, why we have emotions, and how emotions affect our lives. Although emotion research connects with every sub-discipline of psychology, few of these results find their way into standard texts on social psychology, cognitive psychology, and so forth. Researchers now recognize emotion as a central aspect of the human experience, and we believe that a course on emotion can be an important part of the psychology curriculum.

In the Fall of 2001, as one of us (J. W. Kalat) was finishing the sixth edition of his introductory psychology textbook, he contemplated how interesting and challenging it might be to try writing a textbook on emotion … except that he had major gaps in his knowledge of the field. Alas, if only he could find the right co-author. At just that time his editor, Vicki Knight, sent him the latest batch of anonymous reviewers' comments, including one that was unusually insightful and well written, by someone who mentioned being a specialist in emotion! A series of phone calls and e-mails revealed that this anonymous reviewer was Michelle Shiota, a graduate student at UC Berkeley, and that she would indeed be interested in co-authoring a text on emotion. To this date, Kalat and Shiota still have not met face-to-face, although they hope to some day soon! Still, over the years, a rich collaboration developed, and this textbook is the product of two distinct perspectives and areas of expertise, shared and integrated via many, many e-mails and the occasional phone call.

Our emphasis here is on empirical studies of emotion, including its experiential, biological, social, cognitive, and clinical aspects. Because there is no fixed tradition of how to organize a text on emotion, we faced the challenge and opportunity of starting from scratch on the table of contents. One of the major theoretical disputes in the field is whether people have a few discrete "basic" emotions (fear, anger, sadness, and so forth) with qualitatively different effects, or whether emotion is described best in terms of a couple of continuous dimensions, such as positive/negative valence and high/low arousal. Should the structure of the text emphasize research on particular "basic" emotions, or processes that generalize across emotions? Some study results are best explained in terms of processes, and others in terms of specific emotions, depending on the approach favored by a given researcher, so it was a tough call.

In this text we have tried to honor both perspectives. We organized part of the text around specific emotions, in order to include the many studies that address specific emotions rather than processes general to all emotions. If we had discussed emotion strictly in terms of dimensions and processes, we almost certainly would have omitted conceptually important topics such as love, embarrassment, disgust, and amusement. However, we have also included chapters on more general emotion processes, such as the development of emotion, the role of culture in emotion, and the role of emotion in cognition.

People familiar with the first edition will notice significant changes in the second. Cutting-edge research from the last few years has been added for all of the original topics, and we updated the pop culture references (who still remembers *Friends*?). However, the structure of the text has also changed considerably. This edition includes new, full chapters on the evolutionary approach to emotion, central and autonomic nervous system aspects of emotion, the role of emotion in personality, and the role of emotional dysfunction in clinical disorders. Some of the material in these chapters was also in the first edition, but scattered throughout the book. The organization of the second edition reflects Shiota's experience using this text in her own undergraduate courses, as well as advances in the field itself.

College courses on emotion are few today—although more numerous than we had imagined a few years ago—and the ones that do exist are diverse.

No text is equally appropriate for all purposes. We aimed this text at undergraduate students who have had an introductory psychology course, and who remember the essentials about research design, classical conditioning, what a neuron is, and so forth. However, we assume no additional background, and we believe this text is suitable for a course that enrolls mainly sophomores and juniors.

We also know that many professors currently teaching a course on emotion ask their students to read a collection of original articles. Anyone who supplements this text with such articles could certainly raise the level of sophistication and make it suitable for advanced undergraduate or graduate students. For those interested in pursuing specific topics in even greater depth, we include a few suggestions for additional reading at the end of each chapter. Most of these are books written by respected researchers for the general public, and thus balance scientific rigor with an accessible and engaging style. Emotion courses could also be supplemented with independent student projects. Again, we have offered suggestions for simple data-collection projects that do not require expensive equipment.

We are indebted to many people for their support of this project. Our heartiest thanks go to our editor, Jon-David Hague, and our development editor, Kelly Miller, for their encouragement, guidance, patience, and support. We thank Dean Dauphinias for managing permissions for the illustrations, Pamela Galbreath for the design, Lorraine Martindale for copy editing, and Matt Ballantyne for overseeing the production.

We also thank our family and friends for their support, encouragement, and acceptance of "just another minute!" while we finished a paragraph or tracked down an elusive reference. Michelle Shiota especially thanks her mentors Dacher Keltner and Bob Levenson at UC Berkeley, two rock stars in emotion research. They provided outstanding training in the field, and still inspire her every day. James Kalat thanks Paul Rozin, his graduate school adviser, for encouragement and inspiration over the years. Back in 1971, when Kalat received his Ph.D. from the University of Pennsylvania, neither Kalat nor Rozin had any particular interest in emotion, but Rozin encouraged his students to develop broad interests. By the time Kalat developed an interest in emotion, Rozin had become a key contributor to the field, especially in the field of disgust.

We welcome comments from our readers, both students and faculty. We'll update this text again in a couple of years, and your suggestions can help. Our e-mail addresses are: lani.shiota@asu.edu and james_kalat@ncsu.edu. Until then, we hope you enjoy the book!

M. N. Shiota and J. W. Kalat

PART I

General Principles and Issues

1

The Nature of Emotion

Many textbooks begin by explaining why you should care about their subject. Do you need to be convinced that emotions are important and interesting? Probably not. We routinely ask one another, "How are you feeling today?" We care about other people's emotions, and we often want to share what they are feeling. Indeed, it is hard to imagine what the words "want" or "good" would mean if we had no emotions. As Antonio Damasio (1999, p. 55) has written, "Inevitably, emotions are inseparable from the idea of good and evil."

From a scientific standpoint, emotion is central to the field of psychology. Clinical psychologists often want to help people control their harmful or dysfunctional emotions. Cognitive psychologists consider how emotions influence people's thought processes and decisions. Social psychologists and personality theorists consider how emotions impact our relationships with other people.

Although the importance of emotion is intuitively obvious, emotion is also a difficult topic to research. We hope you are starting this book with healthy skepticism about whether a productive study of emotion is even possible. For decades, experimental psychologists virtually ignored emotion because it is so subjective, and even today, anyone with behaviorist inclinations has misgivings about scientific research into private, internal experiences. Scientific progress depends on good measurement, and as we shall emphasize repeatedly throughout this book, accurate measurement is difficult for emotions. The challenge to emotion researchers, therefore, is to make the best use of measures that are currently available, and to keep developing even better techniques.

In this chapter, we begin with attempts to define "emotion." Then we briefly review general approaches to measuring emotion—more detailed discussion will emerge in later chapters. Next we discuss classical theories of how different major *aspects of emotion*, such as emotional feelings, physiological responses, and behaviors, relate to each other. Finally, we will introduce three models researchers have used to classify emotions, asking how *kinds of emotion* are related to each other: the Basic Emotion model, Dimensional models, and the Component Process model.

WHAT IS EMOTION?

In 1884, William James, the founder of American psychology, wrote an important article titled "What is an Emotion?" A century and a quarter later, psychologists continue to ask that question. As with several other important concepts, emotion is difficult to define with precision. According to Joseph LeDoux (1996, p. 23), "Unfortunately, one of the most significant things ever said about emotion may be that everyone knows what it is until they are asked to define it." Emotion is hardly the only important concept that is difficult to define. St. Augustine (397/1955, Book 11, Chapter 14) once wrote, "What, then, is time? If no one asks me, I know what it is. If I wish to explain it to him who asks me, I do not know." William James (1892/1961, p. 19)[1] said about consciousness, "Its meaning we know so long as no one asks us to define it." However, in order to study some phenomenon, we need at least a tentative definition.

Imagine you have accepted a job in your nation's space program. They send you as a psychologist/astronaut to a newly discovered planet. Previous astronauts have learned much about the animals on this planet. Their evolutionary history is separate from ours and their body chemistry is entirely different, but their behavior resembles ours. They see, hear, and smell. They eat, drink, and reproduce. They can learn to approach one color and not another to get food, so evidently they have color vision, motivation, and learning. Now it's your job to determine whether they have emotions. What will you do?

Try to answer before you read further.

La de dah, dah dah ta dah. (We're pausing while you figure out your answer.)

You have an answer? Okay.

We find that our students' most common answer is to put the animals in a particular situation that we consider "emotional" and then watch their behavior. For example, you might swing a weapon at these animals and see whether they scamper away. Or you might damage their nest and see whether they attack you or not. Suppose they do. Could you then conclude that they have emotions?

Return to earth. If you wave your arm at a housefly, it flies away. Do you conclude that the housefly feels fear? We don't know what a housefly feels, if anything. You might not assume it feels fear. If you damage a beehive, the bees come at you to sting you. Are they angry? Again, you could quite reasonably answer either "no" or "I don't know."

If running away or attacking doesn't demonstrate emotion in insects on this planet, these behaviors won't demonstrate it for animals on another planet. Is there any other way to determine the presence or absence of emotion? A physiological measurement won't work. Their physiology is entirely different from ours, so we have no idea what physiological change might correspond to an emotional state.

Ordinarily, when we talk about emotions, we refer to internal feelings as well as observable behaviors, and we often invoke feelings as explanations for behaviors ("Don't mind him, he's just cranky today"). In some cases we actually care more about people's feelings than about their behaviors, so we ask them how they feel. Let's say these alien animals are able to learn our language, so you ask them if they have emotions. Sorry, that won't work either. How are you going to teach them the meaning of the word *emotion*, or the meaning of *fear, anger*, or other emotional states? Might you explain, "*Fear* is what you feel when you are in danger"? That's not fair. You can't tell them they feel fear unless you already *know* they have that feeling, and we're trying to find out whether they have that feeling!

In short, the question of emotions in extraterrestrial animals may be unanswerable. At best you could say that in certain situations these animals act *as if* they are fearful or angry. Here is a key point: *We never observe emotions. We only infer them.*

How did you learn the meaning of words like *frightened, angry, happy*, and *sad*? At some point in your childhood you heard a loud noise and started

---

1. A date shown with a slash indicates a publication first printed in the first year (1892) and reprinted in the second year (1961).

crying. Your parents or someone else said, "Did that scare you? It will be okay. Don't worry." At another time you were upset because you broke your favorite toy, and someone told you that you were sad. People inferred your emotion from the situation and from your reactions. Similarly, you infer other people's emotions. You might also infer emotions for animals (on Earth). If a dog wags its tail, you infer happiness. If it barks at a stranger, you infer fear or anger. We make this inference because we identify to some extent with dogs and many other animals, and because we've seen when they exhibit these behaviors. But for animals less like ourselves—insects, for example—it's a lot harder to make this inference. This doesn't make emotions impossible to study; after all, physicists study extremely large phenomena, such as black holes, and very small phenomena, such as atomic sub-particles, by observing the movement of nearby entities and inferring the existence of these things. It does, however, introduce special challenges for researchers.

A Couple of Attempts to Define Emotion.   People studying emotion often disagree about how to define it, and some doubt it refers to any natural category. James Russell (2003) has suggested that the concept *emotion* is just a convenient label for experiences that seem to share common ground, much as *art* and *music* include many dissimilar items. According to Russell, the border between emotion and not-emotion is as arbitrary as the border between art and not-art, or music and not-music. Some languages do not have a word for "emotion" at all (Hupka, Lenton, & Hutchison, 1999), and those that do have such a word vary in what it includes (Niedenthal et al., 2004).

However, many researchers have tried to define "emotion," proposing that all the things we call emotions do have something meaningful in common. Let's consider two proposed definitions. One of these is a relatively early attempt to define emotion from a psychological perspective, and the other is more recent. Both include elements shared with several other widely recognized definitions (e.g., Ekman, 1992; Frijda, 1986; Izard, 1992;

Lazarus, 1991; Tooby & Cosmides, 2008). They are a little long-winded, but bear with us:

> [Emotion is] an inferred complex sequence of reactions to a stimulus [including] cognitive evaluations, subjective changes, autonomic and neural arousal, impulses to action, and behavior designed to have an effect upon the stimulus that initiated the complex sequence. (Plutchik, 1982, p. 551)

> An emotion is a universal, functional reaction to an external stimulus event, temporally integrating physiological, cognitive, phenomenological, and behavioral channels to facilitate a fitness-enhancing, environment-shaping response to the current situation. (Keltner & Shiota, 2003, p. 89)

What do these definitions have in common?

(1) Both agree that emotions have an effect, that they are "functional" in the evolutionary sense. That is, emotions are useful. Our tendency to feel emotions has evolved because in past generations, those who experienced emotions were more likely to survive, reproduce, and become our ancestors. Many philosophers, including Aristotle and Buddha, considered emotional behaviors to be disruptive or dangerous. Extremely emotional behaviors—panic, for example—are undeniably disruptive. However, under many circumstances, emotions guide us to quick, effective action. For example, when we feel fear, we try to escape. When someone commits an injustice against us, we strike back. When people take care of us, we stay close to them. We shall address this point in more detail in Chapter 2.

(2) Also, according to both definitions every emotion is a reaction to a stimulus—a specific event that takes place. Ordinarily our experiences support this idea: we are happy *about* something, we are angry *at* something, or we are afraid *of* something. The second definition even states that the stimulus must be external, or outside the person. This aspect of the definitions distinguishes emotions from **drives** such as hunger and thirst. If there is a distinction

between drives and emotions, it might be that emotions require a cognitive **appraisal** of the situation—an interpretation of what the situation means. For example, you feel distressed if you hear that someone was injured, but your degree of distress depends on how much you care about that person (Lazarus, 2001). Seeing people smile can make you happy or sad, but your response depends on why you think they are smiling. If you think people are smiling because they are making fun of you, you feel distress, not pleasure. In short, emotions depend on evaluations of external events and their meaning, whereas a drive such as hunger arises from the body's needs.

However, this aspect of the definition of emotion is controversial. Many researchers classify sexual arousal as a drive, not an emotion, but your sexual arousal depends on your appraisal of the social situation (hot or not?) and not just your body's status. Also, many psychologists insist that you can feel an emotion without a conscious appraisal of the situation (Berkowitz & Harmon-Jones, 2004; Parkinson, 2007). Perhaps you see something briefly without paying attention to it. You can't even say what it was, but because of it you feel a little more frightened, happy, or disgusted than you were a moment earlier (Ruys & Stapel, 2008). Or perhaps for some strictly physiological reason your heart starts beating faster and you breathe more heavily. You might feel frightened—even panicked—without knowing why. We will discuss this point in more detail in Chapters 7 and 15.

(3) These definitions, and several others, also agree that an emotional state includes four aspects—cognition, feeling ("subjective changes" or "phenomenology"), physiological changes, and behavior. However, this aspect of the definitions opens a big can of worms. The implication is that emotion is like a square: If something has only three sides, it's not a square. If someone has three aspects of emotion but the other one is missing, it's not an emotion. A "real" emotion has all four aspects.

Is that true? Not necessarily (Russell, 2003). Imagine your professor hands back a test and you get a higher grade than you expected. You have the cognition (good news), a feeling (happiness), and

some physiological changes (excitement), but suppose you don't do anything about it. You don't jump up and down and brag to the other students. You don't even smile. If there was no behavioral change, do we conclude that you didn't really have an emotion?

Suppose your heart suddenly starts pounding for no apparent reason, as it does in a panic attack. You can't explain this physiological change—that is, you have no cognition—but you feel frightened, you are sweating and trembling, and you want to run away to be by yourself. Do we call this an unemotional state because no cognition led to it? Or do we count "I'm panicking" as the cognition? If so, it's not much of cognition.

We shall return to this complicated issue repeatedly throughout the text. Often we shall assume that cognitions, feelings, physiological changes, and behaviors hang together in emotions, as proposed by the definitions above. There are important theoretical reasons for this assumption, which we shall discuss in more detail in Chapter 2. However, we'll also challenge this assumption in several places.

A Different Type of Definition: The Prototype Approach. Some items can be defined precisely and others cannot. For example, we can precisely define *equilateral triangle*: It is a figure with three sides of equal length. Given any object, we can say for certain whether it is or isn't an equilateral triangle. In contrast, try to define *classical music*. You would do best to provide a few good examples and say "music like that." Not every composition is or isn't classical music. Something can be a borderline case, not exactly a member or a non-member of the category.

Perhaps the same is true for emotion. Psychologists agree that fear and anger are good examples of emotions. So we might define emotion as "fear, anger, and things like that." Some researchers have proposed that we think of emotions in terms of "prototypes." The definitions above describe a prototypical emotion, and other psychological states can be more or less like that prototype (Fehr & Russell, 1984; Shaver, Schwartz, Kirson, & O'Connor, 1987). Psychologists have debated whether disgust is or isn't a real emotion (Royzman & Sabini, 2001) and whether confusion, surprise, and interest count as emotions (Rozin & Cohen, 2003). Perhaps we don't need a yes or no answer—"sort of" or "in some ways" can still be helpful in advancing research. We can decide that these states are imperfect examples of emotion, just as some of Philip Glass' compositions are imperfect examples of classical music.

We do not need to settle on a final definition of emotion. However, in any given discussion, we do need to state clearly what definition we are using. When different definitions are used, and this isn't acknowledged up front, confusion is likely. Throughout this text, we will continue to discuss different ways of defining "emotion," as well as implications of the definitions used by various researchers.

RESEARCH METHODS: INDUCING EMOTION

Suppose you want to study the effects emotions have on people's behavior, or their relationships, or another outcome. How would you start? You might begin by finding people who are already happy, frightened, or angry and see if they differ from people not feeling an emotion on your outcome of interest. However, that would not be very convincing research. Maybe the people who tend to be happy (or whatever) are different from not-happy people in some other way causing your outcome, and happiness has nothing to do with the effect. Happy people might tend to be healthier than not-happy people, for example, and the differences in your outcome may be caused by differences in health, rather than happiness. As with any other research, the only way we can be confident of a cause-and-effect relationship is to experimentally manipulate the variable we think is the cause, while holding other factors constant, and then see if the outcome changes in predictable ways.

How do researchers experimentally manipulate emotion, especially in controlled settings like psychology laboratories? Emotion researchers use several methods to elicit feelings in research participants. For

example, researchers may ask participants to think of a time in their life when they experienced an emotion (such as anger or disgust) very strongly, to remember that experience vividly, and then to talk or write about the experience (e.g., Bless, Clore, Schwarz, Golisane, Rabe, & Wölk, 1996; Ekman, Levenson, & Friesen, 1983; Tsai, Chentsova-Dutton, Freire-Bebeau, & Przymus, 2002). Alternatively, researchers may ask participants to read and vividly imagine themselves in a story designed to evoke a strong emotion, such as fear or pride (e.g., Griskevicius, Shiota, & Neufeld, 2010; Keltner, Ellsworth, & Edwards, 1993). Still others evoke emotions by showing participants photographs (e.g., Bradley, Greenwald, Petry, & Lang, 1992) or short film clips (e.g., Gross & Levenson, 1995; Maner, Kenrick, Becker, Robertson, Hofer, Neuberg, et al., 2005; Papousek, Schulter, & Lang, 2009) with emotional content.

These four methods are used most often by researchers to elicit emotions in the laboratory. One advantage of all of these methods is that they are *face valid*—researchers typically use stories or images (such as a story about receiving a high grade on an exam, or a photograph of a spider) with emotional meaning on which most people can agree. Another advantage is that these methods target fairly specific emotion states, such as fear, sadness, and disgust. However, these methods have limitations as well. All evoke emotion through a memory or imagined situation, rather than a "real" event happening in the present moment. In some studies researchers have evoked emotions by putting participants directly into emotional situations, such as giving them small gifts (e.g., Isen, Daubman, & Nowicki, 1987), or asking them to give a speech while the "audience" is behaving rudely (e.g., Taylor, Seeman, Eisenberger, Kozanian, Moore, & Moons, 2010). Although these strategies are *ecologically valid*, resembling the real-life situations in which people feel emotions, they may not be very specific, and people may respond to them in quite different ways. In the end, the best research tries to evoke emotions using a number of different methods in different studies, to see whether the effects of emotions are the same regardless of which method is used to elicit them.

THE NATURE OF EMOTION

Other methods of eliciting emotions are controversial, and although researchers do use them in some studies, it's not always easy to agree on what the results of such studies mean. As we shall see, some researchers have elicited emotions by asking participants to pose specific facial expressions, giving muscle-by-muscle instructions (e.g., Levenson, Ekman, & Friesen, 1990). Although participants are more likely to report feeling the intended emotion after posing a facial expression (an effect we will discuss in more detail shortly), it is possible that any other effects are due to the muscle movements themselves, rather than emotions. Researchers have also used music to elicit emotions in the laboratory (e.g., Zentner, Grandjean, & Scherer, 2008). People are able to reliably identify the emotional quality of some pieces of music, perhaps because the acoustic properties of music can sound like people's voices when feeling a particular emotion, but this technique is not always effective in actually eliciting emotion.

A serious problem in emotion research is that we are rarely, if ever, able to elicit emotions in the laboratory that are as strong as those people experience in their real lives. It is one thing to watch a film clip of a person acting offensively, and seeing such a clip may even remind one of a personal experience, but it is not the same as *actually* being insulted by someone. It is difficult to elicit powerful emotions without violating important ethical principles for research (for example, we can't lie and say a participant's best friend has just been hit by a bus). Researchers must remember that the states studied in the lab may be only a reflection of the emotions people experience in their real lives.

RESEARCH METHODS: MEASURING EMOTION

"Whatever exists at all exists in some amount."
—Edward Thorndike (1918, p. 16)

"Anything that exists in amount can be measured."
—W. A. McCall (1939, p. 15)

"Anything which exists can be measured incorrectly."
—Douglas Detterman (1979, p. 167)

Research on emotion ordinarily requires some kind of measurement. If emotions exist, we should be able to measure them. Unfortunately, if we have trouble defining emotions clearly, we will also have trouble measuring them.

You don't always need to understand something thoroughly to measure it. For example, you might not understand temperature at a theoretical level, but you can measure it with a thermometer. You could also measure magnetism, electrical resistance, and many other physical variables without deeply understanding them. Similarly, psychologists do their best to measure intelligence, motivation, memory, and many other processes that they cannot completely define or explain. Psychologists who study emotion rely mainly on these kinds of methods:

- **Self-reports** are the participant's descriptions of his/her emotional feelings. Participants may also self-report their cognitions, behaviors, and other aspects of emotion.

- **Physiological measurements** include measures of blood pressure, heart rate, sweating, and other variables that fluctuate during emotional arousal. Researchers also measure brain activity and hormones.

- **Behaviors** are actions we can observe, including facial and vocal expressions, running away, or attacking. Although behavior may be reported by participants, it's best if some objective observer assesses behavior.

Look familiar? We noted earlier that the definition of a prototypical emotion includes four aspects: cognitions, feelings, physiological changes, and behaviors. Researchers emphasize these four aspects in measuring emotion as well.

Each method has its strengths and weaknesses. For each method, and indeed for any kind of measurement, researchers want to know whether a measure is reliable and valid before they trust research that uses that measure. The **reliability** of a measure reflects the consistency or repeatability of its scores, and is typically measured on a scale from 0 to 1. If the reliability is high (close to 1), then people who are tested repeatedly under the same conditions get nearly the same score each time. If the reliability is close to 0, scores fluctuate randomly from one test administration to another. If reliability is low, then the test is not really measuring *anything*. For example, a questionnaire might have low reliability if the items are worded in a confusing way, because participants end up giving a different answer to the same question each time it's asked. Similarly, if a physiological sensor is not attached correctly, then an estimate of heart rate will contain a lot of random noise.

Going beyond reliability, **validity** is an assessment of whether the scores represent what they claim to represent. A questionnaire that gives the same score each time a person takes it is reliable, but it might not be valid if it measures something other than what it is supposed to measure. For example, one scale of self-esteem includes this true–false item: *There are lots of things about myself I'd change if I could.* If you say "yes," does that answer indicate low self-esteem, or high ambition? A questionnaire could also be invalid if many people answer it untruthfully.

There are several kinds of validity, and researchers often try to make sure a new measure is valid in all of these ways (Joint Committee on Standards, 1999):

- The content of the measure should match the stated purposes, in a reasonably obvious way.

- If a task is supposed to measure some psychological process or skill, it should be necessary to use that process/skill in order to succeed, instead of taking another route to completing the task.

- All the sub-components of the measure should correlate positively with one another. For example, separate items on a questionnaire should correlate with each other, as should measures of change in heart rate and blood pressure in a physiological index.

- Most important, scores on the measure should accurately predict some conceptually related outcome. For example, scores on a valid test of anger should accurately predict who gets into fights and arguments.

Self-Reports

Self-reports are easy to collect, although not necessarily to interpret. For instance, participants might rate their nervousness, happiness, or level of some other emotion on a scale such as this:

Not at all nervous		Somewhat nervous			Very nervous	
1	2	3	4	5	6	7

Self-reports cannot be precise, simply because each person's standard differs from anyone else's. Many centuries ago, people measured distances in cubits and spans. A cubit is the distance from the elbow to the tip of the middle finger; a span is the distance from the end of the thumb to the end of the little finger when extended. The obvious problem is that your cubit or span is different from someone else's. Self-reports of emotions have the same problem; if you rate your nervousness "5," your 5 may differ from someone else's 5, or even from your own 5 at some other time.

Suppose you ask a crying person, "Why are you sad?" and the person replies, "I'm not sad. I'm fine." Do you believe that self-report? It might be true. People sometimes cry from joy, amusement, or relief (see Figure 1.1). When in doubt, however, we assume that a crying person is probably sad. That is, we usually trust objective behavioral observations more than subjective self-reports.

A further limitation of self-reports is that emotions are sometimes studied in infants, brain-damaged people, nonhuman animals, or others who cannot speak. With people who speak different languages, translation is sometimes uncertain, especially for fine distinctions.

Despite these serious problems, self-reports are useful for many purposes. For example, if you rated your nervousness 5 yesterday and 2 today, the change probably means your nervousness has decreased, even if your 5 means something different from someone else's. Also, there is really no other way to measure the feeling aspect of emotion except through self-reports.

FIGURE 1.1 It is possible to cry for extreme joy. However, if we don't know the reasons for someone's crying, we assume sadness.

Physiological Measurements

Consider the statement "17 + 33 = 50." When you contemplate that thought, do you feel anything physical? Do you get any body sensations at all? Probably not. It is a purely factual statement. However, many of our emotional experiences, perhaps even our choices, include a physical component. If emotions include behaviors, as suggested by our definitions earlier, then any emotional state should include a readiness for action, or "action tendency." For example, anger implies readiness to attack and fear implies readiness to flee. If you are a predator, and you see your possible lunch some distance away, you have to get ready to chase it or go hungry.

Physiological measures of emotion examine the way the body prepares for these kinds of behaviors.

Many emotional conditions are states of intense arousal—your heart beats faster, your stomach tightens up, and your hands start to sweat. Increased activation of the **sympathetic nervous system (SNS)** is important for producing this arousal, readying the body for "fight or flight" emergency actions. Many of the physiological changes prompted by the SNS increase the flow of blood and oxygen to your muscles, so you're prepared for hard physical work. SNS arousal also decreases digestive activity (which would take energy away from skeletal muscle contractions) and sexual arousal (while you are fighting for your life, sex would be a pointless distraction). In contrast, the **parasympathetic nervous system (PNS)** facilitates growth and increases maintenance functions that conserve energy for later use.

Like self-reports, physiological measures of emotion have some limitations. Think of it this way—is emotion the *only* time your heart beats faster? How about when you're walking up the stairs? Your heart rate definitely speeds up then—if not, you're going to feel pretty awful by the time you reach the top. But are you feeling an emotion? Not necessarily. When you are cold, the blood vessels in your hands constrict just like they do when you are afraid. Does that mean you're scared? Again, not necessarily. One of the authors of this book (MNS) has to remove data from her study every time a research participant sneezes, because that messes up her physiological measures. Researchers using physiological measures have to ask whether the changes they're seeing are due to emotion, or to movement, or something else unrelated to emotion.

Also, like self-reports, physiological measures of emotion differ widely from person to person. If you were to measure your own heart rate right now, and that of your best friend, and that of your romantic partner, and so on, you would get different numbers. Some of this variation would arise because you're all engaged in different activities, but even in the same activity people's bodies are different. For these reasons, researchers usually look at the effects of some emotion in terms of *change* in physiology from an unemotional (or at least less emotional) baseline period, usually in response to some instruction or stimulus.

Physiological measures offer some big advantages over self-reports. If someone says their nervousness went from 5 to 2, we're not quite sure what that means, except that it's lower now than it was before. If someone's heart rate increased from 75 beats per minute to 110 beats per minute, however, that is more specific. Also, the definition of heart rate is unambiguous, whereas we're never completely sure whether someone else's definition of "nervousness" is exactly the same as ours.

Researchers also examine brain activity as a measure of emotion. One technique is **electro-encephalography (EEG),** in which the researcher attaches electrodes to the participant's scalp to measure momentary changes in the emotional activity within the brain. An EEG is relatively inexpensive,

and provides millisecond-by-millisecond information about the activity of cells in the brain area closest to each electrode. EEG is especially useful when researchers care about the precise timing of an experience. After a pleasant or unpleasant stimulus, the brain's electrical response can be detected within a split second (Delplanque et al., 2009). In contrast, it is virtually impossible to measure split second changes in people's feelings.

However, an EEG is best for recording activity from neurons nearest the electrodes on the scalp. As we shall see in Chapter 5, much of the neural "action" in emotion occurs much deeper in the brain. Another limitation is that each electrode summates activity over a fairly large area, so an EEG supplies precise information about the time of brain activity, but not its location. A closely related method is magnetoencephalography (MEG), which records momentary changes in brain cells' magnetic activity instead of electrical activity. (The passage of an electrical current generates a magnetic field.)

An increasingly popular method, **functional magnetic resonance imaging (fMRI),** measures brain activity based on changes in oxygen uptake (Detre & Floyd, 2001). A brain area that increases its activity uses more oxygen, and therefore the hemoglobin molecules in the nearby blood vessels release their oxygen. Hemoglobin molecules with oxygen respond differently to a magnetic field than do hemoglobin molecules without oxygen, and an fMRI scanner surrounding the head detects this difference. An fMRI image taps into changes in brain activity within around a second after it happens—not on the order of milliseconds as with an EEG, but excellent for many purposes. It also indicates the location of these changes to within 2 or 3 mm, even deep in the brain—far greater spatial accuracy than an EEG (Figure 1.2). The procedure poses no known risks. In fact, most people who undergo one particular type of fMRI (echo–planar magnetic resonance spectroscopic imaging) say it improves their mood, and some researchers have begun testing this procedure as an antidepressant (Rohan et al., 2004).

An FMRI does have important practical disadvantages. The person must lie motionless in a very noisy device that surrounds the head. Most young to which what happens in the study reflects what really happens in everyday life—for more precise measurement.

Aside from practical disadvantages, the results of any brain scan study must be interpreted cautiously. Let's say that you put someone in an MRI, and you scan her brain while showing her pictures of spiders, as well as pictures of flowers and pencils as a control. Looking at the results, you find that activation in an area called the amygdala (Figure 1.3) is increased while viewing the spider pictures relative to the other pictures. What does this mean? Maybe the amygdala is the fear area of the brain. Maybe it's the spider area of the brain. Maybe the amygdala is specialized for detecting animals. Maybe the amygdala doesn't detect anything, but prepares the brain to track movement. You get the idea—there are *lots* of ways that spiders differ from flowers and pencils, and lots of ways our brains might process those objects differently. With any one study we have no idea which of these differences matters to the amygdala (Baxter & Murray, 2002). However, by comparing several studies, researchers can detect a pattern.

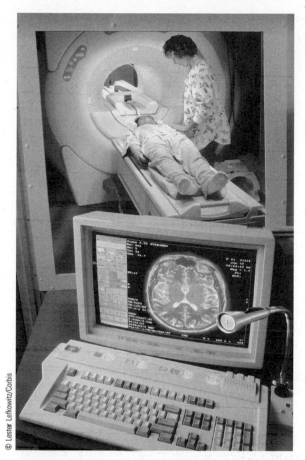

© Lester Lefkowitz/Corbis

F I G U R E 1.2 An fMRI scanner records blood flow from all areas of the brain showing areas of recent neural activity. However, the person must be motionless in a tight, noisy device.

children are unable or unwilling to do so, as are people with claustrophobia (fear of closed-in places). Also, fMRI technology is extremely expensive, and few researchers outside hospitals or major research centers have access to it. Furthermore, the procedures restrict the kinds of experiences an investigator can test. Most of our everyday emotional experiences occur while we are walking around and interacting with other people, not while lying motionless in a noisy machine, looking through a small window at pictures on a monitor. As with so many areas of research, we sometimes have to sacrifice the **ecological validity** of a study—the extent

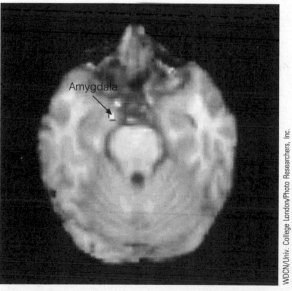

WDCN/Univ. College London/Photo Researchers, Inc.

F I G U R E 1.3 The amygdala is a small, almond-shaped structure in the temporal lobe of the brain.

Authors of an extensive review compared many studies of brain activation during emotional experiences. Figure C.2 on the inside cover shows their results (Phan, Wager, Taylor, & Liberzon, 2002). You will note that the areas activated by emotion are scattered over wide regions of the brain. Much of the variance in results stemmed from the methods used to elicit emotion, rather than emotion per se. For example, studies that aroused emotions by showing pictures activated the visual cortex in the occipital lobe, whereas studies that relied on the spoken word activated the auditory cortex in the temporal lobe. Ultimately, researchers might be able to use brain scans to determine the type or intensity of someone's emotion, but at this point we cannot do so with much confidence. We will discuss the role of the brain in emotion in much more detail in Chapter 5.

Michelle Shiota

FIGURE 1.4 Researchers often use facial expressions to measure the emotions people feel during a study.

Behavioral Observations

When people jump and scream at the sight of a spider, we infer that they are afraid. When they make a fist and shout, we infer anger. Researchers necessarily rely on behavioral observations like these when dealing with nonhuman animals or with human infants too young to talk. Do nonhuman animals experience emotions? Many psychologists dismiss the question because we cannot ask animals to describe their feelings. However, your parents taught you the words for emotions by inferring your emotions from your actions and then telling you "you are afraid" or "you are sad." If we could not infer emotions from behavior, we could not learn the words to make self-reports. If a human infant and a dog both howl after hearing a thunderbolt, we would say, "Oh, you're afraid," and if the dog could learn to talk, it too would learn to give self-reports of fear.

Researchers supplement self-reports by examining behavior, because people often cannot or do not wish to report their own emotions with complete accuracy. In particular, researchers are often interested in contractions of particular sets of muscles in the face, producing emotional facial expressions. For example, when people are angry, they often lower their eyebrows, scrunch them together,

squint their eyes, and tighten their lips (Figure 1.4). Using a behavioral coding system called FACS (Ekman & Friesen, 1984) researchers record which facial muscles contract, and how long and how intensely. Certain patterns of muscle contraction, such as the one illustrated in Figure 1.4, are likely to occur when people say they feel a particular emotion or when they are in a situation likely to elicit a certain emotion (Ekman & Friesen, 1975). For example, people reliably make an expression like that shown in Figure 1.4 in response to an injustice or insult. Researchers sometimes use the patterns of muscle contraction as a nonverbal measure of people's emotions.

As with the other measures of emotion, coded facial expressions have their limitations. First, people can try to fake or conceal their emotions, with varying degrees of success (Ekman, 2001). Second, coding facial expressions is extremely time intensive. The muscle movements can be subtle, and it takes much training and patience to distinguish all the movements correctly. Also, a typical emotional expression lasts only one or two seconds, so to catch every instance, you have to watch videotapes of a person's behavior many times, slowing down to catch the exact start and stop of each movement. It typically takes 30 to 60 minutes to code a single minute of videotape! Third, although most researchers agree on the interpretation of certain expressions, they disagree or express uncertainty about others. Still, with time and effort, researchers can classify many facial expressions with high enough rates of agreement.

So, which of these measures is best? To some researchers, feelings are the most important aspect of emotion, so self-reports are the gold standard. Others consider feelings too subjective to trust as the ultimate criterion for emotion; these researchers tend to emphasize physiological and/or behavioral measures. As with so many things we can study, the more kinds of evidence we have, the better. For example, if we include behaviors, self-report measures, and physiological measures in a study, we can note areas of agreement or disagreement. When measures disagree we have a bit of a problem, because we have to decide which measure we're going to trust most. However, that situation can itself lead to interesting new research ideas. In any case, the strength of any conclusion is no better than the quality of measurements that led to it.

THEORIES OF EMOTION

Earlier we proposed that emotional states include cognitions/appraisals, feelings, physiological changes, and behaviors. Some of the most fundamental questions about emotion concern the relationships among these four aspects, and how they relate to events in the environment. Do they arise separately, or does one of them lead to the other two? If so, which one is primary? Let's consider the most famous theories.

The James-Lange Theory

The scientific approach to psychology began in Germany in 1879 when Wilhelm Wundt established the first laboratory to investigate issues of the mind. A few years later, the founder of American psychology, William James (Figure 1.5), put forth the first major theory of emotions, indeed one of the first general theories in all of psychology. The Danish

Paul Thompson/FPG/Getty Images

FIGURE 1.5 William James, founder of American psychology. He theorized that emotion requires sensations, usually from the muscles or internal organs.

psychologist Carl Lange ("LAHNG-uh") (1885/1922) proposed a similar idea at about the same time, and the theory came to be known as the **James-Lange theory**. According to this theory, emotions are the labels we give to the way the body reacts to certain situations (James, 1884, 1894). In James's words, "The bodily changes follow directly the perception of the exciting fact, and ... our feeling of the same changes as they occur IS the emotion" (James, 1884, p. 190). That idea contradicts the common-sense view that you feel angry and *therefore* you attack, or you feel frightened and *therefore* you try to escape. The James-Lange theory reverses the direction of cause and effect: You notice yourself attacking and therefore you feel angry. You notice yourself trying to escape and therefore you feel frightened.

Common-sense view:
Event → Feeling → Behavior

James-Lange Theory:
Event → Physiological Change & Behavior →
                    Feeling

More specifically, according to the James-Lange theory, a sensation from the muscles or the internal organs is necessary for the full experience of emotion. Any decrease in the sensation decreases the emotion. One example Carl Lange offered in support of this theory was the common observation that drinking wine decreases anxiety. The wine decreases your body's response to a stressor, and as you feel your body become calmer, you feel less emotion. Moreover, James (1884) thought it possible that every "shade of emotion" in terms of feelings would have a unique physiological profile (p. 15), although across his writings he is not always consistent on this point.

The James-Lange theory is easily misunderstood, partly because James at first did not state the theory clearly enough (Ellsworth, 1994). James used the example of the fear of a bear: He said that you don't run away because you are afraid of the bear; rather, the sight of the bear itself causes you to run away, and you feel fear because you run away. Critics pointed out that this statement is obviously wrong: You do not automatically run away from a bear. You would not run away from a caged bear, a trained bear in a circus, or a sleeping bear. True, James (1894) conceded: The cause of your running away is not really the bear itself, but your interpretation or appraisal of the situation (e.g., dangerous animal coming toward you). Still, he argued, when you assess that situation as one calling for escape, you start trying to escape (and your body prepares for escape), and your perception of the physiological changes and behavior is your fear.

James did not clearly distinguish between all the various aspects of emotion, but using the terminology of today, we would say that James's theory applies to the feeling aspect of emotions, not the cognitive appraisal. So, the proper statement of the James-Lange theory is that the *feeling aspect* of an emotion is the perception of the body's actions and physiological arousal:

James-Lange theory, clarified:
Event → Cognition/Appraisal → Physiological
        Change & Behavior → Feeling

The Cannon-Bard Theory

Walter Cannon, a physiologist of the early 1900s, was famous for discovering that the sympathetic nervous system is responsible for fight-or-flight responses. He and another leading physiologist, Philip Bard, also proposed an alternative to the James-Lange theory (Bard, 1934; Cannon, 1927). Cannon argued that the responses of the muscles and organs are too slow to contribute to the feeling aspect of emotion. According to the **Cannon–Bard theory**, emotional cognitions and feelings are causally independent of physiological arousal and behavior, even though these aspects all occur at the same time. Restated in modern terms, the cognitive/appraisal, feeling, and physiological/behavioral aspects of an emotion arise independently:

Cannon-Bard theory:

$$Event \Longleftrightarrow \begin{array}{l} Cognition/Appraisal \\ Feelings \\ Physiological\ Change\ \&\ Behavior \end{array}$$

For example, the sight of a mad killer chasing you with a chainsaw would cause you to decide that you were in danger, and independently cause feelings of fear and the action of running away. Note that the assumed causal independence of cognitions, feelings, and actions has several implications: Your fear does not cause you to run away, and the fact that you are running away does not increase your fear.

This theory is even further from common sense than the James-Lange theory, and much evidence argues against it. For example, a sudden loud noise evokes muscle tension, increased heart rate, and increased sweating within a second or two, surely fast enough to contribute to the feeling of an emotion. Furthermore, as we shall soon see, emotional behaviors can alter feelings even when you are not in an emotional situation. The Cannon-Bard theory was the forerunner to many modern theories that emphasize the cognitive aspects of emotion. However, virtually no one in recent decades has defended this theory in its original form. We include it here for historical completeness.

The Schachter-Singer Theory

Recall that according to the James-Lange theory, different emotional feelings may be caused by different patterns of physiological changes and behaviors. In short, we know *what kind of* emotion we are feeling by the specific way our body is responding. According to the **Schachter-Singer theory** (proposed by Stanley Schachter and Jerome Singer), the physiological arousal that often accompanies emotion is essential for determining how strong the emotional feeling will be, but it *does not* identify the emotion. The Schachter-Singer theory assumes all emotions evoke such similar physiological responses that you cannot recognize which emotion you are feeling just by observing your body's reactions. Instead, you identify which emotion you feel on the basis of all the information you have about a situation (Schachter & Singer, 1962). In other words, the difference between one emotion and another is in the cognitive appraisal aspect, not the feeling or physiology aspects. Figure 1.6 contrasts the James-Lange, Cannon-Bard, and Schachter-Singer theories.

Could you, in fact, recognize one emotion from another, based only on feedback from your heart rate, breathing rate, sweating, and so forth? We will address the research on this question in detail in Chapter 5, but for now consider a thought experiment: Suppose a researcher puts you in one room and your friend in another. The researcher attaches wires to record your friend's heart rate, breathing rate, and other physiological responses and connects those wires to a machine attached to you. Whenever your friend's heart rate increases or decreases, the machine will cause your heart rate to

FIGURE 1.6 According to the James-Lange theory, physiological arousal and behaviors determine emotional feelings. According to the Cannon-Bard theory, physiological/behavior and feelings are independent. According to the Schachter-Singer theory, physiological changes determine the strength of the feelings, but appraisals of events determine specific feelings and behaviors.

increase or decrease equally at the same time. It similarly links your other physiological responses to your friend. Now your friend watches an emotionally gripping movie. You experience exactly the same physiological changes at exactly the same times as your friend, even though you are not watching the movie. Will you say you experience the same emotion?

The James-Lange theory suggests that you should. The Cannon-Bard theory says your physiological changes are irrelevant to your emotional feelings. According to the Schachter-Singer view, the physiological changes determine the strength of your feelings, but not which feelings you experience. This view presumes that all emotions produce sufficiently similar changes that the differences are uninformative. According to this theory, if you are just sitting alone in a room, you have no event to which you can attribute your arousal, so you may or may not report the same emotion as your friend.

The experiment just described is not feasible, but Schachter and Singer did something else that they thought might answer the question: They induced physiological arousal in participants and then put them into different situations. If physiological changes are different for each emotion, and lead to emotional feelings, the participants should all report feeling the same emotion. However, if people interpret the arousal differently depending on the situation, then people in different situations should report feeling different emotions, even though they have the same arousal.

Because this experiment has been so influential, let's examine it in some detail. It is an interesting study, but it also has serious flaws. Schachter and Singer (1962) gave one group of participants an injection of epinephrine (also known as adrenaline), a hormone that increases physiological arousal. Another group received a placebo injection—that is, one with no pharmacological effects. Of those receiving the epinephrine injection, half were told that the injection would increase their heart rate, make them sweat, and so forth. The other participants receiving epinephrine were not told about these effects.

At that point, some participants were put into a "euphoria" situation and the others into an "anger" situation. In the euphoria situation, the experimenters had each participant wait with a young man who was supposedly also a participant, but who was in fact paid to play the role of "happy, playful person." He flipped wads of paper into a trash can, sailed paper airplanes, built a tower with manila folders, played with a hula hoop, and tried to get the other participant to join in his play.

The "anger" situation is diabolically clever. The experimenters simply asked participants to fill out a lengthy questionnaire, which was full of personal, insulting, and downright rude questions. Examples:

1.   What is your father's average annual income?

2.   Which member of your immediate family does not bathe or wash regularly?

3.   Which member of your immediate family needs psychiatric care?

4.   With how many men (other than your father) has your mother had extramarital relationships? 4 or fewer   5–9   10 or more

Again, each participant in this condition had a partner posing as another participant, who was in fact paid by the experimenters. In this case, he muttered in annoyance at the questions and ultimately ripped up the questionnaire and stormed out of the room.

Schachter and Singer did not report ratings of happiness and anger separately, but instead reported the ratio of the two. This makes the results somewhat difficult to interpret, but let's try. All participants reported being more happy than angry, though the ratio varied from condition to condition. Participants given the placebo were not affected much by the situation—they reported about the same ratio of happiness to anger whether they were in the euphoria or anger condition. Those who were given epinephrine without knowing what to expect differed in the hypothesized way. People in the epinephrine-euphoria condition often joined in the play and reported being more happy than angry. Their ratings were about the same as people in the placebo-euphoria condition, so the epinephrine seems not to have affected them at all. Of those in the epinephrine-anger condition, people did not report being more angry than happy, but the two ratings were closer, and some muttered angry comments or refused to complete the questionnaire.

The overall picture is a bit confused because of the results for the people who were told what to expect from the epinephrine. Those in the euphoria situation reported less happiness (relative to anger) than in any other condition, suggesting that the epinephrine made them relatively upset even though they knew what sensations to expect. Those in the anger situation reported the greatest bias toward happy feelings, relative to angry ones. The main finding from the study seems to be that people's interpretation of their arousal in terms of emotional feelings is slightly influenced by the situation, but that telling people to expect arousal detaches the link between people's emotional feelings and the situation. In two later studies, Maslach (1979) and Marshall and Zimbardo (1979) found that participants experiencing unexplained sympathetic arousal defaulted to reporting negative affect (that is, unpleasant mood) compared with control participants who received placebo injections, or those who were told to expect the injection to have "physiological side effects."

Perhaps Schachter and Singer were only partly right, and certain emotions can be confused with each other more easily than others. Here's a later experiment based on the Schachter and Singer theory: The idea was that if one aspect of a situation triggers intense arousal, you might be more likely to associate that arousal with other aspects of the situation as well. In this experiment, young men were asked to participate in a study of "the effects of scenic attractions on creative expression." The men were taken to a bridge and asked to cross it; halfway along the bridge, they were stopped by an attractive female experimenter. Participants looked at pictures on some cards and told short stories about the pictures. At the end of the questions, the experimenter gave each man her telephone number in case he wanted to find out more about the experiment.

The critical variable was the type of bridge the men crossed. Some men talked with the experimenter while standing on a wide, sturdy bridge 10 feet (3 meters) above a river. The other interviews took place on a narrow, wobbly wooden bridge 230 feet (70 meters) above a canyon. Presumably those on the wobbly bridge felt greater arousal due to their precarious situation, and the research question was whether these men might interpret their arousal as attraction toward the experimenter. Evidently many of them did. Of those on the wobbly bridge, 39 percent called the experimenter after the study, compared with only 9 percent of those on the sturdier bridge (Dutton & Aron, 1974).

In a related study, young heterosexual men examined women in the *Sports Illustrated* swimsuit issue and rated the attractiveness of each one (in the name of science, of course). Meanwhile, they heard sounds, which were in fact random. Some were told that they were random sounds, but others were told that the sounds were playbacks of their own heartbeat. Men who thought they were hearing their own heartbeat gave high ratings to whichever photograph they were examining while their heartbeat seemed to be increasing (Crucian et al., 2000). Presumably, they thought, "Wow! Listen to my heart racing! What a beautiful, exciting woman!"

These experiments on people misattributing their arousal to sexual excitement are entertaining, to say the least. However, the effect works only when attraction was present already. That is, a man who thinks he hears his heart beating faster will attribute his excitement to the woman only if he regarded her as attractive in the first place. Similarly, feeling excited might cause you to regard some leader to be viewed as "extremely charismatic" only if he was in fact somewhat exciting (Pastor, Mayo, & Shamir, 2007).

RELATIONSHIPS AMONG COGNITION, FEELING, PHYSIOLOGY, AND BEHAVIOR

Let's return to the question of how the four aspects of emotion relate to one another, and to eliciting events. The James-Lange hypothesis suggests several research questions: How fast is cognitive appraisal? Fast enough to cause other aspects of emotion, as proposed by the revised James-Lange theory, or relatively slow, as suggested by the Schachter-Singer theory? Are physiological sensations and behaviors necessary for emotional feelings? Are they sufficient to cause such feelings?

The Speed of Emotional Appraisals

When you experience an event, how quickly do you identify it as good, bad, or neutral? According to the James-Lange theory and others that emphasize appraisal, you begin by assessing the overall situation and classifying it as calling for some kind of action (escape, attack), or no action at all. This classification triggers physiological changes and behaviors. The term *appraisal* is used here in a broad sense. You don't necessarily analyze the situation well enough to put it into words. What is necessary is that your brain identifies certain implications of the object, such as "dangerous" or "insulting," right away. From an evolutionary standpoint, we should expect this appraisal to be quick. In the presence of a threat, the faster you react, the greater your chance of survival. According to the Schachter-Singer theory, however, we may not bother to appraise the situation at all unless we feel unexplained arousal.

As predicted by the updated James-Lange theory, the brain shows signs of identifying the emotional quality of a stimulus extremely fast. In one case, physicians studied a man who was undergoing brain surgery for severe epilepsy. As is often the case, the surgery was conducted with local anesthesia to the scalp, so the man was awake and alert throughout the procedure. (Keeping the patient awake during brain surgery is helpful. As surgeons probe one brain area after another, eventually the patient says, "That makes me feel the way I do when I'm about to have a seizure." The surgeons then know they are close to the area causing the seizures.) In this particular study, while they had the patient's brain exposed, the physicians inserted electrodes into his prefrontal cortex, an area important for certain aspects of memory and emotion. Then they asked him to look at pictures of pleasant and unpleasant scenes, as well as happy and frightened faces. Cells in the prefrontal cortex responded within 120 milliseconds, and they showed a different pattern of activity to happy faces and pleasant pictures than to frightened faces and unpleasant pictures (Kawasaki et al., 2001). This quick response is consistent with the idea that cognitive appraisal precedes the reactions of the body, which take a bit longer.

In another study, college students looked at photographs of faces with happy, angry, or neutral expressions while the investigators recorded brain activity with an EEG. Looking at an angry, threatening face evoked a strong response 200 to 300 milliseconds after the onset of the photograph, whereas seeing a happy or neutral face did not evoke that response (Schupp et al., 2004). Again, the evidence indicates that the brain categorizes

the emotional quality of a scene quickly, at least for certain kinds of emotions (Robinson, 1998).

In other studies, researchers have recorded movements of facial muscles while participants looked at photos of people with various facial expressions. A smiling face slightly activated the muscles responsible for smiling, and an angry face activated the muscles responsible for frowning. The muscles reacted briefly within less than half a second after onset of a photo, even if the viewer was paying attention to something other than the expression (Cannon, Hayes, & Tipper, 2009; Dimberg & Thunberg, 1998). Another experiment found that a photo of a fearful face caused slight sweating and trembling, even if the photo was presented so briefly that people did not report consciously seeing it at all (Kubota et al., 2000; Vuilleumier, Armony, Driver, & Dolan, 2001). These results imply that the brain classifies the emotional quality of a photo rapidly, but that people need not even be aware of the appraisal in order to show appropriate behaviors and physiological changes. When you think about it, these results are stunning, even hard to believe. They reveal that before you have figured out what you are seeing, in fact before you realize that you have seen anything at all, your brain has already begun to classify images as good or bad, threatening or harmless.

The research just described indicates that classification as good versus bad is often quick enough to precede and guide emotional actions and feelings. However, we are not in a position to say that emotional appraisal is always that fast, or that it always causes feelings and actions. Suppose you are in a bad mood because of an event a few hours ago. Then, someone takes your chair where you wanted to sit, and you yell angrily. Your anger is way out of proportion to the offense, so you look for an explanation—an appraisal—to explain your anger. You say, "You're always so inconsiderate!" or something similar. In such cases, the appraisal apparently comes *after* the feeling and action, or "carries over" from one emotional situation to an unrelated one. That is, cognitive appraisals may lead to behaviors and feelings, but sometimes the feelings may influence future appraisals too.

Are Body Sensations Necessary for Emotional Feeling?

If you had no sensations from your organs, would you still feel emotions? According to the James-Lange theory, and to some extent the Schachter-Singer theory, you might still appraise the situation cognitively (for example, "this situation calls for anger"), but you should not *feel* an emotion. Furthermore, if physiological sensations are critical for emotional feelings, then people with weak feedback from their organs would experience only weak emotions, and people who are especially sensitive to feedback from their organs might experience especially intense emotions. We can examine these issues by comparing various kinds of people.

In one study, people were asked to report whether they thought their heart rate was increasing or decreasing, while researchers measured the actual heart rate. The participants also reported how sensitive they were to visceral (gut) sensations in general, and how intensely they felt moments of fear and sadness. The people who were in fact the most accurate at judging their heart rate tended to be those who reported high sensitivity to visceral sensations and great intensity of unpleasant emotions (Critchley, Wiens, Rotshtein, Öhman, & Dolan, 2004). That is, the more you notice your own arousal level, the more intensely you feel emotions, especially the negative ones.

At the opposite extreme are people with diminished responses. **Pure autonomic failure** is a medical condition in which the autonomic nervous system ceases to influence the body. The causes of this uncommon, incurable condition are unknown. Usually its onset occurs when people are middle-aged. One prominent symptom occurs when people stand up: The blood sinks rapidly from the head to the trunk, and the person faints. (The medical term for this symptom is "orthostatic hypotension.") This would happen to everyone without the action of the sympathetic nervous system. When you stand up, you reflexively trigger mechanisms that increase heart rate and constrict (tighten) the veins leading from your head back to the heart. People with pure autonomic failure lose this reflex and therefore have to stand up

very slowly to prevent blood from sinking out of their head. Physical or mental stresses also have no effect on their heart rate, breathing rate, sweating, and other autonomic responses.

What about emotions? In objectively emotional situations they report the same type of emotions as other people, but feel them less intensely (Critchley, Mathias, & Dolan, 2001). Presumably the appraisal part of their emotion is intact but the feeling part is weakened. Even someone with few or no emotional feelings can say, "I recognize this as a situation that calls for fear" (or anger or whatever). But as the without autonomic changes, they may have nothing to *feel*.

Locked-in syndrome is an even more extreme condition in which people lose almost all output from the brain to the muscles and the autonomic nervous system, although they continue to receive sensations. The cause is a stroke or other damage to the part of the brainstem (see Figure 1.7). Most people with spinal cord damage retain control of some of their muscles, depending on the location of the damage. Even those who

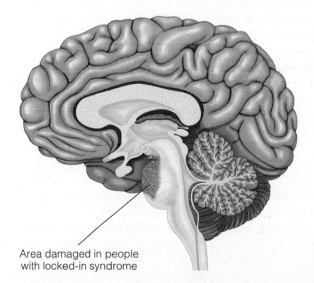

Area damaged in people with locked-in syndrome

FIGURE 1.7 The stippled area shows the location of brain damage in people with locked-in syndrome. Axons in this area provide the communication between the brain and nearly all the nerves controlling muscles. The only muscular control these people retain is of their eye movements, controlled by cells above the area of damage.

are paralyzed from the neck down have output to the heart and other organs because the nerves of the parasympathetic nervous system originate in the pons and medulla, not the spinal cord. In locked-in syndrome, however, key areas of the pons and medulla themselves are damaged. In these areas axons travel from the brain to the spinal cord. A few clusters of neurons above the damaged area control eye muscles, so the person retains the ability for eye movement. Otherwise, the person is totally paralyzed while remaining intellectually alert and capable of surviving for many years.

What happens to their emotions? They can tell us, although not easily. First, a specialist has to teach them to spell out words by a code in which different patterns of eye movements or blinks represent different letters of the alphabet. When they give their first message, you might expect a message of terror or despair. After all, the person is permanently paralyzed except for the eye muscles, and most of us imagine that we would feel overwhelming distress at that prospect. The James-Lange theory, however, predicts greatly weakened emotion, because of the virtual lack of feedback from the body.

Unfortunately, the results are sparse on this point. Communication with these people is slow and laborious. Most of what they say is remarkably unemotional, certainly without any sign of panic or despair. One woman's first message after learning an eye-blinking code was, "Why do I wear such an ugly shirt?" (Kübler, Kotchoubey, Kaiser, Wolpaw, & Birbaumer, 2001). Many of the reports by locked-in patients are described as "tranquil," or calm (Damasio, 1999). A likely interpretation is that they do not experience fidgeting, heart palpitations, stomach churning, or any of the other bodily responses that ordinarily accompany emotions.

However, an autobiography by a locked-in patient (dictated by blinks of one eyelid) does refer to sadness, disappointment, frustration, and similar emotional terms (Bauby, 1997). Two websites by or about locked-in patients also assert that they feel emotions, including at least sadness and frustration. (See www.strokesafe.org/resources/locked-in_

syndrome.html or www.locked-in-syndrome.com/pages/5/index.htm.) We would like to know more: Do they really *feel* emotions, and do they feel them as intensely as before, or are they talking about the cognitive/appraisal aspect of emotions? This distinction is theoretically important to psychologists studying emotions, although obscure to anyone else. The few research studies currently available simply do not provide enough information to answer our questions about emotional feelings.

Are Emotional Behaviors Necessary for Emotional Feeling? Do They Determine Emotional Feelings?

Remember William James' example of running away from a bear as a cause of feeling fear. Are emotional behaviors necessary for emotional feeling? If not, would the behaviors at least strengthen emotional feeling?

Several researchers interested in this question focus on people who have become paralyzed by spinal cord injuries. Although they still have changes in heart rate and activity of other organs, they cannot move their muscles, so emotional behaviors are limited. The results vary depending on how one phrases the question, but most people with spinal cord injuries report that they experience their emotions as strongly as before, especially fear and sadness (Chwalisz, Diener, & Gallagher, 1988; Cobos, Sánchez, García, Vera, & Vila, 2002; Lowe & Carroll, 1985).

Although some psychologists argue that these results contradict the James-Lange theory, it would be better to say they put constraints on the theory. People with spinal cord injuries lack many or most muscular responses, but they will still feel changes in heart rate, breathing rate, sweating, digestion, and so forth. So, given that these people continue to report more or less normal emotional feelings, we can conclude that the feeling aspect of emotions does not require *overt* behaviors—including those of running away, which was William James' primary example.

What about more subtle actions? If you could not make facial expressions, would you feel your emotions less intensely? Researchers temporarily paralyzed some people's frown muscles with botulinum toxin ("Botox"). Until the toxin wore off, people had weaker than normal brain responses to the sight of other people's angry expressions, apparently because they could not frown back at people frowning at them (Hennenlotter et al., 2009). However, this study assumes that the brain responses reflect feelings of anger, which may not necessarily be true. People

with a permanent paralysis of facial muscles adjust to their condition, and they report feeling normal emotions (Keillor, Barrett, Crucian, Kortenkamp, & Heilman, 2002). People with *Möbius syndrome* (a rare congenital condition) are unable to smile. You can imagine how that condition impairs their social relationships. They nevertheless report feeling happy or amused about the same as other people do. The girl in Figure 1.8 underwent surgery to give her an artificial smile (G. Miller, 2007). So, facial expressions are not necessary for emotional feelings.

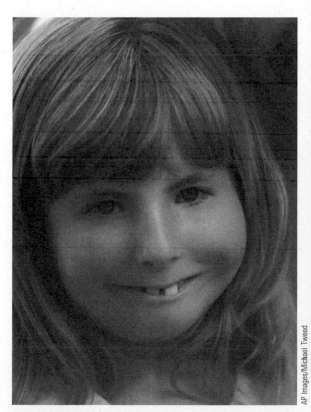

FIGURE 1.8 This girl with Möbius syndrome could not smile before surgeons gave her an artificial smile as shown. She nevertheless could feel happiness, and she showed a sense of humor.

Facial expressions and other behaviors may not be necessary for feelings of emotion, but they could still help create such feelings. For example, does smiling make you feel happy or amused, and does frowning make you feel annoyed? To test these hypotheses, researchers can't simply tell people to smile or frown and then ask them how they feel. Well, they could, but it wouldn't be a good idea. If you were in that study, you would probably guess what hypothesis the experimenters were testing, and you might say you were feeling an emotion just because it was what you thought they wanted you to say. Psychological researchers call this problem one of "demand characteristics," meaning the cues that tell participants what the experimenter hopes to see.

To avoid demand characteristics, researchers use methods that disguise the intention of the study. Here is one clever procedure they have used, which you could try yourself, or ask a friend to try: Hold a pen with your lips, as Figure 1.9 illustrates. Later repeat the procedure holding the pen with your teeth. In each case go through a stack of newspaper comic strips, rating each one as very funny (+), somewhat funny (√), or not funny (−). When holding the pen with your teeth, you are virtually forced to smile; when holding it with your lips, you press your lips together in a way that people do when they are angry or annoyed. In one study, participants holding the pen in a "smiling" position rated cartoons slightly funnier than did those who held it in the "annoyed" position (Strack, Martin, & Stepper, 1988). That is, the sensation of smiling apparently increases amusement. Another study found similar results using ratings of movies instead of cartoons (Soussignan, 2002).

This experiment is a bit more complex than it might seem. Changes in facial expression induce additional changes in heart rate, breathing, and so forth, so it is not certain that the facial expressions by themselves led to emotional responses (Levenson, Ekman, & Friesen, 1990). Also, not

Kathleen Olson

FIGURE 1.9 Holding a pen with your teeth forces a smile; holding it with your lips prevents one. A smiling position tends to enhance reports of amusement.

everyone is convinced that this procedure completely avoids demand characteristics. Might an occasional participant in this study guess what the experimenters were hoping to find? In any case, the results do not indicate that smiling by itself induces happiness. These participants were reacting to cartoons. The results indicate that smiling facilitates happiness or amusement that was already present.

If smiling increases amusement, frowning might decrease it. How could we get people to frown without saying "frown"? Researchers told their participants they wanted to study "divided attention." The participants were to do two things at once: One was to rate the pleasantness or unpleasantness of various photos. The other activity was a motor task: The experimenters attached golf tees above the participants' eyebrows. The participants were instructed to keep the tips of the two golf tees touching each other. The only way to do that was to frown, so the instructions sneakily got them to frown without mentioning frowning. While participants were frowning, they rated most photos less pleasant than at other times, when they were not instructed to touch the golf tees together (Larsen, Kasimatis, & Frey, 1992). Several other studies have also found that facial expressions can elicit or at least strengthen the corresponding emotional feelings, although the effects vary considerably from one person to another (Duclos & Laird, 2001; Hess, Kappas, McHugo, Lanzetta, & Kleck, 1992).

When you feel fear, anger, or sadness, you express it not only with your facial expression but also with your body posture. (See Figure 1.10.) If you adopted both the facial expression and the posture, would you start to feel that emotion? To find out, researchers asked 54 college students to adopt certain postures and facial movements. They concealed the point of the experiment by describing it as a study of how people's movements affected their thinking. They went on to say that sometimes feelings influence the relationship between movements and thinking, so they would have to ask about emotional feelings as well as thoughts. Then they gave detailed instructions about what muscles to move and postures to adopt (Flack, Laird, & Cavallaro, 1999).

Their instructions follow. Try each of them and see whether you start to feel any emotion. Unfortunately, unlike the participants in the experiment, you know the hypothesis, so your results are contaminated by your expectations. However, you could try reading these procedures to a friend without telling him the hypothesis.

1. Push your eyebrows together and down. Clench your teeth tightly and push your lips together. Put your feet flat on the floor directly below your knees, and put your forearms and elbows on the arms of the chair. Now clench your fists tightly, and lean your upper body slightly forward.

2. Lower your eyebrows down toward your cheeks. With your mouth closed, push up lightly with your lower lip. While sitting, rest your back comfortably against the chair, and draw your feet loosely in under the chair. You should feel no tension in your legs or feet. Now fold your hands in your lap, just loosely cupping one hand in the other. Drop your head, letting your rib cage fall and letting the rest of your body go limp. You should feel just a slight tension up the back of your neck and across your shoulder blades.

3. Raise your eyebrows, and open your eyes wide. Move your whole head back, so that your chin is tucked in a little, and let your mouth relax and hang open a little. Scoot to the front edge of your chair, and draw your feet together and underneath the chair. Now turn your upper body toward the right, twisting a little at the waist, but keeping your head facing forward. Now dip your right shoulder a bit, and lean your upper body slightly backward. Raise your hands to about mouth level, arms bent at the elbow, and palms facing forward.

4. Push the corners of your mouth up and back, letting your mouth open a little. Sit up as straight as you can in your chair. Put your hands at the ends of the armrests, and make sure that your legs are straight in front of you, with your knees bent and feet directly below your knees.

FIGURE 1.10 We express emotions with body posture as well as facial expression.

Instruction #1 was intended to induce anger. On the average, participants did report higher than usual anger levels and also somewhat elevated levels of disgust. Instruction #2 was intended to induce sadness, and it did, without elevating other emotions. Instruction #3 was meant for fear. Here the results were less clear. People reported an elevated fear level, but an even more elevated feeling of surprise. This result makes sense, because the facial expressions and postures associated with fear and surprise are similar. Finally, instruction #4 was intended for happiness, and people following this instruction did report greater happiness, on the average.

The graph in Figure 1.11 shows the results for four instructions, arranged left to right: anger, sadness, fear, and happiness. For each set of instructions, people reported the intensity of six emotional feelings: anger, sadness, fear, happiness, disgust, and surprise. Note that each set of instructions aroused the intended emotion and sometimes also a related emotion. Unfortunately, the researchers did not report a baseline of how much of each emotion people might feel when given no particular instructions about facial expression or posture. Oops.

In summary, study results suggest that emotional behaviors, such as facial expressions and postures, are not *necessary* for feelings of emotion, but

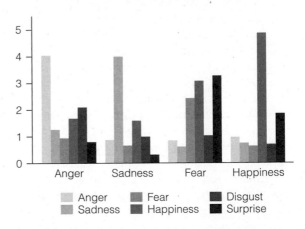

FIGURE 1.11 The instructions intended to arouse anger, sadness, fear, and happiness did indeed arouse those feelings, but in some cases they aroused a closely related feeling also.

Source: Based on data of Flack, Laird, and Cavallaro.

that posing the expression or posture associated with a given emotion can *facilitate* feeling that emotion. All of these effects are small. The fact that these effects occur at all is important for emotion theory, but if you're dealing with someone who is deeply depressed, don't say "Smile; it will make everything better!" Facial feedback doesn't have that strong an effect.

Overall Evaluation of the
James-Lange Theory

Here we are, a century and a quarter after William James proposed one of the first theories in psychology. According to the James-Lange theory, appraisal of an event comes first, then physiological changes and behaviors, and specific emotional feelings arise from the perception of physical sensations and actions. Later, Schachter and Singer proposed that physiological arousal explains the intensity of emotional feelings, but *not* the type of feeling, and that appraisal of the situation may come after the physical sensations and feelings rather than before. Isn't it about time we decided who was right?

We contend that the James-Lange theory is more or less correct, if described in modern terms and understood in the form of James's later writings. The data indicate that at least some emotional appraisal is quick, preceding physiological changes and observable behavior. Furthermore, feedback from behaviors such as facial expressions and postures is sufficient to produce at least mild feeling of specific emotions. In the absence of all feedback from the body, what emotional feelings would someone have? On this key point, the best answer is "we're not sure," based on data from pure autonomic failure and locked-in syndrome. Exactly how much emotional feeling these patients have is hard to say, and no patient has a complete absence of feedback. However, people with very limited feedback do seem to have a low intensity of emotional feeling.

We suggest a modification of James-Lange theory, to which we believe James and Lange would have agreed: The chain of events does not go entirely in one direction. After appraisal leads to physiological changes/behaviors, and behaviors to feelings, the behaviors and feelings can influence subsequent appraisals. For example, if something makes you angry, your anger changes your interpretation of new events, so that a new event that might otherwise seem unimportant now seems like yet another offense (Lerner & Keltner, 2000).

CLASSIFICATION OF
EMOTIONS

We conclude this chapter with an issue that has been controversial among emotion researchers from the start: How many emotions are there, and how should we classify them? In his book *The Expression of the Emotions in Man and Animals*, published in 1872, Chares Darwin described the similarity of facial expressions of happiness, sadness, fear, anger, and several other emotions by people throughout the world. In doing so, he implied that we should think of emotions in terms of a few distinct categories. Some psychologists have proposed a short list of "basic" emotions, including happiness, sadness, anger, fear, disgust, and surprise. Other psychologists add more candidates, such as contempt, shame, guilt, interest, hope, pride, relief, frustration, love, awe, boredom, jealousy, regret, and embarrassment (Keltner & Buswell, 1997). Hindus include heroism, amusement, peace, and wonder (Hejmadi, Davidson, & Rozin, 2000).

An alternative view is that emotion consists of two or more continuous dimensions, such as pleasant vs. unpleasant and aroused vs. calm. Wilhelm Wundt, famous for founding the world's first psychology research laboratory, emphasized how one emotion grades into another, rather than the lines between different kinds of emotions (Wundt, 1907/1977). Since Darwin and Wundt, psychologists have lined up on one side or the other—a few distinct categories of emotion, or continuous gradations. Three major models of emotion have emerged. For now we will just introduce these models, but we shall return to them repeatedly throughout the text.

The Basic Emotions Model

Researchers who emphasize emotion categories such as anger and fear typically refer to these as "basic" or "discrete" emotions. In this view, **basic emotions** are fundamentally distinct entities, like chemical elements or different species of animals. The basic emotions model leads to certain kinds of assumptions.

For example, if anger is a naturally occurring basic emotion, we might propose three things. First, anger is probably an evolved characteristic, like language or walking upright, which means it has a distinct function separate from the functions of other emotions. Second, except for people with brain damage, genetic mutations, or other abnormalities, everyone should have the capacity to experience anger. Third, the various aspects of anger—eliciting events, appraisals, feelings, physiological changes, and behaviors—should "hang together" wherever you go, even if people talk about their feelings in different ways.

If basic emotions do exist, how do we know which ones they are? Several criteria have been proposed. We focus here on the criteria that are the most widely discussed and that have provoked the most research.

One criterion is that *basic emotions should be universal* among humans, and we will probably see signs of basic emotions in other species as well. If an emotion is an evolved part of human nature, then we should see something like it in nearly all people. Finding an emotion in all societies is no guarantee that it is basic, but if we can only find evidence of it in a few societies, that finding would imply that it is socially constructed rather than a built-in aspect of human nature.

A second criterion that has inspired much research is that *if an emotion is basic, people should have a distinct, built-in way of expressing it* including facial expression, tone of voice, and other behaviors. Furthermore, in accordance with the first criterion (similarity across cultures), it is important to demonstrate that people in all cultures show the same or similar facial expressions, and interpret them in approximately the same way. We shall consider this topic in some detail in the next chapter.

A third criterion is that *a basic emotion should be evident early in life.* For example, we would not consider nostalgia or patriotism to be basic emotions, because they emerge in adulthood, or not at all. However, exactly how early must an emotion occur to qualify as basic? Newborns show distress, but not much else. They do not smile or laugh, although they do respond to a parent's happy tone of voice by opening their eyes wider (Mastropieri & Turkewitz, 1999). Perhaps they feel happiness, perhaps not. Smiling and frowning begin to emerge within two or three months (Izard, 1994). Fear expressions become distinct from distress by age six months, but anger expressions emerge gradually over a much longer time. Which of these are early enough to qualify as "basic" emotions? We will return to this issue again in Chapter 12.

Potentially the most persuasive criterion would be that *each basic emotion should be physiologically distinct,* such as increased activity in a particular brain area, or a particular pattern of effects in the body. William James first suggested that different emotional feelings might correspond to different physiological profiles in 1884, and this is still considered important by many researchers today. However, this criterion is also very difficult to study. We shall consider this matter in detail in Chapters 4 and 5.

Dimensional Models of Emotion

As you may have noticed, the basic emotion model assumes the four aspects of emotion (cognitions/ appraisals, feelings, physiological responses, and behaviors) are all equally important, and will hang together in consistent ways. However, several researchers have noted that the four aspects *don't* always hang together predictably, especially when you consider the experience of people in different cultures. As a result, these researchers have proposed that we identify one aspect of emotion as primary, and then ask how that aspect relates to other aspects as an empirical question rather than a theoretical assumption (e.g., Russell, 2003). Researchers who have taken this approach typically focus on the feeling aspect of emotion, and their findings suggest that categories may not do the best job of describing feelings.

Instead of thinking of emotional feelings in terms of categories, an alternative is to arrange them along dimensions. For example, if you were displaying diamonds at a store, you might arrange them in columns from largest to smallest, and in rows from most to least sparkling. We can also describe emotions as positions along continuous dimensions (e.g., Cacioppo,

Gardner, & Berntson, 1997; Russell, 1980, 2003; Watson & Tellegen, 1985). In order to derive these dimensions, researchers can offer people various emotion-related words and ask them to rate the similarity among each pair of words, or they can ask people to report how strong their emotions are at various moments and note which emotions tend to occur together. These data can be analyzed with a method called multidimensional scaling that allows us to see what dimensions emerge from peoples' ratings of their experience. The question is whether the dimensions that emerge reflect discrete categories, such as "sadness," "anger," and so forth, or a more abstract dimensional space in which the supposed basic emotions are just particular points.

Without discussing the mathematics of multidimensional scaling, let's illustrate with an example. Consider color. Suppose we show people various pairs of colors and ask them to rate how similar

they look. Someone might rate two shades of purple as very similar, purple and blue as less similar, and purple and green as still less similar. A mathematical model would put the first two colors close together, the second pair intermediate, and the third pair farther apart. After collecting ratings on many pairs of colors, we might present the results graphically, putting purple near blue, then bluish green, then green, and so forth. If we used multidimensional scaling to analyze these data, we would probably get one "wavelength" dimension representing the color rainbow, and another "brightness" dimension reflecting how light or dark each color is. These two dimensions would do a very good job of describing the colors and how they are related to each other, and would be more precise than categories such as "yellow" and "blue."

Using this method, James Russell (1980) reported the arrangement of emotional terms shown in Figure 1.12. Studies using other languages have

FIGURE 1.12 The terms that people rated as similar to each other appear close together, whereas those rated as dissimilar appear far apart.

Source: From "A Circumplex Model of an Affect" by James A. Russell In *Journal of Personality and Social Psychology*, 39, pp. 1161–1178. © 1980 American Psychological Association. Reprinted with permission from the author.

produced similar outcomes (Yik & Russell, 2003). Russell has generalized from these results to propose the **circumplex model**, in which the emotions form a circle defined by the dimensions of pleasantness and arousal. Using this model, we can describe excitement as a combination of pleasure and arousal, contentment as a combination of pleasure and inactivity, and so forth. Keep in mind that this model emphasizes the feeling aspect of emotion, not cognitive, physiological, or behavioral aspects. For example, anger and fear are close to each other on this graph, even though we associate anger and fear with different cognitions and behaviors. In the circumplex model, the feeling aspect of emotion in terms of pleasantness and arousal is called **core affect** (Russell, 2003).

Other researchers, starting from a different theoretical basis and using different procedures, have proposed a somewhat different pair of dimensions. According to the circumplex model of emotion, an emotional stimulus is either good or bad, or somewhere in between, so it should not be possible to feel strong positive emotion and strong negative emotion at the same time. According to the **evaluative space model** (Cacioppo, Gardner, & Berntson, 1997), our evaluations of some target's "goodness" and "badness" are actually independent of each other, such that something can be good and bad at the same time. As a result, positive and negative affect should be independent dimensions of feeling, rather than opposite ends of a single dimension.

Examine the model presented in Figure 1.13. This model, which was proposed by David Watson and Auke Tellegen (1985), allows for the possibility that positive and negative affect are independent. Each axis has a built-in arousal or activation scale, so that being high on either positive or negative affect is very activated, and being low on both positive and negative affect means being low on activation. However, unlike the circumplex model, being low on positive activation is not the same as being low on negative activation. As a result, "calm" is distant from "sleepy."

So which model of emotional feelings is right—the circumplex model or the evaluative space model? Because of a variety of complicated measurement

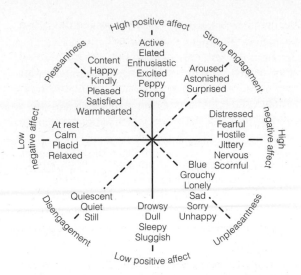

FIGURE 1.13 In this model of emotional feelings, the main dimensions are Positive Affect and Negative Affect.

Source: From "Toward a Consensual Structure of Mood," by D. Watson and A. Tellegen, *Psychological Bulletin*, 98, pp. 219–235. © 1985 American Psychological Association. Reprinted by permission of D. Watson

problems, different sets of researchers get different results on the relationship between positive affect and negative affect. Some find them to be nearly independent of each other (Tellegen, Watson, & Clark, 1999; Watson, Clark, & Tellegen, 1984, 1988). Others find that positive and negative affect are polar opposites—you can feel one or the other at a time, but not both (Remington, Fabrigar, & Visser, 2000; Russell, 1980). According to one study, positive and negative affect are opposites in most situations, but in a few "bittersweet" situations (such as graduating from college), people do feel both (Larsen, McGraw, & Cacioppo, 2001).

One potential explanation of these varied findings is that researchers do not always measure emotion on the same time scale. For example, asking participants to report how much positive and negative affect they feel overall in their lives (e.g., Watson et al., 1988) is very different from asking them how much positive and negative affect they are feeling *right now* (e.g., Barrett & Fossum, 2001). As noted earlier, however, it is very difficult to measure emotional feelings on a moment-to-moment basis, so this debate is likely to continue for some time.

Let's not get too embroiled in this controversy. Here are three points of agreement among the theories that describe emotions as points on continuous dimensions:

1. Emotional feelings are best described in terms of two dimensions.

2. The feeling aspect of emotions is considered primary, not the cognitive or behavioral aspects. Several emotions—such as disgust, guilt, and embarrassment—might *feel* nearly the same, even though we distinguish among them in other ways.

3. The dimensional models contradict any theory that requires each basic emotion to have a distinct physiological profile. According to dimensional models, the underlying biology of emotion is well represented by two or perhaps three dimensions rather than several discrete categories (Russell, 2003).

4. The dimensional models suggest that what people think of as "basic" emotions are psychologically and socially constructed, rather than evolved and universal. That is, the categories (such as "anger") we use to combine emotional feelings with other aspects of emotion are based on the stories we tell about human feelings, and the words our language provides to describe such feelings (Barrett, 2003; Neimeyer, 1995; Russell, 1991). Other cultures may tell different stories, and thus recognize different "basic" emotions. We will discuss this issue extensively in Chapter 3.

Emotions as Compounds of Underlying Processes

Another view challenges the existence of basic emotions. Some researchers disagree that any two dimensions are enough to capture the range of emotional feelings. In one study investigators found that they needed either three dimensions or four,

depending on whether they included surprise as an emotion (Fontaine, Scherer, Roesch, & Ellsworth, 2007). In addition to dimensions of pleasantness and arousal, these investigators proposed a dimension of control, where anger rates high and sadness rates low. Surprise differed from all other emotions in a dimension of unpredictability.

According to **Component Process Theory**, the appraisal aspect of emotion is particularly important, and what we might consider to be a basic emotion reflects a compound of more elementary appraisals. Consider, for example, the display of anger in Figure 1.14. Instead of calling this a single expression, we could analyze it as a combination of

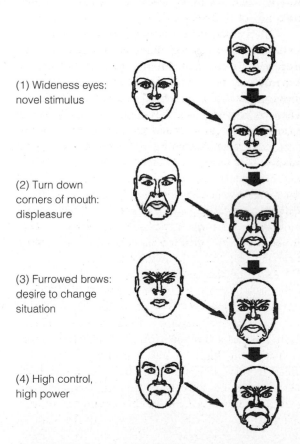

(1) Wideness eyes: novel stimulus

(2) Turn down corners of mouth: displeasure

(3) Furrowed brows: desire to change situation

(4) High control, high power

FIGURE 1.14 The expression we describe as anger could be a compound of several elements.

Source: Reprinted from K. R. Scherer (1992), What does facial expression express? In K. T. Strongman (Ed.), *International Review of Studies on Emotion*, Vol. 2 (pp.139–165). Chichester: Wiley.

at least four components (Ortony & Turner, 1990; Scherer, 1992). First, the widened eyes indicate that the stimulus is unexpected. This part of the anger expression is also a component of surprise and fear.

A second element is turning down the corners of the mouth. According to component process theorists, this movement indicates displeasure, which also occurs in sadness and disgust. Third, the furrowed brows indicate a desire to change the situation. People often furrow their brows when they are frustrated or concentrating, as well as when they're angry. Fourth, the tightened lips indicate a sense of control. That movement is characteristic of anger, but also contributes to the expression of pride—another emotion that involves feelings of power and control (Shiota, Campos, & Keltner, 2003).

The key point is that what we call anger could be a compound of several appraisal components, each pertaining to a different aspect of the situation. A given situation might involve just one or more of these components. Even when a situation does involve several components, they develop in sequence, not all at once (Grandjean & Scherer,

2008). When all components occur, we recognize a clear example of anger, but "parts" of anger can arise without the full profile. Furthermore, some of the components of anger could combine with other components to make different emotions, which we might describe as frustration, determination, surprise, and so forth. Similarly, we could describe fear or any other emotion as a compound of several components.

The component approach to emotion may seem unfamiliar because we are in the habit of thinking about prototypical examples of fear or anger, where all the components are present. However, from a research standpoint, the component approach has much potential. Instead of studying what causes "anger" in general, we could analyze the causes of different components: What causes the element of unexpectedness? What leads to the feeling of displeasure? What influences our perception of control over the situation? If different components of anger have different causes, we will understand them better by studying them separately.

SUMMARY

What have we learned so far? Emotion is complex, elusive, and hard to define. Many psychologists define emotion in terms of four major aspects—cognitions/appraisals, feelings, physiological responses, and behaviors. Ordinarily, an emotion-producing event is cognitively appraised, and the appraisal leads to physiological responses and a readiness for behavior. The feeling aspect of emotion is closely related to feedback from the body. In some cases the feelings and behaviors go on to influence later appraisals. Although these four aspects of emotion are thought to "hang together" most of the time, they don't always do so. As a result, controversy persists about which aspects of emotion are most important, and whether the structure of emotion consists of a few basic emotions or continuous dimensions.

You may notice that we raised a lot of big questions in this chapter, and didn't give many answers. Welcome to emotion research. Emotion is an exciting field—many of the big questions are still being addressed, and researchers are actively debating all of these issues. The different perspectives are important, because different perspectives lead us to ask different kinds of research questions, all of which help us understand emotion better. We hope that you will try to keep an open mind about these issues as you work your way through this text, and consider all of the evidence. Perhaps you'll think of a way to integrate perspectives that have been treated as distinct or opposing in the past. At the end of the text, we hope you'll be able to answer the question "what is emotion?" in a way that satisfies you, while knowing that the question itself is very complex.

KEY TERMS

appraisal: how a person interprets the meaning of a situation, with implications for whether an emotion is felt, and if so what emotion (p. 5)

basic emotions: emotion categories such as "fear" and "anger" that are thought to be fundamentally distinct, universal, adaptive responses to particular kinds of threats and opportunities (p. 25)

Cannon-Bard theory: view that the cognitive experience of emotion, occurring in the cerebral cortex, is independent of the arousal and other actions of the muscles and glands, even though the cognitive experience occurs at the same time as the actions (p. 14)

circumplex model: theoretical model that emphasizes positive-negative valence and degree of arousal as the key aspects of emotional experience; when arranged according to this model, emotions form a circle (p. 28)

Component Process Theory: idea that what we typically consider an emotion consists of underlying elements that could be combined in different ways (p. 29)

core affect: a way of describing the feeling aspect of emotion, that emphasizes the dimensions of pleasantness and arousal (p. 28)

drives: motivations such as hunger and thirst that arise from the body's needs, rather than an external situation (p. 4)

ecological validity: extent to which what happens in a study reflects what really happens in everyday life (p. 11)

electroencephalography (EEG): procedure in which the researcher pastes electrodes on someone's scalp to measure momentary changes in the electrical activity under each electrode (p. 10)

evaluative space model: a model of attitudes, proposing that evaluations of some target's "goodness" and "badness" are independent rather than opposites (p. 28)

functional magnetic resonance imaging (fMRI): procedure that measures brain activity based on changes in oxygen uptake (p. 10)

James-Lange theory: view that emotions (especially the feeling aspects of emotions) are the labels we give to the way the body reacts to certain situations (p. 13)

locked-in syndrome: condition in which people lose almost all output from the brain to both the muscles and the autonomic nervous system, although they continue to receive sensations (p. 19)

parasympathetic nervous system (PNS): branch of the nervous system that increases maintenance functions that conserve energy for later use and facilitates growth and development (p. 9)

pure autonomic failure: medical condition in which the autonomic nervous system ceases to influence the body (p. 19)

reliability: the repeatability of the results of some measurement, expressed as a correlation between one score and another (p. 7)

Schachter-Singer theory: view that the arousal and other actions that are part of any emotion are essential for determining how strong the emotional feeling will be, but they do not identify the emotion; you identify which emotion you feel on the basis of all the information you have about a situation (p. 15)

sympathetic nervous system (SNS): branch of the nervous system that readies the body for "fight-or-flight" emergency actions (p. 9)

validity: whether a test measures what it claims to measure (p. 8)

THOUGHT QUESTIONS

1. Each chapter will offer one or more "thought questions," designed for you to contemplate and perhaps discuss in class. In each case, we do not believe the evidence to date offers a "right" answer. We hope you will consider not only what would be a good answer, but also what research would help improve our ability to answer each question.

   We have proposed different definitions of emotion. Can you offer any way to improve on them?

2. Do non-human animals on earth have emotions? Their physiology is somewhat similar to ours (especially for other mammals), but they cannot tell us about their thoughts and feelings. How would each of the major theories of emotion answer this question?

3. Suppose we discover animals on another planet. They have an entirely different physiology from ours, but their behavior seems similar in many ways. According to each of the theories outlined in this chapter, is it possible to determine whether or not *they* have emotions? If so, how? If not, why not?

SUGGESTIONS FOR RESEARCH PROJECTS

At the end of most chapters, we shall suggest possible research projects that a student could conduct in a limited amount of time, with little or no equipment and no major ethical limitations. In this chapter, we have already mentioned two possibilities:

1. Measure people's ratings of the funniness of cartoons while they hold a pen between their teeth or between their lips, as described on page 22.

2. Ask people to adopt the postures described on page 24 and then describe what emotion, if any, they feel. If you have hypotheses about other emotions that might be associated with specific postures, try those as well.

SUGGESTIONS FOR FURTHER READING

Damasio, A. R. (2003). *Looking for Spinoza*. Orlando, FL: Harcourt. A well-known neurologist's discussion of the relationship between emotional physiology, feelings, cognition, and behavior.

Ekman, P., & Davidson, R. J. (1994). *The Nature of Emotion: Fundamental Questions*. New York: Oxford University Press. Major emotion researchers offer their answers to core theoretical questions about emotion.

2

The Evolution of Emotion

In Chapter 1, we asked whether a housefly has emotions. Although we don't know how you answered, you could quite reasonably have said "no," and most emotion researchers would agree with you. But let's move up the food chain a bit. Does a snake have emotions? How about a pigeon? A mouse? A housecat? A dog? A chimpanzee?

Obviously your answers to these questions depend on how you define "emotion." Since we couldn't give you an agreed-upon definition in Chapter 1, you won't be surprised to learn that researchers disagree about whether any non-human animals have emotions, and if so, which ones do and which do not. But if you said, "no way does a snake have emotions," and then were more inclined to say "yes" as the animals above got smarter and furrier, you'd be pretty typical.

Researchers adopting an evolutionary perspective on emotion believe that this says something important about what emotions are, why we have them, and how we can study them. Soon after developing his theory of evolution, Charles Darwin (1872/1998) noted that the expressions of many animals and small children in emotional situations are similar to those of adult humans, and he proposed that emotional expressions are part of our evolutionary heritage (see Figure 2.1). Since Darwin's time, psychologists have debated the role of evolutionary processes in producing the emotions experienced by modern humans. For many psychologists, thinking of emotions as adaptations has strong implications for the kinds of research questions that they ask. Both of the definitions we presented in Chapter 1 proposed that emotions are functional in the evolutionary sense—that at some time far in the past individuals with emotions were more likely to pass their genes on to future generations than individuals without emotions, so over time genes that enable emotions spread through the population. If we think of emotions in terms of their functions, we can generate specific predictions about the effects of those emotions in several domains.

In Chapters 7–11 we will consider the possible adaptive functions of several specific emotions, and we'll examine research emerging from these functional

Spencer Arnold/Getty Images

FIGURE 2.1 Charles Darwin first developed the idea of natural selection after traveling around the world on the ship H.M.S Beagle. During that five-year trip, Darwin was fascinated by the similarities and differences he saw among animals living on different islands. His theory of natural selection which grew into the theory of evolution was an attempt to make sense of these similarities and differences.

accounts. In this chapter, we will introduce the broad principles of an evolutionary approach to emotion, and we'll consider implications of this approach for how we define and study emotions. We will explain what it means to posit that emotions are functional in the evolutionary sense, and we will contrast two ways in which emotions can be adaptive—by helping the individual survive and thrive, and by facilitating the relationships on which humans (and many other species) depend. We will also examine some of the evidence regarding one of the main predictions of an evolutionary perspective,

that at least certain aspects of emotion should be universal throughout the human species.

AN EVOLUTIONARY PERSPECTIVE ON EMOTION

When we talk about an "evolutionary perspective," what does that actually mean? Although scientists consider the evidence supporting evolutionary theory to be overwhelming, the basic tenets and implications of this theory are commonly misunderstood. Let's clear up some basics, and then turn to implications for emotion.

Basic Principles of Evolutionary Theory

Our story starts with genes. Genes are lengths of DNA—deoxyribonucleic acid—that each person inherits from her parents (Figure 2.2.a). Each gene is like a recipe, describing the ingredients and cooking instructions for a protein used by your body. You can think of your whole genome as a cookbook describing how your body should be put together, or if you're more mechanically inclined, as an instruction manual for do-it-yourself furniture.

An interesting point—when Darwin developed the theory of evolution, he didn't know about genes! The chemical structure of DNA, and its role in heredity, were not understood until the 1950s. Darwin knew there must be some way that traits were passed down from parents to their offspring, but he had no idea how this took place. It wasn't until the 1920s and 1930s that biologists combined Darwin's idea of natural selection with Gregor Mendel's research on the inheritance of traits, and started looking for some kind of physical substance that would explain both. The subsequent research on DNA allowed for Darwin's and Mendel's theories to be combined into modern evolutionary theory.

Chromosomes—long strands of DNA with many genes—come in pairs. In sexual reproduction,

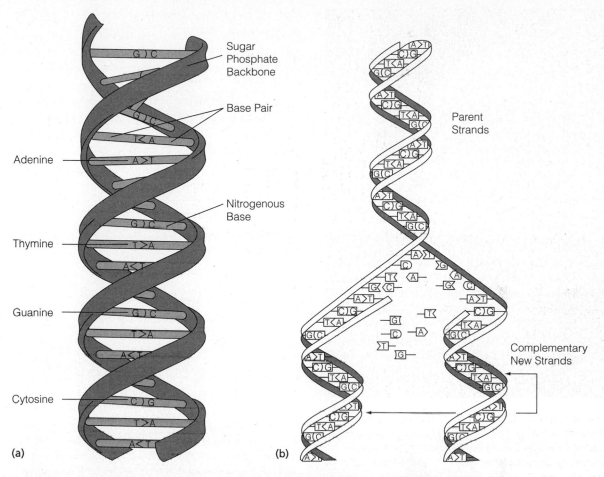

F I G U R E 2.2 Genes are units of Deoxyribonucleic Acid or DNA that provide assembly instructions for how your body should be put together. (a) The double-helix structure of DNA was discovered by James Watson, Francis Crick, Rosalind Franklin, and Raymond Gosling in 1953. (b) In the process of reproduction, strands of parents' DNA are copied via a process called replication. When a copying error takes place during DNA replication, a mutation occurs.

chromosomes are copied from parents in a process called replication (Figure 2.2.b), and then recombined so that each individual ends up with a half-copy of the mother's genes and a half-copy of the father's genes. Thus for each gene, you could have two copies alike, or two different versions (called *alleles*). A traditional example of a genetic effect is eye color. Someone with two genes for blue eyes will have blue eyes, and someone with two genes for brown eyes will have brown eyes. Someone with one of each type will have brown eyes. We say therefore that the gene for brown eyes is dominant. This is a

nice, simple example, but a bit misleading, because most of the characteristics that psychologists care about—such as personality, intelligence, or a predisposition to mental illness—depend on many genes and many environmental influences. Furthermore, many aspects of the environment—such as exposure to stressful experiences or prolonged inhaling of cigarette smoke—can alter the effect of genes, turning some on and turning others off (Launay et al., 2009; Tsankova, Renthal, Kumar, & Nestler, 2007). Genetics is a far more complex field than we once thought.

Sometimes the gene-copying process goes awry, and the copy is a bit off, just by chance. This is called a mutation. Some mutations are a real problem—they mess up a process that is so important, that survival is impossible and the genes aren't passed on to the next generation. To stay with our cooking analogy, if the cook forgets to put baking soda into a recipe for chocolate chip cookies, they won't rise, and they will be hardly edible. Other mutations don't make much difference. If walnuts are left of out a chocolate chip cookie recipe, the cookies will taste different, but still good.

Occasionally a mutation leads to an improvement, just as accidentally adding a bit more vanilla to the cookies might make them taste better than if the recipe were followed exactly. Maybe a mutation makes the muscles a little more efficient, so the next time you are facing a predator, you can run away faster and have a better chance of surviving than anyone else. Maybe the mutation makes neurons communicate with each other more efficiently, so this person is a little smarter than everyone else, and thus catches more food, attracts better mates, and so on. When this happens, there's a good chance that this person will have more offspring than someone without that mutation, so this version of the gene (which is passed on to the kids) becomes a bit more common in the next generation. If this keeps up, that mutation ends up in more and more people, until sometime down the road, almost everyone has it.

That's it. To recap, **natural selection** is the process by which random genetic mutations that happen to be problematic are removed from the population (because they cause the individuals with them to die or under-reproduce), whereas mutations that happen to be beneficial spread through the population (because they cause the individuals with them to have more offspring or to take better care of their relatives, who share their genes). Beneficial characteristics that spread as a result of natural selection are called **adaptations**. Once the genes for an adaptation spread throughout the population that adaptation tends to persist. Evolution is very conservative—only a new mutation that happens to improve upon the previous version will replace what's already there, and even that will spread through the population very, very slowly in most cases. Of course, if the environment changes so that a previously helpful adaptation becomes harmful, natural selection will start to remove the gene for it.

As we noted in Chapter 1, many psychologists' definitions of emotion emphasize that emotions are functional. From an evolutionary perspective, the term "functional" has a very specific meaning. A gene-based characteristic (whether it's a physical feature or a behavior) is functional if it meets one or more of the following criteria:

(1) The characteristic increases the probability that you will survive long enough to reproduce.

(2) The characteristic increases the probability that you will have more offspring than the next guy, and these offspring survive and reproduce.

(3) The characteristic increases the probability that your relatives will survive and have more offspring. For example, if your genes prompt you to take better care of your relatives, you help them pass on their genes, which are mostly the same as your own. By helping them survive and reproduce, you indirectly spread your own genes.

This is a very strict definition of "functional." A characteristic is not functional because it makes you happy, or because it makes you feel good about yourself, or because it makes you a better person. These effects are great, of course, but from an evolutionary perspective a characteristic is functional only if it leads to increased representation of your genes in future generations.

This has been the source of much confusion! When scientists propose that some characteristic is functional, they are *not* necessarily arguing that it is desirable, or morally right. A gene that made you happy, rich, and sterile would be extremely disadvantageous, from an evolutionary standpoint. A gene that helped you produce many children (who were healthy enough to survive) would be adaptive in the evolutionary sense, even if it seemed undesirable in other regards. In such cases it is helpful to explore the mechanism by which some characteristic is "adaptive." Understanding the adaptive function of an otherwise undesirable characteristic can even help researchers study ways to alter its expression, so that it doesn't interfere with the other goals that are important to people.

Also, if we're proposing that some characteristic is an adaptation, it doesn't necessarily mean that characteristic is functional *now*. The characteristic would have been functional in its **Environment of Evolutionary Adaptedness (EEA)**, the time and place in the past when that characteristic spread throughout the population due to natural selection. Functionality during a characteristic's EEA is enough to explain why it would have spread through the population, even if its effects seem neutral or harmful now.

For example, humans really, really like fatty foods (mmm, cheeseburger!). We know there's a genetic basis for liking fatty foods, and it's an important adaptation. After all, throughout most of the history of life highly nourishing food has been scarce. You never knew when you'd go hungry for a while, so storing energy in the form of fat was a good plan. In that environment, fatty foods—which contain many calories per unit of volume—were precious resources, to consume whenever you got the chance. It's only in recent years, when a high-fat meal is as close as the fast food restaurant on the next block, that our love of fat has become a health problem. Liking the taste of fats was adaptive in the EEA in which this characteristic evolved, but it may be harmful in modern, resource-rich societies.

This is the end of the detour into the basics of evolutionary theory. Now we can see how all this applies to emotion.

Emotions as Adaptations

To return to our original question, what does it mean to say that emotions evolved? When researchers say this, they are proposing that emotions are adaptations. Thus:

- Emotions have some basis in our genes;
- The genes needed for us to experience emotions started out as random mutations long ago;

- On average, individuals with emotions had more offspring than individuals without emotions, and/or took better care of their genetic relatives in such a way that their relatives had more offspring;
- Because of this process of natural selection, the genes supporting emotions spread through future generations to become typical of the whole population.

The proposal that emotions are adaptations has huge implications for how we define and study them. One implication would be that emotions are part of human nature—that at least some aspects of emotion are shared by people everywhere. It is possible for a characteristic to be an adaptation, while *not* being a human universal. For example, people in many tropical areas of Africa and Asia evolved genes for sickle-shaped blood cells, because these cells are malaria-resistant. Unfortunately sickle-shaped blood cells also break easily, so if malaria isn't a problem where you live, they're not so great. Even in malaria-infested areas, having one gene for sickle cell is helpful, but having two is fatal. Thus, sickle-cell anemia is an adaptation only seen in a small proportion of humans. However, researchers taking an evolutionary perspective generally propose functions that are relevant for all humans to some degree, so emotions are expected to be universal.

If emotions are the product of natural selection, then we have to consider the possibility that other animals have them as well. Remember that evolution is conservative. If some emotion evolved in an ancestor we share with other animals, then we probably have that emotion too. We share many features with other animals because of shared evolutionary history—like all female mammals, human women produce milk to feed their infants, and like most other primates people have opposable thumbs that allow us to pick up objects easily. The functions proposed for some emotions are relevant to other animals as well as humans, and these emotions could have ancient roots. If the function of fear is to help you escape from predators (Öhman & Mineka, 2003), then fear would be adaptive for any animal that could become some other animal's lunch—in other words, almost all animals. If the function of pride is to claim high status within one's group (Shariff & Tracy, 2009), then we should see pride in group-living animals with a social hierarchy, but not solitary animals. If we inherited the same mechanisms for emotion as did some other animals, this means that animals are fair game (so to speak) for research. As we shall see, this has led to a lot of interesting work.

The proposal that emotions are adaptations need *not* imply that every emotion is functional in every situation. You may be asking yourself, "If emotions are adaptive, why do people do such stupid things when they're angry?" This is a good question! From an evolutionary perspective, saying that some characteristic is adaptive is saying that *in the EEA* that characteristic led to increased representation of one's genes in future generations, *on average*. Researchers have proposed that the function of anger is to reclaim something that has been taken from you, whether that thing is a physical object or something intangible like power or respect (Lazarus, 1991). Anger typically makes us want to threaten the person who offended us. In the modern world, where the offense is often trivial and we have weapons at our disposal to seriously hurt people (guns, cars, etc.), we can do damage that is way out of proportion to the original offense, and either get hurt ourselves or end up in prison. Neither of these outcomes is great for fitness. However, anger presumably evolved during a time when offenses like stealing food or disrespecting a person's place in society could threaten survival and chances of reproducing. In this situation, on average, showing anger might have helped regain your possessions and reputation, so that people would know not to mess with you again.

Saying that emotions are adaptations also doesn't mean that emotions are exactly the same everywhere in the world. It is possible for an adaptation to be universal, and yet to manifest differently in various cultures. For example, although humans evolved to like high-fat foods, different cultures satisfy this craving in different ways depending on what's available. In some cultures, such as the United States, red meat supplies a lot of fat. In other cultures dairy products meet this need, and in yet other cultures it's high-fat vegetables such as avocadoes, olives, and nuts. Dietary preferences vary so much from culture to culture you might easily think humans hadn't evolved any food preferences at all. Once this theme was identified, though, scientists were able to learn a lot more about the chemical structure of fats, and how people respond to them. The evidence for cultural differences in emotion is just as rich as the evidence for cross-cultural similarities, so something similar is probably going on.

Also, some aspects of our emotions could be universal without actually being adaptive. A single mutation typically has several different effects. Some of those effects may be beneficial, some harmful, and some neutral. All that matters for natural selection is the average cost-benefit ratio associated with the mutation over the course of a lifetime (Tooby & Cosmides, 2008). A characteristic that is neutral, but happens to be linked to a mutation that also causes some beneficial trait, is going to get carried along into the population as though it were adaptive. These characteristics are referred to as **by-products** of natural selection (Buss, Haselton, Shackleford, Bleske, & Wakefield, 1998).

For example, infants of all mammalian species share certain physical features—big heads, stubby limbs, big cheeks, and tiny noses—that adult mammals respond to with tenderness and caregiving (Figure 2.3; Lorenz, 1971). The technical term for this set of features is "cuteness"—we're not making this up. Mammals, including humans, are thought to have evolved emotional responses to cuteness, because those responses facilitate taking care of one's own offspring (Hildebrandt & Fitzgerald, 1979). At least in humans, these care giving responses are also easily elicited by cuteness in other species.

FIGURE 2.3 Although you may have a strong emotional reaction to these baby animals, the reaction is probably a by-product of natural selection rather than an adaptation.

Our emotional responses to kittens, puppies, and the like prompt the sale of millions of calendars and posters every year, not to mention a huge industry in products for pets. This doesn't mean that humans have a kitten-loving gene, or that loving kittens is adaptive in the evolutionary sense. These emotional responses are more likely to be by-products of responses that prompt caring for our offspring and young kin, who look a bit like kittens. In discussing any aspect of emotion from an evolutionary perspective, the possibility that it is a by-product, rather than an adaptation, should always be considered.

Emotions as Superordinate Neural Programs

The earliest psychological theories of emotions emphasized their evolutionary origins, and many modern theories still share this emphasis (Ekman, 1992; Frijda, 1986; James, 1884; Lazarus, 1992; Plutchik, 1982). The psychologist Leda Cosmides and the anthropologist John Tooby have taken the evolutionary approach a step further, offering a definition of emotion that reflects cutting-edge thinking in evolutionary psychology (Tooby & Cosmides, 1990; 2008). Their model of emotion is closely related to a few others sharing a strong focus on adaptive function (e.g., Levenson, 1999; Tomkins, 1962), and has become especially prominent in recent years.

In the simplest terms, the goal of evolutionary psychology is to understand human nature. According to Tooby and Cosmides (2008, p. 114), human nature is "the evolved, reliably developing, species-typical, computational architecture of the human mind, together with the physical structures and processes (in the brain, in development, and in genetics) that give rise to this information-processing architecture."

You're going to see a bunch of really long definitions in this book. Sorry.

The key part of this definition is "computational architecture of the human mind." This phrase emphasizes the information-processing aspect of the brain, an organ that is specialized to take in information from the outside world, process that information, and decide what to do about it. In this way the brain has much in common with a computer, hence the term "computational model." Like a computer, the brain exists to gather data and manipulate those data according to some established principles in order to provide output—in our case that output is behavior. This is just a fancy way of saying that our brains exist to help us understand the situation we're in, and decide how to act. This is not too controversial.

The question of where the information-processing principles come from is a bit more controversial. According to evolutionary psychologists, many of these principles (though by no means all of them) are part of human nature—they are encoded into our genes in such a way that almost everybody develops them. This explains the terms "reliably developing" and "species-typical" in Tooby and Cosmides' definition. Of course, we learn many information-processing principles as we go through life. For example, it's unlikely that we are born with a principle that says "green means go." People in the United States simply learn that cultural convention from such an early age that we don't even think about it any more. However, the evidence is growing that certain ways of processing information, including some aspects of language, person perception, causal attribution, and kin detection, are innate (Pinker, 1997).

What does this all mean for emotion? According to evolutionary psychologists, the brain is packed with many little information-processing programs, each serving a specific purpose. We seem to have such a program for detecting faces (Kanwisher, 2000), another for noticing when we've made a mistake (Hajcak & Foti, 2008), another for risk evaluation (Tooby & Cosmides, 2006), one for figuring out what other people are thinking (Baron-Cohen, 1995), and so on.…

Tooby and Cosmides propose that in certain kinds of situations, it is extremely important to coordinate all of these little programs in order to accomplish some major goal quickly and efficiently, and emotions serve this purpose. They define emotions as **superordinate neural programs** activated in particular kinds of situations with serious implications for fitness. The job of these superordinate programs is to activate any little programs (we'll call them "subroutines" from now on) that will help resolve the situation, and to inhibit any subroutines that would interfere with resolving the situation.

This is where the computer analogy becomes helpful. Let's say that you're on your computer, writing a term paper. You're probably using a word processing program. Given that the function of word processing programs is to help people write documents such as letters, essays, textbooks, and so on, it is useful for those programs to make sure you spell words correctly. When you open up word-processing software, it activates a spell-checker that is in your operating system (this depends a bit on your computer—just go with us here). The spell-checker is activated by other programs as well, such as web browsers and presentation software. However, the spell-checker is a waste of resources in accounting software, since you're probably working with numbers anyway. In this analogy, the spell-checker is the subroutine, which is activated by the word processing program, but is not activated by the accounting software.

Taking this analogy back to emotion, let's consider possible subroutines the human mind might contain. Some of these might be: calculate route to home; calculate route to place where you found your last meal; prioritize self-protection goal; prioritize caregiving goal; kin-detection algorithm; animal-detection algorithm; distance measurement algorithm; mating preference algorithm; eye-contact detector; physiological arousal mechanisms (which supply energy to your muscles); and physiological calming mechanisms. We could keep going, but you get the idea.

Let's consider a prototypical situation with powerful implications for survival and reproduction—you're walking through the forest alone, and you hear footsteps behind you. This is a great time to activate a superordinate neural program called "fear." First you need to find out whether you're really in danger. An animal-detection algorithm would be helpful here. You might be more biased toward interpreting some subtle image as a threat than you would if you felt safe and secure (Maner et al., 2005). If you definitely see a predator, you need to know how far away it is, so the distance measurement algorithm should be activated right away. In contrast, the algorithm for mating preferences is not useful at the moment, and should be inhibited. Your favorite sex symbol could flash a smile at you, but unless that person is carrying a handy weapon, you probably won't notice.

Certain memories should be activated, others inhibited. You may suddenly find yourself thinking about home and how to get there, or about people who have taken care of you in the past (Mikulincer, Gillath, & Shaver, 2002). You're probably not thinking about where you last had lunch—that is not a terribly helpful memory right now. Your self-protection goal will become very salient. Your kin-detection algorithms may kick in to help you decide which relatives you should try to assist, and who can fend for themselves (Burnstein, Crandall, & Kitayama, 1994).

If you are definitely in the presence of a predator, what should you do? Your options are to stay hidden and hope it doesn't see you; to run away; to fight it out; and to play dead. Which of these options is your best bet depends on the exact situation, and the superordinate fear program should help you figure out what to do. An eye-contact detector might kick in to help figure out whether the predator sees you (Carter, Lyons, Cole, & Goldsmith, 2008). If not, then staying very still is a good plan, and you may feel as though you were frozen in place. If the predator sees you, but is still far away (there's that distance detector), you'd better run. In this case, physiological arousal mechanisms will kick in to deliver extra sugar and oxygen to your muscles (Sapolsky, 1998). If the predator sees you and you are cornered, you'd better get ready to fight, and you may feel a powerful urge to attack. If none of these seem like options, your body may just give up and pass out, in the hope that this predator won't eat something that's already dead.

A few interesting points emerge from this way of thinking about emotion. First, you'll notice that in order to explain what we meant by "superordinate neural program" we had to focus on a specific basic emotion—fear. Tooby and Cosmides' model strongly emphasizes the discrete emotion approach, rather than the dimensional approach. In fact, in this model there is no such thing as "emotion" generally speaking; there are only separate superordinate emotion programs, each of which has its own properties. The superordinate program model is not totally inconsistent with the component process model described in Chapter 1, because different superordinate programs can "call up" some of the same subroutines. However, in the component process model all emotions are defined by the output of a common set of appraisals, which can combine in any number of ways. In the superordinate program model, different emotion programs may have some overlap in the subroutines they use, but each will also have unique subroutines, and there is only a small number of superordinate programs. Dimensional approaches are also compatible with an evolutionary perspective. These often emphasize the value of deciding quickly whether some event or stimulus is good or bad, and activating cognitive and behavioral processes that facilitate repeating good events and avoiding bad ones (Russell, 2003). However, the majority of researchers who emphasize an evolutionary perspective on emotions focus on discrete emotions.

Another implication of the superordinate program model is that no one aspect of emotion is the "gold standard" for measurement. According to Tooby and Cosmides (2008), emotion is not reducible to one single aspect, such as feeling, physiology, or behavior. Instead, emotions are defined as the entire package of effects elicited by certain kinds of situations, and serving an adaptive function in those situations.

Finally, the superordinate program model emphasizes adaptive function as a key part of each emotion's definition. Identifying the likely function of some emotion allows researchers to predict the situations in which that emotion should emerge, as well as its effects in many different domains (as we did above for fear). In the sections that follow, we'll consider two different types of adaptive functions that emotions might have.

INTRAPERSONAL FUNCTIONS OF EMOTION

In many theories adopting an evolutionary perspective, psychologists have emphasized the **intrapersonal functions of emotion**. The term "intrapersonal" means "within-person," so an intrapersonal function is one that directly benefits the individual experiencing the emotion. In the example we gave earlier, fear is functional because it helps save the life of the frightened person, facilitating that person's escape from a predator (or some other physical threat). Fear does this by changing things within the person, including cognitive biases, physiological conditions, and behavioral responses.

When the function of an emotion is intrapersonal, then the situation eliciting the emotion poses a problem for the individual's fitness, and the effects of the emotion within that individual increase the chance that she will behave in a way that solves the problem. The problem might be a roommate who steals your food. If you get angry, and reclaim the food, that solves the problem. Or perhaps the food has begun to rot, and would make you sick if you ate it. If you feel disgust when you smell the food, and don't eat it, problem solved. Of course, the process is more complicated than that. Between detecting the problem and resolving it lie dozens of more specific processes, including perceptual shifts, activation of relevant memories, biases in cognitive processing, and physiological changes, all of which facilitate an appropriate behavioral response (Levenson, 1999). But the idea here is that the behavioral response facilitated by the emotion *directly* resolves the problem, or at least has a good chance of doing so.

Many negative emotions are explained well in terms of intrapersonal functions. The most widely accepted explanations of anger, disgust, and sadness involve intrapersonal functions, just as for fear.

However, researchers came to notice that intrapersonal functions fail to account for a number of emotions, including positive emotions such as love and pride, and "self-conscious" emotions such as embarrassment and shame. This observation prompted researchers to consider another kind of function.

SOCIAL FUNCTIONS OF EMOTION

Although earlier in the chapter we emphasized how much humans have in common with other animals, humans also have some distinctive qualities. One of these is the extent to which we rely on each other for our most basic survival needs. Like ants and bees, humans are *ultrasocial*, conducting almost all of the business of life in highly cooperative groups (Campbell, 1983). Paleoanthropological evidence, as well as studies of modern hunter-gatherers, show that until recently the human way of life included acquiring food, raising and educating children, and protecting against predators and other threats using carefully coordinated teamwork among dozens of people or more (Eibl-Eibesfeldt, 1989; Sober & Wilson, 1998). Even now, in big, industrialized cities where one can go days at a time without talking to anyone, it would be impossible to survive without relying on hundreds of other peoples' efforts. Humans simply are not built to survive alone.

In other ultrasocial species, cooperative groups generally consist of closely related individuals. For example, in a bee colony nearly all bees are the offspring of the same queen. They are so closely related that from a genetic standpoint, they have more to gain by working together than by trying to fend for themselves. Among humans, though, typical groups include individuals who are less closely related. Moreover, throughout most of human history people spent their entire lives in a tribe of, say, a hundred people. If you break out in a sweat when you consider spending more than a week with your extended family, think about the implications this has for survival and reproduction.

The need to cooperate with many unrelated individuals over long periods of time poses interesting challenges. A number of researchers have suggested that emotions help solve these problems. Whereas some emotions serve intrapersonal functions, helping the individual to solve her own adaptive problems directly, the **social functions of emotion** support the committed, interdependent, and complex relationships among people that, in turn, help us to survive and pass on our genes (Keltner & Haidt, 1999; Keltner, Haidt, & Shiota, 2006).

Consider love. Humans feel strong emotions toward the people we depend on and who depend upon us—our families, romantic partners, children, and close friends. What on earth is the function of love? This question had emotion theorists stumped for a long time. Sure, it feels nice some of the time, but as we said earlier, "feeling nice" isn't a valid function from an evolutionary point of view. In a series of studies, Beverly Fehr and Jim Russell (1991) asked people to describe targets toward which they felt love, and to describe what "love" meant to them in that context. Fehr and Russell found that when people talk about loving someone, they typically mean that they are committed to that person's well-being. In this analysis, we might say that the function of love is to help build a sense of commitment in our important relationships, so that we're prepared to help each other out the next time a group effort is needed.

Even negative emotions may serve important social functions. Think about the last time you felt embarrassed. What function could embarrassment possibly have, other than making you miserable? We don't know what happened to make you feel embarrassed, but you probably violated a social convention. Maybe you slipped and fell in front of a bunch of people. Maybe you accidentally knocked something over. Maybe you burped loudly in public. Your display of embarrassment lets people know that you realize you messed up, you didn't do it on purpose, and you feel bad about what happened (Keltner & Buswell, 1997). This display makes people more inclined to like and trust you, ensuring that you won't be ostracized by the group for whatever weird thing you did.

In these examples, love and embarrassment have something in common. Both emotions help establish and stabilize relationships with other people in your community. These emotions may not directly influence your survival or reproductive output (although a well-timed display of embarrassment might protect you against a beating). However, sometime in the future, your survival may depend on the relationships that these emotional displays supported.

We have distinguished social functions from intrapersonal functions conceptually, but a given emotion can be functional in both ways. Earlier we described an intrapersonal function of anger—protecting your own resources against theft or vandalism. However, anger may have a relationship-building function as well. Not every episode of anger leads to a violent attack. Suppose someone close to you does something hurtful or offensive, making you angry. If you show that person your anger, he will realize what he has done. If he values the relationship he may apologize or find a way to repair the damage. At the very least, he can avoid repeating the mistake. These "constructive" expressions of anger can be good for relationships (Tafrate, Kassinove, & Dundin, 2002).

In summary, emotions can be functional (in the evolutionary sense) in many ways. They can benefit the individual directly, by promoting behavior that will solve a problem. Emotions can also benefit the individual indirectly, by supporting relationships with other people. Both types of function stand in stark contrast to the image of emotions as irrational, destructive forces, and explain why they play such important roles in our lives.

ARE SOME ASPECTS OF EMOTION UNIVERSAL?

There's one little problem with the evolutionary perspective on emotion. It's awfully hard to prove! When a researcher proposes that an emotional response is an adaptation with a specific function, how does she go about providing evidence for that claim? She can't go back in time and experimentally manipulate the conditions that supposedly led to the evolution of fear. She can't just show that fear involves the package of effects she predicts, because college students (the typical participants in psychology research) might have *learned* a cultural definition of fear starting in early childhood (Russell, 1991).

One kind of evidence used to support evolutionary models illustrates that some aspect of emotion is *universal*—that it plays out in a similar way wherever you go in the world. Just as Darwin invoked similarities between species of finches on different islands as evidence that they must have shared a common ancestor, finding a common psychological process in people throughout the world suggests that the process is part of human nature. Researchers have examined cross-cultural similarity in a few aspects of emotion, and their findings have had a huge impact on theory and research. The first of these findings goes all the way back to Darwin's initial observation about the similarity of emotional expressions in humans and other animals.

Facial Expressions of Emotion

After Charles Darwin developed his theory of evolution by natural selection, he became curious about the expression of emotional states (Darwin, 1872/1998). He had noticed similarities in the physical behaviors exhibited by animals of many species when they were threatened, angry, sad, or excited. For example, many species react to a threat by changing their posture to appear larger; birds raise their feathers and spread their wings, cats arch their backs and their hair stands on end, and primates stand on their hind legs and lift their arms. Darwin also noted that some of the most common human expressions of emotion occur in monkeys and apes as well (see Figure 2.4).

In his classic book *The Expression of the Emotions in Man and Animals* Darwin (1872/1998) argued that expressions of emotion probably evolved because they conferred some kind of survival or reproductive advantage on individuals who displayed them. For instance, animals that react to threats by making themselves look larger increase their chance of survival, because the change in appearance might scare off the attacker. In much of the book, Darwin argues that human expressions of emotion are also

FIGURE 2.4 Nonhuman primates have some facial expressions that clearly resemble those of humans and use them in similar situations.

© Eibl-Eibesfeldt

FIGURE 2.5 People throughout the world greet one another by raising their eyebrows, sometimes also slightly opening their mouths.
Source: Eibl-Eibesfeldt (1973).

the result of evolutionary processes that link us to our closest primate relatives.

Darwin recognized that if facial expressions were inherited from primate ancestors, they should be the same in all human cultures. He lived in an era, the mid-1800s, when photography was awkward and expensive, so he had to test his hypothesis by relying on written reports from missionaries and others who had traveled to other continents. Darwin wrote to anybody he knew of living in another part of the world, described "typical" facial expressions of particular emotions, and asked his correspondents if natives of that culture expressed each emotion in the same way.

Darwin's correspondents replied that people throughout the world show similar expressions of many feelings. When surprised or astonished, they open their eyes widely, and sometimes their mouths as well. When puzzled or perplexed, they frown. When determined, they frown and close their mouths tightly. When they feel helpless, they shrug their shoulders. Even some people who were born deaf or blind show these same expressions. When embarrassed, people use their hands to cover their face. Again, even people born blind do the same— amazingly, as they have never experienced what it means to see or be seen. People throughout the world also pout, mostly in childhood. (When was the last time you saw an adult pout?)

About a hundred years later, the Austrian biologist Irenäus Eibl-Eibesfeldt (1973) made extensive visits to remote cultures, photographing people's facial expressions. He too reported remarkable

similarities in the expressions across cultures. Eibl-Eibesfeldt recorded one expression that Darwin had not considered: People often exchange a friendly greeting by raising their eyebrows and slightly opening their mouths (Figure 2.5). Symbolically the gesture says, "I am glad to see you. I open my eyes wide to see you better." Throughout the world, the average duration of the expression, from eyelids relaxed to raised position to down again, lasts about a third of a second.

Darwin documented important similarities in the non-verbal gestures and expressions people use around the world. There were, however, some problems with his research strategy. First, consider the nature of the questions he asked his far-flung assistants. The question was not: "Can you describe the way people's faces typically look when they are astonished?" A typical question read more like: "Is astonishment expressed by the eyes and mouth being opened wide, and by the eyebrows being raised?" Darwin's correspondents simply said "yes" or "no." Today, most researchers would avoid such a suggestive question and let the correspondents describe expressions in their own words. Alternatively, they might offer a series of choices without implying that one is the correct answer. People sometimes agree with a description even if the description is not quite accurate, or if they are not sure, especially when it is clear what hypothesis the researcher is testing. Also, Darwin's question required that his correspondents infer people's emotions by some other means than facial expressions, and it's not clear how they did so.

In the early twentieth century, prevailing theories in the social sciences favored strong environmental influence, and Darwin's conclusions about emotion fell into disregard. By the middle of the twentieth century, ethnographic reports of cultural differences in expression had persuaded most social scientists that the whole concept of emotion must be socially constructed. In the 1960s, however, Paul Ekman and Carroll Izard returned to Darwin's proposal that people from different cultures should agree on the interpretations of a few, prototypical facial expressions, and went out to test this hypothesis.

The basic test was this. Imagine that you are one of the research participants. Someone shows you the six photos shown in Figure 2.6 and asks you to identify which one represents each of the following emotions: anger, disgust, fear, happiness,

sadness, and surprise (Ekman & Friesen, 1984). If you speak a language other than English, then the researchers would first get someone to translate those six words into your language.

Versions of this study have been conducted dozens of times, in countries all over the world. In some of the studies participants lived in small, isolated agricultural villages where they seldom encountered people from the Western world, and did not watch television or movies. In one case the participants had never even seen Caucasians before the researchers arrived in their village! Figure 2.7 shows the results, averaged across many studies and almost two thousand people (Russell, 1994). The light gray bar represents the proportion of times, on average, that non-Western observers chose the "correct" emotion word for the facial expression of

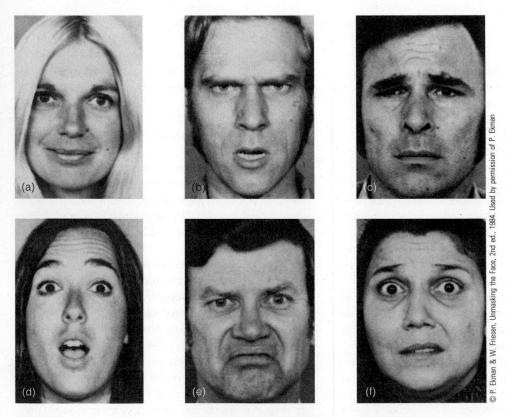

© P. Ekman & W. Friesen, Unmasking the Face, 2nd ed., 1984. Used by permission of P. Ekman

FIGURE 2.6 People in many cultures have been asked to identify which face goes with which emotion: anger, disgust, fear, happiness, sadness, and surprise.

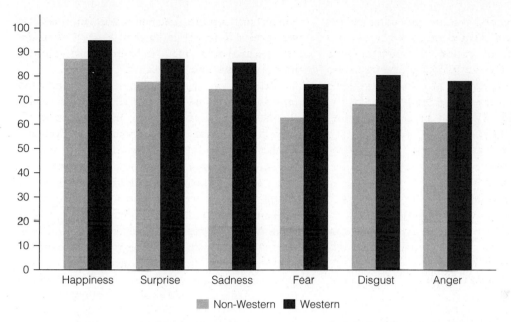

FIGURE 2.7 Mean accuracies for pairing the expressions in Figure 2.6 with their labels.
Source: Based on data of Russell (1994).

an emotion. The black bar represents the corresponding statistic for Western participants. Random guessing would produce 1/6 to 1/3 correct for each emotion (depending upon the exact study), and clearly people did better than that. Even though the photographs were of people of European ancestry, people from other societies throughout the world identified most of the expressions correctly. These findings strongly suggest that most people throughout the world give similar interpretations to certain facial expressions of emotion. To some extent, people recognize expressions from their own ethnic group better than those of outsiders (Elfenbein & Ambady, 2002).

Like Darwin's original study, this study has limitations. One is that the photos were carefully posed to be extremely strong examples of six facial expressions. With such photos, recognition accuracy is high (Tracy & Robins, 2008). However, in everyday life we seldom encounter such complete expressions. Most expressions show a mixture of emotions, and sometimes people try to hide their emotions. With everyday expressions, our accuracy of identifying emotions is less impressive (Naab & Russell, 2007).

Another problem is that the matching procedure probably overestimates people's accuracy (Russell, 1994). When you look at Figure 2.6, presumably you identify face (a) as happy. Almost everyone does. Now you are left with five faces to pair with five labels. Suppose you are unsure whether face (d) represents surprise or fear. If you decide that face (f) is a better expression of fear, you choose (d) for surprise. Suppose you have no idea what to call face (e). If you identify (b) as anger and (c) as sadness, you label (e) as disgust just by process of elimination.

One way to get around this limitation is to present photos one at a time and ask what emotion (if any) each face expresses. The difficulty of this method is that people sometimes give answers that are not exactly what the researchers expect (Ekman, 1994a). For face (f), the intended answer is "fear." Various people call this expression terror, horror, panic, or "she looks like she just saw a ghost." Presumably we would count all those answers as correct, as near-synonyms for fear. But what if someone called the expression "worry"? Is worry close enough to fear that we should consider it correct?

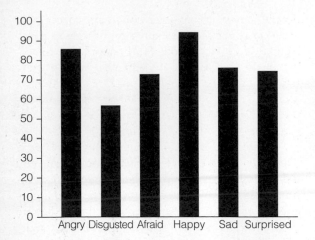

FIGURE 2.8 Accuracy of one group of college students in correctly labeling six emotional expressions. The students were not given the labels or any other suggestions about their answers.

Source: Based on data of Ekman (1994a).

A similar problem arises with the anger expression: Is the description "frustrated" right or wrong? Despite these difficulties, researchers find that people are reasonably accurate at freely labeling facial expressions, even in faces from other cultures, although they can match faces to given labels more accurately and more confidently (Frank & Stennett, 2001). Figure 2.8 shows the accuracy of one group of college students in free-labeling the emotions portrayed by six faces (Ekman, 1994a).

On the other hand, the typical procedures in many ways *underestimate* people's ability to interpret emotional expressions. In everyday life, we do not try to read someone's emotion entirely from a static facial expression. We notice changes over time, such as eye-blinks, trembling, shoulder shrugging, head turns, speed of walking, hand gestures, and direction of gaze (Ambadar, Schooler, & Cohn, 2005; Bould, Morris, & Wink, 2008; K. Edwards, 1998). We note people's posture (Van den Stock, Righart, & de Gelder, 2007). For example, who is more likely to be sad—someone who is slouching, or someone who stands erect? You might not recognize an expression of "pride" from facial expression alone, but with the addition of body posture, most people can (Tracy & Robins, 2004). Consider Figure 2.9. The facial expression is the same for both parts, but most people interpret the expression as sadness on the left and fear on the right, because of the difference in posture (Aviezer et al., 2008).

People can also assess someone's emotion moderately well from just hearing the tone of voice (Adolphs, Damasio, & Tranel, 2002), and they gauge emotions much faster and more accurately if they see and hear the person than if they just see or just hear the person (de Gelder, 2000).

From Angry, disgusted, or afraid? by Aviezer, H., Hassin, R. R., Ryan, J., Grady, C., Susskind, J., Anderson, A., et al. (2008). Psychological Science, 19, 724–732. Reprinted by Permission of SAGE Publications.

FIGURE 2.9 Posture is an important cue to someone's emotion. The same facial expression can look like sadness (left) or fear (right).

people almost always gaze down and to the side, and you recognize the expression of sadness partly from that head position. Furthermore, sad people cry. If you see tears, you assume the person is sad (although in some contexts you might interpret them as tears of joy). Without tears, the same expression may be hard to interpret, as in Figure 2.10 (Provine, Krosnowski, & Brocato, 2009).

In which direction do frightened people look? They look at whatever is frightening them. You will seldom see someone with a frightened expression looking straight at you, unless they are frightened of you! (Or, perhaps, something right behind you, in which case you should check behind yourself immediately.) Although people recognize an angry expression equally well in a face looking at them versus looking away, most people identify a fearful expression more easily in a face looking to the side, as shown in Figure 2.11 (Adams & Kleck, 2003).

In short, measuring people's accuracy at identifying facial expressions is complicated, and the

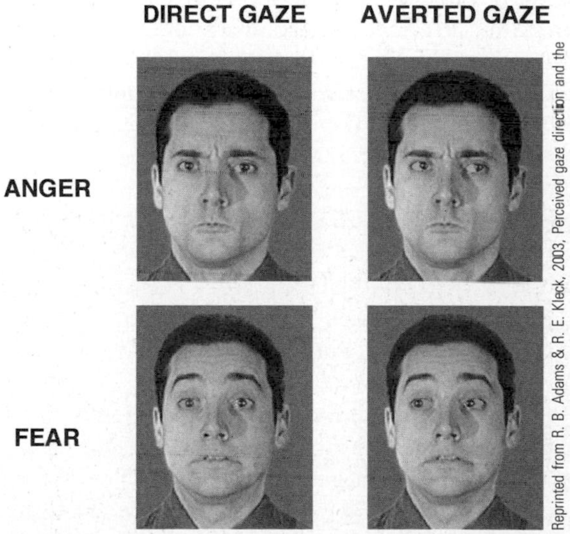

FIGURE 2.10 Tears identify an expression of sadness. Without tears the same expression would be hard to interpret.

Even when people listen to someone speaking an unfamiliar foreign language, they easily identify anger or sadness in the voice, and can also identify happiness, fear, and tenderness (Juslin & Laukka, 2003). Our ability to detect emotions from tone of voice is probably what makes it possible for music to convey emotion (Scherer & Zentner, 2001). Sometimes we even infer people's emotions from their smell (K. Edwards, 1998; Leppänen & Hietanen, 2003; Zhou & Chen, 2009).

The task in Figure 2.6 is artificial in another way also. Notice that the researchers posed all the faces to look directly at you. In real life, happy people look straight at you, and so do angry people, especially if they are angry at *you*. However, sad

DIRECT GAZE   AVERTED GAZE

ANGER

FEAR

FIGURE 2.11 How quickly can you identify these expressions? Most people identify fearful expressions more easily when the person is looking away than straight ahead. However, people recognize expressions of anger about equally well in either direction.

results vary depending on details of procedure. Nonetheless, it is clear that several facial expressions convey roughly the same meaning from culture to culture. Many researchers interpret these findings as evidence that humans have a few innate, universal templates for producing and interpreting certain facial expressions. That conclusion supports the idea of emotions as a product of our evolution, and not just of our culture.

Appraisals and Emotion

If emotions are evolved adaptations, we should also expect to find cross-cultural similarities in how emotions relate to appraisals. Recall from Chapter 1 the idea that emotions depend upon cognitive appraisals—interpretations about events. From an evolutionary perspective, appraisals should be functionally related to the emotional feelings, physiology, and behavior that follow. For example, if you appraise an event as a physical threat, you should take steps to protect yourself, and you should feel fear. Researchers conducting cross-cultural studies on emotional appraisals typically ask two questions. First, do particular emotions accompany the same appraisals, or different ones, from culture to culture? Second, do people in different cultures apply certain appraisals to the same situations, or different ones? Said another way, do emotional responses to the same event differ across cultures mainly because we *interpret* that event differently?

The first question has been addressed by Klaus Scherer (1997), with the help of dozens of colleagues around the world. In his study, participants in 37 countries on 5 continents were asked to think of a time they felt each of the following emotions: joy, anger, fear, sadness, disgust, shame, and guilt. (These emotion words were translated and back-translated[1] to try to get the best word possible in each language). Then participants were asked to describe a situation in which they felt the emotion, and to rate that situation on several dimensions

indicating how they interpreted the situation. In this case, the term "appraisal" refers to the dimensions in the component process model, rather than categorizing the event as a discrete threat, loss, etc. The appraisal dimensions were: novelty/expectedness, pleasantness, goal conduciveness, fairness, responsible agent (self vs. someone else), coping potential (how much control the participant felt in the situation), morality, and relevance for self-concept.

Scherer then examined whether participants around the world associated the same patterns of appraisals with each emotion. Figure 2.12 shows the average appraisal pattern associated with each emotion by people in seven major cultural regions studied: Northern/Central Europe, the "New World" (the United States, Australia, and New Zealand), Asia (including India), the Mediterranean countries, and Africa. Each of these regions is represented by a line. When the lines are on top of each other, people in different regions offered very similar appraisal ratings, on average, for situations in which they had felt that emotion.

Overall, this study suggests that certain appraisal patterns are associated with the same emotions throughout the world. Across regions, similarities were much greater than differences regarding which appraisal pattern fits a given emotion. For example, people said they felt happy in response to an event that was somewhat expected, very pleasant, consistent with their goals, fair, and that made them feel good about themselves. We will go into greater detail regarding the specific appraisal patterns associated with each emotion in later chapters.

Although the similarity in the overall pattern of appraisals across cultural regions is striking, it is also interesting to note where cultural differences emerge. In terms of the dimensions, people in different cultural regions often disagreed about the role of morality in the appraisal of emotional events. Situations eliciting most negative emotions

---

1. The procedure for back-translation is that one person translates something from language A to B, and then someone else translates it from B to A, to see how closely it matches the original.

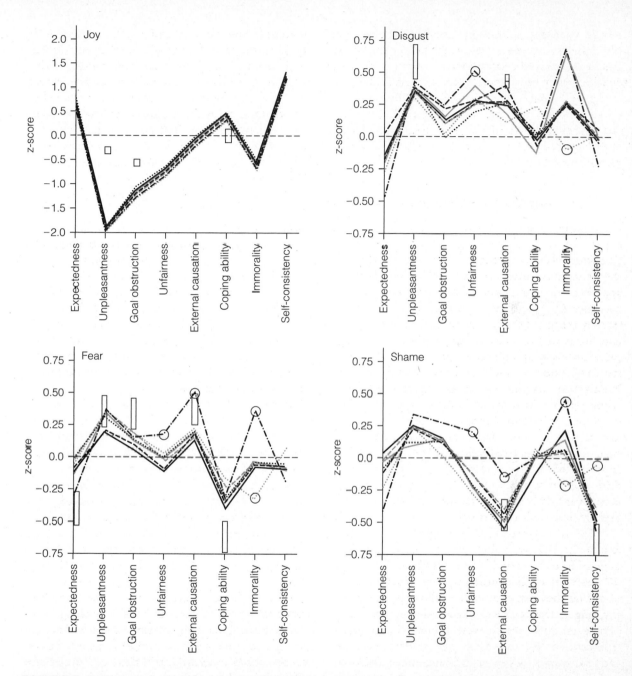

FIGURE 2.12 Appraisal patterns associated with the experience of seven emotions by people of major geographical regions in the world.

Source: From K. S. Scherer, "The Role of Culture in Emotion-Antecedent Appraisal," Journal of Personality and Social Psychology, 73, pp. 902–922.
© 1997 American Psychological Association.

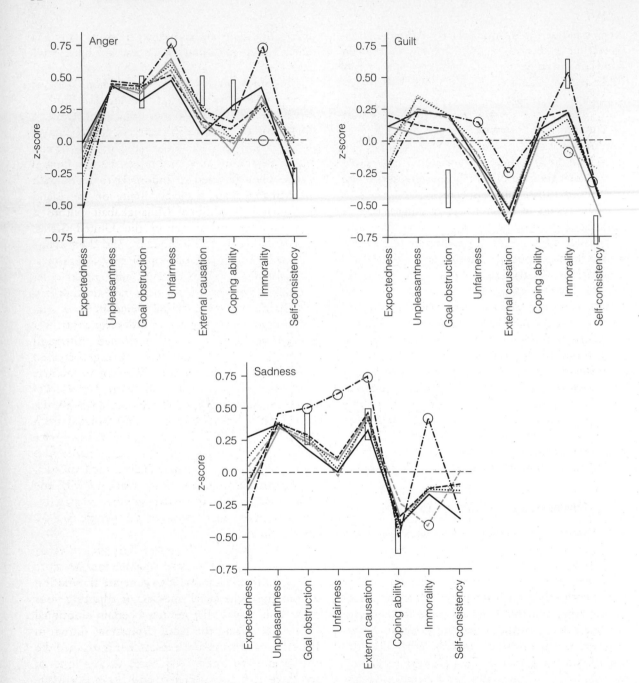

were rated as highly immoral by African participants, but were rated as more morally justified by Latin American participants, with participants from other regions falling at various points in between. Compare this with coping ability—participants from different regions gave nearly identical ratings of this appraisal dimension for each emotion. Perceptions of what is moral and what is not vary a great deal from culture to culture. These results suggest that the role of morality in emotion is also less universal than culture-specific.

The results of Scherer's study suggest that, as with facial expressions, the appraisal profiles associated with a few specific emotions are remarkably similar in most of the world. Just as with facial expressions, cross-cultural agreement is not perfect—people in different cultures agree more strongly about some appraisal dimensions than about others. Keep in mind that we do not know what actual events participants described. For example, participants thinking of a sad event may have reported appraisals of unpleasantness, goal obstruction, external causation, and low coping ability, but that doesn't necessarily mean they were describing losses, or that the situations were similar in any objective way. Further work is needed to study whether categorical appraisals and eliciting situations show comparable similarity across cultures.

Physiological Aspects of Emotion

If emotions are evolved adaptations, we should also expect people to be similar at the physiological level—the way emotions affect our bodies. The facial expression and appraisal studies described above both relied on participants' verbal responses to questions, and this is always cause for concern. On one hand, participants may try to please the researchers, giving "desired" answers rather than the ones they actually believe. On the other hand, participants who are unfamiliar with Western testing procedures may not understand what researchers are asking. Physiological measures are less vulnerable to either of these problems. Do people around the world show similar physiological responses

during the same emotional experiences? This is a difficult question to study, but a few researchers have tried.

In one major study, researchers Robert Levenson, Paul Ekman, Karl Heider, and Wallace Friesen (1992) asked whether participants from an indigenous community in Indonesia showed physiological responses in emotional situations similar to the responses of young adults in the United States. They traveled to Indonesia to work with the Minangkabau, a society living on the island of Sumatra. Traditional Minangkabau culture is very different from that of the United States. Residents live in the mountains, and their economy is based largely on community agriculture. The primary religion is Islam, and gender roles are strictly observed. However, the Minangkabau are also the largest matrilineal society in the world, meaning that property was traditionally controlled by and passed down through women. Although at the time of the study the Minangkabau had been visited several times by Western researchers (including Heider, who had learned the local language and developed a relationship with the community), they were still fairly isolated from the Western world. Despite heavy rains, power outages, and other problems, the researchers were able to study 46 Minangkabau men (cultural rules prohibited women from working with the male researchers), and to compare their physiological responses with those of 62 people in the United States.

In both samples, the researchers elicited emotion in a somewhat unusual way. Remember from Chapter 1 that it is possible to generate an emotion by moving your facial muscles, or adjusting your posture, in a way that mimics a certain emotional expression. Using the facial expressions shown in Figure 2.6 as a template, a researcher instructed the participants to make the facial expressions of anger, fear, sadness, disgust, and happiness while recording their physiological responses. Importantly, researchers did not use the actual emotion words in the instructions. Instead, they gave people instructions such as "wrinkle your nose" and "stick your tongue out a little bit." (Of course, the instructions were translated into the local language.) Although many people in both the United States and Sumatra did not have enough control over their facial muscles to produce the right expressions, the people included in the analyses were able to do so.

The results of the study are shown in Figure 2.13. The top row shows the average physiological changes while the Minangkabau participants posed each emotional expression; the bottom row shows data from the United States participants. We will discuss the various measures used in this and similar studies carefully in Chapter 4, and will also go into greater detail about specific results.

For now, the important thing to notice is the overall similarity between responses in the two samples. For example, in both groups, heart rate increased significantly while participants posed expressions of anger, fear, and sadness, but not while they posed disgust or happiness. In both groups finger temperature increased most while posing anger. A statistical analysis called multivariate analysis of variance, which allows researchers to compare two or more groups on several different outcome variables, did not detect a difference in the two groups' patterns of physiological responding across the five emotions and three physiological variables.

However, as with the facial expression and appraisal studies, there were some cultural differences.

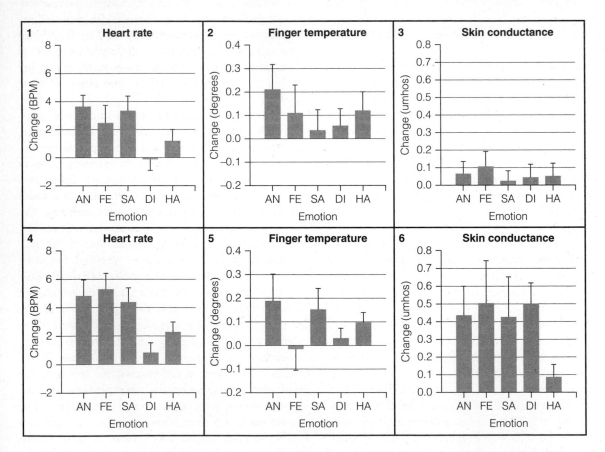

FIGURE 2.13 Physiological reactivity among Minangkabau and United States participants while posing expressions of anger, fear, sadness, disgust, and happiness.

You may have noticed that the bars in the top row of Figure 2.13 are generally smaller than those in the bottom row. Indeed, statistical tests suggested that the magnitude of responses during the facial expression task was smaller among the Minangkabau than among the Americans. This may be because the Minangkabau have smaller physiological responses during emotion, or because the facial expression task was less effective at eliciting emotion in this group—there's no way to know.

Another interesting difference emerged when the researchers asked the participants to describe how they felt during each expression. Americans reported feeling the target emotion most strongly on about a third of trials—not great, but more often than chance. Minangkabau participants reported feeling the target emotion most strongly on only 15 percent of trials, less than half as often. The researchers concluded that physiological sensations and facial expressions may be sufficient for an American participant to conclude that he is experiencing a particular emotion, but that Minangkabau participants are less likely to interpret their feelings this way in the absence of a reasonable emotion-eliciting situation.

These results are exciting, but the study did have some limitations. Researchers had to translate their instructions, and this always poses problems. Also, the Minangkabau participants had more trouble following the instructions than the American participants, and reported that the task was more difficult. Most important, asking people to move their facial muscles is a funny way to elicit emotions. These researchers tried using more traditional ways of eliciting emotions, such as asking people to relive emotional experiences, or watch emotional film clips, but the cultural and language barriers proved problematic. Thus, these results are promising, but far from definitive.

To continue exploring this issue, Jeanne Tsai and colleagues (2002) examined several aspects of emotional responding—including physiology—in two different cultural groups in the United States. One sample consisted of college students of European-American descent. The other sample consisted of students who were ethnically Hmong (pronounced with a silent h)—a distinct Southeast Asian culture originally from Laos. The Hmong students were either born in Laos or Thailand, or born in the United States to two parents born and raised in Laos. Hmong participants also had to be fluent speakers of both Hmong and English. (Language fluency is a common criterion for cultural affiliation.)

Each participant was asked to describe and try to relive experiences in which they felt happiness, pride, love, anger, disgust, and sadness. Participants briefly described a specific event in which they felt that emotion, and then tried to re-experience the event as vividly as they could. Throughout the study Tsai and colleagues measured participants' skin conductance—a measure of electrical activity that increases when people sweat. Tsai found that skin conductance increased slightly during all six emotions, and that these increases were similar between the European-American and ethnic Hmong groups.

It's best to think of these two studies as intriguing first steps on a very long and difficult road. Unlike the facial expression and appraisal studies, which each included dozens of cultures, each of these studies only included people from two groups. The two studies showed some similarities in physiological responding across cultures, but this does not constitute a full test of universality. Some researchers have proposed that if different emotions really serve different evolved functions and reflect qualitatively different superordinate programs, they should also have qualitatively different physiological profiles, and these profiles should be similar everywhere in the world. As we shall see in Chapter 4, this has been quite controversial, not just in cross-cultural research but even in the United States and other Western nations. We can say with some confidence that the physiological responses in emotion show similar patterns for a few emotions in a few cultures. However, a great deal of work must still be done before a claim of universality in physiological aspects of emotion can be justified.

SUMMARY

Emotion is an incredibly complex phenomenon, and yet some aspects of emotion seem familiar to everyone. If you have ever traveled to a very different culture, or read a book or seen a reasonably authentic movie about people from a different place, you may have been struck by vast differences in what people think and how they behave. Yet sometimes our emotional responses show us how much we have in common, with reactions to situations such as danger, loss, insult, reunion with a loved one, and the smile of a child highlighting what it means to be human.

To researchers interested in the evolutionary origins of emotion, the aspects of emotion that we share with people around the world, and even with some other animals, are extremely important. Emotional universals likely reflect ways in which emotions helped our ancestors survive and thrive over time. Understanding these functions allows researchers to predict and understand many specific effects of emotions that might not be apparent without an evolutionary perspective. An evolutionary perspective also suggests that in studying the emotions of other animals, we can learn a lot about ourselves.

Proposing that emotions have functions in the evolutionary sense does not mean that emotions are always good, that they are pleasant, that they invariably make us do the right thing, or that we should not seek to limit their effects in some situations. It also does not mean that people's emotions are exactly the same throughout the world. As we shall see in the next chapter, culture has tremendous implications for how emotion is experienced and expressed. However, an evolutionary perspective has helped researchers to organize huge amounts of information about emotions into some useful, consistent principles, and these principles have generated a great deal of important research.

KEY TERMS

adaptation: a beneficial, genetically-based characteristic that has become species-typical as a result of natural selection (p. 36)

by-product: a genetically-based characteristic that is neutral, but is due to a mutation that also causes some beneficial trait, and becomes species-typical as that mutation spreads through the population (p. 38)

Environment of Evolutionary Adaptedness (EEA):   the time and place in the past when an adaptation spread through the population as a result of natural selection (p. 37)

intrapersonal functions of emotion: ways in which emotions directly benefit the reproductive fitness of the individual experiencing the emotion (p. 42)

natural selection: the process by which problematic genetic mutations are removed from the population, whereas beneficial mutations spread through the population, because of the mutation's effect on reproduction (p. 36)

social functions of emotion: ways in which emotions support committed, interdependent, and complex relationships among people that in turn help us to survive and pass on our genes (p. 43)

superordinate neural program: a hypothesized neural "program" that coordinates the activities of many smaller programs, activating those that will be useful for the function of the program and inhibiting those that will interfere (p. 40)

THOUGHT QUESTIONS

1. What aspects of emotion do you think are most likely to be universal? What aspects should be strongly influenced by culture?

2. Can you think of a kind of emotional experience that is probably a by-product, rather than an adaptation? To what adaptation do you think that by-product might be linked?

SUGGESTIONS FOR RESEARCH PROJECTS

1. The evolutionary perspective suggests that humans share certain ways of expressing emotions with animals. Take pictures of your pet (or borrow a friend's pet) in different situations such as stalking prey (or a toy), seeing its owner come home, being scolded or punished, and just after eating, but make sure the picture doesn't include the situation. Ask people to try to guess what the pet is responding to in each picture.

2. To test people's ability to recognize emotional displays across cultures, rent a film from a different culture, in a language you do not speak. Then ask several people to watch it and record what emotion, if any, they detect at particular times. How closely do they agree? Does someone from that culture, who speaks the language, also agree?

SUGGESTIONS FOR FURTHER READING

Ehrlich, Paul R. (2000). *Human Natures: Genes, Culture, and the Human Prospect*. Washington, D.C.: Island Press.

Pinker, Steven (1997). *How the Mind Works*. New York, NY: W. W. Norton and Company.

Each of these books offers an accessible and engaging introduction to evolutionary psychology, considering ways in which natural selection might have shaped human language, cognition, social behavior, emotion, and even culture itself.

3

Culture and Emotion

According to an evolutionary perspective, as emphasized in Chapter 2, we have emotions because they help us to deal with universal problems related to survival and reproduction. Researchers who emphasize an evolutionary perspective look for universal aspects of emotion—ways in which emotion is similar among humans everywhere, and perhaps in other animals as well.

On the other hand, anthropologists find that people in various societies differ in how they experience, express, and talk about emotion. These differences have led many researchers to emphasize the **social construction of emotion**, processes by which cultures develop and communicate about emotional concepts. In Chapter 2, we suggested that the words "fear," "anger," and so forth might map onto complex, innate behavioral adaptations—evolved solutions to common problems faced by our ancestors. Researchers emphasizing the social construction of emotion propose that certain aspects of these and other emotions may be culturally defined rather than innate or universal. From this perspective, "basic" emotions can be thought of as stories our culture uses to make sense of our experience; other cultures may have other stories, and therefore may have different basic emotions.

At one level, the evolutionary and cultural perspectives might appear to be opposites, such that only one or the other can be true. There is, however, a way to resolve the conflict: Perhaps some *aspects* of emotion are evolved, innate, and universal, whereas other aspects are socially constructed in different ways by different cultures. Even if some of the underlying mechanisms of emotion are the same across cultures, the ways those mechanisms are expressed can differ dramatically. Remember the analogy to human food preferences—people throughout the world like the taste of fats, but different cultures emphasize different sources of fats, and different ways of combining the fats with other foods, so different cultures have very different cuisines.

Here's an example in the domain of emotion. According to research we examined in Chapter 2, the appraisal profiles and facial expressions associated with certain emotions are highly similar across cultures, suggesting that they may be influenced by human nature. If something pleasant and conducive to your goals happens, you are happy. If something unpleasant, externally caused, and unfair happens you are likely to feel angry. Happy people smile, whereas angry people frown and tighten their lips, and people throughout the world interpret these expressions similarly.

However, the way we interpret actual events depends on the norms of our culture and on our personal experiences. For example, if a large dog barks loudly at you, you could interpret the situation in one of several ways. If you think all dogs are dangerous and you feel unable to protect yourself, you might be frightened, and try to get away from this threat. If you think the dog is just badly trained, and the owner is not controlling it, you might feel angry. If you think of dogs as friendly pets and don't feel threatened by them, you might smile and laugh, while feeling affection or amusement.

This is where culture comes in. Any culture encourages certain interpretations of a situation and discourages others (Scherer & Brosch, 2009). Thus, the same event may typically elicit amusement in one culture, but anger or fear in another. Culture also sets standards for the emotions we should display in different situations—for example, whether it is acceptable to cry in public, or how much pride you can show before it seems like obnoxious bragging. In this chapter we discuss what it means to talk about "culture" at all, we ask how culture can have such a powerful influence on our understanding of the world, and we consider the implications of all this for human emotion.

WHAT IS CULTURE?

If you look up the term *culture* in a dictionary, you may find five to ten distinct meanings. Clifford Geertz (1973) complained that one article offered 11 definitions of human culture within 27 pages! To be fair, those 11 definitions had a number of common themes. Still, it helps to focus on a single definition.

A Definition and Its Implications

Here is a well-known definition, offered by the anthropologist Richard Shweder (1993, p. 417): **Culture** consists of "meanings, conceptions, and interpretive schemes that are activated, constructed, or brought "on-line" through participation in normative social institutions and practices (including linguistic practices) … giving shape to the psychological processes in individuals in a society." Yes, we know, that's a mouthful, but the idea is not as complicated as it sounds. Let's break it down a bit, and highlight some key points.

First, cultures are *systems of meaning*—ways of interpreting, understanding, and explaining what is going on in the world around us. Units of meaning are often represented in words—the labels we use to symbolize certain categories of experience. Some categories reflect real distinctions in the natural world, and we would expect almost all cultures to define them the same way. For example, the term *cat* refers to a particular family of animals (the *Felidae*), and even though a particular cat may be atypical in some way, virtually everything in the universe either is or isn't a cat. Other categories are more arbitrary, less clearly defined, and therefore culture-specific. For example, the English language distinguishes among bottles, jars, jugs, flasks, canisters, and other kinds of containers, but other languages draw more, fewer, or different distinctions (Malt, Sloman, Gennari, Shi, & Wang, 1999).

Language distinctions are only one example of how a culture expresses meaning. Think also about religious rituals, holidays, graduations, and marriage ceremonies. Consider several objects: the national flag, an autograph by a celebrity, or a monument commemorating a historical event. In each case something has a certain meaning or significance in the context of a particular culture's history and social structure.

Second, culture activates or constructs meaning *through social participation*. For example, in one class you might sit quietly throughout the lecture, while in another you discuss your own ideas and argue with others. How did you know to behave differently in the two classes? You might sit quietly during a symphony, but not sit at all during a rock concert. Again, why? In each case you learn largely by imitation. You watch what other people do, and you do the same. But according to Shweder, the behaviors also express how we are expected to think about these events.

Third, cultures *give shape to the psychological processes in individuals*. Shweder means that how we think about the world and behave in it depend on the concepts we have learned, and how those concepts relate to each other. For example, most Americans think of a cat as a "pet." Many less wealthy cultures have no such concept. They think of animals as food, workers, or a source of danger, but not as friends or members of the family. They would be baffled by the idea of "cat food." At best it would make no sense; at worst it would seem immoral to buy food for a cat instead of a needy person. Still other cultures have classified cats as holy beings, worshipped them and offered them the choicest food and shelter. To many Americans this degree of care would seem wasteful or even sacrilegious. In short, differences in concepts and meanings can translate into substantial differences in behavior.

CULTURAL DIFFERENCES IN CONCEPTS OF EMOTION

Cultural differences in the ways people think about, classify, and find meaning in emotion can be quite dramatic. If you and your classmates try to define "emotion" or list some typical emotional experiences, you will probably find that you agree, for the most part, on what the term means. If we ask the same question to people from some other culture, however, they may have quite a different answer. You may not even be able to ask the question in some cultures, because not every language has a word corresponding to "emotion" (Russell, 1991).

Even when a language *does* have a word that translates as "emotion," it might not refer to the same set of concepts that the English term does. For example, the Japanese term *jodo* includes "angry,"

"happy," "sad," and "ashamed," which are states that most American psychologists readily identify as emotions (Matsuyama, Hama, Kawamura, & Mine, 1978). However, it also includes states that translate as "considerate," "motivated," and "lucky," which would not classify as emotions in English. Keep in mind that these English terms are inexact translations as well. What the Japanese mean by "lucky" may not be what Americans mean by "lucky," so it is hard to say whether "lucky" in Japanese would count as an "emotion" in English!

Other languages have words that seem to correspond to the English word emotion, or to a particular emotion, except that they refer to the situation rather than the internal feeling that the situation produces. For example, the Fulani word *semteende* denotes a social situation in which an American would probably feel embarrassment or shame. The term is often translated as "embarrassment," but it actually refers to the situation and not how the person feels (Riesman, 1977). A better translation might be "embarrassing." The Ifaluk of the South Pacific also tend to emphasize social situations over internal states in their emotion lexicon (Lutz, 1982).

Here's another example. You walk into a friend's house, because no one has seen him in a couple of days and you wonder how he's doing. He seems droopy and lethargic, sighs frequently, and lowers his eyes. He says he doesn't really feel like doing anything. He also tells you that his girlfriend recently left town for a long trip, and he won't see her again for a while. In one word, how would you describe him?

An anthropologist studying life in Tahiti found himself in a similar situation (allowing for a bit of literary license), and drew the conclusion most Americans would draw—the man was sad because he missed his partner (Levy, 1973). The man himself, however, did not describe his state as an emotion, and in fact Tahitians don't have a word for what we call "sadness." Instead, he described himself as *pe'a pe'a*, which means sick, fatigued, or troubled. In short, he described his condition as an illness, not an emotion. Here we see the differences and similarities between the concept of illness in Tahitian and

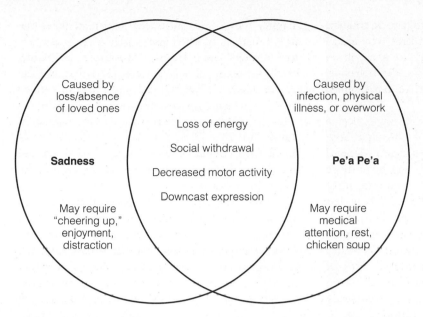

FIGURE 3.1 The conceptual territory of "sadness" in English corresponds closely, though not exactly, with the conceptual territory of illness or fatigue in Tahitian.

sadness in English. They have much in common, but belong in different categories. See Figure 3.1 for a visual diagram of the relationship between these words. In China, also, people often describe their reaction to a situation in body terms—"sick"—rather than emotional terms—"sad" (Tsai, Simeonova, & Watanabe, 2004). Even if the physiological and behavioral aspects of emotion are highly similar around the world, culture influences how we talk about our emotions.

It's easy to think of culture as something other people have, and to define culture in terms of how other societies differ from the American mainstream. However, our own concepts of emotion are shaped by culture as well. When you think about "love," what images come to mind, what stories, what memories? According to Ann Swidler (2001), people's answers to this question reflect their culture's network of meanings, ideas, and beliefs about intimate relationships. In her study, Swidler interviewed 88 middle-class Californian men and women of many ages. She asked these people what "real love" means, what their experiences with

love had been, where their ideas of love came from, what makes a romantic relationship good or bad, and so forth.

Swidler found that American culture promotes two distinct concepts of romantic love, and that the same individuals within our culture often struggle to reconcile them. One concept is the Hollywood, bolt-of-lightning kind of love that turns your world over in an instant and lasts a lifetime. As Swidler summarizes it, "They met, and it was love at first sight. There would never be another girl (boy) for him (her). No one could come between them. They overcame obstacles and lived happily ever after." In this image of love, the beloved is "the one," there is a feeling of destiny, of being meant for each other, and the beloved is completely irreplaceable.

The other concept of love is more prosaic and practical. This kind of love, often espoused by people who are skeptical of the Hollywood version, grows slowly over time rather than happening in an instant. The couple's story revolves around compatibility of personality, social connections, and activities, rather than obstacles to overcome. This kind of love does

Walt Disney/Everett Collection

(a)

Warner Bros./Everett Collection

(b)

FIGURE 3.2 Two versions of "romantic love" in middle-class American culture.

not require finding your one perfect mate. You may find many people with whom this kind of love has the potential to develop, given the opportunity. People who advocate this image of love say it is slow to grow, but deep and sure, whereas "Hollywood" love is flashy and shallow.

The important point, to Swidler, is that neither of these versions of romantic love is objectively more "real" or valid than the other. Both are socially constructed narratives, stories we tell about how romantic relationships are supposed to work, and what experiences and feelings should be involved. Many American movies emphasize the "love at first sight" version, but in societies where arranged marriages are the norm, and among Western couples who have been together for many years, people tend to talk more about the slow-growing, steady kind of love. Swidler also points out that many Americans include both of these concepts of love

in their worldview, and move back and forth between them as needed to explain their experience (Figure 3.2). The key point is that each of these ways of thinking about love is a social construction.

Do All Cultures Have the Same "Basic" Emotions?

Recall from Chapter 1 that one criterion for a "basic" emotion is that it should occur among people everywhere. The data we reviewed in Chapter 2 suggest a few possibilities, including sadness, fear, anger, and disgust; researchers are considering still others. A social construction perspective leads researchers to ask a different question, however: Are there emotions that occur in some cultures but not others?

There are certainly emotion *words* that exist in some languages, but not others. The English language offers more than two thousand emotion words, although most of them are seldom used (Wallace & Carson, 1973). Taiwanese includes about 750 emotion words (Boucher, 1979). The Chewong language of Malaysia only includes seven words that could be translated into English emotion words (Howell, 1981). However, the number of words in a language is not quite the same as the number of emotion concepts. English has many synonyms or near-synonyms for emotions (English dictionaries have accumulated more words than other languages for almost everything). A culture with fewer words could recognize and even discuss an emotion without having a word for it; for example, someone with no word for "embarrassment" could say, "the way you feel when you have made a mistake and others are staring at you." Still, to study cultural differences, one place to begin is to examine the emotions identified by one language and not another.

James Russell (1991) reviewed dozens of ethnographies that described the emotional lives of different cultures. He identified English emotion concepts that various other languages lack, and emotion terms in other languages that English lacks (Table 3.1). We have already mentioned one example: The Tahitian language has no word for sadness, so the Tahitian man whose family was away described himself as ill or fatigued instead.

T A B L E 3.1   **English Emotion Words "Missing" in Other Languages (Summarized from Russell, 1991).**

Sadness	Surprise	Guilt	Love	Anxiety	Depression
Chewong (Malaysia)	Chewong (Malaysia)	Chewong (Malaysia)	Nyinba (Nepal)	Eskimo	Chewong (Malaysia)
Tahitian	Ifaluk (Micronesia)	Ifaluk (Micronesia)		Machiguenga (Peru)	Eskimo
		Ilongot (Philippines)		Yoruba (Nigeria)	Fulani (Africa)
		Pintupi (Australia)			Kaluli (New Guinea)
		Quichua (Ecuador)			Malay
		Samoan			Mandarin
		Sinhalese (Sri Lanka)			Xhosa (Africa)
		Tahitian			Yoruba (Nigeria)

Many languages also contain emotion words that have no English counterpart. Consider the description of *litost* offered by Milan Kundera (1979/1980) in the *Book of Laughter and Forgetting* (pp. 121–122; edited version from Russell, 1991):

Litost is a Czech word with no exact translation into any other language. It designates a feeling as infinite as an open accordion, a feeling that is the synthesis of many others: grief, sympathy, remorse, and an indefinable longing…. Under certain circumstances, however, it can have a very narrow meaning, a meaning as definite, precise, and sharp as a well-honed cutting edge. I have never found an equivalent in other languages for this sense of the word either, though I do not see how anyone can understand the human soul without it…. *Litost* is a state of torment caused by a sudden insight into one's own miserable self…. *Litost* works like a two-stroke motor. First comes a feeling of torment, then the desire for revenge.

Litost is hardly the only example. English also has no equivalent to the German word, *schadenfreude*, meaning the enjoyment of another person's suffering (Leach, Spears, Branscombe, & Doosje,

2003). The Ilongot speak of the emotion *liget,* which, like anger, can be a response to insult or injury, but can also be evoked by mass celebrations, by a successful hunt, or by the death of a loved one (Rosaldo, 1980). Also unlike anger, *liget* is considered a positive force that contributes to society.

Another emotion that researchers often describe as culture-specific is the Japanese feeling of **amae**. This feeling has been described as pleasurable dependence on another person, like the feeling an infant has toward its mother (Doi, 1973). In Japan, one feels amae when one receives a gift, or is cared for, or is allowed to be dependent and childlike (even childish), without any obligation to reciprocate. It is a core characteristic of relationships between spouses, and among family and close friends.

In his description of amae, Doi (1973) says it is a foundation of the Japanese social structure, and that Japanese individuals expect this unconditional nurturance in their close and potentially close relationships. It shows up in many situations. Japanese people rely on social support for getting through a stressful experience more than Americans do (Morling, Kitayama, & Miyamoto, 2003). Japanese mothers talk with their infants more about relatedness than American mothers do (Dennis, Cole, Zahn-Waxler, & Mizuta, 2002). Japanese people define happiness and success in terms of interpersonal relationships, not in terms of individual accomplishments. That is, happiness relates more to intimacy than it does to pride or self-esteem (Kitayama, Markus, & Kurokawa, 2000; Uchida, Norasakkunkit, & Kitayama, 2004).

To many Americans, however, the concept of enjoying dependence on other people seems alien. Americans expect adults to take care of themselves without depending on others. Imagine yourself as a guest in an American home. Your host says there are snacks in the refrigerator and invites you to "help yourself." An American might like that message, interpreting it as an invitation to treat the host's home as one's own. A Japanese might take it as the slightly insulting message, "No one is going to help you!"

Is *amae* really a culture-specific emotion? Or perhaps a culturally defined situation for feeling a pleasant, loving emotion? Not necessarily. In fact, according to Doi, amae is a basic, universal emotion, but one that Americans refuse to acknowledge and Japanese may encourage too much.

The Sapir-Whorf Hypothesis

What, if anything, do these language differences mean for emotional experience? One extreme possibility is that without a word for some emotion, people cannot feel that emotion at all. This seems unlikely, however. For example, even without having an English word for *schadenfreude,* don't you sometimes enjoy seeing someone suffer? Never? Not even when a rich person is arrested for fraud? Not even when a political figure is caught in a scandal? Maybe you are a saint and never feel this way, but most people can relate to the concept, understand that it differs from other types of enjoyment, and are pleased to learn a word for it. Some researchers have now begun to study schadenfreude in English-speaking participants as well as those speaking German (Combs, Powell, Schurtz, & Smith, 2009). Similarly, Russell (1991) describes an Arab woman who was delighted to learn the word "frustration." Because her language did not include a corresponding word, she had never been able to label the feeling before.

Let's consider a broad, related issue: To what extent does emotion vocabulary reflect or limit the emotions we feel? Edward Sapir (1921) and Benjamin Whorf (1956) each proposed what came to be known as the **Sapir-Whorf hypothesis**: Humans require language to think, and therefore we have only those experiences, thoughts, and perceptions for which we have words. In the emotion domain, the consequence would be that people cannot experience an emotion for which they have no word. Or, according to a weaker form of the hypothesis, people might more readily experience or express an emotion for which they have a word than one for which they lack a word.

Researchers have tested the Sapir-Whorf hypothesis in many ways over the last 50 years, but have found little evidence for the strong version. For example, this hypothesis implies that people whose languages lack a word for the color green would be unable to see that color, or to distinguish it from, say, blue. This prediction is simply false. People do discriminate among colors even if they have no words for the differences (Ludwig, Goetz, Balgemann, & Roschke, 1972). Language may have a subtler effect: Perhaps the color words of a language influence how easily we remember colors or what boundaries we draw between one area of the color spectrum and another (Özgen, 2004). This research raises complex methodological issues, however, and researchers do not yet agree on the exact relationship between language and thought and perception (Heider, 1972; Roberson, Davies, & Davidoff, 2000).

A more subtle influence of language on perception, memory, or reasoning is consistent with Shweder's definition of culture, as discussed earlier in this chapter: Culture (including language) helps define the categories of experience we use to make sense of the world around us. It influences the ways in which we communicate our experience to others, but it does not restrict our perception of the world, and we may make conceptual distinctions that are not reflected explicitly in our vocabulary.

A study by Jonathan Haidt and Dacher Keltner (1999) offers evidence to this effect. Haidt and Keltner showed photographs of several emotional facial expressions to participants in the United States and in Eastern India, where people speak the Oriya language. The posed expressions included an embarrassment display (a smile with the lips pressed together, averted glance, and a face touch) as well as a photo of a person covering her face with one hand, suggesting shame. Researchers then asked participants to tell a story about what event caused the person to make each face.

As expected, American participants labeled one expression embarrassment and the other shame, and they described different situations in which each would be felt. But Oriya has only a single word—"lajya"—that combines the meanings of both embarrassment and shame. Accordingly, most Indian participants labeled both of the facial expressions *lajya*. Nevertheless, they typically said the person covering her face (in what Americans called shame) had probably done something wrong, or had failed at something. They said the person smiling and looking away (in what Americans called embarrassment) had done nothing wrong, but was the focus of awkward social attention, such as public praise or winning an award. These descriptions are consistent with the different meanings of shame and embarrassment in English (Tangney et al., 1996). The implication is that even though the Indian participants did not have separate words for embarrassment and shame, they still recognized the different situations that prompted different expressions. They knew the difference and could describe it, even if it was not explicit in the Oriya vocabulary.

Hyper- vs. Hypo-cognized Emotions

If emotion vocabulary does not define or constrain our emotional experience, what does it do? In addressing this question, Levy (1984) invoked his extensive field research on Tahitian life and language. The Tahitian language has 46 words for anger, yet not a single word for what we call sadness (Levy, 1973). After getting to know this culture, Levy concluded that Tahitians do experience sadness.

Levy proposed that cultures **hyper-cognize** emotions that are important in that society, creating an elaborate network of definitions, associations and distinctions, and leading to an increase in vocabulary. For example, the 46 Tahitian words for anger probably distinguish among different degrees of

anger: anger at someone in particular versus general irritability; anger at a fish that got away from you versus anger at the jerk who bumped into you while you were trying to catch the fish; anger that makes you storm home in silence (with no fish) versus anger that makes you yell at the guy who bumped into you, and so on. You get the idea.

Other emotions in a culture might be **hypo-cognized**, lacking much cognitive elaboration or detail. In Tahiti, sadness may be a "real" emotion in the sense that it is a coherent package of responses to loss or separation, but of so little social interest that it is lumped linguistically with illness and fatigue. The lumping of "unrecognized" emotions with other kinds of states is not totally arbitrary. For example, Tahitians are not entirely wrong in lumping sadness in with sickness, as the two states have much in common.

Cultural differences in emotion vocabulary do lead to a tricky methodological problem. How can researchers study emotions in different cultures, if the emotion words of one language don't translate into the other language? One solution is to try to understand the concepts beneath the words. For example, Usha Menon and Richard Shweder (1994) studied the Oriya Hindu emotion "lajya" (a concept combining shame and embarrassment, discussed earlier in the study by Keltner and Haidt) by asking participants to describe the meaning of a well-recognized facial expression of that emotion by the goddess Kali, a core cultural symbol. This approach allowed researchers to examine differences between the Oriya concept of lajya and the English concept of shame, as well as similarities between the two concepts.

What if researchers want to study a proposed "basic" emotion in some culture with no word for that emotion? In this case they can move away from emotion vocabulary to study whether the hypothesized emotion "packages," as described in Chapter 2, can be observed in the other culture. For example, if we wanted to study sadness in Tahiti, we might ask the following questions. When does one feel *pe'a pe'a*? How does one behave? What does one's face look like? The more these features of *pe'a pe'a* resemble those of sadness, the more confident we might be that the two words refer to approximately the same state. The more differences we find, the more we might suspect that *pe'a pe'a* does not really refer to sadness.

Even if sadness and *pe'a pe'a* showed serious differences, if we found that Tahitians reliably look sad, sound sad, have sad physiology, and act sad when a loved one dies, we might conclude that Tahitians experience a universal form of sadness, whether they have a word for it or not. Such research might also help us to understand which aspects of emotion are universal, and which more influenced by culture.

CULTURAL DIFFERENCES IN EMOTION PROCESSES

In Chapter 2 we considered some evidence that certain aspects of emotion may be universal. Emotions also differ across cultures in many important ways. Let's take a look at some of those differences.

Culture and Emotional Appraisals

Recall the study of emotional appraisals by Klaus Scherer, described in Chapter 2 (Figure 2.13). In that chapter we focused on similarities between different cultural regions in the appraisal patterns people associated with the experience of different emotions. The study also documented some cultural differences in appraisal patterns, however. One major difference involved the roles of fairness and morality in emotional appraisals. African participants were most likely to describe any sadness-eliciting event as unfair and immoral—an idea that sounds odd to most Americans, Europeans, and Asians. Think of it this way: You are sad when your dog passes away, but how does fairness come into it? In what way is the event morally wrong? In general, African participants rated the events eliciting most negative emotions as immoral, externally caused, and unfair. By contrast, Latin American participants typically rated events that elicited negative emotions as *less* immoral than participants from other continents.

Interpreting these differences among cultures is difficult, but we can imagine a few plausible explanations. Scherer notes that among all of the regions studied, those in Africa were the least urbanized, and the most traditional. Rural communities are often close-knit and interdependent, with strict conventions for how to go about daily life. In urban communities people of diverse experience and philosophy interact a great deal, but more superficially, so shared morality is not as crucial. It may be that rural communities depend more on shared morality to survive, so issues of fairness and morality may generally be more prominent in rural than in urban communities.

Also, Africa is the least powerful and most politically unstable of the six regions in the study. Although all of the participants in all of the regions were college students, and therefore relatively high-status within their cultures, their sense that negative events were outside their control might reflect a general sense of powerlessness and unpredictability. Because Scherer and colleagues did not measure appraisals of unemotional situations, it may be that these cultural differences in appraisal are not specific to emotions. Perhaps African cultures place greater emphasis on the immorality and unfairness of all situations, emotion-producing or not, whereas Latin American cultures are generally more likely to think of the world as morally right.

Importantly, the Scherer study did not examine the specific events that participants appraised in their descriptions of emotional experiences. One major influence culture can have on emotion lies in the meaning we attribute to various events. People in different cultures may appraise the same event in very different ways, depending on each culture's system of meaning. Think back to the example of being a guest in someone's home, and being invited to "help yourself" at the refrigerator. An American would probably interpret this as pleasant (an invitation to feel at home), fair (it is reasonable to ask you to get the food for yourself), goal conducive (allowing you to eat), and controllable (you can choose whatever you want). Thus, an American might feel happy in this situation.

By contrast, a Japanese might interpret the event as unpleasant (the host has just told you he will not take care of you), unfair (what did you do to be treated in this rude way?), uncontrollable (surely there are things in the refrigerator the host does not wish you to eat—how are you supposed to know what they are?), and goal obstructing (now you cannot eat anything!). Thus, using the same formula for converting appraisals into emotion, but appraising the event in a different way, a Japanese person might experience sadness or anger. Recently, some researchers have suggested that culturally-encouraged "biases" in emotional appraisal may help explain differences in emotional aspects of personality—the frequency with which people experience various emotions (Scherer & Brosch, 2009).

Cultural Differences in Expressing Emotions

The studies by Ekman, Izard, and their colleagues (discussed in Chapter 2) strongly suggest that people throughout the world interpret a few facial expressions of emotion in similar ways. At the same time, certain expressions are clearly culture-specific. The prototypical facial expression of *lajya*, the Orissa Hindu emotion described earlier in this chapter, includes biting one's tongue—not a commonly observed display in the United States (Menon & Shweder, 1994). Whereas clapping the hands usually indicates joy or delight in the United States, it suggests worry or disappointment in Chinese culture (Klineberg, 1938). In most cultures, people indicate "no" by shaking their heads back and forth, and "yes" by nodding it up and down. In Greece and Turkey, however, people typically indicate "yes" by tilting their heads back, and in Sri Lanka they express "I understand" by shaking their heads back and forth. In the United States, people often give a gesture of joining the tip of the thumb with the tip of the index finger to make a circle, to indicate "we're in agreement," or "OK." In many other cultures, however, that gesture is meaningless, and in some it is considered a vulgar invitation to have sex! These are just a few examples.

At the simplest level, cultures vary in the intensity of their facial expressions of emotion.

People in some cultures (such as the United States) tend to show very strong facial expressions, whereas people in other cultures (such as Japan) tend to show more subtle expressions (Matsumoto, 1990). Some researchers have suggested that differences in the intensity of expression are due to differences in intensity of sympathetic nervous system arousal. When young adults in the United States are exposed to a brief stressful experience, on average those of African ancestry show the greatest changes in blood pressure, those of Asian ancestry show the least, and those of European ancestry are intermediate, consistent with observed cultural differences in expressivity (Jackson, Treiber, Turner, Davis, & Strong, 1999; Shen, Stroud, & Niaura, 2004). Keep in mind, however, that correlations do not always indicate causal relationships— if people with bigger changes in blood pressure also show the strongest expressions, it does not necessarily follow that the blood pressure *causes* the expressions.

Another explanation is that people learn from their culture that it is appropriate to amplify or conceal certain emotional expressions. Just as you do not always say in words everything that you are thinking, you sometimes feel emotions without wanting to display them. Cultures differ somewhat in their rules for which emotions should be shown and which hidden, and under what circumstances. These cultural **display rules** are an important tool for any society. We learn at an early age when and where we can express our emotions freely, and when it is best to hide them. For example, when you are in a job interview, you try not to act nervous. If a guest spills something on your carpet, you try not to show anger. If a friend says something stupid, you try not to laugh. Other display rules require us to express emotions even if we do not feel them. Have you ever laughed politely at a joke that wasn't especially funny, or displayed more sorrow than you really felt over someone else's loss?

We learn all of these rules from the people around us, and cultures vary somewhat in their rules and expectations. For example, European and American adults, especially men, are discouraged

© Mark Richards/PhotoEdit

© Antoine Gyori/AGP/Corbis

FIGURE 3.3 Cultures differ in how strongly people are expected to express their emotions, and in the situations where expressions are considered appropriate.

from crying in public (see Figure 3.3), but this prohibition is even stronger in other cultures, such as China. Public laughter is generally acceptable in Europe and America, but customs vary from one locale to another. One of us (JWK) recalls having dinner at a restaurant in Spain when the people at another table broke into uproarious laughter. One of the Spanish people said, "They must be Americans. No Spanish person would laugh that loudly in public." Some cultures discourage emotional expression in general. One study of Hmong immigrants to the United States found that the immigrants who were more assimilated into U.S. culture expressed a number of emotions more visibly than did those who were more traditional (Tsai, Chentsova-Dutton, Freire-Bebeau, & Przymus, 2002).

Wallace Friesen (1972) conducted a classic study of display rules, comparing the behavior of Japanese and American participants while they watched disgusting videos of surgical procedures. Undergraduate participants first watched the videos alone, and then watched them again in the presence of an experimenter, introduced as a graduate student and wearing a lab coat. Although participants from both countries showed considerable disgust when they watched the video alone, Japanese participants masked this disgust with a polite smile when the experimenter was in the room (Friesen, 1972). Japan emphasizes the social hierarchy much more than the United States, and the Japanese consider it inappropriate to show negative emotion to a high-status person. American participants were evidently less intimidated by the experimenter, and saw no reason to hide their feelings.

A number of other display rules also differentiate American and Japanese culture. One study found that Americans expressed their emotions more visibly than either Japanese or Russian people. Japanese and Russians were more likely than Americans to "qualify" their display of negative emotions. That is, when displaying fear, anger, or sadness, Japanese and Russian people often added a slight smile to soften the impression, to indicate that "although I am distressed, it isn't really that bad" (Matsumoto, Yoo, Hirayama, & Petrova, 2005). In the United States moderate displays of anger are fairly common. In Japan, a high-status person can display anger toward subordinates, but almost any other display of anger is considered shockingly inappropriate (Matsumoto, 1996). In Japan it is more appropriate to show negative emotions to acquaintances than to close friends and family, whereas the reverse is true for Americans (Matsumoto, 1990).

Here is another kind of display rule: An American might ask a friend or acquaintance for a favor. For example, "I am feeling sick, I need some medicine, and I don't feel well enough to go the store myself. Could you get the medicine for me?" Asians and Asian-Americans are much less likely to ask for such support, because in that culture the other person would feel obligated to say yes, even if it presented an impossible burden at the time. The Asian would not ask for help, because asking might *force* the other person to say yes. An American does not assume the other person will automatically say yes, and therefore feels less reluctance about asking (Kim, Sherman, & Taylor, 2008).

When we learn a display rule, we may superimpose it onto built-in, biological tendencies. Researchers videotaped facial expressions after various competitors won or lost judo matches at the 2004 Olympics, and at the Paralympic Games (for people with a disability) in the same year. The observation was that people smiled after a victory and frowned after a defeat, and the immediate expression was about the same for sighted or blind competitors, and for people from different cultures. However, a moment or two later, participants from certain cultures—mostly Asian—restrained their expressions (Matsumoto & Willingham, 2009; Matsumoto, Willingham, & Olide, 2009).

Display rules raise particular difficulties for **bicultural** people, those who are members of more than one culture (Harrison, Wilson, Pine, Chan, & Buriel, 1990; LaFramboise, Coleman, & Gerton, 1993). Immigrants and their children are bicultural, unless they settle in an area populated entirely by other immigrants from the same country. In one study, East Asian immigrants to Canada filled out the same questionnaire at three times on each of ten days. At each time they recorded whether they were with other Asians and speaking an Asian language, or with Canadians of European ancestry and speaking English. They also answered questions about their beliefs and attitudes toward emotion. When immersed in Asian culture, they answered the emotion questions in ways typical of Asians. When immersed in Canadian culture, they answered in ways more typical of other Canadians (Perunovic, Heller, & Rafaeli, 2007).

You might get the impression from these examples that only other cultures have display rules, whereas Americans show exactly what they feel. Americans typically think they are *supposed* to show their feelings honestly, and emotional authenticity is valued as a desirable trait (Kim & Sherman, 2007). However, Arlie Hochschild (2003) offers a rich description of some American display rules in her book *The Managed Heart*. In her research on the United States airline industry, Hochschild found that companies make explicit demands for employees' emotional behavior, especially that of flight attendants. As the "front line" of customer service, flight attendants are expected to communicate pleasure, warmth, concern, enthusiasm, and sometimes even sexual attraction as part of their daily work. Those applying for flight attendant positions may be put through an explicit test of their sociability and perkiness, asked to chat lightly with other applicants while recruiters evaluate their social style. Any failure to express the appropriate feelings on the job typically leads to disapproval from supervisors.

Worse yet, changes within the airline industry since the events of September 11 have led to mixed messages about the emotions flight attendants should express. Flight attendants are supposed to be friendly, but not fake. Expressions of emotion should seem natural. They should talk with customers, but not enough to slow down the performance of their duties. They are expected to be warm and nurturing, yet make it clear that they are ready to discipline an unruly passenger or control a dangerous situation at a moment's notice. What we see here is a complex network of rules about feelings, as well as emotional expressions.

As we have seen, every culture has display rules. However, the American combination of professional display rules with cultural values for emotional authenticity puts flight attendants (and others in similar service professions) in a particular bind. A number of cultures encourage posing of appropriate emotional displays, without demanding that individuals actually feel what they express. In the United States, however, people put a high premium on emotional genuineness. In one study, researchers asked pairs of European-American and Asian-American women to view an upsetting film about World War II, and then to discuss the film (Butler, Lee, & Gross, 2009). Among the European-Americans, those who were less expressive showed greater increases in blood pressure, suggesting higher levels of stress in people who were trying to conceal their emotions. In contrast, less expressive Asian-Americans did not show an increase in blood pressure, consistent with the proposal that this culture encourages more restrained emotional displays.

So far we have emphasized cultural differences in the intensity of emotional expressions, but the actual content of expressions also varies somewhat from culture to culture. This even appears to be true of the emotions studied by Ekman, Izard and colleagues. In one well-known article, Hilary Elfenbein and Nalini Ambady (2002) conducted a **meta-analysis** of existing expression recognition studies. This statistical technique combines the results of many different studies into a single analysis. They found that accuracy was consistently higher when participants rated people of the same national, ethnic, or regional group than when the photo was of someone from a different group. This difference was especially noticeable when the photograph was of a posed expression ("now show me an expression of disgust") or a spontaneous expression, rather than an expression defined by specific muscle movements. This strongly suggests that people from different cultures show somewhat different facial expressions, even of possible basic emotions such as anger, fear, sadness, and disgust.

You may be puzzled by this. If people have evolved innate "templates" for facial expressions of emotion, shouldn't those emotions look exactly the same around the world? To take an analogy from language, people in different regions of a country pronounce the same words somewhat differently, and even use some different words. For example, people in some parts of the United States refer to carbonated soft drinks as "pop," whereas people in other regions call it "soda." Both words are technically correct, and in fact, the term "soda pop" is the origin of each. The regions simply have different dialects and accents. People from different regions understand each other, but people who live in the same region might understand a little bit better.

Hilary Elfenbein proposed that people who live in different cultures may also have different "dialects" of facial expressions. To test this hypothesis, Elfenbein and colleagues asked participants from two French-speaking regions—Quebec in Canada and Gabon in sub-Saharan Africa—to pose expressions of anger, fear, sadness, disgust, happiness, surprise, contempt, shame, embarrassment, and serenity (Elfenbein, Beaupré, Lévesque, & Hess, 2007). Rather than asking the posers to move specific facial muscles, the researchers gave posers each emotion word, and asked them to pose an expression their friends could easily understand. All of the emotion words were in French, in order to avoid translation problems.

As expected, expressions posed by people from the two cultures had subtle but consistent differences. For example, displays of happiness by the Quebecois were more likely to include constriction of the muscles surrounding the eyes (try this in front of a mirror—if "crow's feet" wrinkles appear then you're doing it right), whereas displays of the same emotion by the Gabonese were more likely to involve an open mouth. In expressing anger, the Quebecois were more likely to tighten their lips and squint, whereas the Gabonese were somewhat more likely to widen their eyes. Importantly, the elements of each posed expression across the two cultures were characteristic of the "prototypical" expressions identified in prior research; it's just that some muscle movements were more pronounced in one culture than in the other. In a follow-up study, the researchers showed these posed expressions to new participants in each culture, along with expressions that were matched to be morphologically identical. They found an ingroup bias in recognizing the free poses of the expressions, but *not* the matched poses. Both of these findings are consistent with the notion of dialects in facial expressions of emotion.

Cultural Differences in Interpreting Facial Expressions

Because people from various cultures differ somewhat in how they express emotions, we should expect that they also differ in how they interpret emotional displays. For example, if you and those around you ordinarily restrain your public displays of emotion, and now you see someone showing a fairly strong expression, it may seem even more extreme to you than it would to someone accustomed to seeing such displays.

In one study, David Matsumoto and Paul Ekman (1989) examined this phenomenon. They showed photos of several prototype emotion expressions, using Caucasian and Japanese posers, to participants in the United States and Japan. Regardless of ethnicity of the poser, Japanese raters tended to rate both the negative emotions and happiness expressed by the posers as less intense. In another study, when people looked at photographs of relatively *weak* expressions, as in Figure 3.4, Japanese people estimated a *stronger* underlying emotion than Americans did (Matsumoto, Consolacion et al., 2002).

Several factors might explain these confusing and contradictory findings. One possibility is this: Japanese people are accustomed to inhibiting public emotional displays, so when they see a weak emotional expression, they may infer that the person felt the emotion strongly and partly inhibited it. With expressions of average or strong intensity, Americans may be more inclined to trust the authenticity of the display, whereas Japanese guess that such exaggerated

displays are probably feigned. Also, as a general rule, when Japanese people fill out rating scales, they tend to answer toward the middle of the scale, whereas Americans are more apt to give extreme (either high or low) ratings. Because we cannot experimentally assign people to one culture or another, it is difficult to tease these explanations apart.

ASPECTS OF CULTURE THAT PREDICT DIFFERENCES IN EMOTION

The various cultural differences in emotional appraisal, expression, and interpretation can be difficult to keep track of, and even more so to explain. Many early studies of cultural differences in emotion (and in other domains as well) simply noted a difference between the United States and some other culture, and left it at that. Frustrated with the hodgepodge of findings produced in this way, several researchers suggested a new approach. They argued that, although every culture is unique, researchers can nevertheless compare cultures to one another along a few dimensions that are relevant to social behavior and emotional experience. We will discuss the three cultural dimensions that are most emphasized in research on emotion.

Individualism vs. Collectivism

First, cultures have been described as varying along a continuum from individualism to collectivism (Markus & Kitayama, 1991). According to many cultural psychologists, people in Western cultures (especially Americans) tend to be high on **individualism**, which emphasizes individual uniqueness, personal rights, being true to one's self, and independence from others. People high in individualism generally agree with statements like the following:

- *I take pride in accomplishing what no one else can accomplish.*
- *I am unique—different from others in many respects.*

Photo courtesy of Dr. David Matsumoto

FIGURE 3.4 When people examine faces showing relatively low-intensity emotional displays, as in this one, Japanese observers tend to infer slightly higher emotional feelings than do Americans.

In contrast, many other cultures, including most South and East Asian cultures, emphasize **collectivism**, or prioritizing the group over the individual, valuing group identification, deference, social harmony, and interdependence. Each person has a role, knows that role, and tries to fulfill duties rather than compete with others. People who have a collectivist attitude tend to agree with statements like these:

- *To understand who I am, you must see me with members of my group.*

- *Before making a decision, I always consult with others.*

China is generally taken as an example of a collectivist culture, and one indication is that Chinese people talk more about their friends and family, whereas Americans talk more about themselves. A natural question is whether that tendency really reflects the way people think, or just some difference between the Chinese and English languages. In one study, investigators studied young Chinese American adults, all of whose parents had been born in China, Hong Kong, or Taiwan. All the participants were fluent in English, but some were more acculturated (Americanized) than others in terms of their activities, attitudes, food, and social life. The investigators conducted systematic interviews with each, always in English, and found that the less acculturated Chinese Americans spoke significantly more than the others did about friends, family, receiving advice, and other social or collective activities (Tsai, Simeonova, & Watanabe, 2004).

In another study, when people were asked to describe experiences from memory, North Americans usually described how *they* felt, whereas Asians described how they thought the people around them felt (D. Cohen & Gunz, 2002). In one classic study, Chinese and American participants were simply asked to complete the phrase "I am …" 20 times, in any way they wanted (Triandis, McCusker, & Hui, 1990). The researchers found that Chinese participants were three times more likely than Americans to list group membership as part of their identity. Whereas Americans tended to list things that made them different from others, Chinese participants listed similarities. Obviously, these differences pertain to

FIGURE 3.5 Chinese people are more likely than Americans to say the group to the left is chasing the fish on the right; most Americans say the fish on the right is leading the others.

averages across many people. Americans do list group memberships, and Chinese participants describe unusual aspects about themselves.

In another study, researchers asked people to describe the behavior of the fish on the right in Figure 3.5. Most Americans say this fish is leading the others. Among Chinese people, a common answer is that the other fish are chasing this one (Hong, Morris, Chiu, & Benet-Martinez, 2000). That is, the Chinese put more emphasis on group influences and context in interpreting ambiguous situations. Such differences in appraisal can lead to differences in emotional experience. Someone who thinks the fish is a leader would probably think the fish is happy, whereas someone who thinks the fish is being chased would probably infer that it is afraid!

It is an oversimplification to equate Western cultures with individualism and Eastern cultures with collectivism. Even within a culture, individualist and collectivist attitudes vary from region to region, person to person (Fiske, 2002), and even from one situation to another (Bond, 2002). Furthermore, several studies have used Chinese participants to represent "Eastern" cultures, but Eastern cultures are not all equally collectivist. Researchers find that the Japanese people of today are about as individually competitive as Americans, and in some ways more so (Bond, 2002; Oyserman, Coon, & Kemmelmeier, 2002; Takano & Osaka, 1999). Japanese culture was described as highly collectivist shortly after World

War II, but almost any country develops collectivist attitudes in the face of danger or after a disastrous loss (Takano & Osaka, 1999). For example, people in the United States were strongly united shortly after the terrorist attacks of September 11, 2001. Japan today has vastly different customs and attitudes from those of the late 1940s, and vastly different from those of today's China.

How might cultural differences in individualism vs. collectivism affect emotional life? Such differences have been proposed as an explanation for many of the differences in displaying and interpreting facial expressions we discussed earlier in the chapter. For example, if Japan is a collectivist society, then the Japanese may inhibit expressions of negative emotion as a way of preserving group harmony and prioritizing group needs over one's own.

Some researchers have proposed that collectivism also facilitates the *experience* of certain kinds of emotion, whereas individualism discourages such emotions. One striking example occurs in what situations arouse the "self-conscious" emotions such as pride, shame, and guilt, which require an appraisal of one's self as good or bad. Research in the United States suggests that people experience pride when they have accomplished something, and their social status is on the rise (Seidner, Stipek, & Feshbach, 1988; Tiedens, Ellsworth, & Mesquita, 2000). Americans experience shame and guilt after doing something wrong, when others are likely to express disapproval (Tangney, Miller, Flicker, & Barlow, 1996). Thus, pride, shame, and guilt all appear to require an interpretation of whether the self is good or bad. However, "self" means different things to people in different cultures. In individualistic cultures, my "self" is distinct from the people around me. In collectivistic cultures, "self" is more closely tied to group memberships and relationships with friends and family (Triandis, McCusker, & Hui, 1990). Therefore, we might predict that people in collectivist cultures would experience pride and shame in response to their friends' and relatives' actions, not just their own.

Deborah Stipek (1998) tested this hypothesis in a study of American and Chinese university students.

She asked participants in each culture to read several scenarios, and to rate how proud, guilty, and ashamed they would feel in each situation. In two of the scenarios someone was accepted to a prestigious university, but in one scenario it was the participant and in the other it was the participant's child. In two other scenarios a person is caught cheating, but in one scenario it was the participant and in the other it was the participant's brother. Americans reported that they would be equally proud if they or their child were accepted to a prestigious university, but Chinese participants reported that they would be *more* proud to have their child accepted. Chinese participants reported that they would feel more guilt and shame than Americans in the cheating scenario regardless of who did it, and participants in both cultures said they would feel more guilt and shame if they were caught than if the brother were caught. However, Chinese participants reported that they would feel more guilt and shame in the "brother cheated" scenario than did Americans.

Note that this study suggests both similarities and differences between Chinese and American culture. In both cultures, participants expected to feel pride if they accomplished something, and guilt and shame if they did something morally wrong. The difference is that Americans felt the emotions more strongly if they did these things themselves, whereas in China, the activities of one's family reflect strongly enough on one's own identity that those activities can produce strong self-conscious emotion. In fact, participants in China said that it is *more* appropriate to feel pride for other people's accomplishments than for one's own (Stipek, 1998).

Power Distance: Vertical vs. Horizontal Societies

Another major difference among cultures is the degree to which they emphasize power distance, or social hierarchy. David Matsumoto (1996) defines a **vertical society** as one that emphasizes the social hierarchy, and encourages emotions and behaviors that advertise and reinforce status differences. By contrast, a **horizontal society** is one in which people typically minimize attention to status differences and seldom acknowledge those differences publicly. For illustration, contrast various nonhuman species: Most monkey troops have a rigid vertical structure in which one monkey, usually a large male, dominates the others. Deer and cattle have a more horizontal structure, in which all members of the herd have approximately the same status.

Nancy Much (1997) contrasts the social structure she observed in Hindu Indian households with typical American social interaction. Traditional Indian society is a prototypical vertical society, with a firm class structure, and detailed rules for how people interact with others within and between classes. Even within a family, people observe rules of hierarchy, often addressing one another by title (such as "older brother") rather than by name. Younger family members are expected to prostrate themselves (touching their head to the feet of a higher-ranking, older family member) as a standard display of respect. Failure to use the proper title or gesture of respect is a breach of propriety, reflecting badly on both parties. Your father's friend would never invite you to call him by his first name, and you would never agree to do so.

American culture is more horizontal, although no human society is completely status-free. Americans recognize status differences, and acknowledge the authority of parents, bosses, elected leaders, and such, but this authority is limited to certain domains. A worker acknowledges the boss's right to give orders at the office, but not to command what meal to order at a restaurant or how to interact with one's spouse. Status differences in wealth or education are seldom made explicit. The United States has no hereditary aristocracy, and Americans treasure the idea that someone born poor can ascend to a position of power and success. Canada is similar in this regard.

The vertical versus horizontal dimension can influence emotional experience in several ways. Like individualism/collectivism, power distance can facilitate or discourage the experience of certain kinds of emotion. For example, certain vertical societies have an emotion concept that the English language does not recognize, although it is often

translated as "shame." In the Orissa language in India, this is the *lajya* we discussed earlier, and among the Bedouin it is called *hasham*. It's helpful to think of this concept as a combination of embarrassment, shame, admiration, shyness, and gratitude (e.g., Abu-Lughod, 1986; Menon & Shweder, 1994; Russell, 1991). People feel this emotion in the presence of a higher-status person, and show their respect by displaying it. It may seem unfamiliar, but imagine meeting in person an actor, musician, political figure, or someone else you deeply respect. The feeling you would have toward that person might be something like *lajya* or *hasham*.

The emphasis on power distance in a society can also predict who displays what emotions. In Japan, for example, it is appropriate for a high-status person like a coach of a sports team to express anger at a player, but deeply offensive for the player to show anger to the coach (Matsumoto, 1996). Anger implies high status, and for the player to show anger to the coach would be a direct threat to the hierarchy (Matsumoto, 1990). By contrast, group leaders are expected not to show sadness or fear, which might convey weakness. Note that this is a prescription for emotional *display*, not necessarily for emotional *experience*. Inevitably, players will sometimes feel angry toward their coaches, and group leaders will sometimes feel sad or afraid. They can, however, stifle expression of these feelings to maintain the harmony of the group.

Similarly, investigators found differences among Nepali children in their willingness to express anger, based partly on status. In rural Nepal, Brahman Hindu children have relatively high status compared to Tamang children, who follow Tibetan Buddhism. When psychologists interviewed children about how they would feel and act in various difficult situations, the Brahman children said they would feel and express anger in many situations; the Tamang children almost never said they would feel anger. In contrast, the Tamang children were far more likely to say they would feel shame or "just okay." These contrasts relate partly to status and partly to religion; Buddhism praises a calm, balanced attitude as highly desirable (Cole, Bruschi, & Tamang, 2002; Cole & Tamang, 1998).

Of course, these differences among cultures are relative, not absolute. The United States is not a purely horizontal culture, and a coach is more likely to yell at a player than a player to yell at a coach. Similarly, an employer will show anger toward an employee, and a professor toward a student, more often than the reverse. However, the implications of status for emotional expression are less pronounced than in many other cultures.

Linear Versus Dialectical Epistemology

Cultural differences in individualism-collectivism and power distance emphasize different ways to think about the relationships between people. Cultures can also differ in *epistemology*, or theories about what it means to know or understand something. According to Kaiping Peng and Richard Nisbett (1999), Western cultures such as the United States have a very different epistemology than East Asian cultures such as China and Japan. In Western culture, epistemology has been heavily influenced by the theories of Aristotle. In this **linear epistemology**, "knowing" something means knowing what is constant and unchanging about it, knowing how it differs from other things, and knowing what is true and what is false. In contrast, East Asian epistemology has been heavily influenced by Confucianism, Taoism, and Buddhism. This **dialectical epistemology** emphasizes that true knowledge involves understanding that reality is changing rather than constant, that all things are interrelated rather than separate, and that the same proposition can be both true and false, from different perspectives. Although not many people in a given culture actually read the works of Aristotle or Confucius, psychologists believe that their ideas have become part of the broader culture.

What implications might this have for emotion? Remember from Chapter 1, in our discussion of dimensional models of emotion, the debate about whether positive and negative emotions can be experienced at the same time. Mixed emotions are uncommon among Americans, though

people do report them occasionally. Researchers have asked whether this infrequency might be due to linear epistemology, which encourages Westerners thinkers to think of positive and negative emotion as mutually exclusive opposites. In contrast, people from cultures emphasizing dialectical epistemology may be less likely to think of emotions in terms of opposites such as "happy *or* sad" and "loving *or* angry," and therefore may feel mixed emotions more often.

A number of studies suggest that this may be the case. For example, in one study researchers asked participants to report on their emotions frequently as they went about their daily lives, and found that participants in East Asia were more likely than Americans to report feeling positive and negative emotions at the same time (Scollon, Diener, Oishi, & Biswas-Diener, 2004). Another study found that Asian-American biculturals who had been encouraged to think about the Asian aspect of their identities reported more mixed emotions in diaries over a two-week period, compared with those who were encouraged to think about the American aspect of their identities (Perunovic, Heller, & Rafaelli, 2007).

In each of these studies, it is difficult to know whether participants in different cultures had different experiences with mixed emotion because of the way they saw the world, or because they were encountering different experiences. In one study, researchers asked whether Americans of East Asian ethnicity would experience more mixed emotions than those of European ancestry, when engaged in the same task (Shiota, Campos, Gonzaga, Keltner, & Peng, 2010). They invited same-ethnicity Asian-American and European-American dating couples to come into the laboratory and have a series of structured conversations while being videotaped. After every conversation, each member of the couple rated her emotions during the conversation.

In the first conversation, each partner teased the other, making up a nickname and telling a story explaining the nickname. In the second conversation, each partner shared a concern or worry about something outside the relationship. In the third conversation, each partner talked about a previous romantic partner. In the fourth conversation, the couple talked about their first date. During these conversations, participants might reasonably have felt loving toward their partners, but could also have felt particular negative emotions—shame at being teased, anger at hearing about the partner's ex, and contempt when listening to a current concern or talking about the first date. (As we shall see in Chapter 9, contempt is the "anti-love.") The question was: would Asian-American dating partners be more likely than European-American partners to report feeling love and a negative emotion *at the same time* during these conversations?

The actual conversations were very similar. For example, couples from the two cultural groups showed similar patterns of criticizing each other versus praising each other during the teasing task, taking responsibility versus acting helpless during the current concern conversation, and so forth. However, participants in the two groups reported very different patterns of emotional experience. In almost every conversation, European Americans reported *either* love *or* the target negative emotion, but not both—love and negative emotion were negatively correlated. In contrast, the Asian-American participants were more likely to report feeling love and a negative emotion at the same time; in some conversations more love actually predicted *more* negative emotion. Although it is hard to be certain that these differences were due to cultural differences in epistemology rather than some other aspect of culture, it was consistent with predictions suggested by the linear versus dialectical distinction.

METHODOLOGICAL ISSUES
IN STUDYING CULTURE

In this chapter we have asked how culture molds our emotions, in terms of language, experience, and expression. Most of the studies presented in this chapter studied culture by looking at differences (or similarities) between people in two or more countries, or people of different ethnicities within the same country. This is the typical strategy used in

cultural psychology, and it can be a good start to a program of research. There are, however, several limitations to this strategy, and to the way it has been applied so far.

The first limitation is a practical one. The vast majority of psychological researchers come from prosperous, first-world countries—especially the United States—and when they study culture it usually involves going to some other country and comparing that place with home. They might choose the other country because of its theoretical significance, such as being a good example of a collectivist culture, but they also consider how easily they can gain access. A great many cross-cultural studies contrast Japan versus the United States, Japan versus Canada, Japan versus Australia, and so forth. The reason is that Japan is a prosperous, modern country with many psychological researchers of its own. It is the easiest to study of all "non-Western" cultures (with China now a close second). Certainly, there is nothing wrong with comparing Japan or China to the United States, but many other cultures are completely overlooked. This tendency makes it difficult to understand "culture" as something distinct from "how East Asia is different from North America."

A second problem is that cultures do not follow national boundaries. Within the United States, cultures differ greatly between people of different ethnic backgrounds, religions, and regions of the country (A. Cohen, 2009). For example, studies have documented differences between the American South versus the Midwest in the "culture of honor," with important implications for how people experience and express anger after being insulted (D. Cohen, Nisbett, Bowdle, & Schwartz, 1996). People moving from one part of the United States to another often experience "culture shock" as if they had moved to another country! Beliefs, attitudes, and behaviors also depend on birth cohort; being an American child today differs nearly as much from being a child 50 years ago as it does from growing up in a different country (Twenge, 2002). Even within one city at one point in time—Minneapolis, Minnesota—researchers found that young adults of Scandinavian ancestry expressed their emotions with more restraint than those of Irish ancestry (Tsai & Chentsova-Dutton, 2003). Cultural or subcultural differences are probably even greater within many other countries, where transportation and communication are more difficult. For example, the constitution of India recognizes 18 official languages.

Odd though it sounds, culture itself is the third major difficulty in interpreting differences between two countries: Suppose researchers collect self-report measurements, as emotion researchers often do. They ask people of various cultures, for example, to rate themselves on a 1-to-7 scale for how happy they are, or how nervous, or how open in expressing their emotions. Rating yourself on such a scale implies a comparison of how happy (or whatever) you are *in comparison to others*. So if you rate your happiness "4" (average), you mean average with respect to the other people you know, presumably of your own culture. Suppose the mean happiness rating for people in your culture is 4 (as it should be, theoretically) and the mean rating in some other culture is also 4. Can we conclude that people in the two cultures are equally happy? Of course not. Suppose people in one culture rate their happiness *higher* than those of another country. Even then we cannot compare the results with confidence; perhaps people in the two cultures differ not in happiness, but in how they use the rating scales. In short, cultural comparisons based on self-ratings are shaky evidence (Heine, Lehman, Peng, & Greenholtz, 2002).

Aside from these practical concerns, there is an important conceptual problem with studying culture by comparing two countries or other groups. Look back at the definition of culture offered at the beginning of the chapter. Is studying the differences between two groups the same as studying culture? Not really. When we compare, say, China and the United States, we measure some outcome in each country and try to infer the cultural process behind any differences that we find. We can't even be sure that anything about culture is the reason behind the differences we find, because we can't randomly assign people to one culture or another.

Or can we? One clever technique in cultural psychology involves **cultural priming**—studying bicultural people, and using an experimental manipulation to make one of each person's cultural identities especially salient before conducting the rest of the study. For example, a researcher might ask some Asian-American participants to think of a time when they felt very Asian, and others to think of a time when they felt very American. This approach can also be used to examine the effects of particular aspects of culture on various psychological processes, including emotion. For example, researchers might ask some participants to think about a time they accomplished a goal alone, to highlight individualism; other participants would be asked to think about a time they accomplished something as part of a team, to highlight collectivism. This helps to isolate the particular aspect of culture that is important for the process, and the experimental approach also allows researchers to draw conclusions about cause-effect relationships that would not be possible in a correlational research design.

Researchers are still looking for better ways to define and measure culture. Ideally, researchers studying culture and emotion would look directly at the process by which different cultures construct emotion concepts, display rules, and so on, but that will be a difficult task. The proper response to all these problems is not to give up in despair, but to proceed with caution and to use a variety of research methods.

INTEGRATING EVOLUTIONARY AND CULTURAL APPROACHES

On one hand, certain aspects of emotion appear to be universal, but on the other hand, culture has a powerful influence on our emotional lives. Although both of these positions are supported by research, some researchers mainly emphasize the universal aspect whereas others emphasize the cultural differences. Is there any way to integrate both aspects in one theory? Three major proposals have been offered to meet this goal.

Ekman (1972): Neuro-Cultural Theory of Emotion

Paul Ekman's (1972) Neuro-Cultural Theory was the first explicit attempt to articulate where and how culture might influence universal emotion processes. In this model (see Figure 3.6), events in the environment (as well as fantasies and memories) may elicit particular appraisals or interpretations that then lead to an emotion. That emotion involves several biological features, including autonomic nervous system changes, cognitive biases, and automatic facial expressions generated by an innate and universal "facial action program." If conditions are right then these biological features, as well as consciously felt motivations, lead to prototypical emotional behavior.

The Neuro-Cultural Theory was intended to explain universality and cultural variation in facial expressions of emotion. According to Ekman it is possible, with effort, to override expressions triggered by the facial action program. Over time, when one has negated the "natural" expression enough times in the same kind of situation, this overriding can even become habitual. Thus, the Japanese participants in Friesen's study of display rules need not have been thinking "uh oh, high-status person present, can't display negative emotion, must fake smile to cover real feelings." They had probably just learned over countless situations with high-status people what was and was not appropriate emotional behavior, and enacted the appropriate behavior without much thought. Sometimes these display rules are specific to a particular family or other group. For example, although we noted earlier that display rules generally prevent laughing when a friend says something stupid, one of us (MNS) shares with a group of college friends a display rule of laughing at each other whenever possible. Display rules are also prominent parts of the larger cultural system, helping to guide a consistent pattern of social interaction.

Figure 3.6 also suggests that cultures provide feeling rules as well as display rules. Culture has an impact on how different situations are interpreted, so that a given emotion can be elicited by different kinds of situations in different cultures. We saw an example of this in Deborah Stipek's (1998) work on the events that might elicit self-conscious emotions like pride

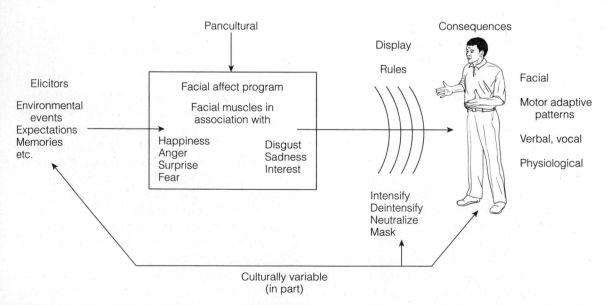

FIGURE 3.6 Paul Ekman's Neuro-Cultural Theory of Emotion.

and shame in China and the United States. Because behavior is so subject to conscious control, the actions that follow upon the experience of an emotion can vary a great deal from culture to culture as well.

Russell (1991): Emotion Episodes as Socially Constructed Scripts

Another way to integrate universal and cultural aspects of emotion has been offered by James Russell (1991). To understand his explanation, it will help to think back to the definition of emotion we tentatively proposed in Chapter 1. This definition included several events: Person X perceives some event in the environment and interprets it in a certain way; X's physiology changes, perhaps with increased heart rate and blood pressure; X reports having a certain feeling; X displays a particular facial expression; X wants a certain outcome in the situation, and takes action to try to bring about that outcome. We called this series of events an emotion, as have many researchers.

Researchers working from the assumption that emotions are evolved responses to the environment think of sequences such as these as innate and universal. Russell has offered a somewhat different interpretation—that such sequences are socially constructed scripts, or cultural beliefs about what events, thoughts, feelings, and behaviors "go together." Some combinations are inherently more common than others, thereby forming a "natural" pattern that is likely to receive universal recognition. On the other hand, there is plenty of room for cultures to tinker with individual components of the scripts, defining and encouraging less common combinations. According to Russell, emotion scripts can be broad or precise, can emphasize some components over others, and any given components or combination of components may be culture-specific or universal.

Based on this framework, Russell proposes that it is possible to identify aspects of emotion scripts that are more likely to be universal, and those more likely to be culture-specific. The former include such components as prototypical antecedents or *actual* eliciting situations, facial expressions, physiological changes, and action tendencies. The *perceived* cause of the emotion, however, may vary tremendously from one culture to the next. In some societies the perceived "cause" may be an interpersonal event, in others it may be a physical illness, in yet others supernatural events such as curses, possession, or ghosts. Note the difference between a "prototypical antecedent," or actual emotion-eliciting event as discussed in Chapter 1, and the "perceived cause" embedded in the meaning system of the person in some culture. Russell says they may be very different.

Also, the expected consequences of emotion in the script may vary considerably. This statement takes Ekman's concept of display rules, and says that they are incorporated into the very emotion concepts recognized by a society. As an example of these differences we can take *litost*, the Czech emotion described by Milan Kundera earlier in this chapter. Litost is caused by a sudden insight into one's own misery—a completely internal event that may or may not reflect some universally recognizable or objective event in the environment. The outcome of litost is a desire for revenge—a consequence that might manifest very differently in another society with another set of feeling and display rules.

Keltner and Haidt (1999): Levels of Analysis

Dacher Keltner and Jonathan Haidt (1999) built upon Ekman's Neuro-Cultural Theory and Russell's Emotion Script theory by specifying the levels of analysis at which one might expect universality versus cultural variation in emotion. The term "levels of analysis" refers to whether one looks at the "big picture," the details that compose it, the details within the details, and so forth. For example, one might study human respiration through research on breathing rates during exercise, research on the structure of the lungs, or studies of how hemoglobin molecules absorb oxygen. Each of these lines of research is valid and important, but people doing one kind of research may not know the other lines especially well, and one may have a somewhat different understanding of what "respiration" means, depending on one's level of analysis.

According to Keltner and Haidt, any apparent evolution vs. social construction conflict reflects confusion over levels of analysis. Much of this argument has centered on the "real" function of various emotions, with some researchers arguing in favor of evolutionary functions that aid survival and reproductive fitness, and others emphasizing the role of emotion in social and cultural life. Keltner and Haidt propose that emotions need not have a single function, and that the emotion literature makes the most sense if you think about function at four different levels of analysis.

The first of these is the intra-individual level—how does an emotion help the individual survive and reproduce? An example is fear, which makes you hide or run from a predator, thereby saving your own hide. The second is the dyadic level—how do emotions help two people to form and maintain a relationship in a way that benefits them both? An example is nurturant love, which motivates parents to care for their offspring, thereby preserving the life of the latter and the reproductive success of the former. A third level is that of small groups, where emotions are used to negotiate everybody's social roles. Examples of this were discussed earlier, where emotions were used to express and reinforce the social hierarchy in vertical societies. Fourth, emotions are functional at the level of the culture, in that we use stories, legends, gossip, and other narratives, intended to evoke emotion, as ways of teaching a society's values.

Keltner and Haidt propose that functions at the first two levels—individual and dyadic—are largely innate and universal, but that the group and culture levels allow much room for variation. This idea implies that all cultures should have similar relationships among appraisals, biological changes, and behavioral urges. However, groups and cultures will encourage those emotions that support the overall social structure (including individualism/collectivism, power distance, etc.) and will discourage experience and display of those emotions that interfere with the social structure. Within a culture, emotions may be experienced and/or expressed only by certain people or in certain situations, again in ways that support the social structure.

SUMMARY

Some aspects of emotion seem to be universal, or nearly so, but cultures differ in what emotions they encourage or discourage, in who is expected to express what emotions in what situations, and in the typical causes and effects of emotions. Most important, cultures vary in how they *talk* about emotion, carving up emotion space in ways that make the most sense for a particular society, and assigning word labels to each slice. According to all three proposals for integrating the evolutionary and social construction approaches to emotion, culture influences emotion because emotion is inherently social, and different cultures endorse very different patterns of social interaction.

Which of the three proposals—Ekman's, Russell's, or Keltner and Haidt's—is right? A good deal of research is yet to be done before we can answer this question, so right now it helps to focus on the things the three proposals have in common. Each suggests that once an emotion-eliciting appraisal has taken place, the corresponding emotional experience and nervous system changes are pretty sure to follow no matter what culture you grew up in (although the proposals differ as to the nature and specificity of these changes), and the changes in emotional experience and physiology make some behaviors more likely than others. This idea is pretty consistent with the research we have seen so far. But each proposal also says that the frequency of various appraisals can differ substantially from culture to culture, so that a given emotion may be experienced quite a lot in one culture, but not much in another. Furthermore, behavior is under conscious control, so different cultures can have their own rules about how people should act when they experience an emotion, depending on the exact situation.

We hope we have convinced you that the evolutionary and social construction approaches to emotion are fully compatible. We still have much to learn about the effects of culture and evolution, but clearly both make massive contributions to our emotional lives.

KEY TERMS

amae: Japanese term describing the feeling of pleasurable dependence on another person, like the feeling an infant has toward its mother (p. 63)

bicultural: the ability to alternate between membership in one culture and membership in another (p. 69)

collectivism: prioritizing the group over the individual, valuing group identification, deference, social harmony, and interdependence (p. 72)

culture: the meanings, conceptions, and interpretive schemes that are activated by participation in social practices (including language) (p. 59)

cultural priming: an experimental manipulation that makes one of a bicultural person's cultural identities especially salient for a short period of time (p. 77)

dialectical epistemology: belief that reality is always changing, that all things are interrelated, and that the same proposition can be both true and false from different perspectives (p. 75)

display rules: policies about when and with whom it is appropriate to display certain kinds of emotional expressions (p. 67)

horizontal society: one in which people typically minimize attention to status differences and seldom acknowledge those differences publicly (p. 74)

hyper-cognize: to create an elaborate network of associations and distinctions that lead to an increase in the vocabulary for some emotion (p. 65)

hypocognize: to fail to give an emotion much cognitive elaboration or detail (p. 65)

individualism: emphasis on individual uniqueness, personal rights, being true to one's self, and independence from others (p. 71)

linear epistemology: belief that "knowing" something means knowing what is constant and unchanging about it, how it differs from other things, and what is true and what is false about it (p. 75)

meta-analysis: a statistical technique that combines the results of many different studies into a single analysis (p. 70)

Sapir-Whorf hypothesis: proposal that humans require language to think, and therefore we have only those experiences, thoughts, and perceptions for which we have words (p. 64)

social construction of emotion: process by which societies create culture-specific ways of thinking about, experiencing, and expressing emotion (p. 58)

vertical society: one that pays particular attention to the social hierarchy, and encourages emotions and behaviors that respect status differences (p. 73)

THOUGHT QUESTIONS

1. How many words can you think of relating to anger? (angry, livid, peeved …) How many can you think of relating to sadness? Embarrassment? Other emotions? Can you conclude which emotions are hypercognized or hypocognized in English?

2. Of the various subcultures and sub-subcultures in which you participate, such as clubs and organizations, do some have a more horizontal social structure and others a more vertical structure? Does this affect the way emotions are expressed in those groups?

3. Talk with friends born in different countries or to immigrant parents, who are fluent in different languages as well as English. Do those languages have emotion words not present in English? Does English have emotion words that do not translate? How does emotional life in other countries differ from that in mainstream American culture?

SUGGESTIONS FOR RESEARCH PROJECTS

1. The text discussed airlines' rules on how flight attendants should display friendly emotions toward customers. Observe and describe the emotional displays of employees in stores and restaurants. Do they show similar tendencies?

2. Keep a record of times when you inhibit an emotional display, or express one more strongly than you feel it. What display rules are in action?

SUGGESTIONS FOR FURTHER READING

Abu-Lughod, L. (2000). *Veiled Sentiments: Honor and Poetry in a Bedouin Society*. Berkeley, CA: University of California Press. A rich description of the relationship between social structure and emotion in Bedouin culture, as observed by a Palestinian-American anthropologist.

Matsumoto, D. (1997). *Culture and Modern Life*. Pacific Grove, CA: Brooks/Cole. An excellent review of how culture relates to all aspects of psychology.

Shweder, R. A. (2003). *Why Do Men Barbecue? Recipes for Cultural Psychology*. Cambridge, MA: Harvard University Press. An insightful and sympathetic discussion of cultural differences, combining psychological and anthropological perspectives.

4

Emotion and the Body
Autonomic Nervous System and Hormones

Think about a time in your life when you were really nervous about something. Maybe you were about to take a test of some kind, or maybe you had to stand up in front of a lot of people to give a speech. Perhaps you were working up the nerve to ask someone out on a date. Remember that experience vividly. How did your body feel?

People in these kinds of situations typically report similar physical sensations. See how well this describes your experience: your heart was pounding, your hands were ice cold, and damp. Your stomach churned and felt a little queasy. Your mouth was dry. Your muscles were tense, and your hands trembled a bit. Sound familiar?

In his book *The Feeling of What Happens*, Antonio Damasio (1999) wrote that "emotions use the body as their theater" (p. 51). As we noted in Chapter 1, many other emotion theorists have also emphasized the body's central role in emotional feelings. William James (1884) went so far as to say that physiological and behavioral changes *are* the feeling of emotion. Think back on all of the intensely emotional experiences you've had throughout your life. How did your body feel during those experiences? Can you think of any strong emotions that did not involve your body at all?

According to many researchers, emotions exist to prepare us for action. Some of this preparation involves changes in sensory perception and cognitive processing, but emotions also help to get our bodies ready for whatever behavior is most likely to be adaptive under the circumstances. The physical changes associated with emotion are controlled by a branch of the nervous system known as the autonomic nervous system, as well as by hormones running through the bloodstream. In this chapter, we will describe these systems that communicate commands from the brain to the body. We'll also consider some evidence about the importance of physiological aspects of emotion for emotional feelings, and we'll ask whether different emotions have different physical effects. Finally, we will discuss the physiological aspects of stress, and explain why long-term stress can pose serious problems for physical health as well as emotional well-being.

THE AUTONOMIC NERVOUS SYSTEM

Think back to the physical sensations associated with nervousness, described above. Although these diverse sensations are spread throughout your body, a single branch of the nervous system controls them. The **autonomic nervous system** consists of neurons extending from the spinal cord to organs such as your heart, lungs, stomach, intestines, genitals, even the smooth muscle surrounding your arteries.

The autonomic nervous system plays an important role in keeping the body alive and functioning. We become especially aware of its effects during strong emotions, but this system is constantly adjusting conditions inside the body to keep the environment just right for your cells. When you stand up after sitting down for a while, your autonomic system adjusts your blood pressure to prevent you from fainting. When you walk up a flight of stairs, you're able to make it to the top because the same system has increased your heart rate to deliver more blood sugar and oxygen to your muscles. When you get cold, the autonomic system reduces blood flow to your extremities to help conserve body heat, and the hairs on your body stand up to trap warm air close to your skin (not that this does much for humans, but if you're a dog it's really effective).

The structure of the autonomic nervous system is depicted in Figure C.1 on the inside cover of this book. The autonomic nervous system has two branches: the sympathetic and parasympathetic branches. As you can see from the figure, these two branches influence many of the same organs,

and they usually have opposing effects. Let's examine each of these branches, and then see how they work together.

"Fight or Flight": The Sympathetic Nervous System

The sensations we associate with nervousness, and with several other negative emotions, reflect increased activation of the **sympathetic nervous system**. It is called "sympathetic" because the clusters of neurons that comprise this system usually act at the same time, in "sympathy" with one another. Overall, the effects of sympathetic nervous system arousal prepare the body for intense muscular activity. This system is especially responsive during dangerous situations; after years of studying how animals react physically to threat, Walter Cannon (1915) first referred to the combined effects of sympathetic activation as the "fight or flight" response in his book *Bodily Changes in Pain, Hunger, Fear, and Rage*. The idea is that if you are in danger, you need to be ready to fight off an enemy or run for your life. This effort demands much of the body's resources, and the sympathetic nervous system makes sure those resources are delivered.

One key aspect of this work is providing your skeletal muscles with the oxygen and glucose (blood sugar) they need for intense effort. This means circulating more blood, which delivers these resources throughout the body as well as picking up carbon dioxide and other waste products. One of the most noticeable effects of sympathetic activation is an increase in heart rate. Not only does the heart beat faster but it also beats harder, pumping more blood with each beat. Another effect of sympathetic activation is to increase respiration rate, or the speed of breathing, and to expand the sacs in the lungs ("bronchioles") so that breathing is more efficient.

When you are in danger your muscles need more blood, but you have only a certain amount in your body, so more blood to the muscles means less blood for something else. Your arteries are surrounded by smooth muscles that tighten (vasoconstrict) and relax (vasodilate) to guide blood to where it is most needed. When the sympathetic nervous system is more active, your arteries reduce the delivery of blood to your internal organs, and increase delivery to your skeletal muscles. They also allocate more blood to your brain, so you can think quickly and clearly. You also want to avoid losing too much blood if you are wounded. The sympathetic nervous system constricts tiny muscles around the arteries leading to your hands, feet, and skin—this "peripheral vasoconstriction" is why your extremities may feel cold when you are anxious. Overall, the changes in arterial constriction and the increase in the heart's output lead to an increase in blood pressure.

Muscle effort generates heat, and the body of a mammal or bird can operate only within a very narrow temperature window. (Reptiles, amphibians, fish, and invertebrates tolerate a wider range.) Another effect of sympathetic nervous system activation is to increase output from the sweat glands, cooling the body. As soon as you become angry or frightened, you may begin to sweat immediately—in what people call a "cold sweat"—to prevent overheating from the activity likely to ensue.

Have you ever tried to exercise right after a big meal? Bad idea, right? Digestion demands physical resources, and the body can't handle digestion and intense muscular activity at the same time. Several actions of the sympathetic nervous system serve to shut down digestion, further re-directing the body's resources to large skeletal muscles:

- salivary glands turn off, leading to a dry mouth
- the smooth muscles in your intestines stop the pulsing, called **peristalsis**, that keeps food going in the right direction
- your stomach stops secreting enzymes that digest food
- if you're *really* upset, sympathetic activation constricts muscles needed to kick food out of your stomach (vomiting), slightly decreasing body weight.

If you're being threatened by a panther, it's also not a great time to mate. As we discussed in Chapter 2, fear probably has effects that decrease interest in fooling around when we're in danger,

but sympathetic nervous system activation also reduces blood flow to the genitalia, which is necessary for erection in men and part of sexual arousal in women as well. In fact, chronic stress is a common reason for reduced interest in sex.

One effect of sympathetic nervous system activation that is striking in other mammals, though not so noticeable in humans, is **piloerection**—when hairs stand up on end. Piloerection has a number of effects, but the most important one may be that it makes most animals look larger and more intimidating. This may be the animal world's equivalent of "don't mess with me" (Figure 4.1). People also get "goose bumps" (erected hairs) when frightened, as an evolutionary relic from our hairier ancestors.

Leslie Keating/iStockphoto.com

FIGURE 4.1 This cat is showing many signs of sympathetic nervous system activation, including piloerection.

One of the subtlest observable effects of sympathetic nervous system activation is on the eyes—the pupils dilate, allowing more light to hit the retina. The effect of this change is similar to opening the aperture in a camera, increasing the overall brightness and detail of the visual image, and increasing focus on whatever is in the center of the visual field. Pupil dilation helps focus visual attention on a target, while blurring the periphery. This can be useful if one is carefully watching a predator, or checking out a possible meal.

Sympathetic activation leads to further effects important for long-term activity. Sympathetic innervation of the liver stimulates the release of more glucose to the bloodstream, supplying plenty of energy to the hard-working skeletal muscles, brain, and heart. Other changes increase the breakdown of fats to create more energy and stimulate overall cellular metabolism. Finally, sympathetic activation changes the chemicals in the blood to promote coagulation—again preparing for a possible wound.

"Rest and Digest": The Parasympathetic Nervous System

If the effects of sympathetic nervous system activation help prepare the body for intense activity, diverting resources away from digestion, reproduction, and maintenance, activation of the **parasympathetic nervous system** has largely opposite effects. Think of how you feel when you have just finished a big, delicious meal, and you are relaxed. Many of the sensations we have at this time reflect parasympathetic activation. For this reason, researchers often refer to the parasympathetic branch as the "rest and digest" system.

Whereas sympathetic activation stimulates the heart to beat faster and harder, parasympathetic activation slows down the heartbeat. Because the heart is not working as hard, and resources (glucose and oxygen) needed by smooth muscles in the digestive system, parasympathetic activation constricts the blood vessels feeding the heart. Similarly, whereas sympathetic activation increases the speed and efficiency of breathing, parasympathetic activation slows

down breathing and constricts the bronchioles. Sympathetic activation expands the pupils, allowing in more light. Too much light can damage the retina, however, so constricted pupils are a better default setting; parasympathetic activation constricts the muscles of the iris to make the pupil smaller.

Many effects of parasympathetic activation are geared toward facilitating digestion—this is why parasympathetic effects are so noticeable right after a large meal. Even during a meal, parasympathetic activation promotes the secretion of saliva, helping to process the food while you chew (Figure 4.2). Have you ever noticed that many cats and dogs drool when they are relaxed? Salivation reflects increased parasympathetic activation associated with that contentment. Parasympathetic activation also stimulates the secretion of various digestive chemicals into the stomach, and stimulates peristalsis so that food moves through the intestines. Since extra energy is coming into your body, changes stimulated by parasympathetic activity facilitate energy storage in fatty tissues.

Parasympathetic activity has no direct effect on the muscles around the blood vessels. (There is no such thing as "unstimulating" a muscle.) However, if sympathetic activation decreases at the same time parasympathetic activation is rising (typical just after finishing a meal), then blood will be diverted away from the muscles and brain and toward the digestive system—hence the "food coma" many people experience after a feast. Increasing sympathetic activation

Jesse Karjalainen/istockphoto.com

F I G U R E 4.2 This dog's appearance is consistent with strong parasympathetic activation.

would interfere with digestion; this is probably why so many cultures encourage a "siesta" or nap after meals. This also suggests that going for a strenuous walk after a big meal, while showing an admirable concern for fitness, is not really a great idea. Best to get the exercise first, and then enjoy your meal and some rest.

Parasympathetic activation also promotes body conditions favorable for sexual activity. In men, parasympathetic activation dilates the blood vessels leading into the penis, causing an erection. In women, dilation of vessels in corresponding tissue facilitates sexual arousal as well. Again presuming that sympathetic activation is low (at least in the early stages of sexual arousal—a point we will discuss shortly), the skin will be warm and flushed because blood vessels leading to the skin are relaxed. Conversely, sympathetic activation interferes with the early stages of sexual arousal. A man who is nervous or frightened will lose his erection.

How the Sympathetic and Parasympathetic Systems Work Together

It is easy to think of the sympathetic and parasympathetic nervous systems as two light switches that are either on or off. In fact, since the effects of the two systems mostly oppose each other, it's easy to think of them as the up-versus-down settings on a single switch. Although this image reflects our common experience (the "rush" that comes with sudden sympathetic activation does feel as though a switch had been flipped), it is misleading. A more accurate image is of two rheostats, the sliding controls that allow you to turn a light up and down gradually, rather than on or off. Both the sympathetic and parasympathetic nervous systems are "on" continuously, but their activation can be stronger or weaker at any point in time. Furthermore, it is possible to activate some parts of the parasympathetic system without activating other parts.

Because the systems are like two rheostats, they change somewhat independently of each other. The balance between the two systems is continuously shifting to compensate for the current state of the body, as well as to try to predict what the body will need next (as in emotion). Many psychological processes involve a distinct combination of sympathetic and parasympathetic activation (Wolf, 1995). For example, nausea is characterized by increased sympathetic stimulation of the stomach, producing a tendency to vomit, plus parasympathetic stimulation to the lower intestines, speeding up the excretion of waste. As we noted earlier, parasympathetic activation is needed for the early stages of sexual arousal. However, sympathetic activation *also* increases as arousal increases, and sympathetic activation promotes vaginal lubrication as well as the muscle contractions involved in orgasm and ejaculation.

You may be wondering—if the sympathetic and parasympathetic systems have largely opposing effects, why do we need them both? One answer is that the effects of the two systems are not perfectly opposed. For example, the parasympathetic nervous system has no effect on the muscles that stand your hairs up, sweat gland activity, or the state of most of your blood vessels. Only the sympathetic system can control these outcomes. In contrast, the parasympathetic system is geared toward increasing activities associated with digestion; sympathetic activation can *inhibit* these activities in an emergency, but it won't actually promote them. Thus, the two systems facilitate different goals, and their interaction defines a number of emotional and other states.

Even where both systems have opposing effects on the same organs, their combined input increases the precision of control the autonomic nervous system can exert. A common analogy here is to the gas pedal and brake in a car. Sure, the amount of pressure you apply to the gas pedal can control your speed; if you want to slow down, you can just take some pressure off, right? But this is not a recommended way to stop your car if you are about to hit something—in that case, you apply the brake. There are certain circumstances when using both the gas pedal and the brake in quick sequence is very handy. For example, one of us (MNS) spends a lot of time driving up and down hills in San Francisco. Sometimes she gets stopped at a traffic light while her car is still pointed uphill, with another car behind her. Anyone who lives in that city knows a trick: apply the brake (the parking brake is fine), and when you're ready to go, release the brake quickly while stepping on the gas at the same time. This way the car gets momentum quickly, so you don't roll into the car behind you.

This is a long example, but it resembles what the body may be doing when you encounter an unexpected threat (Porges, 1997). Imagine a rabbit at rest, nibbling happily on some grass, when it suddenly hears a noise. It freezes, and looks around to find out whether a predator is nearby. At this time, aspects of parasympathetic activation may increase—slowed heart rate and breathing help the rabbit concentrate, and also help conceal the rabbit if it hasn't yet been spotted. Once the rabbit knows it's in danger, though, the parasympathetic "brake" is released while the sympathetic "gas pedal" kicks in strongly to prepare the rabbit to run. The key thing here is that *both* the sympathetic and parasympathetic nervous systems are always active, and the degree of activation in each is constantly being fine-tuned to meet the body's needs.

The same is true for people. If you are in a risky situation, your heart rate may actually *decrease* at first. Imagine yourself in this experiment: You are playing a video game in which you sometimes have an opportunity to win money, and sometimes face the threat of losing money. When you see an image of a gun, it means you are at risk of losing, unless you react very quickly when a signal appears. As the gun gets larger, you know the need for action is approaching. You pay close attention to the gun, but while it is small, representing a distant threat, your heart rate decreases. When the gun grows large, indicating immediate danger, you shift to increased sympathetic activation, and your heart rate increases to prepare for a vigorous response (Löw, Lang, Smith, & Bradley, 2008).

HORMONES AND THE ENDOCRINE SYSTEM

The effects of the autonomic nervous system on the body depend on neurons that allow the brain to communicate directly with specific visceral organs. However, the body's activities are also controlled by **hormones**, chemicals assembled by glands in one part of your body, and carried through the bloodstream to communicate with organs in other areas. This process affects a wide range of physiological functions. For example, the hormone insulin, produced and released by the pancreas, causes cells throughout the body to take in more glucose as a source of energy. Growth hormone, which is manufactured by the pituitary gland, promotes cell reproduction throughout the body.

Some hormones are more important than others for emotional responses. Emotion researchers are especially interested in the hormones epinephrine (a.k.a. adrenaline) and cortisol, which play central roles in our responses to stress. However, anyone who has experienced puberty, pregnancy, and/or menopause is also aware of how estrogen and testosterone affect emotions. Higher levels of estrogen appear to have mood-enhancing effects (Walf & Frye, 2006), and sharp drops in estrogen have been shown to trigger depressive symptoms (Payne, 2003). Importantly, it appears to be the *change* in estrogen levels that triggers mood effects, rather than absolute levels. This is why the intense fluctuations in estrogen typical of puberty and menopause are associated with mood swings, and why mood disorders are less common during stages of women's lives (such as childhood and post-menopause) when estrogen levels are low but consistent.

Testosterone also has a wide range of emotional implications. Testosterone plays an important role in promoting sexual desire in both men and women (e.g., Shifren, Braunstein, Simon, Casson, Buster, Redmond, et al., 2000; Wagner, Rabkin, & Rabkin, 1997). In addition, testosterone appears to have mood-enhancing effects for men similar to those of estrogen for women, although these effects are less well understood (e.g., Seidman, Orr, Raviv, Levi, Roose, Kravitz, et al., 2009). Finally, testosterone has been proposed as a factor in anger and aggression (Kuepper, Alexander, Osinsky, Mueller, Schmitz, Netter, & Hennig, 2009), although the evidence for this is not always consistent.

MEASURING PHYSIOLOGICAL ASPECTS OF EMOTION

Measuring physiological aspects of emotion poses some tricky challenges. Consider the alternatives. Self-reports sound easy; you just figure out what questions to ask, and ask them. The challenge with self-reports lies in figuring out exactly *what* questions to ask, but once you have a questionnaire it's easy to use. Behavioral measures are more complicated, but still comparatively easy to collect. If you have a video camera, you can record people as they participate in your study and look for specific behaviors later.

If we want to measure changes in autonomic nervous system activation, or in hormones, we seek to measure processes going on *inside* the body. This limits our options—for example, emotion researchers rarely try to measure gastrointestinal processes as an index of parasympathetic activation. Some researchers have tried asking people to report on their physiological state. Unfortunately, most people are terrible at assessing their own heart rate, blood pressure, and so forth, although some individuals are better than others, and people can improve with training (Katkin, 1985). Researchers can measure some effects at the level of the skin, however, as well as using techniques to measure electrical activity associated with underlying autonomic processes.

Commonly Used Measures

Researchers use a wide range of measures to estimate autonomic nervous system activation. Because each measure has strengths and weaknesses, several are typically used in a given study. Almost all of these involve attaching some kind of sensor to the skin, and measuring transmission of electricity, pressure, or light at those points.

The best-known physiological measure of emotion is heart rate. Although most people know what "heart rate" means (number of beats per minute), and many people can measure their own heart rate at the wrist or neck, getting an accurate measure of heart rate in the laboratory is a different process. When you take your own heart rate (say, by laying your pointer finger against the inside of your wrist), you are relying on pressure changes to let you know when each heartbeat happens. In the laboratory, researchers detect electrical signals generated by the heart while it contracts.

We won't go into too much detail here, but basically, your heart generates small but detectable electrical signals when it contracts. These signals can be detected by putting sensors that detect changes in electrical potential on a person's chest, on a diagonal line across the heart. The signal measured using this approach is called an electrocardiogram, or ECG ("EKG" is often used as well). A typical ECG signal, showing electrical activity associated with the heartbeat, is shown in Figure 4.3a.

Cardiologists can describe the parts of the ECG signal in great detail (see Figure 4.3b), but for our purposes we care about just a few points. Note the big spike in each heartbeat, followed by a dip, and then a return to the straight line. This sequence is called the "QRS" complex, and it indicates the contraction and relaxation of the ventricles. The "Q" point indicates the beginning of the contraction, the "R" point indicates the peak of electrical activity, and the "S" point indicates recovery. Look familiar?

Emotion researchers can analyze these signals in one of two ways. One option is just to measure heart rate, in terms of number of beats per minute. However, changes in heart rate associated with emotion in the laboratory can be subtle, just a couple of beats per minute on average, so this measure is a bit crude. Emotion researchers are more likely to measure the average **interbeat interval** for the period of interest instead. To do this, they calculate the time in milliseconds between each of the R-peaks in the ECG signal, and then average those numbers for the time period of interest. This finer measurement allows researchers to detect much more subtle changes.

Another well-known physiological measure is blood pressure, which is influenced by the volume of blood in each heartbeat as well as the constriction of the muscles surrounding the arteries. You've probably had your blood pressure measured

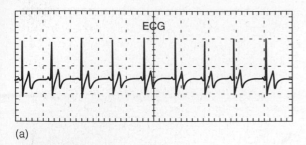

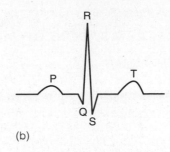

(a)   (b)

FIGURE 4.3 This electrocardiogram (ECG) signal reflects patterns of electrical activity associated with heartbeat, and allows researchers to calculate heart rate. Panel (a) shows a series of beats as they would look on an ECG; panel (b) shows the components of the electrical signal generated by a single heartbeat in detail.

many times before. Unfortunately, researchers can't just keep taking a new blood pressure every few seconds using a sphygmomanometer (isn't that a great word?) and stethoscope, like your doctor. This would clearly interfere with any emotion manipulations the researcher is trying to use! However, computer-controlled blood pressure monitors control a sensor strapped to the wrist or finger, taking a new measure every several seconds. Just like the system in your doctor's office, these monitors apply and release pressure to your pulse, and then examine the effects on blood flow. Researchers often distinguish between **systolic blood pressure**, while your heartbeat is actively pushing blood through your arteries, and **diastolic blood pressure**, while the heart is between beats.

Patterns of vasoconstriction can also be assessed by measuring people's finger temperature. As we noted earlier, sympathetic nervous system activation tends to reduce blood flow to the hands, feet, internal organs, and skin, shunting blood toward the skeletal muscles, heart, and brain instead. Because less blood is being delivered to the hands, they get cold—an effect measured with a temperature-recording sensor.

Respiration rate, or breathing rate, is also typically measured using a pressure-sensitive device. In this case, researchers strap an elastic belt with a tension- or pressure-sensitive component around the participant's diaphragm, and measure changes in pressure associated with breathing. This allows measurement not only of respiration *rate* but also of respiration *depth*, or the volume of each breath.

You'd think it would be easy to measure pupil diameter, because it is one of the few effects of autonomic nervous system activation that you can actually see at the surface of the body. Unfortunately it is actually very challenging. A regular video camera can't detect subtle changes in the size of the pupil, especially if the head is moving. However, researchers who are interested in measuring where an individual is looking, as well as the size of the pupil, can use an eye-tracking device that provides a chin-rest for the participant, as well as a camera that closely follows the eye (Figure 4.4).

Unfortunately, all four of these measures provide ambiguous information about the sympathetic and parasympathetic systems. Recall that sympathetic activation increases heart rate, whereas parasympathetic activation decreases it, and both systems are always being adjusted. If a participant's heart rate increases, is that because the sympathetic nervous system became more active, or the parasympathetic system became *less* active, or both? We have no way of knowing. The same is true of some other measures, such as respiration rate (which people can also control consciously), and pupil diameter.

Fortunately, a few techniques also allow more precise, separate measurement of the sympathetic and parasympathetic branches. One measure, **skin conductance level**, taps into the increased sweat gland activity resulting from sympathetic activation (but not influenced by parasympathetic activation). The human body is full of water, and water does a great job of conducting electricity. When someone

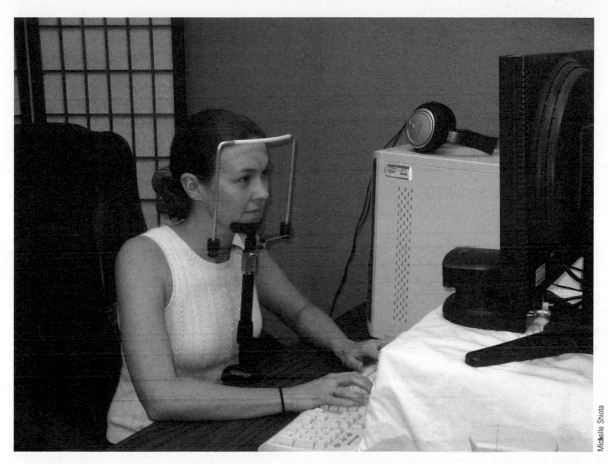

Michelle Shiota

FIGURE 4.4 Researchers can measure changes in pupil diameter with a device that also measures gaze direction. A small camera in front of the computer screen records the participant's eye movements.

sweats, this conductivity increases by a small, but measurable, bit. As a result, researchers can put two sensors on a participant's fingers, send a varying electrical signal through one sensor, and see how long it takes to reach the other sensor. Don't worry, the electrical signal is tiny. In fact, people don't even feel the electricity. The time it takes for the signal to travel from one sensor to the other indicates skin *resistance*, but researchers can just take the inverse of resistance (1/resistance) to get conductance.

Cardiac pre-ejection period is another relatively pure measure of sympathetic activation. Recall that sympathetic nervous system activation not only increases the number of beats per minute, it also

makes the heart beat more forcefully, pushing blood harder through the vasculature. It does this in part by speeding up every contraction of the ventricles, just as a fast kick against a wooden board is more likely to break it than a slow kick. Look back at Figure 4.3, which shows a single heartbeat on an ECG signal. The "Q" point indicates when the ventricles *started* to contract. However, the ventricles need to build up enough pressure to push blood out through the valve leading to the rest of the body; this takes a few milliseconds. Again by measuring electrical signals, researchers can measure when blood has actually been expelled through the aortic valve. The time in milliseconds

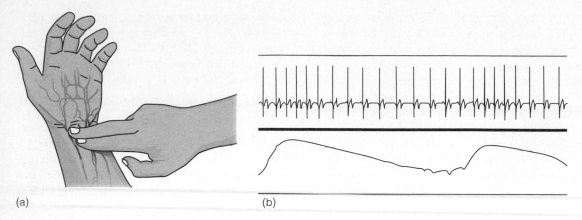

(a)   (b)

F I G U R E   4.5   (a) How to take your pulse at the wrist. (b) The variability in heart rate (upper panel) associated with breathing (lower panel) is called respiratory sinus arrhythmia.

between the Q-point and the expulsion of blood into the aorta is pre-ejection period, which shortens with increasing sympathetic activation.

Although it is technically quite challenging, and still controversial, researchers also have a way to tease parasympathetic activation apart from sympathetic activation. You can actually detect this effect, called **respiratory sinus arrhythmia**, by yourself. If you're sitting quietly and comfortably, use your index/pointer and middle fingers of one hand to measure your pulse on the other wrist, as in Figure 4.5a. Then, take several slow, deep breaths in and out. Notice anything? Many people find that their heart rate speeds up a little while they are inhaling, and slows down while they exhale, as shown in Figure 4.5b. This is because the expansion of the lungs actually interferes with the parasympathetic system's influence on the heart, so it briefly speeds up. The extent of the difference in heart rate between inhalation and exhalation indicates how strongly the parasympathetic system is trying to slow the heart down at any given time.

Think of it this way. Have you ever used a light switch with a switch *and* a rheostat, where the switch controlled whether the light was on at all, and the rheostat controlled the amount of light when it was on? If the rheostat is low, then flipping the switch on

and off doesn't have much impact. If the rheostat is high, flipping the switch on and off has a more dramatic effect, right? In this analogy, the rheostat reflects the degree of parasympathetic input, and the lungs are the switch alternately blocking that signal, or allowing it to pass. The exact method for calculating respiratory sinus arrhythmia is still controversial, but it is an increasingly popular measure.

Hormones are even more complicated to measure than autonomic nervous system activation, because they are in the bloodstream. Fortunately, some hormones (including cortisol) also wind up in saliva in amounts that parallel the amount in the bloodstream, so researchers can take salivary samples and conduct a chemical assay for this substance. It's not as gross as it sounds. Although participants used to have to spit a bunch of saliva into a tube, new techniques allow the participant to roll a wad of cotton around inside the mouth, and then spit *that* into the tube instead. For hormones that do not make it into the saliva, blood must be drawn, so emotion researchers rarely use these measures.

Measurement Challenges

As with any kind of measure in psychology, physiological measures present some challenges. One is that people differ widely in all of the measures discussed above; individual differences in resting heart rate, blood pressure, cortisol level, and so forth are quite dramatic, far outweighing the effects of most laboratory emotion stimuli. (We're not allowed to upset our participants *that* much.) This means that if we want to measure the physiological response associated with an emotion, we need to compare a measurement during the emotion with a measurement taken just beforehand, called a "baseline." This way the effect of the emotion stimulus can be defined as the *change* from baseline to the target period. If the session includes multiple trials, such as a fear trial and a disgust trial, then a separate baseline is needed for each trial to account for any changes between trials that have nothing to do with emotion.

Which brings us to our next point. As we've noted before, the autonomic nervous system is constantly adjusting in response to all kinds of events, both within and outside the body. The various measures listed above change when people stand up, when they jiggle their feet, when they move, and especially when they talk. A researcher has to remove data from a study every time a participant coughs or sneezes, because this messes up the signals. In a study with multiple trials, the greatest effect on participants' physiology is often seen *between* trials, when participants interact with researchers! This is another reason why a baseline before each trial is important, but it also seriously limits the kinds of emotion-eliciting tasks we can have people do.

Third, physiological measures are intrusive. At best, you are attaching sensors to people's hands; at worst, you are placing sensors under people's shirts or inserting needles. Obviously an intrusive procedure makes people nervous, so "baseline" in a physiology study usually means "mildly anxious" rather than emotionally neutral.

Finally, the time course of physiological measures is rather slow. The autonomic nervous system typically takes one to two seconds to react measurably to an emotional stimulus, depending on the stimulus and the type of measurement. Changes in salivary hormones can take 15 minutes or more to detect.

Despite these limitations, physiological measures have one big advantage: you don't have to rely on people to report them, and they're not easily controlled. Someone's heart rate is what it is. If your equipment is in good working order and the sensors are properly placed, your measurement should be correct. Moreover, it will not be biased by your participant's social desirability concerns, interpretation of emotion words, and so forth. Although a few, highly-trained people can change certain aspects of their physiology with great concentration, they are so rare that researchers seldom worry about them.

THE SYMPATHETIC NERVOUS SYSTEM AND EMOTION

Studying autonomic nervous system and hormonal activity as measures of emotion requires a huge assumption—that emotions include physiological changes at all! Recall from Chapter 1 that this was a central tenet of our proposed definitions of emotion, as well as the James-Lange and Schachter-Singer theories. Recall also the assertion in Chapter 2 that emotions exist in order to prepare us for action. All of these suggest that physiological responses should be closely tied to emotional experience. Basic emotion theory even predicts that different emotions will have different physiological signatures, and that these signatures play a crucial role in our own experience of emotion. In contrast, the Schachter-Singer theory and dimensional theories suggest that all strong emotions simply involve "arousal" in the sense of sympathetic activation, and that distinctions between emotions are illusory.

Clearly the relationship between the physiological and feeling aspects of emotion is important for emotion theory, as well as for valid measurement. There are really two questions here: (1) How well do physiological and feeling aspects of emotion hang together in terms of the overall intensity of emotion; and (2) Do different emotions have qualitatively different physiological profiles?

"Coherence" of Physiological Aspects with Feelings and Behavior

Let's start with the first question. Focusing just on the intensity of emotion, how well do the feeling and physiological aspects hang together? Even the Schachter-Singer and dimensional theories of emotion suggest that the intensity of physiological arousal should be related to the intensity of emotional experience, and that there are more-arousing and less-arousing emotions. Unfortunately, initial studies of **emotional response coherence**, or the extent to which self-reports of emotion actually predict physiological changes and simple behaviors like facial expressions, offered pretty weak evidence for this claim (Bradley & Lang, 2000). In these studies, researchers measured people's sympathetic nervous system arousal while they performed a task, like watching an emotional film, and then asked them to rate how strong their emotional feelings were during the task. They would then study whether the people who had the strongest sympathetic nervous system reactions were the same people who reported feeling the strongest emotion. Many studies found little relationship—self-reports of emotion and physiological arousal only weakly predicted each other, and sometimes they were inversely related.

Think about this for a minute, though. Let's say that Iris, for example, reported very strong feelings while watching an emotional film, relative to all of the other participants, but she showed only relatively weak increases in physiological arousal. Is that the same as saying that her arousal did not go up *at the same time that her own self-report of emotion increased?* Not at all! Here we run into one of the big problems in emotion research—self-reports are one of the "gold standards" we use for other measures, but we know they are subjective! Iris's idea of "strong" feelings may be different from other participants, but as long as her own self-reports of emotion and her arousal seem to hang together over time, the coherence hypothesis is in good shape.

A study actually tested this "within-subject" approach to emotional response coherence (Mauss et al., 2005). A within-subject approach is helpful because it avoids comparing each participant's self-rating to everyone else's; instead, each participant's self-rating at one time is compared to her own self-ratings at other times (the same is true for physiological arousal). In the Mauss et al. study, participants watched a five-minute film clip that went from funny, to sad, and back to funny again, three times. Each time, their cardiovascular activation (a composite of heart rate and several other measures) and skin conductance level were measured throughout the film. Once they just watched the film; another time they used a hand-held rating dial to indicate, continuously, how amused they felt throughout the film; another time they used the same dial to indicate, again continuously, how sad they felt throughout the film.

Afterward, the researchers asked whether people's physiological responses and self-reports of emotion tended to "hang together," or travel consistently together over the course of the film. Self-reported amusement showed a moderate positive correlation with cardiovascular arousal and a strong positive correlation with skin conductance, suggesting that amusement was consistently accompanied by sympathetic activation. Self-reported sadness was unrelated to cardiovascular activation over the course of the film, but it was negatively related to skin conductance, suggesting that sadness was associated with decreased sympathetic activation (Figure 4.6).

There are a couple of puzzling aspects to these findings, and more research is definitely needed. One surprise involves the directions of the relationships between the physiological variables and the self-reports. As we shall see in the next section, there is much controversy regarding the physiological aspects of specific emotions, but several studies have suggested that amusement should *reduce* sympathetic arousal, whereas sadness should *increase* it (Fredrickson & Levenson, 1998; Cacioppo et al., 2000). Also, you might interpret these data somewhat differently if you look at the slopes of change during each section of the films than if you look at correlations between physiology and self-report across the entire period. For example, although cardiovascular activation was uncorrelated with self-reports of sadness, that activation generally drops during the funny parts of the film

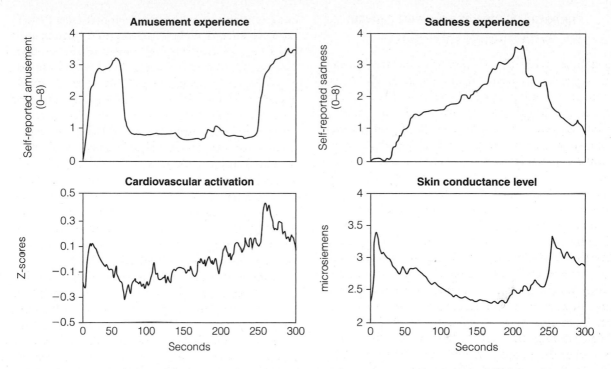

FIGURE 4.6 A within-subjects approach to measuring response system coherence is ideal for assessing the relationship between physiological and feeling aspects of emotion.

SOURCE: From Mauss et al. (2005). "The Tie That Binds? Coherence Among Emotion Experience, Behavior, and Physiology". *Emotion*, vol. 5(2), pp. 175–190. Reprinted by permission.

and rises during the sad parts. Even given these lingering questions, however, the researchers found much better evidence of coherence using the within-subject approach than had been found before.

Autonomic Nervous System Differences Among Emotions

Finding that emotional feelings are often accompanied by physiological changes does not necessarily mean that physiological changes define specific emotions. Consider the Schachter-Singer theory of emotion, presented in Chapter 1. According to these researchers, the extent of physiological arousal should determine the *intensity* of your emotional feelings, but the *type* of emotion you feel (anger, elation, or others) depends on the situation and your appraisal of it. Similarly, dimensional hypotheses of emotion such as the circumplex model and

the evaluative space model suggest that the same level of "arousal" can be part of many emotions that we label with different words. Each of these perspectives accounts for the coherence findings discussed above, but without making claims about basic emotions.

The strong version of the James-Lange theory offers a somewhat different claim—that different patterns of physiological responding will be experienced as different emotional feelings (James, 1884). As we noted in Chapter 2, evolutionary approaches also tend to emphasize the different adaptive functions served by specific emotions, suggesting that different emotions should have different physiological effects (Tooby & Cosmides, 2008). Researchers taking a strong "basic emotions" approach have been the most explicit on this point, stating clearly that discrete emotions should involve different physiological profiles (Ekman, 1992; Levenson, 1992). Where do the data stand?

Early studies of the **autonomic specificity hypothesis**—the hypothesis that different emotions involve different physiological profiles—were inconclusive. An individual study might show specific patterns associated with different emotions, but different studies would find completely different results. One major criterion scientists use to decide whether to take a finding seriously is whether it can be *replicated* in multiple studies, ideally by different researchers. Autonomic specificity failed to meet this criterion, and many researchers abandoned the idea.

However, these early attempts had a number of flaws. As we saw in the "coherence" study described above, it is important to measure changes in emotional physiology along with changes in feelings, during a reasonably strong emotional stimulus. The physiological changes associated with emotion can be quite brief—sometimes lasting just a few seconds—and early studies of the autonomic specificity hypothesis did not always measure physiological changes during the time when emotional feelings were most likely. Also, researchers often failed to make sure that the research participants had felt the intended emotion at all—what is now called a "manipulation check."

In a first attempt to correct these problems, Paul Ekman, Robert Levenson, and Wallace Friesen (1983) conducted a study asking whether anger, fear, sadness, happiness, surprise, and disgust could be differentiated in terms of their autonomic nervous system effects. Does the list of emotions look familiar? Right, it's the same list of emotions Ekman and colleagues used in their studies of facial expressions. In this study, the researchers had sets of participants engage in two emotion-eliciting tasks: (1) Posing facial expressions of each emotion, following muscle-by-muscle instructions; and (2) reliving strong emotional memories. In an interesting twist, the researchers used professional actors and researchers who study facial movements as participants, to ensure that they would be able to follow the facial movement instructions accurately. Only data from trials where the participant reported a moderately strong experience of the target emotion were used. Physiological variables in the study were heart rate, finger temperature, skin conductance, and muscle tension.

The researchers found that in both tasks, the six emotions showed different results for heart rate and finger temperature. The results for these variables are shown in Figure 4.7. Each graph shows baseline-to-trial change scores on a physiological variable, for each of the six emotions. As you can see, heart rate increased substantially from baseline during anger, fear, and sadness, but not during happiness or surprise. During disgust, heart rate actually decreased slightly. Also, finger temperature increased dramatically during anger, and somewhat during happiness, but decreased a little during fear and disgust. This pattern across the two variables suggests that at least anger, fear, and disgust can be differentiated from each other in terms of their autonomic effects, although the status of sadness, happiness, and surprise is still uncertain.

This is only one study, of course. The same team of researchers found almost identical effects of the six emotions in future studies, all using facial expression instruction to elicit the emotions (Levenson, Ekman, & Friesen, 1990). However, other researchers again found different patterns. One problem is that different researchers used different techniques to elicit emotion, and these techniques may themselves have had implications for physiological responding (Christie & Friedman, 2003). For example, exaggerating facial expressions of emotion has physiological effects that would have blurred the effects of emotion in the studies described just above (Demaree, Schmeichel, Robinson, & Everhart, 2004). Looking at the body of new data, some researchers concluded that the evidence for autonomic specificity was strong (Levenson, 1992), whereas others argued that it was inconclusive (e.g., Zajonc & McIntosh, 1992).

In an attempt to resolve this confusion, John Cacioppo and several of his colleagues conducted a meta-analysis of the existing studies of autonomic specificity (Cacioppo, Berntson, Larsen, Poehlmann, & Ito, 2000). As we mentioned in Chapter 3, this technique allows researchers to consolidate the results of many studies by different researchers into one, large statistical analysis. One advantage of meta-analysis is that if studies use different techniques (such as eliciting emotions

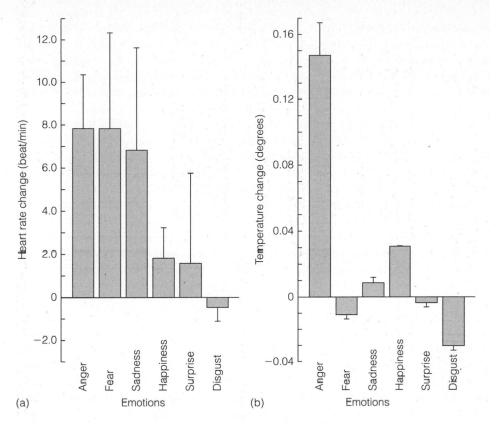

FIGURE 4.7 These baseline-to-trial change scores in (a) heart rate and (b) finger temperature suggest different physiological profiles for a few different emotions.

SOURCE: Ekman, Levenson, and Friesen (1983). Autonomic Nervous System Activity Distinguishes among Emotions. *Science,* New Series, Vol. 221(4616): 1208–1210.

via facial expressions, relived memories, and so on), the analysis can control for these differences. The results of the meta-analysis confirmed some of the original findings about differences between emotions, failed to support others, and found some new differences as well.

Some differences confirmed in the meta-analysis were: (1) Happiness generally involves less physiological arousal than the negative emotions of anger, fear, sadness, and disgust. (2) Heart rate accelerates more during anger, fear, and sadness than during disgust. (3) Anger involves higher blood pressure than fear, smaller increases in heart rate and stroke volume, and greater finger pulse volume and temperature. These patterns do a pretty good job of distinguishing the negative emotions from happiness, of disgust from the other negative

emotions, and of anger and fear from each other, although the status of sadness is still uncertain.

One thing to note about the meta-analysis is that, although it included multiple physiological variables, the results emphasized differences between emotions on one variable at a time. The autonomic specificity hypothesis does not necessarily claim that every emotion will differ on every physiological variable; rather it suggests that emotions should differ in their patterns, or profiles, *across* measures (Larsen, Berntson, Poehlmann, Ito, & Cacioppo, 2008). This is important because, as we noted earlier, the sympathetic and parasympathetic branches of the autonomic nervous system are adjusting constantly, and even within each of these branches, certain sub-branches adjust independently of the others.

Some have taken a more explicit approach to measuring profiles of autonomic activity in different emotions. Often these studies involve complicated statistical techniques. For example, Gerhard Stemmler and colleagues compared the effects of anger and fear on 24 different physiological variables, and distinguished the two emotions using a technique called *multivariate analysis* that examines all of the variables at once (Stemmler, Aue, & Wacker, 2007). Israel Christie and Bruce Friedman (2003) used a technique called *pattern classification analysis* that works backward from the usual analysis. Instead of asking whether different emotions produce different physiological profiles, this analysis asks whether the program can identify the emotion in each trial based upon the pattern of physiological effects, in data from the whole study. Christie and Friedman found that their analysis correctly classified just over a third of trials across seven emotions—significantly better than chance, but far from perfect.

So, after hundreds of studies on the autonomic specificity question, where do we stand? Who wins—the basic emotion camp, or the dimensional camp? As is so often the case in science, just as in the rest of life, it's not that simple. Negative emotions generally seem to involve greater sympathetic activation, or "arousal," than happiness, and it has proved difficult to find strong, consistent evidence clearly differentiating among negative emotions. This is consistent with the general perspectives of the Schachter-Singer and dimensionalist camps. On the other hand, the Cacioppo et al. (2000) meta-analysis did document a few, specific distinctions among anger, fear, and disgust, and more complex analyses looking at many variables at once tend to find better evidence for differences among emotions.

The existing studies still have many limitations. For one thing, few studies include a neutral-emotion condition, and without such a condition it is difficult to tell whether effects are due to *emotion,* or to whatever task you gave to participants. Even an emotionally neutral visual stimulus has powerful effects on physiology, called the "orienting effect" (Stekelenburg & van Boxtel, 2002). Worse yet, the results vary depending on the task used for eliciting an emotion. For example, whereas reliving a sad memory typically makes heart rate increase, listening to sad music can make heart rate *decrease* (Etzel, Johnsen, Dickerson, Tranel, & Adolphs, 2006). The best we can say now is that the data do not seem to support the strong version of the Schachter-Singer theory, which suggests complete physiological similarity among emotions. However, autonomic specificity is still a "viable but unconfirmed hypothesis" (Russell, 2003, p. 163), and physiological evidence for basic emotions theory has a long way to go. Future studies will probably need to integrate these perspectives in order to make sense of the research.

Physiological Aspects of Positive Emotions

You probably noticed that the last section focused on negative emotions. In the Cacioppo et al. (2008) meta-analysis, happiness was easily distinguished from the four negative emotions, by virtue of showing little physiological effect at all. Are positive emotions not "physical" in the same way as negative emotions? Are they emotions at all? As we shall see in Chapter 10, this is a complex set of questions. With regard to emotion physiology, however, the effects of positive emotion are not as bland as they might seem.

It is true that some studies find little or no effect of positive emotion on autonomic physiology (e.g., Ekman et al., 1983; Levenson et al., 1992). Other studies, such as the "coherence" study discussed above, have found that positive emotions involve increased sympathetic arousal (Christie & Friedman, 2003; Demaree et al., 2004; Giuliani, McRae, & Gross, 2008; Mauss et al., 2005; Neumann & Waldstein, 2001). On the other hand, several studies of the **undoing effect of positive emotion** suggest that positive emotions help people recover from the sympathetic arousal associated with negative emotion. In these studies, participants watch a frightening or sad film clip, and then watch either a neutral clip or a clip eliciting contentment or amusement. The first film clip reliably elicits increases in heart rate, blood pressure, sweating, and so forth, and these effects tend to last for a while. However, participants who subsequently watch a more positive film recover faster, returning more quickly to their baseline physiology, than participants who watch the neutral film (Fredrickson & Levenson, 1998; Fredrickson, Mancuso, Branigan, & Tugade, 2000).

So, do positive emotions increase arousal, reduce it, or have no effect at all? The limitations of the existing studies make it very difficult to answer this question, and there probably is not a single answer anyway. Most studies of autonomic specificity have included only "happiness" as the positive emotion, although a couple of studies have included one or two others as well. It's not very clear what "happiness" is, in these studies. Think about the last time you felt very, very happy. Was it when you graduated from high school? Did you suddenly receive a lot of money you weren't expecting? Was it the first time your romantic partner said he or she loved you? Was it a party with lots of friends, or a quiet day luxuriating on a sunny beach? People say they feel happy at all of these times. However, basic emotion theorists suggest that these events might be distinct in both their subjective aspects and their physiology (Shiota, Campos, Keltner, & Hertenstein, 2004). More research is needed to address this question.

STRESS AND ITS HEALTH CONSEQUENCES

You might be wondering—"what is a section about stress doing in a textbook on emotion?" Stress is not on any psychologist's list of emotions of which we are aware. Nevertheless, it has enormous impact on people's emotions. Think of it this way: if stress is not a distinct emotion, is it *emotional*? Very! Perhaps what we call "stress" really reflects a common feature of emotions such as fear, anger, and grief. This common feature appears to involve physiological aspects of emotion—after all, the term "fight-or-flight" was first coined by Walter Cannon to describe the physical reactions many animals have

to a variety of stressful conditions. In the medical field, the concept of stress has received a great deal of attention, with thousands of studies asking whether stress is associated with greater susceptibility to various health problems.

Have you ever noticed how often people say they are "under stress?" We seem to be surrounded by stressed-out people, and sources of stress are to be found everywhere you look. As Robert Sapolsky (1998) has pointed out, the prime stressors for humans today are different from those of our ancestors. Stressors for our remote ancestors were probably much like those of nonhuman animals today—immediate, life-and-death crises. If a fox is chasing a rabbit, the next few seconds will determine whether the rabbit lives or dies, and whether the fox eats today or not. It is a crisis, but at least when it's over, it's over, and if the critter survived (or got his meal) he can relax.

For people today, the most common stressors are less immediate and life-threatening and more prolonged, such as difficulty paying the bills, dealing with a troubled romantic or family relationship, or coping with a stressful job. Instead of resolving quickly one way or the other, these problems can persist for weeks, months, or years. Because the human "fight-or-flight response" evolved to deal with scenarios like the fox-rabbit chase, our bodies react to these prolonged, daily problems as if we were running or fighting for our lives. Our reactions are sometimes inappropriate, and our health suffers.

What exactly is stress? What are the biological effects of short-term stress? What happens when these effects add up over time?

Hans Selye and the Discovery of Stress

Unlike the concept of emotion, the biological and psychological concept of stress is relatively recent. Like many advances in science, it was discovered largely by accident. The story is a great one, and offers lessons about the importance of observation and ingenuity in science, as well as about stress (Sapolsky, 1998).

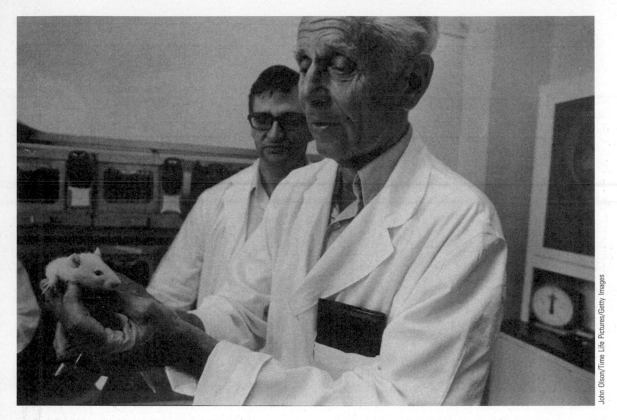

John Olson/Time Life Pictures/Getty Images

F I G U R E 4.8 Hans Selye (1907–1982), an Austrian-born Canadian physician who became a great pioneer in the study of stress.

Hundreds of years ago, medical doctors treated most illnesses in the same way. When someone was ill, they would recommend bed rest, perhaps apply leeches to withdraw "excess" blood, and prescribe herbs or "cure-all" tonics. The great progress of scientific medicine over the last century or so depended on distinguishing one disease from another, so that today the recommended treatment depends on which disease one has.

In spite of the differences among diseases, when Hans Selye (Figure 4.8) was in medical school, he noticed that almost all patients had many symptoms in common. Regardless of their specific symptoms, most had a fever, loss of appetite, sleepiness, decreased activity levels, decreased sex drive, and various changes in their immune systems. Years later, Selye was doing research

with laboratory rats, testing whether a particular kind of substance tended to cause cancer. He administered the substance (by injection) into half of the rats on a regular basis and injected a saline solution into the remaining rats as a control group. When he checked the rats for cancer after some months, he expected that the group given the experimental treatment would have an unusually high rate of cancer. He was right, but was surprised to find that his control rats *also* had a remarkably high rate of cancer!

It turns out that Selye, though a brilliant scientist, was not especially good at giving injections to rats. When trying to administer the shots to both groups of rats he would frequently miss the injection spot, get bitten, drop the rat, chase it around the room, and generally (though unintentionally) torment the poor creature. When he compared rats he had injected with the rats a more skilled research assistant had injected, it turned out that Selye's rats were more likely to have developed cancer. In following up on this lead, Selye noticed that either prolonged heat or prolonged cold increased the rats' heart rate and breathing rate, enlarged their adrenal glands, weakened their immune system, and increased their risk of stomach ulcers and other illnesses. He found the same pattern after rats were exposed to pain, poisons, enforced activity (such as confinement to a motorized running wheel), or frightening stimuli (such as a cat, a more aggressive rat, or an inept researcher chasing it around the room).

Selye concluded that each kind of challenge to the body produced its own specific effects, but also produced more general effects, which were due to the body's efforts to fight the problem. He described the body's reaction to any threat as the **General Adaptation Syndrome,** which he said progressed through three stages—alarm, resistance, and exhaustion. **Alarm** is a brief period of high arousal of the sympathetic nervous system, readying the body for vigorous activity. **Resistance** is a stage of prolonged but moderate arousal. During resistance, the adrenal cortex secretes the hormones cortisol, epinephrine and norepinephrine, which enable body cells to maintain high, steady levels of activity, heal wounds, and fight infections. With even more severe challenges, the body enters the stage of **exhaustion,** characterized by weakness, fatigue, loss of appetite, and lack of interest. The body's prolonged fight against its threats has weakened its ability to do anything else. The immune system becomes less active and the individual becomes more vulnerable to illness. Exactly when someone moves from one stage of response to another is difficult to predict, and the transition between one stage and the next is gradual, but the data now strongly confirm the idea that short-term responses to stress differ from long-term responses.

Eventually Selye introduced the term *stress* to refer to the General Adaptation Syndrome. Selye was not the first to use the term stress, but he greatly popularized it, and changed what people meant by the term. **Stress**, according to Selye's definition, is the nonspecific response of the body to any demand made upon it. The analogy is to a metal: Every time you bend a metal, you weaken it. After you have bent it, bending it *back* also weakens it. Similarly, according to Selye, any major change in your life stresses you by demanding that *you* change, like bending a metal. Changing in any direction—pleasant or unpleasant—stresses you, and changing back stresses you also.

Defining and Measuring Stress

If Selye's definition is a useful one, then a good way to measure stress is to examine all the changes that have occurred in someone's life. Researchers have developed several questionnaires based on this assumption, each with its own strengths and weaknesses (Sarason, Johnson, & Siegel, 1979). We shall consider one of them in detail, as an example of the others.

An influential pioneering study devised a checklist to measure people's stress by how many life-change items they checked (Holmes & Rahe, 1977). The researchers began by assembling a list of major life changes. Based on Selye's concept, the authors included both undesirable events (such as death of a loved one, divorce, or losing one's job) and desirable events that cause upheaval (such as marriage, birth of a child, or taking a vacation). They also included items such as "change in financial state" where *change* could refer to either an increase or a decrease. Again, the assumption was that changing something in life is like bending a metal—a movement in either direction is stressful.

Because various life changes are not equally stressful, they should not count equally. The researchers asked more than 300 people to assign 100 points to "death of a spouse," and then to rate how stressful each of the other life changes would be in comparison. They computed the averages, developing the Social Readjustment Rating Scale (SRRS); a version of this scale (Hobson et al., 1998) is shown in Table 4.1. The instruction is to check the items

TABLE 4.1   The Revised Social Readjustment Rating Scale (Hobson et al., 1998).

Rank	Life Event	Points	Rank	Life Event	Points
1.	Death of spouse/mate	87	27.	Experiencing employment discrimination/sexual harassment	48
2.	Death of close family member	79	28.	Attempting to modify addictive behavior of self	47
3.	Major injury/illness to self	78	29.	Attempting to modify addictive behavior of close family member	46
4.	Detention in jail or other institution	76	30.	Employer reorganization/downsizing	45
5.	Major injury/illness to close family member	72	31.	Dealing with infertility/miscarriage	44
6.	Foreclosure on loan/mortgage	71	32.	Getting married/remarried	43
7.	Divorce	71	33.	Changing employers/careers	43
8.	Being a victim of a crime	70	34.	Failure to obtain/qualify for a mortgage	42
9.	Being the victim of police brutality	69	35.	Pregnancy of self/spouse/mate	41
10.	Infidelity	69	36.	Experiencing discrimination/harassment outside the workplace	39
11.	Experiencing domestic violence/sexual abuse	69	37.	Release from jail	39
12.	Separation or reconciliation with spouse/mate	66	38.	Spouse/mate begins/ceases work outside the home	38
13.	Being laid off/fired/unemployed	64	39.	Major disagreement with boss/co-worker	37
14.	Experiencing financial problems/difficulties	62	40.	Change in residence	35
15.	Death of close friend	61	41.	Finding appropriate child care/day care	34
16.	Surviving a disaster	59	42.	Experiencing a large unexpected monetary gain	33
17.	Becoming a single parent	59	43.	Changing positions (transfer, promotion)	33
18.	Assuming responsibility for sick or elderly loved one	56	44.	Gaining a new family member	33
19.	Loss of or major reduction in health insurance/benefits	56	45.	Changing work responsibilities	32
20.	Self/close family member arrested for violating the law	56	46.	Child leaving home	30
21.	Major disagreement over child support/custody/visitation	53	47.	Obtaining a home mortgage	30
22.	Experiencing/involved in auto accident	53	48.	Obtaining a major loan other than home mortgage	30
23.	Being disciplined at work/demoted	53	49.	Retirement	28
24.	Dealing with unwanted pregnancy	51	50.	Beginning/ceasing formal education	26
25.	Adult child moving in with parent/vice versa	50	51.	Receiving a ticket for violating the law	22
26.	Child develops behavior or learning problem	49			

SOURCE: From "Stressful Life Events" by Charles J. Hobson et al. in International Journal of Stress Management, 5 (1998), pp. 1–23. Reprinted with permission of the author.

you have experienced in the last 12 months, and then add up the corresponding points.

For a large representative sample of U.S. adults, the median total score was 145 (Hobson & Delunas, 2001). However, the distribution of scores is not a neat bell-shaped curve. About one-fourth of all people report scores of zero, and more than 5 percent report scores above a thousand. Although the median is 145, the mean is 278.

The scale does not include every stressor we could imagine—no questionnaire of reasonable length could—but it includes enough that it probably applies to most people. However, it contains a number of problems. One mixed blessing is that the instrument adds points for various minor stressors, and may weight them too heavily. Suppose you graduate from college (26 points), get some unexpected money (33), move to a new address (35), and then start a new job (43). Those events give you a total of 137 points—far more than you would get for a divorce (71) or the death of a husband or wife (87). Should a series of minor stressors count as much as or more than one major stressor? Probably not (Birbaum & Sotoodeh, 1991).

Another problem is the ambiguity of certain items. Consider, for example, the item "Major disagreement with boss/coworker." What you consider a friendly disagreement may seem like a major conflict to someone else. The stressfulness of an event also depends on individual circumstances. For example, being laid off from work could be a catastrophe for a 50-year-old who loved the job and expects to have trouble finding another one; it means almost nothing to an 18-year-old who was planning to quit next week anyway to start college. As Richard Lazarus (1977) pointed out, the stressfulness of an event depends on how people interpret the event and what they think they can do about it. Measuring the stressfulness of an event *to the individual* is obviously critical, but virtually impossible with a brief questionnaire.

Because of all of the conceptual issues raised by these problems in measuring stress, some contemporary theorists have been moving away from Selye's definition. According to Bruce McEwen (2000, p. 173), **stress** is "an event or events that

are interpreted as threatening to an individual and which elicit physiological and behavioral responses." Note three key points about this definition: First, Selye defined stress in terms of the body's reaction to change in a person's life; McEwen defined it in terms of the event itself. This difference in the meaning of the word "stress" sometimes causes problems. Second, Selye's definition included all kinds of changes in life, including pleasant ones. McEwen's definition is limited to threatening events. Third, McEwen's definition emphasizes that stress depends on how the individual *interprets* an event, not just the event itself. For example, not getting a promotion might or might not be stressful, depending on someone's expectations. Suppose you see your professor sitting in the library grading term papers. On one paper, the professor scowls and writes lots of red marks to indicate errors. If you think the professor is reading *your* paper, you will be stressed. If you think it is someone else's, you won't be bothered at all.

How Stress Can Affect Health

Selye's original definition of stress reflected the context in which he studied it—the effect of certain kinds of experiences on physical health. Much, if not most, of the later research on stress has also emphasized its role in illness. Researchers have often bypassed issues of the subjective aspects of stress. In this way, researchers can identify stressful situations, and then examine the mechanisms by which the stressors alter physiology and health. Some of these mechanisms relate to how people think about the situations they face, but researchers also sometimes focus purely on the body's reactions, regardless of what caused them.

There is little question that stress is associated with increased risks to health. People have long observed that if a couple has been together for many years, the death of one leaves the other vulnerable to a wide variety of illnesses, ranging from dental problems (Hugoson, Ljungquist, & Breivik, 2002) to cancer (Lillberg, Verkasalo, Kaprio, Teppo, Helenius, & Kostenvuo, 2003). After the death of one spouse, the other has a 40-50 percent higher than usual probability of also dying in the next six months, compared to other people of the same age (Manor & Eisenbach, 2003). People also tend to get sick after other, less severe life changes. For example, many students describe their first year of college as a stressful time (Gall, Evans, & Bellerose, 2000), and many of them develop health problems (Fazio & Powell, 1997). Research suggests two ways this might happen.

The first has to do with the cumulative effects of repeated, intense, short-term stress on the cardiovascular system. A casual observation gave rise to a hypothesis about stress and heart disease: An upholsterer repairing chairs in a physician's waiting room noted that the fronts of the seats were worn out, but not the backs. The physician started watching the patients and reported that most of his heart patients sat on the front edges of the seats, impatiently waiting for their appointments. The hypothesis therefore arose that heart disease was linked to an impatient, high-achieving, success-driven personality (Friedman & Rosenman, 1974).

That type of personality became known as **Type A personality,** marked by competitiveness, impatience, and hostility. Since the mid-1970s, many studies have sought a link between Type A personality and heart disease. Although most studies fail to find much relationship between heart disease and the competitive, success-seeking aspect of Type A personality (Kawachi et al., 1998), results are stronger for the hostility aspect—the more emotional characteristic of Type A people. With a few exceptions (O'Malley, Jones, Feuerstein, & Taylor, 2000; Sykes et al., 2002), most studies have found a significant link between self-reports of anger or hostility and the risk of heart disease itself, or heart conditions that are precursors to disease (Eaker, Sullivan, Kelly-Hayes, D'Agostino, & Benjamin, 2004; Iribarren et al., 2000; J. E. Williams et al., 2000; Yan, Liu, Matthews, Daviglus, Ferguson, & Kiefe, 2003). In particular, frequent intense but inhibited anger is associated with greater risk for heart disease (Vella & Friedman, 2009). Many of these studies rely on self-reports of hostility. However, another promising study used behavioral observations to measure hostility, instead of questionnaires.

The researchers videotaped people's facial expressions during an interview while recording their *transient myocardial ischemias*—brief periods of inadequate blood flow to the heart muscles of the heart. Transient myocardial ischemias are usually painless, but they can be precursors to heart attacks. People who showed many facial expressions of anger were more likely than others to have transient myocardial ischemia during the interview (Rosenberg et al., 2001).

Recent studies suggest that any frequent or prolonged stress, not just hostility, might have long-term implications for cardiovascular health. One study found that high levels of anger, anxiety, or depression predicted later onset of high blood pressure, although the effect size was small (Rutledge & Hogan, 2002). One longitudinal study found that women with five or more symptoms of post-traumatic stress disorder were more than three times as likely to develop heart disease over the next 14 years as women with no such symptoms at the beginning of the study, even after controlling for pre-existing physical and psychological risk factors (Kubansky, Koenen, Jones, & Eaton, 2009). Unfortunately, the exact pathway through which repeated stress leads to heart disease is still poorly understood (Miller & Blackwell, 2006).

The second mechanism by which stress might affect health has to do with the distinction between short- and long-term stress, and implications for immune system functioning. A sudden stressful event arouses the sympathetic system—the alarm stage of the stress response. That "fight or flight" response readies the body for vigorous actions, but the body cannot maintain emergency readiness for long. Even in an ongoing tense situation, sympathetic arousal fades.

With continuing arousal needed to combat some challenge, the resistance system kicks in: the **HPA axis,** composed of the hypothalamus, pituitary gland, and adrenal gland. Like the sympathetic nervous system, the HPA axis readies the body for vigorous action, but it responds more slowly and lasts longer. That is, it readies the body for a more prolonged struggle, such as a difficult job, a tense relationship with someone you meet every day, living near a war zone, or simply worrying about everything that might go wrong. Although the HPA axis prepares the body for a prolonged struggle, people fighting a prolonged struggle do not feel constantly vigorous. Frequently they feel withdrawn or depressed, their performance is inconsistent, and they complain of decreased quality of life (Evans, Bullinger, & Hygge, 1998).

The HPA axis is illustrated in Figure 4.9. The hypothalamus reacts to a stressful event by sending a releasing hormone to the anterior pituitary gland, which in turn secretes adrenocorticotropic hormone (ACTH). ACTH travels through the bloodstream to the adrenal gland (located adjacent to each kidney). The adrenal gland responds to ACTH by releasing the hormone **cortisol**, which enhances metabolism and increases the availability of fuels. The body stores fuels in the form of carbohydrates, fats, and proteins; cortisol mobilizes all three types of fuel to come out of storage and enter the bloodstream. That activity is helpful up to a point, but muscles are the source of protein. When cortisol provides you with extra protein, it does so by breaking down your muscles. You don't want that process to continue for too long.

A brief or moderate elevation of cortisol not only elevates blood sugar levels but also stimulates parts of the immune system, helping to fight off illnesses ranging from viruses to tumors (Benschop et al., 1995; F. Cohen et al., 1999; Connor & Leonard, 1998). For a given individual, the levels of various kinds of immune cells and their activity are fairly consistent over long periods of time (Burleson et al., 2002), but they can fluctuate temporarily as a result of injury, illness, or stress. To be more precise, brief stress activates certain parts of the immune system, such as the natural killer cells, the leukocyte scavengers, and the secretion of cytokines (Segerstrom & Miller, 2004). The ongoing immune response leads to a variety of physical and behavioral effects that also help fight disease. Among these responses are sleepiness (Ram et al., 1997), fever (Ek et al., 2001), inactivity, decreased appetite, and decreased sex drive—the very symptoms originally identified by Hans Selye as a medical student.

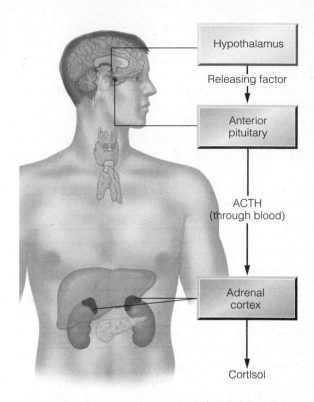

FIGURE 4.9 The hypothalamus-anterior pituitary-adrenal cortex axis. Stress leads to secretion of the hormone cortisol from the adrenal gland. Cortisol elevates blood sugar and increases metabolism.

These adaptations help to conserve energy, so the body can devote more of its resources to fighting the disease.

The immune response also causes a fever, or increase in core body temperature. Perhaps you have thought of fever as something a disease does to you, but in fact it is something your body does to fight the disease. Many kinds of bacteria reproduce faster at normal body temperature than at feverish temperatures, and a mild fever (up to 39°C/103°F) increases someone's probability of surviving the infection (Kluger, 1991).

Even brief bouts of fear or anger stimulate many aspects of immune system response (Mayne, 1999). Many college students have increased immune system activity during final exams, generally a stressful time (Liu et al., 2002). Rats subjected to inescapable shocks develop a fever, sleep much more than usual, and decrease their appetite and sex drive. People who feel much stress, such as those who are nervous about giving a public speech, show some of the same signs (Maier & Watkins, 1998). So, if you have been under a great deal of stress and start to feel ill, the problem may be the stress itself; the stress simply makes you *feel* sick. Is the body "making a mistake" by acting sick when it is merely under stress? Perhaps not: Most highly stressful events throughout the animal kingdom, including the stressors our own ancestors faced, have been situations in which an injury is likely. When your brain identifies some situation as intensely stressful, in effect it tells the immune system, "Get ready for a probable injury!"

The problem comes with long-term stress, when the body enters the exhaustion stage of the General Adaptation Syndrome. Although your initial response to a stressor activates your immune system, prolonged stress weakens it (Segerstrom & Miller, 2004; Zorrilla et al., 2001). For example, production of natural killer cells is suppressed in women taking care of a husband with terminal cancer, women who became widows recently, survivors of a major earthquake, and medical students during final exams week (Glaser, Rice, Speicher, Stout, & Kiecolt-Glaser, 1986; Inoue-Sakurai, Maruyama, & Morimoto, 2000; Irwin, Daniels, Risch, Bloom, & Weiner, 1988). The result? Increased chance of illness. In one study volunteers reported their recent stressful experiences before being injected with a common cold virus. People who reported seriously stressful experiences lasting more than a month were more likely than others to become ill, presumably because their prolonged stress had weakened their immune response (S. Cohen et al., 1998).

Ironically, this effect may be due at least partly to cortisol. Short-term changes in stress levels or cortisol release do not impair immune responses (Bodner, Ho, & Kreek, 1998). However, because prolonged cortisol directs more energy toward producing blood sugar, less energy should be available for the synthesis of proteins needed by the immune system. The data are mixed on this last point,

however. On one hand, many studies do find that prolonged high stress elevates cortisol levels, decreases immune function, and impairs health. That pattern has been reported for elderly people caring for a demented spouse (Vedhara et al., 1999), daughters of breast cancer patients (M. Cohen et al., 2002), and people traumatized by an earthquake (Fukuda, Morimoto, Mure, & Maruyama, 2000). On the other hand, people suffering from posttraumatic stress disorder—the ultimate in stress exhaustion—present a puzzling pattern. Because of their extreme stress, we would expect to find elevated cortisol levels, but many studies find that their cortisol levels are *lower* than average (Bremner et al., 2003; Glover & Poland, 2002; Yehuda, 1997). Nevertheless, their immune response is weakened, according to most studies (e.g., Kawamura, Kim, & Asukai, 2001). The results vary from one study to another, and several aspects of immune response are actually stronger than average in war veterans suffering from very long-term PTSD (Laudenslager et al., 1998; Spivak et al., 1997). More research is needed to track the relationship between cortisol and changes in immune response over moderate and long periods of stress.

Although the relationship between prolonged cortisol and immune functioning is unsettled, other harms from prolonged cortisol are better established. Prolonged cortisol elevation magnifies the effects of toxic chemicals on the hippocampus, a brain area essential for memory (Sapolsky, 1992). High cortisol levels therefore lead to gradual damage to the hippocampus and associated decline of memory (Cameron & McKay, 1999). In one study, baby rats were separated from their mothers (very stressful for infant mammals) for three hours each day for the first two weeks of life. They were treated normally from then on. As adults, they showed less than the normal amount of production of new neurons in the hippocampus (Mirescu, Peters, & Gould, 2004). Other studies have found that a stressful experience in adulthood, such as placing rats in a location where they have previously received electrical shocks, also temporarily reduces their production of new hippocampal neurons (Pham, McEwen, LeDoux, & Nader, 2005).

Apparently the cortisol damages the hippocampus by increasing excitation to the point of overstimulation, thereby shrinking dendrites and interfering with repair processes (McEwen, 2000). Even if hippocampal damage were the only cost of prolonged stress, it would be enough reason to make us try to avoid extreme stress.

THE PARASYMPATHETIC NERVOUS SYSTEM AND EMOTION

You've probably noticed that, although we began this chapter by describing the sympathetic nervous system, the parasympathetic nervous system, and hormones, so far we have only addressed the role of two of these in emotion. What happened to the parasympathetic system? Historically, emotion researchers have been far less interested in the "rest and digest" system than in "fight or flight," for fairly obvious reasons.

However, researchers have become increasingly interested in the role of parasympathetic activation in emotion. This interest has taken two forms. First, researcher Steve Porges (1997) has proposed that one branch of mammals' parasympathetic nervous system has the specific function of facilitating social relationships, and is responsible for the positive emotions associated with attachment and affection. Thus, we might expect positive emotions (at least those experienced in the context of our relationships) to relate to increased parasympathetic activation. A few studies have found that individuals with higher resting parasympathetic activation (as measured using respiratory sinus arrhythmia) report more positive affect in their daily lives (e.g., Bhattacharyya, Whitehead, Rakhit, & Steptoe, 2008; Oveis, Cohen, Gruber, Shiota, Haidt, & Keltner, 2009). However, research is still needed to determine whether parasympathetic activation *increases* during positive emotion in the way that sympathetic activation clearly increases during most negative emotions.

Second, a wide body of research links **vagal tone**, the degree of parasympathetic influence on the heart while a person is at rest, to emotion regulation. Several studies suggest that people with higher vagal tone are better at regulating their emotions (e.g., Eisenberg et al., 1989; Gyurak & Ayduk, 2008; Vasilev, Crowell, Beauchaine, Mead, & Gatzke-Kopp, 2009), and less vulnerable to depression (e.g., Rechlin, Weiss, Spitzer, & Kashcka, 1994), than those with low vagal tone. Still other studies have found that respiratory sinus arrhythmia increases when people are given a task that requires emotion regulation (Butler, Wilhelm, & Gross, 2006). The exact meaning of all this is still unclear, however. One study found that depressed individuals with stronger vagal tone at the beginning of the study were *less* likely to have recovered six months later, not more likely (Rottenberg, Wilhelm, Gross, & Gotlib, 2002). Also, parasympathetic activation increases with the regulation of attention and cognition as well as emotion, and the relationships among these variables is complex (Feldman, 2009). In sum, the emotional significance of parasympathetic nervous system activation is yet to be fully understood.

SUMMARY

When we describe or imagine emotional feelings, we invariably refer to body sensations. Despite the apparently obvious role of the body in emotion, researchers have long struggled with core questions about the relationship between physiological changes and emotional experience. How strongly do changes in physiology predict changes in feeling, or other aspects of emotion? Do different emotions really have different physiological signatures? We hope we have shown you that despite a great deal of research, we have no definitive answer to either of these questions. The available evidence does not yet fully support the autonomic specificity hypoth-esis—that every emotion will have a distinct physi-ological profile—yet it also rules out the strong version of Schachter and Singer's hypothesis that arousal is arousal, with no differences at all. As we have already seen in other aspects of emotion, the right answer is likely to lie somewhere between these two extremes. The good news is that tech-nology for measuring physiological aspects of emo-tion is becoming more sophisticated all the time, and more researchers are studying these processes than ever before.

KEY TERMS

alarm: a brief period of high arousal of the sympathetic nervous system, readying the body for vigorous activity (p. 101)

autonomic nervous system: a branch of the peripheral nervous system, by which the central nervous system influences the visceral organs (p. 84)

autonomic specificity hypothesis: the hypothesis that different emotions involve qualitatively different autonomic nervous system physiology profiles (p. 96)

cardiac pre-ejection period: the time in milliseconds between the beginning of ventricular contraction and the expulsion of blood into the aorta (p. 91)

cortisol: an adrenal gland hormone that enhances metabolism and increases the availability of fuels in the body (p. 105)

diastolic blood pressure: the pressure exerted by blood against the arteries while the heart is not contracting (p. 90)

emotional response coherence: the extent to which self-reports of emotion, physiological changes and behaviors like facial expressions are intercorrelated (p. 94)

exhaustion: the final stage of reaction to a prolonged stressor, characterized by weakness, fatigue, loss of appetite, and lack of interest (p. 101)

General Adaptation Syndrome: Hans Selye's term for the body's reaction to any threat (p. 101)

hormone: a chemical produced by an endocrine gland and released into the bloodstream, with effects on one or more organs elsewhere in the body (p. 88)

HPA axis: a stress-reponse system including the hypothalamus, pituitary gland, and adrenal gland (p. 104)

interbeat interval: the average time in milli-seconds between heart beats (p. 89)

parasympathetic nervous system: the "rest and digest" branch of the autonomic nervous system, that diverts resources to maintenance and growth activities (p. 86)

peristalsis: smooth muscle contractions that move food through the digestive system; caused by parasympathetic nervous system activation (p. 85)

piloerection: contraction of smooth muscles around the base of hairs, making them stand up; caused by sympathetic nervous system activation (p. 85)

resistance: the stage of prolonged but moderate arousal in response to some stressor (p. 101)

respiratory sinus arrhythmia: the change in heart rate associated with breathing in versus out; used as a measure of parasympathetic nervous system activation (p. 92)

skin conductance level: the speed at which the skin transmits an electrical signal from one sensor to another; used as a measure of sweat gland activity (p. 90)

stress (McEwen's definition):   an event or events that are interpreted as threatening to an individual and which elicit physiological and behavioral responses (p. 103)

stress (Selye's definition):   the nonspecific response of the body to any demand made upon it (p. 101)

sympathetic nervous system: the "fight or flight" branch of the autonomic nervous system, that supports and prepares the body for intense muscular activity (p. 84)

systolic blood pressure: pressure exerted by blood against the arteries while the heart is contracting (p. 90)

Type A personality: personality marked by competitiveness, impatience, and hostility (p. 104)

undoing effect of positive emotion: an effect where positive emotions facilitate recovery from sympathetic arousal associated with negative emotion (p. 98)

vagal tone: the degree of parasympathetic influence on the heart while a person is at rest (p. 107)

THOUGHT QUESTIONS

1. The English language includes many physical metaphors for emotion, such as "blowing your top" and "melting." Think of several more such metaphors. What do they imply about the physiological changes we should expect to see in particular emotions?

SUGGESTIONS FOR RESEARCH PROJECTS

1. Ask people to try to estimate their heart rate under several different conditions (such as sitting quietly, remembering an emotional experience, and just after jumping up and down). After each estimate, actually take each person's pulse. In general, how good are people at estimating their heart rate? Are some people better than others, and what variables might predict this?

SUGGESTIONS FOR FURTHER READING

Damasio, A. (1999). *The Feeling of What Happens: Body and Emotion in the Making of Consciousness*. Fort Worth, TX: Harcourt College.

Sapolsky, R. M. (1998). *Why Zebras Don't Get Ulcers: An Updated Guide to Stress, Stress-Related Diseases, and Coping*. New York: W. H. Freeman.

5

Emotion and the Brain
The Central Nervous System

In Chapter 4, we considered the role of the body's visceral sensations in the experience of emotion. That topic is important for a number of reasons, but perhaps most important is that the major theories of emotion described in Chapter 1 emphasize the role of autonomic responses in emotion. According to basic emotion theory, different emotions should have qualitatively different physiological profiles. According to strong dimensional theories, we should only be able to identify physiological markers for a couple of aspects of emotion, such as overall arousal and valence. For all of these reasons, researchers have studied how emotion plays out in the body for a century or more.

Ultimately, however, theories about the structure of human emotion come down to the way emotion is represented in the brain. For much of the twentieth century, most social scientists thought the human brain was a "blank slate," a general-purpose learning organ with little innate architecture. By the early 1990s, technological advances in brain imaging during experimental tasks, combined with a growing body of evidence from patients with localized brain damage, made it clear that the slate comes with some content already engraved, as well as open "fields" where specific pieces of information should be filled in based on experience (Pinker, 2003).

In an early attempt to define the emotional brain, Paul MacLean (1952) proposed that a region he called the "limbic system" was the source of emotion. In his **triune brain model**, MacLean divided the brain into three regions controlling "reptilian" sensory, survival, and reflex actions; "mammalian" emotion; and a neocortex responsible for complex cognition and reasoning in humans and other primates (see Figure 5.1). Later evidence has failed to support the triune brain model as MacLean conceived it, showing that sensory, emotional, and

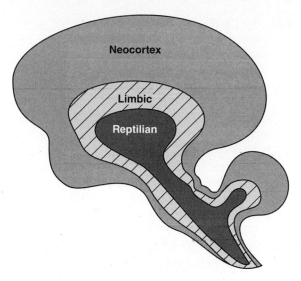

FIGURE 5.1 In the 1950s, Paul Maclean proposed that a "limbic system" located between the brain stem/cerebellum and the neocortex is the source of emotions. Although the limbic brain proposal is no longer widely accepted by neuroanatomists, some of the specific structures in this area of the brain do play important roles in emotional processes.

higher cognitive processes each involve activation distributed across all three regions. However, some of the specific structures in MacLean's limbic system are important in emotional processes, as we shall see shortly.

Theorists on all sides of the basic/dimensional/component process debate now acknowledge the existence of a universal emotional human nature, at least partly pre-wired into our neural systems. They disagree, however, about what that wiring should look like. Early brain imaging studies sought spatial chunks of brain responsible for producing discrete emotions, or for evaluating dimensions such as valence and arousal. More recently, researchers are asking whether distinct networks of activation spread throughout the brain might produce emotional experiences and emotion-related processes. As you've probably come to expect by now, none of these theories unambiguously matches the data. Along the way, however, we are learning a tremendous amount about the relationship between

emotion and cognition, about the similarities and differences among various emotional events, and about the role of the brain in emotion-related problems such as mood disorders and addiction.

The goal of this chapter is to introduce the major techniques and issues in emotion neuroscience, paving the way for additional discussion of this approach in later chapters. We will first introduce the methods used to study the neural foundations of emotion, examining the strengths and limitations of each. We will then discuss the history of research on a particular brain structure—the amygdala—as an example of the challenges faced by emotion neuroscience. After this detailed example, we will review some specific brain structures and neurotransmitters that appear especially important for emotion, before backing up again and looking at the overall state of the field.

METHODS USED TO STUDY EMOTION AND THE BRAIN

If studying the autonomic nervous system presents methodological challenges, studying emotion in the brain is even trickier. Sympathetic and parasympathetic nervous system activation have effects that can be detected reliably at the skin, with simple electrical sensors and reasonably priced equipment. Hormones can be assayed from saliva and, if necessary, from blood. Brain activity is—in the brain! For a long time, the only way to study the neuroanatomy of any human behavior was to wait around for someone to get a brain injury, see how their behavior changed, and then wait for them to die so someone could do an autopsy and examine the exact location of the damage. Researchers conduct experimental lesion studies with animals, but that work is sometimes hard to interpret, especially with regard to emotions.

Recent technologies allow us to take a picture of the brain while it is in action, opening up huge possibilities for human neuroscience. However, each of these technologies has limitations, especially in the context of emotion. When researchers achieve real understanding of the neural substrates of some psychological process, it is usually due to convergent evidence from many studies using several different methods. Let's take a look at some of those methods now.

Lesion Studies

If you want to know whether a behavior depends on activation in a certain area of the brain, there's a logical way to find out. Just cut that part of the brain out, and see whether the behavior goes away. Ta da! This is drastically oversimplifying the **lesion method**, of course, but it does convey the basic idea. In non-human animals lesions can be created surgically, or chemically by injecting cell-toxic substances into particular areas of the brain. In humans, researchers study individuals who have brain damage due to accidents, or patients with neurodegenerative disorders such as Alzheimer's disease. In both humans and other animals, researchers compare the behavior of lesioned individuals to non-lesioned individuals in response to standardized tasks, and ask what deficits occur in those with the lesions. Although somewhat brute-force, this approach was instrumental in refuting "blank slate" theories of the brain. The evidence was too strong that when trauma or surgical lesion damaged a particular part of the brain, the resulting psychological damage could be restricted to quite specific functions (e.g., Sacks, 1985). Lesion studies offer a powerful way to document the necessity of some brain structure for a certain aspect of emotion.

We discussed the limitations of lesion-based approaches to studying emotion in animals earlier—animals can't report their thoughts or feelings. There are also problems with lesion patients in humans. First, the researcher has no control over the location of the lesion. Second, brain lesions resulting from trauma or neurodegenerative disease rarely confine themselves neatly to one structure. Third, some brain structures are more likely to be harmed by trauma than others.

Researchers often deal with these lesion-location problems by doing a structural brain scan

of all research participants, and examining the correlation of brain volumes in a particular target area with some behavior of interest, rather than just comparing patients with non-patients. However, even using this approach, the research has not experimentally manipulated the location of the lesion, so another problem is that causal inferences are harder to justify with lesion-based techniques. Here's an example of the concern. Let's say that patients with damage to the ventromedial prefrontal cortex (VMPFC), Figures 5.2 and 5.3, show greater risk-taking behavior in a gambling task than patients with no lesion, or with a lesion in another area (e.g., Clark, Bechara, Damasio, Aitken, Sahakian, & Robbins, 2008). Damage to this area of the brain is often observed in people who have had head trauma. Well, what kind of person is especially likely to have head trauma? People who take a lot of risks, such as motorcycle riding and extreme sports, right? So, it may be that the people who have lesions to the VMPFC tended toward risk-taking *before* the trauma, and it has nothing to do with the brain damage itself.

We noted earlier that real gains in knowledge come from using multiple methods that cancel out each other's weaknesses. In this case, neural imaging studies with non-lesioned participants also support the role of the VMPFC in mediating caution in the face of risky situations (e.g., Eshel, Nelson, Blair, Pine, & Ernst, 2007), so the inference drawn from the lesion studies seems valid. However, in other cases, the limitations of the lesion method are more worrisome.

Electroencephalography (EEG)
Measures

We briefly introduced **electroencephalography (EEG)** measures in Chapter 1. This method relies on the fact that neurons generate an electrical potential (or "charge") when they depolarize, in the process of communicating from one neuron to another. The potential generated by one neuron is very weak, but if many neurons depolarize at the same time, and they are close enough to the skull,

Image copyright JULIE LUCHT. Used under license by Shutterstock.com

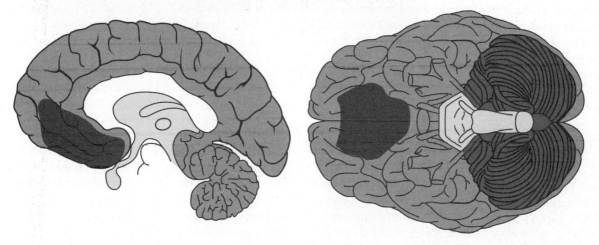

FIGURES 5.2 AND 5.3 The ventromedial prefrontal cortex is an area of the brain easily damaged by head trauma, such as that resulting from motorcycle accidents and extreme sports.

then you can detect a change in potential at the scalp. Researchers take advantage of this by placing electrodes at many points on a research participant's head, and measuring electrical potentials between each of those electrodes and a reference electrode placed elsewhere (Figure 5.4). They can then measure either overall patterns of electrical activity in the brain, or they can examine responses called **event-related potentials** to particular stimuli.

Most research using EEG methods examines early-stage sensory and cognitive processes taking place within a half-second after some new stimulus, rather than emotional processes. This is partly because the areas of the brain where activity can be detected must be fairly close to the scalp, and as we shall see, many structures important for emotion are located deeper in the brain. However, EEG methods have been used in some emotion research. For example, researchers can

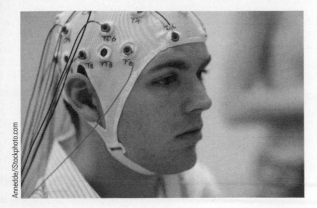

Annedie/iStockphoto.com

F I G U R E 5.4 Electroencephalography (EEG) allows researchers to detect when large groups of neurons depolarize at the same time.

detect a distinctive change in the electrical potential at frontally placed electrodes about 100 milliseconds after a person makes a mistake on some task, an effect called the "error-related negativity." This negative deflection in the waveform is greater in individuals with anxiety disorders than in other people, (e.g., Hajcak, McDonald, & Simons, 2003; Figure 5.5). Many researchers are interested in the overall ratio of activation between the left and right frontal parts of the brain, which correlates in important ways with emotional experience (e.g., Wheeler, Davidson, & Tomarken, 1993).

One advantage of EEG/ERP methods is their excellent temporal precision. This technique allows researchers to detect neural activation happening less than a second after some stimulus, much faster than effects would be seen in autonomic physiology measures, functional MRI scans discussed below, or overt behavior. One limitation is the inability to assess neural activation deep in the brain. It is also difficult to locate exactly where the signal arose. Electrodes on the scalp are recording the average of activity over a substantial area, mostly from cells close to the surface, but also from farther away. Although an increasing number of researchers use complex statistical techniques to try to figure out the origin of potentials based on the pattern of distribution across all sensors, this technique is controversial, and best used in combination with imaging

methods that measure the location of neural activity more directly.

Finally, like all brain imaging methods, participants must remain still during testing, which can go on for hours. In ERP studies, the electrical signal generated in any single trial is so messy that each participant must complete dozens, or in some cases hundreds, of trials. Simple eye movements generate so much electrical activity that they overwhelm the signal the researcher is looking for, so participants are instructed to keep their eyes still, and trials with eye movements are usually discarded. The data from the remaining trials are then averaged together to reduce noise and detect the potential in which the researcher is interested. This is less of a problem in EEG studies comparing overall regions of the brain, but the sensors still limit movement and natural behavior.

Functional Magnetic Resonance Imaging (fMRI)

The next method also seeks to take a snapshot of the brain in action, but in this case it is possible to look at activation deeper in the brain, and with greater spatial resolution, than is true with EEG methods. The physics of this technique are complicated, but **functional magnetic resonance imaging (fMRI)** measures changes in blood oxygen levels in the brain as a way of assessing where neurons have recently been active.

The MRI equipment used in psychology research is the same as used by medical doctors to image other areas of the body. What an MRI does is turn on and off an extremely strong magnet surrounding the participant's body, while also providing pulses of electromagnetic energy. When the magnet is turned on and energy is pulsed, the axes of all of the protons in the person's body line up to point in the same direction, and take on extra energy (making them spin around the axis faster). When the magnet is turned off, the protons begin to release that extra energy, and also fall out of unison with each other. During this latter phase, researchers can "read" pictures of the energy as the protons release it. Because different molecules release energy

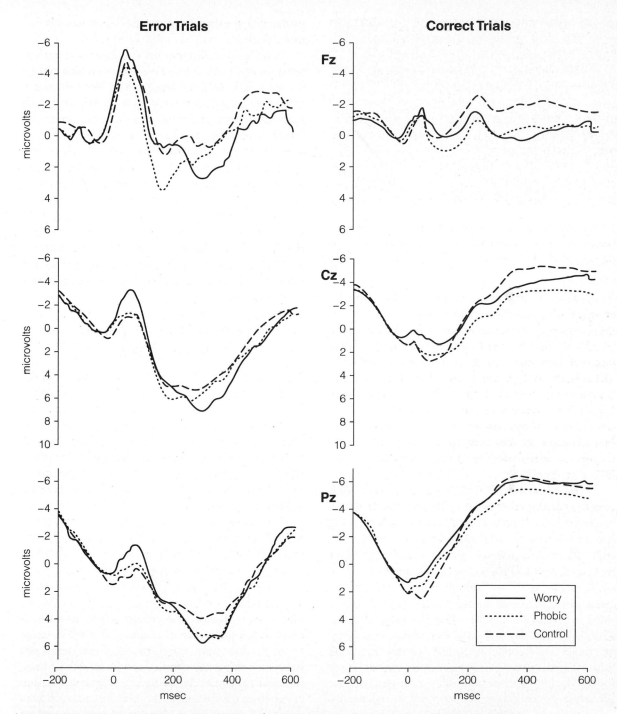

FIGURE 5.5 The negative deflection (note that the negative is up, not down) in the electrical wave form about 100 milliseconds after a participant makes an error is stronger in participants who report strong anxiety-related symptoms (the "worry" group).

SOURCE: From Hajcak, McDonald, and Simons (2003). 'Anxiety and error-related brain activity'. *Biological Psychology* 64 (2003) 77–90. Copyright © 2003. Reprinted with permission from Elsevier.

in somewhat different ways, medical doctors and researchers can adjust the readout parameters to highlight a particular kind of body tissue.

When neurons "fire," they use up most of their stored oxygen, and need more to be delivered right away. As a result, blood cells release more oxygen in areas where neurons have just been active, shortly after the burst of firing. In most functional MRI (fMRI), researchers set readout parameters to maximize the contrast between hemoglobin (a blood chemical) that still has its oxygen, and hemoglobin that has released its oxygen. Researchers read one very thin "slice" of brain at a time, breaking this slice into little cubes called **voxels**, typically 2-3 millimeters thick on each side. Thus, fMRI methods can assess changes in oxygen uptake from the blood for each separate voxel.

Once the technology was discovered in the early 1990s for using fMRI to detect regional changes in blood oxygen levels, psychologists finally had a tool for looking at neural activity within the brain of a living person. Researchers began using this method to address basic questions about the structure of emotion. Functional MRI imaging has many advantages over prior techniques, including terrific spatial resolution. However, fMRI methods also have some serious limitations, and it is important to keep these in mind when evaluating the research.

Perhaps most important is the ecological validity problem we described in Chapter 1. The inside of an MRI machine is a weird place to be. It's extremely loud, and although participants usually wear headphones the noise is still distracting at best. Any visual stimuli are typically presented on a small screen inside the magnet. As with any imaging (such as photography), the slightest movement by the subject will cause the image to blur, so those tested have to stay very still. Behavioral responses are typically limited to pushing small buttons. Although a few recent studies have included either actual human contact (e.g., Coan, Schaefer, & Davidson, 2006), or virtual reality simulations of social interaction (e.g., Eisenberger, Lieberman, & Williams, 2003), in most fMRI studies the participant is alone. Thus, in a typical study the "emotion" condition means you are inside the scanner looking at a picture of a person showing an emotional facial expression. Is this emotion? Researchers debate the extent to which this task evokes real emotional processes, but at best it is a weak copy of the situations in which we ordinarily experience emotion.

Functional MRI methods have other limitations as well. Individuals differ greatly in the amount of blood typically flowing to different parts of the brain, so experimental manipulations need to compare the same participant in different conditions (the "within-subject" design we first discussed in Chapter 4), rather than different participants in different conditions. Individuals also differ in the size and precise location of particular neural structures, so averaging across participants can be challenging. Furthermore, a researcher may examine many thousands of voxels in the same study, increasing the probability that statistical analyses will turn up a few significant "effects" just by chance.

Despite these limitations, fMRI technologies can be used to address many specific and important questions in the psychology of emotion. A good study is clear about what aspect of emotion is being targeted, and makes a strong case for that aspect being elicited despite the strange setting. A good emotion neuroscience study also examines one or a few particular regions of the brain that have already been studied extensively, rather than "fishing" for effects anywhere in the brain. We shall see some examples of strong fMRI studies later in this chapter, and throughout the book.

Neurochemistry Techniques

The three techniques discussed above emphasize neuroanatomy—the roles of different spatial regions of the brain in various psychological processes. An alternative approach emphasizes particular **neurotransmitters**, the chemicals neurons use to communicate with each other. The human brain uses dozens of different neurotransmitters, and some of these appear important in mediating aspects of emotion. A particular neurotransmitter may connect processes located in different places throughout the brain, rather than being confined to a single location, so neurochemistry approaches have been useful in identifying networks of brain activity underlying psychological phenomena.

Neurochemistry techniques fall into a few basic categories. First, you can *increase* the apparent effects of some neurotransmitter by adding more of that neurotransmitter to the brain, by adding a chemical that mimics the neurotransmitter (activating its receptors), by adding a chemical that helps the neurotransmitter bond with its receptors, or by adding a chemical that prevents neurotransmitters already in the synapse from being reabsorbed back into the presynaptic neuron. Second, you can *reduce* the apparent effects of a neurotransmitter by speeding up the natural decomposition or reuptake of this chemical from the synapse, or by adding a chemical that blocks the neurotransmitter's access to its receptors. In each of these cases, a researcher compares the behavior of individuals whose chemistry has been manipulated with individuals in a control group. There are also ways of measuring genetic differences between individuals that affect the number or type of receptors they have for some neurotransmitter, and seeing if these genetic differences predict some aspect of emotion.

These techniques have produced exciting findings about the neurochemistry of various emotional processes. However, the techniques also have limitations. For one thing, the same neurotransmitter may be involved in several brain processes, so it is difficult to manipulate one effect of a neurotransmitter without affecting the others as well.

Also, neurochemistry approaches are used more often with non-human animals than with humans, for several reasons. Many chemicals used to alter neurotransmission must be injected directly into the brain—if swallowed or injected into the blood, they will not cross the blood–brain barrier. There are exceptions. European researchers have studied the effects of oxytocin in the brain by giving participants a nasal spray containing this neurotransmitter (e.g., Kosfield, Henrichs, Zak, Fischbacher, &

Fehr, 2005; Theodoridou, Rowe, Penton-Voak, & Rogers, 2009), though this technique is not yet allowed in the United States (darn!). And of course, a long history of human drug use shows that some psychoactive chemicals can be taken by mouth. However, that same history shows that the brain can change permanently in response to such drugs, so researchers are understandably cautious about giving drugs to people just for research purposes. Studies of neurotransmitter receptor genes are feasible in humans, but the researcher must know which genes to look at, and much of this information is still being gathered (e.g., Iidaka, Ozaki, Matsumoto, Nogawa, Kinoshita, Suzuki, et al., 2005).

THE AMYGDALA AND EMOTION: A HISTORY

The section above highlights the strengths and limitations of several neuroscience methods. Although the strengths are exciting, the limitations make it difficult to understand what psychological processes are supported by any one structure or neurotransmitter—the goal of much emotion neuroscience research. To illustrate why this is so problematic, we will consider the history of research on one brain structure associated with emotion.

In early studies of emotion neuroscience, attention quickly converged on a structure called the **amygdala** ("uh-MIG-duh-luh," plural = amygdalae), an area within the brain's temporal lobe (Figure 5.6). *Amygdala* is the Greek word for almond, and the amygdala is shaped somewhat like an almond, if you use a little imagination. Like nearly all brain areas, the amygdala is a bilateral structure; each hemisphere contains one. The amygdala receives input representing vision, hearing, other senses, and pain, so it is in a position to associate various stimuli with outcomes that follow them (Uwano, Nishijo, Ono, & Tamura, 1995). It sends information to the pons and other areas controlling the startle reflex (Fendt, Koch, & Schnitzler, 1996), as well as to the prefrontal cortex

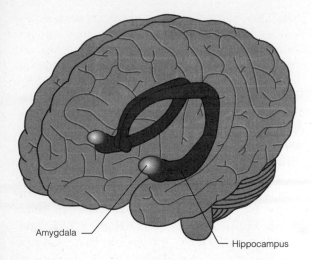

Amygdala

Hippocampus

FIGURE 5.6 The amygdala is located within each temporal lobe of the brain with one in each hemisphere. It is connected with the hippocampus, a structure important in the formation of episodic memories.

(Garcia, Vouimba, Baudry, & Thompson, 1999) and other brain areas (Gifkins, Greba, & Kokkinidis, 2002). Let's see why this little structure got the attention of emotion researchers so early on.

Observations of Animals and Humans with Amygdala Lesions

As is the case for several other structures, the amygdala first began to interest researchers because of the behaviors shown by individuals in whom it had been damaged. In the 1930s, two researchers who were studying monkeys identified what came to be known as the **Klüver-Bucy Syndrome (KBS)**, a pattern of emotional changes accompanying removal of both anterior temporal lobes, including the amygdalae. Animals with such damage seemed not to recognize the emotional implications of objects. For example, they would approach snakes, try to pick up lighted matches, and put feces into their mouths (Klüver & Bucy, 1939). Monkeys with damage to the amygdala would also fearlessly approach aggressive monkeys and unfamiliar humans (Kalin, Shelton, & Davidson, 2004), sometimes

getting injured as a result (Rosvold, Mirsky, & Pribram, 1954).

Research with other animals shows a similar pattern. Normal rats and mice stop whatever they are doing if they smell a cat. After a tranquilizer has decreased activity in the amygdala, however, rats become almost indifferent to a cat's odor (McGregor, Hargreaves, Apfelbach, & Hunt, 2004). After destruction of the amygdala, some rats and mice will fearlessly approach a cat (Berdoy, Webster, & Macdonald, 2000).

Humans with damage only to the amygdala are rare. Many stroke patients have damage to the amygdala and surrounding areas in at least one hemisphere, but stroke damage is never limited to just this one structure. In a rare condition called Urbach-Wiethe disease, however, calcium accumulates in the amygdala and damages it, generally without much damage to surrounding tissues. Much of our understanding of the human amygdala depends on these few patients.

Humans with amygdala damage have some of the same symptoms as monkeys with Klüver-Bucy syndrome, such as putting inedible or disgusting substances into their mouths. Much like the monkeys that fearlessly approached larger, more aggressive monkeys, people with amygdala damage will approach strangers virtually at random when they need help, instead of trying to choose someone who looks friendly or trustworthy. In fact, if asked to look at faces and rate which ones look friendliest or most trustworthy, they rate all faces as almost equal (Adolphs, Tranel, & Damasio, 1998).

Laboratory Studies of Fear Conditioning

One striking feature of individuals with amygdala damage is that they seem not to be afraid of anything! This led researchers to ask whether the amygdala might be especially important for behaviors associated with fear. In one of the earliest studies addressing this question, Joseph LeDoux and his colleagues (1990) used a **fear conditioning** paradigm employed by behaviorist researchers for decades. The basic protocol is this: you put a rat in a cage by itself, and several times over the course of a couple of hours you play a distinctive tone, followed immediately by an electrical shock to the floor of the cage. After being exposed to this pairing several times, rats will tense up or "freeze" when they hear that tone, as though they are waiting for the shock to come. They also show physiological effects, such as increases in blood pressure, consistent with fear. Thus, they seem to have learned that the tone predicts the shock. In a control condition, rats who hear the tones and get the same shocks, but in such a way that the tones *don't* predict when the shocks will come, show no apparent reaction to the tones.

LeDoux and colleagues operated on half of the rats in their study before this procedure, and used an electrical current to damage the amygdalae. Rats in the control group also received operations, but without amygdala damage. Thus, researchers could be sure that any differences between the two conditions were due to the amygdala damage, and not to the effects of surgery per se. After the animals had healed, they were put through the fear conditioning paradigm described above. The results of the study are shown in Figure 5.7. After the same "training period" in which the tones predicted electrical shocks, the amygdala-damaged rats showed much weaker freezing responses and increases in blood pressure after hearing the tone than did brain-intact rats.

This effect has been replicated dozens of times (Antoniadis, Winslow, Davis, & Amaral, 2007; Wilensky, Schafe, Kristensen, & LeDoux, 2006). Subtle variations on the basic design have also supported the role of the amygdala in fear conditioning. The effect holds when chemical injections are used to temporarily disable the amygdala, so that full-blown damage is not necessary (e.g., Schafe, Atkins, Swank, Bauer, Sweat, & LeDoux, 2000). The effect holds with other operational measures of fear as well. For example, if an animal

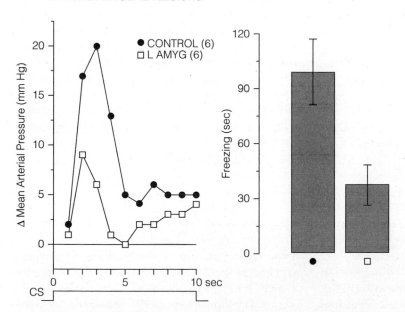

LATERAL AMYGDALA LESIONS

FIGURE 5.7 Rats with intact brains (black dots) quickly learn that a sound tone means an electrical shock is coming, and show physiological and behavioral responses suggesting fear when they hear the tone. Rats with amygdala damage (white squares) show a much weaker response to the tone.

SOURCE: J.E. LeDoux, P. Cicchetti, A. Xagoraris and L.M. Romanski. The lateral amygdaloid nucleus: sensory interface of the amygdala in fear conditioning. *Journal of Neuroscience*, Vol 10, 1062–1069. Copyright © 1990 by Society for Neuroscience.

has learned that a certain tone means a foot shock is coming, it will jump or "startle" more intensely if it hears an unexpected loud noise after hearing the tone. Even in humans, the intensity of this startle response is used as an index of fear (e.g., Lang, Bradley, & Buthbert, 2002). If an animal has damage to the amygdalae, the startle response is no greater after a shock signal than after a safety signal (Heldt, Sundin, Willott, & Falls, 2000; Hitchcock & Davis, 1991; Phillips & LeDoux, 1992). Rats with amygdala damage not only fail to learn new signs of danger, but they also lose fears they had learned from this kind of training *before* the brain damage (Gale et al., 2004). One study reported greater deficits after damage to the right amygdala than the left amygdala (Baker & Kim, 2004), but damage to both produces the strongest effect.

These results suggested to many researchers that amygdala activation might be responsible for the feeling of fear. However, this opens up a lot of possibilities. In the strongest form of this hypothesis, amygdala activity *is* fear, and any person or animal lacking an amygdala has no fear. In milder forms, amygdala activity might be necessary to perceive situations as dangerous, or to display behavioral responses associated with fear, but it might not be necessary for *feeling* fear. This highlights the limitations of working with laboratory animals—they are convenient subjects, but they can't tell us what they are thinking or feeling. For that, you need humans.

Studies of the Amygdala and Human Fear

What is the role of the amygdala in human fear? If the amygdala is damaged, what aspects of fear are compromised? As we noted earlier, patients with selective amygdala damage are very rare, however a few patients have been observed in this regard. In a conditioning paradigm, one patient with bilateral (both sides) amygdala damage failed to show a normal skin conductance response to a color slide that had previously predicted a loud and aversive noise (Bechara, Tranel, Damasio, Adolphs, Rockland, &

Damasio, 1995). Other patients with amygdala damage are found to show reduced distress-related startle facilitation, as in the study described above for rats (Angrili, Mauri, Palomba, Flor, Birbaumer, Sartori, & di Paola, 1996; Funayama, Grillon, Davis, & Phelps, 2001). Functional MRI studies have also found that the amygdala becomes more active during fear conditioning (e.g., LaBar, Gatenby, Gore, LeDoux, & Phelps, 1998), and in general when people see or hear signals of danger (Phelps et al., 2001). The amygdala even becomes more active when we learn from someone else that a new stimulus predicts an electric shock, rather than experiencing the fear conditioning directly (Phelps, O'Connor, Gatenby, Gore, Grillon, & Davis, 2001).

Several studies report that people with amygdala damage are particularly impaired at recognizing facial expressions of fear (Adolphs, Tranel, Damasio, & Damasio, 1994; Hayman, Rexer, Pavol, Strite, & Meyers, 1998; Lilly et al., 1983). One woman with Urbach-Wiethe disease was asked to draw faces showing various expressions. She drew good representations of happy, sad, surprised, disgusted, and angry faces, but then said she didn't know what a frightened face looked like (Adolphs, Tranel, Damasio, & Damasio, 1995). Again, fMRI studies confirm that the amygdala becomes more active when viewing a fearful face than when viewing a neutral face, even when the faces are presented subliminally (e.g., Kubota et al., 2000; Vuilleumeier, Armony, Driver, & Dolan, 2001). The amygdala also becomes more active when viewing an angry face, which could reasonably elicit fear as well. In one fascinating study, seeing an angry expression facing the viewer produced a stronger amygdala response, and greater self-reports of emotion, than seeing an angry face looking to the side (Sato, Yoshikawa, Kochiyama, & Matsumura, 2004). People can recognize an angry expression equally well in either direction, but seeing it facing you tends to be more upsetting.

However, patients with amygdala damage report that they continue to feel fear and other emotions more or less normally in their everyday lives (Anderson & Phelps, 2002). One study compared stroke patients whose damage included the amygdala and stroke patients who had damage elsewhere. Each person rated a series of pictures for pleasantness or unpleasantness, and reported how aroused the photos made them feel. People with amygdala damage made normal reports of pleasantness or unpleasantness, but they reported almost no arousal to the unpleasant pictures (Berntson, Bechara, Damasio, Tranel, & Cacioppo, 2007). Another patient studied by Bechara and colleagues (1995) reported *knowing* that the color slide meant that the loud noise (the unconditioned stimulus) was coming, even though he did not show physiological signs of fear. So, the amygdala does not seem to be necessary for all aspects of fear.

Beyond Fear: The Amygdala and Other Emotions

So far the case seems strong for thinking of the amygdala as the "fear area of the brain," or at least as an area playing a role in some fear-related processes. However, in order to conclude that a brain structure *is* responsible for one distinct kind of process, it is important to show that it is *not* associated with other, unrelated processes. For example, is the amygdala only involved in fear, or do we see similar effects of amygdala damage, and similar amygdala activation, with other negative emotions?

Studies suggest that the role of the amygdala is not limited to fear. For example, nearly everyone pays more attention to emotionally charged words than to other words. If you watch a screen that displayed many words, each for less than a tenth of a second under conditions of distraction, you are more likely to notice a word like *bitch* than one like *birch*, and would report seeing more of such words to an experimenter. People with amygdala damage report the emotionally charged words of several kinds and the everyday words about equally, as though they do not recognize the difference (Anderson & Phelps, 2001). The effect was not limited to fear-related words.

In general, people with amygdala damage have trouble naming the expression in a face, or even determining whether two faces are expressing the same or different emotions (Boucsein, Weniger, Mursch, Steinhoff, & Irle, 2001). Functional MRI studies find that the amygdala responds strongly to faces expressing sadness (Wang, McCarthy, Song, & LaBar, 2005) and disgust, neither of which should frighten the viewer. This response is strongest to a new photo and weakens after repeated presentations, so novelty seems to be important in triggering amygdala activation (Breiter et al., 1996; Büchel et al., 1998). The amygdala's response to happy expressions has been more controversial. Some studies have found a clear response to happy faces, whereas others have not. Part of the problem is that most studies report the average for a small group of people, and individuals differ rather widely on this task, so a group with a few highly reactive people can differ substantially from another group. One study found a strong amygdala response to happy faces only in viewers who had an extroverted personality—that is, a strong tendency to enjoy meeting new people (Canli, Sivers, Whitfield, Gotlib, & Gabrieli, 2002). Presumably these people react more strongly than others to the sight of a stranger's smiling face.

All of these findings raise new questions. If the amygdala is not required for fear or the detection of danger per se, what exactly is it doing? Researchers have offered a number of suggestions. One interesting study found an alternative explanation for why people with amygdala damage have trouble recognizing facial expressions of emotion in general: When they look at a face, they focus almost entirely on the nose and mouth, unlike normal people, who spend much of their time looking at the eyes (Adolphs et al., 2005). Other research shows that when the amygdala is highly activated, people tend to shift their attention toward someone's eyes (Gamer & Büchel, 2009).

The reason for that attentional focus is unknown, but the consequences are enormous for recognizing fear. The eyes are very important for

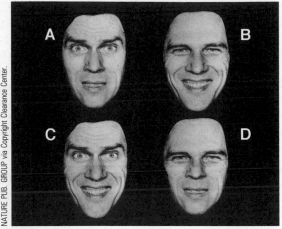

FIGURE 5.8 Parts A and B show normal expressions of fear and happiness. Parts C and D combine the eyes of one expression with the mouth of the other.

SOURCE: Vuilleumier (2005).

communicating emotion in general (Matsumoto, 1989), and especially fear. Frightened eyes, combined with a neutral mouth, still look frightened (Morris, deBonis, & Dolan, 2002). Even a combination of frightened eyes and a happy smile gives some impression of fear. Examine Figure 5.8 (Vuilleumier, 2005). Part a shows an expression of fear; part b shows happiness. In part d, with the eyes of happiness and the mouth of fear, most people perceive little emotion. However, contrast that reaction to part c, which shows fear in the eyes and happiness in the mouth. If you focus on the eyes, you perceive fear; if you focus on the mouth, you perceive happiness. Overall, fear is probably the dominant impression.

The Amygdala and Emotional Memory

Researchers have now proposed a number of possible roles that the amygdala might play in emotion. However, one especially promising school of thought emphasizes the importance of the amygdala for memory formation. Think back to the fear conditioning studies by LeDoux and colleagues. Perhaps the amygdala was not crucial for *fear* as much as for *learning* that a particular situation was dangerous. Studies of memory

for emotional events are consistent with this hypothesis. For example, if you heard a story that included commonplace, unemotional details plus a gruesome description of a child's injury, you would remember the gruesome part far more than the rest. People with amygdala damage do not show this memory bias (Cahill et al., 1995; LaBar & Phelps, 1998). Moreover, fMRI studies find that the degree of amygdala activation while a person views emotional stimuli predicts later memory for those stimuli (Canli, Zhao, Brewer, Gabrieli, & Cahill, 2000; Canli, Zhao, Desmond, Glover, & Gabrieli, 1999).

So, does the amygdala have *anything* to do with emotion? Yes! The amygdala appears to be important in the formation of emotional memories, but not neutral memories. Amygdala activation while viewing neutral stimuli does *not* predict later memory—this is only the case for emotional stimuli (Canli et al., 1999). Also, the amygdala does not seem to be important for all aspects of memory. Recall the study described above, in which an amygdala-damaged patient did not show physiological responses to a conditioned fear stimulus, but was able to say that the stimulus meant a loud noise was coming (Bechara et al., 1995). The amygdala damage did not interfere with the patient's ability to learn facts, just to respond emotionally to those facts.

Elizabeth Phelps (2004; 2005) has noted the amygdala's connections with a structure called the **hippocampus** (see Figure 5.6), thought to mediate the formation of vivid "episodic" memories for events as distinct from memory for factual information. As an example of the difference, think of your last birthday. First, state what activities you did that day—that is factual information, such as you could read off a daily planner. Next, try to vividly remember the best part of that day, using your sense memory to "relive" the experience. This latter kind of memory is episodic, and is more likely to involve feelings of emotion.

According to Phelps, the amygdala serves two functions. First, the amygdala helps to direct our attention toward stimuli we already know to have emotional implications. This includes emotional faces and particular regions of faces (such as the eyes) that are important for conveying emotion, as we saw in a previous study. Second, amygdala activation associated with the experience of a strong emotion facilitates the consolidation of long-term episodic memories by the hippocampus. In this way, amygdala activation might "tag" particular memories as having strong emotional significance, and instigate processes that enhance these memories for future reference.

Researchers are beginning to find support for this hypothesis. One study assessed U.S. soldiers who were wounded in combat. Of those who suffered brain damage outside the amygdala, 40 percent developed post-traumatic stress disorder, defined in terms of vivid, intrusive memories of a traumatic event. Of those with brain damage that included the amygdala, *none* developed the disorder (Koenigs et al., 2008). New research has even documented changes in synapses within the rat amygdala that might reflect new "memories" in the context of fear conditioning (Kwon & Choi, 2009).

Can we now say, with confidence, that we know exactly what the amygdala does? No, although we're closer than we were ten years ago. As we hope this example has shown, identifying the psychological process(es) mediated by a particular brain structure is a long and complex task. A researcher can show that one laboratory task elicits more activation from that structure than other tasks, or that ability to perform the task is diminished in individuals who lack that brain structure. However, any single task relies on several psychological processes. Researchers can guess which specific process is associated with the structure, but they can't be sure until they have ruled out all of the other options, usually by comparing results across many tasks. As we have seen with the amygdala, this takes considerable time and patience, but it eventually pays off.

EMOTION NEUROANATOMY: SOME IMPORTANT STRUCTURES

The amygdala is, by a wide margin, the most-studied brain structure among neuroscientists interested in emotion. One might almost conclude from this emphasis that the amygdala is the primary emotion area of the brain, whose activation distinguishes emotion from not-emotion. Whether this turns out to be justified is still an open question, but it is clear that many other neural structures are also involved in emotional experience, physiology, and behavior. Here we introduce a few structures that are particularly prominent in emotion research.

The Hypothalamus

We met the **hypothalamus**, a small structure located just above the brain stem and below the larger thalamus (see Figure 5.9), in Chapter 4. For such a little structure (in humans it is about the size of an almond, like the amygdala), it is extremely important, essentially responsible for regulating the overall internal environment of the body. Mammalian bodies are picky—we can function only when our internal temperature, sugar levels, hydration, and other factors are all within a narrow range. The job of the hypothalamus is to monitor all of these

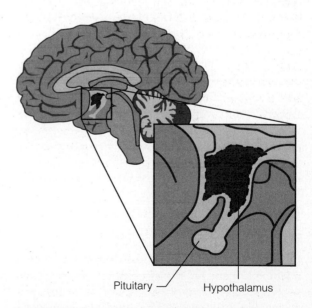

Pituitary   Hypothalamus

FIGURE 5.9 The hypothalamus serves as the "thermostat" of the brain in many ways, regulating the homeostatic balance of temperature, blood chemistry, hydration, and other factors via influence on the autonomic nervous system and endocrine system.

factors continuously, and then initiate corrective change when a factor is out of range—to maintain **homeostasis**. The hypothalamus is often described as the body's thermostat, and it functions in exactly that way, but regulating much more than temperature. The hypothalamus also collects sensory information coming from outside the body (e.g., pheromones in the air) as well as neural input relaying sensations within the body itself (e.g., stomach fullness), and helps promote behaviors appropriate given the situation (e.g., mating, cessation of eating).

This probably doesn't sound very emotional. However, the hypothalamus sets off change in the body via the two physiological systems we discussed in Chapter 4—the Autonomic Nervous System (ANS) and the Endocrine/Hormone system. The hypothalamus certainly uses the ANS for non-emotional regulation: When your temperature is too high, it activates sweat glands, and when temperature is too low, it constricts blood vessels to the extremities so you lose less heat. When you exercise, and muscles consume more oxygen and glucose, you breathe faster to bring in more oxygen, organs release more glucose into the bloodstream, and the heart beats faster and harder to move all this stuff around. The hypothalamus initiates these changes when it detects that homeostasis has already been disrupted. However, the hypothalamus also receives cues that homeostasis is *likely* to be disrupted by upcoming activities, and prepares the body accordingly. This preparation appears to be one of the salient features of emotion.

Hypothalamic control of the endocrine system has similar flexibility. When the hypothalamus detects that your blood pressure is too low, it instructs the pituitary gland to release an antidiuretic hormone called vasopressin, which encourages the kidneys to reabsorb fluid into the body rather than expelling it into the bladder. However, with prolonged psychological stress the hypothalamus will trigger the pituitary's release of cortisol, with all of the effects discussed in Chapter 4. So, the hypothalamus is the central structure controlling changes in the body that we experience during strong emotion.

Because it directs "fight or flight" autonomic nervous system activation and the release of stress hormones, it might seem that the hypothalamus is only involved in negative emotions. However, the hypothalamus is important for at least some positive emotions as well. The hypothalamus plays an important role in sexuality, by controlling the profile of autonomic nervous system activation associated with sexual arousal and orgasm (see Chapter 4), and also by triggering the pituitary gland's release of sex hormones into the bloodstream.

One particular sub-structure within the hypothalamus appears to be important for sexual behavior, and is sexually dimorphic—different in males and females of the same species. The sexually dimorphic nucleus (SDN) (yes, that's its real name) is nearly twice as large in most males than in females (Swaab & Fliers, 1985), due to higher testosterone exposure during fetal development (Pei, Matsuda, Sakamoto, & Kawata, 2006). Lesion studies with rats and mice suggest that this area is very important for male sexual behavior, but this has not been demonstrated for female rodents, and less is known about the role this area plays in human sexual behavior (Balthazart & Ball, 2007). Data also suggest that the SDN may help direct males' sexual orientation—whether they are more interested in female or male sex partners. Studies with both sheep and humans have found that the SDNs of homosexual males (in the non-human animals, males that preferred to mount other males rather than females when given the choice) were much more similar in size to the SDNs of females than those of males (Roselli, Larkin, Resko, Stellflug, & Stormshak, 2004; LeVay, 1991). However, the size of the SDN does not appear to distinguish heterosexual from homosexual females.

Another sub-structure, the paraventricular nucleus (PVN), appears to be important for maternal behavior. Although the PVN has a number of effects, one is to prompt pituitary gland release of oxytocin into the bloodstream (oxytocin is used by the body as a hormone as well as a neurotransmitter), where it facilitates maternal bonding and caregiving behavior (Lévy, Kendrick, Piketty, & Poindron, 1992).

The Insular Cortex

The **insular cortex,** or **"insula,"** is a region of the cortex tucked inside the fold between the temporal and parietal lobes (Figure 5.10). In terms of emotion research, the story of this region is a bit like the story of the amygdala—it's taken a while to figure out what this structure does, and it is still far from clear. Some initial studies associated activation in this area with the experience of disgust. In one study, investigators asked people to look at various facial expressions while undergoing an fMRI scan. The researchers found that the anterior insular cortex was especially activated while viewing the expressions of disgust (M. L. Phillips et al., 1997).

Later studies have also confirmed that viewing disgusting photos activates the insular cortex.

The link between the insular cortex and disgust is interesting, because the insular cortex is also the primary receptive area of the cortex for the sense of taste, and disgust literally means "bad taste." An exclusive relationship between emotional disgust and activation of the insular cortex would suggest a discrete brain region associated with a single emotion—with huge implications for theories of the structure of emotion. Evidence does not, however, support an exclusive relationship. Another study using fMRI found that insula activity increased not only when people looked at disgusting

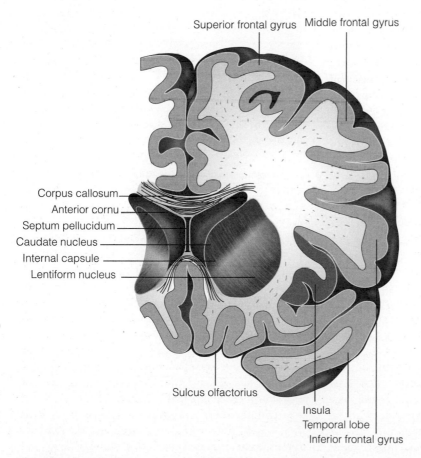

Superior frontal gyrus Middle frontal gyrus

Corpus callosum
Anterior cornu
Septum pellucidum
Caudate nucleus
Internal capsule
Lentiform nucleus

Sulcus olfactorius

Insula
Temporal lobe
Inferior frontal gyrus

FIGURE 5.10 The insular cortex is tucked in a fold between the temporal and parietal lobes of the brain. It appears to mediate awareness of one's internal physical state, and is strongly activated during disgust and fear.

pictures (vomit, maggots, a dirty toilet, a man eating a grasshopper), but also when people looked at frightening pictures (lions, pistols, fire, car accidents). So, it appears that the insular cortex also responds during emotions other than disgust.

The best bet right now is that the insular cortex acts as a "map" of visceral sensations, much as the primary somatosensory cortex acts as a map for the skin's sensory experience of touch. One study found that people with more gray matter volume in the insular cortex were better at detecting and estimating changes in their own heart rate, and these individuals also reported feeling very strong emotions in general (Critchley, Wiens, Rotshtein, Ohman, & Dolan, 2004). Neuroimaging studies find that the insula becomes more active when people experience non-painful changes in temperature (Craig, Chen, Bandy, & Reiman, 2000), when the stomach is full (Ladabaum, Minoshima, Hasler, Cross, Chey, & Owyang, 2001), when the colon is full (Hamaguchi et al., 2004), and during muscular pain (Schreckenberger et al., 2005). If visceral sensations are an important aspect of the feeling of emotion, and if some part of the insula acts to map these sensations, then we would expect insula activation to be an important part of emotional experience.

The Prefrontal Cortex

The **prefrontal cortex**, the part of the brain forward of the motor and premotor areas of the frontal cortex, is often associated with advanced cognitive functions such as planning, working memory, and the inhibition of impulses rather than emotion (Fuster, 2008; Miller & Cohen, 2001). "Higher" cognitive processes of judgment and decision-making are not always distinct from emotion, however, and a wide body of research suggests that the prefrontal cortex facilitates the use of emotional information in making good decisions (Damasio, 1994).

A famous early case bringing attention to this area of the brain was that of Phineas Gage, who in 1848 survived an explosion that sent an iron pole flying into his left cheek and right out the top of his forehead. In the 1990s, researchers studied Gage's skull (which is now on exhibit in a Boston museum)

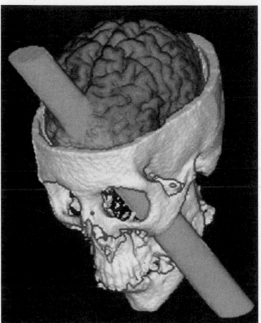

Reprinted with permission from Damasio, H., Grabowski, T., Frank, R. Galaburda, A. M. & Damasio, A. R. (1994). The return of Phineas Gage: The skull of a famous patient yields clues about the brain. Science, 264, 1102–1105. © 1994, AAAS.

FIGURE 5.11 A modern, computer-based reconstruction of the path the iron bar took through the brain of Phineas Gage in 1848. Gage survived, but he became unreliable, lost self-control, and made poor decisions.
SOURCE: H. Damasio et al. (1994).

and reconstructed the pole's probable route through his head, as shown in Figure 5.11 (Damasio, Grabowski, Frank, Galaburda, & Damasio, 1994). Gage's prefrontal cortex suffered severe damage, particularly the **ventromedial prefrontal cortex** (VMPFC), sometimes called the "orbitofrontal" cortex because it lies just above the bone encasing the eyes. This is the area we mentioned earlier in the chapter, easily damaged in motorcycle accidents and other trauma to the front of the head—the brain smashes against the eye bones and is crushed. Gage survived the accident and seemed to be in perfect physical health, but for some time his personality seemed to have changed.

In the 1990s, researchers reported extensive tests on a new patient with prefrontal damage (A. Damasio, 1994; H. Damasio, 2002). This patient, known in the literature as "Elliot," suffered prefrontal damage from a surgical operation to remove a tumor. Afterward he seemed normal in many regards, but he consistently had trouble making decisions. He would deliberate endlessly about unimportant details, only to end with what appeared to be a haphazard (and often harmful) decision. He could neither plan for the future nor follow plans that others suggested. He would interrupt an important task to do something trivial, or continue doing something unimportant when he should quit. For example, at work, when he was supposed to be sorting documents, he once stopped to read one of the documents for the rest of the afternoon. All of us get distracted occasionally, but for Elliot this event was part of a pattern. As a result, he kept losing jobs. He divorced his first wife, married a woman who was clearly a bad choice, and then divorced her. He invested all his savings in a project that seemed sure to fail, and it did.

Of course, many people make terrible life decisions, even lots of them, without having brain damage. How do we know Elliot's problems with decisions are related to the surgery, and what does that mean for the relationship between emotion and decision making? Part of the answer to this comes from the difference between Elliot's behavior before and after the surgery. Eventually these differences seemed serious enough to other people that he was brought to psychologists for testing (A. R. Damasio, 1994). He was relatively normal in tests of vision, memory, language, and intelligence. Even on memory tests that are sensitive to damage in certain parts of the prefrontal cortex, he performed surprisingly well. His only prominent abnormality was a lack of emotional reactivity. When he described terrible events from his own life, he was calm and relaxed. Even when he looked at photos of people injured in gory accidents, he showed none of the revulsion or distress that most people display.

The researchers tried to identify more precisely where Elliot's decision-making process went wrong. They presented him with a variety of hypothetical situations, such as "Imagine you went to a bank and the teller gave you too much change," or "Suppose you broke someone's flower pot," or "Suppose you owned stock in a company and you learned that it was doing badly." In each case Elliot was asked to suggest various actions that he might take, and then to predict the consequences of each. In another set of scenarios he was also asked what was the morally right thing to do. To all these questions he gave normal answers; he seemed to understand the possible courses of action and their consequences as well as anyone else. There was no problem with Elliot's logic—he could reason through scenarios like these easily, as long as they weren't actually happening. The explanation of his problems with real-life decisions came from Elliot's own words. In one case, after describing all the possible actions he might take and all the probable consequences, he remarked, "And after all this, I still wouldn't know what to do!" (A. R. Damasio, 1994, p. 49).

Beyond Gage and Elliot, Damasio (1994) has described a dozen patients with prefrontal damage whose symptoms included flat emotions and poor decision-making. People with damage in this area often act impulsively, taking the first choice that looks reasonable instead of checking for a better one. They also express less empathy than average for other people in distress (Shamay-Tsoory et al., 2004). Two patients who suffered prefrontal damage during infancy never developed any sense of right and wrong; they frequently stole, lied, and hurt other people, without any signs of guilt (Anderson, Bechara, Damasio, Tranel, & Damasio, 1999).

Researchers have tried to specify the ways in which the prefrontal cortex relates to decision-making. According to some researchers, many decisions are based upon the magnitude of possible rewards and punishments, their likelihood, and how soon they will occur. The VMPFC and adjacent areas are activated by taste, smell, and touch stimuli (which are generally experienced as either "pleasant" or "unpleasant") as well as by rewards and punishments of all kinds, including winning or losing money and gaining or losing social approval (Clark, Cools, & Robbins, 2004; Krawczyk, 2002; Rolls, 2004). One possibility is that patients with VMPFC damage are insensitive to the possible consequences of their decisions (Berlin, Rolls, & Kischka, 2004). Several studies have documented a difficulty in shifting decision-making strategy based on rewards and punishments. For example, suppose your task is to choose button A or button B. Button A produces a monetary reward on 70 percent of trials and a loss on 30 percent; button B produces a reward on 40 percent and a loss on 60 percent. By trial and error you learn to choose A. Then (without your being told), the rules change so that B produces a reward more often than A. Every time you learn which button to choose, the rules switch to favor the other one. Most people learn to reverse their preferences quickly, but people with damage to the orbitofrontal cortex are slow to do so, and over the course of many trials, they choose the wrong stimulus more often than the right one (Berlin et al., 2004).

Also, suppose you had to choose between two decks of cards, each of which produces a gain or loss of money. At first you try both decks, and you discover that deck A has larger rewards than deck B. Soon, however, it becomes clear that deck A also has larger and more frequent losses, so in the long run you would do better with the slow, steady gains from deck B. Most people gradually shift their preference to deck B, but people with orbitofrontal damage continue choosing mostly from deck A (Bechara, 2004; Bechara, Damasio, Damasio, & Lee, 1999).

As we saw with Elliot, however, the problem seems not to be with *knowing* the rewards and punishments that are likely to follow from one's actions. Like Elliot, most patients with VMPFC damage can tell you what the likely consequences of their behavior are, even if they do not act in a way that seems to make any sense. A plausible alternative is that those with orbitofrontal damage do not anticipate the *feelings* associated with the consequences of their actions, and therefore have no motivation to behave in one way or another. According to this interpretation, the patient "Elliot" cannot make decisions because he has a difficult time anticipating how he might feel after various outcomes. Think of it this way: In response to the question about getting extra change at the bank, you could say that you could return the extra change and have the bank thank you, or you could try to walk away with it, probably get caught, and

get a reputation for dishonesty. You prefer the first outcome because you anticipate feeling bad if you get caught running away with extra money. Your decision would be based in part on the emotions you anticipate feeling as a result of each possible action. Elliot doesn't know what to do because he does not anticipate his future emotions, especially the negative ones. Without the ability to imagine future feelings, one outcome seems as good as another.

In recent years, researchers have used fMRI approaches to ask whether the VMPFC becomes more active when people are making emotional decisions, and have found some support for this theory in non-patients. In one study, individuals who showed greater activation in the VMPFC while considering a real financial gamble were especially responsive to the size of the potential loss (Tom, Fox, Trepel, & Poldrack, 2007). In other studies, VMPFC activation was found to track the subjective value of a possible reward, as it was reduced from the objective size of the reward due to delay or probability of winning (Peters & Büchel, 2009; Pine, Seymour, Roiser, Bossaerts, Friston, Curran, & Dolan, 2009). This suggests that the *feeling* of possible reward was more strongly associated with VMPFC activation than the actual, or logically relevant, likelihood of reward. Of course, much work remains to rule out other psychological processes that might explain this effect, but so far the findings are compelling.

Nucleus Accumbens and Ventral Tegmental Area: The "Reward Circuit" of the Brain

Perhaps the strongest case for a particular brain structure (in this case, a network of structures) mediating a particular kind of emotional experience is for a kind of positive emotion. The structures in question are sometimes referred to as the "reward circuit," including the **ventral tegmental area (VTA)** and the **nucleus accumbens** as well as part of the frontal lobes (Figure 5.12). This circuit is activated by a signal that a reward is on the way.

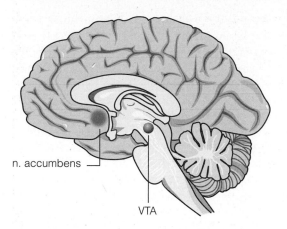

FIGURE 5.12 The nucleus accumbens and ventral tegmental area are part of a neural circuit that appears important for anticipating rewards.

Researchers have found that these brain areas, especially the nucleus accumbens, show enhanced release of the neurotransmitter dopamine both during a reinforcing experience and during anticipation of the reinforcer. The nucleus accumbens becomes more active in response to a wide range of reinforcers, including drugs (such as cocaine), sex, food, and video games (Giuliani & Ferrari, 1996; Harris, Brodie, & Dunwiddie, 1992; Hull et al., 1992; Koepp et al., 1998).

Studies of rats and other mammals have shown that cells in the nucleus accumbens and ventral tegmental area rapidly learn about the relationships between events that predict rewards and the rewards themselves. Activity in these cells then predicts behavior involved in going to get the reward (such as moving toward a chute that will deliver a tasty snack). In brain imaging studies with human participants, this system becomes active in all kinds of rewarding situations, from eating chocolate, to eye contact with an attractive person, to humor, to listening to one's favorite music (Blood & Zatorre, 2001; Kampe, Frith, Dolan, & Frith, 2002; Mobbs, Grecius, Abdel-Azim, Menon, & Reiss, 2003; Small, Zatorre, Dagher, Evans, & Jones-Gotman, 2001).

An important distinction here is between the emotion associated with *anticipating* or wanting something, and the emotion associated with actually *consuming* and enjoying that thing (Berridge & Robinson, 1995). The reward circuit is associated with anticipation rather than consumption or enjoyment. The system becomes highly active if you see something that you want just within your reach. As soon as you consume the reward, the reward circuit quiets down again. In one study, researchers found that people's reward circuits were active when they were first offered pieces of chocolate, but over time, as they ate more and more chocolate and reported getting tired of it, their reward circuits "turned off" as the offers continued (Small et al., 2001).

Moreover, different structures in the circuit appear to respond to different aspects of a potentially rewarding situation. In one study, Brian Knutson and colleagues asked participants to complete a gambling-type task while they were in an MRI scanner (Knutson, Taylor, Kaufman, Peterson, & Glover, 2005). In each trial, the participant first saw a complex shape where the overall shape (circle or square) indicated whether a gain or loss was going to take place, the position of a vertical line across the shape indicated the amount of money at stake, and the position of a horizontal line indicated how likely the gain or loss was (see Figure 5.13). Then the participant saw a delay screen, a white

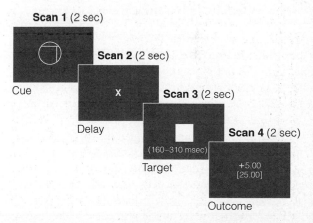

FIGURE 5.13 A typical trial in the Knutson et al. (2005) study showed a figure indicating the magnitude and probability of a monetary gain or loss followed by a delay, a target requiring a response, and then the outcome.

SOURCE: From Knutson, B., Taylor, J., Kaufman, M., Peterson, R., & Glover, G. (2005). 'Distributed neural representation of expected value'. *Journal of Neuroscience*, 25(19), 4806–4812. Reprinted by permission.

target (at which point the participant pressed a button to show she was paying attention), and the outcome of the trial. The researchers were especially interested in brain activity during the delay screen, while participants were presumably mulling over the likelihood of gaining or losing money, and experiencing the appropriate emotions. They found that activation in the nucleus accumbens increased proportionally to the *magnitude* of a possible reward (there was no response to possible losses), and activation in the prefrontal cortex (another part of the reward circuit) increased proportionally to the *probability* of reward on that trial.

These structures are not the only ones involved in the experience or implications of emotion. Throughout the book we will discuss several other structures that play important roles—sometimes in particular emotions, sometimes in more general processes across different emotions. In each case, keep in mind that we have some good evidence for current theories about the function served by a structure, but this is still a very young field, so there are more questions than answers, and much more data is needed before we can rule out alternate explanations.

EMOTION NEUROCHEMISTRY: SOME IMPORTANT NEUROTRANSMITTERS

The neuroanatomical approach to emotion relies on a certain assumption—that specific psychological processes are mediated by activity in clusters of neurons located in the same physical space, or at least in a few discernible regions. If this were not the case, we would not expect some areas to become more active than others while a research participant completes certain tasks, nor would we expect that lesions to particular brain structures would interfere with specific abilities. As we have seen, this assumption appears to be justified for some emotion-related processes. There is, however, an alternative. Rather than thinking of the neural underpinnings of psychological processes in terms of spatial chunks of brain tissue, many researchers emphasize the activity of neurotransmitters used by neurons

to communicate with each other, sometimes across regions of brain space.

Humans have recognized that certain chemicals can change psychological experience for thousands of years, ever since the first person tried drinking some sugary juice that had fermented, or ate a particular kind of mushroom or other plant. The systematic study of the effects of such chemicals is, however, more recent. As with the neuroanatomy section above, we introduce here a few neurotransmitters that seem to play key roles in emotional experience, with others discussed throughout the rest of the book.

Dopamine

Dopamine is probably responsible for more enjoyment, and more trouble, than any other neurotransmitter. Recall the description in the previous section of the brain's reward system. The different structures in this system communicate with each other through dopamine. Dopamine is manufactured in the ventral tegmental area (as well as a couple of other areas elsewhere in the brain), and neurons with cell bodies in the VTA use this neurotransmitter to communicate with neurons in the nucleus accumbens and prefrontal cortex. Thus, dopaminergic neurotransmission appears to be crucial for feelings of anticipation and reward. This is a good thing—dopamine is probably instrumental in motivating goal-oriented activity.

Consistent with this interpretation, many recreational drugs have their effects by altering the dopaminergic reward system. Cocaine binds to the transporters that would normally facilitate re-uptake of dopamine into the axon of the presynaptic neuron, so that dopamine hangs around longer in the synapse and has a longer effect. Amphetamines (such as "meth") actually enter the axons of reward circuit neurons, and push dopamine into the synapse. Alcohol also increases dopamine activity in the reward circuit, although the mechanisms are indirect. Even caffeine increases the release of dopamine by neurons in the VTA.

The implications of each of these drugs for the dopaminergic reward system explain why they become addictive. Studies of laboratory animals and people addicted to alcohol, cocaine, amphetamines, and several other drugs find that they have fewer dopamine receptors in the reward circuit, presumably as the brain compensated for the floods of dopamine that kept happening after repeated drug use (Martinez, Gil, Slifstein, Hwang, Perez, Kegeles, et al., 2005; Volkow, Fowler, Wang, Swanson, & Telang, 2007). As a result, non-drug experiences that would normally elicit a pleasurable sense of anticipation have a much reduced effect. These receptor changes also mean that larger and larger amounts of the drug are needed to produce the same effect—a common feature of addiction.

People often speak of being "addicted" to certain behaviors, such as gambling, shopping, playing video games, and sex. This may be more than a convenient metaphor. Gambling tasks are used routinely by researchers to activate the dopamine reward circuit (Breiter et al., 2001; Knutson et al., 2005), and the nucleus accumbens reponds to video games, as well as cues of sex and food (Giuliani & Ferrari, 1996; R. Harris et al., 1992; Hull et al., 1002; Koepp et al., 1998). Addiction to these behaviors may share some of the same neural mechanisms as addiction to drugs. For example, one study found that gambling addicts were twice as likely as non-addict controls to have the gene for a dopamine receptor variant common among drug and alcohol addicts (Comings, Rosenthal, Lesieur, Rugle, Muhleman, Chiu, Dietz, & Gade, 1996). This suggests that certain genes for dopamine receptors may increase the risk of addiction to any substances or behaviors that strongly activate this system.

Dopamine is not only involved in communication within the reward circuit. This neurotransmitter is also important for complex cognitive operations taking place in the frontal lobes, as well as for fine motor control mediated by an area called the basal ganglia. As a result, drugs used to alter dopamine in any one of these regions will end up altering the other regions as well. For example, some antipsychotic drugs used to reduce frontal lobe dopamine activity in the treatment of schizophrenia tend to induce the tremors and motors characteristic of Parkinson's disease, caused by inadequate dopamine in the basal ganglia (Tandon & Jibson, 2002).

Antipsychotics also tend to make those taking them feel emotionally dull and flat (Arana, 2000). Studies have even found that dopamine-increasing treatments for Parkinson's disease can increase the risk of gambling problems (Dodd, Klos, Bower, Geda, Josephs, & Ahlskog, 2005), presumably due to altered dopamine activity in reward circuits.

Serotonin

The neurotransmitter **serotonin** also appears important for emotional experience, although the exact reasons for this are still unclear. Serotonin is manufactured in the raphe nuclei of the brainstem, and is distributed from there throughout the central nervous system. As a result, serotonin transmission is involved in a wide range of psychological processes, including memory, appetite control, and sleep. However, emotion researchers have been interested primarily in two aspects of serotonergic function.

First, the effects of anti-depressant medications that alter serotonin transmission suggest a strong role in mood. The class of drugs known as **Selective Serotonin Reuptake Inhibitors** (SSRIs) do just what their name suggests—they interfere with the molecules that would normally "recycle" serotonin in the synapse by moving it back into presynaptic axons. This has the effect of keeping serotonin in the synapse for a longer period of time, thereby increasing stimulation of serotonin receptors.

However, some major complications stand in the way of concluding that depression is related to serotonin activity. For one thing, in randomized, controlled studies where the participants don't know whether they're taking the real drug or a placebo, SSRIs do not start having a significant effect on mood until some weeks after treatment begins (Gelenberg & Chesen, 2000; Gourion, 2008). If the effects of SSRIs were due simply to increasing serotonin receptor activation, then SSRIs should begin to improve mood within hours. Also, if depression is caused by inadequate serotonin, we might expect people with depression to show low levels of serotonin and its metabolites in their blood and spinal fluid. Tests of this hypothesis have shown inconsistent results (Leonard, 2000). It gets worse: Most research on antidepressants is sponsored by drug companies. When Irving Kirsch (2010) reviewed all of the unpublished data from studies of antidepressant drugs, he concluded that their effects may be explained entirely via placebo effects. Thus, the role of serotonin in mood is still very uncertain.

Serotonin has also been linked to aggressive behavior, suggesting a possible role in the experience of anger. Laboratory research since the 1970s has demonstrated that rats and mice with low levels of serotonin release (as measured by the concentration of serotonin metabolites in the blood or spinal fluid) are more likely to fight with one another (Saudou et al., 1994; Valzelli, 1973; Valzelli & Bernasconi, 1979). One long-term observation of young male monkeys also found that those with the lowest levels of serotonin metabolites were the most likely to start fights, including fights with larger monkeys. Many of these low-serotonin monkeys sustained repeated injuries and died within the first few years of life (Higley et al., 1996).

Researchers have examined the implications of serotonin levels for human aggression as well. Low levels have been found in people convicted of arson and other violent crimes (Virkkunen, Nuutila, Goodwin, & Linnoila, 1987). Studies of inmates being released from prison found that those with low serotonin levels are the most likely to be convicted of additional violent crimes within the next few years (Virkkunen, DeJong, Bartko, Goodwin, & Linnoila, 1989; Virkkunen, Eggert, Rawlings, & Linnoila, 1996). Similarly, of children and adolescents being counseled because of aggressive behavior, those with the lowest serotonin levels are the most likely to commit additional violent acts (Kruesi et al., 1992). Of people who survive violent attempts at suicide, those with the lowest serotonin levels are the most likely to attempt suicide again within the next five years (Roy, DeJong, & Linnoila, 1989). A thorough review of the available human literature found that the relationship between decreased serotonin and increased violent behavior was consistent, although only moderate in size (Moore, Scarpa, & Raine, 2002).

As with depression, however, the role of serotonin in aggression is also complicated. When researchers have used drugs or other methods to lower people's serotonin levels suddenly, the people with a previous history of violence became violent, those with a history of depression became depressed, and those with a history of substance abuse reported a sudden craving for drugs (Van der Does, 2001). It is as if low serotonin removes inhibitions against various negative impulses, but different people have different impulses. Furthermore, the exact role of serotonin in aggression remains unclear. Neurons actually release serotonin *during* aggressive behavior, not while the individual is preparing for or refraining from aggression (van der Vegt et al., 2003). According to one hypothesis, those who usually have low levels of serotonin release react more strongly than usual to events causing its release, and therefore those with the lowest serotonin turnover have the highest likelihood of violence. In any case, drugs that elevate serotonin do not reliably decrease aggressive behavior.

The research on depression and aggression all emphasize the possible correlates of *low* levels of serotonin. What happens when people's serotonin activity is suddenly increased? Psychedelic drugs such as LSD, psilocybin (the psychoactive chemical in hallucinogenic mushrooms), and mescaline all stimulate a particular kind of serotonin receptor, and all induce dramatic sensory and perceptual changes. These changes are not by definition emotional, although people typically experience strong emotions in response to the hallucinations, and some people experience distress or paranoia.

The drug MDMA, also known as "ecstasy," causes serotonergic axons to dump their contents into the synapse, overwhelming serotonin receptors. The subjective effects are consistent with the wide-ranging importance of this neurotransmitter throughout the brain, and include a sense of peacefulness, intimacy toward others, intensified sensory experience (especially of touch), reduced anxiety and aggressiveness, increased energy and alertness, and decreased pain sensitivity (Verheyden, Henry, & Curran, 2003). Serotonin receptors come in many different subtypes located in different parts of the brain, and these varying effects may reflect the increased stimulation of all the different receptors.

Beta-Endorphins and the Opioid Peptides

The opioid peptides are a third class of neurotransmitters with clear importance for emotion. The best known of these is **beta endorphin**, a neurotransmitter that serves as the body's natural painkiller. The term endorphin is a contraction of "endogenous morphine," because it acts like a self-produced morphine. Physical trauma does not always release endorphins, but when it does, endorphin activity in a region of the brainstem called the periaqueductal gray area helps to curb the pain.

Some studies have linked changes in beta-endorphin activity to the experience of emotional pain, as well as physical pain. Social loss and grief decrease endorphin release, in both humans and laboratory animals. In one study, infant guinea pigs cried when separated from their mothers (presumably indicating distress and low endorphin release), but if they were given a mild dose of morphine (replacing the decreased endorphins), they stopped crying. If given naloxone, a drug that blocks endorphin activity, they cried even harder than usual (Herman & Panksepp, 1978). In another study, young women were asked to describe various life events, including some that were sad and some that were neutral. PET scans indicated decreased endorphin release in several brain areas while the women were describing sad events, but not other kinds of events (Zubieta et al., 2003). In short, the emotional pain that often accompanies grieving or separation from loved ones may be mediated by changes in the same neurotransmitter that responds to physical pain.

SUMMARY

The way emotion emerges from neural processes is a central topic in emotion theory and research. For theorists advocating a basic emotions perspective, finding emotion-specific brain structures or neurotransmitters (or even specific receptors!) would be like finding the Holy Grail. In contrast, dimensional theorists insist that the neural underpinnings of emotion generalize across emotions. Although recently developed technologies have allowed researchers to begin addressing each of these possibilities, it will be a long time before any definitive answers will be found.

Still, we have learned a lot. MacLean proposed that the brain contained a large, distinct area for emotion—a "limbic system" located between the neocortex and the brain stem structures. We now know the brain isn't divided up that neatly, that structures important for emotional processes are located in the brainstem and neocortex as well as in between. We have identified structures that appear associated with emotional memory formation, the use of emotions in decision-making, and in the anticipation of rewards, yet it has been difficult to identify brain structures associated with the experience of a particular emotion. There are hints that certain neurotransmitters facilitate the experience of particular emotions, but we have a long way to go before we really understand these effects. New technologies in emotion neuroscience are emerging all the time, and you can expect this area of research to grow dramatically in coming years.

KEY TERMS

amygdala: an area within the brain's temporal lobe, necessary for fear conditioning and thought to facilitate the consolidation of emotional episodic memories (p. 117)

beta endorphin: a neurotransmitter that serves as the body's natural painkiller, and may be involved in feelings of emotional pain (p. 133)

dopamine: the main neurotransmitter in the brain's reward circuit, as well as in cognitive and motor areas (p. 130)

electroencephalography (EEG): a technique that measures electrical potentials (or "charges") generated by neurons when they depolarize (p. 112)

event-related potentials: rapid changes in the EEG signal in response to particular stimuli (p. 113)

fear conditioning: a procedure in which one learns that a new stimulus, such as a tone or color, predicts an electrical shock or other aversive event (p. 118)

functional magnetic resonance imaging (fMRI): a technique that measures changes in blood flow as a way of assessing where neurons have recently been active (p. 114)

hippocampus: a structure attached to the amygdala, believed to mediate the formation of episodic memories for particular events (p. 122)

homeostasis: the body's ability to maintain acceptable levels of temperature, blood chemistry, hydration, and other factors (p. 124)

hypothalamus: a structure located just above the brain stem and below the thalamus; directs the activities of the autonomic nervous system and pituitary gland (p. 123)

insular cortex, or "insula": a region of the cortex tucked between the temporal and parietal lobes; thought to mediate the experience of visceral sensations (p. 125)

Klüver-Bucy Syndrome (KBS): a pattern of emotional changes accompanying removal of both anterior temporal lobes, including the amygdalae (p. 118)

lesion method: a technique that studies the behaviors of individuals with damage to specific parts of the brain, whether experimentally induced or due to trauma or degenerative disease (p. 112)

neurotransmitters: the chemicals used by neurons to communicate with each other (p. 116)

nucleus accumbens: a structure in the reward circuit of the brain; especially responsive to the magnitude of a possible reward (p. 128)

prefrontal cortex: the region forward of the motor and premotor areas of the frontal cortex, associated with advanced cognitive functions as well as some emotion-related processes (p. 126)

selective serotonin reuptake inhibitors (SSRIs): a class of anti-depressant medications; interfere with the reuptake of serotonin from the synapses (p. 131)

serotonin: a neurotransmitter involved in many sensory, cognitive, and emotional processes; low levels may be linked to depression and aggression (p. 131)

triune brain model: a model that divides the brain into three regions: one for sensory, survival and reflex actions; one for "mammalian" emotion; and a neocortex responsible for complex cognition and reasoning (p. 110)

ventral tegmental area (VTA): a part of the brain's reward circuit; one place where dopamine is manufactured (p. 128)

ventromedial prefrontal cortex (VMPFC): the region of the prefrontal cortex just above the bone encasing the eyes; thought to mediate the use of emotion in decision-making (p. 126)

THOUGHT QUESTIONS

1. Review the studies described above on the ventromedial prefrontal cortex. Can you come up with an alternative hypothesis about what psychological process is mediated by this area of the brain? What study could you do, to pit the current hypothesis against your own?

SUGGESTIONS FOR RESEARCH PROJECTS

1. Some research has implicated an area called the "anterior cingulate cortex" in emotion. Using a database such as Psycinfo or Google Scholar, find a few studies that appear to relate activation in this area to some aspect of emotion. Based on these studies, propose a particular psychological process in which the anterior cingulate might be involved.

SUGGESTIONS FOR FURTHER READING

Damasio, A. R. (1994). *Descartes' Error: Emotion, Reason, and the Human Brain*. New York: G. P. Putnam. Includes a rich discussion of Damasio's research with patients with lesions to the prefrontal cortex.

LeDoux, J. (1996). *The Emotional Brain: The Mysterious Underpinnings of Emotional Life*. New York: Touchstone. A great overview of emotion neuroscience, with emphasis on the amygdala.

Sacks, O. (1998). *The Man Who Mistook His Wife for a Hat*. New York: Touchstone. A neurologist's case descriptions of brain damage patients with remarkably specific psychological deficits.

6

Emotion Regulation

When you experience strong emotion it can feel as though some force has temporarily taken over your body and mind. But emotions do not have total control over us: we can also control our emotions. The ways in which we do so have powerful implications for our lives. **Emotion regulation** consists of the strategies we use to control which emotions we have, when we have them, and how strongly we experience and express them (Gross, 2002). A closely related term is **coping**, which refers to people's attempts to reduce negative emotion during and after a stressful event. The distinction between the two is that coping is always an attempt to reduce negative emotion, whereas emotion regulation includes trying to increase or decrease positive emotions, or even trying to increase a negative emotion if it seems like a good strategy in a particular situation.

People use a wide range of strategies to manage their own emotions, and philosophers and psychologists have long been interested in the differing implications of various strategies. Some strategies are more effective than others on the whole, but the most effective strategy also depends on the situation. In this chapter, we examine several kinds of emotion regulation strategies and evaluate their effectiveness.

FREUD'S EGO DEFENSE MECHANISMS:
AN EARLY TAXONOMY OF COPING

Before we begin, make a thorough list of all the ways you can think of to cope with a distressing situation—talking with other people, getting away from other people, thinking about the problem, not thinking about the problem, and so on. Don't worry if some of your suggestions contradict one another; sometimes one strategy is most likely to be helpful, and sometimes its opposite, depending on the nature of the problem. If you compare lists with others, you might find dozens of suggestions.

An early taxonomy of coping mechanisms was constructed by Sigmund Freud (1937), and later elaborated by his daughter Anna, during the early twentieth century. According to Freud, humans by their very nature have fundamental drives and desires (the "id") that they cannot express in a civilized society. The most famous of these, of course, is the supposed desire to have sex with your mother or father (whoever is the opposite-sex parent). The demands, rules, and societal expectations that limit the expression of the id are housed in a socially learned conscience or "superego." Playing referee between these two conflicting forces is the "ego," the conscious self that tries to appease the id within the constraints of the superego. Freud proposed a series of **ego defense mechanisms**, or psychological regulation strategies that serve to resolve the tension between the id and the superego, and keep disturbing wishes and desires hidden from consciousness. Several of these mechanisms are described in Table 6.1.

The advantage of Freud's taxonomy is that it offers a way to describe and categorize different coping strategies. Scientific progress benefits from clearly defined and labeled constructs, so that different investigators can study the same processes and compare their results. The taxonomy also invites comparison among the various ego defense mechanisms in terms of their overall psychological health. For example, George Vaillant (1977) suggested that the ego defense

TABLE 6.1   Some of Freud's Ego Defense Mechanisms

Ego Defense Mechanism	Definition	Example
Denial	Refusing to acknowledge the reality of an unpleasant or threatening situation	Refusing to admit that your close friend has a serious, life-threatening illness
Fantasy	Retreating to fantasy or daydreaming as a way to fulfill desires	Daydreaming about falling in love with a famous actor or actress, instead of seeking a real romantic partner
Projection	Attributing one's own unacceptable desires, motives, or feelings to another person	Accusing your romantic partner of feeling bored with your relationship, when you are really the one feeling restless
Displacement	Directing disturbing feelings toward an alternative target, rather than the person or event that really elicited them	Yelling at your dog when you're really angry with your supervisor at work
Intellectualization	Focusing purely on the abstract, logical aspects of an issue or experience, rather than the personal or emotional aspects	Logically analyzing the motives and explanations for why a friend let you down, rather than feeling hurt
Reaction Formation	Adopting and expressing attitudes/behaviors that are the extreme opposite of the underlying "real" attitudes and behaviors	Being excessively friendly toward a person you intensely dislike
Repression	"Forgetting" or "blocking" memory of unpleasant or intolerable events; repression is automatic, rather than conscious and intentional	Blocking out memory of a car accident
Suppression	Making a conscious, deliberate decision not to think about a disturbing topic at a particular time	Deciding not to worry about an upcoming deadline at work while you see a movie Friday night
Sublimation	Expressing socially unacceptable desires or impulses in a manner that is constructive and socially condoned	Writing a song or poem that captures your anger toward a parent, rather than arguing with the parent

mechanisms could be organized into four categories, reflecting different stages of emotional maturity as well as differing effects on psychological and life outcomes.

Vaillant proposed that "psychotic" defenses such as denial are common in young children, but indicate trauma or psychopathology in adults. His "immature" category included defenses that avoid dealing with reality, such as fantasy and projection, typical of adolescents but unhealthy for adults. The "neurotic" category includes defenses such as displacement, intellectualization, reaction formation, and repression. According to Vaillant, these defenses are used most often by adults, as they are socially acceptable while also alleviating distress. However, Vaillant considered "mature" defenses such as suppression and sublimation to be the healthiest, as they are intentional and/or lead to prosocial, constructive behavior.

The specifics of Freud's ego defense proposal raise serious problems. Freud defined the defense mechanisms as ways people deal with socially unacceptable sexual and physical desires, and the guilt and anxiety they cause. This emphasis was based on Freud's interpretation of the "real" reasons behind his patients' psychological symptoms, but he never offered anything that would qualify as solid evidence to support this interpretation. In fact, the evidence is now quite strong that most people feel a sexual *aversion* to family members, and others who were familiar during early childhood (Lieberman, Tooby, & Cosmides, 2003; Shepher, 1971; Wolf & Durham, 2005). Furthermore, the evidence for some actual defenses is shaky. When later researchers attempted to find a scientific basis for mechanisms such as repression and projection, their support for Freud's ideas was, to put it generously, "mixed" (Holmes, 1978, 1990).

Furthermore, as Freud's theory developed through one version after another, in many cases he used the same clinical example to support different and even contradictory conclusions (Crews, 1996; Esterson, 2001). That is, he did not develop theories to fit the data; he reinterpreted data to fit the theories. Freud's theory is now less influential in psychology, although many scholars in literature and philosophy follow his ideas.

Most important, Freud's views do not explain the full range of ways we cope with emotional situations. The defense mechanisms he described were not intended to explain how people would cope with the loss of a job, or a divorce, for example. Because the defense mechanisms were thought to help people alleviate anxiety, they do not address ways in which people might try to increase negative emotions or change their positive emotions. Researchers have renewed the search for a way to describe and categorize the various ways of dealing with all kinds of emotions, as elicited in all kinds of situations.

A PROCESS MODEL OF EMOTION REGULATION

James Gross (2002) has offered the **process model of emotion regulation**—a model that organizes emotion regulation strategies according to their place in the emotion process itself—as an alternative way of thinking about and classifying emotion regulation strategies (see Figure 6.1). Building upon earlier theories of emotion and emotion regulation by Lazarus (1991), Frijda (1986), and Arnold (1960), this model starts from certain assumptions about emotions, and the process by which they play out: (1) we enter a particular situation; (2) we pay attention to certain aspects of the situation, rather than others; (3) we appraise those aspects of the situation in a way that facilitates a particular emotional response; and (4) we then experience a full-blown emotion, including physiological changes, behavior impulses, and subjective feelings. As we discussed in Chapter 1, this theory of emotion is far from conclusive—the order of events can vary, and sometimes we experience some aspects of emotion without others. However, the theory seems to explain enough of emotional experience that it has been helpful in understanding emotion regulation as well.

Using this model, we can classify emotion regulation strategies according to *when* they take place in the emotion process, and this classification

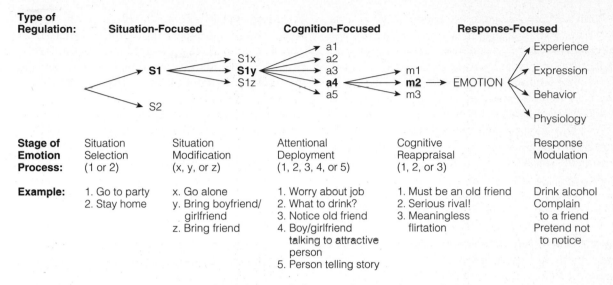

FIGURE 6.1 The Process Model of Emotion Regulation organizes emotion regulation strategies according to their place in the emotion process itself.

SOURCE: Adapted from Gross (2002).

helps us understand why different strategies have different implications and outcomes. The process model highlights three main categories of strategies for regulating emotion. **Situation-focused strategies** are used to control the situation, either by choosing to be in one situation rather than another, or by changing the situation somehow. In **cognition-focused strategies**, we pay attention to certain aspects of the situation or change the way we think about the situation, in order to encourage some emotions and/or deter others. The third category includes **response-focused strategies** that alter the effects of emotions once they have already started. Response-focused strategies presume that a person is already experiencing an emotion and wants some aspect of that emotion to change. This may include "getting it out of your system" by talking about the emotion; attempting to turn off emotional experience, such as by sleeping or consuming drugs or alcohol; or attempting to suppress the expression of an emotion so that other people can't see what you are feeling. Let's take a look at each of these three categories in detail.

SITUATION-FOCUSED STRATEGIES

When possible, a powerful way to control your emotions is to seek out, avoid, or change the situations that elicit them (Gross, 2001). For example, if you are worried about a test next week, you could try to calm your emotions through breathing exercises, but you would do better to spend most of your time studying, so you have less reason for anxiety. If it upsets you that your roommate never cleans the bathroom, you could just be furious every time you have to do it, or you could tell her that sharing housework is important to you, and ask her to help out more often. If a friend repeatedly brings up a distressing topic (an acrimonious political argument, detailed discussion of your worst romantic break-up, the time you accidentally sat on his hamster …), you can simply walk away when that topic comes up, or you could try to redirect the conversation. If these strategies fail, you could tell your friend that you find the topic upsetting and would prefer not to discuss it.

Whenever you manage to avoid or improve a negative situation, you reduce the source of distress. When you seek out positive situations, you are more likely to experience positive emotions.

This point may seem so obvious that you wonder why we bother to make it. After all, why would somebody endure an unpleasant situation if they didn't have to? It is helpful to distinguish here between situation *selection* and situation *modification*. In **situation selection** we simply decide whether or not to enter a situation that is likely to elicit a particular emotion; in **situation modification** we enter the situation, but take steps to change it. Let's consider situation selection first. There's much to be said for choosing to enter situations that will be enjoyable and will likely lead to long-term benefits. (Some activities that are fun in the short-term have negative long-term consequences—those are clearly not good situations to select.) In fact, researchers have found that people who create pleasant events for themselves, such as going for a relaxing walk, or enjoying a nice bubble bath, can be resilient in the face of intense stress (Folkman & Moskowitz, 2000). There's also a benefit to avoiding unnecessary stressors, and many people tend to set themselves up for needless distress.

However, situation selection is not an all-purpose emotion regulation strategy. For one thing, completely avoiding unpleasant situations is not always a realistic option. Sure, you can just decide not to go on job interviews because they make you nervous. You can decide not to ask someone you have a crush on for a date, on the grounds that it will be terrifying to do so, and if you are turned down it will hurt. But is this really a good way to live your life? Extreme use of situation selection limits people's opportunities and relationships. Furthermore, people who consistently avoid anything stressful or unpleasant may fail to keep their lives and health in order. One study found that people who reported more avoidance-based coping in the first year of assessment experienced a greater number of life stressors over the next four years, which in turn predicted increased depressive symptoms (Holahan, Moos, Holahan, Brennan, and Schutte, 2005). Another study found that patients with heart disease who also reported highly avoidant coping styles were more likely to die of heart failure over the next six years (Murberg, Furze, & Bru, 2003). A third study found that kidney disease patients who reported high use of avoidant coping were more likely to die over the next nine years; results suggested that this was due to failure to attend medical appointments (Wolf & Mori, 2009).

In each case, the results suggested that people with avoidant coping styles let their lives fall apart (literally, in the latter studies), rather than dealing openly with their problems. Clearly situation selection is a strategy to be used with careful thought. If you can avoid a stressful situation without negative consequences, by all means do so! However, if tolerating that situation will bring you long-term benefits, or will avert some negative outcome, then there are other emotion regulation options.

In situation modification we take steps to alter the situation we are in, in order to facilitate the desired emotion state. This strategy has often been referred to as "active coping," although as we noted earlier the term coping is limited to negative situations where one is trying to reduce distress. This seems like a pretty obvious approach to emotion regulation, as long as you do actually have some control over the situation. Several studies have found that people who often use situation modification or active coping to regulate their emotions tend to have better than average physical health and psychological well-being (Penley et al., 2002). Although these correlations do not necessarily indicate a causal relationship, it does seem reasonable that taking steps to improve your objective situation would be a healthy long-term way to deal with problems.

Studies suggest that situation modification/ active coping strategies also promote well-being through mechanisms beyond their effects on the situation. Even if something unpleasant is unavoidable, it will feel less disturbing if you take steps to control some aspect of the situation, or if you can at least predict what is going to happen and prepare for it. Conversely, people who feel they have little control over situations are at greater risk for depression than those with a stronger sense of control (Alloy et al., 1999).

Suppose a professor in a large class calls on students at random to answer challenging questions. You would prefer not to be called on, but you have to be ready constantly, because you could be called on next. Now change the situation: The professor still calls on all students, but in alphabetical order. So, if your name is Zoë Zyzzlewicz, you can relax until late in the class; you can predict when you will be called. Change the situation one more time: The professor calls only on students who raise a hand to volunteer. Now you are in complete control. Even if you answer many questions, you feel less stressed because you can choose when to participate.

Even *thinking* you have some control over a situation makes it less stressful. Imagine yourself in this experiment: You are asked to do some difficult proofreading while seated next to a device that will make unpredictable, sudden, loud, annoying sounds. You are told that the point of the study is to examine the effects of that noise on your behavior. Just before you start, you are also shown an "escape button": If the noise becomes unbearable, you can simply press that button to turn it off. You are urged not to press the button unless necessary; after all, the point of the study is to determine the effects of the noise on your behavior. The button is there "just in case." When this study has been done, almost none of the participants actually pressed the button. But participants who had the button and believed they could turn off the noise if necessary performed better on the proofreading tasks than participants who were not offered an escape (Glass, Singer, & Pennebaker, 1977; Sherrod, Hage, Halpern, & Moore, 1977).

In another study, people were given a series of painfully hot stimuli to their forearms. Participants in one group were told that they could decrease the duration of a stimulus from five seconds to two seconds if they manipulated a joystick quickly enough in the correct direction. In fact, they had no control; the duration of the stimulus varied randomly, but because they were trying hard with the joystick, they interpreted every short stimulus as a reward for a "quick enough" response. Moreover, participants who *thought* they had control experienced less pain than other participants who knew they had no control, and measurements of brain activity using fMRI found less arousal in several pain-sensitive brain areas (Salomons, Johnstone, Backonja, & Davidson, 2004).

Consider this stressful situation: You are in a hospital for major surgery. The staff hasn't told you when the surgery will occur, how long it will last, what are your chances for success, or how long it will take to recover afterward. You will feel helpless, and frightened. Now change the situation: The staff tell you what to expect, in as much detail as you wish, and even give you some choices, such as when the surgery will begin and who will be present when you wake up from the anesthesia. When you have some sense of prediction and control, your anxiety is much less severe (Van Der Zee, Huet, Cazemier, & Evers, 2002), and chances are you will even have a better medical outcome (Shapiro, Schwartz, & Astin, 1996).

Hospitals now regularly allow patients to control the administration of painkillers after surgery, using a small button, rather than having a nurse administer the drugs on a fixed schedule. Naturally the device limits how often the patient can self-administer the drug, so the patient receives no more, and frequently less, than if someone else had been controlling delivery. However, patients who control the timing of their doses typically report more satisfaction with their pain management (Lehmann, 1995).

There are limits to the benefits of simply believing that you are in control. Self-help books often encourage people to "visualize success" as a way to gain control over their lives and cause desired outcomes. For example, you might be encouraged to visualize getting your dream job, meeting the perfect romantic partner, winning a contest, or driving a luxury automobile. This advice is extremely misleading. If you simply visualize glorious outcomes, you probably will enjoy the fantasy, but it will not actually improve your situation. It may even deter you from activities that would be truly constructive. What *does* help is to visualize doing the work that would lead to the prizes and honors (Taylor, Pham, Rivkin, & Armor, 1998). If you want to succeed in athletics, visualize yourself practicing the movements of your sport. If you want to write a successful paper, visualize yourself in the library or organizing your notes. (And then go do it!)

Similarly, if you expect to face a challenge in the future, you can gain a sense of control by imagining what you will do when the challenge comes. For example, if you expect to have an unpleasant conversation with someone, you might imagine what you will say, how the other person will reply, and what you might say in return (Sanna, 2000). In one study, first-time pregnant women were asked to imagine and describe going through labor. Those whose descriptions were rated as the most accurate and most detailed showed the least worry about the upcoming delivery (Brown, MacLeod, Tata, & Goddard, 2002). This kind of imagination is not just wishful thinking—it is more like careful cognitive rehearsal for how to handle a stressful situation.

You can also gain a sense of control through psychological "inoculation." To become immunized against a virus, you get inoculated with a weakened form of the virus. To gain **psychological inoculation** against a stressor, you can expose yourself to milder versions of the stressful events (Janis, 1983; Meichenbaum, 1985). For example, armies make soldiers practice combat skills under realistic but non-life-threatening conditions, and police departments ask trainees to practice arresting suspects, intervening in domestic quarrels, and so forth with actors playing the part of the other people. People who practice in this way develop a set of skills for handling the situation, which they can then apply to more serious and challenging versions of the situation.

COGNITION-FOCUSED STRATEGIES

Unfortunately, we sometimes face unpleasant situations over which we have little or no control. In some cases the event has already taken place, and we no longer have any way to change it. For example, you applied for admission to several graduate schools, and all of them rejected you. In other cases the event is still ongoing, but the outcome is uncontrollable, or nearly so. For example, you might be caring for an aging relative with Alzheimer's disease, or a loved one with cancer.

In such cases, you can often control your emotions by thinking about the situation differently. Sometimes this means paying attention to one aspect of the situation while ignoring other aspects. Alternatively, one can attend to a negative aspect of a situation, but interpret its meaning in such a way that it evokes less distress. The benefit of these strategies is that they allow you to tolerate potentially stressful situations, but unlike response-focused strategies they prevent unwanted emotions before they even begin. Cognition-focused strategies have been the focus of much research in recent years, so let's consider each of them carefully.

Attentional Control

Imagine that you have developed friendships with a few of the people in your emotion class, and one evening a classmate invites several of you over to have dinner and watch a movie. When you get there everything seems lovely—pleasant living room, dinner smells good, the television is nice and big—but there's one problem. The classmate did not tell you about his pet tarantula, which lives in a terrarium easily visible on a living room shelf. During dinner and the movie, it sits there in its terrarium. Watching you.

For most people, this situation would cause a fair amount of anxiety. One option is to change the situation, by leaving the party (situation selection) or asking your host to move the creature to another room (situation modification). However, the former strategy means a lost social opportunity, and the latter may seem impolite. Many people in this situation would engage in **attentional control**—they would simply try to avoid looking at or thinking about the thing that is causing distress, in this case the spider.

This is actually a commonly used emotion regulation strategy, and research suggests that it has important outcomes for clinical symptoms. Individuals with anxiety disorders show a strong bias toward attending to threatening stimuli (Cisler & Koster, 2010). Most people attend more strongly to emotional stimuli than to neutral stimuli (Bradley, 2009), but highly anxious people show an especially strong bias. Researchers measure initial attentional biases toward threatening stimuli using a **dot-probe task**. In this task, a participant sees two words (or photographs, or some similar visual stimuli) on a computer screen, right next to each other (see below). One of these words is emotionally neutral, and the other is a threat-related word such as "worry," "danger," or "attack." After a brief interval, the words disappear and one of them is replaced by a large dot on the screen; the participant's task is to indicate the location of the dot. Researchers measure how long it takes for the participant to press the key corresponding to the dot's location. Shorter reaction times mean that the participant's attention was already in the area of the dot. Longer reaction times indicate that the participant's attention was elsewhere.

 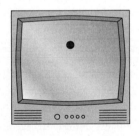

In the dot-probe task, participants use a keyboard to indicate the location of a dot that replaces either a neutral or a threat-related word. Faster responses to a dot replacing threat words indicate that attention had been focused on those words.

In the dot-probe task, most people respond more quickly when the dot replaces a threat stimulus than when the dot replaces a neutral stimulus, indicating that their attention tends to orient toward threat (MacLeod, Matthews, & Tata, 1986). People with anxiety disorders show especially slow reaction times if the dot replaces a neutral stimulus when a threat stimulus was also present, suggesting

that they are having a difficult time pulling their attention away from the location of the threat once it's been oriented there (Salemink, van den Hout, & Kindt, 2007).

Dot-probe studies of attentional control emphasize people's ability to deliberately attend to or ignore stimuli that are right in front of them. However, attentional control can also be used to re-direct attention away from thoughts that might evoke certain emotions. In the novel *Gone With the Wind*, Scarlett O'Hara famously responds to several stressful situations by saying "I won't think about that now—I'll think about it tomorrow, when I can stand it" (Mitchell, 1936). This strategy of not thinking about an emotional situation is similar to Freud's ego defense mechanism of suppression, which differs from the less mature repression in that the individual *decides* not to think about the distressing subject for a while rather than unconsciously denying it. Attentional control is also involved in this approach to emotion regulation.

One great study documents the usefulness of attentional control for emotion regulation. In this study, Ozlem Ayduk and her colleagues (2002) asked participants to vividly remember an experience in which someone else had rejected them—an experience most people find very upsetting. Half of the participants were encouraged to focus their attention on their emotions and physiological sensations during this memory, whereas the other half were encouraged to focus their attention on features of the room in which the rejection took place. After reliving this experience, participants were asked to complete three more tasks: (1) a reaction time task where they decided whether strings of letters were words, or not, as quickly as possible (different kinds of words are used, and the faster you identify a word, the more researchers assume you had that idea on your mind already); (2) self-reported ratings of angry mood; and (3) a written essay about the rejection experience they had just relived. As you can see from Figure 6.2, the attention manipulation had a big effect on people's emotions. Those asked to focus on the characteristics of the room in their memories identified hostility-related words more slowly, reported fewer angry

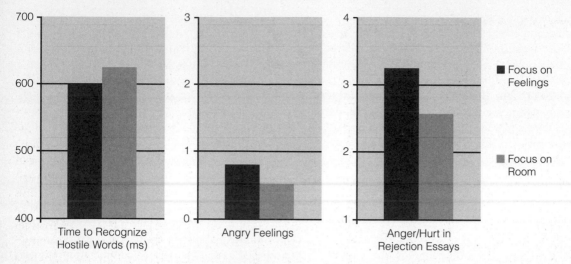

FIGURE 6.2 Participants who focused on features of the room while remembering a rejection experience later detected hostile words less quickly, reported feeling less angry, and used fewer words expressing anger and hurt in essays about the experience than participants who focused on how they had felt at the time.

SOURCE: From Ayduk, O., Mischel, W., & Downey, G. (2002). 'Attentional mechanisms linking rejection to hostile reactivity: The role of "hot" versus "cool" focus'. *Psychological Science*, 13, 443–448. Reprinted by permission.

feelings, and wrote less about feeling angry and hurt in their essays than participants instructed to focus on their feelings and physiology (see Figure 6.2).

In a similar study, children played a game based on the *Survivor* television show. Some of them (randomly assigned) were told they had been voted out of the game—a clear example of peer rejection. Then, during a delay before a second task, various children spent the time quietly thinking or engaging in a distraction such as reading comic books or listening to music. The more time they spent on the distraction, the more their mood improved, as well as their ability to focus on the second task (Reijntjes, Stegge, Terwogt, Kamphuis, & Telch, 2006).

One difficulty with attentional control is that it takes a lot of cognitive energy. As a result, people can run out of ability to control their attention if they are fatigued or have been controlling their thoughts for too long (Engle, Conway, Tuholsky, & Shisler, 2006). In fact, suppressing attention to already-active thoughts and stimuli may be an especially difficult form of cognitive control. In a classic study, Daniel Wegner and colleagues (1987) found that research participants who were asked to avoid thinking about white bears for five

minutes, but to ring a bell if they did, rang the bell more times than a group of participants who *were asked* to think about white bears! However, turning your attention away from one thing is a lot easier if you are also turning it toward something else—a principle reflected in the strategy of cognitive reappraisal.

Cognitive Reappraisal

Let's return to our hypothetical scenario, where you are having dinner with several friends and one tarantula. You just can't keep your eyes off that tarantula. Maybe spiders are a real problem for you. Maybe you studied hard all that day and don't have any attentional control left. Either way, attentional control is not an option. What can you do?

Try imagining the spider as a weak, helpless thing, stuck in some stupid terrarium while everybody else is in the living room having fun and eating something tasty. Then you might feel sorry for the spider, rather than anxious. If that doesn't work, you could try imagining the spider in a funny situation (Figure 6.3). Researchers refer to this strategy as **cognitive reappraisal**—thinking about an

www.Cartoonstock.com

**The Hansons' decision to buy an attack
spider finally paid off.**

FIGURE 6.3 Thinking about feared objects in a way
that makes them seem funny is one kind of cognitive
reappraisal.

event or stimulus in a way that changes your emotional response to it.

Consider the updated James-Lange model of emotion, described in Chapter 1. According to that model, your emotional response to a situation depends on how you appraise or interpret that situation. The assumption here is that there is an automatic link between certain appraisals of a situation and the kind of emotional response you will have. Different researchers think about what "appraisal" means in different ways. For example, Richard Lazarus (1991) proposed that different discrete emotions are evoked by the appraisal of specific **core relational themes** between one's self and the environment. Examples of core relational themes are shown in Table 6.2. In contrast, Klaus Scherer's (1997) cross-cultural study of appraisal, described in Chapters 2 and 3, defined appraisal in terms of a common set of dimensions—expectedness, pleasantness,

external causation, controllability, and so forth (also see Smith & Ellsworth, 1985 for a similar model). In terms of emotion regulation, however, both of these models of appraisal make the same prediction: change your appraisal of the situation, and you will change your emotional response to it (Lazarus, 1991).

Reappraisal doesn't mean pretending the situation isn't happening, or inventing an unrealistic story for how things will turn out. It does mean focusing on a real, but positive (or at least neutral) interpretation of the situation. For example, victims of automobile accidents, hurricanes, and all sorts of other misfortune frequently comfort themselves with the thought, "It could have been worse!" When people change the way they think about a larger emotional issue or frequently occurring situation, the process is called **cognitive restructuring**—a frequent goal in therapies for mood disorders like depression and anxiety. For example, instead of reacting to every unfriendly comment as further evidence that "people don't like me," someone might learn to think, "Oh well, that person is just hard to please," or "I guess my boss is in bad mood again today."

Much research suggests that cognitive reappraisal is both effective and healthy as an emotion regulation strategy. In several studies, participants instructed

TABLE 6.2   Examples of Core Relational Themes (from Lazarus, 1991)

Anger	A demeaning offense against me and mine
Disgust	Taking in or being too close to an indigestible object or idea
Fear	Facing an immediate, concrete, and overwhelming physical danger
Sadness	Having experienced an irrevocable loss
Guilt	Having transgressed a moral imperative
Envy	Wanting what someone else has
Happiness	Making reasonable progress toward the realization of a goal
Compassion	Being moved by another's suffering and wanting to help

to reappraise distressing stimuli have shown reduced self-reports and facial expressions of distress compared with a no-instruction condition (e.g., Gross, 1998; Richards & Gross, 2000; Shiota & Levenson, 2009). Studies have even found that instructed reappraisal reduces amygdala activation to upsetting photographs, compared to trials where participants are asked to simply attend to their emotions (Ochsner, Bunge, Gross, & Gabrieli, 2002). Moreover, people who report using cognitive reappraisal more often also report higher dispositional positive affect, lower negative affect, higher life satisfaction, greater sharing of emotion with others, peer-rated likeability, closer relationships, and lower risk of depression (Gross & John, 2003).

Different Types of Reappraisal

Reappraisal can take many different forms. At the simplest level, one can just ignore the emotional aspects of a situation, and focus on trivial aspects such as the physical setting or what people are wearing. This approach does seem to reduce the experience of negative emotion, as in the study where participants focused on aspects of the room in remembering a rejection experience (Ayduk et al., 2002). As we noted earlier, making a joke about a situation will also improve your emotions (Lefcourt, Davidson, Prkachin, & Mills, 1997). In stressful interactions with another person, taking their perspective can be an important reappraisal technique as well (Gilbert & Holahan, 1982).

We can also consider forgiveness of others as a kind of cognitive reappraisal. Forgiveness often includes finding some acceptable explanation for another person's hurtful behavior. You might decide, "We all have our weak moments. I don't know everything going on in that other person's life. Maybe I should just give him the benefit of the doubt." Getting rid of a grudge releases tension and improves emotional stability (McCullough, 2001; Witvliet, Ludwig, & Vander Laan, 2001). That is, forgiveness helps not only the forgiven, but also the forgiver.

One especially useful reappraisal strategy is to pay attention to a negative event, but try to interpret it in a more benign way. In one study, college students were asked to examine a series of 120 pictures, many of which were unpleasant or disturbing. The participants were asked to suppress their emotional expressions while they viewed the disturbing pictures. Of interest here is the strategy used by the people who were most successful at reducing their emotion displays. When asked how they managed, most said they tried to reinterpret the situation in a positive light. For example, when they saw a wounded soldier, they told themselves the battle was over and the soldier was about to receive good medical care (Jackson, Malmstadt, Larson, & Davidson, 2000).

This strategy of focusing on positive aspects of negative or challenging situations is referred to as **positive reappraisal**, or sometimes "benefit finding." For example, if every graduate school to which you applied rejected you, you might say, "Oh, well. I learned a lot from applying the first time, and next time I'll do better." If you have to care for an aging relative with Alzheimer's disease, you might say, "Here is an opportunity for me to rise to the occasion, to use my skills to help someone who really needs me." Correlational studies suggest that positive reappraisal may be a particularly healthy strategy. For example, people who are **resilient**—those who recover relatively easily from negative events—report thinking about the potential positive effects of negative events more often than less resilient people (Tugade & Fredrickson, 2004).

The utility of positive reappraisal strategies is also evident in research on clinical disorders. Researchers in one study compared the appraisal-focused emotion regulation strategies reported by clinically depressed and anxious Dutch adults, and by a comparable sample of emotionally healthy Dutch adults (Garnefski, van den Kommer, Kraaij, Teerds, Legerstee, & Onstein, 2002). Both groups completed a self-report questionnaire measuring participants' typical frequency of using several cognitive strategies: self-blame, other-blame, rumination, catastrophizing (emphasizing how bad an experience is), acceptance, planning, putting the negative event into perspective, thinking about other positive topics, and positive reappraisal. The one strategy used significantly more often by the healthy sample than by the clinical sample was positive reappraisal. Later studies also found that people who rely on positive reappraisal are less likely than others to report symptoms of depression (Garnefski, Teerds, Kraaij, Legerstee, & van den Kommer, 2004; Kraaij, Pruymboom, & Garnefski, 2002).

One possible explanation for these findings is that positive reappraisal encourages behaviors that improve your life, just like active coping. A meta-analysis of studies looking at the coping strategies used by AIDS patients found that those who used positive reappraisal more often also reported better health behaviors, and showed better actual health outcomes (Moskowitz, Hult, Bussolari, & Acree, 2009).

However, positive reappraisal is not right for every situation, and does not always predict the best outcomes. Another meta-analysis of many studies found that frequent positive reappraisal was unrelated to physical health, and *negatively* associated with psychological health (Penley, Tomaka, & Wiebe, 2002). It may be that some kinds of positive reappraisal are more conducive to health than others. On one hand, seeing the opportunities in a stressful situation may motivate action to take advantage of those opportunities, and may sustain hope. On the other hand, just thinking that things aren't as bad as they seem may reduce a person's motivation to improve the situation, as in Figure 6.4. More research is needed to identify conditions under which positive reappraisal is most helpful.

RESPONSE-FOCUSED STRATEGIES

Suppose the worst has happened. For example, a close relative has died. Nothing you do can undo the loss, and no amount of reappraisal can improve the situation significantly. Once a full-blown emotion is underway, people rely on emotion-focused

FIGURE 6.4 Under some circumstances, positive reappraisal may reduce efforts to improve a negative situation.

regulation strategies to dampen the emotion over time. Many such strategies exist, and we will discuss several that have been subjected to good research. What they all have in common is that their goal is to change the feeling or expression of the emotion, rather than to change the situation or appraisals that led to the emotion.

Expressing Your Feelings

Popular psychology often recommends that you "let it all out"—experience your feelings, and express them to their fullest (Figure 6.5). This strategy dates back to Freud's idea of **catharsis**—the "release" of strong emotions by expressing them. The idea is that the emotions are trapped inside you, and have to come out somehow. As with "visualizing success," the research on this strategy suggests that claims about the benefits of catharsis are partly accurate, and partly bogus.

The bogus part is the idea that deeply feeling and expressing negative emotions will make you feel better. Contrary to the idea of catharsis, research finds that vigorously expressing fear or anger does not reliably reduce the emotion, and often increases

M. Eric Honeycutt/istockphoto.com

FIGURE 6.5 Freud originally proposed that expressing your feelings would "get them out of your system," and make you feel better. For the most part, he was wrong.

it. For example, people who deal with their negative emotions by venting them tend to have more anxiety than average in their interpersonal relationships (Jerome & Liss, 2005). When people are encouraged to cry during sad movies, they end up feeling worse, not better, than people who tried to restrain their tears (Kraemer & Hastrup, 1988). Distressed couples who vent all their anger against each other are taking a major step toward divorce, not reconciliation (Fincham, 2003).

Furthermore, although discussing an emotionally troubling situation does help, dwelling on it for too long can be harmful. It's like medicine: The right amount can help you, but too much can make you sick in a different way. **Rumination** is thinking continuously about a problem for a long time, focusing on negative aspects of the situation instead of possible solutions. Excessive rumination is often a precursor to clinical depression, and may be a contributing factor (Garnefski et al., 2004; Nolen-Hoeksema, 1991). Similarly, attempts to prevent suicide through extensive discussion sometimes lead to rumination that backfires and increases the risk (Moller, 1992).

We are *not* recommending that you try to suppress all thoughts or discussions about negative experiences. Remember what we said earlier, when discussing attentional control—suppressing thoughts is cognitively demanding, and soon the suppression effort takes so much energy that you can't pay attention to anything else. People who try not to think about recent unpleasant experiences perform more poorly than others on tests of working memory (Klein & Boals, 2001). Evidently their efforts to block out unwanted thoughts use up resources that would have otherwise been available.

So … we have cautioned against dwelling on unpleasant experiences and emotions, but also against avoiding all thoughts about them. Somehow you need to find the happy medium between these extremes. One line of research suggests that you can derive substantial benefits from relatively brief exploration of your problems. In one experiment, college students in the treatment group spent half an hour a day for three to five days writing about their deepest thoughts and feelings concerning some intensely upsetting experience. Students who were randomly assigned to the control group spent the same time writing about an unemotional topic. Many in the treatment group wrote about traumatic events, such as the death of a friend or relative, or experiences of physical or sexual abuse. At the end of the week the students could either destroy their journals or hand them in, but no one discussed the content with them. So in these studies, the students were communicating only with themselves.

Afterward, the researchers asked the students for their reaction to the writing experience. Despite becoming very upset while writing, sometimes even crying, nearly all said it was a valuable experience. Follow-up studies later in the semester revealed that, on the average, those in the treatment group had been ill less often, drank less alcohol, and got better grades than those in the control group (Pennebaker, 1997). People get some of the same benefits just by thinking about a stressful event and possible solutions, even if they do not put their thoughts on paper (Rivkin & Taylor, 1999).

Why did the writing task have such positive results, compared with pure emotional expression? According to further research, those most likely to profit from this experience were those who used their writing to try to understand the stressful event and their reactions to it. The more often people used words like *because, reason, realize, know,* and *understand,* the greater their gains in health, academic performance, and overall adjustment (Pennebaker & Graybeal, 2001). That is, the writing helped not because people expressed their emotions, but because they came to understand the situation better in the process of writing.

On the other hand, another study found that a similar amount of writing about an intensely *positive* experience also improved mood and health over the next several months (Burton & King, 2004). Certainly we cannot attribute that benefit to problem-solving, as the positive experience posed no problems. In this case, perhaps the mechanism depends on the positive emotion that comes from writing about and remembering the happy experience.

Expressing your emotions can also have positive benefits through another route—by eliciting social support from other people. In one study, researchers collected reports from thousands of people in 35 countries of the most recent time when they cried, and how crying affected their mood (Bylsma, Vingerhoets, & Rottenberg, 2008). Participants were also asked to report features of the situation, such as who else was present, what event made them cry, what happened afterward, etc. Results showed that crying was most likely to lead to improved feelings when it evoked social support from others, specifically in the form of comforting words or touch, or other friendly behaviors.

Exercise

One of the most successful response-focused coping strategies is physical exercise (see Figure 6.6). Studies have shown repeatedly that exercise is a reliable way to prevent depression (Leppämäki, Partonen, & Lönnqvist, 2002). Over the long term, exercise also helps prevent anxiety (Salmon, 2001). One caveat here is that the benefits come from a consistent program of exercise, not from a single workout. Also, whereas a moderate amount of exercise improves mood, extremely strenuous exercise can actually make one's mood worse (Salmon, 2001).

Why does a steady program of moderate exercise help improve mood? No one is sure exactly, but

FIGURE 6.6 Physical exercise can play an important role in emotion regulation, as well as promoting physical health.

several mechanisms are probably involved. First, exercise is a distraction from the source of stress. Any kind of distraction—such as listening to music or watching television—is one way of dealing with stress, although in most situations not a very powerful one (Fauerbach, Lawrence, Haythornthwaite, & Richter, 2002). Whether distraction makes sense or not really depends on the stressor. If the source of stress is completely out of your control, and reappraisal is not a reasonable strategy, then distraction may be a good idea. On the other hand, if you *do* have some control over a situation, then distracting yourself from it interferes with resolving it and improving your situation in the long run.

Second, exercise improves overall health. People in good physical condition show less tension and sympathetic arousal in response to stressful events, compared to people in worse condition (Crews & Landers, 1987), and we know that muscle tension and arousal are part of the subjective feeling of stress.

Third, any stress readies the body for intense fight-or-flight action, even if the particular stressful situation does not call for physical activity. Once the body has engaged in physical activity after stress, it tends to relax. Studies with laboratory rodents have found that wheel-running exercise, after a separate stressor, can even reduce adrenal stress responses (Mills & Ward, 1986).

Fourth, neurotransmitters called endorphins (see Chapter 5 for a definition) become more active during physical exercise (Thoren, Floras, Hoffman, & Seals, 1990). These chemicals are part of the body's natural pain-killing system, and as we discussed in Chapter 5, opiate activity is generally associated with a strong improvement in mood.

Relaxation

It may seem contradictory to list both exercise and relaxation as ways of controlling emotions, but in fact they may be related. Both help the body reduce muscular tension and autonomic arousal. Having trouble relaxing? Here is some advice (Benson, 1985):

- Find a place that is reasonably quiet.
- Begin by tensing all your muscles so you notice how they feel. Then systematically relax them

one by one, starting with your feet and working upward.

- If at first you find it difficult to relax, don't worry about it. After all, the whole point of relaxation is to stop worrying!
- Shut out as much stimulation as possible by repeating a sound (such as "om") or repetitive prayer, or focusing on some simple object or shape. Choose whatever seems comfortable to you.

This practice is generally known as meditation (see Figure 6.7). People who practice this technique daily report feeling less stress. One study found that

Elena Ray/istockphoto.com

F I G U R E   6.7 People who meditate regularly report less stress. This may be due to cognitive training, or simply to relaxation.

people who went through a 12-week meditation program had a long-lasting decrease in anxiety and depression, as compared with a control group who spent the same amount of time listening to lectures about stress reduction (Sheppard, Staggers, & John, 1997). Although the mechanisms by which meditation reduces stress are not fully understood, one likely hypothesis is that they promote relaxation (Holmes, 1987).

Suppressing Emotional Expression

In some situations, we may feel pressure to control our outward expressions of emotion, regardless of what we feel inside. Imagine receiving an unfair and rudely phrased criticism from a supervisor at work, or a sarcastic comment from a professor. In these situations you might feel offended, but you risk getting into trouble if you express your anger fully. When people try to hide their emotions, so that a person watching them would not know what they are feeling, most are able to do so (e.g., Gross, 1998; Gross, 2002; Gross & Levenson, 1997).

Researchers refer to this strategy as **suppressing emotional expressions**. Note that "suppression" here differs from Freud's meaning of the term. Freud used the term to refer to blocking a thought from consciousness, whereas here the term refers to blocking the behavioral *expression* of an emotion. The ability to suppress emotional expressions is certainly important in some situations. Imagine what it would be like if you could never suppress your displays of emotion! However, as with some other emotion regulation strategies, suppressing emotions indiscriminately is problematic. Many studies have found that suppressing expressions is costly in terms of cognitive resources, with a wide range of negative implications. We will discuss these implications in detail shortly.

Emotional Escape Strategies: Drugs, Alcohol, and Food

If recent events in your life have gone very badly, and you want to escape from the tension—fast—what options would you consider? Go on, be honest.

Many people try using alcohol or other drugs as a quick way to escape their problems, at least occasionally. Many men react to the death of their wife by increasing their consumption of alcohol, sometimes to a dangerous level (Byrne, Raphael, & Arnold, 1999). Many young adults use alcohol to escape from the stresses of work or school. Let's just say that we don't recommend this as a regular strategy. Alcohol by itself is not the problem—huge numbers of people drink alcohol in moderation (a few servings per week) without apparent harm—but relying on alcohol or other drugs to escape from problems can easily develop into a problem itself. Aside from the obvious risks of addiction, and the life problems that typically follow, someone who gets high in order to avoid feeling bad is probably *not* taking constructive action to improve the situation.

Another quick way to make yourself feel good is eating. However, most people who use eating to escape from tension feel worse afterward (Solomon, 2001; Waters, Hill, & Waller, 2001). Also, as with alcohol and drugs, habitual "emotional eating" tends to crowd out more constructive, problem-focused approaches to negative events.

THE NEUROBIOLOGY OF EMOTION REGULATION

Researchers are just beginning to understand the neural bases of emotion regulation, but these kinds of studies can help us understand what cognitive abilities are needed to implement particular strategies. Much of this research has focused on the cognition-focused strategies, partly because it makes sense theoretically, and partly because cognition-focused strategies are easy to elicit in an fMRI magnet. These studies have typically emphasized a point we made above—that cognition-focused strategies require considerable effortful control over thoughts and attention, often referred to as **executive control**. Studies of the neural activation patterns associated with cognitive reappraisal are consistent with this view.

In one study, young men watched a series of short pornographic films while undergoing an fMRI scan. During some of the films, they were instructed to allow themselves to become aroused; during the others they were told to inhibit their arousal. As shown in Figure C.7 inside the back cover of this book, different brain areas became active under the two conditions (Beauregard, Lévesque, & Bourgouin, 2001). While the men were sexually aroused, activity increased in the hypothalamus, right amygdala, and part of the right temporal cortex—areas associated with sexuality and emotion. While they were inhibiting their arousal, activity was lower in the amygdala and hypothalamus, but increased in the prefrontal cortex, an area identified with cognitive control (Tisserand et al., 2004).

In a similar study, participants looked at a series of disturbing photos while undergoing functional imaging. Then they examined the same pictures, while reappraising them to make them less disturbing. While participants examined the photos the first time, they showed extensive activity in the amygdala and the orbitofrontal part of the prefrontal cortex, areas that are often active during emotional experience. When they were reinterpreting the photos those brain areas showed less response, but parts of the prefrontal cortex again became more active (Ochsner, Bunge, Gross, & Gabrieli, 2002).

Cognitive reappraisal is not the only emotion regulation strategy that demands cognitive control. In one study, researchers showed participants several distressing film clips during an fMRI scan. During some clips participants were asked to just watch the clips; during others they were asked to reappraise the clips, and during yet others they were asked to try to suppress their emotional expressions. Both reappraisal and suppression evoked increased prefrontal cortex activation compared with the "just watch" condition. However, reappraisal instruction elicited this activation within a few seconds of the beginning of the clip, whereas suppression instruction evoked activation several seconds later (Goldin, McRae, Ramel, & Gross, 2008). This time difference is consistent with hypotheses based on the process model of emotion regulation, which suggests that suppression actually takes place later in the emotion process than reappraisal.

WHICH EMOTION REGULATION STRATEGIES ARE BEST?

Now that we have reviewed a list of emotion regulation strategies, which ones are best? Before we address this question, note that many strategies are not easily classified as exclusively problem-focused, appraisal-focused, or emotion-focused (Skinner, Edge, Altman, & Sherwood, 2003). For example, we listed "expressing your feelings" as an emotion-focused strategy, but if it elicits help from others it may lead to situation modification as well.

Also, consider the many ways in which social support helps us deal with stressful situations. First, think of all the practical, problem-focused effects of social support: Your friends can give you advice about how to deal with the problem. If you have lost your job, they might help you find a new one. If you are sick, they can drive you to the doctor's office, get your medicine, warn you about side effects, bring you your meals.

Second, think of the ways social support provides emotional comfort. Loneliness hurts, and lonely people are at greater risk for suicide and stress-related diseases (Cacioppo, Hawkley, & Berntson, 2003). Happily married people and those with close friendships report less stress, show a stronger immune response, and stay healthier than average (Kiecolt-Glaser, 1999; Kiecolt-Glaser & Newton, 2001). As with any correlational study, we cannot conclude that there is a cause-and-effect relationship, but the time course is consistent with the proposal that close ties reduce stress. One study found that medical students who married during school reported decreased stress shortly after the wedding. They said their spouse provided care, concern, and encouragement that helped them overcome fatigue and self-doubt (Coombs & Fawzy, 1982).

Although many emotional strategies are difficult to classify, some do fit clearly into one category or another, especially in a specific instance. Studies have observed consistent differences in the apparent effectiveness of the three kinds of strategies. As you might guess, the situation-focused strategies, when successful, have major advantages. If you can actually avoid or reduce the problem, there is less reason for unpleasant emotions in the first place. One study of recently bereaved widows found that those who felt the most control over the events of their lives experienced the least anxiety (Ong, Bergeman, & Bisconti, 2005). Another study found that adults with attention-deficit hyperactivity disorder (ADHD) were less likely than average to use situation-focused approaches to their stressful situation, and therefore more likely to end up in aggressive confrontations (Young, 2005).

However, we cannot apply situation-focused approaches to every situation. Consider, for example, chronic illness, war, or the inevitable fact of human mortality. If you have little control over a problem, your choices are to reappraise the situation or to try to regulate your emotional responses. Ideally, people shift among situation-focused, cognition-focused, and response-focused strategies depending on the situation (Heszen-Niejodek, 1997).

As we noted earlier, several studies have compared the effects of reappraisal with those of suppressing emotional expressions. Some individuals suppress their expressions of emotion habitually, as an overall regulation strategy (Gross & John, 2003). Researchers have consistently found that suppressing facial displays fails to reduce the experience of negative emotion, and can actually increase physiological signs of stress (e.g., Gross, 1998; Gross, 2002; Gross & Levenson, 1997). For example, students who were told to suppress their emotional responses to a series of disturbing slides showed increased blood pressure, compared with those given no instructions (Richards & Gross, 2000). In another series of studies, women watched a very upsetting film about the nuclear bombing of Hiroshima and Nagasaki during World War II. Then they were asked to discuss the film, either naturally or while suppressing their emotions.

Those suppressing their emotional displays showed increased blood pressure (Butler et al., 2003). However, Asians who suppressed their emotional expressions showed fewer of these effects than European-Americans (Butler, Lee, & Gross, 2007), perhaps because Asian cultures encourage suppression more, and people raised in these cultures have more experience at suppression.

Reappraisal and suppression strategies also have different effects on memory. Once people set a reappraisal strategy in motion, they deflect the experience of negative emotion and can attend to other aspects of the situation. Suppressing your emotion requires constant attention, as you monitor your own behavior and think about the instruction to hide your feelings. The cognitive effort involved in the latter strategy leaves less room for other tasks. In studies of participants viewing negative film clips, watching unpleasant slides, and discussing conflicts with a romantic partner, those instructed to suppress their emotion displays consistently showed worse memory for verbal information than those instructed to reappraise, or those given no regulation instructions (Richards, Butler, & Gross, 2003; Richards & Gross, 2000).

Studies also suggest that suppression has a negative impact on relationships, compared with reappraisal. Individuals who report often suppressing their emotional displays rely less on others for social support, and are not as well-liked. By contrast, people who report more frequent use of reappraisal strategies are better liked by their peers (Gross & John, 2003). A recent study found that among individuals who were making the transition from high school to college, those who reported more frequent emotional suppression had a harder time forming new relationships in the new environment (Srivastava, Tamir, McGonigal, John, & Gross, 2009). This trend is especially interesting because the most obvious reason for suppressing negative emotion is to avoid conflict with other people. It is unclear whether suppression has a negative impact on interpersonal relations in all situations. The effect is clear at the dispositional level, however. People who habitually hide their emotions from others are difficult to get close to—they may avoid conflict, but they also avoid intimacy in the process.

So, a convergence of the research suggests that suppressing emotion is a far from ideal regulation strategy. What about the other emotion-focused strategies? As we noted earlier, talking or writing about a problem can have positive effects on emotional and physical health, but only if the person emphasizes resolving the problem, rather than ruminating over negative aspects of the situation. Studies on the long-term effects of exercise and meditation are promising, but because such studies typically use correlational designs rather than experimental designs, we are limited in what we can conclude about cause and effect. Certainly the habitual use of drugs, alcohol, and eating is a poor method of coping with stress, especially in the long run.

SUMMARY

Although we expressed skepticism about Sigmund Freud's methods and theories, he was right on a basic point: People want to avoid anxiety or stress, and they will try one way after another until they succeed. Many people fall into a habit of relying mainly on one method or another, and some strategies work better than others. When possible, the best approach is almost always to try to solve the problem. Even if you cannot fully overcome the problem, exerting any control over it, or even thinking you are exerting some control, makes it seem less overwhelming.

When you have little or no control, reappraisal is usually the next best idea. Consider the distressing situation from a different angle: Can anything good come from it? Can you make it an opportunity to do something worthwhile?

Finally, the response-focused approaches also have their place, either as a supplement to the others or as a final resort when the others fail. Here the research steers us away from a couple of popular ideas: Vigorously expressing your negative emotions does not, as a rule, help reduce them, and suppressing them often backfires also. An intermediate approach is usually best—thinking about the problem and discussing it with others, but without dwelling or ruminating on it. Periodic exercise helps contain the emotions, as does relaxation.

KEY TERMS

attentional control: directing one's attention away from stimuli and thoughts likely to elicit unwanted emotions (p. 142)

catharsis: the "release" of strong emotions by experiencing and expressing them fully (p. 147)

cognition-focused strategies: changing the way we attend to or think about a situation, in order to encourage some emotions and/or deter others (p. 139)

cognitive reappraisal: changing the way we think about a particular situation in order to control emotional experience (p. 144)

cognitive restructuring: changing the way one thinks about a major emotional issue or frequently occurring situation - a frequent goal in therapies for mood disorders like depression and anxiety (p. 145)

coping: the ways that people reduce negative emotion after a stressful event (p. 136)

core relational theme: the appraised meaning of some event in terms of one's relationship with the environment, thought to lead to experience of a "basic" emotion (p. 145)

dot-probe task: a task in which participants indicate the location of dots replacing emotional or neutral stimuli; used to measure attentional control (p. 143)

ego defense mechanisms: psychological regulation strategies that, according to Sigmund Freud, serve to resolve the tension between the id and the superego, and keep disturbing wishes and desires hidden from consciousness (p. 137)

emotion regulation: the strategies we use to control which emotions we have, when we have them, and how strongly we experience and express them (p. 136)

executive control: effortful control over cognitive processes such as attention, working memory, and planning (p. 151)

positive reappraisal: focusing on positive aspects of negative or challenging situations (p. 146)

process model of emotion regulation: a model that organizes emotion regulation strategies according to their place in the emotion process itself (p. 138)

psychological inoculation: dealing with a stressor by exposing yourself to milder versions of the stressful events (p. 142)

resilience: recovering relatively well or easily from negative events (p. 146)

response-focused strategies: trying to change aspects of emotional responding, once the emotion has already occurred (p. 139)

rumination: thinking continuously about a problem for a long period of time, focusing on negative aspects of the situation instead of possible solutions (p. 148)

situation-focused strategies: controlling the situation we are in, either by choosing to be in one situation rather than another, or by changing the situation (p. 139)

situation modification: taking steps to change a situation, typically to improve it (p. 140)

situation selection: deciding whether or not to enter a situation that is likely to elicit a particular emotion (p. 140)

suppressing emotional expressions: attempting to block the behavioral expression of an emotion, such as a facial expression (p. 151)

THOUGHT QUESTIONS

1. Identify one or two problems or difficulties in your life. Describe both a problem-focused and an appraisal- or response-focused approach to dealing with each problem.

2. Either by yourself or with others, make a list of ways to cope with stressful situations. Try to classify each as problem-focused, appraisal-focused, or emotion-focused. How many of them fit into one category or another?

SUGGESTION FOR RESEARCH PROJECT

1. Ask several of your friends to keep a diary for one week, in which they describe the worst thing that happened to them each day, and what they did during and after that event to make themselves feel better. Classify each emotion regulation strategy using the categories described in this chapter. At the end of the week, ask your friends to rate how happy they are, in general, with their lives. Do the happier people seem to use different regulation strategies than the less happy people?

SUGGESTION FOR FURTHER READING

Snyder, C. R. (2001). *Coping With Stress: Effective People and Processes*. New York: Oxford University Press. A collection of chapters by noted researchers.

Some Individual Emotions

7

Fear and Anxiety

With this chapter, we begin a section of this book describing research on several specific emotions. As we discussed in Chapter 1, researchers remain divided on the question of whether people have a limited number of "basic" emotions, or whether we should instead describe emotional states in terms of two or more continuous dimensions. Just as it is useful to discuss Europe separately from Asia, even though the border between them is arbitrary, distinguishing between emotions such as fear and anger can help us to study how they differ and are similar.

Why are we starting this section with fear and (in the next chapter) anger? Fear and anger are prototypical emotions—good examples of what we mean by "emotion"—if a prototypical emotion includes cognition/appraisal, feeling, physiological change, and behavior. Fear and anger are associated with specific appraisals, intense feelings, strong physiological arousal, and fairly clear-cut actions (escape or attack).

Furthermore, we can identify clear examples of fear behavior even in non-human animals. When a mouse freezes at the smell of a cat, a cat runs away from a dog, or a dog barks and cowers at the sound of thunder, we might reasonably infer that they feel fear. Because we can measure fear behavior in laboratory animals, we can also examine the biological changes associated with this behavior.

Fear and anxiety are similar experiences in most ways, but making the distinction between them is sometimes useful. We speak of **fear** when a specific event, such as a snake, provokes dread. Fear is a response to a perceived danger, either to oneself or to a loved one, and it subsides quickly when the threat is gone. By contrast, the term **anxiety** refers to a more general expectation that "something bad might happen" (Lazarus, 1991). If you feel anxiety about a vague possible danger to yourself or your loved ones, you can never be sure the unidentified danger has passed. If you have anxiety about being in public places, or about meeting new people, again you cannot relax for long because the situation arises repeatedly. Many people feel anxiety about the idea of death, and death can only be postponed, not avoided.

Although we experience fear as unpleasant and disturbing, it is nevertheless useful. Evolutionary theory implies that emotions evolved because individuals who experience emotions survive longer or reproduce more successfully than those who don't. Nowhere is the advantage of an emotion more evident than in the case of fear. Fear pulls attention to possible dangers and helps us avoid them. Consider also the facial expression of fear (Susskind et al., 2008): You raise your eyebrows, open your eyes wide, and gasp. Opening your eyes wide increases your ability to see possible threats, even in the periphery of your visual field. Gasping gives you more oxygen, preparing you for possible emergency actions. A fear expression is useful in another way also: The enlarged appearance of the eyes makes the face resemble that of an infant, and most people are highly sympathetic to infants (Sacco & Hugenberg, 2009). If you look like a helpless infant, maybe others will come to your aid.

WHAT DO WE FEAR?

Are we born with any fears? Yes, at least one: Sudden, loud noises frighten virtually everyone, from birth through old age. That fear is also present in virtually all other animal species, except those without hearing. Separation from loved ones may be another built-in fear. In many mammalian species, an infant separated from its mother reacts with distress calls (Shair, Brunelli, Masmela, Boone, & Hofer, 2003). Many old fairy tales, such as "Hansel and Gretel," describe the fear of young children lost in the woods. Today's children are more likely to get lost in a shopping mall or an amusement park, but the idea of separation from one's family is still frightening.

The vast majority of our fears are learned, however. John B. Watson, one of the pioneers of American psychology, was the first to try to demonstrate learned fears experimentally, although by today's standards his research was flawed both scientifically and ethically. He first demonstrated that a young orphan named "Little Albert" was not afraid of white rats. Then, every time Little Albert saw a white rat, Watson struck a loud gong nearby. After a few such pairings, Albert reacted to the sight of a white rat by crying, trembling, and moving away (Watson & Rayner, 1920).

Watson overlooked the fact that we learn some fears more readily than others. Did you ever hit your thumb with a hammer? Probably so. Did you develop a fear of hammers? Probably not. Have you ever been in an automobile accident or witnessed someone badly injured in one? Again, the answer is probably yes. Are you afraid of automobiles? Hardly. In contrast, a great many people fear snakes and spiders, even though few of us have had any personal experience with a serious snake or spider bite.

People learn snake and spider fears, and a few others such as fear of heights, so readily that researchers have suggested a built-in predisposition to learn them (Öhman, Eriksson, & Olofsson, 1975; Seligman, 1971). The reasoning is that snakes have been dangerous to people throughout our evolutionary history. Most of your ancestors stayed away from snakes, and therefore survived long enough to pass on their genes. Evidence for this **preparedness** idea includes several studies with monkeys, which might share that same preparedness. Ordinarily, laboratory-reared monkeys show inhibition and withdrawal from snakes the very first time they see one. If nothing bad happens, their fear habituates (declines), but this initial wariness suggests a predisposition toward fear (Nelson, Shelton, & Kalin, 2003). If a monkey sees another monkey show a fear of snakes, it acquires the fear too, even though the observer has never been bitten or even seen any other monkey bitten (Mineka, 1987; Mineka, Davidson, Cook, & Keir, 1984). These effects are specific to snakes—if a monkey watches a movie of another monkey running away from a snake, it develops a fear of snakes, but if it watches an edited movie showing a monkey running away from flowers, it develops no fear of flowers (Mineka, 1987).

Humans also are quick to learn a fear of snakes. People who get shocks paired with pictures of snakes quickly show a conditioned response (increased heart rate and breathing rate), whereas those who get shocks paired with pictures of houses develop weaker responses (Öhman, Eriksson, & Olofsson, 1975). We can learn such fears even when we're not consciously aware of having seen the snake at all.

All of these results suggest that we may be born with a predisposition to learn to fear certain objects. However, other interpretations are possible. For example, unpredictable, uncontrollable events are more stressful than ones we think we can control. Snakes and spiders pose unpredictable dangers, whereas hammers are unlikely to attack you by surprise. Also, an object becomes less frightening if we have safe experiences with it. You may not have had a negative experience with snakes or spiders, but you also probably haven't had many safe experiences with them. You may have been injured in an automobile accident, but you have also had many safe experiences while driving. People typically develop phobias toward objects that are unpredictable, uncontrollable, and seldom experienced in a safe context.

Most fears arise not just from an object by itself, such as a snake or a gun, but also from an appraisal of the situation. Basic emotion theorists tend to emphasize categorical appraisals, in this case the appraisal that you are in physical danger. For example, your fear of a snake depends on the type of snake and its distance from you. Your fear of a gun depends on whether the gun is loaded, who is holding it, and how that person is acting.

The Component Process Theory approach emphasizes the continuous aspects of appraisal, consistent with our description in Chapter 1. Recall the study by Klaus Scherer (1997), who asked people on five continents to describe a time when they felt sadness, fear, anger, or disgust. He then asked them to rate each of the situations they had described along several dimensions. Consistently across cultures, people described fear-arousing situations as unexpected, unpleasant, externally caused, uncertain, and uncontrollable (Scherer, 1997). Most of those features apply to sad situations also, except that fear situations are high in uncertainty and sad situations are not (Mauro, Sato, & Tucker, 1992). You feel fear if something bad might happen, but you feel sad if it has already happened or is sure to happen.

These features were also similar to those associated with anger. A major difference between anger

and fear was the sense of control. How would you react if someone insults you in a particularly nasty way for no good reason? First imagine that the offender is a peer. Then imagine the same insult from someone bigger and stronger than you are, carrying a gun. The insult likely provokes anger when you are in a position of power, but fear when you are powerless (Keltner, Gruenfeld, & Anderson, 2003).

FEAR AND ATTENTION
TO THREATS

What do you do when you are frightened? Yes, you try to escape the danger. But fear has cognitive as well as behavioral effects. One of the most important aspects of fear is that it focuses your attention on a potential threat. In one clever study, investigators asked young adults to focus on a central spot on a computer screen—and then displayed slides like the one in Figure 7.1. On each trial, a participant was instructed to attend either the top and bottom pictures, or the left and right pictures, and indicate whether the pictures were the same or different. On each trial, one pair showed houses and the other pair showed faces with either a fearful or a neutral expression. On a given trial the participant was supposed to attend to either the houses or the faces and ignore the other pair.

People who reported on a questionnaire that they were feeling low fear and anxiety at the time had no trouble focusing their attention according to instructions. However, those who reported strong fear and anxiety attended strongly to fearful faces even when instructed to focus on the houses, and showed greater activity in the amygdala (Bishop, Duncan, & Lawrence, 2004). Several other studies confirm that fearful faces automatically capture attention, although they are not the only stimuli that evoke this sort of reaction. Angry faces and pictures of babies also capture our attention (Brosch, Sander, Pourtois, & Scherer, 2008). The researchers didn't try pornographic stimuli, but those would probably have captured attention too.

For another example, consider the following task (this "dot-probe" task was also described in

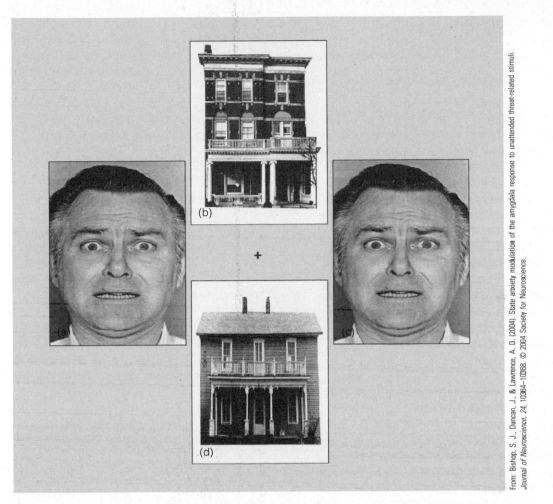

From: Bishop, S. J., Duncan, J., & Lawrence, A. D. (2004). State anxiety modulation of the amygdala response to unattended threat-related stimuli. *Journal of Neuroscience, 24*, 10364–10368. © 2004 Society for Neuroscience.

FIGURE 7.1 People feeling strong fear showed strong brain responses to frightened expressions, even when the instructions were to ignore the faces and attend to the houses.

Chapter 6). Two words are displayed simultaneously on a screen for one second, one above the other, and then a dot is presented in either the up or down position:

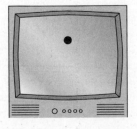

The observer's task is to press a computer key to indicate whether the dot appeared in the upper or lower position. When one of the words is related to anxiety, such as *worry, blush,* or *nervous,* people respond faster if the dot was in the same location as the fear-related word than if it was in the other position; this effect is especially strong among people who report being anxious or worried (Egloff, Wilhelm, Neubauer, Mauss, & Gross, 2002). Presumably, more fearful people direct their attention primarily toward the fear-related words, whereas less fearful people's attention is somewhat less biased.

Physiological measures suggest that we are quick to process frightening objects even when the stimulus is so vague that we cannot identify it consciously. Imagine yourself in this study: You see pictures flashed on a screen for 10 milliseconds, followed by a brief masking image. Under these conditions, people insist they saw nothing, or at most a blur. Some of the photos shown to you—let's say photos of snakes—are followed by shocks, whereas photos of spiders are not followed by shocks. For other participants, it would be the other way around. This procedure continues for a while. All you know is that sometimes you get shocks and sometimes you don't. You certainly don't know the snake pictures predict shock because you don't consciously see any pictures at all.

However, part of your brain does note the difference between the spiders and the snakes, and you gradually develop a conditioned response. When a spider picture flashes on the screen you are calm, but when a snake picture appears your heart rate and breathing rate suddenly increase (Katkin, Wiens, & Öhman, 2001). This response takes place even though you do not consciously recognize the snakes. You might think of this as "unconscious" learning, although researchers prefer the term "implicit" learning.

Would you notice your occasional changes in heart rate and breathing? Some people do and some don't. The experimenters asked participants to report any changes they perceived in their heart rate, and also to predict when they were about to get a shock. All participants said they were just guessing about the shocks. The fascinating result was that people who were the best at reporting sudden increases in their heart rate were also the best at "guessing" when they were about to get a shock (Katkin et al., 2001).

The implications of this study are speculative but potentially important. One implication is that parts of your brain respond to fear-related information, even when the stimuli are so weak that you cannot identify them consciously. Another implication pertains to what people call "gut feelings": Suppose you are very sensitive to your own internal changes, such as those in heart rate. These changes may be for some non-emotional reason, but it is also possible that you were reacting to some danger that you detected "implicitly."

BEHAVIORAL MEASURES OF FEAR AND ANXIETY

Scientific progress almost always depends on measuring some variable more accurately than it has been measured before. Self-reports of fear certainly have their place in research, but with the limitations of all self-report measures. Often researchers disagree about what behaviors indicate an emotion, or the behaviors are too varied and complex to study easily. Most researchers also agree that certain, simple behaviors likely reflect fear, however, even in non-human animals. These measures have allowed researchers to study fear in a variety of interesting ways, so we know more about fear than about other emotions. Let's consider some common measures.

Facial Expression of Fear

One distinctive behavior associated with fear is its facial expression. Paul Ekman and colleagues found that most people in every culture they studied recognized a facial display of fear (see Figure 7.2). This display includes lifting the inner and outer eyebrows, pulling them together; widening the eyes; and contracting the muscles below the corners of the lips, pulling the skin of the lower cheeks down and to the side (Ekman et al., 1987). Typically, the mouth opens slightly.

This appearance is similar to an expression of surprise, and participants often confuse the two when asked to look at a photo and guess how someone is feeling (Ekman et al., 1987). However, expressions of fear and surprise differ in a couple of important ways. When people are surprised, their eyebrows go up and their eyes get wider, as in fear, but only the "fear face" includes the contraction

From Darwin, Charles, *The Expression of the Emotions in Man and Animals* (1872/1998), with permission from Oxford University Press.

FIGURE 7.2 A typical facial expression of fear.

of the eyebrows and lower cheek movement that Figure 7.2 shows.

The expression in Figure 7.2 is a very strong, or "prototypical" one, containing every muscle movement commonly associated with fear expressions. However, expressions of fear (and most other emotions) can also be subtle, including one or a few key movements. As we discussed in Chapter 3, the most common movements may even differ a bit from culture to culture, although they are all typically part of the full prototype. In addition to full-blown, obvious facial expressions that last for a few seconds, people sometimes show very brief expressions—especially when they are trying to hide their emotions. These involuntary, momentary expressions that contradict the intended impression of calmness are called **micro expressions**. We usually overlook micro expressions, but with effort we can learn to notice them. Paul Ekman (2001) found that micro expressions are the most valid guide currently available to discerning people's hidden feelings, especially. (The television series *Lie to Me* is loosely based on this research.)

Facilitation of the Startle Reflex

As already mentioned, a wide variety of animals, including humans of all ages, show a built-in fear response to sudden, loud noises. That reaction is called the **startle response**. The muscles tense rapidly, especially the neck muscles; the eyes close tightly; the shoulders quickly pull close to the neck; and the arms pull up toward the head. All these movements are apparently geared toward protecting the neck, an extremely vulnerable area. Information about the loud noise goes from your ears to a brain area called the *pons* in less than 10 milliseconds, and from there to cells in the medulla and spinal cord that control your muscles (Figure 7.3). The full startle reflex occurs in less than one-fifth of a second (Yeomans & Frankland, 1996).

Although the startle response itself is automatic, input from the rest of the nervous system modifies its intensity. In Chapter 5 we described studies where a rat learns that a tone always precedes an electric shock, called "fear conditioning" studies. If the rat later hears that tone followed by a sudden

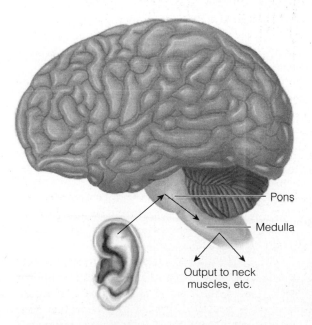

Pons

Medulla

Output to neck muscles, etc.

FIGURE 7.3 The startle reflex depends on a reflexive connection from the ears to the pons to cells in the medulla and spinal cord that control the muscles.

loud noise, it gives a larger-than-usual startle response. However, if it hears a different tone previously associated with pleasant events, then a loud noise after the "safe" stimulus produces a smaller-than-usual startle response (Schmid, Koch, & Schnitzler, 1995).

Similarly, people show a strong startle reflex when responding to unpleasant stimuli and a weaker one when responding to pleasant stimuli (Lang, Bradley, & Cuthbert, 2002). Imagine you are walking alone at night through a dangerous neighborhood, when suddenly you hear a loud sound. Then imagine hearing the same loud sound in the middle of the afternoon among friends in your own home. You will startle in both cases, but much more in the frightening place than in the familiar, safe place. Emotion researchers use this **startle potentiation** to measure fear in non-human animals as well as humans.

Other Behavioral Measures

Another simple behavioral measure of fear is suppression of movement. This measure is especially popular in research with nonhuman animals. In the presence of a smell, sound, or other indicator of danger, most small animals simply "freeze" (Bolles, 1970). When rats are put into an unfamiliar enclosure, some explore freely while others stay motionless in a corner or against a wall. The failure to explore is generally interpreted as an indication of fear or anxiety. (Motionlessness is a good defense for a small animal because predators readily detect anything that moves.) Researchers interested in human emotions occasionally use this measure with children. Children with an "inhibited" temperament tend to be fearful and shy, remaining in the background instead of exploring their environment (Kagan, Reznick, & Snidman, 1988).

Behavioral measures can be used to assess trait fearfulness, as well as the current experience of fear. One approach relies on our knowledge that people tend to focus more on emotional pictures than neutral pictures, especially in the first several seconds of viewing them (Calvo & Avero, 2005). Fearful/anxious people show an especially strong

attentional bias toward threatening information. In this procedure, people read a variety of short passages, some of them with threatening content, such as, "The child went running after his new ball, but while he was crossing the road, a van suddenly appeared without brakes. The van swerved around the child instantly." While people are reading, a device monitors their eye movements. On the average, people with high fear levels have more regressive (backward) eye movements than others do on the threatening sentences. That is, they are more likely than others to stop, go back, and re-read the fear-provoking sentences (Calvo & Avero, 2002). Presumably, people who are dispositionally anxious are especially distracted by threatening content.

THE BIOLOGY OF FEAR AND ANXIETY

The similarity of fear-related behavior in humans and other animals allows us to study emotion-related physiology in lab mammals, as well as in humans. As a result, we know more about the biology of fear and anxiety than is true for any other emotion, and can address more complex questions.

Autonomic Nervous System Responses

As discussed in Chapter 4, much research on the autonomic nervous system grew out of Walter's Cannon's studies of the "fight or flight" sympathetic nervous system response. Thus, the role of autonomic responding in emotion was first studied in the context of fear. Fear responding is associated with signs of full-blown, unambiguous sympathetic nervous system activation. Other negative emotions show many of these signs as well (such as increased heart rate and blood pressure), but also show some unexpected signs (such as increased finger temperature in anger).

The original studies of sympathetic responding in fear all relied on behavioral measures to infer fear. Cannon's original work was on laboratory animals, so he could not ask them if they felt afraid—he had to infer it from their behavior when they were in an objectively dangerous situation. But in order to say that sympathetic activation is really associated with fear, we must also show that it is associated with *feelings* of fear, and with fear-related appraisals.

In a series of studies, Joe Tomaka, Jim Blascovich, and colleagues did just that (Tomaka, Blascovich, Kibler, & Ernst, 1997). Researchers told participants they would spend four minutes doing a "serial subtraction" task: The person would start with a high number, such as 1,528, and then subtract a small number like 7 over and over again (1,521, 1,514, 1,507, …) aloud and as fast as possible. Most people find this task very stressful! Right after describing the task, researchers either emphasized how important it was to do the task well, and said that participants' speed and accuracy would be measured, or they suggested that participants just do their best and "think of the task as a challenge to be met and overcome." Participants receiving the first set of instructions tended to be more threatened by the task—they rated the task as highly threatening and their ability to cope with it relatively low. By contrast, participants hearing the second set of instructions were more likely to interpret the task as a challenge—their rating of their own ability to cope outweighed their rating of the task as threatening.

How did the physiological responses of participants in the "challenge" versus "threat" conditions differ? Heart rate increased in both the challenge and threat groups, but it increased more for the challenge group. Among participants given the "challenge" instructions, the heart took longer to build up pressure needed to pop open the aortic valve with very beat ("pre-ejection period"), and pumped more blood when it did contract ("cardiac output") than was true for participants given the "threat" instructions. Also, total peripheral resistance (a ratio of blood pressure to cardiac output, which indicates how much pressure is being exerted by arteries throughout the body) increased slightly in threat participants but decreased in challenge participants.

In short, the physiological changes observed in the "threat" condition were completely consistent with increased sympathetic nervous system activation. However, the challenge participants showed a more complicated pattern. Although most signs were consistent with sympathetic activation, pressure by the arteries generally decreased, whereas sympathetic activation should have led to an increase in pressure. The "challenge" profile mobilizes the cardiovascular system in the way that is most efficient in delivering blood throughout the body—the heart pumps faster, pumps more blood per heartbeat, and blood meets less resistance from vessels as it moves through the body. Although threat participants' hearts also beat faster, their blood encountered more resistance as it traveled through the body.

This finding has been replicated frequently—it is what researchers call a "robust" effect. However, we should consider three questions. First, is "threat" the same as fear? Certainly the pattern of appraisals reported by participants in the threat condition correspond to the ones we described at the beginning of the chapter—an unpleasant event that has not happened yet, but is about to, and over which one feels little or no control. However, the worst that could happen to people in the threat condition was a blow to their self-esteem. They were in no real, physical danger.

Second, are the cardiovascular responses to threat and challenge limited to those appraisals? Anger is typically associated with sympathetic arousal. When people are angry they tend to think they have more control over the situation, however, suggesting that they should show a "challenge" cardiovascular profile instead. This would be a striking difference between the biology of fear and the biology of anger. Lower peripheral resistance would account for the greater finger temperature observed in anger relative to fear, as we discussed in Chapter 4. In these studies, however, the "challenge" participants felt good, not angry. A study looking at peripheral resistance responses in experimentally elicited anger and fear might answer this question.

Third, what function, if any, does the cardiovascular "threat" response serve? The researchers who performed these studies have described the threat response as an inadequate attempt to mobilize physical resources. Is it actually an ineffective attempt to deliver fuel to the body, or does it produce benefits we have not yet identified? In Chapter 4 we suggested that reduced blood flow to the skin might prevent excessive blood loss in case of a wound, but this hypothesis needs to be tested more carefully.

Despite a general tendency toward constricted blood vessels, frightened people do have increased blood flow to the head, presumably to "wake up" the brain as much as possible so it can choose the best emergency response. Blood flow increases to the face as well. In extreme cases of fear, you may notice someone's face turning red. In milder cases, a researcher can use a thermal camera, which measures heat radiated from the face. Figure C.3 on the inside cover of this book shows one example. Most people increase their blood flow to the face when they are nervous about telling a lie (Pavlidis, Eberhardt, & Levine, 2002).

Very frightened people also sweat, and apparently the sweat of a frightened person is different from other kinds of sweat. Women in one study tried to identify the emotions felt by people in various pictures. Some of the photos were ambiguous.

That is, maybe the person in the photo was frightened, but maybe not. When the researchers occasionally wafted in some sweat odor, it influenced the outcome. If it was the sweat of a frightened person (don't ask us how they got this), participants were more likely to regard the photo as one showing fear. If it was the sweat of someone who felt happy, it had no significant effect (Zhou & Chen, 2009).

Application: Anxiety and Lie Detection

A sudden increase in sympathetic arousal suggests the occurrence of strong emotions, if we have no reason to attribute it to something else, such as pain or exercise. The **polygraph**, popularly known as a "lie-detector" test, is based on the assumption that when people lie they get nervous, and therefore show increased heart rate and blood pressure, rapid and irregular breathing, increased skin conductance, and other signs of sympathetic activation, as Figure 7.4 illustrates. (Side note: the inventor of the polygraph was William Marston, who was also the original writer of *Wonder Woman* comics. Wonder Woman used a "lasso of truth" to force people to respond honestly to her questions.)

(a)

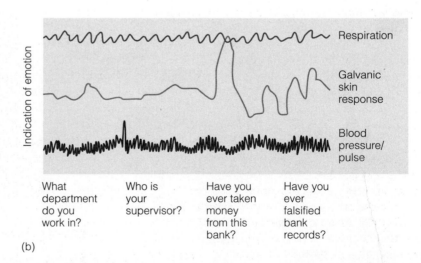

(b)

FIGURE 7.4 A polygraph examiner compares answers to "control" questions and "relevant" questions. Greater nervousness on relevant questions is taken as evidence of lying. The galvanic skin response (a brief spike in skin conductance) is a measure of slight sweating, which, in turn, indicates sympathetic nervous system arousal.

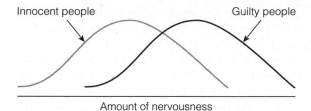

FIGURE 7.5 On a polygraph test, some innocent people appear more nervous than some guilty people. The exact amount of overlap varies.

Is that assumption correct? Well, partly but not entirely. In the "control-question" version of the polygraph test, the examiner asks *relevant questions* such as "Did you steal $500 from the convenience store last night?" and *control questions* such as "Have you ever taken anything that was not yours?" The underlying assumption is that someone who did not rob the convenience store will be at least as nervous about saying "no" to the control question as they are about saying "no" to the relevant question. (Maybe even more so, if you've stolen something else!) However, if you know you have been strapped into a polygraph machine because the police are investigating a robbery at a convenience store, you could still become more nervous about the relevant question, even if you are innocent. In contrast, a habitual liar might not be nervous about either question.

Figure 7.5 shows hypothetical results for two groups of people, some innocent and some guilty. Note that some of the innocent people appear more nervous when telling the truth than some of the guilty ones do while lying. The amount of overlap between the two groups depends on the people involved, the wording of the questions, and so forth. The examiner sets a cutoff score, such that anyone who shows more than a certain amount of nervousness is considered to be lying. However, regardless of where you set that cutoff, you will call some liars innocent ("misses") and some honest people liars ("false alarms"). The more you reduce one kind of error, the more you increase the other.

You may be surprised to learn how few good studies have been done on the accuracy of polygraph tests. Research has not adequately tested how often the test correctly identifies liars, how often it misidentifies innocent people as lying, or what advantages and disadvantages it might have compared to other possible methods (Fiedler, Schmid, & Stahl, 2002; Iacono & Patrick, 1999). What would seem an obvious design is to examine results for people known to be guilty or innocent of serious crimes. However, we seldom know for sure who is guilty. An alternative is to examine people in laboratory conditions, some of whom have been instructed to tell the truth and others to lie. In that case, people have little at stake, so they may not be as nervous about their lies as accused suspects would be in a serious situation.

One of the few good studies of lie detection dealt with 50 criminal cases in which two suspects in a crime were given polygraph tests and one of them later confessed (Kleinmuntz & Szucko, 1984). That is, at the time of the interrogation, the examiners presumably treated every suspect about equally, and later it was possible to determine how accurately they categorized each suspect. Figure 7.6 shows the results. The examiners correctly identified 76 percent of the guilty people as

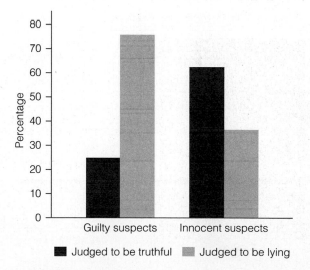

FIGURE 7.6 Results from one study of polygraph accuracy. Note how many innocent suspects were judged to be lying. (Based on data of Kleinmuntz & Szucko, 1984.)

lying, but also identified 37 percent of the innocent suspects as lying.

In other words, polygraph results are neither highly accurate nor utterly worthless. They are more accurate than most people's unaided judgments, because most people overestimate their ability to judge who is lying (Ekman & O'Sullivan, 1991; Ekman, O'Sullivan, & Frank, 1999; Etcoff, Ekman, Magee, & Frank, 2000; Wiseman, 1995). However, most authorities agree that polygraphs are not accurate enough for making important decisions. Therefore, American and European courts almost never permit polygraph results to be entered as evidence (Fiedler et al., 2002; Saxe & Ben-Shakhar, 1999). In the United States, it is illegal for an employer to ask employees or job applicants to take a polygraph test, except under special circumstances (Camara, 1988).

Hand and body gestures can also reveal people's fear, nervousness, or other emotions. Each culture has certain gestures, called **emblems**, with specific meanings. For example, in the United States, a fist or an upraised middle finger indicates anger or contempt, and a shrug of the shoulders means, "I don't know. I'm helpless. What does it matter?" When people intend to make these gestures, they display them openly. People who are concealing an emotion sometimes make a brief, partial emblem. Paul Ekman (2001) found that many people make a brief, partial shrug when they are lying.

The Behavioral Inhibition System

What do animals do when they are afraid? They run away, showing their fight or flight response, right? Not always—the response depends on circumstances. Imagine an impala that spots a lion far away. Lions and other great cats are fantastic sprinters, but they don't have the stamina for long-distance running, so the impala is safe … for now. The impala becomes less active and watches the lion intently. Inactivity is a useful strategy, because the lion is less likely to notice a still object. It is also useful because it enables the impala to concentrate its attention on the lion. The impala's heart rate *decreases*. If the lion approaches, at some point the impala shifts to its alarm reaction. Its sympathetic nervous system becomes highly aroused, heart rate increases, blood flow to the muscles increases, and the impala takes off running. In Chapter 4, we described a similar effect in human research participants playing a video game where they could win or lose money; their heart rate slowed down when the sign of loss (a gun) looked far away, but sped up as the gun appeared to come closer, and immediate action would prevent the loss (Löw, Lang, Smith, & Bradley, 2008).

According to researcher Jeffrey Gray (1982), this slowing of heart rate indicates a second physiological system (other than the sympathetic system) that can be activated in fear. He called this the **Behavioral Inhibition System (BIS)**. Gray proposed that BIS activation increases attention while inhibiting action and decreasing heart rate. The BIS response does prepare the body for flight, however, by increasing muscle tension, just in case. Stephen Porges (1997) has made a similar proposal, arguing further that threat-related decreases in heart rate might be mediated by a branch of the parasympathetic nervous system.

Chronic BIS activation may be responsible for "trait anxiety"—that is, a tendency to experience anxiety and nervous arousal easily and frequently (Knyazev, Slobodskaya, & Wilson, 2002). People high in this trait react strongly to possible threats and dangers. For example, they are likely to become nervous if a boyfriend or girlfriend shows even a slight interest in someone else (Meyer, Olivier, & Roth, 2005). Tranquilizers can weaken the BIS response, and increase approach behaviors, but they have little effect on the tendency to flee from an actual attack or pain (McNaughton & Corr, 2004). At this point, the BIS system remains a largely theoretical construct based on behavior, although researchers are seeking possible neural and other physiological explanations.

The Amygdala and Startle Response Facilitation

We mentioned earlier that feelings of fear appear to increase the startle response to loud noises. It appears that this "startle potentiation" effect relies

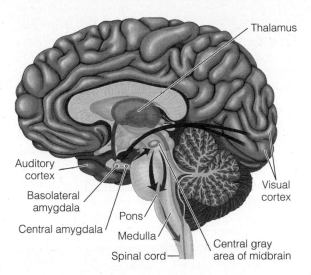

Thalamus

Auditory cortex

Basolateral amygdala

Central amygdala

Pons

Medulla

Spinal cord

Visual cortex

Central gray area of midbrain

F I G U R E 7.7 Although the startle response itself depends just on a reflexive connection through the pons, it can be facilitated or diminished by input from the amygdala. The amygdala processes the emotional content of information, such as "dangerous" or "safe."

in part on activation in the amygdala, a structure we first discussed in Chapter 5. As a quick reminder, the amygdala is an area within temporal lobe of each hemisphere of the brain (Figure 7.7). Each amygdala receives input representing vision, hearing, other senses, and pain, and is also connected with a hippocampus, which is important for memory, so it is in a position to associate various stimuli with dangerous outcomes that follow them. Conditioned fears—that is, fears based on the association of some stimulus with shock—depend on synaptic changes in the amygdala (Kwon & Choi, 2009).

Although in Chapter 5 we emphasized the amygdala's connection to the hippocampus, and thus its apparent role in the formation of emotional memories, the amygdala also "talks to" other areas of the brain. In addition to sending information to the hippocampus, prefrontal cortex (Garcia, Vouimba, Baudry, & Thompson, 1999) and other regions (Gifkins, Greba, & Kokkinidis, 2002), the amygdala sends information to the pons and other areas controlling the startle reflex (Fendt, Koch, & Schnitzler, 1996). Thus, the amygdala is well-placed to modulate the intensity of the startle

response, based on current emotional state. This effect may not be limited to fear, and as we noted in Chapter 5, evidence suggests that thinking of the amygdala as the "fear area of the brain" is an over-simplification. However, the amygdala is part of a system that allows us to use startle potentiation as a behavioral measure of fear.

The Amygdala and Detection of Danger

Amygdala activation may also be necessary for another aspect of fear responding—the detection of danger. In Chapter 5 we described monkeys with temporal lobe lesions, who would play with lit matches, approach snakes, approach strangers indiscriminately, and engage in other risky behaviors. Similarly, patient "SM," a woman with Urbach-Wiethe disease (which selectively damages the amygdalae), approaches other people closely and without caution. During a conversation, most people stand about .6–.7 meters apart (about 2 feet). Coming closer than that feels uncomfortable, except toward a romantic partner or a child. Patient SM approached to within half of the usual distance, and closer than any of the 20 other people the experimenter had tested. When a man she didn't know—a confederate of the researchers—approached SM, she expressed no discomfort, even when he got nose-to-nose with her. (Kennedy, Gläscher, Tyszka, & Adolphs, 2009). (That man said he felt *very* uncomfortable!)

Patient SM seems almost totally lacking in fear. When she watched eight segments from horror movies, each time she rated her fear 0 or 1 on a 0 to 8 scale. People with intact brains rated each segment at least 4. SM claims to hate snakes and spiders. Nevertheless, when researchers took her to an exotic pet store with venomous snakes and spiders, she attempted to touch each of them, and had to be restrained. At a "haunted house," she showed no hesitation in walking down dark hallways. When people dressed as monsters popped out (scaring everyone else), SM showed no fear. In fact, she scared one of the "monsters" by poking it in the head! Her apparent lack of fear often gets her into trouble. She has been raped several times by different men, has been beaten, and has been held up at gunpoint. Evidently she walks right into hazardous situations without detecting danger (Feinstein, Adolphs, & Tranel, 2009).

As we noted in Chapter 5, people with amygdala damage are generally impaired at recognizing others' expressions of emotions, including sadness (Wang, McCarthy, Song, & LaBar, 2005), and in some cases happiness (Canli, Sivers, Whitfield, Gotlib, & Gabrieli, 2002). However, they are especially impaired at recognizing expressions of fear—a sign that you too may be in danger (Fusar-Poli, et al., 2009). When asked to draw faces showing various expressions, SM drew good representations of happy, sad, surprised, disgusted, and angry faces, but then said she didn't know what a frightened face looked like (Adolphs, Tranel, Damasio, & Damasio, 1995). Several studies reported that people with amygdala damage are particularly impaired at recognizing facial expressions of fear (Adolphs, Tranel, Damasio, & Damasio, 1994; Hayman, Rexer, Pavol, Strite, & Meyers, 1998; Lilly et al., 1983). In contrast, people with **social phobia** (a fear of social interactions) show especially strong amygdala responses to the sight of an angry or contemptuous face, presumably a threatening stimulus (Stein, Goldin, Sareen, Zorrilla, & Brown, 2002).

Again, these results do not indicate that the amygdala is specialized for fear responding. One possibility, discussed extensively in Chapter 5, is that amygdala activity facilitates the formation of emotional memories. Despite her series of horrendous experiences, SM shows no trace of post-traumatic stress disorder. Although she knows about her experiences (she does not literally have amnesia), she does not show the kinds of vivid, intrusive, overpowering memories of most people who have lived through such trauma.

Another possibility is that amygdala activation is necessary to feel any strong emotion. Investigators tested Israeli soldiers at the time of induction into the army, showing them unpleasant photos and measuring their amygdala responses with fMRI methods. Later they recorded the soldiers' self-reports of stressful feelings in response to combat. The amygdala responses correlated .67 with later

reports of stress (Admon et al., 2009). A similar study of college students also found a high correlation between daily reports of unpleasant emotional arousal and later amygdala responses to frightening pictures (Barrett, Bliss-Moreau, Duncan, Rauch, & Wright, 2007).

A third possibility is that amygdala activation reflects some kind of value judgment (good or bad) that is particularly salient at the moment. People in one study read a series of names of famous and infamous people. Regardless of the instructions, their amygdalas always responded strongly to the names of disliked people, such as Adolph Hitler. However, if they were instructed to rate how "good" each person was, the amygdala also responded to the names of widely admired people, such as Mother Teresa (Cunningham, Van Bavel & Johnsen, 2008).

A fourth possibility is that the amygdala responds most strongly to ambiguous emotional stimuli, for which the processing takes some effort (Buchanan, Tranel, & Adolphs, 2009). People with amygdala damage have trouble identifying the expression in a face or even determining whether two faces are expressing the same or different emotions (Boucsein, Weniger, Mursch, Steinhoff, & Irle, 2001). They are also impaired at inferring someone's emotion from tone of voice (Scott, 1997). A fearful expression is easily confused with an expression of surprise, and a fearful expression pointed directly at the viewer is especially confusing, because we know that frightened people usually stare at the object that has scared them. Patient SM was asked to examine photos and rate the amount of emotional expression in each. On the faces showing fear, anger, or surprise, she gave lower ratings than any intact participant did. Other Urbach-Wiethe patients have also given low ratings to expressions of fear and surprise (Siebert, Markowitsch & Bartel, 2003).

Our take-home point, here as in Chapter 5, is that it is extremely difficult to pin down the psychological processes mediated by any given area of the brain. In this case, it is also likely that different areas of the amygdala play somewhat different roles in emotional processing. Although the amygdala itself is small, it has semi-distinct sub-regions that could have different functions. You can expect research on this issue to continue intensely for some time.

Neurochemistry: Anxiolytics and Their Mechanisms

One way to learn about the neurochemistry of emotion is to find out what chemicals turn an emotion off. Drugs that relieve anxiety are known as **anxiolytics** or **tranquilizers**. (*Anxioltyic* literally means something that dissolves anxiety.) The most common ones fall into a biochemical class known as the *benzodiazepines* (BEN-zo-di-AZ-uh-peens). Examples include diazepam (trademark Valium), chlordiazepoxide (Librium), and alprazolam (Xanax). These drugs can be given as injections but are more commonly taken as pills. Their effects last for hours, and the duration varies from one drug to another.

Anxiolytics act by facilitating the effectiveness of the neurotransmitter GABA (gamma-aninobutyric acid), the main inhibitory neurotransmitter for all of the brain, including the amygdala. They temporarily produce some of the same emotional effects associated with amygdala damage, beyond suppression of fear. For example, people on anxiolytics have trouble identifying other people's facial expressions of emotion (Zangara, Blair, & Curran, 2002). However, because GABA is the main inhibitory transmitter throughout the brain, the effects of anxiolytics are not limited to the amygdala. They suppress activity in much of the brain, producing drowsiness and memory impairment.

Other chemicals modify amygdala activity also. The neurotransmitter cholecystokinin (CCK) has excitatory effects on the amygdala, acting about the opposite of GABA (Becker et al., 2001; Frankland, Josselyn, Bradwejn, Vaccarino, & Yeomans, 1997; Strzelczuk & Romaniuk, 1996). Cortisol and other stress-related hormones increase the responsiveness of the amygdala, whereas alcohol decreases it (Nie et al., 2004). In that regard, alcohol resembles tranquilizers, decreasing anxiety and, therefore, reducing the social inhibitions that deter people from approaching strangers. Decreased fear may be one reason why people are more likely to become violent after consuming alcohol. As we have seen, however, amygdala activation is not the same thing as fear, so these effects are probably not fear-specific either.

INDIVIDUAL DIFFERENCES IN FEAR AND ANXIETY

What is the "right" amount of fear or anxiety? Obviously, it depends. Do you live in a safe neighborhood or a war-torn country? Even if you live in an apparently safe place, you might have had horrible experiences—a life-threatening accident, a rape or attempted rape, sudden death of a loved one, or discovering a dead body. If so, it makes sense to increase your level of fear (Rosen & Schulkin, 2004). If you were sexually abused as a child, you are more likely than average to develop severe anxieties as an adult (Friedman et al., 2002).

On the average, women report more fear and anxiety than men do, in all countries for which we have data (Fischer, Mosquera, van Vianen, & Manstead, 2004). Why? The research has not yet established an answer, and perhaps several explanations apply. Women are more often the victims of sexual attacks and domestic abuse. However, the gender difference in anxiety appears early in life, beginning before the age of one year, well before such experiences (McLean & Anderson, 2009). It also occurs in nonhumans: female rats show greater fear than male rats in several situations, such as fear of the light (Toufexis, 2007). (Just as many people are afraid of the dark, most rats are afraid of the light.) Males and females do not differ in all situations. For example, men and women show about equal fear responses to a shock or to a cue that predicts shock. However, on the average women show a greater startle response to a sudden loud noise, suggesting greater "background" anxiety (Grillon, 2008). Men and women are about equal in their likelihood of social phobia (avoiding other people), claustrophobia (fear of closed-in places), and fear of injury. Women are more likely to fear various animals, such as spiders, for which the experience is a mixture of fear and disgust (McLean & Anderson, 2009).

Genetics

Genetic differences contribute to the probability of developing anxiety. Differences among individuals are fairly consistent over years or decades (Durbin, Hayden, Klein, & Olino, 2007). Newborn infants who frequently kick and cry are more likely than others to be frightened by unfamiliar events at ages 9 and 14 months (Kagan & Snidman, 1991). At age 7, they tend to be shy and nervous in a playground (Kagan, Reznick, & Snidman, 1988). As adults, they show a strong amygdala response to almost any photograph of a person, especially an unfamiliar person (Beaton et al., 2008; Schwartz, Wright, Shin, Kagan, & Rauch, 2003).

These longitudinal effects suggest a genetic contribution, but other research provides even more direct support. Both panic disorder and phobias are more common among people who have relatives with similar disorders, especially among close relatives such as identical twins (Hettema, Neale, & Kendler, 2001; Kendler, Myers, Prescott, & Neale, 2001; Skre, Onstad, Torgerson, Lygren, & Kringlen, 2000). A gene for *brain-derived neurotrophic factor* (a chemical that aids in learning and memory, among other functions) has several forms that differ among people. One form of the gene is associated with a tendency to form strong learned fears (Hajcak et al., 2009).

Other studies have examined genetic differences in the serotonin transporter protein. Because the neurotransmitter serotonin is strongly affected by antidepressant drugs, it seems likely that genetic variants affecting serotonin should relate to differences in people's emotions. After a neuron releases serotonin, it attaches to its receptor, stimulates it, and then detaches. A protein on the membrane of the presynaptic neuron, called the serotonin transporter protein, then reabsorbs much or most of the released serotonin, to recycle it for further use. Although few people have any genetic variations in serotonin itself, much variation occurs in the gene for the transporter. Portions of the chromosome near the **serotonin transporter gene** regulate the amount of transporter produced. Major portions of each chromosome do not produce any

protein of their own. At one time these portions were called "junk DNA," but we now know that they are not useless junk. They regulate the amount of activity by genes that do produce proteins.

The gene regulating the serotonin transporter comes in two forms, or alleles—*s* (for short) and *l* (for long). The *s* form leads to less production of serotonin transporter, and the *l* form leads to greater production. Many studies (but not all) have found that that people with *s* forms of the gene show greater anxiety and a greater tendency to learn new fears (Aleman, Swart, & van Rijn, 2008; Hariri et al., 2002; Lonsdorf et al., 2009). The inconsistency of results across studies poses a problem. When two variables do not show a strong, consistent correlation, the obvious interpretation is that they are not strongly related. However, another possibility is that we have not measured them accurately. Psychologists know how hard it is to measure anxiety accurately, but some of the research studies also used a controversial method of identifying the *s* and *l* genes (Wray et al., 2009). In short, we need to await more and improved research.

Another interesting line of genetic research focuses on the link between anxiety and *joint laxity syndrome* (popularly known as being "double-jointed"). People with joint laxity syndrome (Figure 7.8) are more likely than other people to develop strong fears, as well as panic disorder and other anxiety disorders (Bulbena et al., 2004; Bulbena, Gago, Sperry, & Bergé, 2006). Recall from Chapter 2 that the same genetic mutation may have a wide range of effects. It may be that trait anxiety and joint laxity are actually influenced in part by a common gene.

Impact of Anxiety on Daily Life

Individual differences in anxiety, genetic or otherwise, obviously influence people's nervousness and likelihood of developing phobias, panic disorder, and so forth. Might differences in anxiety also impact our thinking in ways that seem more cognitive, and less emotional?

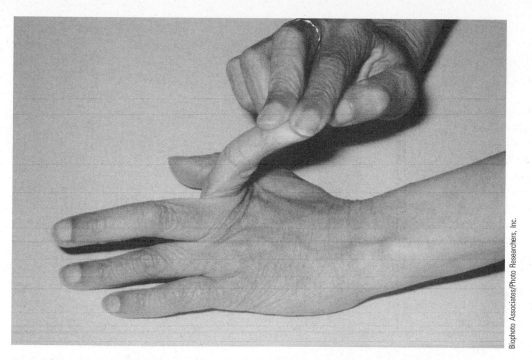

Biophoto Associates/Photo Researchers, Inc.

FIGURE 7.8 Joint laxity syndrome by itself is harmless, but many people with this genetic condition also develop severe anxieties. The two conditions may have overlapping genetic bases.

Researchers identified two groups of people with opposite political beliefs on certain issues. One group favored the death penalty, much use of military force, strong efforts to block immigration, and ready availability of guns. They were also willing to sacrifice personal liberties (such as privacy) in order to fight terrorists. The other group expressed only weak support for the military, blocking immigration, fighting terrorists, and so forth. Then the researchers measured how each person responded to a repeated loud noise, in terms of their startle response. The people with strong support for the military and so forth showed a much stronger response to the noise, and their response declined relatively slowly with repeated trials. Those with weak support showed a weak response to the noise, and it habituated (declined) rapidly (Oxley et al., 2008). Figure 7.9 summarizes the results.

One reasonable interpretation is that people who respond strongly to a fear stimulus, such as a loud noise, also tend to see the world as a dangerous place. They feel a need for

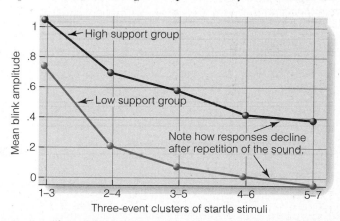

FIGURE 7.9 On the average, people who support strong military, police and anti-terrorism actions tend to show greater tear responses to a sudden loud noise than to people expressing weaker support for such actions.

SOURCE: From KALAT. *Introduction to Psychology, 9/e.* Copyright © 2011 Wadsworth, a part of Cengage Learning, Inc. Reproduced by permission. "http://www.cengage.com/permissions"

strong military protection, personal gun ownership, and strong law enforcement. People who are less prone to anxiety see less need for such protections. Which group is right? Well, sometimes one group is and sometimes the other is, but that is not the point. The point is that our emotions, particularly fear and anxiety, influence our thinking in all aspects of life.

SUMMARY

Fear is like many other things in life: A little is good for you, but too much is harmful. When you are confronted by imminent, serious danger, fear readies the body for quick, vigorous action. Just as important, fear prevents us from doing things that might lead us to real harm, and feelings of fear probably help us remember the warning signs of some trauma after it has happened. All of these effects help us to survive. However, many people are immobilized by constant, excessive fears.

We can find reasons to be optimistic about controlling fear. Researchers have more generally accepted ways of measuring fear than any other emotion, especially in non-human animals, and for this reason we know more about the biology of fear than for any other emotion. Certainly, we do not know nearly as much as we would like to know, but at least the research enables us to help people with extreme fears, and to pose questions for new research clearly.

KEY TERMS

anxiety: a general expectation that "something bad might happen," without identifying any particular danger (p. 158)

anxiolytics: drugs that relieve anxiety (p. 171)

Behavioral Inhibition System (BIS):   neurological system that responds to a frightening situation by increasing attention while inhibiting action and decreasing heart rate (p. 168)

emblems: hand and body gestures that have specific meanings within a given culture (p. 168)

fear: experience in which the dread is directed toward a specific object or event (p. 158)

micro expressions: involuntary, momentary emotional expressions that contradict the intended impression of calmness (p. 163)

polygraph: set of measurements based on the assumption that people get nervous when they lie and, therefore, show increased heart rate and blood pressure, rapid and irregular breathing patterns, increased skin conductance, or increases in other sympathetic nervous system activities (p. 166)

preparedness: proposal that people and other animals are evolutionarily predisposed to learn some things (including fears) more easily than others (p. 159)

serotonin transporter gene: a gene for a protein that "recycles" serotonin after it has been released into the synapse, bringing it back into the presynaptic axon terminal. The "long" form of part of this gene facilitates high transporter protein production; the "short" form less so (p. 172)

social phobia: an intense and overwhelming fear of social interactions (p. 170)

startle potentiation: enhancement of the startle response in a frightening situation as compared to a safe one (p. 164)

startle response: reaction to a sudden loud noise or other strong stimulus in which the muscles tense rapidly, especially the neck muscles, the eyes close tightly, the shoulders quickly pull close to the neck, and the arms pull up toward the head (p. 163)

tranquilizers: see anxiolytics

THOUGHT QUESTIONS

1. Observations on PTSD and other disorders suggest that an experience can reset our anxiety to a higher level, and that we can increase our anxiety level more easily and more quickly than we can decrease it. Why might we have evolved this tendency?

2. Facial expressions of emotion communicate our needs and tendencies to other people. What good does it do us (in both the intrapersonal and social ways discussed in Chapter 2) to communicate our fear? Are there times when it is best to hide our fear instead of expressing it?

SUGGESTIONS FOR FURTHER READING

Elliott, C. H., & Smith, L. L. (2002). *Overcoming Anxiety for Dummies*. New York: Wiley. Written by two practicing clinical psychologists, this is a great introduction to the topic of clinical anxiety.

Glassner, B. (2000). *The Culture of Fear: Why Americans Are Afraid of the Wrong Things*. New York: Basic Books. Well-documented critique of the role that mass media play in constructing targets of fear.

8

Anger and Disgust

Fear and anger have many things in common. Both involve sympathetic nervous system activation, presumably to facilitate physical activity. Both are responses to unexpected, unpleasant events. Yet from the standpoint of a researcher, the contrast is striking. Fear is easy to elicit in the laboratory; anger remarkably difficult. Facial and behavioral expressions of fear and anger overlap little. Although researchers can easily measure aggressive behavior in animals, they are far less likely to call it "anger" than they are to accept freezing and startle facilitation as evidence of fear. As a result, the animal research for anger is not as extensive as it is for fear. For English-language speakers, **anger** can be described as the emotional state associated with feeling injured or offended, with a desire to threaten or hurt the person who offended you. This is very different from the elicitors and behaviors of fear, which were discussed in the last chapter.

This definition suggests that we become angry when we feel that we have been offended or violated in some way. Researchers sometimes distinguish among three negative emotions, each of which might be elicited by some type of violation. According to researchers Paul Rozin, Jonathan Haidt, and colleagues, anger is felt in response to a violation of *autonomy*—that is, individual rights. You are angry when someone takes something away from you, or prevents you from doing something you feel entitled to do. Disgust, they argue, is a response to a violation of your sense of *purity* or *divinity*. To touch—or worse yet, taste—feces, cockroaches, or intestines would bring something impure into your body. Similarly, associating with someone who is morally impure might threaten your feeling of nobility. **Contempt** is a response to violation of *community* standards. For example, you might feel contempt toward someone who cheated on a test, or who did not behave appropriately for his status (imagine a professor who slouched into class wearing ripped shorts and an old, smelly T-shirt, and who seemed hung over—this behavior might be amusing in a fellow student, but not your instructor).

To test this distinction, researchers made a list of actions that seemed to violate autonomy, community standards, or divinity/purity. Then they asked

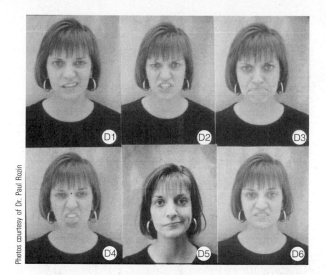

Photos courtesy of Dr. Paul Rozin

FIGURE 8.1 One set of facial expressions offered as choices for how to react to various types of offense. Faces D1 and D5 represent contempt, D2 and D3 represent anger, and D4 and D6 represent disgust. Some participants viewed these American faces, whereas others saw a set of Indian or Japanese faces.

Source: Rozin et al. (1999).

college students in both the United States and Japan to label their reaction to each one as anger, contempt, or disgust, and to choose the proper facial expression from choices like those shown in Figure 8.1. Although participants often confused these expressions when giving them verbal labels (Rozin, Taylor, Ross, Bennett, & Hejmadi, 2005), they typically chose an angry facial expression for the autonomy violations, a disgust expression for the divinity/purity violations, and a contemptuous expression for community violations (Rozin, Lowery, Imada, & Haidt, 1999). In this chapter we will consider evidence regarding anger and disgust as distinct emotions.

WHAT ELICITS ANGER?

Anger poses an interesting problem for researchers, especially those who want to study emotions in a laboratory or other controlled setting. Eliciting fear is easy: a sudden, loud noise will do, a scary movie, or the threat of an electric shock. But imagine trying to elicit anger, in a research laboratory, without overstepping ethical limits. Researchers often elicit emotions such as sadness, fear, amusement, and disgust by showing people film clips, but it is hard to find a film clip that reliably makes most people angry without also eliciting a bunch of other emotions. If you were the researcher, what would you do?

A sharp insult angers most people, but it often produces some combination of fear, sadness, and embarrassment as well. Also, some people fail to notice insults or simply shrug them off, assuming the rude person is just having a bad day. You might promise a nice reward and then refuse to give it; again you manage to anger some participants, but not all. Whereas fear is an almost universal reaction to certain situations, anger is more idiosyncratic—people can be angered by very different kinds of events.

This isn't necessarily a conceptual problem for researchers; after all, many already agree that people's appraisal or interpretation of an event is more important than its objective properties in determining emotion. However, when the objective elicitors of an emotion vary as widely as they do in anger, it is harder to identify their common theme. Although defining the "prototypical" anger situation is not terribly difficult, we must also acknowledge that people show anger in situations that do not fit that prototype well. For this reason, there has been considerable controversy over what elicits anger. Let's take a look at the different sides of this debate.

Prototypical Anger Situations

Richard Lazarus (1991) defined the prototypical core relational theme eliciting anger as a "demeaning offense against me and mine." Consistent with this idea, many studies find that anger arises against someone who has caused harm intentionally or carelessly. If someone steps in front of you and knocks you off balance, your degree of anger depends on *why* you think the person stepped in front of you. You probably would not feel angry with a toddler or a blind person. You might become angry with someone who had no apparent excuse for carelessness. You would become even angrier if you thought someone was intentionally trying to block your way. In one study, American, European, and Asian students all reported anger most strongly when someone treated them unfairly (Ohbuchi et al., 2004). In another study, people reported recent events in which things went badly for them. They reported feeling anger only when they had someone to blame for their misfortune (Kuppens, Van Mechelen, Smits, & De Boeck, 2003).

Studies of appraisal from the Component Process Theory perspective find compatible results. In the cross-cultural study of appraisal by Klaus Scherer (1997), people said they usually felt angry in unexpected, unpleasant, and unfair situations that interfered with their goals, and were caused by someone else. Participants also described anger-inducing situations as potentially changeable. An uncontrollable bad situation elicits more sadness or fear than anger. The "intentionality" factor was not included in this study, so it would be interesting to know whether or not it was really crucial for situations evoking anger.

Scherer's findings suggest that we typically become angry about another person's actions. If *you* did something careless or foolish that caused problems for you later—such as locking yourself out of your house—might you be angry with yourself? Many people say that they are. Self-anger is different from other-anger in several ways. When you are angry toward someone else, you might seek revenge in some way. You don't attack yourself. Self-anger is usually mixed with sadness and guilt or embarrassment (Ellsworth & Tong, 2006).

Much research points to the importance of blame in anger, but the nature of this relationship is unclear. Consider this study: High-school students read descriptions of several situations, rated various aspects of the situations, and then stated how angry they would feel in those situations. They also reported how often they feel angry overall. In general, when students perceived a situation as blameworthy, they said they would feel angry.

The students who tended to feel angry most often in everyday life were also most likely to interpret unpleasant situations as ones in which someone was to blame (Kuppens, Van Mechelen, & Rijmen, 2008). Another study found that participants made to feel angry earlier in the study were more likely to interpret ambiguous words as threats (Barazzone & Davey, 2009). So, does having someone to blame lead to anger? Or does being angry make you look for someone to blame? Research suggests that the causal arrow might go in both directions.

The Frustration-Aggression Hypothesis

Another theory arose among the behaviorists who dominated experimental psychology in the mid-1900s. With their emphasis on observable behaviors and animal models, they avoided concepts like "blame" and "anger," and instead looked for situational determinants of aggressive acts.

According to the **frustration–aggression hypothesis**, interference with one's ability to obtain some expected gratification leads to aggressive behavior (Dollard, Miller, Doob, Mowrer, & Sears, 1939). This implies the possibility of anger and aggression without an appraisal that blames anyone. Imagine you are in traffic. You're in a hurry to get somewhere, but the traffic is moving slowly. Besides that, it's hot out, and your car's air conditioner is broken. You can't logically blame anyone for your distress, but you might start to feel angry anyway. As another example, have you ever found yourself furious with a broken copy machine? The copy machine isn't deliberately trying to annoy you, but you still feel an overwhelming desire to kick it until it does what you want.

The Cognitive-Neoassociationistic Model: Anger Without Attribution?

In Chapter 1 we proposed that emotions result from an appraisal of some event—an attribution about what caused it and what it means for you. Most emotion researchers endorse some form of that proposal, but not all. Does an emotion—anger in particular—always require an appraisal or attribution? Can you feel cranky for no reason at all? The competing view is that anger sometimes arises directly from an unpleasant, uncomfortable sensation, without any appraisal of blame.

According to Leonard Berkowitz's (1990) **Cognitive-Neoassociationistic (CNA) Model of Anger Generation**, any unpleasant event or sensation facilitates anger and aggression. The unpleasant thing might be frustration, but it could also be pain, an aversive odor, or almost anything else. For example, the probability of aggression increases when the weather is hot (Preti, Miotto, De Coppi, Petretto, & Carmelo, 2002), or when people themselves feel uncomfortably hot (Anderson, 2001). If two rats or mice are together when they both get a foot shock, they attack each other. Do they really "blame" each other, or do they feel aggressive just because they are uncomfortable? If a rat gets a foot shock and then sees something unusual, like a plastic hedgehog, it attacks the apparent intruder (Keith-Lucas & Guttman, 1975).

We can observe something similar in human infants. In one study, researchers placed seven-month-olds on a table and restrained their arms so that they could not move (Sternberg, Campos, & Emde, 1983). The babies displayed facial expressions resembling the prototypical anger expression. In another study, infants learned to "call up" a picture of a smiling baby by moving their arms; when researchers turned off the effect so that the babies could no longer make the picture appear, most of them showed an angry face (Lewis, 1993). Many psychologists doubt that infants that young can analyze the situation well enough to blame anyone for their discomfort. The anger—if we can call it that—results from the discomfort or frustration itself.

Note that this proposal contradicts the idea that anger requires an attribution. Berkowitz suggests that being too hot, feeling crowded, having a headache, being in pain, smelling something foul, or any other discomfort *by itself* provokes anger even if you don't attribute it to any one, or interpret it at all. In fact, blame may be something we invent after the fact: You feel angry, you yell at someone, and then you quickly rationalize, "I was angry at that person because...."

Berkowitz's suggestion goes to the heart of what we mean by emotion. Remember two definitions offered in Chapter 1: Emotion is a "complex sequence of reactions to a stimulus" (Plutchik, 1982), or it is a "functional reaction to an external stimulus event" (Keltner & Shiota, 2003). Berkowitz suggests that an emotion can arise directly from a bodily feeling, even hunger or fatigue, without any stimulus at all (Berkowitz & Harmon-Jones, 2004).

What evidence supports Berkowitz's theory? To give just a few examples, study participants who were subjected to physical pain (Berkowitz, Cochran, & Embree, 1981), trapped with an extremely unpleasant noise (Geen, 1978), or exposed to secondhand cigarette smoke (Zillmann, Baron, & Tamborini, 1981) all tended to behave more aggressively toward convenient target people, even though the targets were not responsible for the conditions. Each of these studies did include a stimulus, but not of the kind suggested by most theories of anger. These findings are consistent with the CNA model.

The Impact of Control Appraisals

Frustration, pain, and other kinds of discomfort often lead to anger and aggression, but not always. According to Berkowitz (1990), if you think you are in danger and have no control, fear will trump anger. The study by Scherer and Wallbott also emphasized the importance of control appraisals in distinguishing anger from fear. For example, you might react to an insult with either fear or anger, depending on who insulted you (Keltner, Gruenfeld, & Anderson, 2003), and on the probable consequences if you expressed your anger openly.

In the United States, anger often arises when people are driving (Figure 8.2). Why? One obvious reason is that driving elicits frustration. You are trying to get somewhere in a hurry and some *$#@%& slows down, straddles two lanes, or fails to move when the light turns green. But frustration is not the whole explanation. Another factor is that

Sean Murphy/Getty Images

F I G U R E 8.2 Anger and aggressive behavior are common while people are driving.

in the safety of your car, you can honk, yell, or make a fist without much fear of retaliation (unless you are on a Los Angeles freeway, in which case it's really a bad idea).

If you are not sure what would happen if you express anger, you vacillate between attack and escape. Have you ever watched a cat approach a mouse? If the cat is an experienced mouser and the mouse is small, the cat makes a quick kill. But if the cat is less accomplished and the mouse is large, the mouse hisses and bares its teeth. Under these conditions, the cat retreats. In an intermediate case, the cat approaches cautiously. It bats at the mouse with its paws again and again until it weakens the mouse enough to bite it safely. Observers sometimes think the cat is "playing" with the mouse, but the behavior is in deadly earnest. Give the cat a tranquilizer to reduce its fears, and a cat that would have "played" with the mouse goes for a quicker attack (Adamec, Stark-Adamec, & Livingston, 1980; Biben, 1979; Pellis et al., 1988). Something similar is true in

humans: People who have drunk alcohol or taken tranquilizers sometimes get into fights because they have suppressed their fear. Of course, much larger doses calm them enough to become inactive and cease fighting (Valzelli, 1979).

Putting It All Together: What Elicits Anger?

None of these theories has earned a consensus among researchers studying emotion. On one hand, if appraisal of blame is essential, we cannot explain why people become hostile when they are in an unpleasant situation that is no one's fault. On the other hand, if an emotion, by definition, includes cognition, feeling, physiological changes, and action, then an emotion without cognition (for instance, anger without blame) is impossible, or at least incomplete (Clore & Centerbar, 2004; C. A. Smith & Kirby, 2004). This definition of emotion assumes that these four aspects of emotion hang together as a unit. If one or two of them frequently arise independently, as Berkowitz has suggested, then our definition of emotion should not insist on all four. Another possibility is that anger does require an appraisal of the situation, but hostile intent is not the key factor.

Perhaps appraisal of hostile intent is more important for adult human anger than for that of children or nonhuman animals. Remember that some of the evidence for the frustration-aggression hypothesis came from studies of infants. In another study of the causes of anger, mothers recorded events that had made them or their children angry. Mothers reported feeling anger mostly when their children were inconsiderate, failed to say where they were going or when they were coming home, or did not do their household chores. In short, the mothers were angry when the children hurt their feelings or failed to live up to expectations. Events that angered their children were mostly "goal blockages": They got angry because their parents didn't buy them something they wanted, wouldn't let them spend their own money as they wished, or disciplined them by taking something away (Carpenter & Halberstadt, 2000). Could it be that the very nature of anger somehow changes as we age, or that the frustrated anger of childhood exists side by side with adult anger, with its more complex attributions and appraisals?

Indeed, it is possible that anger has two forms, analogous to fear and anxiety. Fear is related to a specific object and anxiety is more diffuse. One type of anger might be a response to a particular event, whereas another might be due to general discomfort and directed toward whomever happens to be around. The latter "irritability" or "crankiness" is something we can all relate to, but has received little study by emotion scientists. Certainly the relationships among anger, frustration, and irritability are good topics for future research.

Part of the issue in this conflict is the relationship between anger and aggressiveness. In CNA Model of Anger, Berkowitz assumes that pain or other discomfort elicits anger, which leads to reactive aggression. Maybe so, or maybe Berkowitz's

theory applies to aggressive behavior without applying to anger. Here are the two possibilities:

Berkowitz's CNA approach

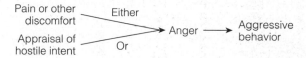

Appraisal approach

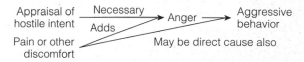

Clearly, the two theories have much in common. Everyone apparently agrees that an appraisal of hostile intent magnifies anger and that discomfort tends to magnify aggressive behavior. The dispute concerns whether appraisal of hostile intent is necessary for anger, and whether aggressive behavior is the best measure of anger.

MEASURING ANGER AND AGGRESSION

As with any other emotion, research on anger is only as good as the methods of measuring it. Much of the research on anger has focused on physical aggression, mainly because aggression is observable and anger is not. However, the relationship between anger and physical aggression is far from perfect. How often do you feel angry? How often do you actually hit someone? Across all the cultures that have been studied, people report feeling angry far more often than they ever consider turning to violence (Ramirez, Santisteban, Fujihara, & Van Goozen, 2002). Also, people can aggress against others without being angry. Here are some measurement options available to researchers.

Self-Reports of Anger

Given a standard definition of emotion as including cognitions, feelings, physiological changes, and actions, a good self-report measure of anger should assess appraisals that lead to anger, angry feelings, and the resulting behavior (Martin, Watson, & Wan, 2000). Researchers often rely on self-reports to gauge cognitions and feelings. Sometimes that approach works well enough, but it has its limitations. As with all self-reports, accuracy is questionable. Also, people sometimes hesitate to admit their anger. In an experiment described in Chapter 1, Stanley Schachter and Jerome Singer (1962) did everything they could think of within the bounds of ethics to make one group of participants angry, but few reported feeling this emotion. Maybe they really felt no anger, but another possibility is that they didn't want to tell their professors how irritated they were.

For many purposes, researchers want to know more than just "how angry" you are. Anger varies along several dimensions, and the Multidimensional Anger Inventory (Siegel, 1986) measures several of them. Some questions relate to how angry you generally become. Another set measures the variety of situations in which you become angry—for example, being delayed, not getting credit for the work you have done, or taking orders from someone less qualified. A third set of questions deals with a hostile attitude—for example, if a person's mere presence is annoying to you. A final set asks how you deal with anger: Do you let the other person know, or do you just keep quiet and let your anger continue to bother you?

The most widely used paper-and-pencil measure of anger is the Spielberger State-Trait Anger Expression Inventory, or STAXI (Spielberger, 1991; Spielberger, Jacobs, Russell, & Crane, 1983). The idea behind this questionnaire is that anger is both a **state** (a temporary condition related to recent events) and a **trait** (a long-term aspect of personality). As an analogy, a state is like a region's current weather, and a trait is like the usual climate. Therefore, the STAXI includes items such as the following:

How do you feel right now?

I feel like yelling at someone.

(1) Not at all   (2) Somewhat
(3) Moderately so   (4) Very much so

How do you generally feel?

I am quick-tempered

(1) Almost never   (2) Sometimes
(3) Often   (4) Almost always

The first item measures anger as a state; the second measures it as a trait. That distinction is useful for many purposes. If we want to know how someone will behave in the next few minutes, we care about her current anger (state), whereas for predicting behavior next week, the important information is the long-term trait.

As with many other measures, the STAXI emphasizes intense, somewhat destructive kinds of anger. Another instrument concentrates on people's ability to handle anger in helpful ways. The Constructive Anger Behavior–Verbal Style Scale (CAB-V) consists of items that can be filled out either as a self-report or by an observer or interviewer, who presumably provides a less biased account (Davidson, MacGregor, Stuhr, Dixon, & MacLean, 2000). Sample items include:

Person discusses his/her anger to see if others can help him/her to come up with constructive solutions.

(1) Almost never   (2) Sometimes
(3) Often   (4) Almost always

Person finds that after discussing his/her anger things don't look as bad as she/he thought they did.

(1) Almost never   (2) Sometimes
(3) Often   (4) Almost always

Generally, people with high scores on this inventory handle stressful situations well and keep their anger under control. The value of having different anger questionnaires is that each measures as a somewhat different aspect of anger, and researchers can choose the one most appropriate for the issue they are investigating.

Facial Expression of Anger

Paul Ekman and colleagues found that people throughout the world recognize a prototypical "angry face" (Ekman et al., 1987). Although angry

F I G U R E 8.3 Facial expressions of anger.

expressions range from mild to very intense, the prototype is clear. Angry people open their eyes wide and force their eyebrows down and toward the middle of their forehead. Their lower eyelids pull up and toward the inner corner of the eyes, and their lips tighten. Figure 8.3 shows examples. In addition to facial changes, body posture shifts, as does the tone of voice. Even in a telephone conversation, you know when someone is angry.

Recall that according to the definition of emotion, any emotion serves a function. Although most people think of anger as destructive, it too serves a useful function. In this case, the display of anger *is* an important part of the function. A quick, mild "constructive" display of anger on your part tells your friend or romantic partner, "Hey, that hurt! Don't do it again." Someone who is reasonably perceptive will detect your irritation, apologize, understand you better, and avoid similar acts in the future. The interchange can improve your relationship (Tafrate, Kassinove, & Dundin, 2002; Kassinove et al., 1997). People confer power and status to people who express moderate amounts of anger (Tiedens, 2001), and people who express mild anger in negotiations tend to get more of

what they want (van Kleef, De Dreu, & Manstead, 2004). Anger lets people know your limits and demands. Under appropriate circumstances, small displays of anger can sometimes improve a social interaction.

If you expect to get into a conflict with someone, might you *want* to be angry? Might it *help* to be angry? People in one study were randomly assigned to play an aggressive video game (striking members of a drug cartel) or a nonaggressive game (trying to spread world peace). Before playing, they could choose between listening to soothing or arousing music, and between recalling experiences when they felt angry or recalling other kinds of experiences. Participants assigned to play the aggressive game were more likely to choose angry memories to recall while preparing for the game, when compared with those preparing for a non-aggressive game. Moreover, those who recalled angry experiences, and felt angry as a result, performed better on the aggressive video game (but not the non-aggressive game; Tamir, Mitchell, & Gross, 2008). That is, we may choose to feel angry when preparing for a confrontational situation, and it may even help us get our way (van Kleef, De Dreu, & Manstead, 2004).

Aggressive Behaviors

Researchers studying anger also observe aggressive behavior. In fact, that approach is the only option when studying nonhuman animals. However, not all anger leads to aggression and not all aggression begins with anger. Psychologists distinguish between hostile and instrumental aggression. **Hostile aggression** is motivated by anger, with the specific intent to hurt someone. **Instrumental aggression** is harmful or threatening behavior used purely as a way to obtain something or achieve some end. Examples include bullying, theft, warfare, and killing prey. Much of human aggression is instrumental. Social psychologists have found that normal, healthy, well-intentioned people sometimes will inflict pain and suffering on someone they've never met, possibly even endanger that person's life, if an authority figure tells them to (Milgram, 1974). Aggression and anger are certainly related, but it would be a tremendous mistake to assume that they are synonymous.

One problem in studying aggressive behavior is that overt fighting is rare even when people are very angry. For that matter, it would be unethical to set up situations in which people *might* actually hurt each other. A clever way to get around these problems is to set up situations in which people *think* they are hurting someone, although in fact they are not. Imagine yourself in this experiment (Berman, Gladue, & Taylor, 1993): You have a discussion with someone you never met before and don't expect to meet again, and this person repeatedly belittles and insults you. Then the two of you are put into separate rooms, and you are told to teach this person something. You should periodically test that person's performance and signal an error by pressing a button to deliver an electric shock. You get to choose among buttons to determine the intensity of that shock.

At least, you think you are delivering shocks; in fact, the other person is a confederate of the researcher, and there are no shocks. The point of the experiment is to find out how intense a shock you choose, measuring your tendency toward aggressive behavior without allowing an actual attack.

In a similar task, people can press a button to take points or money away from another "participant" (Moe, King, & Bailly, 2004).

Psychologists have developed many variations of these tasks, but all of them are subject to certain limitations, including these:

- The rules authorize, even require, people to commit an aggressive act.

- The participants are strangers to each other, with no previous relationship and no expectation of a future one.

- The target of the aggressive act is not visible.

- In many cases, the target of the aggression has no opportunity to retaliate.

- The two people have no way to interact with each other *except* for the designated aggressive act.

- We can't be sure the aggressive act depends on anger. Maybe the motive is competition rather than hostility.

In short, typical laboratory methods of producing aggressive behavior are unlike typical aggression (Ritter & Eslea, 2005). Often psychologists learn a great deal from laboratory procedures that seem distant from the events of the real world, so we should not dismiss this type of research as irrelevant. Still, we should be aware of its limitations.

Implicit Measures of Anger and Aggression

Not all behavioral measures of anger require overt aggression. Implicit measures can be used to detect the emotion in a more subtle way. In one study, people read brief, incomplete stories, some of which included aggressive events. Their task was to write a couple of sentences to finish the story. Researchers then recorded the amount of aggressive content that each person wrote. On average, men included more aggression in their endings than women, and people who described themselves as frequently angry tended to include more aggression than did people who reported less anger (A. J. Bond, Bauer, & Wingrove,

2004). Note the importance of blind observers in such a study. The observers judging the amount of aggressive content must not know which people have already reported being angry or aggressive.

Another measure is called the **themed dot-probe task**. We encountered the dot-probe task in earlier chapters on emotion regulation and fear/anxiety. In this version of the task, two words (one of which might be aggressive) flash briefly on the screen, one above the other. Then a dot appears in the same position as one word, and the person must press a key as quickly as possible to indicate where the dot appeared. The idea is that a violent word will distract attention and slow the response, depending on where the dot appears. People with a history of violence, such as prisoners convicted of violent crimes, are more affected by aggression-related words in this task (P. Smith & Waterman, 2004).

In the **visual search task**, a target word appears briefly in the center of the screen, surrounded by three other words. Then the target word and three new words appear, and the task is to identify the location of the target word. When the target word is surrounded by violent words, people with a history of violence tend to respond more slowly in finding the target word on the second screen (P. Smith & Waterman, 2004). Again, the apparent reason is that violent words attract attention for some people more than others.

Implicit measures are clever and theoretically interesting, and they confirm the idea that aggressive words capture attention more thoroughly for people who are prone to anger and violence than for other people. However, the difference in mean response times between highly aggressive and unaggressive people is just a fraction of a second, with much variation, so these tests are not useful for identifying dangerous individuals.

THE BIOLOGY OF ANGER AND AGGRESSION

Wouldn't it be nice if researchers found that excessive anger and aggressiveness had a simple physiological basis, such as overactivity of one kind of synapse in the brain? Then we could find a medication that suppresses that activity, close down the prisons, and live happily ever after. Right?

The reality is that researchers have found no single biological mechanism responsible for producing anger or aggression. However, they have found that some people have a *deficit* in mechanisms that ordinarily *inhibit* aggression. In that sense, the physiological research meshes nicely with our understanding of anger: Aggression occurs in part when people do not have enough inhibition against it.

The Neuroanatomy of Anger and Aggression

Aggressive behavior is often impulsive, and one basis for impulsivity is damage to the prefrontal cortex (Figure 8.4). People with known damage to certain parts of the prefrontal cortex are impaired at suppressing their emotional expressions after such instructions as "Try not to act startled after the sudden sound you're about to hear." They also are more likely to lose money by making bad gambling decisions, and to choose a smaller reward now over a larger reward later. People with a history of explosive outbursts of anger, including impulsive

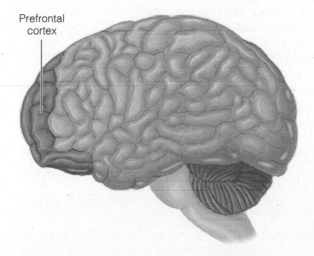

Prefrontal cortex

FIGURE 8.4 Damage to the prefrontal cortex often leads to impulsive behavior, including outbursts of aggression.

murderers, show these same behavioral patterns, even if they have no known brain damage (Best, Williams, & Coccaro, 2002; Davidson, Putnam, & Larson, 2000). The implication is that their prefrontal cortex is intact, but may be less than normally active.

Anger does activate certain brain areas, but researchers face a special problem in trying to measure it in fMRI studies. Emotions are "embodied" in the sense that total body activity is central to the emotional experience. When you are angry, you get ready to attack or threaten. But now picture yourself being insulted while you are lying on your back in an fMRI device, where you are required to remain motionless. People experience much less anger in this position than when they are sitting or standing and free to move about (Harmon-Jones & Peterson, 2009).

Neurochemistry: Serotonin and Testosterone

If the prefrontal cortex is less effective than normal at inhibiting impulses, a disorder in the activity of some neurotransmitter could be the cause. One candidate is serotonin. Only a few clusters of neurons in the brainstem produce serotonin, but their axons spread widely, influencing activity throughout most of the brain, as Figure 8.5 shows.

Laboratory research since the 1970s has demonstrated that rats and mice with low levels of serotonin release are more likely to fight with one another (Saudou et al., 1994; Valzelli, 1973; Valzelli & Bernasconi, 1979). Other studies found that monkeys with the lowest levels of serotonin metabolites in the blood were the most likely to start fights, and to be victims of attacks (Higley et al., 1996; Westergaard, Cleveland, Trenkle, Lussier, & Higley, 2003). Many of these low-serotonin monkeys sustained repeated injuries and died within the first few years of life. However, aggressive monkeys that survived had a high probability of achieving a dominant status within the troop (Howell et al., 2007). That is, low serotonin seemed to be linked to a high-risk, high-payoff strategy.

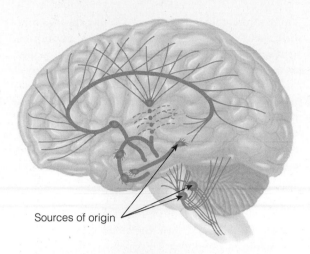

Sources of origin

FIGURE 8.5 Just a few clusters of neurons in the brain stem manufacture serotonin, but their axons influence activity in widespread areas.
Source: Based on Valzelli (1980).

Instigated by these results, other researchers examined serotonin release in humans. Low levels have been found in people convicted of arson and other violent crimes (Virkkunen, Nuutila, Goodwin, & Linnoila, 1987). Studies of inmates being let out of prison found that those with low serotonin levels are the most likely to be convicted of additional violent crimes within the next few years (Virkkunen, DeJong, Bartko, Goodwin, & Linnoila, 1989; Virkkunen, Eggert, Rawlings, & Linnoila, 1996). Similarly, of children and adolescents being counseled because of aggressive behavior, those with the lowest serotonin levels are the most likely to commit additional violent acts (Kruesi et al., 1992). Of people who survive violent attempts at suicide, those with the lowest serotonin release are the most likely to attempt suicide again within the next five years (Roy, DeJong, & Linnoila, 1989).

A thorough review of the available literature found that the relationship in humans between low serotonin and violent behavior was consistent but only moderate in size (Moore, Scarpa, & Raine, 2002). That is, if we examine two large groups of people differing in their serotonin levels, we can confidently predict which group will show more violence, but we could not make confident predictions about any individual. One reason is that the effects of low serotonin depend on other circumstances in the person's brain chemistry, previous experiences, and present life. When researchers have used drugs or other methods to lower people's serotonin levels suddenly, the people with a previous history of violence became violent, those with a history of depression became depressed, and those with a history of substance abuse reported a sudden craving for drugs (Van der Does, 2001). It is as if low serotonin release removes inhibitions against various impulses, but different people have different impulses.

Furthermore, the exact role of serotonin in aggression remains unclear. Neurons actually release serotonin *during* aggressive behavior, not while the individual is preparing for or refraining from aggression (van der Vegt et al., 2003). According to one hypothesis, those who usually have low levels of serotonin release react more strongly than usual to events causing its release, and therefore, those with the lowest serotonin turnover have the highest likelihood of violence (Nelson & Trainor, 2007). Drugs that elevate serotonin sometimes decrease aggressive behavior (Berman, McCloskey, Fanning, Schumacher, & Coccaro, 2009), but not always.

Anger and the Autonomic Nervous System

Anger also manifests itself in physiological arousal, such as heart rate and breathing rate. The physiological state that accompanies anger closely resembles that for fear. Other features of aggression are accounted for by effects of the adrenal gland. At the start of an aggressive attack, part of the hypothalamus sends messages that increase the adrenal gland's release of cortisol and other stress hormones. Those hormones feed back to increase activity in the hypothalamus. Thus, at the start of a fight, the arousal is self-sustaining and self-magnifying (Kruk, Halász, Meelis, & Haller, 2004). A common result is that your anger quickly increases when you are provoked.

The relationship between anger and sympathetic activation has often been invoked to explain the association between high dispositional hostility and cardiovascular disease (Davidson et al., 2000). However, some research has suggested that how anger is expressed, rather than the experience of anger itself, predicts health problems. For example, Siegman (1994) concluded that hostile people who express anger frequently and explosively are more vulnerable to cardiovascular problems, whereas people who experience anger often but express it differently are at less risk. Another study found that people who express their anger verbally while trying to understand the other person's point of view had lower resting blood pressure than people who were less articulate when angry (Davidson et al., 2000). This effect continued to be significant after the researchers controlled for other variables known to predict hypertension, such as sex, weight, and smoking. Although we cannot draw cause-and-effect conclusions from these correlational studies, it may be that the risk of heart disease depends on how people handle and express their anger, not on anger per se.

INDIVIDUAL AND SITUATIONAL DIFFERENCES

One of the most striking features of anger and aggression is that they vary so much. Have you noticed that some people get angry more often than others? Do you sometimes get into an irritable mood yourself, when it takes very little to anger you? As we noted above, people also express their anger quite differently; some becoming loud and aggressive, others becoming cold and aloof, and yet others expressing anger constructively.

Who Becomes Aggressive?

For practical purposes, predicting aggression is easy: The more violent acts someone has committed in the past, the more likely that person is to commit further violence. That statement is a special case of one of the strongest generalizations we can make in psychology: The best predictor of future behavior is past behavior.

From a theoretical standpoint, of course, predicting future violence from past violence is unsatisfactory because it does not explain why some people were more violent in the past. Let's first dispense with a couple of popular explanations that the data do not support. One is that violent behavior is a product of low self-esteem. According to this view, people who see themselves as failures try to raise their own status by attacking someone else. The attraction of this hypothesis comes from observations that many highly violent people are poorly educated, have trouble keeping a job, and in general seem to be the kind of people who *should* have low self-esteem. However, the results do not consistently support the hypothesis if we use standard measurements of self-esteem. Those measurements rely on questions such as these (Blascovich & Tomaka, 1991):

T F At times I think I'm no good at all.

T F I'm a failure.

T F There are lots of things about myself I'd change if I could.

T F I'm often sorry for the things I do.

As you might guess, a "false" on any of these four items counts as a point toward high self-esteem. As measured in this way, most studies find only a weak relationship between self-esteem and violent behavior (Arslan, 2009; Donnellan, Trzesniewski, Robins, Moffitt, & Caspi, 2005). People who are consistent *victims* of violence report low self-esteem, but many perpetrators of violence are confident, self-centered, and arrogant. In one study of elementary-school children, the most aggressive children tended to be those who overestimated how much the other children liked them (David & Kistner, 2000). Of course, not everyone with high self-esteem becomes violent. It may be that some people react violently when other people threaten their arrogant self-esteem. In general, researchers find no strong relationship between violent behavior and low self-esteem (Baumeister, Smart, & Boden, 1996).

Another unsupported hypothesis is that violence results from mental illness. You will sometimes hear reports of a mental patient who acts violently against strangers. However, violent mental patients are a rarity, except for those who abuse alcohol and other drugs. Mental patients who are not substance abusers have about the same crime rate as the rest of the population (Hodgins, Mednick, Brennan, Schulsinger, & Engberg, 1996).

We mentioned a better explanation for violence earlier: Violent behavior is more likely when people have low inhibitions against it. Some people are simply uninhibited in general, and others become that way after drinking alcohol. People also feel less inhibition against aggression if they are (or feel) powerful. If you have managed to push people around in the past, you will likely feel powerful enough to try it again.

Aggression is also common among people who perceive other people's actions as hostile. In one study, highly aggressive and unaggressive boys were shown videotapes of events that could be either accidental or deliberate, such as one child knocking down another's blocks or bumping into the other in the lunch line (Dodge & Coie, 1987). In some cases, the offender's facial expression and verbal cues suggested an intentional offense; in other cases, it appeared accidental; and in yet other cases, the intent was ambiguous. The more aggressive boys usually thought the offense was deliberate, even when the facial expressions and verbal cues indicated an accident. Several later studies replicated the finding that children who attribute hostile intentions to others are more likely than other children to start fights, especially in response to teasing (Crick & Dodge, 1994, 1996). They evidently regard the teasing as hostile, and react accordingly.

In another study, researchers employed a questionnaire to measure people's usual tendency toward anger (anger-proneness as a personality trait). Then they showed each participant a videotape of a person taking someone else's change in a bar, and another videotape of someone driving in front of another car to take a parking spot. Each videotape had two versions, of which each participant saw only one. In one version, the antagonist clearly intended harm.

The other version was ambiguous as to whether the person acted intentionally or absent mindedly. The researchers found that the most anger-prone people were more likely than others to attribute malicious intent to the antagonists, even in the ambiguous situations (Hazebroek, Howells, & Day, 2000).

Genetics and Aggression

As with any other behavior, one hypothesis concerning individual differences is that they result from genetics. Studies of aggressive, delinquent, and criminal behaviors have consistently found greater similarities between monozygotic (identical) twins than dizygotic (fraternal) twins. Studies have also found that adopted children tend to resemble their biological parents in these regards. The degree of resemblance, according to one review of the literature, suggests that genetic factors account for about 40 percent of the variance in aggressive and criminal behavior, whereas environmental factors account for the rest (Rhee & Waldman, 2002).

Various attempts have been made to tie aggressive behavior to a particular gene. Researchers have identified several genes that are somewhat more common among people with a history of violence than in the general population, such as 66 percent versus 57 percent or 51 percent versus 34 percent (Abbar et al., 2001; Manuck et al., 1999; Rujescu et al., 2002). These effects suggest that some people are more predisposed than others to violence, but they also indicate that no one gene has a huge effect. Certain genes linked to aggressive behavior are also linked (weakly) to the probability of a suicide attempt (Giegling, Hartmann, Moller, & Rujescu, 2006). Suicide is a special type of aggressive act—an attack against oneself.

In one study, pairs of dizygotic twins and monozygotic twins showed equal similarity in juvenile offenses, but monozygotic twins showed much stronger similarity in adult crimes (Lyons et al., 1995). Those results suggest that the effects of heredity *increase* as people grow older. A possible explanation is that children have little choice of where or how they live. That is, both members of a twin pair share mostly the same environment.

As adults, they have more choices. Someone predisposed to impulsive violence may choose friends, a neighborhood, and a way of life consistent with antisocial behavior, and thereby magnify a genetic predisposition.

In other words, the effect of the genes depends on the environment. Here is another possible example of that idea: Researchers examined people who differed genetically in how much of the enzyme *monoamine oxidase A (MAO$_A$)* they produced. This enzyme breaks down the neurotransmitters dopamine, norepinephrine, and serotonin, thereby decreasing the amounts available for release. As shown in Figure 8.6, people who had suffered abusive treatment in childhood were more likely than average to engage in antisocial behavior, but that increase was sharper for those with low levels of MAO$_A$ (Caspi et al., 2002). Differences in MAO$_A$ level made little difference for people not abused during childhood. This interaction is fascinating and potentially important, but several other investigators have failed to replicate the finding (Prichard, Mackinnon, Jorm, & Easteal, 2008). Possibly the results depend on the method of

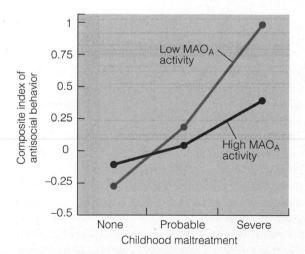

FIGURE 8.6 Abusive treatment during childhood increases the probability of antisocial behavior later, and this effect is greater for people with one set of genes than another.

Source: From Caspi, A., et al. 'Role of genotype in the cycle of violence in maltreated children'. *Science*, 297, pp. 851–854. Copyright © 2002 AAAS. Reprinted by permission from AAAS.

measuring violent behavior, or the method of measuring the enzyme.

Sex Differences in Anger and Aggression

One genetic factor that might come to mind as a possible cause of anger is the Y chromosome—a whole string of genetic material possessed by males, but not females. The common stereotype is that men get angry more often, but the research does not support that view. When people keep records of when and where they become angry, men and women record about the same frequency (Averill, 1983). When the cause is reasonable, women get just as angry as men, and are at least as likely to show their anger in some way (Weber & Wiedig-Allison, 2007).

The difference is in *what* men and women do when they are angry. One of the biggest and best-documented differences between males and females is that males engage in more physically aggressive behavior. Boys get into fistfights far more often than girls do, men get into brawls vastly more often than women, and men commit most of the violent crimes in every culture for which we have data, throughout the world. The sex difference in physical aggression does depend to some degree on what we count as violence. Most fights occur between people who know each other well, not between strangers (Averill, 1983), and much violence occurs between spouses or romantic partners. According to an extensive review of the literature, women commit more than half of this violence (Archer, 2000). Almost everyone finds that statistic surprising because we often hear about battered wives, not battered husbands. The explanation is that researchers defined aggression to include a wide range of minor acts, even slapping or pushing. If we limit attention to acts that could produce serious injury, men clearly commit most of them.

Although girls and women are less likely than males to resort to physical violence, they are more likely than men to attack indirectly, such as by refusing to communicate, spreading unkind rumors, or manipulating one person to hurt another

(Salmivalli & Kaukiainen, 2004; Xie, Cairns, & Cairns, 2002). One woman said that sometimes she felt furious with her husband, but because she felt powerless against him, she attacked in secret ways. Sometimes she put a slug or insect in his food, and felt good about knowing he would eat it unaware (Eatough, Smith, & Shaw, 2008).

One factor that has been proposed to explain men's aggression is the steroid hormone **testosterone**, which is more common in males than females. However, the role of testosterone in violent behavior is not clear. On one hand, violence is most common among males in the age range 15 to 25, which is also the time of highest testosterone levels. Also, in a variety of animal species, aggression is most common in males when their testosterone levels are highest. If you watch birds in the mating season (spring), when testosterone levels are high, you can see repeated threat displays. In the fall, when breeding is over and testosterone levels drop, male birds cluster in large, peaceful flocks.

On the other hand, for a single group and at any particular moment, some males are more aggressive than others, and the correlation between testosterone levels and aggression is weak (Archer, Birring, & Wu, 1998; Archer, Graham-Kevan, & Davies, 2005; Bernhardt, 1997; Brooks & Reddon, 1996). In short, testosterone fluctuations from one time to another for a given individual may predict aggressiveness, but differences between one individual and another do not mean as much.

An interesting way to study testosterone is to examine its effects on women. Researchers injected women with testosterone, temporarily raising their levels to that of young men. Under the influence of testosterone, the women became *less* accurate at recognizing facial expressions of anger (van Honk & Schutter, 2007), but their amygdalae became *more* responsive to angry expressions (Hermans, Ramsey, & van Honk, 2008). That is, consciously they reacted less than usual to the angry faces but emotionally they reacted more.

Given that males of so many species tend to fight more than females, it is natural to suggest that evolution has predisposed males to be more aggressive. Traditionally, evolutionary theorists have pointed out that a male gains in two ways by winning a fight: He forces a competing male out of the way, and he impresses the females. A highly dominant male has the potential to impregnate many females and thus spread his genes.

Anne Campbell (2002) has suggested a different evolutionary explanation, by changing the question to why women are *less* aggressive. She begins with the fact that men take more risks than women under a wide variety of circumstances, including walking through a dangerous neighborhood alone at night—an act that has little chance of impressing females because they are probably not around to watch. Campbell's interpretation is that women are predisposed to value their own lives more than men do. Evolutionarily, that tendency makes sense: If a woman dies before her children are mature, they probably will not survive and she does not pass on her genes. However, a man's children might survive even if he does not.

As Campbell (2002) also points out, whereas males of almost all species compete for the chance to mate with females, almost any female who wants to mate can find a willing partner. Thus, females do not need to fight each other in order to have a chance to reproduce. Certain types of aggressive behavior by females make do sense, however, from an evolutionary perspective. Females will compete to protect or advance themselves and their children. Few animals are more ferocious than a mother bear defending her cubs. Also consider this observation of great reed warblers, European birds (Figure 8.7): A male and female share nesting and infant-care duties, while the male defends the territory against other males. If the male has a particularly good territory, one or more other females will set up "satellite" nests nearby. The male fertilizes their eggs, but otherwise devotes his attention to the nest and young of the primary female. If her eggs fail to hatch, he moves to help one of the satellite females. In fact, the eggs of the primary female frequently fail to hatch, because when they are unguarded, one of the satellite females pecks at them and kills them (Hansson, Bensch, & Hasselquist, 1997).

All of these examples suggest instrumental motives for aggression, rather than hostile motives,

© Mike Lane/Alamy

FIGURE 8.7 Great reed warblers breed in continental Europe. In good territories, satellite females set up nests near the primary nest and, if they get an opportunity, attack the primary female's eggs.

so it's not clear whether evolutionary explanations apply to individual differences in anger. Still, the correlation between anger and aggression makes this a potentially interesting line of research.

Family Environment

Although genetic factors do account for some individual differences in anger and aggression, violence is most common in people whose parents physically abused them, frequently fought with each other, got into trouble with the law, and abused alcohol and other substances (Malinosky-Rummell & Hansen, 1993). Violence is also widespread among those who grew up in a violent neighborhood. It might seem obvious that growing up in such circumstances leads to violence by making the child dispositionally angry and by setting an example of violence. However, we need to consider the alternative possibility that violent and impulsive parents have violent and impulsive children because of shared genes. The best evidence for an effect of family environment independent of genetics comes from studies of adopted children.

Adoption agencies seldom place children with violent or alcoholic parents, but when they do, those children tend to show increased violence. However, that increase in violence is often smaller than you might expect. The greatest incidence of violence occurs in adopted children who had *both* a history of violence in their biological parents *and* exposure to violence by their adoptive parents (Cadoret, Yates, Troughton, Woodworth, & Stewart, 1995).

One of the most remarkable and least understood aspects of human development is **resilience**, the ability of people to overcome the effects of extremely unfavorable environments. For example, only about one third of abused children become abusive parents (Widom, 1989). In some cases, abused children are helped by a relationship with another person; in other cases, they resist harmful influences anyway, without any obvious explanation. Much more work is needed to understand the protective factors that help children to thrive in spite of threatening environments.

One point worth mentioning: The fact that so many people are resilient in the face of abusive or painful experiences does not mean that we should be indifferent to those experiences. One review article (Rind, Tromovitch, & Bauserman, 1998) found that most children subjected to sexual abuse (broadly defined to include such things as seeing a "flasher") recovered reasonably well. That article became the focus of a heated controversy because many critics assumed the authors were implying that childhood sexual abuse is acceptable. They meant no such thing, of course. Studies of this kind tend to look at categorical outcomes, such as whether or not someone who experienced childhood abuse ends up convicted of a crime, or abusing others. Abusive experiences increase the probability of these negative outcomes by some degree, but they also have a wide range of other, less easily categorized effects on people's lives and well-being.

Effects of Watching Media Violence

Do children who grow up frequently watching violent movies, television, and video games become more violent than those who seldom watch them? This kind of argument has been around for eons. The ancient Greeks debated whether violent stories had a bad influence on the young (J. P. Murray, 1998), and people in the early twentieth century worried about whether violent radio programs increased the crime rate (Dennis, 1998). Today the issue is more important because of the quantitative increase in exposure. According to surveys in the United States, the average child spends an average of 40 hours per week watching television, movies, or video games, and most of these programs contain violence. Authorities in this field estimate that by the time a child leaves elementary school, he will have watched depictions of 8,000 murders (Bushman & Anderson, 2001). Many television and movie executives have defended these programs by saying that televised violence does not affect people's behavior. Bushman and Anderson (2001) reply to this claim with the question, "If watching television does not affect behavior, why are so many companies willing to pay for commercials?"

Studies routinely find that people who watch more television or movie violence, or who play more violent video games, also tend to engage in more aggressive behaviors. One study examined 707 families, determined how much violent television the children watched, and measured the children's aggressive behavior. Then, over the next 16 to 18 years, the researchers repeatedly retested the children. They found that, regardless of how aggressive the children were at the start of the study, those who watched more violent programs tended to become more aggressive over the years. They found similar trends when they controlled for potential confounds such as parental education, income, supervision of the children, and type of neighborhood (Johnson, Cohen, Smailes, Kasen, & Brook, 2002).

Of course, these trends do not apply to every individual. One study found that although most adolescents felt increased anger after playing *Quake II* (a popular, highly violent video game), some of the most aggressive youths felt *decreased* anger after playing it (Unsworth, Devilly, & Ward, 2007). Furthermore, the interpretation of correlational results is always problematic. Does watching violence actually cause violence, or is it just that people who tend toward violent behavior also choose to watch violent programs? To examine cause and effect, we need experimental research. Students in one study played a violent or nonviolent videogame for 20 minutes. Afterward, they witnessed a loud fight that was staged in the hall outside the lab. Those who had played the violent game were slower to offer help to the victim (Bushman & Anderson, 2009). This is not the same as actually being aggressive, but the implication is that watching violence dampens our responses to other people's suffering, at least temporarily.

Children who are randomly assigned to watch television episodes containing even mild violence show more aggressive playground behavior a while later than children who watched television episodes without any aggression (Boyatzis, Matillo, & Nesbitt, 1995; Steuer, Applefield, & Smith, 1971). These effects are stronger when the show is live-action (with human actors) rather than cartoon, when the aggressor is the "good guy" rather than the "bad guy," and when the aggressor is similar to the person watching on variables such as sex, age, and ethnicity.

Unfortunately, we do not yet have much information about long-term effects. Does repeatedly watching violence or pretending to shoot people on a video screen increase the probability of actual violence? No one knows, but whether we like it or not, all of us are participants in a very big study as society gradually learns the answer.

Even if we accept that watching violence encourages violent behavior, at least in some people some of the time, an important question remains: what mechanism explains this effect? When we see violence on television and in video games, are we more likely to see the world as a dangerous place, where people are trying to hurt us? If so, the effect of media violence on aggression may indeed involve increased tendency toward anger. Alternatively, does media violence simply desensitize us to the idea of aggression, so that hitting or shooting another person does not seem like such a big deal? Do media presentations of violence teach us that aggression is a good way to get what we want?

To summarize the factors predisposing to anger and aggressiveness: People may vary in their predisposition to anger and aggression because of genetic factors and prenatal environment, but even the influence of those factors depends on later environment. The greatest probability of violence occurs in people from a troubled family in a violent neighborhood who also had a biological predisposition. Exposure to violence in the media increases the risk of aggressive behavior; again, the influence is probably greater in those who were already predisposed for other reasons.

APPLICATION: VIOLENCE PREVENTION

As human technology has developed the ability to make stronger and stronger weapons, the need for violence control has increased accordingly. Many treaties among nations deal with preventing war: "We promise we won't attack you if you promise you won't attack us." "We won't build any more nuclear weapons if you won't either." Unfortunately, many of these treaties are broken. Within a country, a major focus of laws is to deter or punish violent acts. As with international treaties, laws are not always effective, in part because anger is behind so much of the violence. The importance of finding better ways to control anger and aggression could hardly be overstated.

Reconciliation

People who have been quarreling often make an effort to heal the rift afterward. **Reconciliation** is an attempt to restore friendship after a fight and prevent further hostility. For decades, psychologists overlooked reconciliation because so much of the research on aggression examined birds and rodents (which are easy to observe). Most species of birds and rodents have little to lose by driving a competitor out of their territory. Behavior is different among highly social animals such as chimpanzees: After a fight, they remain in a troop together, and neither they nor the other chimpanzees can afford to tolerate continual fighting. After a fight, they spend much time together, hug, hold hands, and so forth. If they don't do so at first, the other troop members push them together. Chimpanzees who have gone through this reconciliation ceremony become less likely to fight in the future (de Waal, 2000). People do the same. With relatives, coworkers, or anyone else you need to deal with repeatedly, you can't afford constant hostility. After a fight, you look for ways to restore harmony.

Controlling Childhood Aggressive Behavior

Most adults who get angry find a way to handle the situation without actually hitting each other. Children, especially little boys, fight more frequently, as you may remember from your own childhood. Most childhood squabbles are minor. A few shootings in schools have been widely publicized, but in general, schools are relatively safe places (Mulvey & Cauffman, 2001).

Although very few fights in school are lethal, many are demoralizing and degrading to the victims. Some children bully others mercilessly. One of the strongest predictors of bullying is simply being larger and stronger than others in early childhood. Apparently some children learn very young that they can push others around, and they get in the habit of doing so. Bullying at age 11 depends more on how large a boy was at age three than how large he is at at the time (Raine, Reynolds, Venables, Mednick, & Farrington, 1998). Most children are consistent over the years in whether they are bullies, victims, or a bit of both (Camodeca, Goossens, Terwogt, & Schuengel, 2002).

Bullies are seldom venting anger. More often, they are using their power for gain or entertainment—what we called instrumental aggression. In fact, researchers who interviewed young bullies found that the bullies enjoyed tormenting other children. They took another child's money or food, forced her to eat grass, and did whatever else amused them. The best way to stop the bullying was to increase adult supervision and enforce rules—that is, to make sure the child did not get away with it (Olweus, 1995).

Controlling Anger in Adulthood

We mentioned early in the chapter that anger can be constructive, by communicating your limits to another person in a close relationship or negotiation. However, displays of anger must be controlled in order to be effective. A strong display of anger may simply drive someone away, temporarily or permanently. The old saying, "Once bitten, twice shy" captures the idea that a brief flare-up of anger produces emotional scars that heal slowly. People who feel frequent anger have few friends and feel dissatisfied with their own lives (Robinson, Vargas, Tamir, & Solberg, 2004). Uncontrolled anger can also evoke aggression from the other person, escalating the conflict.

Anger management training refers to the methods therapists use to try to help people control their anger. Any therapy is most effective for people who are sincerely trying to change, and that statement is especially true for anger control. Getting people committed to controlling their anger is a major first step. Effective progress is likely by means of the following procedures, which are classed as cognitive-behavioral therapy (Dahlen & Deffenbacher, 2001). Well-controlled experimental studies have demonstrated significant benefits for many people (Ireland, 2004), although the results have been disappointing with serious offenders (Howells et al., 2005).

Cognitive restructuring.   The person is taught to reinterpret events as less threatening or hostile, to replace anger-evoking thoughts with calmer ones. For example, if another driver pulls into your lane without signaling, the driver may have been thoughtless rather than deliberately insulting you. A cashier who gives you incorrect change may have miscounted rather than trying to cheat you. Cognitive restructuring is based on the research suggesting that anger is more likely when a person interprets an offense as intentional rather than accidental.

Social skills training. Conflict with other people is probably the major cause of anger, and one reason for conflict is poor communication. Therapists try to teach people to identify when they are starting to get angry, relax themselves, and calm down before speaking. They also try to get people to communicate their needs more clearly to others, so that the others can meet those needs and therefore provoke less anger. They help people practice social skills in real-life situations (Conduct Problems Prevention Research Group, 2002; Farmer, Compton, Burns, & Robertson, 2002).

Distraction. When someone is starting to get angry, a good strategy is to think about something else, such as something pleasant or amusing (Wilde, 2001). In one experiment, also discussed in Chapter 6, people first were asked to recall an emotionally painful experience of feeling rejected. Those who were asked to focus on remembering how they felt reacted with hostility, but those who were asked to focus on what they remembered of the setting were much less upset (Ayduk, Mischel, & Downey, 2002). The idea is to get people to focus on the facts of the situation, not their own distress.

Exposure therapy. A common treatment for phobia is called systematic desensitization: Someone with a fear of something is gradually exposed to that object while remaining relaxed. The same procedure can be applied to someone with extreme anger. The person is told to relax and then is gradually exposed to the kinds of events or insults that would usually provoke anger. The person practices remaining calm in the presence of these insults (Grodnitzky & Tafrate, 2000).

Problem solving. Here the idea is very simple: People who can find a way to solve their problems have less cause to be angry. For example, children with anger problems benefit from academic tutoring.

Other kinds of therapy. Discussing problems of chronic aggression can help, but not always. In particular, group therapy sometimes backfires. People with anxiety problems or substance-abuse problems often profit by meeting with other people with similar problems. However, bringing together a group of violent individuals sometimes aggravates the problem. In one study, groups of seven or eight adolescents with a history of aggression and delinquency were brought together for 12 weekly meetings, in which they discussed their problems and set goals for prosocial behaviors. Over the next year, these participants showed an *increase* in delinquent behaviors, compared to a no-treatment control group (Poulin, Dishion, & Burraston, 2001). Evidently, associating with an all-delinquent group provided bad role models and did more harm than good.

DISGUST

The term *disgust* is literally *dis*, meaning the opposite of, and *gust*, meaning taste or the pleasure of tasting (as in "gusto"). However, disgust is not simply unpleasant taste. If you dislike the taste of spinach, you probably wouldn't call it disgusting. You would not object to seeing someone else eating it, and if you found a tiny piece of spinach mixed into your stew, you might remove the spinach but you would continue eating the stew. In contrast, imagine how you would feel if you found a tiny piece of rat fur in your stew. Your reaction would be stronger and more emotional.

Disgust has been defined as "revulsion at the prospect of oral incorporation of offensive objects" (Rozin & Fallon, 1987). Disgust entails a desire to stay away from something, especially to keep it out of your mouth, but it is also a rejection of the mere thought of touching the object. The evolutionary value of disgust is obvious: Disgust at the prospect of eating feces or rotten meat—what has been called "core disgust"—protects our health. However, people also use the term *disgust* in abstract, sometimes culture-specific ways related to morality (Haidt, Rozin, McCauley, & Imada, 1997).

Is Disgust an Emotion?

Up to now, we have been taking it for granted that disgust is a kind of emotion. Is it?

Many researchers argue that it is. A prototypical facial expression of disgust is recognized throughout much of the world (Ekman et al., 1987), disgust is associated with specific appraisals (Lazarus, 1991; Scherer, 1997), and strong disgust may evoke feelings of physical nausea. Still, some researchers doubt that disgust is an emotion. Edward Royzman and John Sabini (2001) have argued that disgust is substantially different from fear and anger, the prototypical emotions. According to Royzman and Sabini, one important feature of anxiety and anger is that they generate many and varied responses, depending on the circumstances. In contrast, the reaction to disgust is limited: You make a facial expression, you turn away from the offending object, and you refuse to touch or taste it.

Recall also the emphasis on cognitive appraisal in our definitions of emotion from Chapter 1. Another distinction Royzman and Sabini raised is that disgust is not as "cognitively penetrable" than some other emotions. That is, you can sometimes talk someone out of anger or fear, just by getting the person to think about the situation differently. If we accept "cognitive penetrability" as a criterion, we can ask whether thinking differently about cockroaches, rats, feces, or other prototypical elicitors could decrease the disgust they evoke. If not, then perhaps we should not consider disgust to be an emotion. Not much research is available on this point, but it is admittedly difficult to think your way into eating a bowl of soup that just held a cockroach.

Finally, Royzman and Sabini's main point is that emotions can be triggered by abstract information. For example, a spot on a mammogram can evoke fear by suggesting possible breast cancer. An insulting word can evoke anger. In these cases, the emotion pertains to what the information *means*, not the event itself. Disgust, Royzman and Sabini argue, is provoked by a specific stimulus, not by an abstract representation. Are they right or wrong? We need to distinguish two questions. First, do you agree that the ability to elicit a state through abstract appraisal is a good criterion for calling it a "true emotion"? Second, is it true that abstract information cannot evoke disgust?

What Elicits Disgust?

Although the "core" of disgust is bad taste or offensive smell, we extend our rejection to the sight or mere thought of such objects as insects, bloody body parts, and dead bodies. Consider this quote: "Served on toast points, stag beetle larvae are superb. They have a nutty flavor. The head capsules impart a subtle crunchy touch, while the thorax and abdomen have a delicately chewy texture" (Boyle, 1992, p.101). Now that you know how good they taste, would you like to try them? If you find the idea of eating insects repulsive, the taste doesn't matter. However, this reaction depends on culture. In some cultures people grow up accustomed to eating insects—a clear sign that at least some level of interpretation is needed for disgust, rather than some kind of reflex.

Similarly, our reactions to a smell depend mainly on what we think it is, not its sensory quality. Suppose someone asks you to close your eyes and smell a jar containing "a strong cheese." You rate the smell as moderately pleasant. Then you are told, "Oops, I think that jar was mislabeled. It was vomit, not cheese." Now you think it smells horrible. Then the person says, "Oh, no, I'm sorry, I was right the first time. It really was cheese after all." Now you are not sure what to believe. Moreover, you don't know whether you like the smell or not (Rozin & Fallon, 1987).

Suppose a researcher dunks a cockroach in apple juice and asks you whether you would be willing to drink it (see Figure 8.8). Would you? If not, why not? What if someone assures you that the cockroach was carefully sterilized and has no germs? Presumably you still don't want to drink the juice. Why not? No matter how sterile, it is still a cockroach. You are revolted by the very idea of eating or drinking anything that was once in contact with a cockroach (Rozin, Millman, & Nemeroff, 1986).

Similarly, many other disgust experiences depend on the thought of the object, not its sensory qualities or objective implications for health. Suppose someone asks you to put a piece of rubber into your mouth. As you are about to agree to do it, you notice that the rubber is shaped and colored like vomit, from

Photos courtesy of Dr. Paul Rozin

FIGURE 8.8 After you had seen a cockroach placed into a cup of apple juice, how thoroughly would you insist on washing the cup before you would drink from it?

a novelty store (Figure 8.9). Would you still put it into your mouth? Would you drink water from a new, never-been-used toilet bowl? Suppose you are eating something and someone asks you to spit it out onto a plate and look at it. Now could you put it back in your mouth? In each of these cases, we find something disgusting because of the idea, not actual danger (Rozin & Fallon, 1987).

Paul Rozin and his colleagues have noted that nearly everything that we find disgusting is animal in nature—specific animals such as cockroaches and

spiders, body parts such as intestines, body excretions such as feces, dead bodies, and unsavory sexual acts such as incest. Objects such as chocolate fudge or a piece of rubber can be disgusting if they remind us of a disgusting animal or animal part. Rozin has suggested that an item becomes disgusting if it reminds us of our animal nature (Rozin & Fallon, 1987; Rozin, Lowery, et al., 1999). That is, we like to think of ourselves as noble, clean, and pure, and the sight of intestines, feces, or blood reminds us of the most unclean aspects of our existence. Animals in general evoke disgust when they urinate and defecate in public, have sex in public, and in other ways do the things that we like to hide about ourselves.

Disgust and "Magical" or superstitious thinking. Disgust shows the fascinating property of **contagion**, the idea of "once in contact, always in contact." For example, if a cockroach crawls over your food, you might find the food disgusting, even after the cockroach is gone. That idea is part of a type of thinking called "sympathetic magic" (Rozin, Millman, & Nemeroff, 1986). Similarly, you probably would not want to wear a shirt that someone wore while committing a murder, or a hat previously worn by Adolf Hitler or Osama bin Laden. Washing the garment repeatedly does not help; its history fouls it forever.

A second principle of sympathetic magic, also prominent in disgust, is **similarity**, the idea that if something looks similar, we treat it similarly. Recall that many people refuse to put into their mouths a piece of rubber that looked like vomit. People know they are behaving irrationally, but they feel an aversion to tasting something that reminds them of a disgusting object (Rozin, Millman, & Nemeroff, 1986). These tendencies relate to an idea prevalent in many cultures, that "you are what you eat" in the literal sense that you take on characteristics of the objects you eat. That belief does contain a little truth: If you eat garlic, you temporarily smell of garlic. People in many cultures go further, assuming that if you eat a plant that grew fast, you yourself will become quicker, and if you eat the meat of a hedgehog, you will become slow and timid.

© Michael Newman/Photo Edit

FIGURE 8.9 Although this object is shaped and colored to look like vomit, it is actually just rubber. Would you be willing to put it into your mouth?

We "educated" people have outgrown those superstitions, right? Maybe not. Nemeroff and Rozin (1989) asked two groups of American college students to read descriptions of the "Chandoran" people. The descriptions were the same except that in one version the Chandorans ate wild boar and hunted marine turtles for their shells; in the other version they ate marine turtles and hunted wild boar for their tusks. The students were asked to describe their perceptions of the Chandorans. In comparison to students who thought the Chandorans ate turtles, those who thought they ate wild boar rated them as more irritable, excitable, loud, unreliable, fast-moving, bearded, and aggressive. The participants seemed to assume that the Chandorans had personality characteristics associated with their most common food.

Given all of these findings, are Royzman and Sabini (2001) correct in saying that we cannot feel disgust in response to an abstract idea? It depends in part on what one means by "abstract." It appears that one can become disgusted by the idea of feces, or by a plastic representation of feces, but is that the same as seeing a spot on a mammogram and becoming afraid? This may seem like splitting hairs, but such questions have significance for researchers studying emotion. We rely on words such as "emotion" and "disgust" to convey our ideas and research findings. Disagreements about what these and other words mean can cause tremendous confusion and slow down progress in understanding the human experience. Although these disagreements can be frustrating, they are important to hash out, and they usually resolve only with time and extensive research.

The Biology of Disgust

The physiological profile associated with disgust is complicated, and still not completely understood. Although some studies find that disgust is associated with increased heart rate, skin conductance, and other signs of sympathetic arousal, other studies associated disgust with *decreased* heart rate, a sign of parasympathetic nervous system activity. As a result, meta-analysis of the various studies does not show any consistent difference of disgust from a control condition (Cacioppo et al., 2000). We can extrapolate likely features of disgust from nausea, typically felt to a mild degree, although extremely disgusted people occasionally do vomit. Nausea includes decreased heart rate and blood pressure, increased salivation and sweating, and abrupt contraction of the stomach muscles, a pattern that is geared toward evacuating dangerous contents from the stomach. It may be that different studies have examined different phases of the disgust response. If you perceive something revolting, you try to get away from it. This would explain a sympathetic response. If it's too late and you've already consumed the offending substance, you should get it out of your system fast, perhaps accounting for some parasympathetic response. However, more research is needed to test these hypotheses explicitly.

We can learn to feel disgust toward certain foods, just as we can learn new fears or new people to love, and physical nausea is part of this process. Even if a food tastes delicious, people develop a disgust response to it if they vomit after eating it, just once, especially if it was an unfamiliar food (Logue, 1985). It's as though our bodies immediately label a food "dangerous" after a single experience with contamination (Rozin & Kalat, 1971). One of us (MNS) used to love escargot, but after a single, miserable experience can no longer even be at a table where they are served.

In one study using fMRI methods, researchers found that viewing expressions of disgust strongly activated a brain area called the anterior insular cortex, or simply the insula (M. L. Phillips et al., 1997). We introduced this area of the brain in Chapter 5. Your insular cortex responds if you view either disgusting photos or pictures of other people who are feeling disgust (Wicker et al., 2003). The link between the insular cortex and disgust is interesting because the insular cortex is also the primary receptive area of the cortex for the sense of taste, and disgust is literally bad taste. Evidence on this issue is, however, mixed. One young man with damage limited to the insular cortex still described certain objects as "disgusting," such as a dirty toilet, suggesting that he could experience disgust without activity in that brain area. But using the term *disgust* is not necessarily the same as feeling disgust. When this patient looked at photographs of facial expressions of disgust, or listened to retching sounds, he did not recognize them as indications of disgust (Calder, Keane, Manes, Antoun, & Young, 2000). That impairment suggests that the insular cortex may be important for the full experience of disgust.

However, another study using fMRI found that the insular cortex showed increased activity not only when people looked at disgusting pictures (vomit, maggots, dirty toilet, a man eating a grasshopper), but also when they looked at frightening pictures (lions, pistols, fire, car accidents). The amygdala also responded strongly to both kinds of pictures (Schienle et al., 2002). As we noted in Chapter 5, the insular cortex becomes more active when people are aware of their visceral sensations, such as heartbeat as well as gastric feelings. So the insular cortex is related to disgust, but perhaps also any emotions involving the perception of physical change.

Core Versus Moral Disgust

Revulsion at the thought of some unacceptable food is "primary" disgust, or "core" disgust (Haidt, McCauley, & Rozin, 1994). However, people use the term *disgust* more broadly. To map the full meaning of the term, Haidt and colleagues began by asking 20 people to describe all the intensely disgusting experiences they could remember. The researchers then grouped those experiences into these categories:

- Bad-tasting foods
- Body products such as feces, urine, and nose mucus
- Unacceptable sexual acts, such as incest
- Gore, surgery, and other exposure of the inner body parts
- Socio-moral violations such as Nazis, drunk drivers, hypocrites, and ambulance-chasing lawyers
- Insects, spiders, snakes, and other repulsive animals

- Dirt and germs
- Contact with dead bodies

Are all these experiences of disgust similar? If disgust is a single kind of experience, people who feel strong disgust at one kind of item should also feel strong disgust at another. The researchers did find that pattern, with this exception: Disgust ratings about drunk drivers, hypocrites, and the other "socio-moral violations" did not correlate highly with any of the other events (Haidt et al., 1994). That is, someone who called drunk drivers "very disgusting" was not more likely than other people to consider insects, gore, dead bodies, or any of the other items highly disgusting. As many others have pointed out, English-speaking people use the term *disgust* loosely (Royzman & Sabini, 2001; Woody & Teachman, 2000). When we say we are "disgusted" by some immoral act, perhaps we should use the term anger or contempt (Marzillier & Davey, 2004). Or perhaps we should distinguish two types of disgust, **core disgust** that relates to the idea of putting something into your mouth, and **moral disgust** that relates to violations of right and wrong. The two experiences are not the same, but they do overlap. For example, people who easily experience disgust, including core disgust, are more likely than other people to feel extreme antipathy toward criminal behavior. They are more likely than average to vote "guilty" if they are on a mock jury (Jones & Fitness, 2008).

Disgust: Development and Individual Differences

Disgust develops gradually and becomes stronger in some people than others. Young children, up to about age one to one-and-a-half years, will put almost anything into their mouths, and unless it tastes bad, they will chew it and swallow it (Rozin, Hammer, Oster, Horowitz, & Marmora, 1986). As children grow older, they begin to reject foods they believe might be dangerous, and still later reject foods because of the idea of contamination. Suppose you pour a fresh glass of apple juice. Before a child has a chance to drink it, you drop a small piece of dog feces into the apple juice. Will the child drink the apple juice? Even preschool children generally refuse; rejection of feces is probably the first real disgust. (How it develops is an interesting unresolved issue. Do toddlers learn the disgust on their own or from their parents?) Assuming the child refuses apple juice with dog feces in it, what happens after you spoon out the dog feces?

Children less than seven years old generally agree to drink the juice (no, researchers don't let them actually drink it). Slightly older children would not drink that apple juice, but they would accept it if you pour out the apple juice and refill the glass with new apple juice. Still older children insist that you first wash the glass before refilling it. Some adults insist on throwing the glass away (Rozin, Fallon, & Augustoni-Ziskind, 1985).

Expressions of disgust correlate fairly highly (+.45) with the personality trait *neuroticism* (Druschel & Sherman, 1999). That term, easily misunderstood, does not mean mental illness; it refers to a tendency to experience unpleasant emotions relatively easily. In other words, people prone to disgust are also prone to sadness and anxiety. Disgust also shows a negative correlation (−.28) with the personality trait *openness to experience*, the tendency to explore new opportunities, such as trying new or unusual types of foods, art, music, literature, and so forth (Druschel & Sherman, 1999).

"Unlearning" Disgust

If you want to overcome a feeling of disgust, how could you do it? Research on this topic is slim, but here are a few suggestions (Rozin & Fallon, 1987):

- Inhibit yourself from making the facial expression of disgust.

- Change your concept of the object. For example, tell yourself, "This isn't what I thought it was."

- Expose yourself gradually and repeatedly to the disgusting object. Visitors to a foreign country sometimes find certain food items disgusting, but after eating them a few times, at first just in tiny amounts, they begin to find them acceptable. Plumbers and sewage disposal workers manage to overcome their disgust at human waste products.

- When appropriate, lower the psychological boundary between "self" and "other." We generally find our own body secretions and waste products less disgusting than those of others. Lovers come to accept each other's secretions and smells, and parents change their infants' diapers. In effect, they treat the other person as an extension of the self.

SUMMARY

As we consider some specific emotions, a couple of common themes emerge. One theme is that research requires good measurement, and measurement is best when we use a variety of methods. A second theme is that we need to distinguish among different kinds of emotion at different time scales. Just as we distinguish between short-term fear and long-term anxiety, it helps to distinguish among anger over a particular event, longer-term "crankiness," and proneness to anger or aggression as a lifelong personality trait. A third theme is that the consequences of any emotion depend on other emotions that might be present at the same time.

For example, whether anger leads to aggressive behavior depends partly on how much fear someone feels about the possible consequences. Similarly, disgust often combines with fear.

Anger stands out from other emotions because of its social impact. If you are sad or fearful, your emotions are a problem for you and your family and friends but not of great concern to most other people. Angry people, however, are dangerous to everyone, and we need to learn how to predict and control violent behavior. To control violence, we can look to decreasing the causes of people's anger, but we need also to strengthen inhibitions against violence.

KEY TERMS

anger: the emotional state associated with feeling injured or offended, and with a desire to threaten or hurt the person who offended you (p. 176)

Cognitive-Neoassociationistic (CNA) Model of Anger Generation: theory that anger and reactive aggression are enhanced by any unpleasant event or aversive condition (p. 179)

contagion: (as a principle of sympathetic magic) the idea of "once in contact, always in contact" (p. 197)

contempt: emotional reaction to a violation of community standards (p. 176)

core disgust: emotional response to an object that threatens your physical purity, such as feces, rotting food, or unclean animals (p. 199)

frustration-aggression hypothesis: proposal that anything that interferes with one's ability to obtain some expected gratification leads to aggressive behavior (p. 178)

hostile aggression: harmful behavior motivated by anger and the events that preceded it (p. 184)

instrumental aggression: harmful or threatening behavior used purely as a way to obtain something or to achieve some end (p. 184)

moral disgust: experience relating to violations of right and wrong (p. 199)

reconciliation: an attempt to restore friendship after a fight (physical or verbal), and to prevent further hostility (p. 193)

resilience: the ability of people to overcome the effects of extremely unfavorable environments (p. 192)

similarity: (as a principle of sympathetic magic) the idea that if something looks similar, we treat it similarly (p. 197)

state: a temporary experience; in the context of emotion, the experience of an emotion in the present moment (p. 182)

testosterone: steroid hormone more common in males than females, important for male sex-related behaviors (p. 190)

themed dot-probe task: Task in which two words (one of which might be aggressive) flash briefly on the screen, one above the other. Then a dot appears in the same position as one of them, and the person must press a key as quickly as possible to indicate whether the dot appeared in the upper or lower position. (p. 185)

trait: a long-term characteristic of a person; in the context of emotion, one's overall frequency and/or intensity of certain emotional states (p. 182)

visual search task: Task in which a target word appears briefly in the center of the screen, surrounded by three other words. Then the target word and three new words appear, and the task is to locate the target word. (p. 185)

THOUGHT QUESTIONS

1. Researchers have found that people express anger more often at home than when they are at work (Bongard & al'Absi, 2003). Can you suggest an explanation? Might this vary by culture?

2. Compare the Cognitive-Neoassociationistic Model to the James-Lange theory presented in Chapter 1. Are they compatible or contradictory?

3. Do you agree with Royzman and Sabini that one criterion for an emotion is that an emotion can be elicited by abstract information? Recall the discussion of "cognitive penetrability" of emotions. Can you think of anything you could say that would decrease someone's disgust at the idea of, say, eating a cockroach?

SUGGESTIONS FOR FURTHER READING

Beck, A. T. (1999). *Prisoners of Hate: The Cognitive Basis of Anger, Hostility, and Violence*. New York: Harper Collins. Aaron Beck is best known for his research on the cognitive factors in depression; in this book he applies principles of cognitive appraisal to research on anger and violence.

Goldstein, J. H., Ed. (1998). *Why We Watch: The Attractions of Violent Entertainment*. New York: Oxford University Press. In this collection of essays, several mass media researchers offer their thoughts on why violence and aggression are so prominent in human entertainment.

Rozin, P., Lowery, L., Imada, S., & Haidt, J. (1999). "The CAD Triad Hypothesis: A Mapping between Three Moral Emotions (Contempt, Anger, Disgust) and Three Moral Codes (Community, Autonomy, Divinity)." *Journal of Personality and Social Psychology*, 76, 574–586. An important article describing the distinctions among anger, disgust, and contempt.

9

Love

What is love? This question has proved notoriously difficult for emotion researchers (as well as everyone else), and for good reason. In the English language, the word "love" refers to the way you feel toward your romantic partner, parents, children, other family members, close friends, pets, chocolate, a day at the beach, television shows, music, great restaurants, a favorite sweater, and occasionally (we hope) your classes. Our use of the single word *love* for all these targets implies some important similarity among them. Yes, they do have similarities, but the differences are huge also. Certainly the love you feel toward your parents is not the same as love you feel toward a romantic partner, and neither of them is like love of really good Thai food.

To make things even more confusing, love felt for any one target may itself be complex. For example, over the course of a romantic relationship you might feel concern, gratitude, dependence, physical attraction, warmth, and a number of other feelings toward your partner. Which of these are most prominent varies from person to person and from time to time. One couple may be overwhelmed by physical passion, whereas another emphasizes the trust and emotional intimacy they share. No wonder so many people ask "how will I know when I'm *really* in love?" And it is no wonder that the answers tend to be vague and unsatisfying.

In this chapter we explore the research social scientists have produced on love and other emotions in close relationships. We will discuss some of the ways researchers have talked about love, theories about different types of love, biological and behavioral aspects of love, and the role of love in marriage. We will also talk about the ways in which people in close relationships "read" each other's emotions. The goal is not to tell you how to recognize "true love." We didn't set that goal because we knew we couldn't achieve it! We do hope to convey a sense of the issues emotion researchers wrestle with when they approach these important questions.

IS LOVE AN EMOTION?

Before we start analyzing love as an emotion: Is it an emotion at all? If you ask people to write a list of emotions, one of their most common responses is "love" (Fehr & Russell, 1984; Shaver, Schwartz, Kirson, & O'Connor, 1987). However, when psychologists list the "basic" emotions, most do not include love. Love can be an emotional experience without being "an" emotion.

Instead of considering love an emotion, many psychologists consider it an **attitude**—a combination of beliefs, feelings, and behaviors directed toward a person, object, or category (e.g., Rubin, 1970). Attitudes resemble emotions in that they include cognition, feeling, and behavior aspects, but with attitudes, we tend to emphasize the cognitive aspect, and with emotions, the feeling aspect. Also, emotions (or at least the capacity to feel emotions) are functional (useful), whereas an attitude may or may not be. Perhaps the most important distinction is that attitudes are long-lasting, whereas emotions may be brief states. To consider love as an attitude emphasizes that you always wish the best for those whom you love, even in moments when your emotions are not intense.

Others have described love, especially romantic love, as a **script**, or culturally learned set of expectations about events, thoughts, feelings, and behaviors (e.g., Skolnick, 1978). As we noted in Chapter 3, a simple American script for romantic love goes something like, "They met, and it was love at first sight. There would never be another girl (boy) for him (her). No one could come between them. They overcame obstacles and lived happily ever after" (Swidler, 1991). Even if you don't accept that script, you probably accept some other script—some set of assumptions about what happens when people are in love. This script likely includes the experience of certain emotions, but also goes beyond emotions to aspects of the situation and appropriate behaviors.

Both the attitude approach and the script approach attempt to account for the complex feelings of people in close relationships. Both approaches conclude that the whole package of love is too complex to reflect a single "basic" emotion. However, some researchers have asked whether the many different types of love have a common theme.

THE PROTOTYPE APPROACH TO LOVE

Rather than focusing on romantic love, Beverly Fehr and James Russell (1991) used a different approach to untangling the web of relationships, thoughts, feelings, and behaviors associated with the word "love." They proposed that love (like other emotions) is best thought of as a **prototype**—a set of characteristics that describes the ideal example of some category, but that may not be held by every member of that category. Instead of asking what characteristics were necessary to call something love, Fehr and Russell thus asked what the "best examples" of love are, and what those examples have in common.

Fehr and Russell asked their participants to list as many types of love as they could think of, and then the researchers examined which types were listed most often. Although some participants did list love of food, country, music and art, and material things, the most commonly mentioned examples were close relationships—love for parents, children, family members, romantic partners, and very close friends. When Fehr and Russell asked another set of participants to rate how "prototypical" twenty different kinds of love were, again people said the best examples were love for family, romantic partners, and close friends (See Table 9.1).

What do these "best examples" of love have in common? Fehr and Russell asked a third group of participants to rate the prototypicality of each of the 20 types of love listed in Table 9.1, and then asked how natural twenty statements were in describing each type. For example, one statement was "_____ is very painful if not reciprocated." Participants had to rate different versions of each sentence, such as "maternal love is very painful if not reciprocated" and "romantic love is very painful if not reciprocated." People generally reported that the kinds of love they considered most prototypical—such as romantic love—were also the kinds that fit

TABLE 9.1   Although the term "love" describes people's feelings toward many kinds of targets, American participants agree that some kinds of love are more "love-like" than others. This table shows how prototypically love-like Fehr and Russel's (1991) participants considered 20 different types of love.

Type of Love	Prototypicality
Maternal love	5.39
Parental love	5.22
Friendship	4.96
Sisterly love	4.84
Romantic love	4.76
Brotherly love	4.74
Familial love	4.74
Sibling love	4.73
Affection	4.60
Committed love	4.47
Love for humanity	4.42
Spiritual love	4.27
Passionate love	4.00
Platonic love	3.98
Self-love	3.79
Sexual love	3.76
Patriotic love	3.21
Love of work	3.14
Puppy love	2.98
Infatuation	2.42

SOURCE: From "Concept of Emotion Viewed From a Prototype Perspective," by B. Fehr and J. A. Russell, in *Journal of Experimental Psychology: General*, 113, pp. 464–486. Reprinted with permission of Dr. Beverly Fehr.

best with certain statements. For example, consider the statement "love is a giving process, understanding the other, and realizing the other's faults." Clearly, that statement fits romantic love, and to a large extent love between parent and child, but it fits only awkwardly with love of country and not at all with love of chocolate. Similarly, romantic love, parent-child love, and other prototypical examples of love fit well with statements like, "commitment and caring are important components of love," and "love has to be worked at and strived for to truly be achieved."

This study has helped emotion researchers to narrow their focus a bit. People may talk casually about loving material things, but prototypical love is mainly experienced in the context of close relationships. Prototypical love involves commitment to someone else, a willingness to give even under difficult circumstances. Love also includes knowing someone for who they really are, accepting their faults as well as their strengths.

This approach suggests that, if love is an emotion, its function has to do with building and maintaining close relationships. In Chapter 2 we noted the distinction between intrapersonal functions of emotion—the way an emotion coordinates cognitive, physiological, and behavioral responses within an individual, and social functions that facilitate the development of relationships between people. Love for romantic partners, relatives, and close friends may help encourage commitment to them, so that our emotions make it natural to work together as a team. But the prototype approach is not necessarily about identifying basic emotions in terms of evolutionary function. Rather, it emphasizes the meaning speakers of a particular language ascribe to a particular word. Other researchers have taken a more explicit evolutionary approach to love.

THREE TYPES OF LOVE?: BOWLBY AND THE "AFFECTIONAL BONDS"

Fehr and Russell's research emphasized the features that prototypical kinds of love have in common. Another approach is to try to identify qualitatively different types of love that account for our broad use of this English-language term. John Bowlby, who spent his career carefully observing infants and their parents, agreed that emotions in close relationships are an important part of our evolutionary heritage. Based on his observations Bowlby described three distinct "behavioral programs" that he considered the biological foundations of bonding within families (Bowlby, 1979): attachment, caregiving, and sex. He did not call these behavioral programs emotions, but rather described them as complex social instincts. Bowlby was a developmental psychologist interested in the evolutionary basis of parent-child interactions. As a result, much the research described in this section involves finding the correlates of certain kinds of behaviors (like calling for a parent when left alone, or comforting a crying child), rather than finding the correlates of emotional experience. According to Bowlby, however, each of these behavioral programs includes an important, and distinct, emotional component. As we shall see, Bowlby's typology of behavioral programs in close relationships suggests distinctions among three kinds of love (Shaver, Morgan, & Wu, 1996).

Love as Attachment to Parents and Other Caregivers

Most people's first experience of love is for their parents—the people who care for and nurture us on a daily basis from the first moments of life. According to Bowlby, the behavioral program that facilitates this kind of love is also the first to emerge. Newborn infants are not terribly selective about the people with whom they interact. Things change as soon as infants can move around independently, and thus risk getting separated from those who protect and care for them. At this point infants develop the capacity to form selective emotional bonds with a few special people. Emotions associated with the attachment system make it pleasurable for infants to be close to their parents, and prompt cries of distress when caregivers leave or can't be found. A baby who would lie calmly in anyone's arms just a few weeks earlier suddenly becomes hysterical when Mom leaves the room. Rather than playing with every new object or person it encounters, the infant constantly checks with a few people, to see if they're around and paying attention. Developmental psychologists refer to this new pattern of behavior as **attachment**—a long-lasting emotional bond between the individual and a few regular caregivers, producing a desire to be near that person (and

distress when separated), a tendency to turn to that person when threatened, and a sense of being supported in exploring new things.

Attachment in infants and toddlers is usually observed in a research paradigm called the **strange situation** (Ainsworth, 1979). An infant and parent enter a toy-filled room and the infant is allowed to play. A stranger then enters the room. After a couple of minutes the parent leaves the room, and then returns. Next both the stranger and the parent leave the room, the stranger returns alone, and finally the parent returns. All this coming and going may sound tedious, but it creates a good scenario for observing attachment-related emotional behavior. A "securely attached" infant will typically protest when the parent leaves the room, show joy when the parent returns, and "check in" with the parent frequently while playing.

Because the caregiver is an agent in this equation, however, an infant's most effective attachment behavior depends on how the caregiver responds (Isabella & Belsky, 1991). Not all infants show "secure" attachment. If a caregiver is smothering, ignoring the infant's need to explore on its own or decide when to rest, the infant may become especially uncomfortable with being alone, yet need to push away in order to gain some space. These infants, with an "anxious" attachment style, become extremely upset when the caregiver leaves, and simultaneously cling to the caregiver and push her away when she returns. With a distant, rejecting caregiver, an infant may not show much distress when the caregiver leaves or returns. Infants with this "avoidant" attachment style pay little attention to the caregiver when present, and cry when she leaves, but do not go for comfort when the caregiver returns. Thus, intrusive, pushy caregivers are more likely to have anxiously attached infants, and unresponsive caregivers to have avoidant infants.

How do infants even decide who their caregivers are? Sure, they might recognize mom's smell or her voice right after birth, and dad is probably the guy who's around most often, but what about other people? This is an important question—if we can learn what cues infants use to select attachment figures, we can see whether these same cues predict attachment in other kinds of close relationships. Ruth Feldman (2007) has emphasized the importance of synchrony between two individuals' behaviors as a possible trigger for the attachment system. Newborn infants experience alternating periods of alertness and withdrawal. Mothers typically try to interact with their infants when they become alert, but let them rest at other times. Newborns are especially attuned to this contingent responding, and become particularly interested in mothers who are sensitive to their cues for play versus quiet (Feldman & Eidelman, 2007). By the time infants are three months old they contribute to behavioral synchrony as well, matching facial expressions and turn-taking with vocalizations. One study found that greater behavioral synchrony between the infant and its father predicted more secure attachment (Feldman, 2003), although this relationship was not observed for mothers.

So far we have talked about attachment as a way that an infant relates to its caregivers over time—more like an attitude than an emotion. The English language does not really have a single emotion word that applies specifically to feelings of love for caregivers. However, the Japanese word **amae** comes close. Recall from Chapter 3 that *amae* describes the feeling of pleasurable dependence on another person, like the feeling an infant has toward its mother (Morsbach & Tyler, 1986). According to Takeo Doi (1973), the experience of *amae* begins around six months of age, the same time frame as for attachment. The emotion re-creates a sense of oneness with Mom, even as the child's developmental needs lead to increased levels of separation.

This is all well and good when talking about infants and small children, but do adults ever experience *amae*? Imagine having a terrible case of the flu, being barely able to move from your bed, and having a friend or a romantic partner go to the store and get your medicine, bring you hot soup, make you tea, turn on your favorite television show, and throw away the used facial tissues that are piling up nearby. In this situation you might feel *amae* toward your kindly caregiver. Although *amae* is often referred to as a "Japanese" emotion, Doi himself describes it as "a psychological phenomenon that is basically common to mankind" (Doi, 1973, p. 28).

If *amae* is universal, why is there a word for it in Japanese, and none in English? Recall from Chapter 3 the distinction between hyper-cognized emotions, which play important roles in society and are likely to have their own vocabulary, and hypo-cognized emotions, which are discouraged and rarely discussed. In Japan, says Doi, the mother-infant relationship is considered an ideal to which all other relationships aspire, even in adulthood. As a result, Japanese seek the opportunity to *amaeru* (the verb form of *amae*) in many of their close relationships throughout their lives. By contrast, in the United States and similar countries we place such a high value on individual independence that we may deliberately avoid situations that would elicit *amae*. Think back to the flu scenario we described above. How would you feel in that situation? Some people relax and enjoy letting someone care for them. But many Americans are annoyed with this helpless role and uncomfortable troubling another person with their illness. For example, one study of American college students found that ratings of *amae*-related feelings such as "babied" and "relying" correlated only with self-reported experience of negative emotions, whereas Japanese students associated *amae*-related feelings with both positive and negative emotions (Kitayama, Markus, & Kurokawa, 2000).

Perhaps as a result, positive emotion associated with attachment has received relatively little attention from Western scientists. So little empirical research addresses the subject that we are unprepared to say whether attachment love has the qualities of a distinct emotion or not. As we shall see shortly, however, researchers have devoted a great deal of energy to the study of attachment in the context of adult romantic relationships, and the principles suggested by this research may help guide future studies of love for attachment figures.

Nurturant Love and the Caregiving System

Bowlby called the second of his three behavioral programs the **"caregiving" system**, which motivates parents to nurture and protect their offspring, especially while they are young and almost helpless. Throughout the mammalian class of animals, a parent's devotion to offspring is remarkably dependable. Like the attachment system, however, the caregiving system can be activated by a broader range of situations involving someone who is young, helpless, needy, or in distress.

Emotion researchers have described three emotion states that could be associated with activation of a caregiving system. **Sympathy** has been defined as concerned attention toward someone who is suffering (Eisenberg et al., 1989). **Compassion** often functions in a similar way, emphasizing that the recipient is in distress (Shiota et al., 2004). By comparison, **nurturant love** has been defined as an emotion elicited by cues of youth and vulnerability, which motivates caregiving intended to enhance the other's overall well-being (Brown & Amatea, 2000; Griskevicius, Shiota, & Neufeld, 2010).

Although emotion researchers sometimes use these three terms interchangeably, or at least fail to distinguish them clearly, the concepts differ in a subtle but important way. Sympathy and compassion, by definition, are always responses to a distressed person. Feeling sad on that person's behalf is how these responses begin. Both states can be contrasted with **personal distress**, or self-focused anxiety in the face of another's suffering. Nurturant love is not necessarily a response to distress. Because it can be evoked by something helpless or cute, it need not include the component of sadness.

These definitions suggest that sympathy, compassion, and nurturant love all motivate helping another person. Does personal, empathic distress, when faced with another's suffering, also predict helping? Nancy Eisenberg and her colleagues have addressed this question, contrasting the implications of sympathy and personal distress. Earlier studies had found that participants who reported feeling the most sympathy to another's suffering were the most likely to try to help (e.g., Batson et al., 1983; Fultz et al., 1986). In these studies, however, participants were given instructions designed to elicit sympathy or personal distress, or they were simply asked to report which emotion they felt. In either case, participants were likely to say what they thought was the "right thing," or do what was expected of a good person. If so, people might have been motivated by other people's opinions instead of their own feelings.

To get around this problem, Eisenberg measured actual helping behavior as well as other signs of emotion, such as facial expressions and autonomic nervous system changes. She used a multi-method approach: If one measure might have flaws, use several kinds of measures, and see if the same pattern of results emerges with each. If it does, you can feel more confident that the results were not the product of a particular measurement or an overlooked flaw in the experiment's design.

Eisenberg and her colleagues brought elementary-school-aged children and college students into the lab, and showed them a short local community news program (Eisenberg et al., 1989). Participants were told that the researchers were hired by a local television station to find out how people responded to news stories. The program showed a single mom and her two children in a hospital room, and described a car accident in which the two kids had been seriously injured. The mom talked about the kids' fears of falling behind in school, and about her own stressful feelings about supporting the household and still spending time at the hospital. As participants watched this program, experimenters videotaped the facial expressions and measured the heart rates of the participants.

After the news program, the experimenter gave the participants an envelope from "the professor in charge of this study." In the envelope was a letter from the mother portrayed in the news clip, asking for the participants' assistance, along with a note from the professor saying she had encouraged the mother to write the letter. Adult participants were asked to spend some time helping the mother with housework; child participants were asked to help collect the injured children's homework assignments during their own recess breaks. Then, the participants were left alone for a few minutes with a slip of paper. Adults could write the number of hours they were willing to help the mom; children could mark on a calendar the days they would collect homework.

As you've probably guessed, the "news story" was really designed by the researchers to see how people would respond to this opportunity to help.

What did they find? Eisenberg and colleagues split participants into "low helper" and "high helper" groups to see whether their heart rates, facial expressions, and self-reports of emotion were different. They found that high helpers' heart rates dropped when the segment showing the hospital scene began, whereas low helpers' heart rates tended to speed up. Also, high helpers tended to show more sadness (see the photograph in Figure 2.6, p. 46) and more concerned attention (leaning forward with the eyebrows contracted and lowered, as though concentrating) while watching the news story than low helpers. Expressions of personal distress (a mild version of the fear expression shown in Figure 2.9) were not associated with helping. In an interesting twist, facial expressions of sadness were associated with *both* self-reported sympathy and self-reported personal distress. That is, looking sad could mean "I'm sad for you," or "I'm sad that I have to watch this"!

In later studies Eisenberg and her colleagues have asked whether certain stable differences between people can help explain why some people respond to another's suffering with sympathy and aid, while others respond with personal distress. The ability to regulate one's own emotions may be very important here. Recall that sad expressions were associated with sympathy and personal distress, so both emotions seem to start with empathic sadness. In a study of children between four and eight years old, Eisenberg's team found that those who were high on "effortful control" (the ability to regulate one's attention and behavior) reported stronger sympathy to another's suffering, and less personal distress (Valiente, Eisenberg, Fabes, Shepard, Cumberland, & Losoya, 2004). In another study, Eisenberg's team found that high helping was predicted by greater respiratory sinus arrhythmia, the fluctuation in heart rate associated with breathing (Fabes, Eisenberg, & Eisenbud, 1993). In Chapter 4, we noted that this measure of parasympathetic nervous system activation has been linked to emotion regulation ability (e.g., Butler et al., 2006; Vasilev et al., 2009). So it may be that helping someone in distress is most likely when you empathize with that person's sadness,

but are able to regulate the emotion so it doesn't become overwhelming.

Is sympathy an emotion? On one hand, Eisenberg and colleagues' research has identified a facial display (concerned attention), physiological characteristics (decreased heart rate and higher heart rate variability), and behavior tendency (helping) that seem to cluster together in a way that sounds like an emotion. On the other hand, the studies relating effortful control to sympathy and helping suggest that sympathy may consist of well-regulated sadness, rather than being a separate "basic" emotion.

What about compassion and nurturant love? Although there is increasing interest in both of these emotions (Brown & Amatea, 2000; Davidson & Harrington, 2002; Griskevicius et al., 2010), they have not been the subject of much empirical research. The questions are many: Do sympathy, compassion, and nurturant love elicit the same facial expressions and nervous systems patterns? Do they feel different, and if so, how? Do people behave differently in situations eliciting these emotions, or does the helping behavior look the same either way? Far more research is needed to examine the extent to which these states overlap or are distinct.

Sexual Desire

Bowlby's third behavioral program, the **"sex" system**, relates to sexual interest in people who are likely to be good reproductive partners. Who are these people? Well, what constitutes a "turn on" does vary considerably from person to person (Morse & Gruzen, 1976), but most people, even across cultures, agree on a few features that enhance attractiveness (Buss, 1989; Cunningham et al., 1995). One of the most consistent is health. Other things being equal, healthy people are sexier than unhealthy people. In women, features such as long, healthy hair and clear, flushed skin are considered attractive, perhaps because hair and skin are quick to show signs of malnutrition or illness (Rushton, 2002). A waist-to-hip ratio around .70, in which the waist is somewhat smaller than the hips, is also considered most attractive for women in many cultures (Singh, 1993; Streeter & McBurney, 2003). Researchers have proposed that these proportions are ideal for conception and childbearing, suggesting both a healthy level of nutrition and hips wide enough to bear children without extreme risk. Waist-to-hip ratio is not the same thing as thinness—one can have wider hips than waist while being either slim or plump. Preference for overall body weight does not seem to be as universal as preferences for certain proportions—some cultures consider very thin women to be the most attractive, whereas others prefer rather heavy women (Marlowe & Wetsman, 2001; Tassinary & Hansen, 1998; Yu & Shepard, 1998).

Statistically "average" features are also attractive. For example, if you photograph many people with their faces in the same position, and then get a computer to average the faces, most observers rate the resulting average as a very attractive face (Langlois & Roggman, 1990; Langlois, Roggman, & Musselman, 1994). Why? Average features are familiar, so they may make us feel comfortable. They also represent genes that have succeeded in past generations. A nose, mouth, or other feature noticeably larger or smaller than usual deviates from this successful pattern and may be a sign of something wrong. One recent study suggests that the "averageness effect" may explain the waist-to-hip ratio findings discussed above. The researchers drew hundreds of line models of women, systematically varying waist size, hip size, and shoulder width, and asked men to rate how attractive these figures were. They found that waist-to-hip ratio did not predict attractiveness across cultures, but the overall averageness of each factor did (Donohoe, von Hippel, & Brooks, 2009).

All of these studies suggest that attractiveness should be positively correlated with physical health and fertility. The evidence here is somewhat inconsistent. Several studies have examined the relationship between attractiveness (rated from high-school or college photographs) and various measures of health, fertility, and longevity; some find a small but statistically significant relationship; others do not (e.g., Henderson & Anglin, 2003; Kalick, Zebrowitz, Langlois, & Johnson, 1998; Shackelford &

Larsen, 1999). In reviewing this research, Jason Weeden and John Sabini (2005) concluded that only waist-to-hip ratio was significantly associated with actual physical health and fertility, at least in Western cultures. Whether symmetry would be more strongly associated with health in developing countries, which have lower quality medical care, is still an open question.

Do we find different features attractive in men versus women? It seems obvious that we should, and yet research suggests considerable similarity. Many studies that use computer techniques to manipulate photographs find that "femininity" (softer, more rounded features with large eyes and small nose, also characteristic of children) is attractive in both men's and women's faces (Koehler et al., 2004; Weeden & Sabini, 2005). At the same time, another study manipulated photos to exaggerate the effects of testosterone, such as the height of the face and size of the jawbone. Women in this study tended to prefer faces suggesting average levels of testosterone influence (Swaddle & Reierson, 2002). So, the ideal man's face seems to combine somewhat childlike features of softness and eye and nose size with a few features linked to sexual maturity.

In addition to good looks, we are also attracted to people with certain personality characteristics. People seek a happy disposition and kindness toward others (Cunningham et al., 1995; Evans & Brase, 2007; Gross & Crofton, 1977; Langlois & Roggman, 1990). We are also attracted to intelligence (Evans & Brase, 2007; Shackelford, Schmitt, & Buss, 2005), and a sense of humor (Li, Bailey, Kenrick, & Linsenmeyer, 2002; Sprecher & Regan, 2002). Humor may be a sign of high intelligence and good mate value, but humor is also used to show your interest in another person, so it can be an important part of flirting (Li, Griskevicius, Durante, Jonason, Paslsz, & Aumer, 2009). Both men and women value all these features to a comparable degree.

Perceptions of physical attractiveness and personality are not independent (Kniffin & Wilson, 2004; Lewandowski, Aron, & Gee, 2007). After you come to like and respect someone, you might find that person better looking than before.

Similarly, you may find yourself repulsed by the appearance of someone you dislike. Personality has a slightly stronger impact on women's perception of men's attractiveness than the other way around, although the effect occurs in both sexes (Lewandowski et al., 2007).

How do people behave when they feel sexual desire for another person? You probably have some ideas about this—if you've gotten all the way to college without noticing how people flirt, you haven't been paying attention! Researcher Monica Moore (1985) went to an ideal place to observe flirting—a bar near a college campus—and took careful notes recording women's behavior. Women seemed to display initial interest in a man through a "darting glance," looking at him for a couple of seconds, and then quickly looking away. A bolder approach involved gazing at the man for a longer period of time. Some women also tossed their heads and flipped their hair with their hands, tilted their heads, licked their lips, and caressed the objects around them.

Were these behaviors really flirting, or just things young women do from time to time? To check, Moore compared women's behavior in another bar and at other locations where flirting was less appropriate (like the campus cafeteria and the library). She found that women displayed the listed behaviors far more often in the bar than in the other locations. Also, in each location, women displaying more of these behaviors attracted more approaches from men.

Does anything strike you as odd about this study? Moore detailed how women flirt, but did not study men's flirting behavior at all! Some researchers have suggested that men display fewer non-verbal flirting behaviors than women, because when they are interested they simply approach a woman and talk with her (Grammer et al., 2000). Women may prefer a less direct way of expressing their interest. One reason is to slow down courtship while they gather more information. Another is that even when women flirt in subtle ways, men tend to overestimate women's interest, so a more direct approach would certainly invite men to misunderstand (Abbey, 1982). Unfortunately, men are capable of misunderstanding in both directions (Farris, Treat, Viken, & McFall, 2008): Many men think women are flirting when really they are not, and often think women are not flirting when really they are!

Studies of mixed-sex interaction suggest that men and women subtly match each other's non-verbal cues when they are attracted to each other (Lakin & Chartrand, 2003). That is, one signals, the other copies, and so forth (Figure 9.1). Still, it is unclear whether the men, women, or both control this correspondence (Grammer, Kruck, & Magnusson, 1998). We still have much to learn about how men and women express attraction!

FIGURE 9.1 Men and women often show their attraction to each other by matching each other's posture and movements.

Jürgen Reisch/Getty Images

Physiologically, the experience of desire is associated with a complex interplay of relaxation and sympathetic nervous system arousal. As we noted in Chapter 4, parasympathetic activation is needed in order to get sexually aroused in the first place. This makes considerable biological sense—after all, a situation that calls for fight or flight is probably not a great time to be mating. As sexual desire increases, however, sympathetic activation increases leading to increased heart rate and blood pressure, flushing, and overall muscle tension (Masters & Johnson, 1966). This response prepares the body for the physical exertion of sex.

Bowlby, Revisited: Three Kinds of Love?

John Bowlby proposed that intimate relationships reflect three universal behavioral programs, each with a strong emotional component. The prototypical example of the first behavioral program was the attachment of a young infant to its mother. The prototypical example of the second was the nurturant bonding of a mother to her baby. The prototypical example of the third behavioral program was a sexual relationship.

Although distinguishing among these programs is theoretically reasonable, not all examples of love fall neatly into one category or another. For example, a close friendship may include a mixture of attachment and caregiving. A romantic relationship generally includes all three behavioral programs at various times (e.g., Ainsworth, 1989; Fraley & Shaver, 2000). For example, a couple that initially united because of sexual attraction might later develop a relationship dominated by attachment and caregiving. Even over shorter times, you might depend on your partner for support one day and take a nurturant role the next. Which system is activated depends on events in each partner's life.

It is also unclear whether Bowlby's three behavior patterns relate to similar or different emotions. Researchers have gathered some evidence regarding appraisal themes, central and autonomic nervous system physiology, behavioral displays, development, and universality concerning *amae*/attachment,

sympathy/compassion, and sexual desire, but they have not fully described all the differences. You might think of all this research as a puzzle—there are enough pieces now to start fitting them together, and guess what the puzzle will show, but we can't be sure until we put in the rest of the pieces.

OXYTOCIN: THE LOVE TRANSMITTER?

An alternative to the three-types-of-love proposal is that there is really only one type of love, biologically speaking, which plays out in different ways under different circumstances. After all, different kinds of love do overlap. New mothers talk about "falling in love" with their babies in much the same way that they fell in love with the baby's Dad, and nursing a baby provides intensely pleasant physical sensations. In fact, many mothers while nursing a baby experience sexual arousal, which they may find distressing if they have not been told to expect it. Also, consider the affectionate use of the term "babe" or "baby," and the tendency to use "baby-talk," when speaking with a romantic partner (Bombar & Littig, 1996).

Biologically, one major similarity among attachment, caregiving, and sex relates to the pituitary hormone **oxytocin**. Oxytocin stimulates the uterus to contract while a mother is giving birth. It also stimulates the mammary glands to produce and release milk, and the brain uses it as a transmitter to facilitate maternal behaviors. Skin-to-skin touch between mother and child releases oxytocin, which in turn facilitates **maternal bonding**, the attachment behaviors of a mother toward her baby (Feldman, Weller, Zagoory-Sharon, & Levine, 2007; Keverne & Kendrick, 1992; Klaus & Kennell, 1976). Because the hormone makes its way easily into breast milk, and from there into the infant, it may influence the infant's as well as the mother's behavior. Baby rats injected with a chemical that interferes with oxytocin fail to develop preference for their mother's smell (Nelson & Panksepp, 1996), suggesting that the hormone helps mediate infant attachment to the mother. In short, many kinds of evidence link oxytocin to aspects of love.

The role of oxytocin in attachment formation is not limited to parent-infant relationships. Some fascinating studies comparing different animal species have emphasized the link between oxytocin and attachment between mates. In most mammalian species, a male mates with a female and then virtually ignores her and her babies, but in some species, male and female form long-term pair bonds, and the male helps with infant care. Generally, species forming pair bonds show more oxytocin and vasopressin (a closely related hormone) in certain brain areas during sex than do species lacking pair bonds (Carter, 1998; Young, 2002). This result suggests that sexual activity may lead to attachment in mammals with high levels of these hormones.

In particular, consider little rodents called voles, which are similar to mice. Prairie voles and meadow voles (Figure 9.2) are closely related species, but prairie voles develop long-term male-female pair bonds after mating, whereas meadow voles do not. If a male meadow vole is given a choice between the female he recently mated with and some other female, he shows a 50–50 preference. Male prairie voles release much vasopressin during sex and some other social encounters; meadow voles release little. Sue Carter and her colleagues found that injecting oxytocin directly into a female prairie vole's brain caused her to form an attachment to a nearby male, even without a mating experience. On the other hand, blocking oxytocin prevented formation of pair bonds, even after voles did mate (Williams et al., 1994).

Researchers genetically engineered some male meadow voles, which ordinarily do not form pair bonds, to produce more vasopressin receptors. The result: Each male developed a strong attachment to the female with which he mated. He spent as much time with her as possible and even helped take care of her babies (Lim et al., 2004).

You may have noticed that most of the research on oxytocin and bonding has used rodents as subjects. How much does this tell us about the biological processes associated with bonding in humans? Surely our emotional relationships are deeper than those of prairie voles, and our parenting is far more complex. Why should we assume that the chemical systems associated with vole bonding work the same way in us?

Research suggests that oxytocin and vasopressin play important roles in human behavior as well. A study of married couples found that men with more vasopressin receptors have closer relationships with their wives and are less likely to have considered divorce (Walum et al., 2008). In another study, researchers took measures of oxytocin in the blood while participants remembered an experience of strong romantic love. Participants who showed more facial displays of romantic love and affiliation while verbally describing the experience also tended to show greater increases in oxytocin levels while vividly remembering that experience (Gonzaga, Turner, Keltner, Campos, & Altemus, 2006). In yet another study, researchers administered oxytocin nasal spray or a placebo to romantic partners 45 minutes before they had a conversation about a conflict in their relationship. Couples who had received the oxytocin spray showed a significantly higher ratio of positive behavior during the conversation (eye contact, emotional disclosure, caring, validating the partner's perspective, etc.) to negative behavior (e.g., criticism, contempt, defensiveness) than couples who had received the placebo (Ditzen, Schaer, Gabriel, Bodenmann, Ehlert, & Heinrichs, 2009).

Gary Meszaros/Photo Researchers, Inc.

FIGURE 9.2 Prairie and meadow voles are closely related species, but their relationships after mating look very different. Researchers believe that the strong pair bonds formed by prairie voles after mating may be facilitated by the hormones oxytocin and vasopressin.

Oxytocin also predicts people's behavior in non-romantic relationships that require trust. Participants in one study received a nasal spray, containing either oxytocin or a placebo, and then engaged in an "investment" task (Kosfeld, Heinrichs, Zak, Fischbacher, & Fehr, 2005). Imagine yourself in this study: You are given 12 "units," each worth .25 Euro (about 32¢). You can keep it all, or invest any or all of it by giving it to another player, called the "trustee," whom you have never met before. Whatever amount you give the trustee immediately quadruples in value, and then the trustee decides how much to return to you. For example, if you invested all 12, they became 48. The trustee might return 30 to you, keeping 18 as a commission. If so, both of you profited. However, the rules permit the trustee to keep any amount, even all 48! The researchers found that participants who received the oxytocin spray invested more than those given the placebo, suggesting that they were more willing to "trust" a stranger. Why would adult love for romantic partners, and trust for others, depend on a hormone related to the mother-infant relationship? One theory is that over evolutionary time the attachment and sexual types of love evolved out of the caregiving system (Diamond, 2004).

Some evidence also links oxytocin to the relationship between social support and physiological health. Psychological stress interferes with the healing of physical wounds (Kiecolt-Glaser et al., 2002). In studies of hamsters, both experimentally injected oxytocin and the presence of other hamsters were found to block the effects of stress on wound healing, and hamsters given chemicals that interfered with oxytocin did not show the usual social facilitation of healing (Detillion et al., 2004).

THE BIOLOGY OF ATTACHMENT? ENDOGENOUS OPIATES

A number of studies suggest that the endorphins, which have effects similar to heroin and morphine, also play an important role in close relationships. One of the core features of attachment is distress at being separated from the attachment figure. Baby rats, chicks, kittens, puppies, and monkeys all cry in distinctive ways when separated from their mothers, much like human infants do. Researchers have found that these separation distress cries are associated with a sudden decrease in endorphins (Nelson & Panksepp, 1998). When young rhesus monkeys are separated from their mothers, a small amount of morphine reduces their cries, and the drug *naloxone*, which blocks opiate receptors, increases their cries (Kalin, Shelton, & Barksdale, 1988). Francesca D'Amato and her colleagues studied mice that lacked the gene for the μ (mu) type of endorphin receptor. The researchers reasoned that if endorphins are important for attachment, then animals insensitive to endorphins should develop only weak attachments. Indeed, these mice made far fewer than the normal number of cries when they were separated from their mothers (Moles, Kieffer, & D'Amato, 2004).

Endorphins are the body's natural painkillers. The role of endorphins in separation distress may help explain why people find loss of an attachment figure so literally "painful." People who have lost or are separated from a loved one may actually experience something like physical pain! In humans, fMRI studies have found that brain areas associated with physical pain, such as the anterior cingulate gyrus (Figure C.4 on the inside cover), become more active during an apparent social rejection as well (Eisenberger & Lieberman, 2004; Eisenberger, Lieberman, & Williams, 2003).

One key difficulty in this area of research is measuring the positive emotions involved in attachment. It is easy to measure distress cries evoked by separation from the mother. But it is less clear what behaviors indicate *positive* feelings of attachment, which are closer to love as an emotion than love as an attitude. Some studies have attempted to measure the relationship between endorphins and attachment-related love, at least in rodents. Normal mice exhibit some behaviors that suggest they find their mother's presence rewarding. First, when they have been separated from their mother for a while, see their mom briefly, and then are again separated, they will cry more often during the reunion and second separation than during the first, as though they had learned that their calls would be rewarded by the mother's return. This effect is called "maternal potentiation" of the calls. Second, normal mice prefer to spend time in bedding that smells like their own mother than in bedding that smells like another female mouse.

D'Amato and her colleagues (2004) found that the mice lacking the opiate receptor did not show the maternal potentiation effect, and were far less likely than normal mice to choose their mother's bedding over an unfamiliar mouse's bedding. The researchers concluded that the opiate system is important for the pleasurable aspects of attachment, as well as attachment-related distress. Mice lacking opiate responses seem to develop only weak pleasures of attachment.

In another study, researchers examined the behavior of rhesus macaques with different versions of the μ-type endorphin receptor gene, one of which leads to enhanced receptor function. They found that monkeys with the allele for more efficient receptors not only cried more persistently than those with normal receptor genes when separated from their mothers, they also spent more time with their mothers when other monkeys were present, suggesting a strong preference for their mother's company (Barr, Schwandt, Lindell, Higley, Maestripieri, Goldman, et al., 2008).

Does all of this mean that attachment love is a discrete emotion, with a distinct neurological aspect? Not necessarily. Some studies suggest that endorphin activity also plays a role in mothers' bonding to their infants. For example, one study using fMRI methods found increased activation of the periaqueductal gray area of the midbrain—a region rich in endorphin activity—when mothers looked at pictures of their own infants rather than other infants. Even at the neurological level, much research is needed before researchers will be able to decide whether attachment love and nurturant love should be considered different emotions.

EMPATHY

When people think of positive aspects of relationships, empathy often comes to mind. The term has a somewhat muddled history in psychology because people have used it in so many ways, but researchers are finally settling on useful definitions and distinctions. Rather than being a distinct emotion, **empathic accuracy** is the ability to figure out what another person is thinking and feeling (Ickes et al., 1990; Levenson & Ruef, 1992). **Emotional empathy** is actually feeling what another person is feeling, usually including similar physiology and expression as well as subjective experience.

In order to study empathic accuracy William Ickes and his colleagues (1990) brought men and women who had never met into the lab, and (under the pretext that the experimenter needed to copy some forms) left them alone for several minutes. During this period the two participants were videotaped. At the end of this period, the participants were taken to separate rooms, shown the videotape, and asked to stop the tape every time they remembered having a specific thought or feeling. They were then instructed to write down the thought and note whether they were feeling positive, neutral, or negative. Each participant then watched the tape again, but this time the experimenter stopped the tape every time the other person reported having thought or felt something. The participant then had to guess what the other person was thinking and feeling.

Would you guess women were more accurate than men at guessing their partner's thoughts and feelings? If so, you were wrong! Actually, men and women were about equally accurate. This finding is a little difficult to interpret, however, because Ickes and colleagues studied only mixed-sex dyads, and in only this one rather limited situation. It's possible that men and women are equally good decoders, but it's also possible that women are more expressive and that men had an easier task.

Unsurprisingly, people were more accurate when their partners talked more, and specifically when the partners talked more about themselves. Somewhat more interesting was the finding that people were more accurate when rating a physically attractive partner than when rating a less attractive partner! Several explanations are possible: Participants may have spent more time looking at attractive partners, or may have been more motivated to get to know attractive partners, or attractive people may have been somewhat more open in subtle ways that made them easier to read.

People with higher grade point averages tended to be more accurate, and interestingly, people who smiled more tended to be more accurate in evaluating their partners. In interpreting this last finding the researchers asked whether the partners of smilers talked more about themselves, whether the partners of smilers were more physically attractive, and whether smilers spent more time looking at their partners than non-smilers. The data did not clearly support any of these explanations, so the researchers concluded that smilers were just more interested in their partners in a way not picked up by their other measures.

Emotional empathy is a quite different process from empathic accuracy. You can figure out what someone is likely to be feeling, just by thinking logically. If you encounter a person who is staring at a loudly barking dog, who you know has a dog phobia, and who looks frightened, you can (we hope) infer that this person is afraid without actually feeling fear yourself. But by what process do we actually *feel* another person's emotion, without being in the same situation? Although this is still very controversial, some researchers have proposed that emotional empathy is the result of natural mechanisms for matching each other's physiological and behavioral states.

In one study, researchers found that participants were better able to track the emotions of a video-taped stranger if the participant and the stranger showed similar changes in heart rate over the course of the taped sequence (Levenson & Ruef, 1992). Recently, researchers have proposed the involvement of **mirror neurons**—motor neurons that show similar patterns of activity when we observe others' movements and when we make those movements ourselves—in empathy. One study using fMRI measures found that participants who scored higher on a questionnaire measure of empathic perspective-taking showed greater mirror neuron activity when looking at photographs of emotional expressions (Montgomery, Seeherman, & Haxby,

2009). However, the research on the role of mirror neurons in empathy is still at a very early stage. A key question is whether people are born with mirror neurons that help them understand other people, or whether learning to understand other people leads to the development of mirror neurons.

Is empathy good for relationships? Research suggests that the effect of empathy on a relationship depends on at least two things: 1) whether we are talking about empathic accuracy or emotional empathy, and 2) what the "target" is thinking and feeling. Emotional empathy can be hazardous in situations where one or both partners might become upset, perhaps leading to escalation of conflict and distress (Levenson & Gottman, 1983). Several studies have found that people in happy relationships seldom express displeasure toward one another, and when they do, the other person usually doesn't notice (Gable, Reis, & Downey, 2003; Simpson, Oriña, & Ickes, 2003).

The effect of empathic accuracy depends on what the target partner is thinking and feeling. Let's put it this way. You are on a date, and are watching a great new movie in the theater. During the date your partner thinks, "Wow, that actor/actress is incredibly hot!" Do you want to know that your date has this feeling? Would that knowledge help your relationship? Here's another scenario. You are out grocery shopping with your partner, and your partner thinks about you, "He should think twice before buying so much bacon—it's starting to show." Is knowing this helpful for your relationship?

Maybe not. Researchers in one study brought young romantic couples into the lab and told them they were participating in a study of physical attractiveness. The couple was shown 12 photographs of more and less attractive men and women, and told that in a follow-up study they might be asked to talk for a while with the people they rated most attractive. It turns out that the couples who were closest showed the *least* empathic accuracy in guessing what their partners were thinking and feeling when they later watched a videotape of the task, especially if the partners were rating very attractive people (Simpson, Ickes, & Blackstone, 1995). In another study researchers found that empathic accuracy was associated with decreased relationship satisfaction when the target partner was thinking about something that threatened the relationship (Simpson, Oriña, & Ickes, 2003). By contrast, when the target partner's thoughts and feelings were non-threatening, empathic accuracy was associated with higher relationship satisfaction. In short, when your partner is thinking something favorable to your relationship, you want to know about it. If she is thinking something that might annoy you, you might not want to pay too close attention.

ROMANTIC LOVE AND MARRIAGE

For young adults the most salient kind of love is romantic love. Many people wonder, "how will I know when I'm in love?" or "how will I recognize the person who is right for me?" There is no easy answer to these questions, and the fact that about half of all American marriages end in divorce suggests that many people either don't know how to choose the right partner, or don't know how to maintain love once the sparks have died down and they have to figure out whose job it is to clean the garage. Although we wish science had even more well-tested advice to offer on this subject, psychologists studying emotion in marriages and other romantic relationships have identified some features of typical romantic relationships, and found a few predictors of couples' happiness and stability.

The discussion that follows applies mainly to western cultures where young people date many partners, virtually unsupervised. Many Arab, Asian, and Latin American cultures consider it scandalous for an unmarried couple to spend time together without a chaperone, and in some cases parents arrange a marriage between young people who are not even acquainted. So, from the start we must admit that a "typical" romantic relationship varies among cultures. In fact, the relationship between romantic love and marriage itself differs from culture to culture. Romantic love is a widespread, but not universal concept. One study of 166 cultures found that 89 percent showed evidence of romantic love (Jankowiak & Fischer, 1992). In modern Western cultures, romantic love is often given as the motivation for marriage and reproduction (Swidler, 2001). On the other hand, romantic love is *not* considered a prerequisite for marriage and reproduction in all cultures, and it may even be seen as a threat to the extended family relationships that provide the foundation of many cultures' social structures (Dion & Dion, 1993). In many societies, parents arrange young people's marriages for economic or other practical considerations, and virtually ignore romantic love. People in these societies manage to mate and rear their children quite successfully (Figure 9.3).

"Yes," you might say, "but are those marriages happy?" Some are and some aren't. And in the United States, where partners choose each other based on love, some marriages are happy and some aren't. Studies have found that, on average, parent-arranged marriages in India are happier than love-based marriages in the United States (Gupta & Singh, 1982), although parent-arranged marriages in China tend to be less happy (Xu & Whyte, 1990). Also, even if spouses in arranged marriages were not in love at the time of the wedding, they may develop strong, loving feelings for each other once they begin sharing a life.

Our discussion also focuses on heterosexual dating and marriage. The research on homosexual couples is relatively meager. The few available studies suggest that many of the important issues are similar for homosexual and heterosexual relationships. For example, in either case, people seek a partner with similar attitudes, who will be honest, supportive, and trustworthy (Bäccman, Folkesson, & Norlander, 1999). Also, the variables associated with relationship satisfaction are similar for homosexual and heterosexual couples (Kurdek, 2005).

Although (as we noted earlier) love is unnecessary for marriage in many societies, in America it is considered essential. Two people meet and find each other attractive. If initial contacts go well, they see each other more and more often. The early stages of a romantic relationship usually constitute **passionate love**, marked by frequent thoughts

Jupiter Images

Nikhil Gangavane/iStockphoto.com

FIGURE 9.3 Although modern western cultures emphasize romantic love as the main prerequisite for marriage, other cultures encourage arranged marriages based on compatibility.

about the other person, intense desire to be together, and excitement from the partner's attention (Diamond, 2004; Hatfield & Rapson, 1993). At this stage, each person is likely to idealize the other—to be well aware of the other's positive qualities, but less aware of flaws and limitations.

Passionate love is intensely rewarding, even at the neurological level. One study examined 17 young adults who professed to be "deeply and madly in love." Each viewed photographs of friends and of the person she was in love with, while researchers used fMRI to measure brain activity. Viewing the loved person activated a variety of brain areas, including the dopamine-laden reward centers responsive to drugs like cocaine and alcohol. During the stage of passionate love, the sight of the loved one produces euphoric excitement (Bartels & Zeki, 2000).

Many people report that they changed dramatically when they fell in love. Some of this change is the emotional "rush" we just described, but some of the change may be in behavior as well. In one study, Art Aron asked college students five times over the course of a semester to answer the question "who are you today?" (Aron, Paris, & Aron, 1995). At each time point, Aron also asked whether each participant had fallen in love since the last report. People who said they had recently fallen in love described themselves in more diverse ways than they had prior to falling in love, in terms of traits, feelings, and social roles. Why might this be? Aron believes that when people fall in love, they begin to incorporate into themselves various aspects of the partner's personality, activities, and attitudes—a process he describes as "self-expansion."

If the relationship continues, partners typically begin to increase their commitment to the relationship, and their integration into each other's lives. Lovers are introduced to each other's families, they may begin to share resources or live together, and they may decide to marry or make some other long-term commitment. Over the course of this process, relationships are characterized more by **companionate love**, with an emphasis on security and mutual care and protection (Diamond, 2004; Hatfield & Rapson, 1993). Each wishes the best for the other person, and is confident that the other person wishes the best in return. A strong companionate love is usually related to high satisfaction with life, much more so than passionate love is. Passionate love, on the other hand, tends to be related to strong overall emotional feelings (Kim & Hatfield, 2004).

Nobody can make a good impression all the time, hard as they may try during the passionate phase. Pretenses fade, idealization wanes, and each partner begins to see the other's weaknesses, quirky habits, and bad moods. They will also find out about big and small incompatibilities; differences that they need to negotiate in order to get along. In general, people tend to be more satisfied with their relationship if they consider their partner's flaws specific to particular situations, or if they see the flaws as related to virtues (Murray & Holmes, 1999). For instance, a woman may tolerate her boyfriend's occasional impulsiveness or shocking comments if she regards these behaviors as evidence of "spontaneity and honesty" instead of "bad judgment and disrespect."

Physical attraction is still present in companionate love, but each person feels less excitement from the other's presence and less insistence on being together constantly (Bersheid, 1983). Just think how many stories—from fairy tales to Hollywood movies—deal with dating, overcoming obstacles, and eventually getting married. In contrast, think how few stories deal with the couple *while* they are living "happily ever after." Living happily ever after is great, but it's not an exciting story.

However, couples may be able to re-ignite the spark in their lives by doing novel and exciting activities together. Art Aron and his colleagues (2000) brought long-term romantic couples into the lab, and assigned them to work together either on a somewhat boring task, or on an arousing task like having two of their legs tied together and crossing a large room on "three legs." Participants not only reported having more fun with the second task, but they also reported that their relationship improved afterward!

Predicting Romantic Attraction

It is fascinating to see who finds whom attractive. Have you ever tried to pair two people that you think would be good for each other? Friends and family introduce single individuals they believe will find each other appealing, and dating services make phenomenal amounts of money helping people to find "that special someone." Sometimes these matches work well, and sometimes they don't.

What predicts whether or not two people will fall in love? Although people have elaborate ideas about what makes a good match, research suggests that a few simple factors account for a great deal of attraction and satisfaction. Earlier we discussed some of the physical and personality characteristics that most people find attractive, including a healthy body type, a happy outlook, intelligence, and kindness. One of the best additional predictors of a long-term stable relationship is similarity (Caspi & Herbener, 1990). Although "opposites attract" when we are talking about magnets, romantic relationships work best between people with similar values, lifestyles, favorite activities and beliefs. This rule holds especially for people who like themselves in the first place—if you like yourself, you will probably like a partner who is similar (Klohnen & Mendelsohn, 1998).

As a relationship continues, partners grow even more alike (Anderson, Keltner, & John, 2003; Davis & Rusbult, 2001). However, couples often overestimate their similarity in attitudes and preferences, as they emphasize shared feelings over differences and each projects his or her own feelings onto the other partner (Murray et al., 2002). One study found as couples dated, their estimates about each other's attitudes and behaviors became more *confident* without becoming more *accurate* (Swann & Gill, 1997).

The similarity principle also applies to what people are looking for from a relationship. Clyde and Susan Hendrick (1986) identified three major styles of romantic love, giving them Greek and Latin names. The *eros* style is based on passion and physical "chemistry." The *ludus* style is love as a kind of game-playing, with relatively frequent changes of partners. The *storge* style is based mainly on friendship. Of course, most relationships straddle the borders instead of falling exclusively into one category or another. Still, most people identify with one of these styles more than the others, and a romance is most likely to succeed if both partners approach love with the same style.

Attachment in Adult Romantic Relationships

Although attachment was originally described as a set of behaviors observed in infants, attachment remains an important aspect of close relationships throughout our adult lives (Ainsworth, 1989; Hazan & Shaver, 1987). **Adult attachments** are relationships in which one or both people (1) prefer to be in close contact, experiencing distress during extended separation, (2) turn to the partner for support in times of stress or danger, and (3) derive security and confidence from the partner, facilitating a confident approach to the rest of the world (Fraley & Shaver, 2000). Among young children, parents are the primary attachment figures. As people enter their teens they form attachments to a few close friends, and eventually to romantic partners.

Although few psychologists have studied attachment in close friendships, a strong body of research now documents the role of attachment in long-term romantic relationships (Fraley & Shaver, 2000). Many individuals do appear to rely on their romantic partners to provide a safe haven and a secure base, in much the same way that toddlers rely on their parents (Hazan & Shaver, 1987). One study, conducted at a university in Northern California, followed students over the course of a semester (Aron, Paris, & Aron, 1995). A few weeks into the study a devastating earthquake hit the Bay Area. The study found no evidence that more people fell in love after than before the quake. However, people who did fall in love during the couple of weeks following the quake reported being much more upset than most other people immediately after the quake, and significantly less upset ten days later (after they had fallen in love).

What might explain this effect? First, increased overall arousal can enhance your sense of attraction to someone else, and nothing gets your sympathetic nervous system going like a good earthquake. It may be that the people who were more disturbed by the quake were also more likely to transfer those feelings of arousal to a potential romantic partner. Also, keep in mind that threatening situations activate our attachment needs—we actually start looking for someone to take care of us. The earthquake may also have prompted some highly distressed people to develop attachments to those who provided comfort during a time of great stress.

In fact, one of the key features of infant attachment is that an infant who feels threatened or stressed turns to the attachment figure for protection and comfort. Mario Mikulincer and colleagues (2000) wanted to know whether adults showed these same tendencies. People certainly report that they do. But can we measure this tendency? Measuring attachment with toddlers is relatively easy: The mother takes the toddler into an unfamiliar room and then leaves, and researchers measure how hard the child cries. This would not be effective with an adult couple. Mikulincer developed an indirect measurement by asking whether people are quicker to detect words of closeness or separation when they feel threatened. In an ingenious experiment, he asked participants to watch a computer screen. When they saw one word (called a "prime") flash on the screen for a second, they had to decide whether the next string of letters was a word or not. Sometimes the first word was "failure," and sometimes it was a neutral word. The following string of letters might be a proximity-related word like "closeness" or "love," a distance-related word like "rejection" or "abandonment," or a neutral word or a non-word string of letters.

The idea was that if certain kinds of thoughts are already in a person's mind, they should be able to identify words related to those thoughts faster than if they were thinking about something unrelated.

Mikulincer found that, in general, people identified proximity-related words faster after seeing the word "failure" than after seeing a neutral word. It was as though the tiny threat of thinking about failure made people want to feel close to someone. In a later study, the same effect was found using the names of participants' particular attachment figures rather than generic proximity words (Mikulincer, Gillath, & Shaver, 2002).

Adults appear to have different "attachment styles," just like toddlers, which influence their feelings in romantic relationships. Think about how you generally feel in romantic relationships. Then read the three paragraphs in Figure 9.4—which describes you best?

These paragraphs were designed by Cindy Hazan and Phil Shaver (1987) to represent what secure, anxious, and avoidant attachment—the three styles observed in infant attachment to parents—might feel like in the context of adult romantic relationships. Hazan and Shaver had these three paragraphs printed in a local newspaper, along with dozens of self-report items measuring beliefs about relationships, attitudes toward the respondent's most important relationship partner, and characteristics of the respondent's relationships with parents and important romantic partners. Readers were asked to complete the whole questionnaire, cut it out, and mail it back to the researchers.

Hazan and Shaver found that adults classified themselves into attachment styles in about the same proportions observed in studies of infants: 56 percent of the sample said the secure paragraph described them best, 25 percent chose the avoidant paragraph, and 19 percent said the anxious paragraph described them best. (Of course, these labels were not printed in the actual newspaper questionnaire.) People endorsing different attachment styles also had different relationship histories, and different beliefs about relationships. Adults endorsing the "secure" paragraph had longer relationships than adults with other styles, were less likely to have been divorced, and typically described their most important love experience as happy, friendly, and trusting. They tended to endorse the belief that ups and downs are normal in relationships—sometimes the romance will cool down, but then it will flare up again. They were unlikely to say that it was easy to fall in love, or that they fell in love frequently. In a follow-up study, participants with secure attachment styles described themselves as easy to know and likable, and described other people as well-intentioned and good-hearted.

By contrast, people endorsing the "anxious" paragraph described themselves as obsessively preoccupied with their partners, experiencing intense emotional highs and lows in relationships. They were more likely than secure and avoidant individuals to agree that their love experiences constituted "love at first sight," and that an intense feeling of oneness with their partner was important to them. They were most likely to say that they fell in love easily and often. They also agreed most strongly of the three groups that they experienced much self-doubt, were misunderstood or unappreciated, and

---

The following paragraphs were written as descriptions of what attachment "styles" might look like in the context of people's attitudes toward adult romantic relationships. Which best describes you? Which paragraph do you think describes the "secure" style, which the "anxious" style, and which the "avoidant" style? The answers are printed upside-down at the bottom of the figure.

(1) I am somewhat uncomfortable being too close to others; I find it difficult to trust them completely, difficult to allow myself to depend on them. I am nervous when anyone gets too close, and often, love partners want me to be more intimate than I feel comfortable being.

(2) I find it relatively easy to get close to others and am comfortable depending on them and having them depend on me. I don't often worry about being abandoned or about someone getting too close to me.

(3) I find that others are reluctant to get as close as I would like. I often worry that my partner doesn't really love me or won't want to stay with me. I want to merge completely with the other person, and this desire sometimes scares people away.

Answers: (1) Avoidant, (2) Secure, (3) Anxious

FIGURE 9.4 Descriptions of secure, anxious, and avoidant attachment styles.

that they were more able than most people to commit to a long-term relationship.

Finally, people endorsing the "avoidant" paragraph described being afraid of closeness in their most important relationships, and unable to accept their partner's imperfections. They were more likely than secure and anxious participants to agree that romantic love does not last forever, and less likely to agree that romantic feelings grow and wane repeatedly over the course of a relationship. They were also most likely to endorse a statement that they were independent and able to get along by themselves.

How do the three adult styles relate to the attachment types observed in infants? According to Chris Fraley and Philip Shaver, adult styles reflect the same kinds of deeply ingrained expectations about caregiver/partner relationships that are the basis for infant styles (Fraley & Shaver, 2000). Securely attached infants expect that caregivers will be responsive, consistent, and warm; securely attached adults think of themselves as lovable and worthy, and of their lovers as kind, trustworthy, and dependable. Anxiously attached infants seem to expect inconsistency from caregivers, and are highly dependent, yet terrified of separation. Attachment-anxious adults want to be in a deep, intense relationship and think such relationships are possible, but they don't really trust others, don't think of themselves as lovable, and are constantly afraid of being abandoned. Avoidant infants appear to have given up on their caregivers, playing on their own and showing little reaction when the caregiver leaves; attachment-avoidant adults seem to have given up on committed, intimate relationships in a similar way.

Or have they? Have attachment-avoidant people really turned off their attachment needs in the way their self-reports and surface behaviors suggest? In the Mikulincer et al. (2000) word-recognition study described earlier, researchers found that people with more anxious attachment styles were quick to detect proximity-related words regardless of whether the prime was "failure" or the neutral word. They seemed to be thinking about attachment needs at all times, stressed or not. Also, attachment-anxious people

were quicker to recognize distance-related words after the "failure" prime, as though the stress made them worry about rejection.

Since attachment-avoidant people should also expect rejection from others, one might have expected them to show a similar pattern, but they did not. In order to find out whether avoidant people were just suppressing these attachment anxieties, Mikulincer and colleagues (2000) repeated their study, but this time participants had to complete the word-detection task while listening to a loud and annoying story over a set of headphones. This time, the stressful prime had an even bigger effect on the avoidant participants' distance word recognition than it did on the anxious participants. It was as though avoidant participants usually put mental effort into suppressing their fears of rejection, but when they were overloaded these fears were released.

You may be wondering at this point, "Do people really fall that neatly into one attachment style or another? Are adult feelings about romantic relationships that easy to categorize?" It's a good question. Toddlers can't tell us in detail about their feelings, so we have to rely on their behavior in the strange situation in order to measure their attachment to caregivers. Behavior in the strange situation is fairly easy to categorize, so the three-type model is the one used most often in studying small children. Adults, however, may describe themselves as "mostly secure, but kind of anxious," or "somewhat avoidant," or even "both anxious and avoidant." When you read the three newspaper paragraphs used by Hazan and Shaver (1987), you may have identified with two or more paragraphs as well.

According to Kim Bartholomew (1990; Bartholomew & Horowitz, 1991), this is because attachment styles represent the junction between two "working models," or implicit internal beliefs—one about the value of the self, and one about the value of other people. As a result, adult attachment is best measured in terms of two dimensions, rather than three categories (Fraley & Waller, 1998). The anxiety dimension measures whether a person generally has positive or negative feelings of self-worth and desirability as a partner. People who think of *themselves* as less worthy and desirable thus score higher on "attachment anxiety." The avoidance dimension measures whether a person measures whether a person generally has positive or negative beliefs about *other* people. People who think others are less trustworthy, and who see less value in intimate relationships, score higher on "attachment avoidance." Attachment questionnaires based on the two-dimensional model have proved to be reliable and useful in measuring adults' attachment styles (e.g., Brennan, Clark, & Shaver, 1998; Griffin & Bartholomew, 1994).

The critical test of a questionnaire measure, of course, is whether it predicts people's thoughts, feelings, and behavior in the way that it should. In an extremely creative study, Fraley and Shaver (1998) went to a local airport, and surreptitiously recorded the behavior of couples waiting at the gate until either both partners got on the plane, or one got on the plane, and the other left. (Obviously this study was done while you could still go to the gate without a ticket.) If one person was left behind, the researchers asked that person to complete an attachment style questionnaire. The effects were striking for women who were expecting separation from their partners. Women who scored higher on attachment anxiety, as measured by the questionnaire, reported feeling more upset about the separation. Women who scored higher on avoidance showed fewer contact and caregiving behaviors (such as kissing, hugging, gently touching, and whispering to the partner) and more avoidance behaviors (such as looking away from the partner and breaking off physical contact).

One interesting feature of this study is that it demonstrated the independence of attachment anxiety and avoidance as separate dimensions, just as Bartholomew had suggested. Attachment anxiety most effectively predicted how women *felt* when facing a separation, with more anxious women feeling more distress. By contrast, attachment avoidance best predicted women's *behavior* in terms of avoiding contact or closeness when separation was imminent. Thus, a very anxious woman could be feeling very distressed at the idea of separation, but her avoidance score would predict whether she handled the distress by seeking or avoiding contact.

Similarly, an avoidant woman might or might not feel particularly sad about the separation, but was likely to disengage from her partner either way.

The questionnaire measure of attachment did not predict men's behavior or feelings as accurately, and it's not quite clear why. Do men have different attachment systems than women? Are there different kinds of constraints on men's affectionate behavior in public than on women's behavior? There is still a great deal to learn about the role of attachment processes in adulthood, but Bowlby's original ideas have proved remarkably helpful in our understanding of romantic relationships.

Marital Stability and Satisfaction

Most love stories end with the couple getting married. What happens beyond that point? Although some marriages last "as long as we both shall live," the United States is the most divorce-prone country in the world. What predicts whether a marriage will survive and flourish, or end with the spouses parting ways?

First, marriage is not a good way to save or improve a bad relationship. One study examined recently married couples and then followed up years later to see which marriages ended in divorce. The researchers found that most marriages that ended in divorce within seven years were shaky from the start. When a couple got married hoping they could fix the problems in their relationship, the problems only grew worse (Huston, Niehuis, & Smith, 2001).

Some predictors of marital stability involve simple demographic characteristics (Harker & Keltner, 2001; Howard & Dawes, 1976; Karney & Bradbury, 1995; Myers, 2000b; Thornton, 1977; Tzeng, 1992). Marriages are most likely to last if the spouses:

- were over 20 when they married
- grew up in two-parent homes
- dated for a long time before marrying, but did not live together
- have about the same level of education, especially a high level of education
- have a good income

- have a long-term happy disposition
- live in a small town or a rural area
- are religious and of the same religious affiliation
- are approximately the same age and have similar attitudes
- have sexual relations often, and arguments rarely.

Does this list mean that if you don't go to church you are doomed to divorce? Or that you should give up now on the partner you've been living with for a year? Should you move to a farm to keep your marriage alive? Of course not. Keep in mind that each of these factors *correlates* with, or tends to predict, whether a couple divorces or stays married. A correlation does not demonstrate a causal relationship. For example, how would living together before marriage cause divorce? Other things being equal, marriages do better when people have dated for a long time and already know each other's quirks and flaws; living together is certainly a way to learn about each other. Think of it this way. Who *doesn't* live together? A number of religions specifically prohibit living together outside of marriage, and these same religions tend to prohibit (or at least seriously discourage) divorce. Another possibility is that some couples decide too casually to live together, and then drift into a decision to marry. For a couple not living together, the decision to marry is more deliberate.

Here is a related issue: Given that certain religions prohibit or strongly discourage divorce, we should not be surprised that religious people are less likely than non-religious people to divorce. Can we infer that religious people are more happily married? Or are they just more likely to remain married even if they are unhappy? Because duration of a marriage is not the same thing as happiness of a marriage, researchers have turned more to studying the predictors of marital satisfaction.

One important factor relates to people's expectations for their relationship. On average, spouses' marital satisfaction takes something of a dive soon after the birth of their first child, remains low for a while, and then gradually increases, so that they are pretty happy again after the kids leave home

(Feeney et al., 1994). Some parents experience an "empty nest syndrome" (sadness when the last child leaves home), but frankly most are rather pleased. Children are wonderful, but stressful as well! Many couples have trouble finding time for passion and romance while they are taking care of children … including teenagers. Couples who are prepared for these transitions, and know that changes in their feelings probably reflect the stress of raising a family rather than anything inherent in the marriage, may find it easier to survive the challenging years with a young family.

Also, people differ in the extent to which they think passionate love is crucial for a successful marriage, and cultures differ on this issue as well. In the early 1990s, 78 percent of American women agreed that "keeping romance alive" was important for a good marriage, compared with 29 percent of Japanese women (American Enterprise, 1992). People whose motivation for commitment is very strong and who are willing to wait out the less happy periods of a relationship may be rewarded. One national survey in the United States found that, of the people who reported being unhappily married during the first wave of the study, but did not divorce, 86 percent reported being happily married (to the same person) five years later (Popenoe, 2002).

Another factor that predicts marital satisfaction is equity, especially in terms of what skills, effort, and resources each spouse brings to their shared life. People who feel, in general, that they get about as much as they give in their relationships tend to be happier, and people who feel like they are doing all the work are less satisfied (Van Yperen & Buunk, 1990). Individuals tend to feel more trust in a relationship if they perceive that the partner is willing to make some sacrifices for them (Wieselquist et al., 1999). That is, both should feel they are getting a "fair deal."

However, this does not mean that couples should keep "score cards" about who did what for whom. In fact, one sign of closeness in both friends and married couples is that they don't expect instant repayment for favors, or explicit exchanges of one favor for another (Buunk & Van

Yperen, 1991). They long ago lost track of who has done more for the other, and they continue doing nice things just because they want to make each other happy. If necessary, one will nurse the other through a long illness, even knowing that the other will never be able to return the favor. In short, equity is important at the start of a loving relationship, but less important later.

Many other predictors of marital satisfaction (at least in the United States, where most of the research has been done) concern how spouses communicate with each other. Couples with happy relationships generally have high levels of **self-disclosure**, sharing personal, intimate, and confidential information (Hendrick et al., 1988; Sanderson & Cantor, 2001). In strong relationships this process develops gradually over time. As a general rule people like others who self-disclose to them (Aron et al., 1997), although they feel uneasy if someone discloses deep secrets too early in a relationship. We also like more the people to whom we have self-disclosed (Collins & Miller, 1994). Do not infer that you need to tell your partner *everything* about yourself. But anything that you think your partner should know about you, or is likely to find out anyway, you should tell. If your partner discovers that you have lied, or have withheld important information, you will lose a great deal of trust.

Researcher John Gottman (1994; Gottman, Coan, Carrere, & Swanson, 1998) has spent decades studying the ways in which married couples interact with each other. In order to determine which relationships will succeed, he has observed couples at their worst—when they are arguing about some area of disagreement in their lives. Gottman and his colleagues first work with a couple to identify an aspect of their lives that causes conflict—such as money, how to raise the kids, or who is doing more of the housework. Then they videotape the couple during a 15-minute discussion about that topic by themselves. Gottman and his colleagues have identified several emotional components of these conversations that predict the future of the couple's relationship.

You might think that anger would be the biggest risk factor for a relationship. Actually, Gottman and colleagues' research suggests that anger is not always a major problem. Obviously, it depends on how much anger, and how people express it. Think back to our discussion of the constructive aspects of anger in Chapter 8. In some cases, mild anger (not screaming or throwing things) may help to let a partner know that you are serious about your concern, and gives the partner an opportunity to make some changes. Gottman has identified four emotional patterns that do predict serious problems for a relationship, however, that he calls "the four horsemen of the apocalypse." They are:

1. *Criticism:* Suggesting changes in behavior can be constructive, but complaining about personal flaws is destructive. Criticism at its most destructive includes attacking the spouse (or the spouse's relatives!), listing the spouse's flaws, and blaming the spouse for problems in the relationship. ("You never help me with the housework! You're so lazy!")

2. *Defensiveness:* This is usually a response to criticism, in which one defends oneself by denying that the complaint is valid, giving an excuse for the behavior, or counter-criticizing the spouse ("You're such a perfectionist that you think I never do anything right, so why should I try?").

3. *Contempt:* This includes behaviors like rolling one's eyes, being sarcastic, or insulting the spouse—any message suggesting that the spouse is incompetent or beneath the speaker.

4. *Stonewalling:* A spouse stonewalls when (s)he ignores or shuts out the spouse who is trying to communicate something, either sitting stone-faced and not saying anything, or actually looking away or closing his or her eyes.

So what communication patterns predicted happier marriages (see Figure 9.5)? For years therapists have encouraged couples to empathize with each other, try to feel what the other is feeling, and to validate their spouses—to summarize the meaning of what a spouse has said, and convey it back ("I hear you saying that …" or "so you feel that …"). More recently,

Marcus Clackson/iStockphoto.com

FIGURE 9.5 Spouses who are able to emphathize with each other and appreciate each others' perspectives, even during conflict, tend to have happier marriages.

however, Gottman has found that this pattern may not be as effective as researchers had thought, and may even be too much to expect from two people who are really invested in whatever they're arguing about (Gottman et al., 1998). It is difficult to listen sympathetically when one's partner is expressing hostility.

In couples with satisfying relationships, the pattern often looks more like this: 1) The wife (who is usually the one to raise a concern about the relationship) brings up the issue with, at most, mild levels of anger, expressing what she thinks is the problem, when the problem occurs, and what might be a solution. 2) The husband shows willingness to consider the wife's understanding of the problem and to accept the wife's influence in figuring out a solution. 3) The husband remains fairly calm, rather than getting agitated. 4) The wife makes a joke. 5) The husband expresses affection or happiness. Among less happy couples, the wife is more likely to come in charging with high levels of anger, and the husband is more likely to deny his wife's power in the relationship and escalate the negative emotion in the conversation.

What does this mean for you? Well, if you are in a heterosexual relationship in which the woman is usually the one raising concerns, how you can help improve conflict depends on whether you are the guy or the girl. Women might want to think about staying calm when raising an issue, bringing it up when they feel relaxed and trying not to frame the concern as a criticism or accusation. Men can bring a constructive frame of mind to the conflict as well, trying to interpret their partners' concerns as an opportunity to develop the relationship, rather than a criticism or threat, and being open to solutions proposed by the partner. If you are not in this "typical" kind of relationship, you might find it more helpful to think about whether you, or your partner, are usually the one to raise concerns, and act accordingly. For both partners, finding a natural way to introduce some positive emotion into the conversation is a big help. Don't make a joke at your partner's expense, or say something you don't mean, but you might look for something cheerful to say or some way to show signs of love and affection.

ATTACHMENT AND FRIENDSHIP

Do people love their friends in the same way they love parents, children, and romantic partners? Well, not in exactly the same way, but studies suggest that people can develop attachments to their platonic friends as well. People begin to form friendship bonds early in childhood, and as children mature into their teens, friends become an increasingly important source of emotional and practical support (Furman & Buhrmester, 1992). Warm, secure friendships in adolescence may be crucial building blocks for healthy adult lives; in one study, researchers measured the number and quality of friendships in early adolescence, and found that those with more and closer friends had higher self-esteem and fewer symptoms of psychological disorders (such as depression and anxiety) 12 years later (Bagwell, Newcomb, & Bukowski, 1998). As you can probably guess, this was a correlational study (after all, you can hardly randomly assign teenagers to have lots of friends or no friends), so it is difficult to know whether the friendships actually caused people to thrive emotionally in adulthood, or whether people who were already on track for healthy adult lives tended to form more friendships as teenagers. Certainly happy people who feel good about themselves are more pleasant to be around than miserable people who hate themselves.

Some studies, however, suggest that healthy childhood and adolescent friendships do help buffer people from the effects of other negative influences. Theorists have proposed that the functions of attachment transfer from parents to peers during this time, so that as children grow up they come to rely more on friends for a secure base and for support in times of danger or stress. If so, then close relationships with friends may even help compensate for troubled relationships with parents. In one study, researchers found that children from abusive home environments in early childhood were more likely than others to be the victims of bullying in the third

and fourth grade, but that this correlation was weaker among children who reported having many friends (Schwartz, Dodge, Pettit, & Bates, 2000). In another study, researchers asked whether the security of relationships with parents or friends was the better predictor of adolescents' overall adjustment (Laible, Carlo, & Raffaelli, 2000). As expected, adolescents who reported secure relationships with both parents and peers were the best adjusted, and those reporting insecure relationships with both were the worst adjusted. However, teens who had secure relationships with peers, but insecure relationships with parents, were better adjusted than teens for whom the reverse was true. The buffering effect of friendships in adolescence is particularly strong for girls, and is most associated with very close, warm and supportive friendships rather than casual or activity-based friendships (Rubin, Dwyer, Booth-LaForce, Kim, Burgess, & Rose-Krasnor, 2004). These findings suggest that close friendships do confer distinct benefits of their own, and that attachment may be an important part of this process.

SUMMARY

John Bowlby once wrote: "intimate attachments to other human beings are the hub around which a person's life revolves, not only when he is an infant or a toddler or a schoolchild, but throughout his adolescence and his years of maturity as well, and on into old age" (Bowlby, 1980, p. 422). As we have seen, our close relationships are fraught with emotion, and can be a tremendous source of reward, a source of stress and pain, or both. Social contact can be rewarding even at the level of the brain's chemistry, increasing the activity of reward neurotransmitters like dopamine and opiates, and promoting hormonal activity that can improve physical health. On the other hand, intimacy and closeness do entail risk. There are some things we'd prefer not to know about a partner's thoughts and feelings, and if we are so linked that we absorb a

partner's good moods, we may absorb their bad moods as well.

Scientists are just beginning to understand the complex package of emotions that accompanies emotional intimacy. Most research on close relationships has emphasized objective social, developmental, and biological processes rather than emotion. (No surprise there. Researchers naturally start with what is easiest to measure.) Psychologists have not agreed upon a taxonomy of love, much less developed a complete understanding of love as an emotion or set of emotions. One reason is that researchers have long thought of emotion purely as something within the individual. Of late, however, psychologists have begun to recognize the powerful role of emotion and its functions *between* people, so interest in love, compassion, and empathy is growing rapidly.

KEY TERMS

adult attachments: relationships in which one or both people (1) prefer to be in close contact, experiencing distress during extended separation, (2) turn to the partner for support in times of stress or danger, and (3) derive security and confidence from the partner, facilitating an open and engaged approach to the rest of the world (p. 220)

amae: a feeling of pleasurable dependence on another person, like the feeling an infant has toward its mother (p. 207)

attachment: a long-lasting emotional bond to a regular caregiver, producing a desire to be near that person (and distress when separated), a tendency to turn to that person when threatened, and a sense of being supported in exploring new things (p. 206)

attitude: a combination of beliefs, feelings, and behaviors directed toward a person, object or category (p. 204)

caregiving system: according to John Bowlby, the system that motivates parents to nurture and protect their offspring (p. 207)

companionate love: strong attachment with an emphasis on security, mutual care, and protection (p. 219)

compassion: a caring and concerned response to another person's distress (p. 208)

emotional empathy: actually feeling what another person is feeling (p. 215)

empathic accuracy: ability to figure out what another person is thinking and feeling (p. 215)

maternal bonding: the attachment behaviors of a mother toward her baby (p. 212)

mirror neurons: motor neurons that show similar patterns of activity when we observe others' movements and when we make those movements ourselves (p. 216)

nurturant love: an emotion elicited by cues of youth and vulnerability, that motivates caregiving behavior (p. 208)

oxytocin: a pituitary hormone released by female mammals while giving birth and while nursing, and by both males and females during the sex act (p. 212)

passionate love: experience of frequent thoughts about the other person, intense desire to be together, and excitement from the partner's attention (p. 217)

personal distress: self-focused anxiety in the face of another's suffering (p. 208)

prototype: set of characteristics that describe the ideal example of some category, but that may not be held by every member of that category (p. 204)

script: culturally learned set of expectations about events, thoughts, feelings, and behaviors (p. 204)

self-disclosure: sharing of personal, intimate, and confidential information (p. 225)

sex system: according to John Bowlby, the system designed to prompt sexual interest in people who are likely to be good reproductive partners (p. 209)

strange situation: a research procedure for studying attachment, in which a child is repeatedly separated from and reunited with the attachment figure. (p. 206)

sympathy: concern, attention, and empathic sadness for another person who is suffering (p. 208)

THOUGHT QUESTIONS

1. During the stage of passionate love, early in a dating relationship, each person becomes more aware of the other's strengths than weaknesses. Why? (Think about it from the standpoint of both the perceiver and the person being perceived.)

2. The text distinguished sympathy, compassion, nurturant love, and personal distress. Under what circumstances might you experience one of these without the others—for example, nurturant love without sympathy or compassion?

SUGGESTION FOR RESEARCH PROJECT

Psychologists know surprisingly little about the prevalence of love. You might survey people you know, asking how many people they once thought they were "in love" with, and in retrospect, how many times they *now* believe they have really been in love. Do the answers differ for men and women? For older and younger people? For people of different ethnic backgrounds?

SUGGESTIONS FOR FURTHER READING

Coontz, S. (2006). *Marriage, a History: How Love Conquered Marriage*. New York: Penguin.

Hatfield, E., & Rapson, R. L. (1993). *Love, Sex, and Intimacy*. New York: Harper Collins.

Hrdy, S.B. (1999). *Mother Nature: Maternal Instincts and How They Shape the Human Species*. New York: Ballantine.

Parker-Pope, T. (2010). *For Better: The Science of a Good Marriage*. Hialeah, FL: Dutton.

Swidler, A. (2001). *Talk of Love: How Culture Matters*. Chicago: University of Chicago Press.

Tannen, D. (1990). *You Just Don't Understand*. New York: Morrow.

10

Happiness and the Positive Emotions

What is your primary goal in life? Many people in the United States reply, "to be happy." The statement "I just want you to be happy" is a strong expression of personal support, and the phrase "whatever makes you happy" is used to advise another's decisions. The Western philosophy of utilitarianism is based on the moral superiority of whatever course of action results in happiness: "The greatest happiness of all those whose interest is in question [is] the right and proper, and only right and proper and universally desirable, end of human action" (Bentham, 1780/1970, p. 11). The United States' Declaration of Independence states: "We hold these truths to be self-evident, that all men are created equal, that they are endowed by their Creator with certain unalienable Rights, that among these are Life, Liberty and the pursuit of Happiness."

Does anybody *not* agree that the pursuit of happiness is a primary goal, right up there with life itself? People in many Asian cultures prefer a sense of contentment from doing their duty toward family and community, rather than personal exhilaration (Tsai, 2007; Uchida & Kitayama, 2009). Perhaps both cultures value happiness, even if Asians have a different concept of it than Westerners.

A few research questions about happiness are obvious: What makes people happy? Why does happiness sometimes last so long and sometimes so briefly? What can we do to make ourselves happier? Are happy people more productive and more successful than unhappy people? What *is* happiness, anyway? What purpose does it serve? Is it really an emotion, or is it more like an attitude or trait? Alternatively, is "happiness" a general term we use for several distinct emotions, as we have suggested for "love?"

Given people's interest in living happy, fulfilling lives, you might suppose that researchers have devoted enormous effort to these questions. However, research on the positive emotions—feelings that enrich life, such as happiness, love, amusement, hope, compassion, pride, gratitude, and awe—only began receiving serious attention in the 1990s, much later than research on anger, fear, and depression (Seligman & Csikszentmihalyi, 2000). One reason for this delay is that psychologists spend most of their time trying to help people overcome or control their anger, fear, and depression. True, people would like to be happier, but generally their reason for seeking help is to *stop* being *unhappy!* Another reason for the research delay is that happiness is difficult to define and measure, even more so than other emotions.

IS HAPPINESS AN EMOTION?

Fear and anger are prototypical examples of emotions, but happiness fits the definition much less clearly. Let's try applying the criteria we discussed in Chapter 1 to happiness:

1. *Emotion is a reaction to a stimulus.* Happiness can be a reaction to an event, like winning a game or receiving a compliment, but often people are happy for no particular reason. Also, happiness or satisfaction is more persistent than typical emotions; in some ways, it is closer to being a personality trait. If you feel happy about some event, like winning a prize, your emotion fades over time, but people who are happy for no particular reason tend to be happy most of the time, day after day.

2. *Emotion is a complex sequence of physiological, behavioral, and subjective changes.* According to many studies, the autonomic nervous system changes associated with happiness are unimpressive compared to anger or fear. Fear leads to fleeing and anger to fighting or at least threatening. What behavior does happiness evoke? Although studies by Ekman and others have associated a particular kind of smile with genuine happiness, many theorists have had trouble articulating a more specific, functional behavior.

3. *An emotion is a functional response to the situation.* Here "functional" means "adaptive." In what way does happiness help you survive?

The fitness-enhancing benefits of happiness are less obvious than the benefits of fear, anger, or disgust.

In short, happiness—at least in the sense of general satisfaction with life—does not fit most standard definitions of emotion. In the chapters on fear and anger we made a distinction between emotional *traits*, or long-term dispositional aspects of mood or affect, and short-term emotion *states* felt during a particular event. For example, we proposed that fear is an emotional state, whereas anxiety is more of a long-term mood or trait. By this distinction, what most lay people and researchers call "happiness" qualifies more as a mood or affect. People with a happy personality have been described as emotionally stable, conscientious, trusting, and in control of the situation or trying to be in control (DeNeve, 1999; DeNeve & Cooper, 1998). Another description is that happy or satisfied people have autonomy, mastery of their situation, personal growth, positive relations with others, purpose in life, and self-acceptance (Ryff & Singer, 2003). Happy people have their bad moods, too, but they snap back relatively quickly (Diener & Seligman, 2002). They are high in **subjective well-being**, which is an evaluation of one's life as pleasant, interesting, and satisfying (Diener, 2000).

Happiness as a personality trait is important, and we should discuss it in a textbook on emotions. But it is *not* an emotion in the usual sense. Sometimes we do have an intense, pleasant emotional experience in response to a particular event. Some researchers refer to that emotion as **joy** (Lazarus, 1991; Scherer, 1997). It may sound as if we are quibbling about words, but the distinction is important. Joy is evoked temporarily by a wide variety of events, such as doing well on a test, seeing your team win a game, having a good meal, or going shopping (Arnold & Reynolds, 2003). But long-term happiness or life satisfaction is not just the sum of many events producing short-term joy. We will begin by discussing happiness in the trait-like sense, and later in the chapter we'll examine some research on positive emotion states.

Measuring Trait Happiness

If happiness is a trait rather than an emotion per se, then a lot of the assumptions from Chapter 1 about how to measure emotions do not apply. Many researchers define "happiness" in terms of high life satisfaction, frequent experience of overall positive affect, and infrequent experience of negative affect (Diener & Diener, 1996; Diener, Suh, Lucas, & Smith, 1999). These fundamentally reflect the cognition and feeling aspects of emotion—physiological responses and behaviors are potentially interesting as correlates, but it would be difficult to claim that they *are* happiness. Thus, researchers interested in happiness have relied mainly on self-reports.

One of the most frequently used measures of happiness is the Satisfaction With Life Scale (Pavot & Diener, 1993). This measure asks people to rate how much they agree with each of the following statements on a scale from 1 (strongly disagree) to 7 (strongly agree):

_____ In most ways my life is close to my ideal.

_____ The conditions of my life are excellent.

_____ I am satisfied with my life.

_____ So far I have gotten the important things I want in life.

_____ If I could live my life over, I would change almost nothing.

Another often-used measure of overall happiness is the Positive Affect scale of the Positive and Negative Affect Schedule, or PANAS (Watson, Clark, & Tellegen, 1988). The PANAS has 20 items, each of which is a single word. A participant says, on a scale from 1 to 5, how well that word describes his feelings during a certain time (which could be a day, a week, a month, "in general," or any other unit of time). Ten of the 20 items are negative words such as " scared," "upset," "distressed," and "ashamed." The other 10 items, intended to measure Positive Affect, are "enthusiastic," "interested," "determined," "excited," "inspired," "alert," "active," "strong," "proud," and "attentive."

Consistent with the description of happiness as a trait, this questionnaire does not necessarily assess emotion, at least in the sense meant by many emotion researchers. Words like "enthusiastic" and "proud" seem to correspond to emotions, but what about "strong," "alert," and "determined"? These are desirable qualities, and if you feel strong, determined, and alert, then you probably feel good. Many researchers agree that the Positive Affect scale is best thought of as measuring high energy and overall positive mood, which is ideal for measuring trait happiness.

Another strategy for self-report research is to examine the emotions that people mention spontaneously, rather than using a questionnaire. That is, instead of directly asking people how happy or satisfied they are, we can take samples of their speech or writing and count how many times they say something about feeling happy. In one study, researchers examined information about a homogeneous group over time. An order of Catholic nuns asked young recruits in the 1930s and 1940s to "describe themselves," and kept those autobiographical essays. Some had expressed a great deal of positive emotion, whereas others had expressed little positive emotion (and generally little emotion of any types). Here are two examples (Danner, Snowdon, & Friesen, 2001, p. 806):

> [High positive emotion:] God started my life off well by bestowing upon me a grace of inestimable value…. The past year which I have spent as a candidate studying at Notre Dame College has been a very happy one. Now I look forward with eager joy to receiving the Holy Habit of Our Lady and to a life of union with Love Divine.
>
> [Low positive emotion:] I was born on September 26, 1909, the eldest of seven children, five girls and two boys…. My candidate year was spent in the Motherhouse, teaching chemistry and Second Year Latin at Notre Dame Institute. With God's grace, I intend to do my best for our Order, for the spread of religion and for my personal sanctification.

The researchers obtained data on what happened to those women over the rest of their lives. On the average, those who had expressed the most positive emotion in their essays survived the longest. Although this study used a correlational design, and we cannot assume that happiness caused long life, this is a remarkable study in terms of having few confounding lifestyle variables. That is, the nuns all had similar lifestyles and socioeconomic status; none married or had children; and few engaged in risky behaviors that might endanger their health, explaining the apparent effects of happiness.

WHAT MAKES PEOPLE HAPPY?

Are most people happy? One striking finding is that most people in reasonably prosperous countries say they are happy overall—that is, above the middle on a scale from very unhappy to very happy (Diener & Diener, 1996). Some psychologists argue that we evolved to make happiness the "default setting" (Buss, 2000). In general, happy people tend to be more productive than others and are more likely to compete successfully for reproductive opportunities. After all, wouldn't you rather mate with a happy person than an unhappy one? According to this reasoning, happy people are more likely than other people to pass on their genes (Buss, 2000). If so, most of us are descended from a long line of ancestors who tended to be reasonably happy most of the time, and we inherited genes that predispose us toward happiness. Still, even among people who call themselves happy, some report being happier than others, and it is interesting to see what predicts—and what *fails* to predict—these differences.

Self-Reported Causes of Happiness

If we want to know what makes people happy, the most obvious thing to do is to ask them. This method is far from perfect, but it is a reasonable way to start. You might try this yourself. Ask people you know about the causes of their happiness, but ask different people in different ways: "What *makes* you happy?" versus "What *would* make you happier?" The different wordings of this question

tend to give different results. One of us (JWK) has informally surveyed his introductory psychology class using these questions several times. In each case, half of the students received a questionnaire with the first wording and half with the second. For those who were asked "What would make you happier," the most common answers fell into these categories:

- More money or possessions
- A good job and a secure future
- A new boyfriend or girlfriend or a better relationship with the current one
- Better grades in school
- More time with family and friends
- More sleep

Here are a few interesting individual answers:

- "To experience more of what life has to offer."
- "Being in a log cabin in the mountains where there's snow sitting in front of a large fire place on a comfy couch with a blanket."
- "Warm weather or 10 million dollars or both."
- "To understand myself and my reactions to others."
- "If I could know without a doubt that the career I choose is the best one for me so that 20 years from now I will not look back and regret the choice I made."
- "For my mother and father to be happy together like they were when I was small."
- "To have a ~~great~~ social life."

In contrast, here are some common answers to the question "What makes you happy?":

- Friends and family (by far the most common answer)
- My boyfriend or girlfriend
- A feeling of success or accomplishment
- Relaxing
- Playing sports, being active
- Enjoying nature

- Music and humor
- Religion
- Making others happy

Note the contrast: Most of the items people say *would* make them happy are things that could happen *to* them. However, most of what *does* make them happy are their own actions or an appreciation of what is readily available (friends, family, nature).

A more systematic survey of middle-aged U.S. adults also found that most people said that their relationship with family and friends was their main source of satisfaction in life. Other common answers included physical health, financial security, self-development, a satisfactory job, faith, and simply enjoying the activities of life (Markus, Ryff, Curhan, & Palmersheim, 2004). Curiously, when people are asked about the sources of their happiness, few mention music, but if someone suggests it as a possible answer, almost everyone agrees it is a good one.

Although certain answers are very common, people with different lifestyles do tend to give somewhat different answers about what makes them happy. In particular, many of those with a college education cited their accomplishments. Those with only a high-school education seldom mentioned accomplishments and were more likely to cite a "sense of autonomy"—that is, feeling in control of important events (Markus et al., 2004). A sense of control is important to almost everyone, and people who feel a sense of control tend to be healthier as well as happier than others (Lachman & Firth, 2004). College-educated adults presumably took personal control for granted. To less educated people, many of whom probably got bossed around in their jobs, a sense of control was important wherever they could find it.

Personality: The "Top-Down" Theory of Happiness

A quote attributed to Abraham Lincoln is, "Most folks are about as happy as they make up their minds to be." Is that true? To what extent is happiness something we decide or create for ourselves, and to what extent is it a product of the events life has brought us?

This distinction is sometimes phrased as "top down" versus "bottom up," where top down means that your personality determines your happiness and bottom up means life events do (Heller, Watson, & Ilies, 2004). Psychologists initially assumed the bottom-up hypothesis: Good life events make you happy and bad events make you unhappy. To some extent this idea is true. A series of pleasant events can build an overall positive attitude that helps you deal with the occasional unpleasant experiences (Cohn, Fredrickson, Brown, Mikels, & Conway, 2009). However, many people are consistently happier or less happy than we might expect, given events in their lives.

One determinant of happiness is people's natural disposition, or personality. How happy you are now is a good predictor of how happy you will be many years from now (Pavot & Diener, 1993; D. Watson, 2002). Heritability studies suggest that genes play some role in these individual differences. Two studies, each examining thousands of pairs of twins, found that monozygotic (identical) twins resemble each other in life satisfaction more strongly than do dizygotic (fraternal) twins, both in young adulthood and later in life (Lykken & Tellegen, 1996; Røysamb, Harris, Magnus, Vittersø, & Tambs, 2002).

Although researchers do not expect to find a single gene for happiness, probably many genetic factors contribute, possibly by altering production of neurotransmitters or their receptors. One neurotransmitter associated with positive emotionality is dopamine. Some researchers have proposed that people genetically predisposed to high levels of dopamine, or to highly reactive dopamine receptors, end up being both happy and extraverted—a personality trait that correlates highly with happiness (Depue & Iacono, 1989; Gray, 1970). However, research has found only an inconsistent relationship between dopamine receptors and extraversion (Benjamin et al., 1996; Ebstein et al., 1996; Persson et al., 2000; Soyka, Preuss, Koller, Zill, & Bondy, 2002). The endorphin transmitters, which inhibit pain, also contribute to mood. Endorphin release increases during happiness and decreases during sadness (Zubieta et al., 2003).

Wealth and Happiness

When asked what would make them happier, many people answer "more money." If you think more money would make you happy, how much more money would you need? According to one survey, people earning $25,000 per year thought $50,000 would make them happy. People earning $50,000 said $100,000 would be enough. Those earning $100,000 thought they would need about $200,000, and so on ... (Csikszentmihalyi, 1999). Although few people are satisfied that they have "enough" money, we can ask whether wealthier people are happier than poorer people. Researchers have approached this question in several ways, which lead to somewhat different answers.

Here is one way: When people gain wealth, do they become happier? Right after people win a lottery, they rate their happiness very high, to no one's surprise. However, a few months later, their happiness ratings decline to about average (Diener, Suh, Lucas, & Smith, 1999; Myers, 2000a). Unfortunately, the meaning of this result is not altogether certain. The obvious interpretation is that money doesn't buy happiness. Another possibility is that people are happier, but have changed their standard of reference so that a rating of "4" on a 7-point scale doesn't mean the same thing it did a few months ago.

Another way to explore the relationship between wealth and happiness is to survey large groups. Most studies find a low correlation between wealth and happiness, around .20, and for years, psychologists concluded that wealth has little to do with happiness. However, most of the research had what scientists call a "restriction of range" problem: You won't find much influence of a variable if you measure only a small range of its possible values. Think of it this way: If you want to know whether people get happier or sadder as they grow older, could you find out by studying only teenagers? Of course not! What happens between ages 13 and 19 doesn't tell us what might happen between 19 and 99. Similarly, suppose we ask people about their wealth and their happiness, but the vast majority of survey participants have middle-class incomes. The difference between slightly lower and slightly higher middle-class incomes doesn't account for which people are happier than others. However, if we examine people with a wider range of incomes, we find that the wealthiest people report, on the average, significantly more happiness than the poorest (Lucas & Schimmack, 2009).

Impoverished people are particularly unhappy if they are surrounded by friends and relatives who are doing better. Also, the emotional impact of any event depends on whether it was better or worse than expected (Fliessbach et al., 2007). Thus, an impoverished person who never expected a high salary copes better than someone from a rich background who has fallen into poverty. The impact of poverty depends on health as well: It is possible to be poor and happy, but it is hard for someone who is both poor and sick to be happy (D. M. Smith, Langa, Kabeto, & Ubel, 2005).

Perhaps the relationship between wealth and happiness would change if we measured happiness in a different way. Instead of asking people to rate their overall happiness, researchers asked them to record what they were doing at various times during the day and how they felt during each activity. Richer people tend to spend more of their time on work-related activities, and less of it on leisure and recreation. According to this research method, middle-income people experience about as much pleasure as rich people (Kahneman, Krueger, Schkade, Schwarz, & Stone, 2006). However, this method depends on that word *pleasure*. Most people spend much of their time on child care, volunteer activities, and other pursuits that they regard as important and valuable, but not exactly pleasant or joyful. Life satisfaction depends on feelings of accomplishing something worthwhile, and not just on accumulating momentary enjoyment (White & Dolan, 2009).

Another kind of research compares happiness ratings for people from different countries. Figure 10.1 shows the mean results for many countries (Inglehart, Foa, Peterson, & Welzel, 2008). In general, people in wealthier countries report higher life satisfaction than those in poorer countries. However, other variables are important as well. Although exceptions abound,

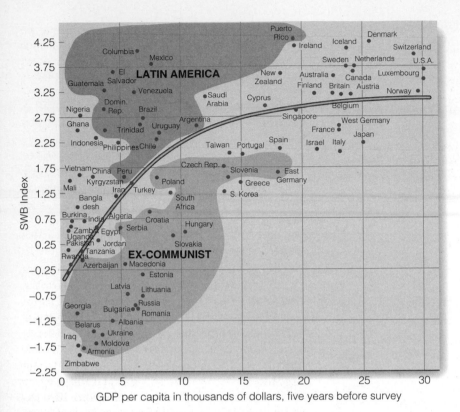

FIGURE 10.1   Each dot represents the mean for one country. The value along the x-axis shows the mean income per person in that country. The value along the y-axis shows the mean rating of subjective well-being. Surveys were conducted in different countries in different years.

Source: From Inglehart, R., Foa, R., Peterson, C., Welzel, C. (2008) 'Development, freedom, and rising happiness'. *Perspectives on Biological Science*, 3, pp. 264–285. Reprinted by permission.

the mean level of life satisfaction is generally higher in very religious countries, such as those of Latin America, then in more secular countries. Happiness also tends to be greater in countries that treat minority groups well, and that provide men and women with approximately equal status (Basabe et al., 2002). Whenever one group prospers at the expense of another group, sooner or later everyone suffers. If you would like to check out more data on happiness, try this website: http://worlddatabaseofhappiness.eur.nl/

Here are some tentative conclusions: Contrary to what psychologists thought at one time, wealthier people do tend to be happier than poorer people, on the average. However, the size of this effect is uncertain, depending on the method of measuring it,

and differences among middle-class people appear to be slight. Certainly life satisfaction depends on a great many other factors. Wealth might be the easiest to measure, but it is probably not the most important. Note also that nearly all the research is correlational, and therefore open to alternative explanations. Although it seems reasonable to assume that wealth increases happiness, it is also likely that a happy attitude increases one's chance for employment success, and therefore wealth. Studies on people who suddenly win a lottery have the best chance of demonstrating a cause and effect relationship—that is, that wealth leads to happiness—but they generally show less long-term benefit from wealth than we might have expected.

Other Correlates of Happiness

A few other factors also correlate with trait happiness. Because the investigator does not control either variable, we cannot draw cause-and-effect conclusions. Still, these findings can help guide ideas for future research. In general, people with more close relationships (close family members and friends) say they are happier than those with fewer relationships. On average, married people describe themselves as happier than unmarried people (DeNeve, 1999), and among college undergraduates, people with strong romantic attachments and close friendships are happier than those without such attachments (Diener & Seligman, 2002).

How shall we interpret this result? One obvious possibility is that friendships and romantic attachments are good for people. A before-and-after study found that young people reported decreased stress in their lives after getting married (Coombs & Fawzy, 1982). Another longitudinal study found that marriage produced long-term increases in happiness for some people, though not for all (Lucas, Clark, Georgellis, & Diener, 2003). The relationship between marriage and happiness varies; an unsatisfying marriage can do a great deal of harm (Heller et al., 2004).

Consider another plausible interpretation: Happy people are more likely than unhappy people to attract friends and partners, develop lasting attachments, get married, and stay married (Lyubomirsky, King, & Diener, 2005). Happy people also tend to have happier friends. One study found that when one person becomes happier, within a few months many of that person's friends become happier too, and later those people's friends as well (Fowler & Christakis, 2008). Happiness appears to be contagious! The correlation between close relationships and happiness almost certainly reflects effects in both directions: Happiness promotes relationships, and relationships increase happiness.

In general, healthy people are happier than unhealthy people (DeNeve, 1999; Myers, 2000a). Here it is hard to doubt that being ill makes people unhappy. However, part of the correlation probably reflects an influence in the other direction also: Being happy decreases the probability of becoming ill (e.g., Danner et al., 2001). Also, happy people are less likely than sad people to *say* they are ill, and they tend to report fewer symptoms, even when they are about equally ill (Salovey & Birnbaum, 1989).

People with religious faith tend to be happier than those without it (Myers, 2000a; Myers, 2000b). The natural assumption here is that religion provides a sense of purpose, comfort in difficult times, stability, and a sense of community. Another possible explanation is that happy people are more likely than unhappy people to accept religion, although people are more likely to experience a spiritual transformation or seek religious conversion when they are going through a personal crisis (Smith, 2006).

Happy people are more likely than others to have a goal in life (Csikszentmihalyi, 1999; Diener, Suh, Lucas, & Smith, 1999). Typical goals of happy people include making the world a better place in some way. The one goal that does not consistently lead to happiness is that of making money. In one study, researchers asked more than 12,000 U.S. college students about their life goals and followed up on them later. On average, those who had expressed the greatest interest in becoming rich were the least happy 19 years later. Of course, most of them did *not* become rich, so the unhappiness may have been due to failure to reach their goal, rather than the goal itself (Nickerson, Schwarz, Diener, & Kahneman, 2003). People whose goal was to make the world a better place usually felt they were accomplishing that goal, at least to some extent.

The importance of having a clear and important goal has been rediscovered by psychologists in one generation after another. The idea goes back at least to Alfred Adler (1927), a personality theorist and rival of Sigmund Freud. Adler proposed that people's primary motivation is "striving for superiority" and that different people seek that goal in different ways. The obvious way is to try to do something especially well, to win at some kind of competition. Another way is to find excuses for your failure, to find other people you can blame. According to Adler, the healthiest way to strive for superiority, and the way most likely to lead to a feeling of satisfaction, is to strive for the welfare of something greater than yourself, such as the betterment of society, world peace, justice, or the advancement of knowledge. Similar ideas were developed by the humanistic psychologists (e.g., Maslow, 1971), and again by researchers interested in self-esteem, who found that life satisfaction depended not on self-esteem itself, but on finding something to strive for—in other words, a worthy goal (Crocker & Park, 2004).

These predictors account for a small amount of individual differences in happiness. Income, age, health, and marital status *combined* account for less than 20 percent of the variance in people's happiness (Heller et al., 2004). These contributions may increase if some variables are measured differently. For example, one reason why marriage has only a small correlation with happiness is that some couples are unhappily married. *Happily* married couples are, on the average, much happier with their lives than are unhappily married couples (Heller et al., 2004). Our ability to predict happiness may improve as these more subtle features are taken into consideration.

Some Variables with Surprisingly Weak Influences

Wealth is not the only variable that has less influence on happiness than we might predict. Would you guess that good-looking people are happier than most others? If you are good-looking, many people smile at you, invite you to parties, and so forth. According to surveys, good-looking people are more satisfied than average with their romantic life, but in other ways no happier than average (Diener, Wolsic, & Fujita, 1995).

What about weather? It certainly makes a difference in the short term. If you have just been through a cloudy, cold, miserable winter, and today's weather is sunny and warm, you will probably rate yourself as happier than usual (Denissen, Butalid, Penke, & van Aken, 2008; Keller et al., 2005). However, people who live in sunny California rate themselves no happier, on the average, than people who live in Michigan, with its long, cold winters (Schkade & Kahnemann, 1998). Evidently people get used to their circumstances. Or perhaps a Californian who reports a certain level of happiness

means something different from a Michigander with the same report.

Would you expect well-educated people to be happier than less-educated ones? Here the answer is a bit more complicated. Better-educated people tend to have more challenging jobs, with higher pay but more stress. Higher pay is an advantage, but stress is a disadvantage. When researchers control for these two factors, by comparing people with similar pay and stress but different education, they find little difference in people's positive affect (Mroczek, 2004). That is, education by itself has little influence on happiness. It does, however, correlate significantly with "interest," which we could regard as a different kind of positive emotion (Consedine, Magai, & King, 2004). Better-educated people tend to have more diverse interests.

Would you expect young people to be happier than old people? Most young people are healthy, active, and attractive. They have a whole lifetime of exciting opportunities to anticipate. However, self-reports of emotions across the lifespan suggest the opposite. In fact, healthy people age 65 or older report more positive affect, and less negative affect, than younger or middle-aged adults (Mroczek, 2004; Mroczek & Spiro, 2005). In many ways they seem to screen out the negatives in life. For example, they deliberately turn their attention toward pleasant photos and objects, and away from disturbing ones (Isaacowitz, Toner, Goren, & Wilson, 2008; Knight et al., 2007). When they buy a product, they are more likely than younger people to say they like it two weeks later (Kim, Healey, Goldstein, Hasher, & Wiprzycka, 2008). If they play a game with a chance to win or lose money, they show as much excitement as young people about winning, but much less distress about losing (Larkin et al., 2007).

The results from self-reports parallel those from other kinds of research. When young adults and older adults look at emotionally relevant photos, fMRI scans of brain activity show that the amygdala of young adults responds more strongly to the unpleasant photos; in older adults it responds more strongly to pleasant photos (Mather et al., 2004). That is, research supports the idea that most people do "mellow" with age.

Events That Decrease Life Satisfaction

Life satisfaction is to some extent a personality trait, but not entirely. Events do make a difference. Most of the events that bring intense joy produce only a brief surge in overall happiness, but certain events can produce lasting consequences.

It is easier to produce a long-term decrease in happiness than a long-term increase. For example, an injury that causes major disability, such as paralysis, produces an immediate drop in life satisfaction, from which most people show little recovery over the next few years (Lucas, 2007). Also, if you lose a job that you care about, one that you take pride in as your long-term career, it hurts badly. One study of more than 24,000 German workers found that their satisfaction dropped sharply when they lost a job. Satisfaction recovered somewhat over time, but on the average did not return to its previous level even after 15 years (Lucas, Clark, Georgellis, & Diener, 2004).

Another powerful influence is loss of a spouse by either death or divorce. Figure 10.2 shows the results of one long-term study, in which people reported their satisfaction repeatedly over years (Diener & Seligman, 2004). The researchers isolated the data from those participants who lost a spouse and lined up their results so that year "0" was the year of the loss. Several points are worth noting in the graph: Life satisfaction declined gradually over the years *before* the loss, presumably because the marriage was deteriorating for those couples who divorced, and because health was deteriorating for the spouses who died. In general, widows and widowers were happier than divorced people, both before and after the loss, though about equal at the time of loss. Life satisfaction recovered slowly after the loss, but on the average, it did not return to its previous peak. Obviously, these average results do not apply to every individual. Some people recover well and others hardly at all; researchers are still trying to understand these individual differences in resilience.

Activities That May Increase
Life Satisfaction

A joyful event increases happiness temporarily, and a major loss can decrease it for a long time, but what

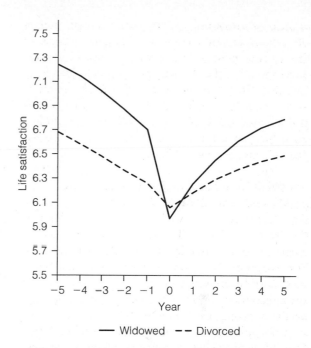

FIGURE 10.2 People reported gradually decreasing life satisfaction during the years prior to losing a spouse by death or divorce and gradually increasing satisfaction in the subsequent years, but on the average, satisfaction did not return to its original peak level.

Source: From E. Diener & M. E. P. Seligman, "Beyond Money," *Psychological Science in the Public Interest,* 5, pp. 1–31. Copyright 2004 Blackwell Publishing. Reprinted with permission.

can increase life satisfaction for more than a short time? Research suggests that events that happen *to* you are less important than what you *do.* Psychologists identified students who recently improved their life circumstances, such as by switching to a more preferred roommate, and others who had improved their activities, such as by joining a new club. The students with a new roommate reported increased happiness for a while, but those with new activities continued to report increased happiness all the way to the end of the semester (Sheldon & Lyubomirsky, 2006).

One particularly helpful activity is "counting your blessings." Researchers found that people improved their life satisfaction, optimism, and overall health if they set aside some time once a week to list five things for which they were grateful. The researchers recommended doing so just once a week, not more often. If you write your gratitude list every day or two, you start getting into a routine of saying the same things, and you don't take the task as seriously (Emmons & McCullough, 2003).

Another helpful activity is to do something to help someone else (Sheldon & Lyubomirsky, 2004). Researchers gave students some money in the morning, instructing some of them to spend the money on themselves, and others (chosen randomly) to buy a surprise gift for someone else, and then to report back to them in the late afternoon. Which do you think you would prefer, spending money on yourself or on someone else? Most people assume they would prefer to spend it on themselves, but in fact those who bought a surprise for someone else reported being happier at the end of the day (Dunn, Aknin, & Norton, 2008). In the words of a Chinese proverb, if you want happiness for an hour, take a nap. If you want happiness for a day, go fishing. If you want happiness for a year, inherit a fortune. If you want happiness for a lifetime, help somebody else.

POSITIVE EMOTION STATES

So far we have talked about happiness more as a mood than as an emotion. This is common among emotion researchers, many of whom have doubts as to whether there really are positive emotions comparable to fear, anger, and so forth. However, some studies have treated "happiness" or "joy" as an emotion state rather than a trait. Still other researchers have asked whether the broad term "happiness" really covers a number of more specific positive emotions, in the same way that there might be multiple basic emotions we call "love." Let's consider positive emotions as short-term states now.

Function: The "Broaden-and-Build" Theory of Positive Emotions

For many years, researchers had a good reason for reluctance in considering happiness as a possible "basic"

emotion. It is easy to propose a fitness-enhancing function for fear, anger, disgust, and even love, but how might happiness increase the representation of your genes in future generations? In Chapter 2, we made the explicit point that "happiness" alone does not make something adaptive. In some cases, theorists proposed that the function of positive emotions was to help relieve us from the physical and behavioral consequences of negative emotion, basically equating positive emotion with relief (Fredrickson & Levenson, 1998; Lazarus, 1991). Other than that, this problem really had researchers stumped.

Eventually researcher Barbara Fredrickson (1998) proposed that we think about the effects of positive emotions in a different way than we think about the functions of negative emotions. Whereas negative emotions are thought to enhance fitness by promoting immediate *actions* that deflect threats in the environment, she reasoned, positive emotions may enhance fitness by changing the way we *think* about the world around us, helping us to gather information and resources that will be helpful in the future. According to the **broaden-and-build theory**, positive emotions promote broadened attention so that we are more likely to notice opportunities in the environment, as well as greater flexibility in the actions we might take to maximize those opportunities.

A number of studies provide support for this general hypothesis. In one study, Fredrickson and her colleague Christine Branigan (2005) used film clips to induce feelings of amusement, contentment, anger, anxiety, and neutral affect in participants. They then gave participants a series of test items that looked something like this:

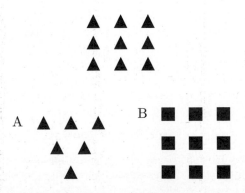

Your task is to look quickly at the image in the upper row, and then decide which of the two images below is more like it. Do it quickly—don't think too hard, your answer should be instinctive. Which did you choose—A or B?

According to the researchers, choosing "A" indicates that your attention is focused on local details of the upper figure (the little triangles), rather than the "big picture" of the shape. Choosing "B" indicates attention to the target figure's overall configuration—a square. Individuals who had just viewed the funny or contentment-inducing film were much more likely to choose "B" and similar options in other items, suggesting that the positive emotion biased their attention toward global features rather than details.

Other studies have found a number of cognitive effects of positive emotions, also associated with big-picture thinking and open-mindedness. In general, people tend to be better at recognizing particular faces of their own race than of other races (the "they all look alike to me" phenomenon). One study found that this bias was reduced in people right after a positive emotion manipulation, compared to a neutral condition (Johnson & Fredrickson, 2005). Another study found that people who reported more positive emotion states in diaries over a one-month period also showed greater increases in trait life satisfaction, and that this effect was accounted for by increased resilience or ability to handle stress (Cohn, Fredrickson, Brown, Mikels, & Conway, 2009).

These studies emphasize a common feature of positive emotions—they help us take advantage of opportunities presented by the environment. Does that mean there is only one positive emotion, with only one function? Not necessarily. According to Fredrickson and others, different "basic" positive emotions may also have more specific functions that involve observable behaviors as well as effects on cognitive processing (Fredrickson, 1998; Shiota, Campos, Keltner, Hertenstein, 2004). We will discuss some candidates for positive "basic" emotion status shortly.

Positive Emotion as a Contrast Effect

What kind of event brings you happiness or joy? Pleasant events do, of course, but not just any pleasant event. The emotional impact depends on a comparison with what was happening previously or with an alternative possible event. How would you feel if a stranger on the street handed you $10 for no reason? Happy, we presume. But if that stranger had been handing out $20 to everyone else until it was your turn, you might feel sad or angry, even though you got something for nothing. In one study people sometimes knew they were going to receive money (but not how much) and sometimes knew they were going to lose (again without knowing how much). When they won smaller amounts than they hoped, they were sad. When they lost smaller amounts than they feared, they were happy (J. T. Larsen, McGraw, Mellers, & Cacioppo, 2004).

In another study, researchers examined videotapes and interviews from the 1992 Olympics (Medver, Madey, & Gilovich, 1995). They found that on the average, bronze medal winners (third place) looked and acted happier than the silver medal winners (second place). The researchers' interpretation was that the silver medal winners reacted, "Ouch! Just a little more and I might have won the gold medal!" The bronze medal winners were thinking, "What a relief! I just barely missed finishing fourth and going home empty-handed!" (See Figure 10.3.) Psychologists refer to this tendency as a **contrast effect**, the emotional influence of whether an outcome was better or worse than some other likely outcome.

Consider your grades. How would you feel about receiving a B in a course? If you had been expecting a C, the B would make you happy. If you had expected an A, then you would be sad and frustrated (Mellers & McGraw, 2001). (See Figure 10.4.) Many professors find that students who receive a B+ are far more likely to complain than students who got Cs or Ds. It seems that "almost A" is very disappointing. Almost any event can be either a reward or a punishment, depending on the alternatives.

Facial Expressions of Positive Emotion

Anger and fear arguably produce observable behaviors, even in nonhuman animals. But what does a happy animal do? Dogs wag their tails at times

FIGURE 10.3 Finishing second is disappointing to someone who thinks, "I came so close to being first!"

when we assume they are happy, and cats purr. According to one study, zookeepers agree with one another fairly consistently about which chimpanzees seem happiest or most satisfied with life

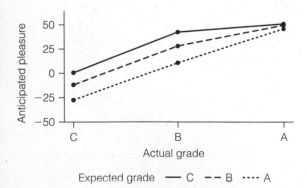

FIGURE 10.4 Students rated how they would feel about receiving various grades. Their emotions depended on whether the grades were higher or lower than they expected.

Source: From Mellers & McGraw, "Anticipated Emotion as Guide to Choice," *Current Directions in Psychological Science*, Vol. 10, pp. 210–214. Copyright 2001 Blackwell Publishing. Reprinted with permission.

(King & Landau, 2003). However, many animals give no obvious signals of happiness.

Behavioral observations of happiness in humans are not much easier. What do people *do* when they are happy? For one thing, they act more optimistically. They approach other people more boldly than usual, they take more chances, and they react less strongly than usual to threats (C. Peterson, 2000). Whereas frightened or angry people focus their attention narrowly on the object of fear or anger, happy people broaden their attention (Fredrickson, 1998; Gable & Harmon-Jones, 2008). They are more open to considering new ideas and trying activities they have never tried before, including those of other cultures (Ashton-Jones, Maddux, Galinsky, & Chartrand, 2009). These complex behaviors certainly have important implications for people's social and practical lives. However, none of them is a good operational measure of happiness for research purposes.

Another consequence of happiness is speed. Sad people slow down in the way they walk and talk, and even in their thinking. Happy people tend to move quickly and speak rapidly. Manipulations that prompt people to speak and act more rapidly generally make people feel happier (Pronin & Jacobs, 2008; Pronin, Jacobs, & Wegner, 2008).

The most easily measurable behavior associated with happiness is smiling. Yet even smiling poses measurement problems. Happy people don't always smile (especially when they are alone), and most smiles don't last long. Furthermore, people learn to smile politely in certain situations, and some cultures encourage public smiling more than others. On average, women smile more than men. Should we conclude that women are also happy more often? Perhaps, but women are also more likely than men to smile even when they are not particularly happy (LaFrance, Hecht, & Paluck, 2003).

Fortunately, there is a fairly reliable way to tell whether a smiling person actually feels happy or is just being polite. Researchers studying facial expressions of emotion have identified a special kind of smile, the **Duchenne smile** (named after the investigator who first described it), which includes raised cheeks and crow's feet at the corners of the eyes plus a smiling mouth, that usually communicates real positive emotion. Figure 10.5 supplies examples of Duchenne and non-Duchenne smiles. Because the eye muscles that contract in the Duchenne smile are difficult to control voluntarily, few people can fake a Duchenne smile convincingly. Try it yourself!

It is important to note that not all emotional smiles are Duchenne smiles. Observers have found that young children usually react to any pleasant event first with a non-Duchenne smile. If the pleasure is strong enough, the non-Duchenne smile gradually grows into a Duchenne smile (Messinger, 2002). Even with adults, many sincere smiles fail to meet the Duchenne criteria. A good way to think of it is this: A Duchenne smile almost always

(a)   (b)

Paul Ekman

F I G U R E 10.5 Very happy or amused people show a Duchenne smile, as in the photo on the left. Note the raised cheeks and the appearance around the eyes. Voluntary smiles usually look like the photo on the right. However, the smile on the right could also be an honest expression of mild happiness or amusement.

indicates genuine happiness, but a non-Duchenne smile can also indicate happiness.

Using the Duchenne smile as an indicator of happiness is more difficult than it probably sounds. We described the challenges of facial expression coding in detail in Chapter 1, but in brief, participants must be videotaped, and then their facial behavior must be painstakingly coded for the presence, frequency, intensity, and duration of Duchenne smiles. The problem is that the Duchenne smile is subtle. Ordinarily, we evaluate the happiness of someone's expression almost entirely by the mouth. Consider the several versions of the *Mona Lisa* painting in Figure C.5 (see the inside cover of this book). Nearly everyone regards B as happy and A as sad because of the differences in the mouth. Many insist that the eyes look happier in B also, even though the eye expressions are in fact the same for A and B. In contrast, the eye expressions differ for C and D, but most people don't notice, because the mouths are the same (Kontsevich & Tyler, 2004).

Despite its drawbacks, the Duchenne smile has proved a very useful measure of happiness—one of the strongest and most reliable in research on positive emotion. For example, one remarkable study looked at the ways young women smiled in their college yearbook photos, and then asked whether the smiles predicted how women's lives played out throughout adulthood (Harker & Keltner, 2001). In this study, women who showed stronger Duchenne smiles in this single photograph were happier in their marriages and less likely to divorce, and they described themselves as more competent and more socially active decades later than women with more "polite" smiles, or no smile at all. Clearly our smiles convey something important about the way we approach the world.

Is the Duchenne smile the only expression of positive emotion? Few studies have addressed this question systematically, but Jessica Tracy and Rick Robins (2004) have identified an expression of pride that is recognized cross-culturally, and that resembles the posture of high-status animals. Researchers have also tentatively identified facial expressions of amusement and awe, but these await further research (Shiota, Campos, & Keltner, 2003).

Physiological Measures of Positive Emotion

So far, autonomic measures have not been particularly helpful in assessing positive emotions. Remembering a moment of joy increases heart rate, but not by much compared to fear or anger (Cacioppo et al., 2000; Levenson, Ekman, & Friesen, 1990). Although some studies do find autonomic effects of positive emotions, these are sometimes in opposing directions. Some studies find that positive emotions are associated with signs of increased sympathetic activation, such as increased heart rate and skin conductance (Christie & Friedman, 2003; Demaree, Schmeichel, Robinson, & Everhart, 2004; Neumann & Waldstein, 2001). Other studies find that positive emotion is associated with *reduced* sympathetic activation, especially when the positive emotion follows a period of arousing negative emotion (Fredrickson & Levenson, 1998; Fredrickson, Mancuso, Branigan, & Tugade, 2000). It may be that these different researchers are actually eliciting different positive emotions in their studies, accounting for the wide range of effects, but more research is needed to explore this possibility. Also, as we noted in earlier chapters, different methods of eliciting emotion have their own physiological effects, so it is hard to tease apart the effects of the emotions from the effects of the methods.

Functional MRI studies find that happiness is associated with increased activity in some brain areas, and decreased activity in others (George et al., 1995). However, the results vary substantially from one study to another, depending on the details of procedure (Esslen, Pascual-Marqui, Hell, Kochi, & Lehmann, 2004; Eugène et al., 2003; Murphy, Nimmo-Smith, & Lawrence, 2003). A more robust finding pertains to differences between the left and right hemispheres of the brain. Most research has linked activation of the frontal cortex of the left hemisphere to approach tendencies (including both happiness and anger) while linking activity of the frontal cortex in the right hemisphere to withdrawal tendencies (including sadness and fear).

This difference takes place in two ways (Coan & Allen, 2004). One is as a predisposition: People who usually have greater left than right activity tend to respond more strongly than others to pleasant events of life, whereas people who usually have greater activity on the right side tend to respond more strongly to events provoking fear or sadness (Urry et al., 2004). The second aspect is as an outcome: Events that elicit happiness tend to activate the left hemisphere more than the right hemisphere, whereas events that elicit fear and sadness tend to activate the right hemisphere more strongly (R. J. Davidson & Fox, 1982; R. J. Davidson & Henriques, 2000; Reuter-Lorenz & Davidson, 1981). For example, researchers used EEG methods to monitor brain activity while ten-month-old infants watched videotapes of someone smiling or looking sad (R. J. Davidson & Fox, 1982). While the babies viewed the happy faces, their left frontal lobes were more active than their right. When viewing the sad faces, the activity was about the same on both sides of the frontal lobes. In most studies with older participants, sadness evoked more activity on the right side than the left (Henriques & Davidson, 2000).

Another study also compared responses of the right and left hemispheres to happy and sad stimuli. This study relies on the fact that the right hemisphere processes information coming from the left side of the visual field (anything to the left of your focus), whereas the left hemisphere processes information from the right side of the field. With the proper equipment, researchers can show different images to your right and left hemispheres at the same time. Participants viewed pairs of images in this way, with either a happy or a sad face on one side and a neutral face on the other. The task was to say as quickly as possible which side had an emotional face. On the average, people responded faster if the right hemisphere was viewing a sad face or if the left hemisphere was viewing a happy face, rather than the other way around (Reuter-Lorenz & Davidson, 1981).

However, the difference between left and right hemispheres is not really a matter of happiness versus sadness. The left frontal lobes seem to be specialized for processes associated with *approach*, including anger as well as happiness (Murphy, Nimmo-Smith, & Lawrence, 2003). So any researcher who uses brain recordings to infer emotions needs to guard against confusing one "approach" emotion with another.

So far we have discussed positive emotions as states rather than lasting traits, but still have treated positive emotion as a single, broad category. Increasingly, researchers are asking whether there are multiple, "basic" positive emotions as well. Although this is still controversial, let's consider a few candidates and look at some of the available evidence.

ENTHUSIASM: THE ANTICIPATION OF REWARD

When we look forward to a pleasurable experience, we experience **anticipatory enthusiasm**—pleasure from expecting a reward. Suppose we could arrange to provide you with a wonderful, romantic kiss from the movie star of your choice. Would you rather have it now or a week from now? Most people prefer to delay it (Loewenstein, 1987), presumably because they want to enjoy looking forward to it. Researchers have also found evidence for the surprising conclusion that commercial interruptions in a television program actually increase people's enjoyment of the program! Why? During the interruption, they look forward to the resumption of the program, and when it returns, people enjoy it more than before the interruption (Nelson, Meyvis, & Galak, 2009).

This kind of positive emotion has been associated with a brain pathway sometimes called the "reward circuit," including the ventral tegmental area (VTA) and the nucleus accumbens, as well as parts of the frontal lobes. We first introduced this circuit in Chapter 5. Researchers have found that these brain areas, especially the nucleus accumbens, show enhanced release of the neurotransmitter dopamine in a way that depends on how a reward compares to what was expected or predicted. An unpredicted reward, or one larger than predicted, releases dopamine. Reward exactly as predicted does not. Reward that is omitted or less than predicted *inhibits* dopamine release to less than its baseline level (Daw & Shohamy, 2008).

The nucleus accumbens reacts to a wide range of reinforcers, including drugs (such as cocaine), sex, food, and video games (Giuliani & Ferrari, 1996; R. A. Harris, Brodie, & Dunwiddie, 1992; Hull et al., 1992; Koepp et al., 1998). It also responds in gambling games when someone has been winning or appears likely to win. The amygdala responds strongly, though in different ways, to both reinforcing and punishing events.

Studies of rats and other mammals have shown that cells in the nucleus accumbens and VTA rapidly learn about the relationships between events that predict rewards and the rewards themselves. Activity in these cells then predicts behavior involved retrieving the reward (such as moving toward a chute that will deliver a tasty snack). For this reason, researchers have called the pathway that includes these brain areas the "Behavioral Activation System" (Gray, 1970). In fMRI studies with human participants, this system becomes active in all kinds of rewarding situations, from eating chocolate to eye contact with an attractive person, humor, and listening to one's favorite music (Blood & Zatorre, 2001; Kampe, Frith, Dolan, & Frith, 2002; Mobbs, Grecius, Abdel-Azim, Menon, & Reiss, 2003; Small et al., 2001).

An important distinction here is between the positive emotion associated with *anticipating* something, versus the pleasure associated with actually *consuming* something (Berridge & Robinson, 1995). Brain activity in the Behavioral Activation System demonstrates the power of the contrast effect. The system becomes highly active if you see something that you want just within your reach. As soon as you consume the reward, however, the reward circuit quiets down again. In one study, researchers found that people's reward circuits were active when they were first offered pieces of chocolate, but over time, as they ate more and more chocolate and reported getting tired of it, their reward circuits "turned off" as the offers continued (Small et al., 2001).

In another study, investigators used fMRI scans to record brain activity while people were playing a game of chance, somewhat like a slot machine (Breiter, Aharon, Kahneman, Dale, & Shizgal, 2001). Each participant was given $50 to start and told that she would have to spin a dial a certain number of times to determine how much money would be added to or subtracted from that total. Different players had different dials, as diagrammed here:

Note that some participants could only win, some could win or lose, and some could only lose, but all had the possibility of a zero on a given spin. The researchers were specifically interested in activity in the nucleus accumbens and the amygdala (Hamann, Ely, Hoffman, & Kilts, 2002). Both the nucleus accumbens and amygdala reacted to an outcome of zero as a reward when the alternatives were −$1.50 and −$6, but they reacted to it as a punishment when the alternatives were +$2.50 and +$10 (Breiter et al., 2001).

We can apply this principle to the happiness rating studies previously described. Immediately after gaining wealth, such as winning a lottery, people's happiness should increase, as indeed it does, because their wealth is higher than usual and higher than expected. After people have become accustomed to their wealth, the contrast is no longer present and their happiness returns to its usual level. Their wealth may still be high, but they now *expect* it to be high.

CONTENTMENT

In describing anticipatory enthusiasm we emphasized the distinction between *anticipating* something that you still don't have yet, and *consuming* something once you have it. Of course, both are pleasurable, and we may enjoy the sensations associated with consumption even though we weren't craving that thing in the first place (Small et al., 2001). According to researcher Barbara Fredrickson (1998), the **contentment** we feel *after* consuming a big meal or other reward should also be considered an emotion.

This is a familiar state for most people. You've just had a nice, big, delicious meal, and although you're not uncomfortably stuffed you are pleasantly full. Your body feels relaxed and warm, and your brain even seems to slow down. These effects can be accounted for by increased activation of the parasympathetic nervous system, discussed in Chapter 4 (see Figure C.1 inside the cover of this book). Recall that researchers often refer to the parasympathetic branch of the autonomic nervous system as the "rest and digest" system. This is because the effects of its activation take resources away from the skeletal muscles and promote digestion. Thus, we would expect to see signs of increased parasympathetic activation when people have just consumed a reward and are feeling contentment. We know this is true after literally eating; whether parasympathetic activation increases during other forms of contentment is yet to be demonstrated.

At the neural level, changes associated with contentment after eating can also be detected. After consumption, dopaminergic activation in the reward circuit calms down, and is replaced by endogenous opiate activity that slows down overall behavior (Depue & Morrone-Strupinsky, 2005).

Fredrickson proposed that post-consummatory contentment should facilitate memory for the pathway one took to reward. After all, whatever you just did must have been successful, so remembering your actions is a good plan. Although little research has addressed this hypothesis, one remarkable study with mice lends some support. In this study, researchers inserted single-cell recording electrodes into "place cells" in rodents' hippocampi—neural structures necessary for memory formation. They then had the animals run a maze to find a snack. After eating the snack the animals went through a typical "satiety sequence" that includes looking around to make sure no predators were nearby, grooming, and hanging out quietly (Bradshaw & Cook, 1996). While the animals were engaged in this contentment-like behavior, their hippocampal place cells fired in the *reverse* sequence from firing while they actually ran the maze, as though they were mentally backtracking their course (Foster & Wilson, 2006). Much more work is needed to examine these processes in humans, and to see whether the characteristics of post-food-consumption contentment generalize to other sources of this emotion as well.

HOPE AND OPTIMISM

Imagine that it is the night before an important exam, and a classmate calls you in terror to say that in previous classes, more than 60 percent of the students failed. You know things look bad, but you also prepared carefully for the exam, believe that if you approach the test the right way you'll do well, and are determined to put in another hour of study before getting a good night's sleep to refresh your mind. How would you describe the emotion you might be feeling? According to Snyder and colleagues, this is the essence of **hope**—high agency in a challenging situation combined with active generation of plans that can facilitate the desired outcome (Snyder, Sympson, Michael, & Cheavens, 2001). People who are hopeful also tend to be optimistic. **Optimism** is generally defined as an expectation that mostly good things will happen. In this sense, optimism is the type of appraisal that facilitates the emotion hope. Monozygotic twins also resemble each other more strongly than dizygotic twins do in their degree of optimism (Schulman, Keith, & Seligman, 1993).

Optimism is often measured by a questionnaire called the Life Orientation Test (Scheier, Carver, & Bridges, 1994). Here are some example items:

In uncertain times, I usually expect the best.

1	2	3	4	5
Strongly disagree				*Strongly agree*

If something can go wrong for me, it will.

1	2	3	4	5
Strongly disagree				*Strongly agree*

Overall, I expect more good things to happen to me than bad.

1	2	3	4	5
Strongly disagree				*Strongly agree*

As you might guess, an optimist is someone who strongly agrees with the first and third items but disagrees with the second. A pessimist, the opposite of an optimist, agrees with the second item but not the other two. Pessimism is related to but not synonymous with **neuroticism**, a tendency to experience fear, sadness, and anger relatively easily.

One common optimistic belief is that "better things will happen to me than to other people." That is, I am more likely than other people to succeed in life, more likely to survive to old age, less likely to have an automobile accident, less likely to get a dreaded disease, and so forth (Quadrel, Fischhoff, & Davis, 1993). That belief is often called "unrealistic optimism" because most people have no reason to believe their chance of success or of illness is any different from the average (Nezlek & Zebrowski, 2001). A mild degree of unrealistic optimism is nevertheless widespread. Most U.S. adults overestimate the accuracy of their guesses on difficult questions (Plous, 1993), their probability of winning a lottery (Langer, 1975), and their ability to explain complex physical phenomena (Rozenblit & Keil, 2002). When asked how conscientious they will be about exercising, saving for retirement, and so forth, they give almost the same answers as when asked how they would be "in an ideal world" (Tanner & Carlson, 2008).

We might assume that unrealistic optimism is a bad thing, and indeed it is when it leads to foolish risks or bad plans. For example, most people severely overestimate how quickly they will finish a difficult task, and don't set aside enough time for it (Buehler, Griffin, & Ross, 1994; Dunning, Heath, & Suls, 2005). Many people ignore warnings about diet, smoking, alcohol, and so forth, confident that they will remain healthy anyway. As a rule, however, a little unrealistic optimism helps people deal with bad news and muster up the energy to go on with life (Taylor & Brown, 1988; Taylor, Kemeny, Reed, Bower, & Gruenwald, 2000). Most people recognize that their estimates are not always accurate, but believe that slightly unrealistic optimism is a good thing (Armor, Massey, & Sackett, 2008).

Another type of belief is that "everything will turn out all right no matter what I do, so I don't have to do anything." That is a calming attitude, but not a productive one. The more helpful type of optimism is the belief that "my problems are solvable, my actions make a difference, and I can control my future chances for success." Optimism in this sense differs from pessimism by the attributions people make for their successes and especially for their failures (Carver & Scheier, 2002; Peterson & Steen, 2002). Pessimists tend to feel that desirable outcomes are beyond their control, whereas optimists believe that their actions make a difference and that effort pays off.

People with an optimistic attitude have advantages in many aspects of life and no known disadvantages, except when overconfidence leads to bad decisions. Optimistic people make friends more easily (Helweg-Larsen, Sadeghian, & Webb, 2002). In tense or trying situations, optimistic people experience less anxiety (Wilson, Raglin, & Pritchard, 2002) and less emotional exhaustion (Fry, 1995). They are less likely than other people to abuse drugs (Park, Moore, Turner, & Adler, 1997). After major surgery, they report less distress and better overall quality of life. One reason for this is that an optimistic person asks questions of the doctors and nurses, reads about the illness and its treatment, and makes plans for overcoming the problem (Carver et al., 1993; Scheier et al., 1989). Generally, a well-informed patient is more likely to follow medical advice, to get proper nutrition and exercise, and to take all the other steps that improve chances for recovery. So optimism provides its benefits in both direct and indirect ways.

AMUSEMENT AND HUMOR

In the final part of this chapter, we explore one of the least studied mysteries of human psychology—laughter and humor. Think how much we value humor. We gladly buy tickets for a show that promises to make us laugh. When people describe the characteristics they want in a dating partner or lifelong mate, "sense of humor" is usually near the top. However, few psychologists have done much research on humor or laughter, and many of the fundamental questions are unanswered.

The good news is that if you want to do your own research, you can find questions that are easy to address without expensive equipment, and you won't have to compete with hundreds of other researchers trying to answer the same questions.

What Makes Something Funny?

George Orwell (2000, p. 284) once said, "A thing is funny when—in some way that is not actually offensive or frightening—it upsets the established order. Every joke is a tiny revolution." According to one theory, people experience humor in response to a **cognitive shift** in the perception of some target—a transition from thinking about the target from one perspective to thinking about it from a completely different, but still appropriate, perspective (Latta, 1999). Consider the following joke:

Q: How do you stop a lawyer from drowning?

A: Shoot him before he hits the water.

If you think this is funny, why? According to the cognitive shift perspective, the humor lies in switching from the assumption that one is trying to save the lawyer's life to a focus on choosing the method of death. The implicit assumption set up in the premise of the joke is shattered and replaced by the punch line, so you have to think about the situation in a new way. Note that the effectiveness of the joke depends upon having some contempt for lawyers, so that the idea of wanting to kill one is plausible. If you are a lawyer, thinking about becoming a lawyer, or have close friends who are lawyers, this joke might not seem funny. Starting with the question "How do you stop a kindergarten teacher from drowning?" will presumably dampen the joke's value.

Humor also depends on surprise. A joke that seems hilarious the first time you hear it probably evokes less or no response the second time. Just seeing someone make a strange face, wear odd clothing, or yell "boo" can seem funny if it catches you by surprise. The same act is hardly amusing if you expected it. However, not all surprises are funny, so it is not unexpectedness alone that determines humor.

One implication of the "cognitive shift" definition is that what strikes one person as funny may not amuse another. Consider puns, bathroom humor, dirty jokes, ethnic jokes, and slapstick. (See Figure 10.6.) In each case, some people laugh uproariously and others consider the joke rude, tasteless, stupid, or at least not funny. In order to understand the premise of a particular joke, and find the punch line surprising, yet appropriate, you need certain cultural reference points and personal attitudes. Few comic movies, plays, or books stand the test of time. Granted, Shakespeare's *A Midsummer Night's Dream* still amuses audiences hundreds of years after it was written, but many comic movies of 10 or 20 years ago miss the mark today. The humor of a different culture often fails completely in translation. By contrast, a well-done serious play or tragedy can deeply move audiences of a different culture or a different point in time. Even old monster movies, such as *Frankenstein, Dracula,* or *Godzilla,* hold much of their appeal over time and place.

Amusement also depends on who presents the joke. You are more likely to say something funny, and to enjoy the other person's attempts at humor, if you like the person than if you don't (Li et al., 2009). That is, humor is a way to indicate your interest in a friendly relationship. Many professors try to liven their lectures with humor, but if you don't like your professor, you won't like her jokes either. Ethnic humor is especially fragile. An Asian person can make fun of other Asians and a Jew can joke about Jews, but an outsider should beware of telling the same joke. Remember that humor relies on a lot of background assumptions and information. If you and your listener have different perspectives, attempts to be funny may fall flat or even seem offensive.

What Makes People Laugh?

Humor and laughter are linked, but not entirely. Laughter is fundamentally a kind of communication, and it occurs mostly in social settings (Provine, 2000). It is a way for even a preverbal child to tell a parent, "Yes, I'm enjoying what you're doing! Keep it up!" It is a way for one adult to tell another, "I'm happy and enjoying your company." People smile more in a social setting than when they are

Bettmann/Corbis

FIGURE 10.6 Tastes in humor may vary by country, culture, gender, age, and historical era. A film that someone else considers hilarious may not amuse you at all.

alone, and the same is true of laughter. If you are alone while watching a comedy on television, you won't laugh much. Surround yourself with friends who are laughing, and you laugh too. Many television shows include a "laugh track" of recorded laughter to prime you to laugh along.

Laughter is contagious, much like yawning. If you hear other people laughing vigorously, you may laugh along with them, even if you don't know why they are laughing. However, the contagion of laughter depends on how it sounds. Some laughs are "unvoiced": they consist of just a single noisy grunt or snort. Someone who makes an unvoiced laugh evokes little emotional response in the listener (Bachorowski & Owren, 2001). A "voiced" laugh includes several puffs of "ha," "ho," or "he." And you almost always continue with whichever sound you start with. You might laugh "ha ha ha ha ha" or "ho ho ho ho ho," but not "he ha ho ha ho." Each puff lasts about 1/15 of a second, and the delay between one puff and the next is 1/5 of a second. The figures are nearly the same for people of all

ages and backgrounds, so they are probably part of our biological heritage (Provine, 2000). They are also nearly the same for people who were born profoundly deaf (Makagon, Funayama, & Owren, 2008). If you hear laughs that fit this pattern, you are likely to laugh along. However, if you hear "ha ... ha ... ha ..." at a noticeably different speed, you don't imitate.

An unanswered question here: Is the contagiousness of laughter built-in or learned? One crying baby in a nursery gets all the others crying. But even when infants are old enough start laughing, at first they hardly react to other babies' laughs. Do they have to learn how their own laugh sounds before they recognize it in others? No one seems to have studied this issue.

When Robert Provine (2000) set out to observe laughter, he assumed, as most of us do, that people laugh mainly when they hear something funny. However, when he and his students spent many hours eavesdropping in malls and other hangouts, they found that people laughed mostly when they were talking, not in response to someone else. Most laughs came after saying something that would not strike a listener as amusing, such as, "I'll see you guys later. Ha! Ha! Ha!" or "I hope we all do well. Ha! Ha! Ha!" If you doubt this observation, listen to laughs yourself at a social gathering. Do people laugh more after their own statements or those of others? And how many of those laughs follow truly witty statements?

Provine has suggested that laughter communicates social support, as much as or even more than humor. This explanation would also account for gender differences in laughter. Men tell more jokes, but women laugh more (Provine, 2000). (See Figure 10.7.) In childhood, boys and girls laugh about equally. By adolescence, men tell more jokes, but women laugh and smile more (Hall & Halberstadt, 1986; Provine, 2000). The fact that women laugh more does not necessarily mean that women are on the average more amused than men. Both laughter and smiling make other people feel comfortable, understood, and appreciated (LaFrance, Hecht, & Paluck, 2003; Provine, 2000). Gender differences in laughter may reflect different social role expectations rather than, or in addition to, differences in emotional experience.

Laughter and Health?

What good is laughter? One function, as mentioned, is social. Laughter indicates that you are having a good time, that you like the people you are with, and that you would like to maintain a friendly relationship with them. You may also hear people claim that laughter is good medicine, that it reduces pain and cures illnesses. Much of the evidence for this idea is anecdotal, from people who used laughter when they felt ill and then recovered nicely. Anecdotes are weak evidence, though. Several studies have found that positive

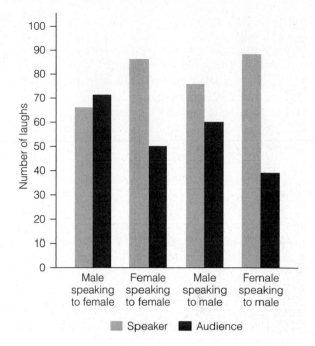

FIGURE 10.7 For each occasion in which at least one person laughed, the graphs show how often the speaker laughed and how often the audience laughed. Note that, in general, speakers laugh more often than audiences, and women laugh more than men.

Source: Based on Provine (2000).

experiences in general, including humor, enhance the activity of the immune system. Humor reportedly enables surgical patients to decrease their use of pain-killing drugs and to decrease their fear of death (Lefcourt, 2002). However, research on humor and health is sparse, and much of it has used only a few participants and questionable control groups. Humor may be good for you medically, and it can't hurt, but the scientific evidence regarding its health benefits is weak (R. A. Martin, 2001).

SUMMARY

Happiness rises and falls with the events of life, but it also depends strongly on someone's disposition or personality, an enduring trait that we bring to the situation. Optimistic people find something to be happy about or they make something good happen. Pessimists are more likely to give up and wallow in boredom or distress.

On the other hand, when people are not happy, it doesn't make sense to say, "Well, too bad, I guess they just don't have happy dispositions." Disposition is part of life satisfaction, but not all of it. Events do matter. Many people remain cheerful despite unpleasant circumstances, but it may be because they make an effort to improve their circumstances, rather than some fixed aspect of their brain chemistry. The way we think about situations is also part of our personality that af-

fects our emotions, but unlike our genes it is a part we can change with practice and effort.

As a society, the United States (along with many other countries) strives for economic prosperity. Why? Presumably because it will make us happy. Why not strive for happiness itself? Most people say they have other goals besides wealth, and some they consider far more important than wealth. Wealth gets more than its share of attention, possibly because it is easy to measure. Diener and Seligman (2004) have proposed that psychologists should try to measure life satisfaction and use that as a guide to public policy, just as economists advise the government based on economic measures. It is an idea worth pursuing and refining, and a likely basis for much future research.

KEY TERMS

anticipatory enthusiasm: pleasure from expecting a reward (p. 245)

broaden-and-build theory: theory that positive emotions promote broadened attention to the environment, as well as greater flexibility in thought/action repertoires (p. 240)

cognitive shift: transition from thinking about some target from one perspective to thinking about it from a completely different, but still appropriate, perspective (p. 249)

contentment: positive emotion felt after consuming a meal or other reward (p. 246)

contrast effect: emotional influence of whether an outcome was better or worse than some other likely outcome (p. 241)

Duchenne smile: expression that includes raised cheeks and crow's feet at the corners of the eyes as well as a smiling mouth (p. 243)

hope: high agency in a challenging situation, combined with active generation of plans that can facilitate the desired outcome (p. 247)

joy: intense pleasant emotional experience in response to a surprising gain or success (p. 231)

neuroticism: tendency to experience fear, sadness, and anger relatively easily (p. 248)

optimism: expectation that mostly good things will happen (p. 247)

subjective well-being: self-evaluation of one's life as pleasant, interesting, and satisfying (p. 231)

THOUGHT QUESTIONS

1. In Chapter 2, we considered the controversy about what (if anything) constitutes a "basic" emotion. Here we have discussed joy, hope, optimism, and amusement. Should we consider any of them a separate (basic) emotion?

2. Presumably we smile when happy because we gain some advantage by communicating our happiness to others. Why is that communication helpful? Is it ever disadvantageous? That is, are there times when we should inhibit our smiles?

SUGGESTIONS FOR RESEARCH PROJECTS

Ask people to list as many words as they can think of for positive emotions. Then ask a new set of people to combine those words into clusters with similar meaning. How many positive emotion categories might there be in the English language?

SUGGESTIONS FOR FURTHER READING

Diener, E., & Suh, E. M. (Eds.) (2000). *Culture and Subjective Well-being*. Cambridge, MA: MIT Press. A review of cultural differences in life satisfaction.

Haidt, J. (2006). *The Happiness Hypothesis: Finding Modern Truth in Ancient Wisdom*. New York: Basic Books. A thoughtful integration of philosophy and modern empirical research on what makes us happy.

Gilbert, D. (2006). *Stumbling on Happiness*. New York: Knopf. The author links happiness (and the lack thereof) to biases in the way we estimate our future feelings.

Seligman, M. E. P. (1991). *Learned Optimism*. New York: Knopf. A book by one of the leaders of the positive psychology movement.

11

The Self-Conscious Emotions

We typically feel happy, sad, frightened, angry, disgusted, or surprised about things that happen *to* us, or in the environment around us. The events that elicit these emotions happen out there in the world. In contrast, the emotions we consider in this chapter all reflect an appraisal of the *self*. You feel embarrassed, ashamed, or guilty if you have fallen short of expectations in your own or others' eyes. You feel proud if you have done something particularly well. You feel jealous or envious if you think you have less than someone else in some domain. These experiences require appraisals of yourself and how you relate to others.

This has a number of interesting implications. First, the need for self-appraisal has implications for the development of self-conscious emotions. An infant doesn't have a sense of "self" yet, so we do not expect it to feel embarrassed or ashamed. Many people insist that their dog acts ashamed at times, but we don't see signs of self-conscious emotions in many other species. As we consider the emotions of this chapter, we explore what it means to be a mature human being. The emphasis on appraisals of self-other relationships also means that the social functions of these emotions should be especially important. Finally, the focus on self-other relationships suggests important cultural variability in these emotions. If "self" means different things to people in different cultures, or if different cultures have different expectations about relationships, then the self-conscious emotions may also play out quite differently. Let's consider some of these emotions and the issues involved.

EMBARRASSMENT, SHAME, AND GUILT:
ONE EMOTION OR THREE?

Embarrassment, shame, and guilt have much in common. They make us feel bad, they reflect the belief that we have done something wrong, and they make us want to hide or withdraw in some way. In one study, investigators used fMRI to monitor participants' brain activity as they read various sentences. One block of sentences dealt with embarrassing experiences (such as "I was not dressed properly for the occasion"), another described experiences of guilt ("I left the restaurant without paying"), and others described unemotional events. As Figure C.6 shows (see inside cover), the areas activated by the embarrassing sentences were almost the same as those activated by sentences about guilt (Takahashi et al., 2004).

In short, the experiences of embarrassment, shame, and guilt overlap heavily. Should we even study them as distinct emotions, or are they just different words for the same thing? Researchers have conducted several studies trying to tease their causes and characteristics apart. One way to do this is simply to ask people when they have felt each of these emotions and see whether they report different kinds of situations. In one study, investigators asked U.S. college students to recall a recent experience in which they felt embarrassment, shame, or guilt (Keltner & Buswell, 1996). The most common experiences associated with embarrassment were:

- Poor performance
- Physical clumsiness (such as tripping or spilling something)
- A cognitive error (such as forgetting an acquaintance's name)
- Inappropriate physical appearance (such as wearing casual clothes when everyone else is dressed formally)
- Failure of privacy (such as accidentally intruding when someone else was naked)
- Being teased
- Conspicuousness (being the center of attention)

That final category, being the center of attention, deserves some comment. Suppose a professor asks whether everyone understands some point, or whether anyone has any questions. You are in fact puzzled and you would like to ask a question. Why don't you? You would likely feel embarrassed to call attention to yourself, or to admit that you need help (Bohns & Flynn, 2010). You might also feel embarrassed by public attention when people mean to honor you. A familiar example is having people sing "Happy Birthday" to you in a public place. For another example, suppose a professor announces to the class that you got the highest score on the midterm exam. She raves about your brilliant answers and calls it one of the most impressive performances she's ever seen. The whole class stares at you. You have done nothing wrong, but you probably want to crawl under your chair anyway.

In contrast, the most common experiences associated with shame were:

- Poor performance (as with embarrassment)
- Hurting someone else's feelings
- Lying
- Failure to meet other people's expectations (such as getting poor grades in school and thereby disappointing one's parents)
- Failure to meet one's own expectations

The most common experiences associated with guilt were:

- Failure to perform one's duties (such as not following through on a promise)
- Lying, cheating, or stealing
- Neglecting a friend or loved one
- Hurting someone else's feelings
- Infidelity to a romantic partner
- Breaking a diet

As you can see, the kinds of experiences that elicit embarrassment, shame, and guilt overlap to some degree. Poor performance is commonly cited as a cause for either embarrassment or shame, and hurting others is a common cause of either shame or guilt. A reasonable conclusion is that embarrassment, shame, and guilt overlap and shade into one another, much as the colors red, orange, and yellow do. However, we can also draw some distinctions. Embarrassment need not imply that you did something morally wrong. It occurs most often when you are suddenly the focus of other people's attention because of an understandable mistake, an accident, or even a positive event. You just had the misfortune to do it in public. Shame is most common when you fail to live up to expectations. Guilt arises when you do something that hurts someone. We could draw a further distinction between guilt and regret: If you harm others, you feel guilt. If you harm only yourself, you feel regret (Zeelenberg & Breugelmans, 2008).

But these are subjective impressions, created by reading many descriptions of specific events and asking what they have in common. Another way to distinguish among emotions is for people to think of an experience in which they felt each emotion and then rate the accuracy of various statements in describing their experience. In one study, June Tangney and her colleagues (1996) asked participants to remember a time they felt embarrassment, shame, or guilt. Then the participants rated how intense the feeling was, how long it lasted, how much they expected the event that caused the emotion, and several aspects of the event itself.

The researchers found that people's rating patterns for the embarrassment experiences were quite different from their rating patterns for shame and guilt. Unlike shame and guilt, embarrassment arose suddenly in response to an unexpected event, lasted briefly, and faded. By contrast, the events that elicited shame and guilt were more expected, and the feelings built up more slowly. Participants reported being angry with themselves during shame and guilt experiences but not angry with themselves (or only slightly) in times of embarrassment.

We noted earlier that shame and guilt seemed to be distinctively associated with doing something morally wrong, and Tangney's results confirmed this point. Participants describing shame and guilt experiences felt strongly that they had violated a moral standard. They regarded the situation as serious, rather than funny, and they felt personally responsible for the event. Participants reporting embarrassment experiences felt less responsible for the event, thought it was as funny as it was serious, and did not think they had done anything morally wrong. Participants were also asked to infer what the people around them thought about the event. People describing embarrassment experiences felt strongly that other people were looking at them

but that the onlookers felt amused by the event. People describing shame and guilt experiences felt that other people were angry with them.

These studies, and others like them, allow psychologists (at least those speaking English) to state somewhat more precisely what they mean by the terms *embarrassment, shame,* and *guilt.* There are enough differences that it seems useful to consider them separately, at least for now. Let's consider each of these three emotions in turn.

EMBARRASSMENT

We can tentatively define **embarrassment** as the emotion felt when one violates a social convention, thereby drawing unexpected social attention and motivating submissive behavior that should appease other people. We noted in Chapter 1 that any emotion is presumed to have a function—a way in which people benefit from feeling and/or displaying the emotion. What function might embarrassment serve? Although the experience of embarrassment is unpleasant, your *display* of it lets other people know you care about their opinion, and that you hope for their understanding after you have done something clumsy, awkward, or inappropriate (Keltner & Buswell, 1997).

To illustrate the usefulness of the embarrassment display, imagine this scenario. You are in a grocery store carrying a large, heavy box of kitty litter. As you walk through a crowded aisle, you trip and knock over a huge display of bottled salsa, breaking several bottles, and spewing a ghastly mixture of salsa and kitty litter on a couple of people's clothes. If you just walk away casually as if nothing happened, how will other people react? Most likely they'll be angry and consider you rude as well as clumsy. However, if you apologize and look embarrassed, they might laugh and tell you not to worry—they might even start to like you a little bit (Semin & Manstead, 1982). People particularly improve their opinion of you if you blush, perhaps because it is so difficult to fake this display (Dijk, de Jong, & Peters, 2009). Overall, your display of embarrassment transforms a potentially tense, aggressive situation into a polite and friendly one.

Research confirms that embarrassment helps repair awkward social situations in just this way. Researchers in one study showed participants videos of a scene like the one above; participants liked the embarrassed klutz more than the unconcerned one (Semin & Manstead, 1982). In a similar study, people said they would be more likely to forgive someone who broke a valuable item if he looked embarrassed (R. S. Miller, 2001b). Children who display embarrassment after breaking a rule are punished less severely than children who don't (Semin & Papadopoulou, 1990). People are also more likely to help a person who looks embarrassed, and to show affection toward that person (Keltner, Young, & Buswell, 1997; Levin & Arluke, 1982).

One limitation of this effect is that embarrassment diverts people's anger only if they think your transgression was truly an accident (De Jong, Peters, De Cremer, & Vranken, 2002). That is, you are not appeased by hearing someone say, "I'm sorry, I didn't mean to do it," if you think the person did mean it. Remember from Chapter 8 that people are more likely to become angry when they think another's harmful actions were deliberate. Embarrassment sends the message that your actions were not deliberate, but if for some reason people don't believe you, they will get mad anyway.

Experiences That Evoke Embarrassment

Let's explore the experiences that evoke embarrassment in more detail. After all, the definition we suggested earlier is vague: What does it mean to "violate a social convention"? Is all social attention embarrassing? Is it more embarrassing for some people than for others, and if so, why? To understand better the kinds of experiences that could cause embarrassment, John Sabini and his colleagues asked college students to read descriptions of several interpersonal scenarios and then asked how embarrassed they would feel in each situation (Sabini, Siepmann, Stein, & Meyerowitz, 2000). The situations fit into three categories: making a social mistake, being the center of attention, and being in a

"sticky situation." Here are examples of each of these categories:

Social Mistake. I had been working with Ellen for about six months on several projects. She was an excellent team member, and we got along well, but she seemed overly friendly, and it made me a bit uncomfortable. When she invited me over for dinner, I realized I would have to talk about it with her. So I accepted the invitation with the plan of clarifying our relationships as "friends only." Just as she let me into her apartment I suddenly felt so nervous that I blurted out, "Ellen, I just need to clarify that my coming here doesn't mean there's anything romantic between us," and just then a man walked into the entrance hall and introduced himself as Ellen's husband [Sabini et al., 2000, p. 237].

Center of Attention. I was attending a cocktail party where I didn't know a lot of people. Just as I started to enter I heard an announcement that the guest of honour was arriving, and a spotlight was turned on the door. It followed my entrance instead of that of the real guest of honour who was just behind me [Sabini et al., p. 238].

Sticky Situation. I had lent my friend a large sum of money, which he had not repaid. I suddenly found myself in a tight spot, and needed the money back in order to pay my rent, so I knew I was going to have to ask my friend to repay the loan [Sabini et al., p. 238].

Sabini and colleagues' results suggest that all of these situations were considered embarrassing, but were they all embarrassing for the same reason? Put another way, if we want to understand what causes embarrassment, should we look for something all three situations have in common, or do different situations cause embarrassment in different ways? One way to address this question is to ask whether the individuals who considered one kind of situation embarrassing also considered the other kinds equally embarrassing. If so, then presumably there is something that all three situations share. If not, then perhaps different people become embarrassed for different reasons.

The results of this study supported the latter proposition. The ratings that students gave to "mistake" situations correlated highly with one another. That is, those who said they would be "highly embarrassed" in one mistake situation generally gave similarly high ratings to other mistake situations. Also, embarrassment ratings on "center of attention" situations correlated with one another, and ratings on "sticky situations" correlated with one another. However, ratings on different kinds of situations did not correlate highly with one another. People highly embarrassed by a mistake were not necessarily highly embarrassed by being the center of attention, and those embarrassed by being the center of attention were not necessarily embarrassed by a sticky situation.

When considering the implications of this study, keep in mind that participants said only how they *thought* they would feel in each situation. The researchers did not measure whether people *actually* felt embarrassed by each of these situations. Thus, these results may reflect people's expectations about embarrassment, rather than what really makes people feel embarrassed. There's no way to know, from this study alone, how well people's ratings reflect what would actually make them feel embarrassed.

Let's also consider a fourth scenario: **empathic embarrassment**, or being embarrassed in sympathy for someone else who is in an embarrassing situation. Imagine yourself in this study: First you come to a psychologist's laboratory, where, among other tasks, you are asked to sing "The Star Spangled Banner" (the U.S. national anthem). A week later, you are asked to return to the lab and to bring a friend with you. At this point, you have no idea what this study is about.

So you and the friend arrive, as does a third person unfamiliar to both of you. The researcher attaches electrodes to one cheek of each person. Again, you don't know why, but in fact the electrodes measure blushing. Now the three of you watch a video on the television screen. All goes smoothly for a while, and

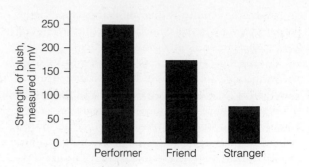

FIGURE 11.1 Mean amount of blushing by the participant watching him- or herself singing, by a friend, and by a stranger.
Source: Based on the data of Shearn et al. (1999)

then suddenly the video shows *you—singing the national anthem.* How do you feel? Most people are embarrassed and blush immediately. The "Star Spangled Banner" is a difficult song, and few people can sing it alone without sounding foolish. Figure 11.1 shows the mean amount of blushing by the singers, the singers' friends, and the strangers. Note that the singer blushes the most, but the friend blushes a lot too, presumably in sympathy with the friend, and the stranger blushes the least (Shearn, Spellman, Straley, Meirick, & Stryker, 1999).

One common feature of all embarrassing experiences may be that we think we are likely to be rejected by others, either because of a social gaffe or simply because we are suddenly the focus of others' attention. Does this really require a sense of self, or simply an awareness of other people? One study of patients with frontotemporal lobar degeneration (FTLD)—a form of dementia that strikes the frontal and temporal lobes—highlights the role of self-awareness in embarrassment (Sturm, Rosen, Allison, Miller, & Levenson, 2006). Patients with FTLD show distinct losses in self-awareness in nonemotional tasks, so we might expect them to show fewer signs of embarrassment as well.

The researchers in this study unexpectedly played a loud blast of white noise, sounding very much like a gunshot, right behind participants' heads while videotaping their reaction. Most people startle sharply when they hear a loud noise, but then show a "secondary" emotional response of embarrassment (and sometimes anger). The FTLD patients startled just like most people, but showed little embarrassment, suggesting a lack of awareness of how they might have looked to others. In a follow-up study using the "singing" task described above, FTLD patients also showed less embarrassment (Sturm, Ascher, Miller, & Levenson, 2008). Although these studies each used a correlational design (self-awareness was not experimentally manipulated), and it is possible that some other variable accounted for the differences in embarrassment, the findings are consistent with the proposed importance of self-awareness in this emotion.

Facial Expression of Embarrassment

If you feel embarrassed, what is the first thing you ordinarily do? Most avoid eye contact and hide their face, either by covering their eyes with their hands or by turning their head down and usually to the left. ("Why left?" We don't know. Good question.) The message is, "I don't want you to see me right now" (see Figure 11.2). People who feel embarrassed often smile, although their lips also tense up as though they were trying to suppress the smile. The expression of embarrassment is highly similar from one human culture to another. Researchers have noted that the display of embarrassment resembles the bashful behaviors of a child or subordinate (Keltner, 1995; R. S. Miller, 2001a). In addition, the most distinctive expression of embarrassment is the **blush**, a temporary increase in blood flow to the face, neck, and upper chest.

As we noted in Chapter 2, many emotion researchers assume that facial expressions of emotion are evolved characteristics, behaviors inherited from our primate ancestors because they serve some function. Psychologists have interpreted the embarrassment expression as an appeasement gesture, analogous to the way a weak, young animal deters an attack from a superior. The gesture says, "I know I made a mistake. I'm sorry. I feel lowly and inferior. Please don't be angry."

This interpretation of embarrassment makes sense, given that people are more likely to forgive someone who looks embarrassed than someone

FIGURE 11.2 The expression of embarrassment attempts to make the person smaller and less conspicuous. The message is, "I don't want you to see me."

who does not. However, it raises many questions as well. How did the experience and expression of embarrassment first arise? Are nonhuman animals ever embarrassed? Even if dogs and perhaps a few other species are capable of embarrassment, no one has ever reported seeing a nonhuman animal blush. If they did, their faces are covered with fur, so presumably other dogs or whatever could not see the response either. As far as we can tell, blushing may have arisen specifically during human evolution (Edelmann, 2001). If we grant that humans evolved a tendency to blush to signal our apologies to others, a question remains: How visible or salient was that expression for our early human ancestors? Most anthropologists believe the original humans were Africans with dark skin, which makes the blush expression difficult to see.

Another issue: Why do we find blushing itself so unpleasant? Most people are embarrassed by the fact that they are blushing. Just telling someone "you are blushing" often causes them to blush, or increases the blush's intensity (Drummond et al., 2003).

We have mentioned in earlier chapters that different ways of measuring emotions have different strengths and weaknesses. This is true of self-reports and displays of embarrassment as well, because the two do not always go together. For example, people in one study were asked to watch a series of slides showing naked people of both sexes. Most of the observers later reported feeling embarrassed while looking at the slides, especially if other people were present. However, they seldom looked away or turned their heads aside—part of the prototypical embarrassment expression. If they were embarrassed, why hadn't they looked away? One explanation is obvious: They knew their task was to continue looking at the slides (Costa, Dinsbach, Manstead, & Bitti, 2001). So in a case like this, self-reports provide emotional information that objective facial expression measurements would not.

Individual Differences in Embarrassment

We can learn much about an emotion by asking who feels it more often or more strongly than others. Certainly, some people are more easily embarrassed than others, and some groups enjoy teasing a person who blushes easily. Our task is to find a reliable way to measure these individual differences. Then we can ask what people who are easily embarrassed have in common, and how they differ from people who are not easily embarrassed.

To measure dispositional experience of embarrassment, researchers usually rely on self-reports. When people are embarrassed—such as when students have to give class presentations—their self-reports of embarrassment correlate moderately well (+.31) with observers' estimate of their embarrassment, so self-reports are at least somewhat valid (Marcus & Miller, 1999). Several self-report scales

of embarrassment are in widespread use, including the Embarrassibility Scale (Modigliani, 1968) and the Susceptibility to Embarrassment Scale (Kelly & Jones, 1997). Each of these questionnaires briefly describes a variety of situations and asks people how embarrassed they think they would feel. One problem is that "how embarrassed you feel" implies a comparison to others, and people do not know exactly how they compare to others. Also, people are only moderately consistent in how they answer the questionnaire when they complete it multiple times (Maltby & Day, 2000).

Scores on embarrassment questionnaires correlate rather highly with scores on neuroticism questionnaires (Edelmann & McCusker, 1986; Maltby & Day, 2000). That relationship should not be surprising. After all, neuroticism is defined as a tendency toward easily experiencing "negative" emotions such as fear, anger, sadness, and . . . embarrassment. Susceptibility to embarrassment also correlates positively with social anxiety, shyness, and loneliness (Neto, 1996) and correlates negatively with extraversion and self-esteem (Edelmann & McCusker, 1986; Maltby & Day, 2000). People who feel confident about themselves in social situations do not become embarrassed often and handle their embarrassment well when they do. People who lack confidence frequently think they have made social mistakes even when they haven't. These findings are consistent with the notion that embarrassment serves to repair our relationships after we have made a mistake. People who are confident and extroverted may consider their relationships to be less vulnerable in general, and thus are less threatened by little social gaffes.

One complication in interpreting these results is that many people misperceive how often they are embarrassed. People who particularly fear being embarrassed in public tend to overstate the frequency of embarrassing experiences (Mulkens, de Jong, Dobbelaar, & Bögels, 1999). Their fear of embarrassment is psychologically important and may even lead to social phobia, a condition of avoiding other people to decrease the risk of embarrassment (Leary, 2001; Miller, 2001a). However, because their reports are objectively inaccurate, they pose a problem for research in this field.

Who do you guess becomes embarrassed more strongly or more frequently, men or women? The common stereotype is that women are more easily embarrassed. A few reports confirm that view (e.g., Neto, 1996), but most indicate no significant difference (e.g., Maltby & Day, 2000). If there is a gender difference in susceptibility to embarrassment, it is not a strong one.

Age, however, does predict susceptibility to embarrassment. At the beginning of this chapter we suggested that embarrassment requires a sense of self, and that infants therefore should not able to feel this emotion (or shame, guilt, or pride, for that matter). The evidence is consistent with this proposal. Infants and very young children don't experience embarrassment at all. Only at about age two do they start to show evidence of self-conscious emotion, right around the time they begin showing signs of self-consciousness—the ability to think about themselves as they think about other people. Signs of embarrassment become more intense and more frequent as children grow older, reaching a peak in the teenage years. Embarrassment occurs less and less often during adulthood (Maltby & Day, 2000). This decline may reflect increased self-confidence and prestige, and/or fewer concerns about the impressions we make on others.

SHAME AND GUILT

In the studies discussed in the beginning of the chapter, embarrassment stood out as a distinct emotion, but shame and guilt overlapped more. Are shame and guilt different, or just two varieties of the same emotion?

As is so often the case, the answer depends on what measures are used and how each study is done. The facial expression of embarrassment is clearly distinct from the expressions of shame and guilt. When college students examine photos of people expressing embarrassment and shame, they correctly classify the expressions more than half the time (Keltner, 1995). As we saw in Chapter 3, this is even the case in the Orissa culture that uses the same word for the two emotions—*lajya*—as long as the expressions

are matched to situations rather than emotion words (Haidt & Keltner, 1999). People do not, however, distinguish reliably between "ashamed" and "guilty" expressions (Keltner & Buswell, 1996). The expression of shame/guilt includes lowered eyes and hunched posture, similar to the expression of embarrassment. However, whereas an embarrassed person might have a little sheepish grin, an ashamed person does not smile and may turn down the corners of the mouth in a display more like sadness (Figure 11.3).

As we saw earlier in the chapter, the *events* that elicit shame and guilt are also not that different. People feel shame or guilt when they think they have done something morally wrong, or when they have failed to live up to their own or others' expectations (Tangney, Miller et al., 1996). The distinction between the two becomes more clear when researchers study how people *interpret* the negative event in question. Studies suggest that you are likely to feel shame when you think of yourself as bad or unworthy. You interpret the negative event as evidence that your entire self is defective or inadequate. Thus, we can tentatively define **shame** as the emotion felt when one does something wrong and focuses on one's own global, stable inadequacies in explaining the transgression. By contrast, you are more likely to feel guilt if you feel bad about a specific action, but not about who you are as a person (Tangney, Wagner, Hill-Barlow, Marschall, & Gramzow, 1996). **Guilt** is the emotion felt when one fails or does something morally wrong, but focuses on how to make amends and how to avoid repeating the transgression.

This distinction is observed mainly in people's descriptions of shame and guilt experiences. When people think about times when they felt shame, they say things like "If only I weren't so stupid." When they think about times when they felt guilt, they say things like "If only I hadn't done such-and-such" (Niedenthal, Tangney, & Gavanski, 1994). The distinction also emerges consistently in self-report measures of shame- and guilt-proneness, in which you read a scenario and then rate the how strongly you would feel bad *about yourself* in that situation versus wishing you had *acted differently* (Tangney, 1996).

© Corbis

FIGURE 11.3 The expression of shame implies a more serious violation than mere embarrassment.

These "bad self" ratings and "bad action" ratings are positively correlated, but not so strongly that shame- and guilt-proneness seem to be the same (e.g., Covert, Tangney, Maddux, & Heleno, 2003).

Dispositional shame-proneness and guilt-proneness are also differentially associated with people's approaches to social interaction. Shame-prone people tend to have more problems with relationships than guilt-prone people. They experience more anger and social anxiety and feel less empathy (O'Connor, Berry, & Weiss, 1999; Tangney, Burggraf, & Wagner, 1995; Tangney, Wagner et al., 1996). The correlation with anger is interesting and worth exploration. Why should shame-prone people, who presumably feel bad about themselves, tend to get angry with *others*? Why should guilt-prone people be immune to this effect? According to June Tangney and her colleagues (Tangney, Wagner et al., 1996), shame-prone people tend to attribute their own negative outcomes to global, stable personal inadequacies, over which they have little or no control. They feel a strong sense of other people's disapproval. At the same time, because shame-prone people do not feel that they have control over their outcomes, they may

feel that this disapproval is unfair. As a result, they are more likely to be angered by the disapproving judgments they perceive in others. In contrast, guilt-prone people take more responsibility for their individual actions and feel more control over whether they will repeat those actions.

The distinction between shame and guilt is supported by a study of the interpersonal problem-solving skills of shame- and guilt-prone people (Covert et al., 2003). In this study, participants read scenarios such as the following:

> Your friend and co-worker has been getting behind in his/her work, and asks you for help in catching up. You know that your friend needs this job. This happens several times, and you notice that you are getting behind in your own work, in spite of putting in extra, unpaid hours [Covert et al., 2003, p. 6].

After reading the scenario, participants described as many suggestions as they could for resolving the situation and stated how effectively they thought they could implement each solution themselves.

Each participant's solution to each scenario was coded by the researchers as: (1) likely to make the situation worse, (2) not even trying to resolve the situation, (3) making a fair attempt to resolve the situation, (4) making a good attempt, or (5) making an excellent attempt to resolve the situation. The researchers found that shame-prone people tended to have a low quality of problem-solving attempts and a low belief in their ability to resolve the problems. In contrast, guilt-prone people tended to be better than average at suggesting solutions.

Consistent with earlier studies of shame and guilt, the researchers interpreted this study as evidence that shame-proneness implies a low sense of control over one's own outcome, combined with the feeling that one is a bad person. Guilt-proneness includes a high sense of control over the outcome and the feeling that if one has done something bad, one can make amends and avoid the negative action in the future.

So, are shame and guilt different emotions or not? Shame and guilt do not appear to fulfill at least one of the proposed criteria for separate, basic emotions—they do not have distinct, recognizable facial expressions. Also, the subjective feelings are similar, as are the actual events that elicit these emotions. However, shame and guilt are associated with somewhat different appraisals, or interpretations of the eliciting situation—at least among English-speaking participants. Researchers have not written much about possible evolutionary functions of shame and guilt, so it is difficult to compare the two on that criterion. Whether you think of shame and guilt as two different emotions depends on which criteria you emphasize in your definition of "emotion," but by most criteria, they appear to be variants of a single emotion.

For practical purposes, it may not matter whether shame and guilt are separate, basic emotions, two variants of the same emotion, or not emotions at all. Research on how the two are related to each other, and on the clinical, social, and personality factors associated with guilt versus shame, has moved along just fine without a consensus on this issue. However, researchers and clinicians would need to be cautious about assuming that the shame/guilt distinction is the same in other cultures as in English-speaking cultures, or even that the distinction exists at all. Unless future evidence suggests that the appraisal differences observed in the United States are common to other cultures as well, it may be that the shame/guilt distinction is largely a social construction.

Guilt and Repentance

If you feel guilty, what do you do about it? Most people want to pay back the hurt person in some way, if possible. That is, guilt serves a useful social function: It punishes a mistake and motivates efforts to repair the damage (Amodio, Devine, & Harmon-Jones, 2007). As you might guess, people who usually don't feel much guilt tend to be selfish and inconsiderate of others (Krajbich, Adolphs, Tranel, Denburg, & Camerer, 2009).

Repentance is the state of feeling bad about one's misdeeds and seeking forgiveness. Repentance and forgiveness are important religious concepts, but so far psychological researchers have not had much to say about them. Psychologists may be underestimating the importance of these processes. Researchers do know that religious people tend to be more forgiving than nonreligious people (Fox & Thomas, 2008). That tendency is moderated somewhat by the type of religion. Jews are more likely than Christians to believe that some offenses are unforgivable (Cohen, Malka, Rozin, & Cherfas, 2006). Jewish teaching emphasizes that some offenses are too extreme to forgive, that repentance must precede forgiveness, and that only the victim can forgive an offense. Christian teaching recommends forgiveness more broadly.

Under non-extreme circumstances, at least, forgiveness serves many purposes. First, the person who forgives feels better. Bearing a grudge is stressful to both mental and physical health. Second, forgiveness promotes reconciliation between people, and enables them to resume a favorable relationship. Occasionally, forgiveness backfires and tells the person "you can get away with this act again." However, in most cases the offender feels kindly toward the forgiver and becomes more cooperative in the future (Wallace, Exline, & Baumeister, 2008). The phrasing of the forgiveness message is important. If someone humbly apologizes after intentionally harming you in a serious way, you could say, "I forgive you." However, someone who harmed you in a minor way might react badly to the message "I forgive you." The person might even feel irritated at you for implying a need for forgiveness. Under those conditions, a more casual comment such as "It's okay" or "Don't worry about it" works better (Struthers, Eaton, Shirvani, Georghiou, & Edell, 2008).

Forgiveness has an additional benefit that is less obvious. People like to think that their own acts are justified. Most people also like to think that life is fair, and that people usually get what they deserve. (Psychologists call this the "Just World Hypothesis.") If you know you have hurt someone and you feel unforgiven, you have to do something to justify your actions. A common way to do so is to convince yourself that the person you hurt deserved it. That belief leads to still more hostility. One experiment demonstrating this process went as follows: German students read a description of the Auschwitz concentration camp. For some, the last paragraph concluded that although these events were horrible, they are just a part of history with little direct impact on anyone today. For others, the last paragraph emphasized that Jews today continue to suffer as survivors or as descendants of survivors. Then both groups of students answered a questionnaire about their attitudes toward Jews. Students who read the second version (implying continuing guilt) were more likely to show anti-Jewish attitudes (Imhoff & Banse, 2009).

What if, for some reason, you can't apologize to the hurt person and can't undo the damage? In that case, people often punish themselves in some way, or pass up opportunities for pleasure (Nelissen & Zeelenberg, 2009). They evidently feel, "If that other person can't be happy right now, I shouldn't, either." This reaction is common after someone dies. Even if you don't have a reason to feel guilty in the ordinary sense—that is, the person's death isn't your fault—you may experience **survivor's guilt**, a feeling of guilt about going on with life, because "there is no logical reason why the other person died instead of me." After a loved one dies, you may feel for some time that you have no right to feel happy. After a plane crash, a military battle, or other disaster in which most people die, the survivors often feel an obligation

to do something especially noble with their lives, in some sense to pay back those who died.

PRIDE

Now let's consider the opposite of shame or guilt—pride. Jessica Tracy and Rick Robins (2004) define **pride** as the emotion you feel when you accept credit for causing a positive outcome that supports a positive aspect of your self-concept. Let's break this definition down a bit. You feel pride when something good happens. That's no big surprise because positive emotions should result from positive events. What makes pride special is (1) when you are proud, you feel that you *caused* the good event, and can take the credit for it, and (2) the good event confirms your positive self-image.

Let's say you win an essay contest at your college. You will probably feel pride if you worked hard on your essay, if hundreds of people submitted essays, and if the judges used strict standards in selecting the winner. You feel even stronger pride if being a good writer is important to your sense of self. You are less likely to feel pride if only a few essays were submitted, or if the judges selected the winning essay by folding all of the essays into paper airplanes and seeing which one flew the farthest. In the latter scenario, you won the contest, but you can't really take credit for it. You might also feel less pride if, say, your music skills are more central to your sense of self than your writing skills.

Would you feel proud if you won a lottery? Surely you would feel happy, but probably not proud—unless you believe that you somehow had control over what is supposed to be a random event. Many chronic gamblers take pride in their wins, because they believe something about their personal character or judgment influences their luck.

Expression of Pride

A few researchers have begun to study the aspects of pride that distinguish it from other kinds of positive emotion, and one of those aspects is expression. In many regards, the expression of pride is the

FIGURE 11.4 Although you can't clearly express pride from facial expression alone, you can from a combination of face and posture. The expression of pride makes you larger, helping others to see and admire you.

Source: Tracy and Robins (2004)

opposite of embarrassment or shame: A person tilts his head back slightly, sits or stands tall, and puts his arms above the head or hands on the hips. (See Figure 11.4.) The message here is, "I want you to see me clearly right now." The prototypical pride expression includes a smile, but only a small smile, not a broad one. Most people—at least in the United States and Italy, the only countries tested so far—easily identify this expression as meaning pride (Tracy & Robins, 2004).

Earlier in the chapter, we noted that the expression of embarrassment closely resembles the expressive behavior of a child or low-status individual. As you might expect, the expression of pride looks like the behavior of high-status people, and people who display pride are assumed to hold high-status positions in society (Cashdan, 1998; Tiedens, Ellsworth, & Mesquita, 2000). Although no one likes pride that

leads to bragging, pride in the sense of self-confidence is generally helpful. In one study, researchers asked people to do two tasks, the first as individuals and the second as a group. After the first task, they privately told certain individuals (chosen randomly) that they had performed unusually well. On the group task, people who believed (rightly or wrongly) that they had done well on the first task took a prominent role in the group activity, and other members of their group described them as "very likeable" (Williams & DeSteno, 2009). Evidently self-confidence based on actual (or perceived) achievement leads to additional success.

CULTURAL DIFFERENCES IN EMBARRASSMENT, SHAME, AND PRIDE

Most research on the self-conscious emotions has been done in the United States, and we noted in Chapter 3 that the United States has some unusual cultural features. Americans are more individualistic—believing that individual rights, achievement, and expression take priority over group needs—than people in almost any other country in the world. On the other hand, American culture tends to downplay issues of social hierarchy. Because the self-conscious emotions reflect people's self-evaluations relative to group standards, and because the expressions of embarrassment, shame, and pride seem to reflect expectations about status, it may be that the self-conscious emotions present themselves very differently in other cultures.

Experiences of embarrassment, shame, and pride occur throughout the world. What varies is the circumstances that provoke these emotions. People feel embarrassed or ashamed when they fail to meet society's expectations, but these expectations vary from one culture to another. For example, the Dusun Baguk of Malaysia say they experience *malu*, roughly corresponding to our embarrassment or shame, whenever they eat during a period set aside for fasting, dress too ostentatiously, or even walk too fast. They also feel *malu* just from being in the presence of a more prestigious person (Fessler, 1999). The Dusun

Baguk also report an experience they call *bangga,* approximately translating as "pride," when they receive attention appropriately for something done well. For example, they feel *bangga* for a display of skill or wit or for hosting a fine feast for guests.

Some cultural differences in events that elicit pride relate to differences in the nature of "self." In the United States and many other Western countries, the self is a unique personality, defined by consistent traits that differentiate you from other people. Individuality is highly valued in the United States, and most people claim to reject conformity. In East Asian countries, the self is defined more by your relationships with other people, and by the groups to which you belong.

If self-conscious emotions are reactions to the good or bad actions of the self, and the nature of "self" differs in the United States and in Asian cultures, then people may feel self-conscious emotions in very different situations. In Chapter 3 we discussed a study in which Chinese and American participants were asked how proud they would be if they themselves were accepted to a prestigious university and how proud they would be if their child were accepted to the university (Stipek, 1998). Recall from that discussion that Chinese participants (unlike Americans) said they would actually be proud of their children's accomplishments than of their own. Does this mean that Chinese and American respondents mean something different by the term *pride?* Probably not—after all, the Chinese respondents said they would feel some pride for their own achievement, and Americans said they would feel some pride for their child's. This study does suggest that, even in terms of the events that elicit self-conscious emotions, the Chinese react to close relatives as though they were part of their own self.

Pride is generally considered a good thing in the United States. Most societies, however, frown on too much pride. The Dusun Baguk consider it rude and immoral to flaunt one's *bangga.* You can feel your pride, but don't show it too much. This is true in the West as well; a study of young German children found that, by about age five years, children would often hide their feelings of pride when they beat their younger siblings at a competitive game (Reissland & Harris, 1991). Calling someone

"proud" in English is not always a compliment, but as a general rule, Americans are more comfortable with pride, and consider it more positive, than people in cultures that emphasize collectivism over individualism. For example, Chinese participants tend to agree far more strongly than Americans that expressing pride is generally a bad thing, and that it is socially appropriate to show pride only for achievements that benefit other in-group members (Stipek, 1998). Americans are much less shy about celebrating their individual accomplishments.

JEALOUSY AND ENVY

We have another category of self-conscious emotions, which arise when we compare ourselves to others who apparently got a better deal. Envy and jealousy both refer to resentment at someone else's good fortune. The distinction between them is that when we refer to anything concerning friendship, sex, or romance, we use the term *jealousy.* If you wish you had someone's job or salary, we could say either that you are envious or that you are jealous. If you wish that you had someone else's boyfriend/girlfriend, or you worry that someone might take your boyfriend/girlfriend, we say you are jealous, but we are less likely to call this feeling envy.

Sexual jealousy often triggers rash behaviors. If you believe your husband, wife, boyfriend, or girlfriend is interested in someone else, the potential loss threatens your happiness and self-esteem. Aggressive behavior is a common outcome. An estimated 40 percent of murders of women involve sexual jealousy (DeSteno, Valdesolo, & Bartlett, 2006). Envy sometimes triggers aggression also. People have been known to destroy something valuable to prevent someone else from having it or enjoying it (R. H. Smith & Kim, 2007).

Envy is not always harmful. If you envy someone else's success, you could be motivated to hurt the other person, to bring him down to your level, or you could be motivated to raise your own level of success. The Dutch language has two words for envy, one corresponding to hurting others, and one corresponding to improving oneself (van de Ven, Zeelenberg, & Pieters, 2009).

SUMMARY

The emotions we considered in this chapter all reflect a sense of self, and awareness of the relationship between self and others. This has implications for who can feel them, and under what circumstances. Although dogs and some other animals may show displays of shame and pride, it is hard to imagine a non-human animal showing embarrassment. Infants and toddlers do not show these emotions, seeming sad or happy in situations where an older person would experience shame or pride. Signs of self-conscious emotion do not emerge until children are old enough to show other signs of self-awareness, such as recognizing themselves in a mirror. To many theorists, this raises questions about whether embarrassment, shame, and pride should be considered "basic" emotions.

Perhaps because of the role of self-awareness, these emotions also show striking cultural influence. The experiences and expressions of embarrassment, shame, and pride appear similar in different parts of the world, but cultural differences modify them nevertheless. You may feel pride if your "self" has done something good, but that has very different implications depending on whether your "self" includes just you, or all of your family, close friends, teammates, and colleagues as well. Feeling pride also depends on interpreting some accomplishments as valuable, and different cultures value very different kinds of achievements. Once you do feel pride, the way in which you show it may vary dramatically depending on the kind of culture you come from—one that encourages displays of status and hierarchy or one that encourages modesty and equality.

Emotions are thought to serve a function, and the self-conscious emotions serve especially important "social" functions in maintaining civilized behavior. Any society has clear expectations of how people within it should behave. Those who fail to meet those expectations are expected to experience embarrassment, shame, or guilt, depending on the nature and extent of the error. The expectation is that people recognize their mistake and try to do better in the future. Pride can be helpful too, up to a point, if seeking a feeling of pride motivates people to work hard to accomplish something.

But what about jealousy and envy? People have long recognized the harm that envy can do. (Consider the tenth commandment, "Thou shalt not covet.") Sexual jealousy sometimes leads to murderous rage. How could we imagine a "function" for these feelings? The answer is that evolution doesn't act for the betterment of society. It simply spreads genes that lead to successful reproduction. In our evolutionary history, people who guarded their mates "jealously" were more successful in spreading their genes, including those that facilitate jealousy, than were any people who encouraged their mates to have dalliances with others. Thus we can imagine how such tendencies might have been established. Nevertheless, knowing more about the origins of jealousy can help us take steps to prevent its more dangerous consequences today.

KEY TERMS

blush: a temporarily increased blood flow to the face, neck, and upper chest (p. 259)

embarrassment: the emotion felt when one violates a social convention, thereby drawing unexpected social attention and motivating submissive, friendly behavior that should appease other people (p. 256)

empathic embarrassment: being embarrassed in sympathy for someone else who is embarrassed (p. 258)

guilt: the emotion felt when one fails or does something morally wrong but focuses on how to make amends and how to avoid repeating the transgression (p. 261)

pride: emotion felt when someone takes credit for causing a positive outcome that supports a positive aspect of his or her self-concept (p. 264)

repentance: feeling bad about one's misdeeds and seeking forgiveness (p. 263)

shame: the emotion felt when one fails or does something morally wrong and then focuses on one's own global, stable inadequacies in explaining the transgression (p. 261)

survivor's guilt: a feeling of guilt about going on with life after other people close to you have died (p. 264)

THOUGHT QUESTIONS

1. Would it be easier to recognize expressions of embarrassment, shame, guilt, and pride from films than from still photos? Why or why not?

2. Would you be less likely to feel embarrassed by a mistake you made if you thought no one would recognize you personally? Imagine, for example, being on a visit far from home or attending a costume party. If so, what are the implications about embarrassment?

3. Researchers have found a moderate correlation between susceptibility to shame and susceptibility to guilt (Covert et al., 2003). What conclusion would we draw if the correlation had been close to 1? What if it had been close to zero?

SUGGESTION FOR FURTHER READING

Miller, R. S. (1996). *Embarrassment: Poise and Peril in Everyday Life*. New York: Guilford. Excellent review of the issues and research by one of the very few who have specialized in the study of embarrassment.

PART 3

Emotion Research in Subdisciplines of Psychology

12

Development of Emotion

Studying the development of emotion is important for several reasons. A practical consideration is that anyone dealing with, say, two-year-olds (or adolescents) needs to understand their emotional reactions. Another reason is that studying development helps us understand the functions of emotions. As we noted in Chapter 11, certain emotions, such as embarrassment, emerge at a particular age. This may tell us something about the nature and function of that emotion. Also, remember the issue that Chapter 1 raised about the possible existence of a few "basic" emotions. One criterion is that basic emotions should emerge early in life. Identifying the age of emergence of various emotions may shed light on that question.

Infants and toddlers display a great deal of emotion. In many ways infants' and children's emotional expressions are more frequent and less restrained than those of adults. However, distinctions among different types of emotion emerge slowly. Newborns cry, showing distress, but they don't display anything that would distinguish between fear, sadness, and anger. They reject bad-tasting foods, but otherwise they don't show anything resembling adult disgust. Within a few months, they start smiling and laughing, sometimes long and loud. However, they do not know embarrassment, shame, or pride until they are at least a couple of years old.

During the course of maturation, different emotional displays emerge at different times. By about three years of age, children express a wide range of emotions. By this time they also seem fairly savvy in understanding their own emotions, and usually understand other people's emotional expressions as well. Even seven-month-olds become uneasy if someone stares at them with an angry face (Hoehl & Striano, 2008). If a parent shows fear at the sight of a new toy, infants and toddlers become frightened too, approaching the toy with caution, if at all (Vaish, Grossman, & Woodward, 2008). The ability to pick up on subtler emotional cues continues to develop throughout life. Even during adulthood, people grow gradually more attentive and more acute in discriminating emotional signals.

The process of learning to regulate emotional displays develops slowly. The cultural rules we described in Chapter 3 for when and how to display emotions do not apply at all to infants, and barely to toddlers. For example, Asian adults restrain their emotions more than Europeans do, but no one expects an infant of any culture to show restraint. As children grow older, we expect gradual improvement in their ability to regulate their displays, but the task is difficult and never ending. Presumably, even your parents and grandparents are still working on it.

To discuss the development of emotions, it helps to distinguish among several aspects of emotion, and the model diagrammed in Figure 12.1 offers one way to do so (Halberstadt, Denham, & Densmore, 2001). According to this model, we develop the capacities to *experience* emotions, *send* messages about our emotions, and *receive* emotional messages from others. The model is shaped like a pinwheel to emphasize the fact that it spins around: One aspect leads to the next one, which leads to the next one. For example, if you (rightly or wrongly) interpret someone else's behavior as hostile, you feel either hostile or afraid, you express that emotion, and your expression modifies the other person's behavior (Crick & Dodge, 1994). Then the cycle continues. Any way in which a child matures in one aspect of this cycle facilitates development in other aspects also.

In this chapter, we shall explore the ways in which emotional experience, display, and perception develop during infancy and early childhood. In the final section, we discuss the emotional changes that continue through adolescence and adulthood and into old age.

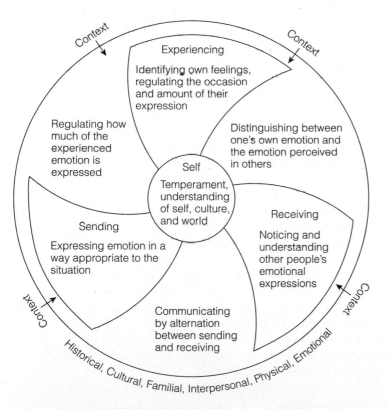

FIGURE 12.1 According to this model, simplified from Halberstadt Denham, & Densmore (2001), emotion includes experiencing emotions, sending messages about them, and receiving other people's emotional messages. Each of these three aspects affects the others.

EMOTION IN NEWBORN INFANTS

What emotions, if any, do newborns have? When and how do other emotions emerge? Unfortunately, newborns are notoriously difficult to study. They sleep most of the day. Most of their waking time is devoted to feeding. For the first couple of days, the doctors and nurses are frequently checking on the baby. Many parents are reluctant to let researchers intrude on their time with a newborn.

Research becomes easier as the child grows older, but not quickly. For the first year children don't talk, and for the next year most of them don't talk much. A few children around two years old do make hand gestures to indicate emotions—for example, drawing the forefinger from an eye down the cheek (like a flowing tear) to indicate sadness (Vallotton, 2008). However, nonverbal gestures convey limited information about emotion, at best. Even after children begin to talk, we can hardly expect them to provide detailed self-reports of their emotions. In fact, we have to guess at infants' emotions before we can even teach them the words they would use for self-reports. That is, a parent has to tell a child, "Oh, you're scared," or "I see you're angry," before the child can learn those words. If we couldn't infer emotions from actions, we couldn't teach the words.

Even ignoring self-reports, many of the other methods we use for measuring emotions in adults are inappropriate with infants and young children. Infants' facial expressions are limited, compared to the rich variety that adults show. We certainly can't ask infants or toddlers to watch films while they sit motionless in an MRI scanner. For the most part, researchers observe infants' spontaneous behaviors or their reactions to simple situations, such as the mother leaving the room. Even then, researchers have to be creative in finding appropriate measures.

Crying

The one emotional expression readily apparent from birth is crying (see Figure 12.2), so a study of newborn emotions is essentially a study of crying. Newborns cry when they are hungry, sleepy, gassy, or uncomfortable in any other way. A newborn's cry expresses **distress**—an undifferentiated protest against anything unpleasant or aversive. Crying has an immediate and powerful effect on people nearby, especially the baby's parents: Suddenly everybody wants to know why this thing is howling and how to make it stop. The advantage to the infant is clear: Crying is at first its only way of getting attention and care. Later, the addition of smiling and laughter offers a second message: "Keep doing that." We can speculate: Did humans evolve

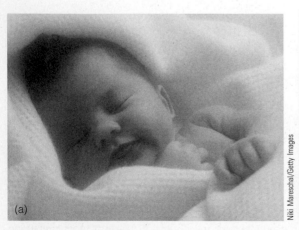
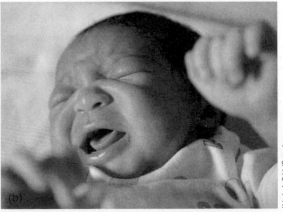

(a) Niki Mareschal/Getty Images   (b) Kristin I. Stith/Getty Images

FIGURE 12.2   At the very least, newborn infants show emotional displays of comfort and distress.

crying and laughter primarily as a way for infants to communicate with their parents?

Newborns also exhibit **sympathetic crying**, or crying in response to the sound of another newborn's cry. It is as if they are thinking, "I don't know what it is, but something is happening that's bad for babies!" One hypothesis about the function of sympathetic crying comes from observations of nonhumans: In a nest of baby birds, the chick that peeps loudest gets fed the most. So, if you're a baby, it may be risky to keep quiet while another baby is demanding attention.

Researchers aren't sure what function sympathetic crying serves, but babies are selective about when they do it. Tape-recorded cries of older children, monkeys, or the infants themselves seldom provoke much reaction. Only the cry of another newborn will suffice (Dondi, Simion, & Caltran, 1999; Martin & Clark, 1982). Sympathetic crying typically stops by about age six months (Hay, Nash, & Pedersen, 1981). One surprising feature of sympathetic crying is that once they are about a year old, babies show no evidence—and even then, only limited evidence—of being distressed by other infants' cries (Blackford & Walden, 1998). Curiously, among somewhat older infants—eighteen months or more—reactions to another child's distress are greater among children who have an older brother or sister (Demetriou & Hay, 2004). Evidently, by interacting with an older sibling, they learn to pay proper attention to emotional displays.

Smiling

The closest newborns come to displaying positive emotion is when they relax. Sometimes they curl up the corners of the mouth. By about age three weeks, their eyelids begin to crinkle as well, and infants may open their mouths into a full grin (Emde & Koenig, 1969; Wolff, 1987). These smiles occur occasionally throughout the day, but most commonly during REM (rapid eye movement) sleep (Dondi et al., 2007). These expressions look like smiles, but they have little or no connection to the social situation, so it's a matter of definition as to whether we want to call them smiles. After the first

three weeks, infants begin smiling in response to their parents' actions, such as a simple game of peek-a-boo, and these smiles increase in frequency over the next few months (Mendes, Seidl-de-Moura, & Siqueira, 2009). Infants vary enormously in this regard, as in almost anything else. With increasing age and cognitive maturity comes the ability to smile at more symbolic or abstract kinds of information. For example, an adult might smile after hearing about improved living conditions in some other country, or a breakthrough in treatment for some disease, or something else that would be of no consequence to an infant and not even any direct benefit to the adult.

At about age six to eight weeks, infants begin **social smiling**—exchanging smiles with another person (Wolff, 1987). Suddenly the infant responds to other people's smiles by grinning in return (see Figure 12.3). This behavior is incredibly rewarding for parents and other people interacting with the infant. Parents find it more pleasurable to interact with infants who reciprocate their smiles, so they are more likely to play with infants who exhibit social smiling. This increased social interaction is crucial for the infant's further cognitive and social development (Bower, 1977). The reward value of the social smile become clear in studies of parents

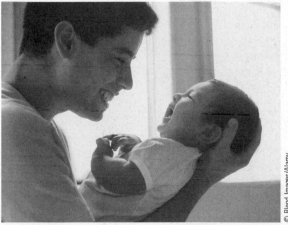

FIGURE 12.3 Social smiling, which emerges in the second or third month of life, makes it more rewarding for adults to interact with babies. This interaction is critical for babies' continued cognitive development.

whose babies show deficits in this behavior, such as babies with Down syndrome (Emde, Katz, & Thorpe, 1978). Parents of Down babies often report feeling less rewarded by interaction with their infants than do parents of healthy babies, an effect that may lead to decreased investment of time and energy. This suggests one reason smiles may have evolved: They help infants get attention and care.

Why does the social smile emerge at this time? Many researchers relate the transition to the development of visual acuity and to changes in how the infant looks at people's faces. For the first few weeks of life, infants have only blurry vision, and they tend to look toward the top of the face (the eyes) rather than the bottom (Cassia, Turati, & Simion, 2004). At about six to eight weeks, infants begin to look more closely at people's features and have a chance of detecting a smile when they see one. However, improved vision alone does not explain social smiling. People blind from birth smile about as much as sighted people do, and in the same situations (Matsumoto & Willingham, 2009). That is, you don't have to see someone else's face in order to learn how to smile.

To study the role of vision development, Selma Fraiberg (1974) studied the emergence of social smiling in blind babies. She worried that parent-child relationships might suffer because blind babies could not respond to parents' smiles with smiles of their own. She noticed, however, that many parents of blind children played physically with their babies (tickling, bouncing, and so on) more than parents of sighted children, and that the blind babies often smiled in response to this play. Fraiberg developed a training program for parents of blind babies, showing them how to maximize the opportunity for their babies to develop social smiles.

Other researchers have confirmed that blind babies smile in response to tactile and auditory social cues (Rogers & Puchalski, 1986). Indeed, tactile cues, especially skin contact, are an important basis of bonding for everyone. Adults who recall that their parents frequently touched them and hugged them when they were children are more likely than average to have good romantic relationships, and less likely than average to become depressed (Takeuchi et al., 2010).

Responses to Danger

Besides crying and smiling, one other infant behavior that we might think of as an emotional expression is the **Moro reflex**—a sequence in which the infant flings out the arms and spreads the fingers, then contracts quickly into a fetal position with fingers bent. The Moro reflex has been described as an "infant startle," and the second part of it does resemble the adult startle response. Babies display the Moro reflex in situations that suggest danger, such as being dropped, hearing a sudden loud noise, or seeing a large figure moving quickly toward them. Infants need not understand that these signals mean danger, and they probably don't, any more than a duck understands why it sits on eggs or why it feels an urge to fly south for the winter. Rather, the human nervous system has developed to produce a startle response in situations that are likely to be dangerous.

The utility of the Moro reflex is clear. In a potentially dangerous situation, an infant reaches out and grabs onto whatever it can, pulling in tightly. Grabbing something might prevent an infant from falling. Grabbing an adult might mean that the adult will carry the infant away from danger.

Does the Moro reflex indicate that newborns feel fear? Possibly, but there are reasons for doubt. Fear and startle are closely related but not quite the same thing. The Moro reflex looks different from the prototypical fear expression. Also, the adult experience of fear depends to some extent on our appraisal of the situation. If a loud noise or sudden flash of light startles us, we might flinch, but if we examine the situation and find no danger, the startle might give way to an expression of amusement, anger, or indifference, rather than fear. Infants just start crying regardless of what else is happening. If they start to cry at the sound of fireworks, for example, their crying continues despite the lack of any other sign of danger. However, they fail to show fear of many situations adults find dangerous. Infants are not afraid of heights until they begin to crawl and have a few experiences of falling (Adolph, 2000; Campos, Bertenthal, & Kermoian, 1992). Even toddlers two or three years old approach snakes and other objects thought to be prototypical elicitors of fear. In short, the newborn's Moro reflex is related to fear, but is not the same as adult fear.

One consistent trend emerges from these lines of research. In newborns, expressions such as crying, smiling, and startle are responses to simple biological states. Newborns cry because they are in pain, not because someone has hurt their feelings or because they miss their stuffed animals. They smile because their bodies feel good and their tummies are full, not because they see a friend coming. They exhibit the Moro reflex, or startle, only in response to sudden bright lights or loud noises or when they are dropped. Emotions in response to cognitive appraisals of events come later.

Do Infants Experience Discrete Emotions?

Crying is newborns' only emotional expression, so at that point we see evidence for only one kind of emotion—distress. Two or three months later, they begin to smile. Over the succeeding months and years, they gradually develop a full range of emotional expressions. What accounts for that change?

One hypothesis is that even newborns possess the full range of basic emotions, or at least the potential for them. By this reasoning, newborns do not display anger partly because they lack the cognitive capacity to assign blame, and partly because they lack the motor capacity to make an angry expression. A second hypothesis is that newborns' distress is a mixture of anger, fear, sadness, disgust, and so forth. As the infant matures, these emotions separate from one another, as if you took a mixed pile of objects and sorted them into different stacks. A third hypothesis is that certain emotions are simply absent at birth. According to this hypothesis, a newborn is no more capable of experiencing anger than of seeing ultraviolet light. The capacities for anger, disgust, and so forth develop later through brain maturation, learning, or both. Presumably, different emotions emerge at the age when they first become useful.

At first glance, these distinctions may seem like splitting hairs. After all, does it really matter whether a crying baby is feeling anger, fear, sadness, or just distress? In either case, aren't you going to check its diaper, try feeding it, and rock it in your arms? The importance of the distinction is theoretical. Someone who thinks that emotions are socially constructed might find support in the idea that infants are not born with specific emotions. A defender of the idea of evolved, built-in emotions might want to find evidence of those emotions in infants as young as possible. Also recall the debate about whether people have a few "basic" emotions or continuous dimensions of emotional experience, such as pleasant/unpleasant, and active/inactive. If we have continuous dimensions, then it is unsurprising that infants fail to show specific emotions such as anger. However, if you accept the idea of discrete, basic emotions, then you have to explain why newborns don't show them.

Unfortunately for theoreticians, the evidence is often ambiguous as to the age at which various emotions first appear. Consider "surprise," for example. Experimenters show an infant two objects, then cover them with a screen and retrieve one of the objects from behind the screen, as shown in Figure 12.4. Then they remove the screen to show either one object (the "possible" outcome) or two objects (the "impossible" outcome). Even infants just a few months old sometimes are likely to stare longer at the impossible outcome (Wakely, Rivera, & Langer, 2000; Wynn & Chiang, 1998). When they do, experimenters infer that the infants were "surprised" by the impossible outcome, suggesting a primitive understanding of number. However, the infants don't *look* surprised. Yes, they stare (sometimes), but they don't show the facial expression of surprise (which includes lifted eyebrows and widened eyes). We only begin to see that expression in toddlers close to two years old.

Follow-up studies examined infants' and toddlers' reactions when an experimenter's voice suddenly changed to a squeaky, metallic sound (because the experimenter was speaking into a microphone connected

Sequence of events 2 − 1 = ?

| 1. Objects placed in case | 2. Screen comes up | 3. Empty hand enters | 4. One object removed |

Then either: possible outcome | **or impossible outcome**

| 5. Screen drops . . . | . . . revealing 1 object | 5. Screen drops . . . | . . . revealing 2 objects |

F I G U R E 12.4 Experimenters show infants a possible or impossible outcome of removing one doll. The question is whether the infants stare longer at the "impossible" and therefore "surprising" outcome.

to a sound distorter). Even up to age 14 months, the children almost never made any vocal or facial expressions resembling adult surprise. They did, however, stop whatever else they were doing and stare at the experimenter (Scherer, Zentner, & Stern, 2004). So do infants feel "real" surprise, or not? We might say they are showing "interest," rather than surprise, but that raises a debate over whether interest is an emotion or not. The point is that it is difficult to conclude whether infants do or do not experience surprise. In some ways they do and in some ways they don't.

THE EMERGENCE OF DIFFERENTIATED EMOTIONS

How do infants progress from just one or two emotions to many? One hypothesis is that newborn infants already have the capacity to feel many distinct emotions, but don't understand the world well enough to experience them fully (e.g., Sroufe, 1996; Witherington, Campos, & Hertenstein, 2001). For example, researchers in one study examined the emergence of anger in infants of one, four, and seven months of age (Sternberg & Campos, 1990). To elicit anger, the researchers gently held down the infant's arm to prevent its movement, and

videotaped the infant's reactions. Later they carefully coded all the facial expressions and changes in gaze direction.

The tiny participants' expressions started out resembling mild annoyance, but looked increasingly distinct in older groups. The one-month-old infants did not show a prototypical anger display, but they did lower their brows and raise their cheeks in an expression somewhat different from mere distress. Their eyes were closed, and their tongues stuck out of their mouths—movements that differ from a prototypical anger display. At four months, infants showed a more characteristic anger expression, narrowing their eyes, pulling back their lips, frowning, and raising their cheeks. At this age they looked primarily at the arm that was being restrained. At seven months, infants showed a prototypical anger expression and looked at the face of the experimenter doing the restraining—and at their mothers, who were in the room.

According to Sternberg and Campos (1990), this sequence reflects development from a fuzzy sense of frustration to prototypical anger, directed specifically at the experimenter. At one month, the infant can't move its arm and presumably doesn't understand why. By four months, the infant localizes this frustration to the arm restraint but still cannot attribute the event to the actions of another person. By seven months, the infant appears to blame the experimenter (and maybe Mom) for the situation. By this interpretation, infants are beginning to feel different kinds of distress even in the first month of life, but they become more prototypically angry as they develop the cognitive ability to attribute their frustration to a particular cause, especially another person. They also develop the motor capacity to display their anger.

Other researchers followed up with variants on this procedure. Under which condition would you guess a six-month-old shows more distress—if a stranger holds down the infant's arm, or if the mother does? We might guess that having a stranger hold the arm down would be more distressing, because the infant trusts the mother and not the stranger. However, infants show significantly more distress when the mother does the restraint (Porter, Jones, Evans, & Robinson, 2009). Why? Perhaps the infant is accustomed to such intrusions by strangers, especially physicians and nurses. Perhaps the infant feels betrayed by the mother's mistreatment. Or perhaps the infant feels less inhibited at expressing anger toward the mother, uncertain how the stranger would react. In any case, an infant's responses show a complex interaction of many influences.

According to another hypothesis, newborns experience only comfort or distress and not a variety of separate emotions. By this view, distress differentiates into more specific emotions later (e.g., Camras, 1992; Messinger, 2002; Spitz, 1965). Again, most of the evidence relies on analyses of infants' facial expressions. One can examine expressions by infants and be impressed by the subtle differences between anger situations and fear situations—or be impressed with the considerable similarity.

In one of the largest studies, researchers obtained photographs of strong facial expressions by dozens of infants ranging in age from 2 hours to 21 months (Oster, Hegley, & Nagel, 1992). The researchers first wanted to know whether untrained adult participants would label negative facial expressions with discrete emotion terms, or whether they would tend to refer to all of the displays as global "distress." Second, they wanted to know whether two separate coding systems, used to classify infant facial expressions of emotion, would interpret the displays in the same way.

The researchers found little evidence that infants less than three months old displayed discrete emotions that adults could recognize. Untrained coders were in agreement about happy and sad expressions, but they tended to label most negative expressions as distress rather than assigning a specific negative emotion word. The two facial coding systems also failed to agree in most cases. Both systems identified expressions of happiness and surprise. However, only 3 of the 19 expressions coded by the first system as displays of a particular negative emotion were coded the same way by the other system.

In a related study, researchers recorded the expressions of 11-month-olds in two situations, one designed to elicit anger and another designed to produce fear. The infants responded differently in terms of body movements, but their facial expressions to the two situations were indistinguishable (Camras et al., 2007).

Even at a later age, children do not clearly distinguish one type of emotion from another. In one study, children were asked to look at pictures of people's faces and put into a box only those faces that looked happy. On other trials, they examined the same pictures and put the sad faces into the box, or the angry or scared faces. Even four- and five-year-old children made many mistakes, and often confused one negative expression with another. Into the "sad" box they might put not only sad pictures, but also pictures that adults would label angry, scared, or disgusted (Widen & Russell, 2008). That is, children do not at first conceptualize emotion in terms of a few distinct categories.

Do infants and young children have distinct emotions or not? We recommend caution on this point. Adults, especially parents, are tempted to overinterpret infants' expressions: "Oh, look, our baby is happy! Ooh . . . now she's angry." Well, maybe so, but maybe not. Psychologists sometimes overinterpret expressions also. We cannot get "inside the infant's head" to know what an infant feels. However, we also should beware of drawing conclusions from the *absence* of facial expressions. Infants' lack of clear facial expressions could reflect motor limitations rather than a lack of distinct emotions.

Regardless of whether young infants have discrete emotions, it is clear that their emotional experience changes enormously over the first couple of years. By age one year or so, infants show clear expressions of happiness, sadness, anger, and fear (Lewis, 2000). To what extent does this development rely on learning and to what extent on physical growth and other maturational processes?

Physical Maturation

The capacity to display emotions requires a certain degree of physical maturation. For example, newborn infants have poor vision, especially in the center of the eye, where adults' visual acuity is best (Abramov et al., 1982). For the first six months, they have trouble shifting visual attention from one object to another. A moving object will capture their attention so thoroughly that they literally cannot look away from it (Clohessy, Posner, Rothbart, & Veccra, 1991; M. H. Johnson, Posner, & Rothbart, 1991). At the very least, their immature vision limits their ability to respond to visual stimuli.

Similarly, developing abilities to crawl and walk introduce new situations with implications for emotion. An infant newly able to crawl must face the risk of getting lost or of encountering danger. An infant newly able to stand and walk suddenly must cope with the risk of falling. These changes in motor ability may trigger the development of new emotion systems, or they may stimulate emotion systems that were present but dormant.

More important, increasing motor maturation enables the infant to express emotions more clearly. A newborn human cannot make a fist in anger or run away in fright, cannot yet laugh, and in many ways resembles a computer that is not attached to a screen or printer. That is, much may be going on inside, but no one knows about it. Muscle control increases greatly in the first year or two of life, and with it the capacity for emotional and other communication greatly increases.

Cognitive Maturation

Recall from the definition in Chapter 1 that one important element of emotion is an appraisal, or cognitive interpretation of some event. Without an adequate appraisal, an emotion is either absent or incomplete. For example, in the Sternberg and Campos (1990) arm restraint study, the one-month-olds and seven-month-olds differed in many ways, and presumably one of them was that the older infants looked for a cause of their distress, whereas the younger ones could not.

Cognitive development is hardly limited to infancy. The frontal cortex of the brain, closely associated with planning and logic, doesn't reach maturity until the late teens (Sowell, Thompson, Holmes, Jernigan, & Toga, 1999; Sowell, Thompson, Tessner, & Toga, 2001), and learning continues throughout life. The first few years of life, however, see the most dramatic transitions in cognitive ability. During this time, humans develop an ability to understand events from another person's perspective, an awareness of how one looks to other people, and many other cognitive abilities that adults typically take for granted. The infant's emotional life is limited without these abilities.

The importance of cognitive development is particularly salient with regard to the self-conscious emotions of pride, shame, and guilt, which require comparing yourself to an abstract standard of behavior. Younger infants clearly do not compare themselves to a set of expectations (Mahler, Pine, & Bergman, 1975), and most psychologists believe that infants lack a clear sense of "self." Lewis and Brooks-Gunn (1979) designed a clever study to determine when children can recognize themselves. They asked the mothers of 9- to 24-month-old children to put a spot of rouge on the children's noses, while pretending to wipe off their faces. The mothers then held the children up to a large mirror. Infants younger than about 16 months of age typically reached out to the mirror, as though it were another child. By contrast, children 18 to 24 months of age consistently did what adults would do—reach up to their own noses to wipe off the spot. (See Figure 12.5.) That is, they recognized, "The child I see in the mirror is me." Modifications of this test have demonstrated apparent self-recognition in just a few non-human species, including chimpanzees, certain monkey species, dolphins, elephants, and magpies (a bird species)

© Anne Dowie

FIGURE 12.5 A child younger than age 1½ to 2 years sees the red dot on the nose or forehead and points at it in the mirror. An older child points to his or her own head, indicating recognition that the child in the mirror is himself or herself.

(Heschl & Burkhart, 2006; Plotnik, de Waal, & Reiss, 2006; Prior, Schwarz, & Gunturkun, 2008).

As we noted in the last chapter, self-awareness and self-recognition open the door to new emotions based on self-evaluation. For example, before age two years, children react to their failures with sadness; after that, they react with shame or guilt (Lewis, 1992; Lewis, Sullivan, Stanger, & Weiss, 1989). These emotions continue to develop over at least the next few years. Around the fourth year of life, children begin to show **theory of mind**, the understanding that other people have minds too, and the ability to discern what other people know or think (Astington & Gopnik, 1991). Once you have "theory of mind," you understand that other people are sometimes watching you, thinking about you, and evaluating you (Witherington, Campos, & Hertenstein, 2001).

Social Interaction

Finally, as social constructivists have pointed out, humans learn a great deal about emotion from their social environment. Infants begin looking to trusted caregivers to find out how they should feel about novel objects or events sometime late in their first year (Klinnert, Emde, Butterfield, & Campos, 1986; Mumme, Fernald, & Herrera, 1996; Sorce, Emde, Campos, & Klinnert, 1985; Walden & Baxter, 1989). From that point on, social interaction has tremendous implications for the person's emotional life (Keltner & Haidt, 1999). Different cultures have different expectations about emotions, and different rules for displaying them. Infants begin learning these expectations very early from day-to-day interactions with family and other people (Much, 1997). They learn much from interactions with other children. For example, children who share their toys with others find that the other children are willing to share their toys in return (Fujisawa, Kutsukake, & Hasegawa, 2008).

DEVELOPMENT OF EMOTIONAL COMMUNICATION: PERCEIVING, SHARING, AND TALKING ABOUT EMOTIONS

Emotional communication is crucial for human survival. Imagine you are visiting somewhere far from home. You go walking through the wilderness, accompanied by people who live in the area, when suddenly you see an animal that you don't recognize. Is it dangerous or harmless? You don't know. If the other people smile and keep walking, you do too. But if they shriek and start running away, so do you. Psychologists refer to this process as **social referencing** (Klinnert et al., 1986; Walden & Baxter, 1989): You base your own emotional reaction to the ambiguous situation on your perception of other people's emotions.

Infants and young children gradually develop the capacity for social referencing, and as they do, they mature in the appropriateness of their own emotions. The age at which it emerges varies across situations. The earliest sign of social referencing appears at about nine months, in the visual cliff: Researchers place an infant on a table with plates of clear glass on either side. On the "shallow" side, the infant sees a floor that is just a short step down. On the "deep" side the floor appears to be much farther (see Figure 12.6). Infants who have had some experience with crawling, and therefore some experience with falling down, usually turn toward the shallow side, indicating the ability to detect depth (and a preference for avoiding injury).

Suppose researchers place an infant on the safe (shallow) side while the mother stands on the other side of the table, beyond the deep end. The mother is instructed either to look frightened or to smile and encourage the infant to cross. Starting at about nine months of age, most infants use their mothers' cues to decide whether to cross. An infant stays put when the mother looks frightened, but tests the glass and then crosses when the mother looks happy (Sorce, Emde, Campos, & Klinnert, 1985).

In other situations social referencing begins later. Imagine an infant who is confronted with one or more unfamiliar toys, such as a remote-controlled robot that makes odd sounds. If the mother says, "Oh, that toy scares me," making a facial expression of fear, children as young as 11 months also act afraid of the toy, with girls generally more responsive to the mother's expression than boys are (Blackford & Walden, 1998). Similarly, if an infant sees two new toys, and someone—even a stranger—reacts to one of them with pleasure and the other one with disgust, the infant becomes more likely to play with the "pleasant" toy (Moses, Baldwin, Rosicky, & Tidball, 2001; Mumme, Fernald, & Herrera, 1996; Walden & Baxter, 1989). An 11-month-old avoids the "disgusting" toy only if tested within a few minutes, whereas a 14-month-old avoids it even an hour later, suggesting that the older child remembers the emotional association learned from the other person (Hertenstein & Campos, 2004).

Intersubjectivity

Social referencing is part of a larger phenomenon, known as intersubjectivity. Social smiling and shared affect are called primary intersubjectivity— the sharing of experience. Parents often make a deliberate effort to share an infant's emotions and let the infant know about the sharing (Jonsson et al., 2001). For example, an infant reaches out to grab a toy, and the parent says, "Ohh, look at that!" In the process, the parent communicates, "I understand what you feel," and the infant gets some idea of what the parent is feeling. Observers find that mother and infant usually match each other's emotions within seconds (Beebe, 2003). Even when infants are very young, they and their mothers learn to coordinate their responses. Infants more or less match their rhythms of babbling and glancing at the mother with the mother's rhythm of talking and glancing at the infant (Beebe et al., 2000; Crown, Feldstein, Jasnow, Beebe, & Jaffe, 2002). In effect,

© Mark Richards/Photo Edit

FIGURE 12.6 Infants late in their first year of life will look to caregivers to decide how to respond to novel situations, such as the visual cliff.

they hold nonverbal "conversations" long before the infant learns any words. These processes constitute a major step toward understanding each other's mental states (Sanefuji, 2008).

Secondary intersubjectivity occurs when the infant and the caregiver share their experience of an object or a third person (Trevarthen & Hubley, 1978). For example, when a child sees a puppy, gets the parent's attention, and points to the puppy, the two of them are engaging in secondary intersubjectivity. The parent and child jointly attend to the puppy and share their feelings. When the object or situation in question is unfamiliar, infants use social referencing to decide how to act. They wait to see someone else's reaction before deciding to enjoy the object or avoid it. Infants as young as five months old look at their parents and other people to evaluate a situation, and this tendency increases as the child grows older (Striano & Bertin, 2005).

Interpreting Facial Expressions of Emotion

When young children see a smile, how do they know that it means "happy"? How do they know what a frown means? Answers here are speculative. One possibility is that an infant automatically knows what a smile and frown means, through some inherited mechanism. That hypothesis is plausible, and from an evolutionary standpoint, this kind of communication is so important for infants that a built-in mechanism would be highly adaptive. However, opportunities for learning occur also. Infants and their parents tend to have similar emotional experiences and expressions at the same time. (See Figure 12.7.) One reason is that they react to the same events at the same time (Kokkinaki, 2003); another is that they sometimes copy each other's expressions. Parents often imitate their infants' expressions, and infants more than nine months old

LWA-Dann Tardif/Surf/Corbis

FIGURE 12.7 Young children and their parents often have the same emotional expression at the same time because they are reacting to the same event. This synchrony provides one opportunity for infants to learn what different expressions mean.

imitate their parents (Feldman, Greenbaum, & Yirmiya, 1999). An infant who smiles, feels happy, and sees someone else smile at the same time has the opportunity to associate a happy feeling with the sight of a smiling face. Separating the roles of heredity and environment is difficult in this case.

Facial mimicry, copying other people's facial expressions, has been observed in the first days of life, although its significance is unclear (Field, Woodson, Greenberg, & Cohen, 1982; Meltzoff & Moore, 1977, 2002). (See Figure 12.8.) How does an infant know which facial muscles to contract to produce the expression it sees? Why does it imitate? Perhaps the newborn's mimicry is closer to being an automatic reflex than a motivated behavior. Although researchers know this behavior exists at a remarkably young age, its meaning is less clear.

Emotional Language

Another way to study the development of emotional communication is to analyze children's language. Soon after children start to talk (around age one and one half to two years), their emotion vocabulary starts to grow. However, the fact that they use words like "angry" or "sad" does not tell us how thoroughly they understand those terms. To test how well toddlers understand emotions as internal experiences, Judy Dunn and colleagues (1987) examined the situations in which preschool children use emotion words. The researchers found that even two-year-old children use emotion words in fairly accurate ways. In play, they attribute emotions to dolls and stuffed animals in appropriate situations. Toddlers also talk about what they and others have felt in the past and what they expect to feel in the future, not just in the present (Wellman, Harris, Banerjee, & Sinclair, 1995). This emotion talk is a good predictor of healthy social development. In one study, three-year-old children who talked more with their families about emotional experiences showed a better ability to figure out other people's emotions when they reached first grade (Dunn, Brown, & Maguire, 1995). This result does not

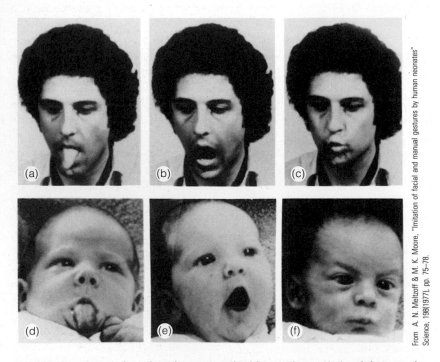

From A. N. Meltzoff & M. K. Moore, "Imitation of facial and manual gestures by human neonates" *Science*, 198(1977), pp. 75–78.

FIGURE 12.8 Infants less than a month old sometimes mimic adults' mouth expressions.

Source: Meltzoff and Moore (1977).

mean, of course, that young children distinguish one emotion from another as clearly as adults do (Widen & Russell, 2008).

Two-year-olds are so aware of how their emotions affect other people that they may begin faking emotion to get what they want (Bretherton, Fritz, Zahn-Waxler, & Ridgeway, 1986). For example, they might pretend to be sad or frightened to get attention. At this young age, children use emotion to "train" their parents just as much as parents use emotion to train their children.

By three years of age, children's ability to communicate about emotions has increased. In one study, researchers noted each time a child displayed happiness, sadness, distress, or anger while playing at a day-care center (Fabes, Eisenberg, Nyman, & Michaelieu, 1991). After each expression, the researcher approached another child, who had seen the expression but was not the cause of it, and asked what the target child was feeling and what event had caused that emotion. In the meantime, an adult observer recorded what she thought the target child felt and why. Even the three-year-old children agreed about two thirds of the time with the adult observer's interpretation of the event. By this stage of development, children clearly recognize emotional expressions and their causes.

DEVELOPMENT OF EMOTIONAL BONDS: ATTACHMENT

In Chapter 9, we first described the selective emotional bond researchers call **attachment**. At first, an infant who has just developed social smiling reacts with a smile to any smile it sees. Beginning at about six to nine months, the infant becomes more discriminating. A baby who would lie contently in anyone's arms just a few weeks earlier now becomes hysterical when Mom leaves the room. Developmental psychologists use the term **attachment** to denote a long-lasting emotional bond between the infant and a few regular caregivers. In infants and toddlers, attachment is measured using a paradigm called the

strange situation, in which the child's behavior is observed as the parent leaves and returns to the child in an unfamiliar room.

A "securely attached" infant more than about six months old will typically protest when the parent leaves the room, show joy when the parent returns, and "check in" with the parent frequently while playing. Why does attachment begin specifically at six months? Several theories have been proposed, and they probably all have some element of truth. First, infants' vision improves substantially from birth to age six months (Banks & Salapatek, 1983). Some researchers have suggested that this is the first time infants can see parents and other caregivers well enough to recognize them and know when they have come or gone. If taken as an absolute, the idea that infants do not recognize their parents until age six months is certainly overstated. Even newborns show signs of recognizing their mother's voice (DeCasper & Fifer, 1980). However, recognizing by voice and recognizing by sight are different, and vision has obvious advantages for monitoring people's movements at a distance.

Another explanation relates to cognitive maturation. During Jean Piaget's sensorimotor stage of development (from birth until almost two years), infants respond mostly to what they see and hear in the present instead of anything they remember. Piaget argued that infants less than nine months old lack **object permanence**—the understanding that objects continue to exist even when we do not see or hear them. For example, infants less than nine months old reach for objects they see, but not for objects that have been covered or hidden (Piaget, 1937/1954). Later researchers using different research methods found indications of object permanence much earlier, even at ages four to six months (Baillargeon, 1986, 1987; Wynn & Chiang, 1998). Still, the tendency by the youngest infants to respond mainly to what they see at the moment would decrease their response to someone leaving the room (Schaffer, 1971).

The final explanation is probably the most commonly accepted. At about six to eight months of age, most babies begin to crawl, and they begin their rush to explore the world. This new skill opens doors to all sorts of new experiences, including, unfortunately, such possibilities as getting lost, tumbling down the stairs, touching sharp or hot items, and encountering less-than-gentle animals. Before the baby could crawl, it could rely on caregivers to keep the immediate environment safe. Now the baby must balance the thrill of exploration with the risk of wandering away and getting into serious trouble. According to John Bowlby (1969), a biological attachment behavior system develops about the time a baby starts to crawl to help regulate these two competing needs. As long as a trusted caregiver is nearby and in regular contact, a child plays happily. As soon as the caregiver is out of sight, the child does something to repair the breach. The emotions and behaviors necessary for this regulation constitute attachment.

This last explanation means that attachment behavior—especially the protest when a caregiver leaves—has the specific purpose of keeping caregivers close enough to help when needed, but distant enough for the infant to do some exploring. Before six months that strategy is unimportant, because the infants are not yet crawling. It gradually becomes less important again as the child grows old enough and competent enough to explore without constant supervision. In the strange situation, children continue protesting the caregiver's departure up to age 18 months and beyond, but their protests become less and less intense (Izard & Abe, 2004).

We also noted in Chapter 9 that an infant's attachment behavior depends to some degree on how the caregiver responds to the infant (Isabella & Belsky, 1991). If a caregiver is smothering, ignoring the infant's need to explore on its own, the infant may develop an "anxious" attachment style, becoming extremely upset when the caregiver leaves yet simultaneously clinging to the caregiver and pushing her away when she returns. With a distant, rejecting caregiver, infants may develop an "avoidant" attachment style, paying little attention to the caregiver when present, and not turning to her for comfort when she returns. Children with an avoidant attachment style are at increased risk for aggressive, antisocial behaviors later in life (Burgess, Marshall, Rubin, & Fox, 2003).

There are three possible explanations for this, which may all be true to some degree: First, infants develop an attachment style that corresponds to their caregivers' typical behavior. Second, the caregivers' behavior depends to some degree on the infants' personality and inherent emotional style. Third, most studies pertain to children and their biological parents, so they can have related behavior patterns for genetic reasons.

Hand in hand with attachment comes **stranger anxiety**—a fear of unfamiliar people (Sroufe, 1977). Not all children experience this sudden increase in fear of strangers, and in most children this fear declines over time (Greenberg & Marvin, 1982). Developmental psychologists relate the fear of strangers partly to advances in memory—a newfound ability to recognize familiar people and therefore to notice when someone is unfamiliar. Fear of strangers may also relate to maturation of the capacity for fear in general. A similar trend is common in the animal kingdom: Baby mammals and birds curiously explore the world, but as they grow older, they become more cautious and more likely to flee from unfamiliar objects. Infants' fear of strangers is especially intense for adult men. Why? One explanation is that adult men tend to be large, and larger is scarier. Another explanation relates to evolution: Adult males have posed a potential threat to infants throughout mammalian evolution. Perhaps we evolved a tendency for infants to be wary of unfamiliar men (Bracha, 2006).

SOCIALIZATION OF EMOTIONAL EXPRESSION

How do children learn when, where, and how strongly to express their emotions? Expectations about emotional expression vary by culture, as we discussed in Chapter 3. In general, however, cultures are similar in their expectations for children. A survey of 48 countries found that parents in all locations wanted their children to be happy, not too fearful, and capable of controlling their anger (M. L. Diener & Lucas, 2004). Most people expect and tolerate occasional impulsive and aggressive behaviors by two- and three-year-olds (as in the expression "the terrible twos"), but after that, they expect children to start restraining themselves, and peers ostracize those who don't (Trentacosta & Shaw, 2009). Those expectations are largely similar in cultures ranging from Javanese society to the more individualist society of the United States (Eisenberg, Liew, & Pidada, 2001; Eisenberg, Pidada, & Liew, 2001; Hanish et al., 2004).

Expectations for emotional expression also vary by gender, although again the differences are not huge. Across cultures, most parents stress control of fear and anger more for their sons than for their daughters, and encourage the expression of happiness more for their daughters than for their sons (M. L. Diener & Lucas, 2004). According to observations of preschool children, parents tend to discuss emotions with their daughters more than with their sons, possibly because girls initiate such conversations more often (Fivush, Brotman, Buckner, & Goodman, 2000). Parents, especially fathers, pay more attention to angry outbursts by sons than by daughters (Chaplin, Cole, & Zahn-Waxler, 2005). Perhaps parents are less worried that their daughters' anger will get out of control.

When do children learn and begin to follow their culture's display rules? By age three years, many children begin to learn to hide their feelings. One study demonstrated this by instructing children not to look at a hidden toy. Their behavior was filmed while the experimenter left the room. Afterward, the children were asked whether or not they had disobeyed (Lewis, Stanger, & Sullivan, 1989). Naturally, many of the children did look at the toy and then lied about it. Although careful behavioral coding revealed that the lying children showed subtle hints of shame and guilt, such as nervous smiles and self-touches, untrained adults could not distinguish liars from the children who really did not look at the toy. Thus, the children in this study seemed successful at hiding their guilty emotions.

Another study found substantial individual differences among children in their ability to conceal their emotions. In the United States, one rule of polite behavior is to express thanks for any gift

and never react with disappointment. Preschool children were asked to rank-order five small presents from best to worst, and experimenters promised to give them one of the presents later, after the children performed a task. When the time came, the experimenters at first gave each child his least preferred gift, waited a few seconds, and then apologized and gave the most preferred gift. During those few seconds' delay, the experimenter recorded the children's reactions. Some children cried, threw the unwanted present, and demanded a better one. Others politely accepted it and hid their disappointment. As you might guess, those who vigorously displayed their frustration were rated by their teachers and others as "lacking social skills," whereas those who hid their disappointment were considered good at controlling their emotions in a variety of situations (Liew, Eisenberg, & Reiser, 2004). Those with better control of their emotions also tended to do better in their schoolwork (Liew, McTigue, Barrois, & Hughes, 2008).

How do children learn the rules for displaying or concealing emotions? Anthropologists emphasize the effect of day-to-day interactions in the home (Much, 1997). Most mothers of 6- to 12- month-old infants in the United States express much joy, interest, and surprise during their interactions with their babies and respond strongly to their infants' displays of interest or surprise (Malatesta, Grigorvey, Lamb, Albin, & Culver, 1986; Malatesta & Haviland, 1982). As a rule, parents who express mostly positive emotions have children who also express positive emotions, whereas parents who express many negative emotions have children who also vigorously express their fears and anger (Cole, Teti, & Zahn-Waxler, 2003; Denham et al., 2000; Valiente et al., 2004). It is tempting to assume that the children react to their parents' displays and copy them. However, these studies are correlational and we cannot draw cause-and-effect conclusions. Perhaps the parents are reacting to their children's emotional outbursts. Perhaps parent and child show similar emotional displays because of their genetic similarity. Studies on parents of adopted children would help to unravel this problem, but few such studies have been conducted.

In one study, researchers asked Japanese and American mothers to yell angrily while their 11-month-old infants crawled toward a toy (Miyake, Campos, Kagan, & Bradshaw, 1986). The American babies typically paused briefly but then kept approaching the toy, whereas Japanese babies paused far longer. According to the researchers, the American babies had heard their mothers yell so often that they did not take them seriously. ("Mom's yelling again. Oh well.") For Japanese babies, however, an angry voice was a rare occurrence and therefore worth much attention. Even in the first year of life, infants learn cultural rules about how to interpret other people's emotions. American babies might also be learning that anger is acceptable and normal, whereas Japanese infants might be learning that anger is rare and generally inappropriate.

Children also learn cultural rules when parents and other caregivers reinforce or discourage emotion displays (Figure 12.9). We noted above that an infant's attachment pattern correlates with caregiver behaviors—responsive but unintrusive caregivers tend to have securely attached toddlers, whereas unresponsive, distant caregivers tend to have avoidant toddlers, and intrusive, always-in-your-face caregivers tend to have anxiously attached toddlers. One can think about these parenting styles as examples of good versus bad parenting, but one can also think of them as reflections of emotional style, which differs from culture to culture. For example, in one study of the strange situation in Germany, nearly half of the infants were classified as attachment-avoidant, compared with an average 23 percent of American infants (Grossman, Grossman, Spangler, Suess, & Unzer, 1985). Many infants did not seem terribly worried about their mother's absence. When researchers observed the mothers' behavior, they did not find that German moms were neglectful or unresponsive. Rather, the mothers expressed a belief that parents should encourage independence in their children.

In Japanese samples, high proportions of toddlers are typically classified as attachment-anxious by U.S. standards (e.g., Miyake, Chen, & Campos, 1985; Rothbaum, Weisz, Pott, Miyake, & Morelli, 2000). Mothers in traditional Japanese families rarely

Ace Stock Limited/Alamy

FIGURE 12.9 Children learn their culture's emotional display rules when parents reinforce or discourage certain emotional expressions.

leave their infants, and they intentionally encourage dependence on others. The strange situation is thus vastly "stranger" for Japanese toddlers than it is for American toddlers. Sometimes experimenters have trouble even persuading Japanese mothers to leave their infants in the presence of a stranger to conduct the research. As a result, emotional responses to this situation are understandably different for Japanese and American infants. As cultures change, so do the emotional lessons conveyed by parents. Among Japanese mothers with careers outside the home, attachment style proportions are similar to those typical of the United States (Durrett, Otaki, & Richards, 1984).

Sometimes parents give lessons in emotional regulation without realizing what they are doing. In one study, researchers asked Japanese and American mothers of three- and four-year-olds how they would respond to various kinds of misbehavior, such as drawing with crayons on the wall or knocking products off the shelves at the supermarket (Conroy, Hess, Azuma, & Kashiwagi, 1980). Mothers in the United States often said they would demand that the child stop the behavior, or that they would physically force the child to stop. These strategies trigger a clash of wills, encouraging the child to argue and become angry. If the parent then gives in to a child's tantrum, the emotional behavior is reinforced—if you don't get what you want, get angry, fight, and you will win.

By contrast, Japanese mothers said they were more likely to explain why the misbehaviors hurt other people, appealing to their children's desire to please and cooperate. In training children to reinterpret such situations from other people's perspectives, Japanese mothers encourage the development of positive social emotions and discourage self-focused appraisals that may lead to anger.

EMOTION IN ADOLESCENCE

Adolescence lasts from the onset of puberty (a biological event) until the onset of adult responsibilities (a social and economic event). When you think of adolescent emotions, what comes to mind? Many people consider adolescence to be a period of "storm and stress." In fact, individuals vary greatly in how much their emotions change during the teenage years. Most adolescents experience a moderate amount of conflict with their parents, especially in early adolescence, plus occasional periods of depression, anxiety, or anger (Laursen, Coy, & Collins, 1998). Some have more serious problems than that, and some have almost none. Part of this variation in outcome is genetic in origin (McGue, Elkins, Walden, & Iacono, 2005), and part relates to the amount of sympathy and understanding that adolescents receive from their parents (R. A. Lee, Su, & Yoshida, 2005).

One reason for increased emotions is a change in activities. Parents and other adults carefully supervise preadolescent children at almost all times. In Western cultures, however, adolescents have more freedom to be with others of their own age. They make their own decisions and take more risks, and may encounter more emotionally intense situations than they did a few years earlier. Adolescence is also a time of increased exploration and risk-taking in many other species as well (Spear, 2000). Biological factors—especially dramatic fluctuations in sex hormones such as estrogen and testosterone—also contribute to increased emotional volatility. Researchers find that the onset of puberty is a better predictor of increased emotional intensity than age itself (Forbes & Dahl, 2010).

Adolescence is also portrayed as a time when emotions and impulses dominate action, rather than rational thinking. Overall, how mature are the decisions made by adolescents? This issue has profound practical consequences as well as theoretical interest. In 1990 the U.S. Supreme Court heard the case *Hodgson v. Minnesota*, concerning whether adolescent women have the right to seek an abortion without parental consent. The American Psychological Association (APA) argued that adolescents reason in a mature enough way to make that decision. The court compromised, ruling that a state could require a woman to consult with her parents, as long as the law had an escape clause for a woman whose parents were difficult to contact. Fifteen years later, the Supreme Court heard *Roper v. Simmons* concerning whether it is constitutional to apply the death penalty to someone who committed a murder while less than 18 years old. In that case, the APA held that adolescents make less mature, more impulsive decisions than adults, and should not be held to the same legal standard.

As you can imagine, the APA was accused of reinterpreting the scientific data for each case to fit psychologists' political beliefs. However, the APA positions were not quite as inconsistent as they might seem: Adolescents are more mature in some ways than in others. With deliberate, cognitive decisions and plenty of time, they reason about as well as adults. The difference comes with emotional and social decisions, especially in situations that call for quick decisions. Most adolescent crimes are impulsive acts, not thought out in advance. Although adolescents make better decisions when they have time to think carefully, they tend to be impulsive, and they have trouble inhibiting strong urges (Steinberg, Cauffman, Woolard, Graham, & Banich, 2009).

Here is one easy laboratory test of this tendency: A light flashes at an unpredictable location, and the viewer's task is to inhibit the tendency to look at it, and instead look the *opposite* direction. The ability to inhibit such automatic responses is weak in childhood and gradually improves throughout the teenage years, concurrent with maturation of the prefrontal cortex of the brain (Luna, Padmanabhan, & O'Hearn, 2010).

Peer pressure also increases adolescents' impulsiveness and risk-taking. Researchers watched people as they played a video game in which the player, driving a virtual car, could gain extra points by driving through a yellow light, but at the risk of a game-ending crash. Adolescents took the risk more often than adults, and even more so if their friends were watching (Gardner & Steinberg, 2005). Could someone decrease adolescents' risk taking by teaching them to think through their decisions and evaluate the risk? Perhaps, but in many cases adolescents already do think about their decisions. Suppose we ask people about possible decisions:

- Swimming with sharks: Good idea or bad idea?

- Eating a well-balanced diet: Good idea or bad idea?

- Setting your hair on fire: Good idea or bad idea?

Ordinarily, adolescents make the same decisions that adults do, but on the average, adolescents take more time thinking about it. Adults know immediately that they don't want to swim with sharks. Adolescents weigh the pros and cons (Reyna & Farley, 2006). In short, adolescents are not always impulsive, but under time pressure they are more likely to take risks and to be swayed powerfully by their emotions.

EMOTIONAL DEVELOPMENT
IN ADULTHOOD

Until now, we have focused on how emotion develops in early life. What happens later? Although most research has focused on emotional development in children and adolescents, emotions change through the rest of a person's life too.

Individual Consistency Across the Lifespan

Emotional characteristics tend to be consistent throughout a person's life. In one study, investigators observed hundreds of seven-year-olds and later followed up on them at age 35. "Proneness to distress" in childhood correlated .24 with adult measures of anger, indicating a moderate relationship (Kubzhansky, Martin, & Buka, 2004). In another study, researchers coded the quality and intensity of smiles posed by young women in their college yearbooks, and then asked whether these single expressions of emotion could predict aspects of the women's lives decades later (Harker & Keltner, 2001). They found that women who had displayed stronger and more "felt" smiles (Duchenne smiles) in the college photographs were more likely to have married and less likely to have divorced. They described themselves as more competent, more emotionally stable, and more agreeable than women with less intense or genuine smiles. A similar study found that both men and women who showed a good smile in their yearbook photos were less likely than average to get a divorce later in life (Hertenstein, Hansel, Butts, & Hile, 2009).

Why should this be? According to the researchers, the yearbook photos were snapshots of people's emotional dispositions as well as of their physical appearance. People who were happier as young adults were likely to carry that cheerfulness throughout their lives, smoothing the way in their activities and relationships. In short, the emotions you feel right now are moderately good predictors of the emotions you will feel throughout life, and those emotions are good predictors of some major life outcomes.

Age Trends in Emotional Intensity

The studies we have just described examined whether people who are above average (or below average) in warmth or some other characteristic remain above average (or below average) years later.

These studies did not consider what happens to the average itself. For example, if you are warmer than average for your age, you could become less and less affectionate over the years and still remain "above average" if others your age declined as fast or faster than you did.

Therefore, a different question is how people's emotions change, on average, between young adulthood and old age. Laura Carstensen and her colleagues have studied this question intensely, finding that emotional experience, the importance of emotion, and people's ability to regulate or control their emotions do change substantially over the course of adulthood.

First, as people grow older, they pay more attention to emotional matters in general. Carstensen asked participants in their 20s through their 80s to read a two-page excerpt from a novel, and then to spend the next hour doing various other tasks (Carstensen & Turk-Charles, 1994). At the end of the hour, participants were asked to recall as much as they could from the story. Although memory for most kinds of material gets worse as people age, the older participants showed a greater memory for the emotional aspects of the story (see Figure 12.10).

Although older adults pay more attention to emotional material in general, they report fewer negative events. Carstensen and Charles (1998) distributed pagers to people ranging from 18 to 94 years of age, paged them several times a day over the course of a week, and asked them each time to rate and describe their current emotional experience. Older and younger adults in the sample reported about the same frequency of positive emotions, but older adults reported feeling negative emotions considerably less often.

Other studies indicate that older adults not only avoid negative emotions, but actually feel happier than young adults, on the average. As long as older adults remain healthy, they rate themselves happier than the average young adult (Mroczek, 2004; Mroczek & Spiro, 2005). Brain recordings show a similar tendency: When people view a series of photographs, the brains of older adults show stronger responses to pleasant photos, whereas those of young

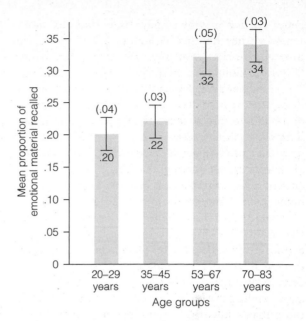

FIGURE 12.10 Emotion seems to become more salient, or important, to people as they age. This graph shows the amount of emotional material participants of different ages remembered from a two-page story.

Source: From "The salience of emotion across the life-span" by L. L. Carstensen and S. Turk-Charles in *Psychology and Aging, 9*, pp. 259–264. © 1994 American Psychological Association. Reprinted with permission from the authors.

adults respond more strongly to sad or frightening photos (Mather et al., 2004).

What accounts for these trends? One explanation is that older people in fact have fewer worries (if their health is okay). Young people worry about whether they will get a good job, get a good salary, and pay the bills. Older people are in or approaching retirement, and it's too late to worry about job success. Young people sometimes worry about whether their husband or wife might be sexually unfaithful. A couple of 75-year-olds won't waste much time on that worry. A young couple may worry about rearing their children. Older people may worry about their grandchildren, but it's not as intense.

Another possibility (which does not contradict the first) is that older adults shift their attention toward positive events and stimuli, rather than negative events. Recall from earlier chapters that emotional images, especially threatening ones, tend to capture and hold our attention strongly. Older adults do not show this bias quite as strongly, and in fact seem to be biased toward more positive stimuli. One study using a version of the "dot-probe" procedure found that photos of smiling faces "pulled" at older adults' attention almost as strongly as photos of angry or sad faces when paired with a neutral face; smiling faces were less attention-grabbing among young adults (Mather & Carstensen, 2003). Another study found that older adults selectively recount positive information from autobiographical memories, to a greater degree than young adults (Kennedy, Mather, & Carstensen, 2004).

Emotional Salience

Carstensen and her colleagues (1999) proposed that people often have to choose between conflicting goals. Sometimes you have to choose between enjoying the present and doing something less pleasant to build resources that will help you in the future (Carstensen, Fung, & Charles, 2003). According to **Socioemotional Selectivity Theory**, midlife triggers an increase in adults' motivation to make the most of their remaining time. Most young adults seek to build resources for the future. Older adults are less motivated to build resources for the future, and more motivated to seek maximum enjoyment now.

Several comparisons of younger and older adults support Socioemotional Selectivity Theory. For example, would you prefer to spend this weekend meeting interesting new people, strengthening relationships with people you know at work, or getting together with friends and family members you have known for most of your life? Younger people are more likely to choose the new relationships, whereas older people prefer to be with family and long-term friends (Carstensen, 1992; Carstensen & Charles, 1998). Older adults also behave differently when interacting with loved ones. For example, when talking about an area of conflict in their marriage, older adults are less likely to quarrel (Levenson, Carstensen, & Gottman, 1994a), and more likely to express affection during the discussion (Carstensen, Gottman, & Levenson, 1995).

The message so far is that as people grow older, they try to maximize their pleasant emotions and minimize their unpleasant emotions. But when they do face unpleasant emotional experiences, do they *feel* them as strongly as when they were young? This is not an easy question. Older and younger adults rate the intensity of their emotions about equally (Carstensen, Pasupathi, Mayr, & Nesselroade, 2000), but we do not know whether they are using the rating scale the same way. That is, a "5" on a 1-to-7 scale of some emotion may mean something different to an 80-year-old than to a 20-year-old. As people grow older, even though their ratings of the emotional experience remain about the same, their heart rate and other physiological responses to an emotional event decline (LaBar, Cook, Torpey, & Welsh-Bohmer, 2004; Labouvie-Vief, Lumley, Jain, & Heinze, 2003; Lawton, 2001). That is, a given emotional rating corresponds to a much less intense physiological feeling for an older person than for a younger one.

Emotion Regulation

You've probably heard the expression "older but wiser." Is it true? One aspect of wisdom is managing one's emotions effectively—entering rewarding situations and avoiding unpleasant ones, thinking about events in ways that facilitate a more positive emotional experience, and maintaining emotional balance in difficult situations. When James Gross and his colleagues (1997) asked American and Norwegian participants about their emotional experience and behavior, they found that older adults rated themselves as less emotionally expressive, less impulsive, and better able to control their emotions than younger adults. These measures rely on self-reports, but at least older adults *believe* that they have gained some emotional wisdom over the course of their lives.

In another study, adults of various ages named up to six people they knew well and then described a recent occasion when they had some irritation or difficulty with each person. Finally, they described how they handled each situation. On the average, older people described their conflicts as less intense than those of younger people, and the older people were much less likely to react with anger (Birditt & Fingerman, 2003). Many other studies have confirmed that older people find less to be angry about than younger people, and when they do become angry, they handle the situation more calmly and with more forgiveness (Blanchard-Fields & Coats, 2008). This trend makes sense if we consider the function of anger. Young people are competing with one another for mates, jobs, job advancement, and so forth. If someone treats them badly, it could have consequences for their long-term success. For older people, the cost of a fight may be more than what they could gain from it.

As we mentioned earlier, older adults seem to be biased toward attending to positive stimuli, and recalling positive aspects of memories. This may have implications for how they use particular emotion regulation strategies, such as reappraisal.

In one study young, middle-aged, and older adults were asked to watch several film clips that were very sad (showing someone reacting to a loved one's death) or very disgusting (showing a person eating horse rectum or cow intestine). After the first few clips, participants were asked to use one of two reappraisal strategies to make themselves feel better—detached reappraisal (thinking about unemotional aspects of the film clip) or positive reappraisal (thinking about positive aspects of the events in the clip). Although older adults seemed to benefit less from the detached reappraisal instructions than young adults, showing smaller decreases in self-reported distress and physiological reactivity, they seemed to benefit *more* from the positive reappraisal instructions (Shiota & Levenson, 2009). So, a positivity bias may help older adults regulate their emotions in particularly effective ways. Something to look forward to!

SUMMARY

Emotions change considerably throughout the lifespan, from early infancy through late adulthood. The emotions of infancy are theoretically interesting because they may shed light on the question of "basic" emotions. If infants have a set of discrete emotions, then those emotions would satisfy one major criterion for being basic. However, as you have seen, the results on this point are inconclusive. Infants' ability to display particular emotions develops gradually over a year or more, and it is hard to identify a particular age when some type of emotion first appears. Even if newborns lack discrete emotions, that need not contradict the idea of basic emotions; after all, language also matures at a later age, and psychologists widely agree that language is a feature of human nature.

Even if the capacity for emotions is evolutionarily built in, many important aspects of emotional development depend on the environment as well.

For example, you were born with the capacity to develop language, but whether you speak English, Chinese, or Swahili depends on social and cultural influences. Similarly, your biological nature gave you the capacity to feel emotions, and your genes influence how intensely you feel them, but you have learned from your culture the appropriate ways to express them and the situations in which you should suppress or modify them.

The topic of emotional development raises deep, hard-to-answer psychological issues. To review a few: How much emotion do infants experience, despite their limited cognition? Why do newborns imitate the facial expressions they see? How do infants learn what various emotional expressions mean? What accounts for the changes in emotion observed between young adults and older adults? These and other issues will continue to challenge researchers for decades to come.

KEY TERMS

attachment: a long-lasting emotional bond between an infant and a caregiver, indicated by distress upon separation, joy upon reunion, and much emotional sharing (p. 283)

distress: an undifferentiated protest against anything that is unpleasant or aversive (p. 272)

facial mimicry: copying other people's facial expressions (p. 282)

Moro reflex: a sequence in which the infant flings out its arms and spreads its fingers, then contracts quickly into a fetal position with fingers bent (p. 274)

object permanence: the understanding that objects continue to exist even when we do not see or hear them (p. 283)

secondary intersubjectivity: a process by which the infant and the caregiver share their experience of an object or a third person (p. 281)

social referencing: looking at the emotional expressions of trusted caregivers before responding to novel objects, people, or situations (p. 279)

social smiling: exchanging smiles with another person (p. 273)

Socioemotional Selectivity Theory: the view that midlife triggers an increase in adults' motivation to make the most of their remaining time and that, consequently, older adults put a high priority on emotional quality of life (p. 290)

strange situation: procedure in which an infant and parent enter a toy-filled room and the infant is allowed to play. A stranger then enters the room; after a few minutes, the parent leaves the room, then returns; next both the stranger and the parent leave the room, the stranger returns alone, and finally the parent returns. (p. 283)

stranger anxiety: a fear of unfamiliar people (p. 284)

sympathetic crying: crying in response to the sound of another newborn's cry (p. 273)

theory of mind: the understanding that other people have minds too and the ability to discern what other people know or think (p. 279)

THOUGHT QUESTIONS

1. Early in this chapter, we noted that crying is an infant's way of getting care and attention from adults. If so, why doesn't it cry all the time, to get even more care and attention?

2. Infants less than two months old respond to the sight of a smiling face by giving a smile of their own. What does this observation imply about an infant? Does the infant respond reflexively without understanding the meaning of a smile? Or does an infant understand that someone else's smile means happiness? What research might help answer such questions?

3. What kind of research evidence would convince you that six-month-old infants feel surprise? What kind of evidence would convince you that six-month-old infants are *not* capable of feeling surprise?

4. In what ways have your emotions changed since your early childhood? How could you design a study that would test whether these changes are true for most other people as well?

SUGGESTIONS FOR RESEARCH PROJECTS

1. Ask several people to describe their earliest emotional memories. Examine when these memories took place, what kinds of emotions people felt, what kinds of situations led to the emotions, and what other people's responses were to these early emotional displays. If possible, ask the same questions of children, whose memories of their earliest emotional experiences should be fresher.

2. Look for examples of intersubjectivity in your own experience. How often do adults use other people's reactions to guide their own emotional responses?

SUGGESTIONS FOR FURTHER READING

Charles, S. T., & Carstensen, L. L. (2010). " Social and Emotional Aging." *Annual Review of Psychology, 61,* 383–409. An article that reviews research on how emotions change over the lifespan.

Erikson, E. H. (1963). *Childhood and Society* (2nd ed.). New York: Norton. An influential classic that discusses the social and emotional crises people face at each stage of life.

13

Emotion and Personality

You might summarize psychologists' concerns in terms of two questions: How are we all the same, and how are we different? Throughout much of the text so far, we have emphasized aspects of emotion that are thought to be similar for most people. In this chapter we focus on differences between people. One of your friends is always cheerful and affectionate, and another tends to be gloomy. One person is emotionally volatile, with intense feelings that change frequently, whereas another is stable and calm. These traits are so striking that some central dimensions of personality can be defined in terms of the kinds of emotions that individuals typically feel.

People also differ in how they manage their own and other people's emotions. Some people are emotionally savvy, read others' expressions well, and handle emotional situations in wise ways. Other people seem clueless. You can probably think of friends or family who fall into that latter category. Some people regulate their emotions effectively, yet others seem overwhelmed by their feelings. Many psychological researchers have studied the extent to which this "emotional intelligence" overlaps with other kinds of intelligence.

In this chapter we examine the role of emotion in several key features of personality, and consider possible genetic and neurological accounts of these individual differences. We also discuss the nature and measurement of emotional intelligence, asking how it relates to academic intelligence, and whether people can learn to be "smarter" in how they deal with emotions in their lives. Chapter 15 will address individual differences in emotion that are extreme, leading to clinical levels of dysfunction, but here we will look at more typical variability in people's emotional traits.

INDIVIDUAL DIFFERENCES IN EMOTIONAL RESPONDING

"Emotional dispositions" are the ways in which people differ from one another in the emotions they typically feel. Emotional dispositions correlate strongly with behavioral differences, so emotion has played an important role in theories of personality that emphasize behavior. More recently, researchers have also asked whether individual differences in emotional experience are associated with different patterns of brain activation, just while people are resting and doing nothing. Let's take a look at this research now.

Emotions and the "Big Five" Personality Factors

If you are going to meet someone for the first time, and during that meeting you have to do something important together—collaborate on a project, go on a date, etc.—what do you want to know about that person? Take a minute to think about the traits that you would most want to find out about before you read further.

You might list something unusual, but most people have roughly the same concerns. Is the person energetic and sociable, or quiet and reserved? Is the person nice, friendly, trustworthy? Is the person reliable? Is the person emotionally stable, or a wreck? Is the person interested in new ideas and experiences, or more comfortable with familiar and predictable events? These concerns appear to be ubiquitous, so much so that they account for many of the words we use to describe people in several languages.

Beginning in the middle of the last century, psychologists began to ask whether patterns of vocabulary could be used to identify the basic dimensions of personality, in much the same way that some researchers have asked whether emotion vocabulary might reflect the basic dimensions of human affect (Shaver, Schwarz, Kirson, & O'Connor, 1987). A study by Lew Goldberg (1990) is a good example. Goldberg identified more than 1,700 adjectives used to describe people in the English language, and asked participants to rate the extent to which each of the adjectives

described them well on a scale from 1 (*extremely inaccurate*) to 9 (*extremely accurate*). He averaged ratings of some of the words that were near synonyms (such as "brave," "venturous," "fearless," and "reckless"), creating 75 word clusters. Even so, many of the cluster ratings correlated highly with one another, suggesting that certain clusters of words were more semantically similar than different. For example, mean ratings on the "sociability" cluster were highly correlated with mean ratings on the "spontaneity" cluster.

Goldberg then used a statistical technique called **factor analysis** to examine the patterns of intercorrelation among these cluster-level mean ratings, to see how many dimensions or "factors" were needed to account for most of the differences between the words. Although the interpretation of factor analysis is always somewhat controversial (there is no absolute rule for deciding how many factors there are), Goldberg found that five factors were enough to explain most of the similarities and differences among the 75 clusters of words.

Psychologists then examined the items associated with each of these five factors to determine how best to describe each factor. The first factor in Goldberg's analysis has typically been called **Extraversion**, defined by word clusters such as talkativeness, sociability, spontaneity, boisterousness, energy, and adventure. The second factor is **Agreeableness**, characterized by amiability, generosity, tolerance, courtesy, warmth, honesty, and trust. The third cluster is **Conscientiousness**, which consists of consistency, reliability, formality, foresight, maturity, and self-discipline. The fourth is **Neuroticism**, marked by self-pity, anxiety, insecurity, timidity, and passivity. The fifth cluster, **Openness to Experience**, relates to wisdom, originality, objectivity, reflection, and art. Whereas Extraversion includes an interest in seeking new adventures, Openness to Experience pertains to an interest in new intellectual stimulation.

In further research, sometimes participants rated themselves on the items, and sometimes participants rated another person. In each study the same five factors emerged, with slight differences in how best to describe them. Hundreds of studies since have supported the usefulness of these **"Big Five" personality factors**. Studies similar to Goldberg's have been conducted in other languages, such as German and Dutch, uncovering the same five factors (Hofstee, Kiers, de Raad, Goldberg, et al., 1997), although the results are a bit different in China (Cheung et al., 1996). A number of questionnaires measuring each of the Big Five factors with several items have been developed, and translated into other languages. Factor analyses of scores on these new instruments also suggest that the Big Five factors are key dimensions of personality in other languages and cultures (e.g., Benet-Martinez & John, 1998; Plaisant, Srivastava, Mendelsohn, Debray, & John, 2005; Trull & Geary, 1997).

Further research suggests that questionnaire measures of the Big Five are associated with real-life behavior. Researchers performed a statistical meta-analysis of 15 studies in which participants completed a Big Five questionnaire, and then reported their activities several times a day for a number of days. Although many have been skeptical about the utility of questionnaires in predicting behavior, the meta-analysis suggested that questionnaire measures of the Big Five showed respectable correlations (between $r = .42$ and $r = .56$) with theoretically relevant behaviors (Fleeson & Gallagher, 2009).

Emotion plays an important role in several of the Big Five factors. Extraversion (Figure 13.1) has been associated with the frequency and intensity of positive emotion experience in dozens of studies (Larsen & Ketelaar, 1991; Lucas & Fujita, 2000; McCrae & Costa, 1991; Lucas & Baird, 2004). People who are highly extroverted are not only happier on average, but they also respond to specific positive stimuli with greater increases in positive emotion than those who are more introverted (Gross, Sutton, & Ketelaar, 1998). This correlation is so robust (meaning that it is observed across many studies using different methods) that some have proposed positive emotionality as the central feature of Extraversion (Watson & Clark, 1997; Wiggins, 1979), or a consequence of it (Costa & McCrae, 1980). One possibility is that Extraverts have especially strong activity in the dopaminergic reward circuit described in Chapter 5 (Depue & Collins, 1999; Depue & Iacono, 1989; Gray, 1970), enhancing the sense of pleasure in rewarding events. Extraverts do show greater neural

Aldo Murillo/istockphoto.com

FIGURE 13.1 Extraverts tend to experience a lot of positive emotion, especially when socializing with other people.

activation than introverts in some parts of the reward circuit during a gambling task than introverts, and these individuals are also more likely to have a type of dopamine receptor that enhances dopaminergic neurotransmission (Cohen, Young, Baek, Kessler, & Ranganath, 2005).

Another study explored a behavioral mechanism linking Extraversion to positive emotionality. Sanjay Srivastava and colleagues (2008) asked college students to report on their activities at the end of each day, and to report their emotions during each of the activities. They found that extraverted and introverted participants reported similar amounts of positive affect during social interactions, but that extraverted college students engaged in social interaction than introverts more often, leading to more positive affect across the day. Thus, extraversion may facilitate positive affect by increasing engagement in fun social activities.

Like Extraversion, Neuroticism has often been defined in terms of emotion—in this case negative emotion. The word clusters on this factor in the Goldberg (1990) study emphasize this point, including self-pity, anxiety, insecurity, and timidity. In fact, this factor is sometimes referred to as "emotional instability" rather than Neuroticism!

However, the explanation for why neurotic individuals are so unhappy is more complicated. One possibility is that neurotic individuals tend to choose or create situations that make them unhappy. In one very interesting experiment, researchers randomly assigned participants to act neurotic ("emotional, subjective, moody, and demanding") or emotionally stable ("unemotional, objective, steady, and undemanding") while having a conversation with another participant. Although participants in these two groups were no different in terms of trait Neuroticism, those instructed to behave more neurotically actually reported more distress during the conversation (McNiel & Fleeson, 2006). The researchers did not report on the actual behavior of their participants, so we're not sure how they truly acted. However, one interpretation is that neurotic individuals tend to engage with other people in a way that elicits unfriendly behaviors in return, and that increases their unhappiness.

Another possibility is that neurotic individuals simply feel more distress than others in the same situations—they are more emotionally reactive. Neuroticism does predict the intensity of people's distress responses to controlled laboratory tasks, such as upsetting film clips (Larsen & Ketelaar, 1991). In Chapter 5 we described the neurotransmitter serotonin, which has been implicated in mood and aggression. Neuroticism has been associated with a "short" version of the serotonin transporter gene that impairs this neurotransmitter's activity in the brain (Munafò, Clark, Moore, Payne, Walton, & Flint, 2003). Another study found that trait Neuroticism mediated, or accounted for, the relationship between having the "short" allele and probability of major depression (Munafò, Clark, Roberts, & Johnstone, 2006). Keep in mind, though, that finding a genetic marker for an emotional trait doesn't rule out effects of situations and behaviors. Given that low serotonin levels have been implicated in aggression, it may be that individuals with the short serotonin transporter gene act more aggressively toward others, eliciting unfriendly responses and thereby causing more distress.

A third possibility is that more neurotic and less neurotic individuals have similar experiences and default emotional reactions to those experiences, but neurotic people are terrible at regulating their emotions. Many studies find that neurotic people rely more on wishful thinking, withdrawal, and emotional response-focused coping strategies, and less on more effective strategies such as problem-solving and reappraisal (Connor-Smith & Flachsbart, 2007). A study in China found that self-reported reappraisal ability partially mediated the effects of Neuroticism on negative emotionality, meaning that neurotic participants reported less use of reappraisal to regulate their emotions, and this in turn (not surprisingly) predicted more negative affect (Wang, Shi, & Li, 2009). Studies by Maya Tamir (2005) even suggest that neurotic individuals *try* to make themselves more worried and upset when they have to perform a difficult task, and that worrying improves their performance! It may be that when forced to choose between feeling good and doing well, neurotic individuals are more concerned with the latter.

Emotion has also been implicated in Agreeableness (Figure 13.2), although not as strongly as for Extraversion and Neuroticism. Agreeableness predicts people's dispositional experience of positive affect, above and beyond the effects of Extraversion (McCrae & Costa, 1991). In particular, Agreeableness is associated with more frequent and intense experiences of love and compassion (Shiota, Keltner, & John, 2006) and forgiveness (Berry, Worthington, O'Connor, Parrott, & Wade, 2005). It is also associated with lower proneness to anger (Kuppens, 2005). We noted earlier that both central (brain) and peripheral

FIGURE 13.2 Agreeableness is associated with frequent experience of love and compassion, and with low experience of anger.

(bloodstream) oxytocin have been implicated in social bonding and feelings of love and trust, so one possibility is that individuals with more effective oxytocin transmission will tend to be more agreeable. Individuals high on Agreeableness are also more likely to have a variant of the serotonin transporter gene that facilitates serotonergic neurotransmission.

Another possibility is that Agreeableness relates to high positive emotion and low negative emotion because all three are associated with effective emotion regulation. More agreeable people say they put more effort into trying to manage their emotions, and one study found that individuals who scored high on Agreeableness showed greater prefrontal cortex activity while viewing distressing photographs in an MRI scanner, consistent with a greater degree of regulation effort (Haas, Omura, Constable, & Canli, 2007). Another study found that people's tendency to think of the world in terms of blame predicted their angry feelings (in daily life and while watching a video in the laboratory) only if they were disagreeable. More agreeable people seemed able to blame someone for a negative event, yet feel less anger toward them (Meier & Robinson, 2004). However, it is still unclear from these studies whether Agreeableness actually helps people regulate their emotions, or is simply the name that we give to someone who is good at regulating their emotions and is therefore likely to be pleasant to others. That is, should we regard Agreeableness as an explanation, or just a description?

The implications of Conscientiousness for emotion might not be immediately obvious, and yet this Big Five trait affects our emotions in several indirect ways. One study found that individuals who reported being highly conscientious also tended to report greater dispositional joy, contentment, and pride (Shiota et al., 2006). As we discussed in Chapter 10, these emotions are typically associated with need fulfillment and personal accomplishment, so this effect may reflect conscientious people's ability to achieve their goals.

Another study suggests that more conscientious people might be better at controlling the behavioral expression of their emotions (Jensen-Campbell, Knack, Waldrip, & Campbell, 2007). Imagine being a participant in an extremely clever study. In one laboratory session, you complete several questionnaires, including a measure of the Big Five factors. When you return to the lab a few days later, you learn that researchers are interested in various aspects of perception, including taste perception and person perception. In this session you will be teamed with another participant, who is in the next room. That individual has been randomly assigned to the "perceiver" role in the study, and your role is to be the target for the person perception task. You are given the choice of a few possible topics (such as "the legality of smoking in public places"), and you are to write an essay explaining your position on that topic. This essay is given to the participant in the next room, who will write comments on the essay and rate his impression of the person who wrote it (you). Several minutes later, you receive the essay back, as well as the ratings. The ratings are highly negative—based on your essay this person thinks you are unintelligent, boring, irrational, unfriendly, and so forth. One example comment is, "I cannot understand why someone would think like this. I hope this person learns something while at [name of University]."

Here comes the clever part. You are told that the next part of the study involves taste perception, and you are asked to select the substance the other participant will taste, so that the experimenter can remain "blind" to or unaware of the participant's experimental condition while actually interacting with him (this is typically called a "double-blind" study). Your options include water flavored with sugar, apple juice, lemon juice, salt, vinegar, and hot sauce. Food coloring has been used to make all options look the same, so until the end of the session only you will know which substance you handed to the experimenter. Whichever substance you choose, the other participant has to drink. At this point you also rate how strongly you are feeling several emotions right now.

As you've probably deduced by now, there is no "other participant," and the drink assignment task was actually a measure of aggressive behavior. (Presumably if you assigned hot sauce, you were hoping to make things unpleasant for that person.) The researchers found that participants with higher Conscientiousness scores reported less anger after apparently being insulted. More important, angry feelings were not as strongly associated with aggressive behavior (assigning a more unpleasant drink) among conscientious people, whereas anger strongly predicted aggression among people who scored low on Conscientiousness. The authors conclude that Conscientiousness reflects an overall tendency toward good self-control, and that this enhances people's ability to regulate their emotions as well as their thoughts and actions (Jansen-Campbell et al., 2007). Thus, both Agreeableness and Conscientiousness may affect emotions in part because of better emotion regulation.

Of all of the Big Five factors, Openness to Experience has been studied the least with respect to emotion. However, Openness does predict dispositional positive affect even when controlling for the other four factors (McCrae & Costa, 1991), and it is especially associated with strong feelings of love, compassion, and awe (Shiota et al., 2006). Although no one has suggested that Openness directly influences emotion, it seems likely that open-minded, curious individuals will respond more compassionately (and less judgmentally) to a wider range of people, and will also seek out new and interesting experiences that elicit positive affect (Figure 13.3).

As we have seen, important aspects of personality involve emotion in many ways. In some cases, it may be that biologically based factors directly affect people's emotional reactivity. The strongest cases can be made for Extraversion and Neuroticism. However, Big Five traits may also relate to emotion indirectly, by facilitating behaviors that alter people's situations, or through individual differences in emotion regulation. Although researchers have known that personality predicts emotion for decades, far more work is needed to understand the mechanisms behind these effects.

Frontal Asymmetry and Individual Differences in Affect

As we mentioned in Chapter 5, there is a growing trend to turn to the brain when looking for the causes of emotion. This is true for personality research as well as for research emphasizing effects of the situation. One substantial body of research has used

Bartosz Hadyniak/istockphoto.com

F I G U R E 13.3 Individuals high on openness to experience often seek out experiences that inspire awe.

electroencephalography (EEG) methods to ask whether people have global patterns of brain activity that predispose them to certain emotional traits. In Chapter 5, we focused primarily on EEG responses to particular stimuli, known as event-related potentials or "ERPs." However, researchers can also study overall patterns of activity when the brain is at rest.

Emotion researchers have shown a particular interest in the extent to which the left or right frontal lobe of the brain is more active in general and during specific tasks—a ratio often called **frontal asymmetry**. In some individuals, the right hemisphere tends to be more active, even when the person is just sitting quietly. In others, the left hemisphere tends to be more active than the right. Building upon research finding that lesions to the left and right hemispheres had somewhat different implications for emotion, researcher Richard Davidson (1984) hypothesized that the two hemispheres might be specialized for different types of emotional experience.

In the intervening years, dozens of studies have supported Davidson's proposal. In one classic study, Davidson's team measured the ratio of right frontal and temporal lobe activation to activation in the corresponding region on the left, while participants rested quietly. Some days later, participants returned to the laboratory and watched several film clips chosen to elicit happiness, fear, and disgust, rating their emotional experience after each clip. Participants who showed greater relative activation on the right reported greater distress while viewing the two kinds of negative films, whereas participants who showed greater relative activation in the left hemisphere reported more intense responses to the positive films (Wheeler, Davidson, & Tomarken, 1993). Other studies have shown similar effects of frontal asymmetry on trait levels of positive and negative affect, as well as responses to stimuli in the lab (Tomarken, Davidson, Wheeler, & Doss, 1992).

One interpretation of these effects might be that the right frontal lobe is specialized for negative emotion, whereas the left frontal lobe is specialized for positive emotion. Although this hypothesis was considered, later research suggested that valence was not the best way to describe the distinction. In one study, frontal asymmetry failed to predict trait positive and negative affect, but did predict scores on questionnaires measuring trait-level **behavioral approach** (a tendency to seek out rewarding experiences and engage with the world) and **behavioral avoidance** (a tendency to withdraw from potential threats). Specifically, participants with greater right frontal activation reported greater behavioral avoidance relative to behavioral activation, whereas the opposite was true for participants with greater activation on the left (Sutton & Davidson, 1997).

Of course, behavioral approach overlaps positive affect, and avoidance resembles negative affect. However, a study by Eddie Harmon-Jones and John Allen (1998) made it quite clear that valence is not the key dimension here. Rather than measuring overall positive and negative affect, they measured trait levels of anger. Anger is the ideal emotion for their purposes, because anger is a negative emotion, yet it promotes approach-related behaviors. If frontal asymmetry reflects the valence of emotion, then angrier people should show greater activation in the right hemisphere. If asymmetry reflects approach/avoidance, then dispositionally angry people should show greater activation on the left. Harmon-Jones and Allen's data strongly supported the latter hypothesis: The left hemisphere is specialized for both types of approach—happiness and anger.

Does this mean that the right frontal lobe contains neural structures specifically devoted to avoidance, and the left frontal lobe contains structures specialized for approach? It may be that new techniques detecting networks of brain cells may be able to detect structural differences, but in general the two hemispheres look very much the same. However, research on other psychological processes has documented the laterality of certain abilities. For example, the left temporal lobe appears to be somewhat specialized for language (Grodzinsky & Amunts, 2006). It may be that what appears to be the same structure has a slightly different function on each side of the brain. Alternatively, a structure may have a similar functional role in both sides of the brain, yet be a bit more powerful on one side. Despite decades of work documenting the emotional implications of frontal asymmetry, we still have a long way to go in actually explaining this effect (Davidson, 2004).

EMOTIONAL INTELLIGENCE

It is fairly easy to describe people in terms of the emotions they typically *feel*. However, another way of thinking about individual differences emphasizes how people *deal with* emotions—their own and others'—in daily life. Beginning in the 1990s many psychologists began discussing **emotional intelligence**, the ability to recognize the meanings of emotions and their relationships, and to use emotions effectively in reasoning and problem-solving (Mayer, Caruso, & Salovey, 2000). The implication is that people's differences in this ability are consistent over time and across situations, and that emotional intelligence resembles academic intelligence in some ways, but also differs in important ways.

Emotional intelligence might be important when dealing with situations like these:

You are walking down the street when you notice a young woman sitting alone and crying on a park bench (Figure 13.4). You pause and look at her. She looks up briefly, curtly says "Hello," and resumes crying. Should you go over and offer to help, or would she prefer to be left alone?

You need to get to an appointment fast, and your roommate has promised to drive you. But your roommate is slow in getting ready, and you are starting to feel tense. Do you try to speed up your roommate or do you try to calm yourself down? In either case, how do you do it?

Someone has just told you a joke that you find insulting. Do you say that the joke offends you, or just fail to laugh and hope the person takes the hint?

An attractive person smiles at you and says hello in a cheerful voice. Was this a flirtation and a signal of a potential romantic relationship? Or was it mere friendliness?

You are sitting quietly with someone you have been dating for months. You are thinking romantic thoughts but you don't know what your partner is thinking. Would this be a good time to say for the first time, "I love you"? Or is the other person about to break up with you?

FIGURE 13.4 If you saw someone quietly crying in public, what would you do? People's answers to hypothetical situations like this are sometimes used to measure emotional intelligence.

In each of these cases, the correct answer is obviously "it depends." In the first example, before you decide whether to offer help to the woman crying on the park bench, you might consider her facial expression, body language, tone of voice, any clues you can see as to why she is crying, and so forth. The right answer also depends on who you are. For example, she might be more willing to talk with a woman her own age than with a child or a middle-aged man. Similarly, in any of the other situations, you would assess the whole situation before deciding what to do. The point, however, is that you probably can think of people you know who usually make good decisions in cases like these. They look at someone and quickly discern that person's emotional state. They usually know the right thing to say or do. On the other hand, no doubt you also can think of people who make consistently bad decisions in emotional situations and invariably ignore or misread other people's emotional expressions.

Beginning in the 1990s, the idea of emotional intelligence began attracting a good deal of attention, both among psychologists and in the popular press. Many people seem to agree that emotional intelligence is important, even though they are not exactly sure what it is. After all, emotions are important and intelligence is good, so emotional intelligence must be valuable too. The term has been used in many ways, however, so we need to work toward a clearer definition (Mayer, Salovey, & Caruso, 2008). Typically, researchers and theorists emphasize three major components (Mayer, Caruso, & Salovey, 2000):

Perceiving emotions in facial expressions, music, art, and so forth.

Understanding and reasoning about emotions.

Managing emotions, such as calming oneself down or relieving someone else's anxiety.

MEASURING EMOTIONAL INTELLIGENCE

As we have seen so often in this textbook, understanding and measuring some concept each facilitates the other: The better we understand the concept, the better we know what to measure; and as we make better measurements, we increase our understanding. Certainly if we find that we cannot measure something effectively, we have reason to question the concept itself. How has emotional intelligence been measured, and what do studies of these measures suggest about the concept?

Self-Report Measures

Psychologists have attempted to measure emotional intelligence in several ways (Ciarrochi, Chan, Caputi, & Roberts, 2001; Conte, 2005). One approach is to treat it like a personality trait and measure it with self-reports. For example, to measure the personality trait *Extraversion,* psychologists ask people questions such as these:

T/F: I have the time of my life at parties.

or

On a scale from 1 to 7, how much do you enjoy meeting new people?

Similarly, some psychologists have tried to measure emotional intelligence with self-report inventories. Here are a few true–false items from one such questionnaire (Austin, Saklofske, Huang, & McKenney, 2004):

I sometimes can't tell whether someone is serious or joking.

Other people find it easy to confide in me.

I know what other people are feeling just by looking at them.

I help other people feel better when they are down.

As you would guess, a "false" answer on the first item counts the same as a "true" on the next three. One problem with a test of this sort is the uncertain accuracy of people's answers. When psychologists measure Extraversion, they generally trust people to report honestly how much they enjoy going to parties or meeting new people. But when someone claims to know people's feelings just by looking at them, how much should we trust that answer? Some people give themselves high ratings on social sensitivity but get low ratings from their friends

(Carney & Harrigan, 2003). It is possible to be socially insensitive and not even realize it. In fact, the more insensitive you are, the less likely you are to notice your mistakes.

The best way to evaluate self-report tests of emotional intelligence is to check their predictive validity. That is, people's scores on a good test of emotional intelligence should predict how well they handle real emotional situations. Most of the research on self-reported emotional intelligence has measured its relationship to how well people *say* they handle emotional situations. That is, the studies compare one self-report to another. This approach is not ideal, but it is better than nothing. According to such studies, people with high self-reported emotional intelligence also rate themselves high on social adjustment (Engelberg & Sjöberg, 2004). They tend to be extraverted and agreeable (Warwick & Nettelbeck, 2004), and they recover better than most people do after a traumatic experience (Hunt & Evans, 2004). Workers with high self-reported emotional intelligence report higher work morale and lower job stress (Dulewicz, Higgs, & Slaski, 2003). Men with low emotional intelligence scores are more likely than others to have psychological disorders (Hemmati, Mills, & Kroner, 2004). Some studies find a significant relationship between overall emotional intelligence and overall positive mood (Schutte, Malouff, Simunek, McKenley, & Hollander, 2002), although other studies do not (Spence, Oades, & Caputi, 2004).

A few studies have related scores to actual (as opposed to self-reported) performance. In one study, people filled out an emotional intelligence questionnaire and also participated in tests of their ability to recognize as quickly as possible the emotional expressions in people's faces. People with higher emotional intelligence scores generally outperformed most other people on this task (Austin, 2004).

In short, the self-report measures do appear to be measuring something, and that something is beneficial. Problems remain, however. One is that, on the average, men in prison have higher self-reported emotional intelligence than men outside prison (Hemmati, Mills, & Kroner, 2004)! The best guess is that some of the questions simply mean something different to prisoners than to others. For example, consider the item, "I know what other people are feeling just by looking at them." Maybe emotional expression in prisons is more intense, and therefore easier to read. An alternative hypothesis is that prisoners are more confident in their ability to "read" other people, even though they are actually reading them wrong. Whatever the explanation, we need to worry about exactly what the test is measuring.

Another problem is that scores on self-report measures of emotional intelligence correlate fairly strongly with measurements of personality traits, such as Agreeableness, Extraversion, Openness to Experience and lack of Neuroticism (De Raad, 2005; Warwick & Nettelbeck, 2004). If emotional intelligence is to be a useful concept, it needs to be more than a new name for personality traits that psychologists were already measuring.

Performance/Ability Measures

The other approach to measuring emotional intelligence is to develop an ability test, comparable to IQ tests or other standardized tests. The best-known and most widely used test of this type is the **Mayer-Salovey-Caruso Emotional Intelligence Test (MSCEIT)**, pronounced "mes-keet". Here are examples, reworded slightly from items in actual use (Mayer, Caruso, & Salovey, 2000):

(1) On a scale from 1 to 5, rate the amount of each emotion in the photos you will see. For each emotion, (1) indicates "Definitely Not Present" and (5) indicates "Definitely Present."

Happiness _____

Anger _____

Fear _____

Sadness _____

Disgust _____

Surprise _____

(2) A middle-aged man says his work has been piling up and he is falling behind. He works late at night and spends little time with his family. His relationship with his wife and daughter has suffered. He feels guilty for spending so little time with them, and they feel left out. Recently a relative moved in with them after he got divorced and lost his job. After a while they told him he had to leave because they needed their privacy, but they felt bad about kicking him out.

On a scale from 1 to 5, where 5 is highest, rate how much this man feels:

Depressed _____

Frustrated _____

Guilty _____

Energetic _____

Liking _____

Joyous _____

Happy _____

(3) A dog runs into the street and gets hit by a car. The driver stops and the dog's owner hurries to check on the dog.

On a scale from 1 to 5, where 5 means "extremely likely" and 1 means "extremely unlikely," how would the driver and the dog's owner probably feel?

The owner would feel angry at the driver _____

The owner would feel embarrassed at not training the dog better _____

The driver would feel guilty for not driving more carefully _____

The driver would feel relieved that it was a dog and not a child _____

(4) Someone you know at work looks upset. He asks you to have lunch with him, alone, in a quiet place. After a few minutes, he confides in you that he got his job by lying on his application. Now he feels guilty and he is afraid of getting caught. *What do you do?*

The crucial issue here is, *what are the correct answers?* On each item you might like to answer, "It depends! I need more information!" However, you're not allowed that answer. You have to do your best with the meager information that is provided. We can imagine several ways of determining the right answers, but each faces serious problems

(Roberts, Zeidner, & Matthews, 2001). One way is **expert scoring**, relying on the answers chosen by experts in the field, just as we would ask outstanding mathematicians to determine the correct answers on a mathematics test. However, we are not sure who the emotional intelligence "experts" are. For want of any better choice, the psychologists doing research on emotional intelligence usually nominated themselves, and decided what they thought the right answers should be.

But something strange happened with the resulting scores. According to the answer key, men showed slightly higher emotional intelligence than women. That result gives us reason to scratch our heads. Most people agree that they can think of more women than men who seem to be good at emotional intelligence, given admittedly casual observations and unsystematic criteria. Also, a variety of studies show female superiority at such diverse tasks as identifying facial expressions of emotion from brief presentations (Hall & Matsumoto, 2004), interpreting other kinds of nonverbal communication (Hall, 1978; Hall & Halberstadt, 1994), foreseeing likely breakups in a dating relationship (Rubin, Peplau, & Hill, 1981), and even guessing people's emotions from their smells (Chen & Haviland-Jones, 2000). On the average, women also score higher than men on self-report measures of emotional intelligence (Van Rooy, Alonso, & Viswesvaran, 2005).

What if the researchers' answers to the various questions were wrong? We shouldn't necessarily assume that researchers themselves have high emotional intelligence. After all, people who do research on vision or memory don't necessarily have outstanding vision or memory. People who do research on marriage are not particularly good at identifying which couples are happier than others (never mind whether they're good at marriage itself!). In one study, people watched videotapes of married couples having short conversations, and then guessed how happy the marriage was. The couples themselves had reported their own marital satisfaction, so there was a reasonably clear "right answer." Of all the groups tested, psychologists who had done research on marriage were *least* accurate in estimating the couples' marital satisfaction (Ebling & Levenson,

2003). People who had recently married or recently divorced did much better, on the average. The point is, if we want to use expert judgment as the criterion for some test, we have to be very careful in deciding who the experts are.

A related problem is that most people doing research on emotional intelligence have been middle-aged white men. Therefore, the "expert scoring" is based on the judgments by one kind of person. A big question is whether emotional intelligence items have any correct answer at all, or whether the answers vary from one group to another. If we are going to rely on expert scoring, we first need to get a diverse and representative group of "experts," and then determine what kind of question, if any, has similar "correct" answers across cultures and subcultures.

A different way to determine the correct answers is by **consensus**—using the answer given by the largest number of people. That is, the most common answer is considered correct. In most cases, the consensus answer is the same as that chosen by the researchers (Mayer, Salovey, Caruso, & Sitarenios, 2003). However, the consensus doesn't always agree with the researchers, and by consensus scoring, women consistently score higher than men (Kafetsios, 2004). If men are motivated to "try harder," their scores improve, but on the average they still don't catch up with women (Ciarrochi, Hynes, & Crittenden, 2005).

The problem with the consensus method of scoring is that if the right answer is whatever the majority says, then the test can't include any difficult items that only "emotional geniuses" get right. For comparison, imagine a mathematics test in which we let people vote to determine the right answer. Because the test could not reward someone who was right when most people were wrong, it could not identify the best mathematicians. It could, however, identify the worst—those who consistently missed even easy questions that almost everyone else got right. Similarly, although the MSCEIT does not identify those with especially outstanding emotional intelligence, it does pick out those with the worst. Some have suggested that we rename it as a test of "emotional stupidity" (Roberts et al., 2001; Zeidner, Matthews, & Roberts, 2001).

In fact, there is merit in identifying people with low emotional intelligence. For example, if we ask people to identify other people's emotions from their facial expressions, as in Figure 13.5, or from their tone of voice, the people whose answers differ most strongly from the majority consist largely of people known to have problems with social relationships, such as:

People with schizophrenia (Edwards, Jackson, & Pattison, 2002; Kohler et al., 2003),

Psychopaths (Blair et al., 2004),

People with brain damage in and near the amygdala (Adolphs, Baron-Cohen, & Tranel, 2002; Rosen et al., 2002),

Alcoholics and recovering alcoholics (who tend to overstate the amount of fear they see in other people's faces) (Kornreich et al., 2001; Townshend & Duka, 2003), and

People who themselves have high anxiety levels (who also tend to overstate the fear they see in others) (Dowden & Allen, 1997; Richards et al., 2002).

Psychologists usually modify the consensus approach as follows (McCann, Roberts, Matthews, & Zeidner, 2004): Suppose on some multiple-choice question, 55 percent choose answer C, 40 percent choose A, 4 percent choose B, and 1 percent choose D. You would get .55 points for answering C, .4 for A, .04 for B, and .01 for D, indicating that C is the best answer, D is the worst, and so forth. In other words, the scoring system acknowledges that no answer is exactly right and some "wrong" answers are better than others. Note a problem: If one question is so easy that 99 percent of all people get it right, you get .99 for the right answer. On the most difficult question, where let's say only 30 percent of people get the consensus answer, you get only .30 for that answer. In other words, the more difficult the question, the *less* credit you get for choosing the best answer.

An alternative to either expert or consensus scoring is to base the correct answers on responses from **targets**—people who have had the experiences described in the test questions. For example, for the item about how a driver would feel after accidentally hitting someone's dog, we could find people who have had that experience and ask them. We could show videotapes of interviews with crime suspects, some of whom were later demonstrated to have been lying. The question then would be, "Can you identify who is lying?" We could show videotapes of discussions between married couples, some of whom later got divorced, and ask which couples appeared

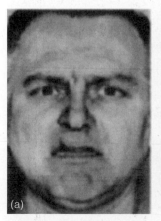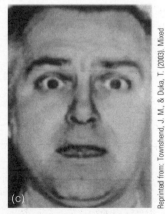

(a) (b) (c)

Reprinted from: Townshend, J. M., & Duka, T. (2003). Mixed emotions: Alcoholics' impairments in the recognition of specific emotional facial expressions. *Neuropsychologia*, 41, 773–782, with permission from Elsevier.

FIGURE 13.5 One way of testing people's ability to interpret facial expressions: Each of these faces is "morphed" (computer combined) between expressions of two emotions. How much happiness, sadness, anger, fear, surprise, and disgust do you see in each of these? Compare your ratings to the answer given at the end of this chapter.

Source: Townshend and Duka (2003).

to be doing better. We could show videotapes of psychiatric patients, some of whom attempted suicide a few days or weeks later, and ask what emotions each patient expressed. Target-based scoring has great potential, but so far it has not been used extensively. So far, the tests are based on pencil and paper (like standard IQ tests), rather than using audiovisual materials or other technologies.

Reliability and Validity of Emotional Intelligence Tests

Evaluating a test requires more than just being sure the answers are correct. Recall from Chapter 1 that psychologists evaluate tests in terms of reliability (the consistency of an individual's scores) and validity (the relationship between the scores and the behaviors we are trying to predict).

According to the authors of the MSCEIT, its reliability is about .9, which is similar to other standardized psychological tests (Mayer, Salovey, Caruso, & Sitarenios, 2001). However, other researchers have reported much lower reliability. One study found that certain scales of the MSCEIT had reliabilities less than .50 (Føllesdal & Hagtvet, 2009). More research is clearly needed. If the reliability is uncertain, no one should use the test for any important purpose.

The issue of validity is a little different. A test has **predictive validity** if a test score accurately predicts people's behavior in another setting. In the case of emotional intelligence, valid test scores might predict how well people make decisions in emotional and social situations. MSCEIT scores do correlate positively—although not always highly—with several outcomes reflecting behaviors, including quality of friendships and romantic relationships (Lopes et al., 2004) and ability to identify the emotion intended by musical compositions (Trimmer & Cuddy, 2008). However, the scores do not correlate significantly with other measures of ability to recognize people's emotions from facial expression or tone of voice (Roberts et al., 2006).

One preliminary study identified teenagers with high or low scores on a test of emotional intelligence, and then asked them to describe an emotional situation in their own lives and how they handled it.

First, here is an example from a 14-year-old girl with one of the lowest scores:

> "We were at a birthday party. A game was played. It was stupid, because it made me look like an idiot." [Question: How did you handle it?] "I cried and left." (Mayer, Perkins, Caruso, & Salovey, 2001, p. 135)

In contrast, here is an example from a 16-year-old girl with a very high score:

> "Once my friends wanted to sneak in someone's room and paint them while he slept. It began as joking around…. Then it slowly evolved into dares…. I felt like it was betraying the trust I had with the other person…. I know how little pranks like this could really hurt someone's feelings." [Question: How did you handle it?] "Told them straight out that it was a degrading thing to do and they shouldn't be so cruel." (Mayer, Perkins, Caruso, & Salovey, 2001, p. 136)

This result is promising, as the person with the higher score certainly appears to be operating at a higher level. However, this was a preliminary study with just a few participants. Also it is not obvious whether the test is specifically measuring emotional skills or verbal skills.

Ideally we would like to determine whether the emotional intelligence scores predict outcomes such as mental health, job performance, successful marriages, and overall life satisfaction. Studies of short-term outcomes are the easiest to complete, but in many ways the least satisfactory. For example, one study found that emotional intelligence scores did not correlate significantly with the impressions people made on others while working together in one brief session (Day & Carroll, 2004). Long-term studies have generally found positive but weak relationships between emotional intelligence and observed behaviors in work situations (Van Rooy & Viswesvaran, 2004). Several studies have found that people with high emotional intelligence scores have decreased probability of violence and criminal activity (Brackett, Mayer, & Warner, 2004; Mayer, 2001). These results are promising, but hardly overwhelming. Psychologists disagree sharply with one another about whether emotional intelligence tests have enough validity to be useful (Daus & Ashkanasy, 2005; Locke, 2005).

Another important criterion for a good test, after reliability and validity, is that a good test should not overlap too much with existing tests, because if it does, it adds nothing new. That is, even if a test predicts some outcome reasonably well, it is not a useful test unless it predicts something *better* than we could have predicted it already, using other measures. Self-report tests of emotional intelligence have a moderately high correlation with measurements of personality traits, such as Extraversion, Agreeableness, empathy, and lack of Neuroticism (De Raad, 2005; Warwick & Nettelbeck, 2004). Ability tests of emotional intelligence, such as the MSCEIT, correlate moderately well with cognitive measures (Mayer, Caruso, & Salovey, 2000; O'Connor & Little, 2003). Do emotional intelligence tests tell us anything that personality tests and cognitive tests don't?

One study found that a self-report scale of emotional intelligence correlated .49 with life satisfaction, but life satisfaction correlated just as highly with Extraversion and lack of Neuroticism. A combination of emotional intelligence and the personality factors predicted life satisfaction slightly—but only slightly—better than the personality factors by themselves could (Gannon & Ranzijn, 2005). In another study, measures of general intelligence and Big Five personality traits predicted psychological well-being, and after controlling for what the intelligence and personality tests could predict, the MSCEIT scores didn't add anything (Rossen & Kranzler, 2009).

In short, emotional intelligence, as currently measured, adds little to what we already know from measures of cognition and personality. Its predictive validity for very general measures of life satisfaction and psychological well-being is positive, but not high. More research is needed to examine more specific life outcomes. These conclusions apply only to current measures. If emotional intelligence is a valuable concept, the key is to improve our measurements. Psychologists have a long history of measuring people's abilities, attitudes, and personalities with pencil and paper tests, but those procedures may not be well adapted for measuring emotional abilities. In a real-life emotional situation

you see, hear, and sometimes even smell information that a pencil-and-paper test cannot capture. Perhaps an adequate measure requires more realistic situations.

IS EMOTIONAL INTELLIGENCE TEACHABLE?

It is certainly easy to detect the harm that results from poor emotional intelligence. A husband or wife says something, the other one incorrectly interprets it as hostile, and suddenly a fight erupts for no good reason (Flury & Ickes, 2001). A child on a playground misinterprets another child's facial expression or tone of voice and retreats from the playground in tears (Halberstadt, Denham, & Dunsmore, 2001). No doubt you can think of other examples.

As the concept of emotional intelligence became popular, many people set up programs to teach it, or urged the schools to teach it (Elias, Hunter, & Kress, 2001). Given that we are not exactly sure what emotional intelligence is or how to measure it, you shouldn't be surprised that the early attempts to teach it produced no apparent benefits (Izard, 2001). Emotional intelligence is not something we can learn by reading or listening to lectures. We probably can learn it, however, in some other way. Measurements of emotional intelligence have found higher scores, on the average, for middle-aged people than for young adults (Derksen, Kramer, & Katzko, 2002; Hemmati, Mills, & Kroner, 2004; Kafetsios, 2004). The research used a cross-sectional design, so conceivably the results could represent a cohort effect. (That is, maybe people who were born in an earlier era developed more emotional intelligence than the current younger generation.) However, the more likely explanation is that as people grow older and more experienced, they learn more emotional intelligence. In contrast, general academic intelligence ("*g*") reaches its peak in the late teens or early 20s, and then starts a long, slow decline. If emotional intelligence increases over the years, it is more like expertise or "crystallized intelligence" (which can be learned) than like fluid intelligence (which is harder to increase).

If emotional intelligence can be learned, how should it be taught? One fascinating study assigned children randomly to receive drama lessons, keyboard lessons, singing lessons, or no lessons at all. Afterward, the researchers tested the children's abilities to identify people's emotions from their tone of voice. The children who had received either drama or keyboard lessons outperformed those with singing lessons or no lessons. The same researchers found that adults who have had musical training also excel, on the average, at recognizing emotion in other people's speech (Thompson, Schellenberg, & Husain, 2004). Presumably either drama or music lessons train people to listen carefully and attend to subtle aspects of intonation. Why keyboard lessons helped and singing lessons didn't, we don't know. Of course, identifying emotion from tone of voice is just one small aspect of emotional intelligence. The main point is that it does make sense to do research on ways of teaching emotional intelligence. Lecturing on "here's how to be emotionally intelligent" probably doesn't work, but other kinds of training might.

SUMMARY

When we think about what characteristics of other people are most important and informative, emotion comes easily to mind. Individual differences in people's emotions are so striking that two of the "Big Five" core personality factors can almost be defined in terms of emotional responding. The newest research in this area asks how and why different personalities have such different emotional experiences—genetic and other biological differences, behaviors, and emotion regulation abilities may all play an important role.

Most of us also agree that some people are better than others at understanding their own and other people's emotions. They control their emotions, judge when to follow their gut feelings and when not to, and so forth. As you have seen, however, things get tricky when we try to go beyond casual observations and specify exactly what we mean. We have dwelt on the measurement issues because they are critical. If emotional intelligence is real, there should be a reliable and valid way to measure it, and it should predict important outcomes in ways independent of academic intelligence and personality. At this point the available measures of emotional intelligence are measuring some aspects of it, but not well enough to live up to the high expectations many people have. Future research will determine whether a better way of measuring emotional intelligence will prove to be more useful.

KEY TERMS

Agreeableness: one of the Big Five personality factors, defined by traits such as amiability, generosity, tolerance, courtesy, warmth, honesty, and trust (p. 295)

behavioral approach: a tendency to seek out rewarding experiences and engage with the world (p. 300)

behavioral avoidance: a tendency to withdraw from potential threats (p. 300)

"Big Five" personality factors: five core dimensions in personality, as identified by factor analyses of trait adjectives (p. 296)

Conscientiousness: one of the Big Five personality factors, defined by traits such as consistency, reliability, formality, foresight, maturity, and self-discipline (p. 295)

consensus-based scoring: defining the correct answer to some question as the answer given by the largest number of people (p. 304)

emotional intelligence: the ability to recognize the meanings of emotions and their relationships, and to use emotions effectively in reasoning and problem-solving (p. 301)

expert scoring: procedure of determining the correct answer by relying on the answers chosen by experts in the field (p. 304)

Extraversion: one of the Big Five personality factors, defined by traits such as talkativeness, sociability, spontaneity, boisterousness, energy, and adventure (p. 295)

factor analysis: a statistical technique that examines patterns of intercorrelation among item ratings, to see how many dimensions or "factors" are needed to account for most of the variability in the items (p. 295)

frontal asymmetry: the extent to which the left or right frontal lobe of the brain is more active in general, and during specific tasks (p. 300)

Mayer-Salovey-Caruso Emotional Intelligence Test (MSCEIT): best-known and most widely used pencil-and-paper test to measure emotional intelligence (p. 303)

Neuroticism: one of the Big Five personality factors, defined by traits such as self-pity, anxiety, insecurity, timidity, and experience of other negative emotions (p. 295)

Openness to Experience: one of the Big Five personality factors, defined by traits such as wisdom, originality, objectivity, reflection, and art (p. 295)

targets: people who have had the experiences described in the test questions (p. 306)

THOUGHT QUESTIONS

1. What are your most important emotional characteristics? How about those of the people you are close to, such as friends and family? Are emotional traits usually easy to see when you meet them, or does it take a long time to learn someone's emotional personality?

2. Think of people you know who you consider emotionally intelligent, but not terribly bright in other ways. What characteristics are you calling emotional intelligence?

SUGGESTIONS FOR RESEARCH PROJECT

1. Get some friends to behave in extroverted versus introverted ways, and record the behavior of people with whom your friends interact. (Or try acting in both ways yourself.) Does extroverted behavior elicit responses from others that might make them happier?

2. Keep a diary of occasions when you observe examples of either good or poor emotional intelligence in those around you. Look for patterns. For example, do certain friends repeatedly show good examples while others show poor examples? Do some situations seem to encourage good emotional decisions more than others?

SUGGESTIONS FOR FURTHER READING

Matthews, G., Zeidner, M., & Roberts, R. D. (2004). *Emotional Intelligence: Science and Myth.* Cambridge, MA: MIT Press. As the title implies, this book evaluates the evidence behind claims of emotional intelligence, separating those that the results support from those that appear unfounded.

Answer Concerning Figure 13.5:

(a) Morphed to show equal parts of disgust and anger.

(b) Equal parts sadness and disgust.

(c) Equal parts surprise and fear.

14

Effects of Emotion on Cognition

You're in a good mood and you decide to walk instead of driving to a store a few blocks away. You notice the sunshine, the trees, the birds singing, the smiling faces of people you see along the way. Ah, what a glorious day!

A few days later, you're walking the same route but you're in a bad mood: You have to walk because someone borrowed your car and wrecked it. Now you hardly notice the trees, birds, or smiling people. Instead you notice the litter on the street, the filthy smell of an uncovered trashcan, and the sounds of the traffic. What a lousy day.

Emotions influence what we notice, what we remember, and how we reason.

When we face an important decision, people often advise us to think calmly and rationally, not to let emotions get in the way of logical reasoning. That advice implies that emotions lead to bad decisions. Sometimes they do. For example, during the first three months after the terrorist attacks of September 11, 2001, many people were afraid to get onto planes, so they drove to their destinations instead. During those three months, the number of people killed in U.S. traffic accidents increased enormously. The *increase* in the number of traffic fatalities during those few months was greater than the number of people killed in the terrorist attacks themselves (Gigerenzer, 2004).

On the other hand, the evolutionary approach to emotion described in Chapter 2 proposed that emotions are *functional*. That is, emotion should lead to productive, useful thinking and action more often than not. For example, fear of snakes, spiders, and grizzly bears keeps us away from unnecessary dangers. As it turned out, avoiding airplane flights after September 11, 2001, was a mistake, but no one could have known that for certain at the time. Sometimes fear is exaggerated, but a total lack of fear would be disastrous. Perhaps the lesson from the increase in automobile fatalities during the months after 9/11 is not that we should fear airplanes less, but that we should fear cars more! So, overall, do emotions help us make good decisions, or do they interfere?

The answer (of course) is "it depends." But "it depends" on what? One hypothesis is that mild or moderate emotion helps reasoning whereas higher amounts hurt.

As we have seen in several earlier chapters, emotion is often accompanied by sympathetic nervous system arousal. According to one of the oldest findings in psychological research, the **Yerkes–Dodson law**, learning is at its best when stimulation or arousal is neither too strong nor too weak (Yerkes & Dodson, 1908). Later psychologists broadened the idea to say that learning, memory, performance, and reasoning are most enhanced under medium levels of arousal, motivation, or emotion (Teigen, 1994). The idea strikes most people as reasonable: "I do my best if I'm a little aroused, but not too much." However, with arousal levels anywhere in the vast middle ground between utter boredom and absolute frenzy, the evidence does not clearly indicate a "best" level of arousal (Bäumler, 1994). In short, the Yerkes-Dodson law is a very broad generalization (Mendl, 1999).

Another way to think about the impact of emotion on cognition is to specify more precisely what we mean by the latter term. Maybe benefit or harm in making decisions depends not on the amount of emotion, but on the type of reasoning we are talking about. Among psychologists, "cognition" is an umbrella term for a wide range of processes. Emotion might have different effects on attention, memory, reasoning and other forms of information processing, and decision-making, all of which combine to influence a single decision. If so, it's best to examine the effects of emotion on each of these aspects of cognition separately. Fortunately, researchers interested in emotion have done just that.

EMOTIONS AND ATTENTION

Almost any emotional stimulus captures attention, at least momentarily, at the expense of attention to other stimuli. Imagine yourself in this study: On each trial, the screen displays a pair of one-digit numbers separated by a word, like this:

5 chart 8

Your task is to press one key if both numbers are odd, or both are even (such as 3 and 5, or 2 and 8), and a different key if one number is odd and the other even (such as 5 and 8). You are supposed to ignore the word between them. However, if that word is an emotional one, such as *kill*, it is hard to ignore, so it takes longer for you to press the correct key. Even though it is irrelevant to your task, that emotional word distracts your attention and slows your response to the numbers more than neutral words like "chart" (Harris & Pashler, 2004).

As discussed in Chapter 7, fear in particular focuses one's attention, and therefore decreases attention to other items. Suppose a poisonous snake is near you and poised to strike. Thoughts that occupied your mind a few moments ago become trivial; your only interest is in how to escape. In another method for studying attention to emotional stimuli, people sit in front of a screen that displays two or more pictures at once, which might include emotional content. Using an eye-tracking device like the one shown in Chapter 1 (see page 18), researchers record people's eye movements to identify which picture holds their attention at any given moment, and sometimes also record their brain activity with EEG or fMRI methods. In these ways researchers have found that pictures of angry faces attract more attention and evoke more cortical arousal than pictures of happy or neutral faces (Schupp et al., 2004). Actively threatening pictures capture people's attention even if they are presented in the periphery of vision. For example, if a particular kind of picture has been paired previously with bursts of loud noise, then a viewer immediately attends to one of those pictures, even if it is far off to the side (Koster, Crombez, Van Damme, Verschuere, & De Houwer, 2004).

Studies of this type have often reported conflicting data, however, and other researchers tried to discover why the results vary. One important reason for the varying results is that different investigators measured people's eye movements for different durations. During the first half second after the pictures are presented, most people look at the more emotionally arousing picture. After that half-second, many people look *away* from distressing pictures, such as a dead body or a starving child, and people who are prone to strong anxieties are especially likely to look away (Calvo & Avero, 2005). That is, a threatening stimulus captures attention quickly, but people then try to avoid it.

(a)

Juniors Bildarchiv/Alamy

(b)

Alexander Scheible/iStockphoto

F I G U R E 14.1 Which of these images captured your attention first? Although many studies have found that positive effect promotes attention to global features of complex figures, pictures like the one on the right may promote more focus on details.

As we noted in Chapter 10, Barbara Fredrickson (2000) has proposed on theoretical grounds that positive emotions should have a somewhat different effect. According to the "broaden and build" theory, positive emotions should expand the focus of our attention, helping us to survey more of the environment and appreciate the "big picture." Indeed, several experimental studies have found that participants in a positive mood are more creative, and will attend more to the global characteristics of complex figures, than people who feel negative or even neutral affect (Bolte et al., 2003; Fredrickson & Branigan, 2005; Fredrickson & Joiner, 2002). In order to refresh your memory of this effect, just look back to the description of the study on page 241.

Some positive emotions may not have this broadening effect. Recall the distinction made in Chapter 13 between behavioral approach and behavioral avoidance. We typically associate positive emotions with approach motivation, although anger is a good example of approach motivation as well. Researchers Philip Gable and Eddie Harmon-Jones reasoned that positive emotions do not all involve approach motivation to the same degree. Furthermore, they proposed that positive emotions involving especially strong approach motivation or reward seeking should actually narrow attention, leading to a focus on local details.

Gable and Harmon-Jones randomly assigned participants to two groups (Figure 14.1): one that watched a short film clip with cats playing (low approach motivation), and one that watched a clip with tasty desserts (high approach motivation). After watching the film clip, all participants completed the global-local attention task used by Fredrickson, described in detail in Chapter 10. (Briefly, the participant is shown a complex figure made up of smaller figures, and then is asked to choose which of two additional figures is more like this target; one option is similar in terms of the target shape as a whole, but the other option is more similar in terms of the smaller figures.) Although participants who had viewed the film of cats playing tended to choose figures on the basis of global similarity, as found in previous studies, participants who had viewed the desserts film based their similarity judgments more on the details (Gable & Harmon-Jones, 2008). These results suggest that the effects of emotion on attention may depend not only on the valence of emotion, but also on the specific emotion and its function. Further research is needed to assess the impact of other positive emotions, and of different negative emotions, on attention.

It is also possible that the global-local attention task measures a somewhat different aspect of "attention" than the other tasks listed above. Studies using eye-tracking and similar methods ask whether people attend more to emotional aspects of a complex

(a)

FIGURE 14.2 On the average, people remember the central aspect of an emotional picture better than that of an unemotional picture. However, they are more likely to remember background details from the unemotional picture than from the emotional one.

(b)

situation than to its neutral aspects. Studies using the global-local similarity task ask whether emotions bias our attention toward the overall theme of a complex image, versus particular details. Results from the two types of studies may not always be the same. For example, if you watched a video that included cats playing as well as a bunch of emotionally neutral objects and events, you would probably spend most of your time looking at the cats, though you might also be attuned to the overall theme of the film. One study did show such an effect, finding that participants typically spent much more time looking at pleasant images than at neutral images with which they were paired (Nummenmaa, Hyönä, & Calvo, 2006).

EMOTIONS AND MEMORY

Not only do we attend to emotionally powerful stimuli—we are also more likely to remember them. To illustrate: Suppose we briefly display a series of complex pictures like those in Figure 14.2, and later test the viewers' memory. Ordinarily, when

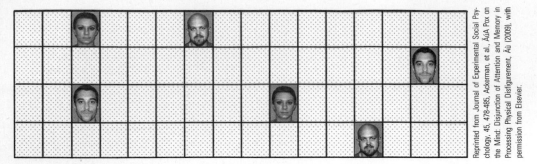

Reprinted from Journal of Experimental Social Psychology, 45, 478-485, Ackerman, et al., ÄúA Pox on the Mind: Disjunction of Attention and Memory in Processing Physical Disfigurement, Äù (2009), with permission from Elsevier.

FIGURE 14.3 In this concetration game, participants had more trouble remembering the exact location of disfigured faces, despite paying more attention to them.

people look at an unemotional picture, they recall some mixture of central objects and background details. However, when they look at a picture with something frightening or distressing at the center, they remember the central object well, and usually forget the details in the background (Adolphs, Denburg, & Tranel, 2001). In some ways, it is as if the person were looking at the emotional scene from a closer perspective, and looking at the unemotional scene from a greater distance (Mathews & Mackintosh, 2004).

Other kinds of emotional arousal also facilitate memory. In one experiment, participants viewed a series of photographs of people, and answered questions later about what they remembered about them. Among the series of otherwise ordinary photos was one photo of a nude. As you can imagine, participants remembered the nude well. However, they remembered almost nothing about the background details of that photo, and they also forgot almost entirely the next two or three photos after the nude. The nude captured their attention so thoroughly that for a while, they lost memory of everything else (Schmidt, 2002). Presumably these memory effects are driven at least partly by attention—after all, if you look at some part of a picture longer, you are probably going to remember it better.

However, a few studies suggest that memory can sometimes be detached from attention. In one study, researchers asked participants to play a computer-based version of the game "Concentration," in which they had to find pairs of matching photographs in a large

matrix while viewing only one photo at a time (see Figure 14.3). The photographs included several people with a striking disfigurement—a large "port wine" discoloration over part of the face—as well as people without disfigurement. Although a prior study found that people paid more attention to the disfigured faces than to the normal faces, they actually made more mistakes in matching the disfigured ones (Ackerman et al., 2009). In particular, participants tended to confuse the disfigured images with each other more than they did the normal images. So, memory is enhanced by attention, but it is also an independent process affected by other factors.

Emotion affects memory in many ways, and at multiple stages of the memory process—encoding memories, storing them, and retrieving them. It is helpful to talk about each of these effects separately, because the effects of emotion on memory depend on which aspect of memory we are talking about. Let's start with the first step in the process—the initial formation of memory during an event.

Emotion and Memory Formation

One particularly robust effect of emotion is to enhance the formation and intensity of memories. We first mentioned this effect in Chapter 5, in our discussion of the amygdala. Strong emotional arousal strengthens memories, even memories of events that were not especially emotional, but just happened to occur during a time of heightened emotions. This effect breaks down at extreme levels of emotion.

Occasionally someone forgets an event that happened during a moment of absolute panic. But such instances are rare. As a general rule, a rousing emotion enhances the initial formation of memories.

In one classic study of this phenomenon, researchers showed participants 60 photographs of all kinds of objects and events, ranging from everyday pictures of hair dryers and umbrellas to emotionally intense pictures of mutilations and extreme sports (see Figure 14.4 for examples). Then they asked the participants to rate each picture on how pleasant or unpleasant it was, and how calm or aroused it made them feel. After viewing all 60 pictures, each participant was asked to name or briefly describe as many pictures as possible. It turned out that people were more likely to remember pictures that they had rated very arousing than pictures they

FIGURE 14.4 When people view large numbers of emotional and nonemotional images like these, they are more likely to remember the emotional ones—even as much as a year later.

had rated as calming, regardless of whether the pictures were pleasant or unpleasant. When the researchers contacted the same participants a year later and asked them to describe as many of the slides as they could, people were *still* more likely to remember the intense, arousal-producing ones than the more mundane ones (Bradley, Greenwald, Petry, & Lang, 1992).

People remember emotionally charged pictures better than neutral ones even when the pictures are presented rapidly and with divided attention, to discourage or prevent people from rehearsing (Harris & Pashler, 2005). Research with word memory has produced similar results. Participants remember emotionally-charged words better than neutral words, and report remembering them more vividly (Kensinger & Corkin, 2003).

How do we know it was the emotionality of the arousal-producing pictures that made them more memorable? Maybe images of guns pointed at us are simply more unusual than images of trashcans, and they stick in our minds for that reason. However, physiological research supports a special role for emotion. Think back to our discussion of the nature of emotion, back in Chapter 1. The James-Lange theory argues that the feeling aspect of emotion is really about visceral, physiological experience—things like a racing heart beat, heavy breathing, and sweaty palms. If so, and if strong emotions really do produce enhanced memory, then we may be able to strengthen or weaken memory encoding by increasing or decreasing physiological arousal of the kind seen in strong emotion.

Emotional arousal leads to increased release of the hormones epinephrine (adrenalin) and cortisol from the adrenal gland. Studies of humans and laboratory animals have found that a direct injection of epinephrine or cortisol strengthens the memory of an event that was just experienced (Cahill & McGaugh, 1998). Epinephrine and cortisol stimulate the vagus nerve, which in turn excites the amygdala. Direct stimulation of either the vagus nerve or the amygdala in lab animals also strengthens memory storage (Akirav & Richter-Levin, 1999; Clark, Naritoku, Smith, Browning, & Jensen, 1999). Even events that arouse our stress response improve memory, if the stress is mild and

doesn't last too long (Abercrombie, Kalin, Thurow, Rosenkranz, & Davidson, 2003).

On the other hand, weakening physiological arousal weakens memory storage. One study examined this hypothesis by giving participants one of two pills— either a **beta-blocker**, a drug that temporarily disables some aspects of sympathetic arousal, or a placebo with no physiological effects. The participants then viewed a slide show depicting some wrecked cars, an emergency room, a brain scan, and a surgery. While watching the slide show, participants heard one of two stories. In the "neutral" version a young boy walks by a junkyard and looks at some wrecked cars, then goes to the hospital where his Dad works, looks curiously at a brain scan, and watches a surgical team doing a practice drill. In to the "arousal" version, the boy is hit by a car on the way to visit his Dad, is rushed to the hospital, has a brain scan that shows his brain is bleeding badly, and undergoes surgery (Cahill, Prins, Weber, & McGaugh, 1994). All participants watched the same set of images, but their emotions were manipulated both by the content of the story that accompanied the pictures, and by the pill that they took before the slide show.

One week later, participants were asked to answer 80 multiple-choice questions about the slides and the stories that had accompanied them. As expected, people who had heard the "neutral" version of the story had mediocre scores on the test—on average, they answered only about two-thirds of the questions correctly. For participants in the "arousal" version, memory depended on whether they had taken the beta-blocker pill or the placebo. Participants who had been given the beta-blocker (and therefore would not have felt a racing heart or similar symptoms, even if they recognized that the story was upsetting) performed no better on the memory test than participants in the "neutral" condition. Participants who had been given the placebo did much better—on average answering more than 85 percent of the questions correctly. (See Figure 14.5.) This suggests that the effects of emotions on memory depend at least partly on the physiological changes observed with strong emotion.

Studies using fMRI, based on changes in blood flow in the brain, confirm that the amygdala is more active when people view emotionally intense slides than when they view neutral ones. These same studies

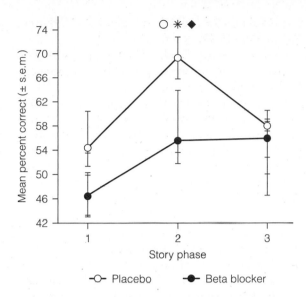

FIGURE 14.5 In this study, the placebo group remembered the emotionally disstressing part of the story (phase 2) especially well. The beta-blocker group, whose physiological responses were blunted, remembered the emotional phase no better than less worrying material.

Source: From L. Cahill, et al. "ß-Adrenergic activation and memory for emotional events". *Nature*, 371, pp. 702–704. © 1994 Nature Publishing. Reprinted with permission.

show that the greater the degree of amygdala activation, the more accurately participants remember the images later on (Canli, Zhao, Brewer, Gabrieli, & Cahill, 2000). People with damage in the amygdala can still form memories, but the strength of their memory formation is no longer affected by emotion. For example, suppose you read a story containing frightening or tragic events, or read a list of words that included "taboo" words like *penis* and *bitch* mixed among more mundane words. You probably would remember the frightening events and the taboo words more than the rest of the material. Amygdala-damaged people remember those elements no better than anything else (LaBar & Phelps, 1998).

Why should strong emotions strengthen memories? We have discussed the physiology of this effect, but why did we evolve in such a way that emotions enhance memory formation at all? One reasonable explanation is that the kinds of events that produce emotion are more important than most other events. After all, emotions accompany events that have serious implications for our lives—a time you were in danger, the day you were accepted into your dream college, a time when someone died, the time someone cheated you out of hundreds of dollars, the day you fell in love. Maybe survival depends on remembering these events—what led up to them, how they played out, which people were helpful or harmful, and what happened after. This kind of memory allows us to predict important events and improve outcomes the next time we face a similar situation.

Emotion and Memory Storage

Emotion has a somewhat different, and considerably less clear, effect on the long-term storage of memories. To illustrate, consider the following. First, think about where you were and what you were doing on September 11, 2001, when you found out about the terrorist attacks on the World Trade Center and the Pentagon. If you were too young at the time for that event to make a big impression, or if you are from a country where that event was not big news, substitute a personal memory of a very emotional nature. For example, you might recall the time when you heard that some relative or close relative had died, or if you prefer a pleasant memory, perhaps the moment of your first kiss.

Whichever memory you have chosen, how vivid and detailed is it? Can you remember where you were, who else was around, what you were doing, how you felt, and what your first thoughts were? Can you remember what happened just before and after this moment? Now in contrast try to remember some unemotional event, like the last time you went to buy toothpaste. How long does it take to remember, specifically, that last time? Were you with someone or alone? What time of day was it, and what was the weather like? What else did you buy? What did the person at the checkout counter say and do? Here's another question—how confident are you that your memory of September 11, 2001, (or whatever your emotional memory was) is accurate? How confident are you that your memory of your last trip to buy toothpaste is accurate?

For most people, highly emotional memories seem drastically different from those of everyday events. Psychologists refer to these emotion-laden, vivid, and highly detailed memories as **flashbulb memories**, because they have such a clear, photographic quality. Flashbulb memories feel detailed and lifelike, and their vividness inspires us to feel confident of their accuracy. The "flashbulb" aspect is not entirely an illusion. In one of the first experimental (as opposed to observational) studies of this topic, students observed colored words displayed at various locations on a computer screen; their task was to ignore the words and just say the color of the ink. Half of the words were names of animals (such as *turtle*) and half were profanities and ethnic insults. Each word appeared repeatedly, and some always occurred in the same location. At the end of this procedure, the students were asked (to their surprise) to identify which words occurred consistently in which locations. Even though they had no reason to pay attention to the meanings of the words, they were much more accurate at identifying the locations of the "taboo" words than the emotionally neutral words (MacKay & Ahmetzanov, 2005). The researchers suggest that emotions (presumably elicited by the taboo words) led to the formation of image-like memories.

Although flashbulb memories are vivid, much research finds that they are no more accurate over the long term than more mundane memories (Weaver, 1993). Shortly after the terrorist attacks of September 11, 2001, researchers asked U.S. students to recall details of what they were doing when they heard that news. At various later times they asked the students to report their memories again. Over weeks and months, their memories changed, presumably becoming less and less accurate (Talarico & Rubin, 2007). However, the students continued to insist that their vivid memories were right. Similarly, Israeli students were interviewed two weeks after the assassination of Israel's Prime Minister, Yitzhak Rabin, and again 11 months later. Students reported their memories confidently at both times, but on the average more than one-third of what they said at the later time contradicted what they said the first time (Nachson & Zelig, 2003). The same general effect has been observed in studies of people's memories of Princess Diana's death (Hornstein, Brown, & Mulligan, 2003).

One laboratory study of people's memories for neutral and unpleasant photographs found that people remembered both kinds of photographs about equally well, but had greater confidence in their memory of the unpleasant, emotional photographs (Sharot, Delgado, & Phelps, 2004). In sum, flashbulb memories of highly emotional events are highly vivid and detailed, but sometimes wrong.

How can flashbulb memories be so vivid, yet inaccurate? If strong emotions enhance the initial formation of memories, why aren't those memories accurate later on? The most likely answer is that the memories are strongly formed at first, but (just like non-emotional memories) are changed or "corrupted" over time. One explanation is that we repeatedly discuss highly emotional events with other people. Most research on flashbulb memories has focused on highly publicized national or international events, such as deaths, assassinations, or terrorist attacks. These are the kind of events we sit around discussing with friends and family. Perhaps we confuse our own reports with what we have heard other people say when they describe their own experiences. We may also adjust our reports somewhat for the purpose of talking with a particular person, perhaps embellishing a bit here, leaving out a detail there, and so forth. Unfortunately, these changes may be confused with the original memory in the long run (Marsh, 2007).

Another implication: Suppose you were a witness or victim of a crime. Later you describe the event to the police, identify the guilty person from a lineup, and testify in court. You remember the event vividly, and feel you can identify the guilty person confidently. Given your testimony, the jury is likely to convict. Unfortunately, physical evidence discovered years after a crime has often shown that eyewitness reports were inaccurate, and eyewitnesses' confidence is not highly correlated with the accuracy of their memories (Wells, Olson, & Charman, 2002).

Emotion and the Retrieval of Memories

When we remember our emotional experiences, we remember them selectively, and sometimes through rose-colored glasses. In one study, college students took personal data assistants (PDAs) with them on a spring-break trip. The PDAs beeped at seven unpredictable times each day, signaling the person to report their emotions at the moment. After returning home, students filled out a questionnaire about how much they enjoyed the trip. On the average, the remembered pleasantness of the trip was substantially greater than the average of all reports during the trip (Wirtz, Kruger, Scollon, & Diener, 2003). Evidently our memory of an experience is not an average of emotions over the whole time, but a reflection of a few highlights.

Current emotions also modify what events we remember. To some extent, when you are in a good mood, you are more likely to remember previous events that happened when you were in a good mood. When you are sad, you are more likely than usual to recall prior events when you were sad. Similarly, when you are frightened you tend to remember frightening information, and when you are angry you remember information consistent with being angry (Levine & Pizarro, 2004). However, the key phrase a couple of sentences ago was "to some extent." Mood-specific memory is not a robust effect. You are most likely to strengthen one set of memories or another if your happy or sad mood is strong and stable over a fairly long time, and if you participate actively in events, as opposed to taking the passive role imposed in many laboratory studies (Eich, 1995).

EMOTIONS AND INFORMATION PROCESSING

Emotions affect not only attention and memory—the contents of cognition—but also how we process the information we have. A useful distinction to make here is one between *what* decision you make (which we will address in the next section), and *how* you go about making that decision. To illustrate: First, how are you feeling right now? If you had to choose, would you say you are feeling more angry or sad, or neither? Second, consider the following situation:

> You and your housemates are having a party for about ten people, one of whom you just met at a coffee house. This person was attractive and seemed interested in you, and was excited by your invitation. You are really looking forward to getting to know this person, and hope that a romantic relationship might develop.
>
> You tell your housemates about this person, hoping they will make him/her feel comfortable and welcome. Your new friend arrives at the party after everyone else is there, and when you open the door, you see that this person has brought a date. To make things worse, the date is a good friend of your housemates.
>
> The room suddenly becomes quiet, and you hear one of your housemates chuckle and say, "So there's the new love." Your new friend is silent, and the date seems upset. You try to create a more relaxed atmosphere, and your housemates attempt to keep everyone entertained, but as you go into the kitchen you hear your new friend and his/her date whispering to each other uncomfortably (adapted from Keltner, Ellsworth, & Edwards, 1993).

A pretty awful situation, certainly, but why was it so uncomfortable? Were your roommates to blame, or was it just the situation itself? On the average, people who have just imagined themselves in an anger-producing situation (in a supposed "warm-up" to the real study) are more likely to blame the roommates, whereas people who have just imagined themselves in a sad situation are more likely to blame it on bad luck. In fact, angry people blame most bad events on other people rather than chance circumstances, whereas the reverse is true for sad people (Keltner, Edwards, & Ellsworth, 1993).

Here's a similar experiment: Two months after the September 11 attacks, more than 1,700 U.S. adults were randomly assigned to three groups who were asked to write short essays. One group was asked to write about how the attacks made them feel angry. A second group was to write about how the attacks made them sad, and a third group was to write about how the attacks made them afraid. Then all were asked how much danger they foresaw for themselves personally and the United States in general for the coming year. Those who had just finished writing about fear estimated greater probabilities of danger for both themselves and the country (Lerner, Gonzalez, Small, & Fischhoff, 2003).

Each of these studies shows that emotions influence how we interpret and reason about situations, as well as what we attend to and remember about them. How can we explain these effects of emotion on reasoning? Keep in mind that part of what causes an emotion in the first place is a particular appraisal, or interpretation, of an event. Maybe once the emotion gets going, that appraisal tendency "carries over" for a while, so that later events are likely to be interpreted in the same way.

Affect Valence and Systematic versus Heuristic Processing

Another way to think about the effects of emotion on reasoning is to ask how carefully people think about the information at their disposal. Do they consider all the facts, weighing the relative importance of each before reaching a decision, or do they base their decision on a few, superficial points? Many researchers have studied the ways in which emotions promote **systematic cognition**—thorough and deliberate analysis of the available information—versus **heuristic cognition**—making decisions on the basis of simple "rules of thumb."

For example, people can process attempts to persuade them of some new position either systematically or heuristically. Think back to the last time you watched a television commercial advertising a product. What techniques did the commercial use? Did it present lots of relevant facts about the product, or did it simply surround the product with pretty people who

were having a great time? How did you think about it? Did you think, "wow, that really seems like a well-crafted X," or "that looks fun—I want an X too!"

Psychologists distinguish between two major approaches to persuading others (Petty & Cacioppo, 1986): The **central route to persuasion** consists of providing facts and logic. The **peripheral route to persuasion** consists of superficial factors such as frequent repetition of a slogan or endorsements by celebrities. For examples of the peripheral route, watch advertisements for soft drinks, beer, or pet food. They will play cheerful music, entertain you, include lots of happy, attractive people, and show the product—but don't expect to hear a list of facts.

Political candidates typically aim for both the central and the peripheral routes to persuasion in their campaigns. A televised spot might show the candidate smiling, shaking hands with voters, and expressing nice generalities such as "I will fight for the citizens of this state." That approach is the peripheral route. The candidate might also say, "I am in favor of greater governmental efforts for environmental protection, and here is why …" Statements of that sort qualify as the central route.

Both approaches can be effective, but their effectiveness depends on circumstances. It takes you almost no energy to watch an ad for cat food and say, "Oh, that was cute!" You need much more effort to understand and evaluate reasoned arguments and economic or scientific data. People can often be persuaded by the peripheral route if they think their decision is unimportant, but if they think their decision will have major consequences and is worth the effort, they respond better to the central route. Also, people who start off with ambivalent attitudes about the persuasive message are less likely to consider the reliability of the message's source—an aspect of systematic processing that has more effect on people with stronger initial attitudes (Zemborain & Johar, 2007).

How does emotion influence the processing of persuasive messages? Several studies indicate that when people are in a happy mood, they are *more* susceptible to peripheral route influences and *less* susceptible to the central route. That is, happy people are more apt to jump to conclusions without critically examining the evidence. Sad people pay more attention to the quality of the evidence.

For example, in one study students were randomly assigned to writing for 15 minutes about either one of the most pleasant or one of the least pleasant events that ever happened to them, to induce a happy or a sad mood. Then they listened to either strong, factual arguments or weak, superficial arguments in favor of raising student fees at their university. As shown in Figure 14.6, the students in a happy mood were about equally persuaded by the strong or the weak argument. In contrast, those in a sad mood were persuaded by the strong argument but not by the weak one (Bless, Bohner, Schwarz, & Strack, 1990). A sad mood appeared to promote more careful analysis of the arguments than did a happy mood.

Stereotypes offer another way to shortcut decision-making, using heuristics to bypass careful analysis of the evidence. Suppose you are given a list of names and asked to identify which ones are famous

basketball players, famous politicians, or infamous criminals. Some of the names (which are in fact neither famous nor infamous) sound like they are probably white people, such as John Olson or Daniel Stuart. Some are names that you would guess are probably black people, such as Leroy Washington or Karanja Jackson. If you resist the stereotypes and answer just on the basis of whether you have heard of these people, you will not classify any of them as famous or infamous, and in fact people who have just watched a sad or neutral movie make few errors.

However, people who have just watched a funny movie make significantly more errors, identifying many of the black names as either basketball players or criminals, and more of the white names as politicians (Park & Banaji, 2000). Several other studies have also found that happy people are more likely than others to apply stereotypes, and to explain people's behavior in terms of personality traits rather than situational factors (Bodenhausen, Kramer, & Süsser, 1994; Forgas, 1998). In contrast, sadness seems to discourage reliance on stereotypes when judging new targets (Bodenhausen, Sheppard, & Kramer, 1994; Krauth-Gruber & Ric, 2000).

Heuristic processing can also influence what we notice and remember about new situations, if they closely resemble situations we have been in many times. When we have repeated experience with some activity, we develop a script for that kind of event—a sort of mental prototype that includes typical features common across specific instances. For example, you probably have a script for what happens when you leave the house each day: grab your backpack or purse, find your keys, go out the door and lock it, and walk to your car/bus stop/first class. This script is so compelling that it can be difficult to remember on any given day whether or how you completed a specific element of the script. One of us (MNS) parks in the same place on the third floor of her parking lot every time she goes to work, even when spaces are available on lower floors; if she parks anywhere else, she is just going to walk up to that third floor location anyway, out of habit, and there is no way she'll remember a different location!

In a study investigating the effects of emotion on the use of scripts, students were again randomly

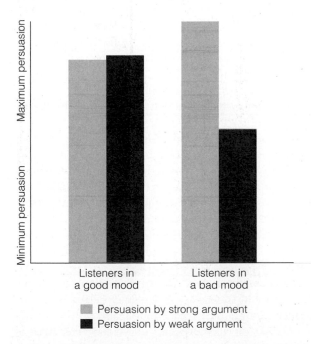

FIGURE 14.6 A strong, evidence-based argument was more persuasive to students in a sad mood, and a weak argument was more persuasive to students in a happy mood.

Source: Based on data of Bless et al. (1990).

assigned to write about a pleasant or unpleasant life event, and then asked to listen to a story titled "Going out for dinner." Later they were given a list of sentences and asked to identify which sentences had been part of the story. Some were part of the story and some were not; moreover, of those not in the story, some were typical going-out-for-dinner items that would have made sense (e.g. "He called a friend of his, who recommended several restaurants") and some were irrelevant or atypical (e.g. "Jack cleaned his glasses"). Students in a happy mood were more likely than the others to make the mistake of "remembering" typical sentences that were not in the story (Bless et al., 1996). That is, they relied more on their "script" of what usually happens or what seems likely, instead of the information they had actually heard.

So far the kinds of outcomes we have discussed are not terribly important. After all, remembering the details of a story about going out to dinner does not have life-or-death implications. Do emotions have less impact on reasoning when we contemplate a more serious issue? One study addressed this question by evaluating the effects of emotions on moral reasoning. For example, imagine that your loved one has a life-threatening disease, and the only way you can get the extremely expensive medicine you need is by stealing it. What should you do? Even if we disagree about what is the right answer to that question, we can agree on what would be a better or worse explanation for a given answer. In one study, students who had just finished watching a sad movie tended to give more sophisticated and principled explanations, whereas those who had just finished watching a light comedy gave more superficial or casual explanations (Zarinpoush, Cooper, & Moylan, 2000).

The evidence presented so far suggests that sad people tend to examine the evidence more carefully, whereas happy people answer more impulsively, follow first impressions, rely on stereotypes, and so forth. If happiness turns people's brains to mush, while sadness makes us think clearly, why is that? One hypothesis is that happiness uses up a certain amount of attention or "mental energy" (whatever that means), leaving less available for other purposes, such as

evaluating evidence. If so, we could predict that a happy mood would interfere with any and all kinds of intellectual activity. Research has refuted that prediction. People in a happy mood perform better than those in a sad mood on some cognitive tasks, worse on others (Bless et al., 1996; Phillips, Bull, Adams, & Fraser, 2002). Shortly we will discuss evidence that people in a happy mood will solve a creativity task faster than those in a neutral mood (Isen et al., 1987). In one study, older adults who were in *either* a happy mood or a sad mood performed worse on problem-solving tasks than those who were in a neutral mood (Phillips, Smith, & Gilhooly, 2002). In short, the evidence does not support the hypothesis that happiness uses up more mental energy than sadness does.

A second hypothesis is that sad people are motivated to decrease their sadness. They buy themselves presents and become more motivated than usual to cheer themselves up (Raghunathan & Pham, 1999). To avoid hurting themselves even further, they become more attentive than usual to details (Gasper & Clore, 2002) and the result is careful attention to evidence. This explanation is plausible, although it does not explain why happy people become *less* attentive than usual to details and evidence.

A third possibility is that sad people interpret their sadness as a signal that they are in a dangerous situation, which calls for attentiveness, whereas happy people infer from their mood that the situation is so safe that they can relax. Larissa Tiedens and Susan Linton (2001) offered an interesting modification of this idea. According to their interpretation, the decisive factor is not really happiness versus sadness, but certainty versus uncertainty. Happy people are usually confident, and therefore prone to accept their first judgments quickly without challenging them. Sad people feel less certain about themselves (and everything else) and therefore question assertions, examine evidence carefully, and delay making a decision until they have enough facts.

To test this hypothesis, Tiedens and Linton (2001) induced two kinds of happy moods and two kinds of unhappy moods in their participants. Each participant was asked to write a short essay about a personal experience. Participants were randomly assigned to write about an experience that made them feel content (a positive, high certainty mood), surprised (a positive but uncertain mood), angry (negative and certain), or worried (negative and uncertain). Then they were asked to read an essay and say whether they agreed with its conclusions. Some of them were told that a community-college student (lower prestige) wrote the essay, and others were told that a college professor (higher prestige) wrote it. Both groups actually read the same essay.

The students in the low-certainty moods (surprised or worried) were about equally persuaded in both cases, suggesting that they evaluated the logic of the argument itself, regardless of the prestige of its author. The students in the high-certainty moods (contented or angry) were more persuaded if they thought that a professor wrote the essay. Evidently they were more vulnerable to "peripheral route" persuasion. Overall the results suggest that highly confident people are more likely than others to make quick decisions based on weak evidence.

Positive Affect and Creativity

Are happy people just useless, cognitively speaking? According to Alice Isen, positive affect confers some important cognitive advantages, as well as disadvantages. In one study, Isen and colleagues examined the effects of positive emotion on creativity. They showed a neutral film clip to one group of participants, and a funny film clip to those in another group. Then, to test creative thinking, they offered participants the items shown in Figure 14.7

FIGURE 14.7 Using just the materials shown here, how could you affix the candle to the wall so that it would burn without dripping wax on the table or floor? Think creatively, and then check the answer at the end of this chapter.

and asked them to find a way to affix the candle to a corkboard on the wall in such a way that it would burn without dripping wax onto the table or the floor (Isen, Daubman, & Nowicki, 1987).

Can you figure out a solution? Here's a hint: In order to complete the task you need to think about using some of the objects in a way that's different from the way they are normally used—a classic aspect of creativity. Think about it and then check the solution given at the end of this chapter.

In this study, people who had watched the funny film clip were more likely to solve the problem (and solved it faster) than people in the neutral condition. This result suggests that positive affect promotes creative thinking (Isen, Daubman, & Nowicki, 1987). One question that still remains is whether all positive emotions promote creativity, or just amusement. After all, humor typically involves changing your perspective on some target and seeing it in a whole new light, just like creativity. In another study, participants who had been given a gift of candy did no better on the creativity task than the neutral group. Although they said they were happy about receiving the candy, the effect may have been weaker than that of watching a funny film. Alternatively, perhaps amusement and happiness produce different effects in this situation.

"Depressive Realism?"

If people who are sad in the current moment process information more systematically and carefully, what happens to people who are actually depressed? Are they generally more thoughtful and accurate? According to the hypothesis of **depressive realism**, people who are mildly depressed are more realistic than happy, optimistic people. They are more likely to perceive themselves and their situation accurately, and therefore to make careful and correct decisions. Although the usual term is "depressive" realism, few studies deal with people who are clinically depressed. Most participants in these studies are **dysthymic**, which means mildly depressed or even having a mixture of happy and depressed characteristics.

In one classic experiment, participants were told to press or not press a key to find the best pattern to make a green light come on as frequently as possible. After a period of trying, they were asked how much control they had over the light. When they actually had partial control of the light—such as 50 percent or 75 percent—they generally perceived their control correctly. The interesting result occurred when people had no true control at all. Non-depressed students estimated that they had about 40 percent control, whereas dysthymic students estimated only about 15 percent control (Alloy & Abramson, 1979). In other words, the dysthymic students more correctly recognized their lack of control.

The idea of depressive realism (or dysthymic realism) is surprising. Psychologists have long agreed that depressed people have cognitive distortions, sometimes to the point of being unable to function. Now we are told that depressed people are right and the rest of us are wrong. Partly because the idea is so surprising, psychologists have scrutinized the evidence carefully, and many find it to be less than compelling. Here's the problem (Ackermann & DeRubeis, 1991; Stone, Dodrill, & Johnson, 2001): You can't be sure how accurate a clock is if you check it at only one time of day. If it said "9:35" when that was in fact the correct time, maybe the clock is accurate, or maybe it is stuck at 9:35. Similarly, if some dysphoric person is tested in an uncontrollable situation and correctly perceives, "I am doing badly and I have no control over my situation," we don't know whether the person is *accurate,* or consistently *negative.*

To illustrate, answer each of the following questions, and next to each one estimate your confidence of being correct. For example, if you are certain you are right, put 100 percent; if you have no confidence at all you could put 50 percent on a true-false item or 20 percent on a multiple-choice item with five choices. Of course, you could also put an intermediate number to indicate 70 percent confidence, 90 percent confidence, and so on.

1. The actor John Wayne appeared in more than 100 movies. (true/false)

2. The largest giant redwood tree in the United States is more than 150 meters (492 feet) tall. (true/false)

3. The leaning tower of Pisa has more than 400 steps. (true/false)

4. In biology, rabbits are classified as (a) monotremes, (b) rodents, (c) lagomorphs, (d) artiodactyls, (e) pinnipeds.

5. The term "serendipity" originally came from (a) a story by Horace Walpole, (b) a society of musical composers in Austria, (c) a Greek word for lightning, (d) an American Indian word for treasure, (e) a contraction of "serene" and "disparity."

6. The word "absinthe" refers to (a) a precious stone, (b) a liqueur, (c) a point in the orbit of a moon, (d) a Caribbean island, (e) an exception to the rules of parliamentary procedure.

7. The most widely consumed fruit, worldwide, is the (a) apple, (b) banana, (c) grape, (d) mango, (e) orange.

Now add your numbers on percent confidence. For example, if you wrote 70 percent , 60 percent, 50 percent , 50 percent , 80 percent , 70 percent , and 100 percent , your total would be 480 percent. The highest possible total is 700 percent, so you would estimate that you would get 4.8 answers correct out of a possible 7. Now turn to the end of this chapter, page 335, and check your answers.

Did you answer as many correct as you predicted? Most people do not. When the questions are difficult, as they were here, most people overestimate how many questions they have answered correctly (Plous, 1993). In contrast, mildly depressed people express less confidence in their answers. Sometimes they even *under*estimate their percent correct (Stone, Dodrill, & Johnson, 2001). Note, however, that underestimating does not support the idea of depressive realism. Rather, it suggests that dysthymic people see themselves in a negative light. If the questions were easier, optimistic people's estimates of their percent correct would become accurate, while dysthymic people's lower estimates would be clearly inaccurate. Results like these confirm that dysthymic people are less likely than others to be overconfident, but they don't really indicate that dysthymic people are consistently accurate (Ackermann & DeRubeis, 1991).

Studies on self-perception also point to a difference in negativity, rather than accuracy. In one study college students wrote predictions of what events they might experience in the next four or eight weeks, and then kept diaries that reported such events. Dysthymic students were slightly more accurate at predicting unpleasant events, such as how often they would cry, but happier students were more accurate at predicting pleasant events, such as how often they would laugh (Shrauger, Mariano, & Walter, 1988). In another study, students were given what they were told was their own individual personality profile, although everyone received the same printout. Then they were asked to rate how favorable it was. Although the profile itself was as close to neutral as the experimenters could make it, most dysthymic students rated it relatively unfavorable, whereas most other students saw it as favorable (McKendree-Smith & Scogin, 2000). In research of this type, dysthymic people are not necessarily more accurate; they are biased to see themselves in a negative light, whereas others tend to see themselves in a positive light.

All of these studies have examined depressed people's biases in the conclusions they reach, rather than the process they used to get there. It may be that depression does facilitate more rational information processing, but with a negative bias. In order to address this possibility, researchers in one study compared the approaches taken by depressed and non-depressed participants in making a simple but meaningful decision. Each participant had the task of choosing a partner for a tedious eight-hour task, and they could ask as many questions as they wanted about five potential partners before choosing one of them. The depressed patients asked more questions and collected more total information before deciding, and considered all candidates about equally instead of focusing mainly on one or two. In those regards they would seem realistic and rational. However, they were no more satisfied with their final decisions than the non-depressed controls, and they were just as likely as the controls to stick with whichever candidate they were leaning toward at the start of the process. All the additional evidence they collected did not apparently improve the quality of their decision. We might therefore characterize the depressed people as "indecisive" rather than "rational" (Lewicka, 1997).

A strong body of research suggests that sad people process information more systematically or carefully, yet another body of research shows that depressed people's reasoning is just as flawed as that of non-depressed people. How can that be? One possibility is that the effects of full-blown depression are different from those of temporary sadness. Recall the Yerkes-Dodson law, described at the beginning of this chapter. It may be that systematic processing increases with moderate levels of sadness, but that pessimistic biases increase with extreme or long-term sadness. Another possibility is that the emotional distress associated with depression is qualitatively different from the sadness elicited in most experiments. As usual, more research is needed to explain the discrepancies in these findings.

You may have noticed that almost all of the studies described above used sadness as the only negative emotion, and were vague about what "happiness" meant. Remarkably few studies have considered the effects of other negative emotions, or more specific positive emotions, on any aspect of cognitive processing. There are a few exceptions, such as one study of persuasive message processing discussed above (Tiedens & Linton, 2001), and a few other studies have examined the effects of discrete emotions on processes such as persuasion and stereotyping (e.g., Dasgupta, DeSteno, Williams, & Hunsinger, 2009; Griskevicius, Shiota, & Neufeld, 2010), but a great deal of work remains before we know which of the effects above can be generalized to all positive or negative emotions, and which are more limited to specific emotions.

EMOTIONS AND DECISION-MAKING

At the end of the day, all of this attending, remembering, and processing should lead to an actual decision. The evidence is quite strong that emotions influence our decision-making, often in ways of which we're completely unaware.

According to the **Affect Infusion Model**, people often use their current emotional state as information in reaching a decision about some target, even if the target did not evoke the emotion (Forgas, 1995). For example, if someone asks you on a sunny day to rate how well your life is going overall, you are likely to give a higher rating than if you are asked on a cloudy day (Cunningham, 1979). The current weather really isn't relevant to the question—after all, you're being asked how satisfied you are with your whole life, so the cloud pattern shouldn't matter, but it does. Evidently people rely on their current mood to help answer broad questions about well-being.

One interesting aspect of this finding is that the "cloudy day" effect disappears if participants pay explicit attention to the weather and recognize that it might be affecting their judgment. When researchers in the previous study prefaced their question about life satisfaction by asking, "how's the weather down there?" the effect of weather disappeared. In a similar study, researchers found that participants who had just written about a sad experience reported lower life satisfaction than those who had just reported a happy experience, *unless* they had been told by the experimenter that the room they were in (a sound-proof room with a separate lighting system) often made people uncomfortable (Schwarz & Clore, 1983). These findings suggest the following interpretation: If you are feeling bad and you are not sure why, you report that you are generally unhappy with life. If you can easily blame your bad feelings on something in the situation, such as the weather or the room, then you discount your current mood when answering questions about your long-term life satisfaction (Clore, 1992).

Decisions about buying and selling also yield to emotions. Suppose we ask you to estimate the value of some object, such as a set of highlighter pens. Perhaps you estimate a value of $10. Now we actually give you the pens to keep, but ask whether you would be willing to sell them back to us for $10, the price you said they were worth. Most people in a neutral or happy mood refuse, saying they would prefer to keep the pens. Sad people are more inclined to sell; they would prefer the money. People feeling disgust estimate lower values for

objects, and they don't seem to care whether they keep the object or the money. It's as if they don't want either one. They are just in a mood to spit things out, to reject, to get rid of whatever they can (Lerner, Small, & Loewenstein, 2004).

So emotions influence your choices. Does anybody ever use this idea for practical purposes? You bet they do! Stores arrange cheerful decorations and play happy music, hoping to entice you into a happy mood so you will be more likely to buy things. Television advertisers try to associate their product with happy scenes, especially if they are advertising something like cola beverages, where there aren't many facts to separate one brand from another. The influences are quick and implicit. If you really thought it out, you wouldn't conclude that one kind of cola or potato chip will make you more fun or popular or attractive than another cola or potato chip. Political candidates often use a similar approach to advertising. In the constraints of a brief television advertisement, they can't explain the complexities of a difficult issue, so they try to associate themselves with smiles and cheerful music, while associating their opponents with frightening, unpleasant images.

The Somatic Marker Hypothesis

It may seem surprising that something as transient and irrelevant as mood should have a noticeable effect on our decisions. What purpose could this possibly serve? Wouldn't we all think more clearly, and make better decisions, if we avoided emotion and just used logic (see Figure 14.8)? According to Antonio Damasio, relying on emotion to guide our decisions is not only helpful, it's necessary. In Chapter 5, we discussed Damasio's work with patients suffering from traumatic lesions to the ventromedial prefrontal cortex. Although these patients were able to describe the consequences of various actions they might take in some situation, they still had a hard time making a decision, and the decisions they finally made tended to be bad ones. Damasio's **Somatic Marker Hypothesis** proposes that when we have to make a decision, our mind quickly estimates the likely outcomes of possible options, generates emotional responses to these outcomes, and uses the emotion to

Photos 12/Alamy

F I G U R E 14.8 Would people make better decisions if their emotions did not influence their reasoning? Perhaps not.

guide the decision (Damasio, 1996). The emotional response includes a neural representation of the physiological changes you would feel in the actual outcome situation, hence the term "somatic marker."

Here's an example. You are driving to campus on a busy day, running late for class, and having a terrible time finding a place to park. You see one place at the end of a block near campus. Unfortunately, there is not quite enough space for your car, and if you park there you will nudge up against a fire hydrant. Dilemma. Your mind runs quickly through the plausible consequences of taking the spot: make it to class on time, check; car gets ticketed, you might be able to live with that; car gets towed. Uh oh. According to the somatic marker hypothesis,

that last option probably evoked a strong response in you, foreshadowing how you *would* feel if your car was actually towed, and this feeling would likely dissuade you from the risky parking spot.

Of course, this process might happen a bit differently. Perhaps you only needed to get to "parking ticket" before an aversive feeling kicked in—it depends on the current state of your bank account. Or perhaps you don't care about getting your car towed, in which case none of these outcomes would generate much emotion. But the key point is that if you *did* feel an emotional response while imagining any of these outcomes, this would guide your decision.

Notice a couple of things about this example. For one thing, we did not mention the relative probability of the various outcomes. It may not be likely that your car will be towed, but to the extent you consider it plausible, you will still have an emotional reaction when imagining it. Also, we acknowledged that different people will have different reactions for a variety of reasons. Your response to the imagined outcomes is presumably related to the response you would actually have if it happened, and that's not the same for everybody. Also, some people may show tighter links between their anticipated and actual emotions than others. Damasio has proposed that people with less-functional prefrontal cortex regions (brain damaged people, teenagers, etc.) may have weak *anticipatory* emotions even if their emotions in the actual situation would be strong. Nonetheless, the Somatic Marker Hypothesis offers a solid proposal for a useful role of emotion in decision making.

One implication of the Somatic Marker Hypothesis is that people who have a stronger emotional reaction while making a decision should actually make different decisions, even given the same information to work with. In one study, investigators asked people how much they would decrease their consumption of beef if they thought it had some small possibility of contamination with Mad Cow Disease. They asked other people how much they would decrease consumption of beef if they thought it had some small possibility of contamination with bovine spongiform encephalopathy (BSE). People expressed a stronger avoidance based on Mad Cow Disease than of BSE, even though these well-educated participants knew quite well that Mad Cow Disease and BSE are the same thing (Sinaceur, Heath, & Cole, 2005). "Mad Cow Disease" just sounds scarier, so it leads to more avoidance.

From these two examples it's clear that emotions sometimes support good decisions, yet at other times they lead us astray. Under what circumstances are outcomes improved by emotion? Research suggests that it depends in part on the kind of decision you have to make. Let's consider some different scenarios.

Choices Based on Preferences and Values

Although computers do an excellent job of figuring out the probability of various events, and determining logically the best way to reach certain goals given current circumstances, they don't *set* the goals. Suppose a computer tells us that some medical patient will probably survive longer with treatment A than treatment B, but will have a better quality of life with treatment B. Can the computer tell us which treatment is "better?" Hardly. "Better" requires a value judgment, and a decision based on values is necessarily based on emotions. Remember the quote from Antonio Damasio (1999, p. 55) cited early in Chapter 1: "Emotions are inseparable from the idea of good and evil."

If the decision you have to make involves competing values or personal preferences, then it might be wise to listen to your "gut reaction." A number of studies suggest that people who make subjective, aesthetic decisions based on their instinctive response tend to be happier with that decision in the long run. Here's a typical study (Wilson, Lisle, Schooler, Hodges, Klaaren, & LaFleur, 1993). Researchers invited participants into the laboratory, and seated them in front of several posters. Half of the participants were instructed to write down their reasons for choosing their major. The remaining participants were instructed to write down the things they liked and disliked about each poster. All participants rated how much they liked each poster.

After the participants completed the writing task, the experimenter returned to the room and encouraged them to choose a poster to take home as a gift. The "reasons" manipulation (encouraging people to systematically list the advantages and disadvantages of each poster) had several interesting effects. First, these participants were less discriminating in rating the attractiveness of the posters. Some of the posters were objectively beautiful art prints, rated by pretest participants and control participants as very likable. The others were cute, moderately funny pictures of animals (see Figure 14.9). Participants in the "reasons" condition rated the two types as equally likable, whereas pretest and control participants considered the funny posters much less likable than the art prints. Those in the "reasons" condition were also far more likely to choose one of the funny posters to take home.

Most important, when contacted three weeks later, participants who carefully listed their reasons for liking and disliking each poster were less satisfied with their choice. In general, those who chose the funny posters were relatively dissatisfied, but even among those who chose the art posters, those who listed their reasons before choosing were less satisfied than those who simply picked the poster they liked on first response.

Why might this be? One possibility is that the process of listing advantages and disadvantages of each option simply made it harder to choose, rather than easier. When we try to list the pros and cons of some set of options we usually do so to highlight differences among the options. However, the number of pros and cons may balance out in each case, making the choice more difficult. A later study suggested that people were less consistent in how they weighted the importance of various features when reasoning through their "liking" ratings for several options—people who simply stated their ratings were actually more consistent (Levine, Halberstadt, & Goldstone, 1996). Another possibility is that the kinds of features we list in an exercise like this are not actually the ones that determine whether we'll be happy with our choice. For example, someone might

Waterlily Pond, 1899 (oil on canvas), Monet, Claude (1840–1926)/National Gallery, London, UK/The Bridgeman Art Library International

Hang in there, Baby!

Nikolay Stoilov/istockphoto.com

FIGURE 14.9 Which poster would you choose to take home? More importantly, how would you choose?

list "fits better on my wall" as a benefit of one poster. This would presumably give that factor weight in the person's choice, even though fit on the wall might not be important for long-term satisfaction.

Does this mean that we should just make preference-focused choices immediately, without thinking about them at all? Another clever study provides evidence that waiting to decide is not the problem; rather, it is the process of logical reasoning that gets in the way (Dijksterhuis & van Olden, 2006). Researchers in this study used the same poster-choice procedure as in the study above. In this case, however, they had three conditions: one group of participants chose their poster immediately, a second group listed pros and cons of each poster, and the third group viewed the posters, but then completed an unrelated word-finding task for a comparable amount of time before choosing a poster. Who liked their poster best? The people who were distracted by another task between viewing the options and making their choice! The researchers concluded that it's good to wait before deciding, but logically analyzing your options disrupts the subconscious mulling that would otherwise be going on, and that the latter process actually leads to a better decision in this kind of task.

In sum, although listing pros and cons of various options can be useful for practical decisions, such as which health insurance program to choose, or whom to vote for, your gut reaction may be the best piece of information for choices involving what you like.

Emotions and Moral Reasoning

Choosing a poster is not a terribly weighty decision. Given the link between emotions and our values about good and bad, however, we should also expect emotions to be important in moral reasoning. Let's begin with two examples of difficult moral decisions, which have been of interest to both philosophers and psychological researchers.

The Trolley Dilemma. A trolley car's brakes have failed, and it is plunging toward five people who cannot move. You are standing at a switch that controls which track the trolley will enter at a junction. If you leave the switch alone, the five people will be killed. If you pull the switch, you send the trolley onto another track, where only one person is standing. Then that person will be killed. Should you pull the switch? Compare this dilemma to …

The Footbridge Dilemma. An out-of-control trolley is, again, plunging downhill toward five people. Again, there is no hope that they will jump out of the way. This time there is no switch and only one track, but you are standing on a footbridge above the track. For a split second you consider diving onto the trolley track to stop the trolley, sacrificing your life to save the other five. Unfortunately (or fortunately, depending on your point of view) you are not heavy enough to stop the trolley, so your sacrifice would accomplish nothing. However, standing right next to you is a very large wrestler, whose mass would surely stop the trolley. Should you

push this person off the bridge to stop the trolley, and save the five people's lives? (See Figure 14.10.)

From a purely logical standpoint, these scenarios are the same dilemma, as you would be killing one person to save five, yet far more people say it is okay to pull the switch in the first scenario than will say it is okay to push the stranger off the bridge in the second. Even those who decide it is morally right to push the stranger in the footbridge dilemma are slow to make that decision, as if they are fighting hard against an impulse to say no (Greene, Sommerville, Nystrom, Darley, & Cohen, 2001). Why is pulling the switch morally better than pushing the stranger? Of course, you may hesitate to push a stranger off the bridge for a number of reasons, including being less certain that doing so will save the others. But Joshua Greene and colleagues have emphasized the importance of

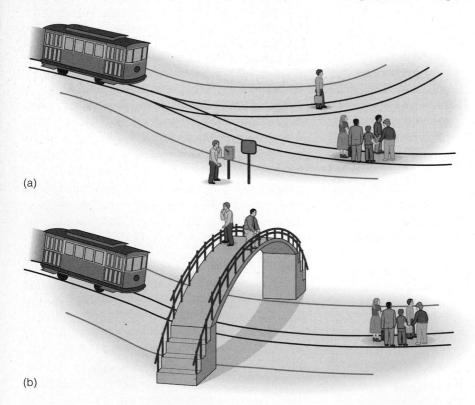

(a)

(b)

F I G U R E 14.10 (a) Would it be right to flip a switch to divert the trolley to a different track in the trolley dilemma? (b) Would it be right to push a stranger off a bridge to block a trolley in the footbridge dilemma? In either case, your action would kill one person but save five others.

"personal force" in our judgment of morality in these situations—using physical force in a way that directly causes someone harm *feels* immoral, whereas incidental harm that results from our manipulation of some inanimate object is less problematic (Greene, Cushman, Stewart, Lowenberg, Nystrom, & Cohen, 2009).

This may seem like a silly distinction to make under the circumstances. After all, either way the person in the train's path is dead, and you were the agent. However, our reluctance to lay hands on someone and hurt them directly may have very old and deep origins, and probably serves us well most of the time. Situations in which we might harm someone as a result of a complex mechanical trick are pretty rare, whereas opportunities abound to hurt someone directly. The notion that some part of our emotional nature protests against such an action, even in the service of helping others, is actually pretty heartening if you think about it.

Let's consider yet another moral decision. Here you don't have to decide what *you* should do, just whether *other people* have made an acceptable decision: Mark and Julie are brother and sister, college students, traveling together on a summer vacation. One night they are staying alone in a beach cabin, and they decide to have sex with each other. Julie is already taking birth control pills, but Mark uses a condom anyway. They both enjoy the experience, although they decide they will not do it again. They keep this night as their special secret, and neither one feels hurt by the experience. In fact, they grow even closer together. So, what do you think? Was it okay for them to have sex?

By the second sentence of this story, most people scream, "Oh, no!!! Wrong, wrong, wrong!"

Well, okay, but *why* was it wrong? When asked, people begin searching for rational explanations of their reaction (Haidt, 2001). "It's wrong because if Julie got pregnant, that kind of inbreeding would probably produce a deformed child." But the scenario specified that they used two dependable forms of birth control, so pregnancy is not a realistic worry.

"Well, but surely they would be emotionally scarred by the experience." This objection doesn't seem fair, either. The scenario explicitly stated that they both enjoyed it and neither was emotionally hurt. It is understandable that you might be skeptical, but if you accept the scenario, then Mark and Julie enjoyed the experience and were not hurt. Do you still think their act was wrong?

Even then, nearly everyone insists it was morally wrong. If you try long enough, you might propose some new, better explanation for why Mark and Julie were wrong. However, if you are honest you will admit that emotionally it just *feels* wrong, whether it is logically acceptable or not. The idea of sex between siblings is repulsive to most people in every culture, and a number of anthropologists have suggested that it is an instinctive taboo that evolved to protect people against inbreeding, before reliable birth control was available (Westermarck, 1891/1922; Wolf & Durham, 2005). Recent experimental work by psychologist Debra Lieberman and colleagues suggests two important cues that people use to determine how closely related they are to others, and that predict aversion to a sexual relationship (Lieberman, Tooby, & Cosmides, 2007). The first is how long you lived together as children. The second is whether or not you saw your own mother caring for this person right when he was a newborn. The point is that our emotional reactions often have a "logical" origin, even if we're not aware of the logic, or if the logic doesn't apply in this exact situation.

Emotions also enter into many political attitudes. Consider the death penalty. Are you for it or against it? How much do you actually know about it? Is the murder rate lower in states that have the death penalty? Does the murder rate drop after a highly publicized execution? How often have people been sentenced to death and later found to be innocent? How much more likely are poor people to get the death penalty than rich people, for similar crimes? On questions such as these, most people admit they "don't know" on many of the questions, and when they think they do know, they are almost as likely to be wrong as right. Moreover, most say that the facts do not matter; they could not imagine any fact that would change their attitude (Ellsworth & Ross, 1983). Even when people do cite facts, it is as if they made up their minds first and then looked for facts to back up their opinion (Haidt, 2001).

Scott Olson/AFP/Getty Images

F I G U R E   14.11   The emotinal anticipation of reward may scale to the size of the reward, without considering its probability, or any risks involved.

Is it wrong to rely on emotions in decisions like these? That is really a philosophical question, rather than a scientific one. If you think the "right" moral decision is the one that a computer would have reached, then emotions are just getting in the way. If you think the right decision is the one you can best live with as a human being, even if it seems a bit illogical, then emotions will sometimes help. Scenarios like the footbridge dilemma describe unusual situations, designed so that carefully reasoned logic opposes our instincts. Presumably emotions evolved because they provide benefits in *most* situations, and one major benefit is that they help us make quick decisions when we do not have time to analyze all the relevant data. It *feels* wrong to push someone off a bridge or to have sex with your brother or sister, and almost all the time it really *is* a bad idea. Your emotions are not always right, but often enough they prepare you for a quick, probably useful response.

The Down Side of Relying on Emotions

We have considered two ways in which emotions might help us to make better decisions. When we must make a decision purely based on liking and

preference, subconscious, affective processing may lead to a better decision than systematic analysis of the options (Dijksterhuis & van Olden, 2006). When we face important moral decisions, our emotional responses may reflect evolved instincts that served our ancestors well, even though they are illogical in a few, odd situations. After discussing the benefits of emotions in decision-making, it is time to consider some disadvantages. As we said above, people typically choose the course of action that they expect will bring them the greater happiness or the least distress. Provided that we have good information about the probabilities involved, our emotions are likely to guide our choices well. However, people can pay so much attention to the potential payoff of some event that they overlook how likely or unlikely the event may be.

Consider gambling. Would you risk $1 on a 50 percent chance of winning $2? Most people would not. What about betting $1 on a 1 percent chance of winning $100? Statistically this is the same as the first bet, as you should come out even in the long run. But most people find this second bet more appealing, because winning $100 sounds like much more fun than winning $1. Would you bet $1 on a one in a million chance of winning $1 million? Again, statistically this is a break-even bet in the long run; however, far more people are willing to make this bet than the 50 percent chance of winning one dollar.

In fact, almost half of U.S. college students say they would bet $10 on a one-in-a-million chance of winning $1 million (Rachlin, Siegel, & Cross, 1994). Statistically this is a terrible bet. You would have to take a one-in-a-million bet about 700,000 times to have a 50 percent chance of winning at least once, and by that time you would have already lost close to 7 million dollars. People in other countries show the same tendency to prefer bets with a very small chance of a very high pay-off (Birnbaum, 1999; see Figure 14.11). The low-probability, high-payoff bet seems appealing because we anticipate enormous pleasure from the possible win, and the low probability of the win (and high probability of loss!) does not weaken our emotions.

Curiously, people who are in a happy mood become less interested in gambling, especially if they see a possibility of incurring large losses (Nygren, Isen, Taylor, & Dulin, 1996). One interpretation is that they try to protect their current happiness by avoiding anything that might weaken it. However, in Chapter 5 we discussed a dopaminergic "reward circuit" in the brain that is associated with emotional feelings of wanting, such as wanting to gamble, wanting to shop, or wanting to take a drug. Although one part of this circuit appears sensitive to probabilities, the part of the circuit that seems to have real emotional kick (the nucleus accumbens) only cares about the size of the reward. As a result, this emotion can drive us into some very foolish decisions.

SUMMARY

We started the chapter by stating that there is no simple way to describe the effects of emotion on cognition, because "cognition" means too many things. What have we learned by considering different aspects of cognition separately? First, emotional stimuli grab our attention. Second, other things being equal, emotional arousal does improve memory.

Third, emotions influence how we interpret information. If you are already frightened, you tend to see new events as frightening also. If you are angry, it doesn't take much to get you angry again. If you are in a good mood, you might tend to make careless, even sloppy decisions based on a few "heuristics" or simple rules of thumb. If you are in a sad mood, you tend to be more cautious, processing the available information carefully or "systematically."

Fourth, emotions have a direct impact on our decisions. We can easily attribute our current feelings to whatever is in front of us, whether that thing caused our emotions or not, and we may act accordingly. In some cases, such as simple personal preferences and moral decisions, emotions may be a good guide. But when you feel craving for something, watch out—you may have to put extra effort into thinking through the consequences of your actions and probabilities of success before making a good decision.

If one theme runs throughout this chapter, it is that emotion is part of our thinking, not something separate. Your thoughts influence your emotions, but your emotions alter what you remember, how intensely you remember it, what aspects of the environment you notice, whether you blame yourself or others for misfortunes, what events you consider likely in the future, and how much effort you put into making a decision.

If you have a major decision to make—what job to take, where to live, whom to marry—how should you make it? Should you sit down and make a careful list of the pros and cons of all of your options? Or should you put it in the back of your mind for a while, and then let your instincts guide your choice? Perhaps our best suggestion is to do both. Make sure you have a realistic understanding of the facts relevant to your decision, but also take some time to process this in the back of your mind, and then listen to your heart.

KEY TERMS

Affect Infusion Model: theory that people use their emotional state as information in reaching a decision about some target (p. 325)

beta-blocker: drug that temporarily disables the stress hormone system responsible for some aspects of emotional arousal (p. 316)

central route to persuasion: persuasion based on facts and logic (p. 320)

depressive realism: proposed tendency for people who are mildly depressed to be more realistic than happy people, to perceive themselves and their situation accurately, and therefore to make careful and correct decisions (p. 323)

dysthymia: being mildly depressed or having a mixture of happy and depressed characteristics (p. 323)

flashbulb memories: recollections of highly emotional events that are vivid and detailed with a clear, almost photographic quality (p. 318)

heuristic cognition: making judgments on the basis of simple "rules of thumb" (p. 320)

peripheral route to persuasion: persuasion based on superficial factors such as frequent repetition of a slogan or endorsements by celebrities (p. 320)

Somatic Marker Hypothesis: when we have to make a decision, our mind quickly estimates the likely outcomes of possible options, activates emotional responses to these outcomes, and uses the emotion to guide the decision (p. 326)

systematic cognition: thorough and deliberate analysis of the available information (p. 320)

Yerkes-Dodson law: learning is at its best when arousal is neither too strong nor too weak (p. 311)

THOUGHT QUESTIONS

1. Research has demonstrated that intense negative emotions such as fear focus attention more narrowly than usual. On the other hand, people report flashbulb memories including details of weather and so forth concerning highly emotional events, such as hearing about some disaster. Do these two findings contradict each other? How might you explain the difference?

2. As reported on page 319, students' reported enjoyment of a spring-break trip is usually higher than the average of how happy they reported being at various times during the trip. What result would you expect if we asked about a predominantly unpleasant experience, such as a visit to a funeral or a stay in a hospital? Would people report the total experience as happier, or less happy, than the average of individual moments within this experience? What leads you to this prediction?

SUGGESTIONS FOR RESEARCH PROJECT

1. Keep a diary of personal events, recording as much detail as possible and categorizing events as highly emotional or not emotional. A month or more later, test your own memory of each event. Do you remember the more emotional events more clearly than the others? Are your memories more accurate?

2. Ask some of your friends to make predictions about their grades for the current semester, their prospects of getting a good job, the

direction of the national economy, or whatever else you wish to include. Ask some of them for their predictions just after your college team has won a big victory, and others just after a disappointing loss. Evaluate the predictions and see whether people make more optimistic predictions when they are in a good mood than when in a sad mood.

SUGGESTIONS FOR FURTHER READING

Damasio, A. R. (1994). *Descartes' Error: Emotion, Reason, and the Human Brain*. New York: Avon Books. This popular book includes a detailed yet easy-to-read description of Damasio's work with frontal lobe lesion patients, and their problems with decision-making.

Reisberg, D., & Hertel, P. (Eds.) (2004). *Memory and Emotion*. New York: Oxford University Press. A collection of chapters by noted researchers studying the interplay of emotion and memory.

Solution to the Problem Posed on Page 323

Dump the matches out of the box, use tacks to pin the side of the box to the corkboard, light the candle, and use melted wax to stick the candle into the box.

Answers to Questions on Page 324

1. True. John Wayne was in 153 movies.
2. False. The tallest redwood was measured at 112 meters (367.5 feet).
3. False. The leaning tower of Pisa has 294 steps.
4. c. Rabbits are lagomorphs.
5. a. The term came from Walpole's story *The Three Princes of Serendip*.
6. b. Absinthe is a liqueur.
7. d. Mangoes are the world's most widely eaten fruits, thanks mainly to the people of India and Pakistan.

Emotion in Clinical Psychology

Do you know anyone whose emotions seem dysfunctional in some way? Do you sometimes feel this way yourself? What is the nature of the problem? Do they seem to have too much emotion, especially when there seems to be no reason for it? Or not enough emotion? Is the problem limited to one particular emotion, or does it generalize across emotions? Think for a moment about people you know, or even fictional characters in books or films, whose emotion systems do not work quite right.

Clinical psychologists are interested in emotion for many reasons. The most obvious of these is that several psychiatric disorders involve problems with emotion (Kring, 2008). Emotional aspects of disorders can be obvious, as in the excesses of distress that characterize depression and anxiety, or they can be more subtle, as in the apparent disjunction of emotional feelings, physiology, and expression in patients with schizophrenia (Kring & Neale, 1996). Researchers interested in basic emotion processes also have a great deal to learn from clinical research. Have you ever tried to fix a piece of equipment that has stopped working, such as a photocopy machine or computer printer? If so, you know that you can learn a lot about how something works by figuring out why it's *not* working in a particular situation. The same is true of emotion—if we can find out what has gone wrong in people who have emotional problems, we will learn more about how emotions work "normally." These "basic" and "applied" lines of research are not exclusive. The more we know about emotional disorders, the more we learn about emotion systems. The more we understand how healthy emotions work, the better able we are to develop treatments for those with problems.

We have used the terms "disorder" and "normal" as though this were a clear-cut distinction—you either have a disorder or you don't. The definitions of specific disorders presented in this chapter come from the ***Diagnostic and Statistical Manual of Mental Disorders, 4th edition*** (DSM-IV; American Psychiatric Association, 1994). This publication lists the criteria to be used by clinical practitioners in diagnosing their patients, and it treats diagnoses as categories. However, many psychologists now acknowledge that most symptoms associated with mental disorders are a matter of degree. Certainly the cut-off point between normal and pathological emotion is far from obvious.

Also, what the DSM considers "pathological" changes periodically. The DSM is revised by a team of psychiatrists every several years (in case you're wondering, psy*chiatrists* are medical doctors who attend med school and residency, and are authorized to prescribe drugs; psy*chologists* are Ph.D.s whose doctoral training focused on research and/or talk therapy, rather than medical intervention). These practitioners discuss new evidence, and decide how to re-define the various disorders. For example, homosexuality used to be a DSM diagnosis, but as researchers learned more about sexual orientation, and as social norms changed, the team decided that same-sex preference should not be considered a disorder. In the DSM-IV, the team considered the possibility that there are two types of depression with somewhat different symptoms and causes. The DSM is being revised again as this textbook goes to press, with a number of controversies regarding possible changes to the diagnostic criteria.

The upshot of all this is that the distinction between normal, healthy emotion and pathological emotion is not always black-and-white. However, one consistent criterion across many diagnoses and editions of the DSM is reduced ability to function and quality of life. Whatever is going on with a person, it must cause "clinically significant distress or impairment in social, occupational, or other important areas of functioning" in order to be diagnosable. For example, if someone is extremely frightened of airplanes, this would not qualify for diagnosis unless it really interferes with that person's life—perhaps he can't go on necessary professional travel or visit family because he is too afraid of flying. Although we acknowledge that the line between normal and pathological emotion is somewhat arbitrary, in this chapter we will emphasize emotional problems that seriously disrupt people's lives.

DEPRESSION

Generally speaking, depression is an unhappy mood that persists for a long time, without any clear precipitating event sufficient to merit such a severe reaction. Mood disorders are described in terms of "episodes" when one experiences depressive symptoms (or mania, to be discussed in the next section) for a certain period of time. A **major depressive episode** is defined as the experience of five or more of the following symptoms (including one or both of the first two) nearly every day for at least two weeks (American Psychiatric Association, 1994):

- Depressed mood most of the day
- Markedly diminished interest or pleasure in all, or almost all, activities
- Significant weight loss (not due to dieting), or weight gain
- Insomnia (not sleeping enough) or hypersomnia (sleeping too much)
- Motor retardation (slowing) or agitation
- Fatigue or loss of energy
- Feeling of worthlessness or excessive or inappropriate guilt
- Diminished ability to think or concentrate
- Recurrent thoughts of death or suicidal thinking, with or without a specific plan

Clinicians and researchers can diagnose depression in a number of ways. A clinician may simply talk with a client, gather reports of the symptoms above, and conclude that a diagnosis of depression is warranted. A more formal method relies upon the **Structured Clinical Interview for DSM disorders (SCID)**, an interview protocol that elicits information needed to diagnose a new patient according to DSM standards (First, Spitzer, Gibbon, & Williams, 1997). Researchers may also use questionnaire measures to identify depressed individuals. The most widely used is the **Beck Depression Inventory**, a multiple-choice questionnaire about sadness, guilt, self-blame, suicidal thoughts, loss of interest, sleep problems, fatigue, and so forth. People answer in terms of how they have felt over the previous two weeks. A score above 15 on this scale indicates moderate depression, and a score above 30 indicates severe depression.

As a general rule, clinicians do not count extreme sadness as depression when it is part of a normal grieving process, as with the death of a loved one. A normal response to bereavement looks very much like depression. You are sad no matter what good events happen, for weeks or months. You can still react with brief pleasure to a bit of good news, but that momentary pleasure does not take away from your deep grief. Normally distress is greatest shortly after the loss, and it gradually dissipates over time. People vary greatly in how fast they recover, however, and severely prolonged, intense grief may still be diagnosable as depression.

Many depressive episodes are precipitated by a severe loss, such as the loss of a job or an important relationship (Tennant, 2002). However, people vary in their tendency to become depressed after such an experience (Figure 15.1). Most of us will experience a major loss at least once in our lives, but only about 10 percent of people will suffer from diagnosable depression (Riolo, Nguyen, Greden, & King, 2005). Why are some people more vulnerable to depression than others? Some of this variation can be predicted by people's "default" mood. One study took advantage of the fact that a group of college students had filled out personality questionnaires shortly before a major earthquake struck their city in California. Researchers found that virtually everyone felt sad or depressed in the first weeks after the damage.

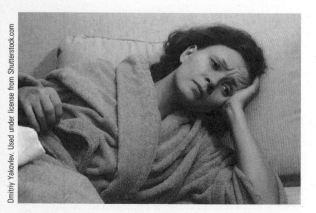

FIGURE 15.1 Approximately 10% of people will experience major depression at some point during their lives.

Dmitriy Yakovlev. Used under license from Shutterstock.com

However, those who already had been mildly depressed before the earthquake reacted more strongly to it, and remained strongly depressed longer than the other students (Nolen-Hoeksema & Morrow, 1991).

Still, the question remains as to why people have different default moods, or why some react more strongly than others to a given event. One hypothesis is genetics. Depression tends to run in families (Erlenmeyer-Kimling et al., 1997). That evidence by itself is inconclusive, but better evidence reveals that when an adopted child develops depression (after reaching adulthood), depression is generally more common among that person's biological relatives than among the adoptive relatives (Wender et al., 1986). The risk of depression is highest for people whose relatives became depressed early in life, and higher for those with depressed female relatives than those with depressed male relatives (Bierut et al., 1999; Kendler, Gardner, & Prescott, 1999; Lyons et al., 1998). The interpretation is that many people who become depressed early in life may have genes predisposing them to depression. One candidate is the serotonin transporter gene, discussed in Chapter 13. Individuals with certain versions of this gene are more likely to experience depression after a stressful life event (Bukh, Bock, Vinberg, Werge, Gether, & Kessing, 2009).

We mentioned in Chapter 2 that a single gene is likely to have many effects, and the genes that confer vulnerability to depression likely have other effects as well. Major depression runs in the same families with alcohol dependence, other substance abuse, antisocial personality disorder, bulimia, panic disorder, migraine headaches, attention-deficit disorder, and a variety of other problems (Dawson & Grant, 1998; Fu et al., 2002; Hudson et al., 2003; Kendler et al., 1995). That is, if you have a relative with any of these disorders, your risk is above average for developing the same disorder, or any of the others. The predisposition interacts with other factors including gender. Within a given family, on the average more men will have issues with alcohol and more women will have problems with depression (Dawson & Grant, 1998). The underlying genetic predisposition may be the same.

Another hypothesis about the causes of depression is that having gone through previous bad experiences may predispose people to react more strongly to new bad experiences, and therefore become depressed. Some of these early experiences are more likely to happen to women than men. For example, several studies have found that women who were sexually abused during childhood are at increased risk for adult depression and suicide after stressful life events (Brent et al., 2002; Buzi, Weinman, & Smith, 2007; Davidson, Hughes, George, & Blazer, 1996). One difficulty in interpreting those results is that many of those growing up with sexual abuse may also have been exposed to poverty, various kinds of nonsexual abuse, and other problems that would also predict depression. To control for these other influences, researchers examined people who reported childhood sexual abuse, and among them identified those who had a twin that did not report childhood sexual abuse. As a rule, the twin reporting sexual abuse had the greater risk of depression and suicide attempts, although the other twin also had more than the average for the rest of the population (Kendler, Kuhn, & Precott, 2004; E. Nelson et al., 2002). The implication is that the overall family life predisposed both twins somewhat to depression, but sexual abuse added to that predisposition.

The Reward Insensitivity Hypothesis of Depression

When we think of depression, we typically think of someone who is extremely sad. Sadness and depression share many features in common, and research using fMRI scans has found that depressed people show larger than normal responses when they see a picture of a sad face (C. Fu et al., 2004). However, some researchers have argued that for many depressed people, the main symptom of depression is not extreme sadness, but a lack of pleasure. For example, in one study, depressed and non-depressed people watched several kinds of films and reported their responses. The two groups responded about equally to the sad and frightening films, but the depressed people reported much less amusement while viewing the comedies. In fact, they sometimes reported mild

sadness during the comedies (Rottenberg, Kasch, Gross, & Gotlib, 2002).

In another study, depressed and non-depressed women viewed a series of pictures and reported their emotional responses, while researchers observed their facial expressions. The depressed and non-depressed women reacted about equally to the sad pictures, but the depressed women showed significantly less response to the pleasant pictures. (See Figure 15.2.) In the same study, the participants were asked to rate how well 12 pleasant words and 12 unpleasant words applied to themselves. Afterward, they were asked (to their surprise) to recall the 24 words. The depressed women recalled fewer of the pleasant words than the non-depressed women did; the two groups recalled equal numbers of the unpleasant words (Sloan, Strauss, & Wisner, 2001).

In a third study, depressed and non-depressed participants viewed words on a computer screen, and then completed a second task as a distraction.

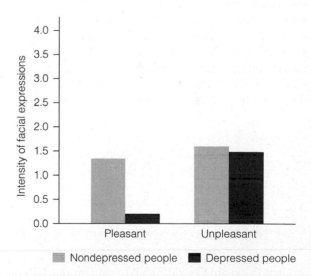

FIGURE 15.2 Depressed and nondepressed people showed about equal intensity of facial expressions when viewing unpleasant slides, but the depressed people showed much less response to the pleasant slides.

Source: From "Diminished response to pleasant stimuli by depressed women". *Journal of Abnormal Psychology*, 10, pp. 488–493. © 2001 American Psychological Association. Reprinted with permission from Dr. D. Sloan.

Then the researchers presented a longer list of words and asked participants to identify which ones had been on the original list. There were two types of trials, however. On some trials, participants were simply told to answer as accurately as possible, without any opportunity for a reward. On a different set of trials, all "hits" (correct identifications of previously viewed words) gained the participant 10 cents, with no penalty for saying "yes" incorrectly (a "false alarm"). If you were a participant, what would you do? Presumably, on the no-reward trials, you would do your best to answer correctly. On the rewarded trials, you would change your strategy: "When in doubt, say yes." Most non-depressed participants showed just this pattern, but depressed participants failed to change their strategy. That is, they did not increase their "yes" answers when those answers had a chance of being rewarded. Evidently they were less responsive than other people to the potential rewards in the situation (Henriques & Davidson, 2000).

If depression involves insensitivity to reward, we should expect people with depression to show some kind of dysfunction in the dopamine circuits of the brain that mediate reward. Some investigators have reported decreased levels of dopamine metabolites in people with depression (Reddy, Khanna, Subhash, Channabasavanna, & Rao, 1992). Studies with rodents also suggest that manipulations of dopamine activity in the reward circuit discussed in Chapter 5 can produce depression-like behavior (Nestler & Carlezon, 2006). Fewer studies have addressed this issue in humans, but one recent fMRI study asked whether depressed individuals show less activation in the reward circuit during gambling tasks that typically elicit such activation (Knutson, Bhanji, Cooney, Atlas, & Gotlib, 2007). Although depressed participants showed fairly normal activation in the nucleus accumbens (a core part of the reward circuit) than non-depressed controls, they showed *greater* activation in an area called the anterior cingulate cortex (see Figure 15.3), thought to mediate conflict or uncertainty. Thus, depressed people may still feel the "wanting" associated with potential reward, but may perceive greater risk in trying to reach those rewards.

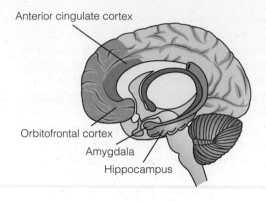

Anterior cingulate cortex

Orbitofrontal cortex

Amygdala

Hippocampus

F I G U R E 15.3 Although depressed people do show activation in the brain's reward circuits while gambling they also show greater than normal activation in the anterior cingulate, an area thought to mediate feelings of risk.

Two Types of Depression?

The DSM criteria for depression require depressed mood *and/or* lack of pleasure, most of the day nearly every day for two weeks. Which is the real defining feature of depression? If you look at the other diagnostic criteria, you may see other contradictions. Weight gain *or* loss? Sleeping too much *or* too little? Psychomotor retardation *or* agitation? What is going on here?

Clearly the symptoms clinicians associate with depression include opposite ends of the same spectrum. One potential explanation is that there are actually two distinct types of depression, with different sets of biological and psychological features. Peter Maas (1975) was among the first to propose distinguishing two types of depression. Type "A" depression, he suggested, was associated with a deficiency of dopamine and norepinephrine, whereas Type "B" was characterized by serotonin deficiency. If Maas was right, then these two neurochemical patterns should correspond to different sets of symptoms. In particular, Type A should involve reward insensitivity, whereas Type B might involve intense feelings of sadness.

Building on these ideas, the DSM-IV has tentatively identified two types of depression: **Typical or melancholic depression** (roughly corresponding to Maas's Type B) is characterized by decreased appetite and weight loss, insomnia, and psychomotor agitation—such as trembling and moving around compulsively. **Atypical depression** (corresponding to Maas's Type A) is characterized by increased appetite and weight gain, sleeping too much, and psychomotor retardation (Posternak & Zimmerman, 2002). In a recent study, researchers found that people reported more fatigue and pessimism after a personal failure, suggesting atypical depression, whereas people reported more crying and sadness after a social loss, perhaps suggesting typical depression (Keller & Nesse, 2006). Of course, this study examined short-term feelings of distress after an event rather than full-blown, diagnosable depression, but the findings are still suggestive.

Distinguishing different subtypes of depression helps to account for some strange features of the diagnostic criteria. There is also some support for multiple kinds of depression at the neural level, as the serotonin and dopamine systems have both been implicated, and treatments intervening in both systems can help alleviate symptoms. However, the distinction between typical and atypical depression is still quite controversial (Davidson, 2007). The symptoms do not necessarily cluster well statistically into the proposed subtypes, so many individuals cannot be classified easily into one subtype or the other. For example, a depressed person who is losing weight may also sleep too much. It may be that even more subtypes are needed, or that the two sets of symptoms have different causes but can still overlap. Researchers are working actively in this area, and you can expect to see further progress in the coming years.

Cognitive Aspects of Depression

Earlier we discussed possible genetic profiles and life experiences that might make people vulnerable to depression. However, depression is also related to the ways people think about the world. People feel sad when they believe they are helpless or without control in some negative situation. Similarly, they become depressed if they feel helpless or hopeless in general (Lazarus, 1991).

The classic study of this effect documented a phenomenon called **learned helplessness** (Seligman & Maier, 1967). In this study, dogs were first harnessed in place on a floor that would give an electrical shock a few seconds after a sound tone. Half of the dogs were harnessed in front of a panel that would de-activate the shock, as long as the dog pressed the panel right after hearing the tone. These dogs learned quickly that they could control the shock. The remaining dogs were placed in a similar position, but could do nothing to stop the shock. Later, all of the dogs were placed in new structures where the tone still predicted a shock in one part of the floor, but if the dogs responded quickly they could jump into another section where they would not be shocked. The dogs that had previously been able to prevent the shock learned to do so quickly in this new situation. However, dogs that had no control in the earlier part of the study just gave up. Most of them never found out that there was a way to escape the shocks in the new structure, because they never even looked for one. Although there is no way to know what these dogs were feeling, their behavior looked a lot like depression.

Versions of this study have now been conducted many times with humans, suggesting that learned helplessness is an important part of clinical depression (Peterson, Maier, & Seligman, 1993). One consistent feature of depression is a tendency toward a pessimistic explanatory style for negative events. An **explanatory style** is a characteristic way of making attributions for success or failure. Most people recognize that their successes depend on some combination of luck, skill, and hard work. In contrast, people differ more in how they explain their failures. Some tend to blame their failures on themselves, some generally blame bad luck, some blame other people, and so forth. A person's explanatory style for failures tends to be consistent across situations and over long periods of time, even decades (Burns & Seligman, 1989). Blaming failure on your lack of effort is a somewhat optimistic style; it implies that you have the skill to succeed and next time, with more effort, you will. Blaming failure on your lack of ability ("I'm stupid") is the most pessimistic style. It implies that the reason for failure is internal (within yourself), stable (consistent over time), and global (consistent across situations). Most depressed people have a pessimistic explanatory style (Alloy et al., 1999).

In addition to a pessimistic explanatory style, most depressed people have unrealistic beliefs about what they "must" become or what they "must" accomplish in order to be satisfied. One example is, "Failing at something means I am less worthy as a person." Aaron Beck (1973, 1987) has reported that depressed people find failures in the most ordinary events because of these beliefs. Every minor defeat seems further evidence of their weakness or stupidity. If someone walks by without smiling or talking, they take it as further evidence of their unpopularity. People who interpret almost every event as a failure quickly become discouraged, as you can imagine, and one of the main hallmarks of depression is a lack of motivation and activity. Dysfunctional beliefs are clearly related to pessimistic explanatory style, but correlate even more strongly with depression than pessimistic explanatory style does (Spangler & Burns, 1999).

Women are far more likely to be diagnosed with depression than men. Studies suggest that this may be due in part to the fact that women are more likely than men to ruminate, or think repeatedly and nonconstructively about negative events. In general, people who ruminate more about negative events are more likely to become depressed (Rood, Roelofs, Bögels, Nolen-Hoeksema, & Schoouten, 2009). Studies find that men tend toward higher senses of mastery or control, and that only those women who ruminate extensively and have lower mastery scores show greater susceptibility to depression (Nolen-Hoeksema, Larson, & Grayson, 1999). If a pessimistic explanatory style predicts depression, it may be that women are more likely to have learned this explanatory style than men. An alternative interpretation is that rumination does not cause later depression; it just precedes it as an early symptom. That is, those who ruminate extensively are already a little depressed. However, teaching people not to ruminate does help prevent depression, so rumination appears to be a causal factor leading to depression (Morrow & Nolen-Hoeksema, 1990).

Treating Depression

Clinicians and scientists have tried a number of possible treatments for depression. In extreme cases, when symptoms do not respond to treatment with talk therapy and/or drugs, psychiatrists may suggest electroconvulsive therapy (administering a strong electrical current to the brain) or brief periods of complete sleep deprivation, each of which alters brain chemistry in a way that can help alleviate major depression (Gorgulu & Caliyurt, 2009; Medda, Perugi, Zanello, Ciuffa, & Cassano, 2009). However, these treatments are not commonly prescribed, and are reserved for the most severe cases. Most depression will be treated with some form of talk therapy and/or medication. Each of these treatments has proved effective in randomized, controlled experimental trials, and although many clinicians will emphasize one or the other, research suggests that a combination of the two is most effective in many cases (Keller, McCullough, & Klein, 2000).

Therapists have many different strategies for helping people work through issues related to depression. However, the most effective of these appears to be **cognitive therapy**, an approach that seeks to alter the explanatory styles and dysfunctional biases that characterize disordered individuals (Arnow & Post, 2010; Beck, 1975). A therapist using this technique will typically ask clients to talk about events in their daily lives (perhaps keeping records in a diary) and will then help the client challenge assumptions and beliefs that promote distress. For example, if a depressed client has a tendency to interpret every negative event as a personal failure, even when this is unrealistic, the therapist may point out this bias in a particular situation, and suggest other possible attributions. The idea is that over time, the client will internalize new ways of interpreting events that are less likely to cause depression. However, this takes a long time (months or even years), so it is not unusual for a therapist to recommend antidepressant medication to help reduce symptoms in the meantime.

Antidepressant drugs have become remarkably popular in the last decade or so, and some medical doctors will prescribe them based on very little information from the patient, without discussing alternative or complementary options. This is especially problematic with general practitioners and other non-psychiatrists, who are legally authorized to prescribe these drugs, but who do not have training in psychological disorders. However, when prescribed and supervised properly antidepressants can be an important part of treatment.

Most antidepressant drugs increase the availability of serotonin and/or dopamine at their synapses. One of the most popular antidepressants, fluoxetine (trade name Prozac) is fairly specific to serotonin, with little effect on other neurotransmitters. After serotonin is released at a synapse, it attaches to its receptors, activates them, breaks away, and then in most cases becomes reabsorbed by the cell that released it, via a membrane protein called the serotonin transporter. Fluoxetine blocks the serotonin transporter, and therefore allows released serotonin to remain longer in the synapse, where it can reattach to its receptors. Antidepressant drugs with this type of effect are referred to as **selective serotonin reuptake inhibitors, or SSRIs**. Some other antidepressant drugs block the dopamine transporter as well as the serotonin transporter, prolonging the effects of both neurotransmitters. A few antidepressants, such as buproprion (Wellbutrin), act only on dopamine synapses. The fact that different people respond to different drugs supports the idea that depression comes in several types, as discussed above.

Most antidepressant drugs increase serotonin activity, which suggests that depression is associated with, perhaps even caused by, a deficit in serotonin. However, other kinds of evidence offer mixed support for this hypothesis. For example, we might predict that depressed patients would show low levels of serotonin or its metabolites in their blood and other body fluids. Multiple tests of that hypothesis have found only inconsistent results (Leonard, 2000). Low levels of serotonin metabolites in the blood generally correlate better with aggressiveness and suicidal tendencies than with depression (Mann, McBride, Anderson, & Mieczkowski, 1992; Spreux-Varoquaux et al., 2001). However, the research has been more consistent in finding that depressed people have abnormalities of the serotonin transporter proteins discussed in earlier chapters (Leonard, 2000), and people with certain variants of the gene for these proteins respond better to treatment with SSRIs (Kraft, Slager, McGrath, & Hamilton, 2005).

Another relevant type of research tests the effects of decreasing or increasing someone's serotonin levels. One way to deplete the brain of serotonin, quickly and temporarily, is by a diet that is rich in most amino acids but lacking in tryptophan, the amino acid that the brain converts into serotonin. That procedure triggers a bout of depression in people with a history of depression, but not in people without such a history (Neumeister et al., 2004). Evidently low serotonin by itself does not automatically cause depression; it has that effect only in people who are already predisposed to it.

In short, serotonin is not the "anti-depression" neurotransmitter. Still, SSRIs seem to work for many people, even though we don't entirely understand why.

People suffering from major depression should be encouraged to seek professional treatment. However, people can also take some fairly simple steps to prevent sadness from overwhelming them or developing into depression. Much of the advice is the same as that for coping with stress, discussed in Chapter 6. One recommendation is to try to reappraise negative events in a way that is less hurtful and catastrophic. In one study, college students who were at risk for depression were randomly assigned to receive no treatment or a series of eight workshops on how to combat negative thoughts about themselves. For example, if you fail a test, it doesn't mean that you should give up on yourself academically. It might be a message to rethink your educational plans and take different types of courses. In any situation, the idea is to interpret unfavorable events in a way that avoids excessive discouragement and self-blame. The students who received this kind of training reported significantly fewer episodes of anxiety and depression over the next three years (Seligman, Schulman, DeRubeis, & Hollon, 1999).

Exposure to a moderate amount (30 minutes to an hour) of sunlight or other full-spectrum light can also help alleviate depression (Even, Schröder, Friedman, & Rouillon, 2008). Light therapy can be especially effective for individuals with seasonal affective disorder—depression that is limited to the winter months when days are short and skies often cloudy—but may be helpful for other kinds of depression as well (Lavoie, Lam, Bouchard, Sasseville, Carron, Gagné, et al., 2009). Also, try to get some exercise on a regular basis (Figure 15.4). Moderate aerobic exercise such as jogging, brisk walking, or dancing—just enough to speed up the blood flow—is one of the most reliable ways to combat mild depression (Leppämäki, Partonen, & Lönnqvist, 2002). Another recommendation is to adhere to a regular sleep schedule. Although short periods of sleep deprivation are sometimes used to treat extreme depression, chronic sleeplessness may facilitate more garden-variety depression, and just getting to bed at a more consistent time can help reduce risk (Wehr et al., 1998).

Many studies suggest that the prevalence of depression has been rising over the decades, especially in the United States (Murphy, Laird, Monson, Sobol, & Leighton, 2000). No one knows why, but it may be related to a shift in lifestyle. One obvious change is that people today are more sedentary. We sit at desks instead of working in factories or farms, we drive instead of walking, and take elevators instead of climbing the stairs. We spend much less time outdoors, and don't get enough exposure to natural light and fresh air. Most of us are sleep deprived. We don't want to suggest anything so simplistic as that a little more sleep, exercise, and sunlight will prevent all depression. We definitely do not suggest that people experiencing depression should take these steps instead of seeking professional help. However, if you want to boost your mood during a time of stress, these steps will probably help somewhat, and they sure can't hurt.

MANIA AND BIPOLAR DISORDER

Some people experience major depressive episodes as one part of their disorder, but at other times swing to the opposite extreme. It may seem odd to think of "excessive pleasure" or "insufficiently depressed mood" as pathological emotion states. However, a quick look at the DSM criteria for a **manic episode** points out the problem:

- Inflated self-esteem or grandiosity
- Decreased need for sleep (e.g., feels rested after only three hours)

F I G U R E 15.4 Regular exercise and exposure to sunlight may help prevent or alleviate moderate depression.

Tyler Olson. Used under license from Shutterstock.com

- More talkative than usual, or pressure to keep talking
- Flight of ideas, or subjective experience that thoughts are racing
- Distractibility, difficulty focusing attention
- Increase in goal-oriented activity and/or psychomotor agitation
- Excessive involvement in pleasurable activities that have a high potential for painful consequences (shopping, sexual indiscretion, gambling, poor business investments, etc.)

The first six criteria may not sound too bad. Many of us feel a bit hyperactive sometimes, and these bursts of energy can be pleasurable (if a bit annoying to others). People who experience mild levels of mania may describe it as a fun state, as long as it doesn't go on too long or become extreme. However, pressured speech, racing thoughts, and distractibility can quickly become uncomfortable. People in manic episodes often seem irritable, as though they wish either (a) everyone else could keep up with their pace instead of slowing them down, or (b) their brains would shut up for a few minutes. And of course, the last criterion is the one that causes the real damage. Remember that in order to qualify as a disorder, the person's symptoms need to interfere with well-being and ability to function. In mania, people may do a great deal of damage in the process of seeking rewards: spending thousands of dollars on gambling or shopping, engaging in risky and dangerous thrill-seeking, or harming close relationships through careless sexuality.

Mania is pretty unusual on its own, and the DSM does not have a diagnostic category for manic disorder without accompanying depressive episodes. **Bipolar disorders** are those in which the person alternates between episodes of mania and depression. Because the treatment for depression is different when mania is or is not involved, it is important to find out whether a depressed person might sometimes experience mania, so the DSM includes a description of **hypomania**—a state in which several symptoms of mania are present, but the symptoms are not severe enough to cause problems in life.

The depression experienced in bipolar disorder is more likely to be of the atypical kind than the typical kind (Aksikal & Benazzi, 2005). Considering the symptoms associated with atypical depression, this makes some sense—lethargy, sleeping too much, and lack of interest in things seems more the opposite of mania than agitation and crying. This effect provides further evidence for multiple, biologically distinct kinds of depression. However, the relation between bipolar disorder and atypical depression is not perfect—some bipolar individuals experience more typical depressive symptoms—and researchers continue to seek explanations for the various aspects of mood disorders.

Patients with bipolar disorder are at high risk for attempted suicide. Approximately half of people with untreated, diagnosable bipolar disorder will attempt suicide at least once in their lives, and about 15 percent will succeed (Rihmer, 2009). These rates are higher than for unipolar depression, suggesting that bipolar affective disorder confers particular risk for suicide (Raja & Azzoni, 2004). Suicide attempts typically occur during depressive episodes, especially involving feelings of hopelessness, although they may also occur during mixed episodes with depressive and manic symptoms (Hawton, Sutton, Haw, Sinclair, & Harriss, 2005).

The treatment for bipolar disorder is different than for unipolar depression (with no manic episodes). For one thing, bipolar disorder is not as strongly linked to explanatory style, so although some talk therapy may be helpful in managing problematic behavioral symptoms, medication is much more central to treatment. Antidepressants may only kick a bipolar person from a depressive episode into a manic episode, and this is not helpful at all. The most effective pharmacological treatment for bipolar disorder is lithium (Berghöfer, Alda, Adli, Baethge, Bauer, Bschor, et al., 2008). As with SSRIs, it is not clear how exactly lithium affects the nervous system, but one possibility is influence on the receptors for the neurotransmitter glutamate. Glutamate generally speeds up neural activation throughout the brain, and in mice lithium appears to stabilize glutamate levels so they don't bounce around too much (Dixon & Hokin, 1998).

ANXIETY DISORDERS

Generally speaking, anxiety disorders are defined in terms of "excessive" fear and avoidance. Of course, the line between excessive or pathological fear/avoidance and normal or healthy fear is not easy to define, and varies from situation to situation. As we discussed in Chapter 7, not having fear responses at all would be extremely problematic, and "normal" fear should track the objective level of danger in the environment. Do you live in a friendly, safe neighborhood or a war-torn country? If you have had some horrible experiences, it makes sense to increase your level of fear and caution; your world really *is* a dangerous place (Rosen & Schulkin, 2004). So we need to define "excessive" fear in terms of what seems appropriate under someone's circumstances.

The DSM-IV lists more than a dozen psychological disorders in which the main symptom is excessive anxiety. The simplest example, **generalized anxiety disorder (GAD),** is characterized by almost constant nervousness and a wide range of worries. People with GAD worry intensely about their health, finances, job, and even minor matters such as household chores or car repairs. Their worries make them irritable, restless, and fatigued, and consequently they have trouble doing their jobs and getting along with their families. About 5 percent of all people qualify for a diagnosis of GAD at some point in life (Wittchen, Zhao, Kessler, & Eaton, 1994). However, because anxiety is a symptom of many other disorders, few people have GAD alone; most people with GAD qualify for one or more additional diagnoses (Bruce, Machan, Dyck, & Keller, 2001).

Panic disorder is characterized by repeated attacks of panic, with sharply increased heart rate, rapid breathing, sweating, trembling, and chest pains. About 1-3 percent of people experience panic disorder at some time during their lives, with greater frequency in women than men (Weissman et al., 1997). People having a panic attack often fear they are having a heart attack. Most panic attacks last only a few minutes, although some last longer.

Not everyone who has a panic attack goes on to develop panic disorder. Some people have one or more panic attacks, shrug them off, and go on with life (Wilson & Hayward, 2005). Ironically, the problem escalates when people worry too much about their panic attacks. This fear of fear itself increases their anxiety level, and thereby increases the probability and severity of future attacks (McNally, 2002). After having a few panic attacks, people begin to associate them with the events and circumstances that accompanied them. Later, similar circumstances may evoke new panic attacks as a conditioned response (Bouton, Mineka, & Barlow, 2001). Also, whenever people with panic disorder begin to notice rapid breathing or other signs of arousal, they tend to interpret the signs as the start of an attack; the resulting anxiety then triggers an actual panic attack (Battaglia, Bertella, Ogliari, Bellodi, & Smeraldi, 2001; Gorman et al., 2001).

Many people with panic disorder also develop a condition called **agoraphobia**, a term based on the Greek words *agora* (market place), and *phobia* (fear) that refers to an excessive fear of public situations that would be difficult to escape in the event of a panic attack. Those situations include open, public places, but also include tunnels, buses, and so forth. Agoraphobia is uncommon in people without panic disorder (Wittchen, Reed, & Kessler, 1998), and likely develops because people with panic disorder fear that they could be embarrassed by a panic attack in public.

A phobia is an extreme fear that interferes with everyday life. It should not necessarily be defined as an unrealistic fear. Many people are afraid to fly in an airplane—a demonstrably unrealistic fear. The statistics say that airplane travel is so much safer than automobile travel that, depending on how close you live to the nearest airport, you may be more likely to die in an automobile accident on the way to the airport than you are to die in the airplane itself (Sivak & Flannagan, 2003). However, an unrealistic fear of airplanes does not qualify as a phobia unless it interferes with your everyday life (perhaps your job requires air travel). On the other hand, fear of snakes and spiders is realistic, but when this fear is so intense that it interferes with daily life, it qualifies as a phobia. Phobias usually begin in the teens or young adulthood and are more common among women than men (Burke, Burke, Regier, & Rae, 1990).

Whereas GAD is almost constant fear, and panic disorder is extreme anxiety at largely unpredictable times and places, a **specific phobia** (sometimes also known as a *simple phobia*) is characterized by excessive fear of a particular object or situation. The presence of that object or situation can provoke extreme fear, as can a film depiction (Sarlo, Palomba, Angrilli, & Stagagno, 2002), and sometimes even a thought about the object. Some common objects of phobias are (Cox, McWilliams, Clara, & Stein, 2003):

- Public speaking
- Heights (including elevators, being on a high floor of a building)
- Not being on solid ground (being in the air or on the water)
- Being with or being observed by strangers (*social phobia*)
- Being alone
- Threats or reminders of threats (snakes, spiders, other animals, blood, injections, storms, etc.)

One of the key characteristics of phobia is the ability of the feared object to dominate attention. Recall the research from Chapters 7 and 14, showing that fear increases attention to threatening objects. That tendency is magnified in people with a phobia. In one study, people were asked to try to find the one picture of a mushroom among many pictures of flowers, or to find the one mushroom among many pictures of flowers and one picture of a spider. People with a phobia of spiders had no trouble finding the mushroom in the case without a spider, but had much trouble, relative to other people, if one spider picture was present (Miltner, Krieschel, Hecht, Trippe, & Weiss, 2004). Evidently the spider picture grabbed their attention quite strongly.

Finally, in **post-traumatic stress disorder (PTSD)**, someone who has experienced a traumatic event has frequent distressing recollections (flashbacks) and nightmares about the traumatic event, avoids reminders of it, and shows an exaggerated startle reflex. PTSD victims also report outbursts of anger, guilt, and sadness. PTSD lasts for months and sometimes years (Pitman, van der Kolk, Orr, & Greenberg, 1990). One study examined 94 Iraqi children who were in a shelter when it was bombed during the 1991 Gulf War, killing more than 750 people. Those children continued to show fear and sadness two years later (Dyregrov, Gjestad, & Raundalen, 2002).

The various anxiety disorders have much in common, but they also differ in important ways. In one study, researchers recorded people's sympathetic nervous system responses and frowning expressions when they heard brief reminders of their fears. People with specific phobias showed the strongest responses. For example, if someone is deathly afraid of snakes, even the slightest reminder of snakes provokes severe distress. People with GAD showed the weakest responses. They are a little afraid of almost everything, but not much afraid of any one item, so no brief reminder elicits much response. People with panic disorder were intermediate (Cuthbert et al., 2003). That is, anxiety disorders vary from being intensely frightened by a few items to being mildly frightened by many items.

Causes of Anxiety Disorders

Some people are more prone than others to strong fears. Children who show excessive anxieties are more likely than others to become adults with anxiety disorders (Otto et al., 2001). Even when people are in the same dangerous situation, and even when they seem to be equally powerless, some seem more frightened than others. Of people exposed to virtually the same traumatic experience, some develop problems such as PTSD, and some do not. Why?

Many people develop fears after painful experiences. For example, sexually abused children are, on the average, more likely than others to develop both fear-related disorders (Friedman et al., 2002) and depression (E. Nelson et al., 2002). John B. Watson, one of the pioneers of American psychology, was the first to try to demonstrate learned fears experimentally, although by today's standards his research was flawed both scientifically and ethically. He first demonstrated that a young orphan named "Little Albert" was not afraid of white rats. From then on, every time Little Albert saw a white rat, Watson struck a loud gong nearby. After a few such pairings, Albert reacted to the sight of a white rat by crying, trembling, and moving away (Watson & Rayner, 1920).

A few people can trace the onset of their phobias to a personal experience—such as one person who found a dead body in a lake and thereafter had a phobia of water (Kendler et al., 1995)—but most people do not recall any experience that led to their phobias. Investigators in one study identified people with a phobia, each of whom had a twin. Some individuals with a phobia could trace their phobia to a frightening experience; others could not. Researchers found the same elevated risk of phobia in twins of those who could and those who could not recall an experience that started their phobia (Kendler, Myers, & Prescott, 2002). In other words, there was no evidence that having a shocking experience increased the risk of phobia beyond whatever risk already was present, based on genetic factors. This does not mean that environment is irrelevant. However, as with loss and depression, most people will encounter a frightening experience that *could* lead to a phobia, and only some people develop them. Genetic predispositions may be important in determining people's responses.

Both panic disorder and phobias are more common among people who have relatives with similar disorders, especially if those with the disorders are close relatives such as identical twins (Hettema, Neale, & Kendler, 2001; Kendler, Myers, Prescott, & Neale, 2001; Skre, Onstad, Torgerson, Lygren, & Kringlen, 2000). Those results imply a genetic predisposition. But how might such a predisposition act? One of the neurotransmitters found in the amygdala (as well as elsewhere in the brain) is serotonin. We have previously discussed a gene that controls production of the serotonin transporter protein, implicated in neuroticism and depression. Several studies found that people with the "short" form of this gene were more likely to develop

various anxiety disorders than were people with the "long" form of the gene. One study used fMRI to measure amygdala responses as people examined photographs showing expressions of anger or fear. Those with the "short" form of the gene showed stronger responses in the amygdala (Hariri et al., 2002). Another study found that people with the short form of the gene learned cues of danger more quickly in a fear-conditioning paradigm (Lonsdorf, Weike, Nikamo, Schalling, Hamm, & Öhman, 2009). Presumably, alteration in serotonin activity led to an over-responsive amygdala, which is related to anxiety disorders (Rosen & Schulkin, 1998). However, not everyone with this gene develops a disorder, and some people without it do. This is presumably not the only gene that influences disposition to experience fear, and its influence by itself is limited.

At one time, PTSD seemed like a perfect example of a disorder caused purely by experience, but now PTSD too appears to be influenced by genetic predispositions. Long-term studies of people who were severely injured in automobile accidents have found that the intensity of anxiety and stress early after the accident has almost no relationship to the probability of developing PTSD later (Harvey & Bryant, 2002; Shaley et al., 2000). That is, even if two people have the same experience and react about the same way to it immediately, one might develop PTSD while the other one does not.

One reason for the difference relates to brain anatomy. On the average, people with PTSD have a smaller than average hippocampus, a brain area responsible for control of stress hormones in addition to its more widely known role in memory (Garfinkel & Liberzon, 2009; Stein, Hanna, Koverola, Torchia, & McClarty, 1997). To determine whether that brain difference developed as a result of PTSD or prior to it, investigators examined pairs of identical male twins. One member of each pair had developed PTSD during war, whereas the other had not been in battle and thus had not developed PTSD. The investigators found that *both* twins had a smaller than average hippocampus

(Gilbertson et al., 2002). That is, the hippocampus was probably smaller than average before development of PTSD; it was a predisposing factor, not a result of PTSD.

Treating Anxiety Disorders

As with depression, treatment for anxiety disorders often involves talk therapy and/or medication. Cognitive therapy, described above for depression, can also be effective in treating generalized anxiety disorder and panic disorder (Dugas, Brillon, Savard, Turcotte, Gaudet, Ladouceur, et al., 2010; Marchand, Roberge, Primiano, & Germain, 2009; McLean & Woody, 2001). In GAD, the therapy may emphasize identifying feelings of worry, developing greater tolerance for uncertainty (recall that low certainty appraisals have been strongly associated with feelings of fear), and learning to solve problems constructively rather than ruminating about them. In panic disorder, treatment may also emphasize reinterpreting physiological symptoms so they are perceived as less threatening and more tolerable.

Specific phobias are often treated using a technique called **exposure therapy**. Imagine that you, like one of the authors of this textbook, are deathly afraid of spiders. A therapist would first make sure you are comfortable and feel safe, in a nice comfy chair and a cheerfully lit room. Then, she would ask you to imagine a small spider, minding its own business several feet away. This might make you nervous at first, but the therapist would encourage you to hold the image in place until you get used to it. During the next session things escalate a bit— you are asked to imagine a larger spider nearby. After a few sessions, you dispense with the imagined spiders and bring in some real ones—first a small one, on the other side of the room. Again, you sit quietly and focus on staying calm until the spider no longer bothers you. In subsequent sessions the spider will be brought closer, and you may even get to where you can cope with touching it.

The idea here is that you are exposed to the object of your fear in increasing doses that you can just tolerate, until you get used to it and are ready to move up a level. If you can put up with some discomfort along the way, this treatment is extremely effective. One study using EEG methods found that arachnophobic women who had completed exposure therapy showed reduced signs of attention to photographs of spiders, compared with a non-treated control group (Leutgeb, Schäfer, & Scheinle, 2009). Another study found that exposure therapy for arachnophobia led to reduced self-reported distress while viewing spider pictures, and that this distress reduction was correlated with levels of activation in the amygdala (Scheinle, Schäfer, Hermann, Rohrmann, & Vaitl, 2007).

Most drugs that relieve anxiety are in a class known as **tranquilizers**. The most common ones fall into a biochemical class known as the *benzodiazepines* (BEN-zo-di-AZ-uh-peens). Examples include diazepam (trade name Valium), chlordiazepoxide (Librium), and alprazolam (Xanax). These drugs can be given as injections, but are more commonly taken as pills. Their effects last for hours, and the duration varies from one drug to another.

Tranquilizers act by facilitating the effectiveness of a neurotransmitter known as GABA.[1] GABA is the main inhibitory neurotransmitter throughout the nervous system, including the amygdala. Thus tranquilizers suppress activity in the amygdala, decreasing the response to threatening or otherwise emotional stimuli. However, they also suppress activity in much of the rest of the brain producing drowsiness and memory impairment. Tranquilizers temporarily produce some of the same emotional effects that amygdala damage produces permanently. For example, people on tranquilizers have trouble identifying other people's facial expressions of emotion, such as anger or fear (Zangara, Blair, & Curran, 2002). It's important to recognize, therefore, that GABA is not exclusively an "anti-fear" neurotransmitter—it is the main inhibitory neurotransmitter throughout the brain for a huge variety of functions.

---

1. GABA is an abbreviation for gamma-aminobutyric acid. Mercifully, people almost always use the abbreviation, not the whole term.

Other chemicals modify amygdala activity also. The neurotransmitter cholecystokinin (CCK) has excitatory effects on the amygdala, acting about the opposite of GABA (Becker et al., 2001; Frankland, Josselyn, Bradwejn, Vaccarino, & Yeomans, 1997; Strzelczuk & Romaniuk, 1996). Cortisol and other stress-related hormones increase the responsiveness of the amygdala, whereas alcohol decreases it (Nie et al., 2004). In that regard, alcohol resembles tranquilizers, decreasing anxiety and therefore reducing the social inhibitions that deter people from approaching strangers. As we have seen, however, amygdala activation is not the same thing as fear, so these chemicals are probably not fear-specific either.

OBSESSIVE-COMPULSIVE DISORDERS

Unlike mood disorders such as depression, and the anxiety disorders, obsessive-compulsive disorder is not defined primarily in terms of emotion. The DSM-IV defines **obsessions** as recurrent and persistent thoughts, impulses, and images that are experienced as intrusive and inappropriate, and cause marked anxiety or distress. **Compulsions** are repetitive behaviors, such as hand washing or ordering, or mental acts, such as counting things or repeating words, that a person feels internal pressure to perform in response to obsessive thoughts. In order to qualify for diagnosis, the obsessive thoughts must not be exaggerated but reasonable worries, and compulsions must not be connected realistically with some practical outcome. For example, persistent worry about how you are going to pay your bills this month is not technically an obsession if this is a realistic concern for you. Washing your hands is not a compulsion if you are around a lot of sick people, and the frequency is consistent with what is needed to keep you healthy.

Although the core symptoms of obsessive-compulsive disorder (OCD) mainly involve thoughts and behaviors, diagnosable obsessions must cause anxiety or distress, and a true compulsion will cause anxiety until the action is taken. In the fourth edition of the DSM, obsessive-compulsive disorder is classified as an anxiety disorder. For a number of reasons, however, researchers are considering removing OCD from the anxiety disorder category and creating a new category with a greater emphasis on the compulsive symptoms (Hollander, Braun, & Simeon, 2008).

Anxiety is not the only type of emotion distinctly associated with OCD. Feelings of disgust also tend to be especially strong among people with this disorder, as well as people with strong but sub-clinical obsessive symptoms (Olatunji, Tolin, Huppert, & Lohr, 2005). This is especially true for those whose obsessions involve contamination concerns, consistent with the theory that the function of disgust is to prevent contact with disease (Olatunji, Lohr, Sawchuck, & Tolin, 2007).

ANTISOCIAL PERSONALITY DISORDER AND EMPATHY

So far we have focused mainly on disorders in which people feel too much emotion, or feel emotion in inappropriate circumstances. However, some psychological disorders may be characterized by insufficient emotion. One diagnosis of particular interest here is **antisocial personality disorder**, defined by failure to conform to social norms, deliberate deceitfulness, impulsivity, aggressiveness, reckless disregard for one's own and others' safety, consistent irresponsibility, and lack of remorse for harm one has caused to others. This set of symptoms overlaps with characteristics of "psychopathy" and "sociopathy," although these commonly used terms are not actually DSM-defined disorders. All three terms share a theme of willingness to harm or manipulate other people, with no concern for their well-being, and no signs of remorse.

Much research has noted profound deficits in empathy among people who exhibit psychopathic behavioral traits (Kirsch & Becker, 2007). In Chapter 9 we distinguished between empathic accuracy and emotional empathy, and this distinction turns out to be important in describing people with psychopathic traits. Although psychopathic adults are very good at *knowing* what other people are feeling, or empathic accuracy, they do not show signs of *feeling* what other people are feeling, or emotional empathy (Dadds, Hawes, Frost, Vassalo, Bunn, Hunter, & Merz, 2009).

In an interesting twist, children with psychopathic traits show deficits in empathic accuracy as well, suggesting a possible developmental trajectory for these kinds of problems. It may be that in normal development, emotional empathy is an innate ability (consistent with some proposals about the role of mirror neurons in empathy) that facilitates empathic accuracy at a young age. Individuals who lack innate emotional empathy may eventually learn to infer others' emotions on the basis of facial expressions, behaviors, and so forth, but empathic feelings will still be missing. Researchers studying twins have found that psychopathic personality symptoms are highly heritable, so genetic influence on this trait may be strong (Larsson, Andershed, & Lichtenstein, 2006).

If psychopathic behaviors are due partly to a lack of empathy for other people, then interventions that encourage empathy toward others may help reduce symptoms. One study with children showing psychopathic characteristics found that they were less aggressive against a supposed opponent in a computerized game (aggression was defined in terms of blasting the "other player" with a loud noise) if they received a written message communicating that person's distress (van Baardewijk, Stegge, Bushman, & Vermeiren, 2009). Given the findings described above, this intervention may have increased empathic accuracy without affecting emotional empathy. Unfortunately, such interventions may also teach people to manipulate people's emotions more effectively, increasing psychopathic symptoms in the future. More research is needed to determine whether emotional empathy can be affected by psychological interventions, or whether empathic accuracy interventions are enough to decrease antisocial behavior even in the absence of empathic feelings.

SUMMARY

Although we have emphasized the functional aspects of emotions repeatedly throughout this book, our emotion systems can go haywire. "Normal" variability in emotional responding is great, as we saw in Chapter 13. But when emotions become so extreme that they interfere with a person's ability to function effectively and have a satisfying life, treatment is needed. Treatment can include talk therapy and behavioral intervention as well as medication, and a combination of these is sometimes most effective.

KEY TERMS

agoraphobia: an excessive fear of public situations that would be difficult to escape in the event of a panic attack (p. 346)

antisocial personality disorder: failure to conform to social norms, deceitfulness, impulsivity, aggressiveness, disregard for safety, irresponsibility, and lack of remorse (p. 350)

atypical depression: depression characterized by increased appetite and weight gain, sleeping too much, and psychomotor retardation (p. 341)

Beck Depression Inventory: a multiple-choice questionnaire assessing symptoms of depression (p. 337)

bipolar disorders: mood disorders in which the person alternates between episodes of mania and depression (p. 345)

cognitive therapy: an approach that seeks to alter the explanatory styles and other dysfunctional cognitive biases that characterize disordered individuals (p. 342)

compulsions: repetitive behaviors or mental acts that a person feels internal pressure to perform in response to obsessive thoughts (p. 350)

Diagnostic and Statistical Manual of Mental Disorders (DSM): a publication that lists criteria to be used by clinical practitioners in diagnosing their patients (p. 336)

explanatory style: a characteristic way of making attributions for one's successes and failures (p. 341)

exposure therapy: a treatment for specific phobias in which the client is exposed to increasingly intense versions of the feared object, becoming comfortable with each version before proceeding to the next (p. 349)

generalized anxiety disorder (GAD): a disorder characterized by almost constant nervousness and a wide range of worries (p. 346)

hypomania: a state in which symptoms of mania are present, but these are not severe enough to cause problems in life (p. 345)

learned helplessness: failure to try to improve one's current situation, resulting from actual lack of control in a prior situation (p. 341)

major depressive episode: the experience of five or more of the symptoms for at least two weeks (p. 337)

manic episode: a period of time characterized by increased sense of energy, goal-directed activity, rapid thoughts and speech, and

pleasurable activity without regard for harmful consequences (p. 344)

obsessions: recurrent and persistent thoughts, impulses, and images that are experienced as intrusive and inappropriate (p. 350)

panic disorder: disorder characterized by repeated attacks of panic, with sharply increased heart rate, rapid breathing, noticeable sweating, trembling, and chest pains (p. 346)

post-traumatic stress disorder (PTSD): flashbacks and nightmares about a traumatic event, avoidance of reminders of it, and an exaggerated startle reflex (p. 347)

selective serotonin reuptake inhibitors, or SSRIs: antidepressant drugs that increase the amount of time serotonin remains in synapses (p. 343)

specific phobia: excessive fear of a particular object or situation, strong enough to interfere with normal life (p. 347)

Structured Clinical Interview for DSM disorders (SCID): an interview protocol that elicits information needed to diagnose a patient according to DSM standards (p. 337)

tranquilizers: drugs that slow overall brain activity, sometimes used to treat anxiety (p. 349)

typical or melancholic depression: depression characterized by decreased appetite and weight loss, insomnia, and psychomotor agitation (p. 340)

THOUGHT QUESTIONS

1. Depression is fairly common, and some researchers have suggested that such a common psychological response may have an evolutionary function. Given what you know about sadness and depression, can you think of a way that depression might be adaptive?

2. Some medications, including SSRIs, can be used to treat either depression or anxiety. What do depression and anxiety have in common? Can you think of a shared mechanism that might account for both?

SUGGESTIONS FOR RESEARCH PROJECTS

1. Identify people you know who have had a loss experience (such as a romantic breakup) or have failed at something important to them (such as an exam). Ask them about changes in their sleeping, eating, and motor activity after the event. Do the different events predict the types of symptoms people report?

SUGGESTIONS FOR FURTHER READING

Smith, L. L., & Elliott, C. H. (2003). *Depression for Dummies*. New York: Wiley. Written by two practicing clinical psychologists, this is a great overview of clinical depression.

Epilogue

We've now reached the end of our journey through the psychological research on emotion. On the one hand, we hope you are impressed with how much you learned along the way. On the other hand, we hope you have even more questions about emotion now than when you began! Emotion research has come a long way in the last couple of decades. It would be hard to appreciate the extent of that progress unless you looked at what introductory psychology texts said about emotion 20 years ago (there weren't any textbooks on emotion). Despite all this progress, however, the biggest challenges for researchers still lie ahead.

At the beginning of this textbook we posed several big questions, and although we offered tentative answers, we also noted that researchers still wrestle with those issues today. Now that you've had a chance to immerse yourself in emotion research, let's revisit those questions.

WHAT IS EMOTION?

The first question we addressed was the most fundamental: What is emotion? We offered the following, tentative definition as an example: "An emotion is a universal, functional reaction to an external stimulus event, temporally integrating physiological, cognitive, phenomenological, and behavioral channels to facilitate a fitness-enhancing, environment-shaping response to the current situation" (Keltner & Shiota, 2003, p. 89).

We hope you find this definition easier to understand at the end of the book than it probably was at the beginning. It shares common elements with definitions offered by dozens of other theorists, including the notion that emotions have several aspects that work together. According to this perspective, emotions are not just subjective feelings—they reflect measurable changes in our bodies, they are predictable responses to events in the environment (or at least our interpretation of those events), and they have meaningful effects on our thoughts and behavior. Although we often think of emotion as the most private part of our experience, emotions have a tremendous impact on how we interact with the world around us.

A core feature of this definition is its emphasis on function. Far from being damaging or disruptive, emotions serve us well, on average, facilitating sensible, helpful responses to certain kinds of situations. In Chapter 2 we proposed that emotions served adaptive functions in the evolutionary sense, helping our ancestors to survive threats and to pass on their genes. For example, individuals who feared large, quickly moving objects—such as attacking tigers or stampeding elephants—did not have to think carefully about whether to hide from them or get out of their way. In other cases, emotions may have increased our ancestors' reproductive success by cementing and smoothing interpersonal relationships. From this perspective, different "basic" emotions likely evolved to facilitate adaptive responses to several, qualitatively different threats and opportunities. Because emotions would have solved adaptive problems faced by our ancestors long ago, before humans became a distinct species, researchers working from an evolutionary perspective tend to seek out universal aspects of emotion—our emotional human nature.

When we talk about evolutionary functions of emotion, we are talking about function in the hunter-gatherer environment our ancestors lived in tens or hundreds of thousands of years ago. Those of you reading this textbook live in a very different environment today. Our social networks are far larger, yet often more distant. Modern urban, and even suburban and rural, ways of life present very different threats and opportunities. Are our emotional responses still functional? Are some emotions more functional than others? Are emotions more functional in some kinds of situations than others? If you could change anything about your emotions, what would it be, and what effect would it have on your overall life?

Although we have emphasized the definition above (and others like it) throughout much of the textbook, we also noted that it poses serious difficulty for researchers. If emotions are defined as "packages" of appraisals, feelings, physiological changes, and behaviors, then is a combination of any three of these aspects without the fourth *not* an emotion? How often do you really get all four aspects, anyway? A number of researchers have proposed that the feeling aspect of emotion should be considered primary. Many studies find that emotional feelings can be explained well in terms of two or three dimensions, such as positive versus negative valence and degree of arousal, rather than the "basic emotion" categories implied by English-language emotion words.

From this "dimensional" perspective, the relationship of emotional feelings to other aspects becomes an empirical question. Rather than proposing that basic emotion packages will be similar across cultures, reflecting "human nature," researchers working from a dimensional perspective may ask how emotional feelings relate to appraisals, physiological changes, and observable behaviors in different cultures. Emotions are still thought to be functional, but the emphasis is on function in the context of a particular society with particular values and norms, rather than on situations faced by all humans.

The "basic emotion" and "dimensional" perspectives each posit a particular structure for the substrates of emotion in the brain, and also offer hypotheses about the physiological aspects of emotion. Does the body simply experience undifferentiated arousal, which it then interprets as pleasurable or aversive depending on the situation? Or do different emotions have qualitatively different profiles of physiological responding? Are there networks supporting a few universal, basic emotions in the brain, or is our emotional hard-wiring limited to distinguishing good from bad? As we saw in Chapters 4 and 5, researchers have no definite answers to these questions. Although the technologies for measuring emotion-related changes in the body and brain are astounding, they are still too new to allow for a sure answer either way. As Jim Russell (2003) has put it, the autonomic specificity hypothesis and hypotheses about discrete emotions in the brain are still "viable but unconfirmed."

After everything you've read in this textbook, how would you define "emotion?" Do any of the definitions proposed by earlier researchers ring true? Do you gravitate toward the basic emotion approach, or toward a more dimensional approach? Can you think of a way to reconcile these two perspectives? Alternatively, does Component Process Theory seem more plausible to you? What kinds of studies might you conduct if you were to adopt each perspective, or if you wanted to pit the perspectives against each other?

HOW DO WE MEASURE EMOTION?

Measurement is an important and contentious issue in any area of science, and we have returned to this point repeatedly. Measurement is especially challenging for emotion researchers. First, if researchers do not agree on how to define emotion, then they will have trouble agreeing on how to measure it. Second, according to all of the definitions we have considered, emotion is something we have to *infer* in other people; we cannot observe it directly. Whether you define emotions primarily as subjective feelings, or as functional packages of feelings with appraisals, physiological changes, and behaviors, there is no clear, objective criterion for when an emotion has occurred.

For this reason, researchers may try to use multiple measures of emotion, and see whether they agree with each other. Each strategy for measuring emotion has strengths and weaknesses. Self-report measures may be subjective and inconsistent, but they travel well. Physiological and behavioral measures usually require observing research participants in a laboratory or other, very controlled situation. But in the lab we elicit mild emotions, at best— strong emotions happen in real life. We can't measure people's heart rate and blood pressure when they have just escaped an automobile accident or as they are falling in love, at least not with current technologies. So, researchers using these more objective measures are often studying "emotion lite," and we have to make certain assumptions in generalizing the findings to more powerful situations.

When it is possible to take multiple measures of emotion, what if the different measures disagree? Which kind of measure should be the "gold standard?" In most studies presented in this textbook, self-reported emotion was the primary or only measurement, even though many researchers question the validity of self-reports. For the last several years research on emotional brain activity has been hugely popular, suggesting that the ideal measure might be activation in some emotion-specific brain area. This is a huge oversimplification, however, saying that certain areas of the brain become more active during an emotion is not the same as saying that the area becomes active *only* with emotion. Besides, how do we know it becomes active during emotion, except by correlating it with another measure—such as self-report?

Why do we care so much about measurement? First, scientific progress almost always depends on improved measurements. Second, results of emotion research vary with different measures. For example, researchers studying the causes of anger offer different explanations depending on whether they are explaining self-reports of anger or aggressive behavior. Even different kinds of self-report measures may lead to different conclusions. For example, guilt and shame look quite similar when people are simply asked to describe experiences that made them feel one of these emotions, but dispositionally shame-prone people react to social situations quite differently than guilt-prone people.

When reading through the studies we've described in this textbook, did you ever find yourself questioning the methods used to elicit emotion, or the way in which emotion was measured? Which studies did you find most convincing, and what kinds of measures did they use?

WHAT CAUSES EMOTIONS?

Another major question is: What causes emotions? In Chapter 1 we compared a few major theories of emotion, each with a different answer to this question. The James-Lange theory proposes a fairly specific sequence to the emotion process: an event takes place; we interpret or "appraise" the event in a particular way, that appraisal leads to specific patterns of physical changes, the physical changes facilitate certain behaviors, and the physical changes and behaviors in turn create our "feelings" of emotion. The Cannon-Bard theory also emphasized events as causes of emotion. In contrast, the Schachter-Singer theory proposes that emotions start with non-specific physiological arousal, which may or may not be due to current events. Feelings of arousal make us look to the situation for an explanation, and we conclude that we are feeling an emotion (as well as which emotion we are feeling) based upon what is going on around us.

Of these three, the current literature best supports some version of the James-Lange theory. You had to take our word for this in Chapter 1, but by now you've seen for yourself how much this theory has influenced emotion research over the last couple of decades. Throughout the chapters on specific emotions, we saw how people's interpretation of situations seems to predict their emotional responses. The cross-cultural study of emotional appraisals found remarkable similarity around the world in how people interpreted situations that evoked particular emotions. Several studies, like the studies of physiological reactions to subliminal photos of spiders, snakes, and people's facial expressions suggest that we sometimes appraise an event's emotional significance before we're even consciously aware of the event! In Chapter 6, we noted that re-appraisal is a particularly effective way for people to alter or change their emotions.

However, the Schachter-Singer perspective has also given birth to strong research challenging the assumption that emotional appraisals are necessary for emotion. In Chapter 8, we examined evidence that people tend to become angry and aggressive whenever they experience unexplained physiological arousal. We've also seen evidence that people show physiological signs of emotion even without being consciously aware of the stimulus as when people show skin conductance responses and heart rate changes to subliminal pictures of spiders. This suggests that appraisal (at least conscious appraisal) may not be needed for an emotion to occur.

Much of this debate may depend on how a given researcher defines "appraisal." We have discussed two major approaches in this text: Component Process Theory, which emphasizes a common set of appraisal dimensions, and Lazarus's (1991) Core Relational Themes, which are more categorical and should lead to the experience of particular basic emotions. In each of these approaches "appraisal" is fairly complex and abstract. However, "appraisal" may be as simple as the awareness that your heart is beating faster, or a quick classification of some event as good or bad for you. Whether you think appraisal is necessary for emotion depends in part on which definition you are using. However, the possibility that physiological changes can lead to emotions independent of what is going on around us is still largely unexplored.

HOW DO EMOTIONS AFFECT OUR LIVES?

We hope that by now you agree that emotions affect every aspect of our lives! In Chapter 4, we discussed implications of stress and related emotions for physical health. In several places, especially Chapters 8, 9, and 11, we discussed the implications of emotions for our relationships with other people. In Chapter 14, we showed that emotions affect every aspect of our cognition from what we remember to how we solve problems. This means that emotions are important in just about every sub-field of Psychology.

Perhaps the most obvious application of emotion is to Social Psychology, and in fact many emotion researchers were trained primarily as social psychologists. This is increasingly true as researchers acknowledge that emotions have social functions, as well as intrapersonal ones. Four emotions that are widely accepted as "basic" (fear, anger, disgust, sadness) all have something in common: their function is to keep you alive and out of danger. But researchers are increasingly interested in another function of emotion, that of developing and maintaining relationships with other people. For the various kinds of love, and the self-conscious emotions, social functions are the main or only ones.

Social psychologists are also interested in the role of culture in emotion. The definition of emotion we offered in Chapter 1 emphasized universal aspects of emotion. In Chapter 3 and beyond, however, we've emphasized how people's day-to-day emotional experiences can differ, depending on their culture. Universality and cultural differences may seem like opposing claims, but they don't need to be. Even if the "foundation" of emotions consists of universal links among certain appraisals, physiological reactions, and behavior impulses, much room remains for cultural influences. People in different cultures can find different meaning in the same event. Cultures may use very different conceptual categories when thinking about emotion, and can talk about emotion in different ways. Cultures may also have quite different rules for what emotions to express or conceal in various kinds of situations. Although the majority of research on emotion still emphasizes what is universal, or nearly so, researchers are becoming more interested in explaining the aspects of emotion that differ between cultures.

An understanding of emotion is also critical in Developmental Psychology. Some of the most carefully studied processes in early development—learning about the world, developing relationships with others—are driven largely by emotion. Since very young children can't tell us what they're thinking, we often use their emotional reactions to get a sense of how they interpret their world. Researchers also learn a lot about emotions by looking at how they develop in children—for example, some of the most illuminating research on the self-conscious emotions has come from psychologists interested in the development of self-awareness and the ability to guess what others are thinking and feeling.

Although Western philosophy typically separates emotion from reason, treating these as conflicting forces, psychologists now recognize how intertwined feeling and thinking are. We've seen how pervasive the effects of emotion are on all aspects of cognition, from attention, to memory, to

judgment and decision-making. We've seen that even when brain-damaged people retain the ability to reason their way through simple problems, a lack of emotional responding can destroy their judgment. And we've seen that emotions can prompt sensible or lasting decisions even in the absence of rational logic. Of course, emotions can bias our thinking as well as guide it. Fear makes everything around us look like a threat, and we may pass up important opportunities because of fear alone. Conversely, an opportunity for reward can feel so compelling that we ignore the low probability of success, or even the serious risks involved. By learning when emotions may guide us to better decisions, as well as how they bias our judgment, we gain greater control over our lives.

Clinical psychologists spend most of their time dealing with people's emotional difficulties. Many clinical diagnoses, such as depression, mania, and anxiety disorder, are based primarily on excessive amounts of one emotion or another. In learning about the biological characteristics of these disorders and in finding effective ways to treat them, we also learn much about the emotions themselves. At the same time, knowing more about "normal" versions of these emotions may help guide treatment more effectively, where in the past treatments have often been identified through trial and error.

Finally, and most important, emotion is a part of our everyday lives. Sometimes the emotions we feel contribute to our quality of life, and sometimes they interfere with it. We deal with other people's emotions—pleasant and unpleasant ones—all the time. Emotions help us make our way through the world effectively, and listening to them is generally a good idea. In the modern world, however, our instinctive emotional responses may sometimes lead us astray. Fortunately, emotions are not beyond our control. With practice, we can learn to manage our own emotions, and to understand and respond to other people's emotions more effectively. We hope that you've learned some things from this text that improve your life, and we wish you great happiness—however you define it!

References

Abbar, M., Courtet, P., Bellivier, F., Leboyer, M., Boulenger, J. P., Castelhau, D., et al. (2001). Suicide attempts and the tryptophan hydroxylase gene. *Molecular Psychiatry, 6,* 268–273.

Abbey, A. (1982). Sexual differences in attributions for friendly behavior: Do males misperceive females' friendliness? *Journal of Personality and Social Psychology, 42,* 830–838.

Abercrombie, H. C., Kalin, N. H., Thurow, M. E., Rosenkranz, M. A., & Davidson, R. J. (2003). Cortisol variation in humans affects memory for emotionally laden and neutral information. *Behavioral Neuroscience, 117,* 505–516.

Abramov, I., Gordon, J., Hendrickson, A., Hainline, L., Dobson, V., & LaBossiere, E. (1982). The retina of the newborn human infant. *Science, 217,* 265–267.

Abu-Lughod, L. (1986). *Veiled sentiments.* Berkeley: University of California Press.

Ackerman, J. M., Becker, D. V., Mortensen, C. R., Sasaki, T., Neuberg, S. L., & Kenrick, D. T. (2009). A pox on the mind: Disjunction of attention and memory in the processing of physical disfigurement. *Journal of Experimental Social Psychology, 45*(3), 478–485.

Ackermann, R., & DeRubeis, R. J. (1991). Is depressive realism real? *Clinical Psychology Review, 11,* 565–584.

Adamec, R. E., Stark-Adamec, C., & Livingston, K. E. (1980). The development of predatory aggression and defense in the domestic cat (*Felis catus*): 3. Effects on development of hunger between 180 and 365 days of age. *Behavioral and Neural Biology, 30,* 435–447.

Adams, R. B., & Kleck, R. E. (2003). Perceived gaze direction and the processing of facial displays of emotion. *Psychological Science, 14,* 644–647.

Adler, A. (1927). *Understanding human nature.* New York: Greenberg.

Admon, R., Lubin, G., Stern, O., Rosenberg, K., Sela, L., Ben-Ami, H., et al. (2009). Human vulnerability to stress depends on amygdala's predisposition and hippocampal plasticity. *Proceedings of the National Academy of Sciences (U.S.A.), 106,* 14120–14125.

Adolph, K. E. (2000). Specificity of learning: Why infants fall over a veritable cliff. *Psychological Science, 11,* 290–295.

Adolphs, R., Baron-Cohen, S., & Tranel, D. (2002). Impaired recognition of social emotions following amygdala damage. *Journal of Cognitive Neuroscience, 14,* 1264–1274.

Adolphs, R., Damasio, H., & Tranel, D. (2002). Neural systems for recognition of emotional prosody: A 3-D lesion study. *Emotion, 2,* 23–51.

Adolphs, R., Denburg, N. L., & Tranel, D. (2001). The amygdala's role in long-term declarative memory for gist and detail. *Behavioral Neuroscience, 115,* 983–992.

Adolphs, R., & Tranel, D. (1999). Preferences for visual stimuli following amygdala damage. *Journal of Cognitive Neuroscience, 11,* 610–616.

Adolphs, R., Tranel, D., & Damasio, A. R. (1998). The human amygdala in social judgment. *Nature, 393,* 470–474.

Adolphs, R., Tranel, D., Damasio, H., & Damasio, A. (1994). Impaired recognition of emotion in facial expressions following bilateral damage to the human amygdala. *Nature, 372,* 669–672.

Adolphs, R., Tranel, D., Damasio, H., & Damasio, A. R. (1995). Fear and the human amygdala. *Journal of Neuroscience, 15,* 5879–5891.

Ainsworth, M. D. S. (1989). Attachments beyond infancy. *American Psychologist, 44,* 709–716.

Akirav, I., & Richer-Levin, G. (1999). Biphasic modulation of hippocampal plasticity by behavioral stress and basolateral amygdala stimulation in the rat. *Journal of Neuroscience, 19,* 10530–10535.

Akiskal, H. S., & Benazzi, F. (2005). Atypical depression: A variant of bipolar II or a bridge between unipolar and bipolar II? *Journal of Affective Disorders. Special Issue: Bipolar Depression: Focus on Phenomenology, 84* (2-3), 209–217.

Aleman, A., Swart, M., & van Rijn, S. (2008). Brain imaging, genetics and emotion. *Biological Psychology, 79,* 58–69.

Alloy, L. B., & Abramson, L. Y. (1979). Judgment of contingency in depressed and nondepressed students: Sadder but wiser? *Journal of Experimental Psychology: General, 108,* 441–485.

Alloy, L. B., Abramson, L. Y., Whitehouse, W. G., Hogan, M. E., Tashman, N. A., Steinberg, D. L., et al. (1999). Depressogenic cognitive styles: Predictive validity, information processing and personality characteristics, and developmental origins. *Behaviour Research and Therapy, 37,* 503–531.

Ambadar, Z., Schooler, J. W., & Cohn, J. F. (2005). Deciphering the enigmatic face. *Psychological Science, 16,* 403–410.

American Enterprise (1992, January/February). Women, men, marriages, and ministers (p. 106).

American Psychiatric Association. (1994). *Diagnostic and statistical manual of psychiatric disorders* (4th ed.). Washington, D.C.: Author.

Amodio, D. M., Devine, P. G., & Harmon-Jones, E. (2007). A dynamic model of guilt. *Psychological Science, 18,* 524–530.

Anderson, A. K., & Phelps, E. A. (2002). Is the human amygdala critical for the subjective experience of emotion? Evidence of intact dispositional affect in patients with amygdala lesions. *Journal of Cognitive Neuroscience, 14,* 709–720.

Anderson, C., Keltner, D., & John, O. P. (2003). Emotional convergence between people over time. *Journal of Personality and Social Psychology, 84,* 1054–1068.

Anderson, C. A. (2001). Heat and violence. *Current Directions in Psychological Science, 10,* 33–38.

Angrilli, A., Mauri, A., Palomba, D., Flor, H., Birbaumer, N., Sartori, G., & di Paola, F. (1996). Startle reflex and emotion modulation impairment after a right amygdala lesion. *Brain: A Journal of Neurology, 119*(6), 1991–2000.

Antoniadis, E. A., Winslow, J. T., Davis, M., & Amaral, D. G. (2007). Role of the primate amygdala in fear-potentiated startle. *Journal of Neuroscience, 27,* 7386–7396.

Arana, G. W. (2000). An overview of side effects caused by typical antipsychotics. *Journal of Clinical Psychiatry, 61*(Suppl. 8), 5–11.

Archer, J., Birring, S. S., & Wu, F. C. W. (1998). The association between testosterone and aggression in young men: Empirical findings and a meta-analysis. *Aggressive Behavior, 24,* 411–420.

Archer, J., Graham-Kevan, N., & Davies, M. (2005). Testosterone and aggression: A reanalysis of Book, Starzyk, and Quinsey's (2001) study. *Aggression and Violent Behavior, 10,* 241–261.

Armor, D. A., Massey, C., & Sackett, A. M. (2008). Prescribed optimism: Is it right to be wrong about the future? *Psychological Science, 19,* 329–331.

Arnold, M. B. (1960). *Emotion and personality* (Vols. *1–2*). New York: Columbia University Press.

Arnold, M. J., & Reynolds, K. E. (2003). Hedonic shopping motivations. *Journal of Retailing, 79,* 77–95.

Arnow, B. A., & Post, L. I. (2010). Depression. In D. McKay, J. S. Abramowitz & S. Taylor (Eds.), *Cognitive-behavioral therapy for refractory cases: Turning failure into success.* (pp. 183–210). Washington, D.C., U.S.: American Psychological Association.

Aron, A., Melinat, E., Aron, E. N., Vallone, R. D., & Bator, R. J. (1997). The experimental generation of interpersonal closeness: A procedure and some preliminary findings. *Personality and Social Psychology Bulletin, 23,* 363–377.

Aron, A., Norman, C. C., Aron, E. N., McKenna, C., & Heyman, R. E. (2000). Couples' shared participation in novel and arousing activities and experienced relationship quality. *Journal of Personality and Social Psychology, 78,* 273–284.

Aron, A., Paris, M., & Aron, E. N. (1995). Falling in love: Prospective studies of self-concept change. *Journal of Personality and Social Psychology, 69,* 1102–1112.

Arslan, C. (2009). Anger, self-esteem, and perceived social support in adolescence. *Social Behaviour and Personality, 37,* 555–564.

Ashton-Jones, C. E., Maddux, W. W., Galinsky, A. D., & Chartrand, T. L. (2009). Who I am depends on how I feel. *Psychological Science, 20,* 340–346.

Astington, J. W., & Gopnik, A. (1991). Theoretical explanations of children's understanding of the mind. *British Journal of Developmental Psychology. Special Perspectives on the Child's Theory of Mind, 9*(1), 7–31.

Augustine. (1955). *Confessions* (A. C. Outler, Trans.). (Original work written 397.) Retrieved Jan. 13, 2005, from www.ccel.org/a/augustine/confessions/confessions.html

Austin, E. J. (2004). An investigation of the relationship between trait emotional intelligence and emotional task performance. *Personality and Individual Differences, 36,* 1855–1864.

Austin, E. J., Saklofske, D. H., Huang, S. H. S., & McKenney, D. (2004). Measurement of trait emotional intelligence: Testing and cross-validating a modified version of Schutte et al.'s measure. *Personality and Individual Differences, 36,* 555–562.

Averill, J. R. (1983). Studies on anger and aggression: Implications for theories of emotion. *American Psychologist, 38,* 1145–1160.

Aviezer, H., Hassin, R. R., Ryan, J., Grady, C., Susskind, J., Anderson, A., et al. (2008). Angry, disgusted, or afraid? *Psychological Science, 19,* 724–732.

Ayduk, O., Mischel, W., & Downey, G. (2002). Attentional mechanisms linking rejection to hostile reactivity: The role of "hot" versus "cool" focus. *Psychological Science, 13,* 443–448.

Bäccman, C., Folkesson, P., & Norlander, T. (1999). Expectations of romantic relationships: A comparison between homosexual and heterosexual men with regard to Baxter's criteria. *Social Behavior and Personality, 27,* 363–374.

Bachorowski, J. A., & Owren, M. J. (2001). Not all laughs are alike: Voiced but not unvoiced laughter readily elicits positive affect. *Psychological Science, 12,* 252–257.

Bagwell, C. L., Newcomb, A. F., & Bukowski, W. M. (1998). Preadolescent friendship and peer rejection as predictors of adult adjustment. *Child Development, 69,* 140–153.

Baillargeon, R. (1986). Representing the existence and location of hidden objects: Object permanence in 6- and 8-month-old infants. *Cognition, 23,* 21–41

Baillargeon, R. (1987). Object permanence in 3 1/2- and 4 1/2-month-old infants. *Developmental Psychology, 23,* 655–664.

Baker, K. B., & Kim, J. J. (2004). Amygdalar lateralization in fear conditioning: Evidence for greater involvement of the right amygdala. *Behavioral Neuroscience, 118,* 15–23.

Balthazart, J., & Ball, G. F. (2007). Topography in the preoptic region: Differential regulation of appetitive and consummatory male sexual behaviors. *Frontiers in Neuroendocrinology, 28*(4), 161–178.

Banks, M. S., & Salapatek, P. (1983). Infant visual perception. In P. H. Mussen (Series Ed.), M. Haith & J. J. Campos (Vol. Eds.), *Handbook of child psychology: Vol 2. Infancy and developmental psychobiology* (4th ed., pp. 435–571). New York: Wiley.

Barazzone, N., & Davey, G. C. L. (2009). Anger potentiates the reporting of threatening interpretations: An experimental study. *Journal of Anxiety Disorders, 23,* 489–495.

Bard, P. (1934). On emotional expression after decortication with some remarks on certain theoretical views. *Psychological Review, 41,* 309–329.

Baron-Cohen, S. (1995). The eye direction detector (EDD) and the shared attention mechanism (SAM): Two cases for evolutionary psychology. In C. Moore, & P. J. Dunham (Eds.), *Joint Attention: Its Origins and Role in Development* (pp. 41–59). Hillsdale, NJ: Lawrence Erlbaum Associates, Inc.

Barr, C. S., Schwandt, M. L., Lindell, S. G., Higley, J. D., Maestripieri, D., Goldman, D., et al. (2008). Variation at the mu-opioid receptor gene (OPRM1) influences attachment behavior in infant primates. *Proceedings of the National Academy of Sciences of the United States of America, 105*(13), 5277–5281.

Barrett, L. F., & Fossum, T. (2001). Mental representations of affect knowledge. *Cognition and Emotion, 15*(3), 333–363.

Barrett, L. F., Bliss-Moreau, E., Duncan, S. L., Rauch, S. L., & Wright, C. I. (2007). The amygdala and the experience of affect. *Social Cognitive & Affective Neuroscience, 2,* 73–83.

Bartels, A., & Zeki, S. (2000). The neural basis of romantic love. *Neuroreport, 11,* 3829–3834.

Bartholomew, K. (1990). Avoidance of intimacy: An attachment perspective. *Journal of Social and Personal Relationships, 7,* 147–178.

Bartholomew, K., & Horowitz, L. M. (1991). Attachment styles among young adults: A test of a four-category model. *Journal of Personality and Social Psychology, 61,* 226–244.

Basabe, N., Paez, D., Valencia, J., Gonzalez, J. L., Rimé, B., & Diener, E. (2002). Cultural dimensions, socioeconomic development, climate, and emotional hedonic level. *Cognition and Emotion, 16,* 103–125.

Batson, C. D., O'Quin, K., Fultz, J., Vandeplas, M., & Isen, A. (1983). Self-reported distress and empathy and egoistic versus altruistic motivation for helping. *Journal of Personality and Social Psychology, 45,* 706–718.

Battaglia, M., Bertella, S., Ogliari, A., Bellodi, L., & Smereldi, E. (2001). Modulation by muscarinic antagonists of the response to carbon dioxide challenge in panic disorder. *Archives of General Psychiatry, 58,* 114–119.

Bauby, J. D. (1997). *The diving bell and the butterfly* (J. Leggatt. Trans.). New York: Knopf.

Baumeister, R. F., Smart, L., & Boden, J. M. (1996). Relation of threatened egotism to violence and aggression: The dark side of high self-esteem. *Psychological Review, 103,* 5–33.

Bäumler, G. (1994). On the validity of the Yerkes-Dodson law. *Studia Psychologica, 36,* 205–209.

Baxter, M. G., & Murray, E. A. (2002). The amygdala and reward. *Nature Reviews Neuroscience, 3,* 563–573.

Beaton, E. A., Schmidt, L. A., Schulkin, J., Antony, M. M., Swinson, R. P., & Hall, G. B. (2008). Different neural responses to stranger and personally familiar faces in shy and bold adults. *Behavioral Neuroscience, 122,* 704–709.

Beauregard, M., Lévesque, J., & Bourgouin, P. (2001). Neural correlates of conscious self-regulation of emotion. *Journal of Neuroscience, 21,* RC165.

Bechara, A. (2004). The role of emotion in decision-making: Evidence from neurological patients with orbitofrontal damage. *Brain and Cognition, 55,* 30–40.

Bechara, A., Damasio, H., Damasio, A. R., & Lee, G. P. (1999). Different contributions of the human amygdala and ventromedial prefrontal cortex to decision-making. *Journal of Neuroscience, 19,* 5473–5481.

Bechara, A., Tranel, D., Damasio, H., & Adolphs, R. (1995). Double dissociation of conditioning and declarative knowledge relative to the amygdala and hippocampus in humans. *Science, 269*(5227), 1115–1118.

Beck, A. T. (1973). *The diagnosis and management of depression.* Philadelphia: University of Pennsylvania Press.

Beck, A. T. (1987). Cognitive models of depression. *Journal of Cognitive Psychotherapy, 1,* 5–37.

Becker, C., Thiébot, M.-H., Touitou, Y., Hamon, M., Cesselin, F., & Benoliel, J. J. (2001). Enhanced cortical extracellular levels of cholecystokinin-like material in a model of anticipation of social defeat in the rat. *Journal of Neuroscience, 21,* 262–269.

Beebe, B. (2003). Brief mother-infant treatment: Psychoanalytically informed video feedback. *Infant Mental Health Journal, 24,* 24–52.

Beebe, B., Jaffe, J., Lachman, F., Feldstein, S., Crown, C., & Jasnow, M. (2000). Systems models in development and psychoanalysis: The case of vocal rhythm coordination and attachment. *Infant Mental Health Journal, 21,* 99–122.

Benet-Martínez, V., & John, O. P. (1998). *Los cinco grandes* across cultures and ethnic groups: Multitrait-multimethod analyses of the big five in spanish and english. *Journal of Personality and Social Psychology, 75*(3), 729–750.

Benjamin, J., Li, L., Patterson, C., Greenberg, B. D., Murphy, D. L., & Hamer, D. H. (1996). Population and familial association between the D4 dopamine receptor gene and measures of novelty seeking. *Nature Genetics, 12,* 81–84.

Benschop, R. J., Godaert, G. L. R., Geenen, R., Brosschot, J. F., DeSmet, M. B. M., Olff, M., et al. (1995). Relationships between cardiovascular and immunologic changes in an experimental stress model. *Psychological Medicine, 25,* 323–327.

Benson, H. (1985). Stress, health, and the relaxation response. In W. D. Gentry, H. Benson, & C. J. de Wolff (Eds.), *Behavioral medicine: Work, stress and health* (pp. 15–32). Dordrecht, Netherlands: Martinus Nijhoff.

Bentham, J. (1970). *An introduction to the principles of morals and legislation.* London: Methuen. (Original work published 1780.)

Berdoy, M., Webster, J. P., & Macdonald, D. W. (2000). Fatal attraction in rats infected with *Toxoplasma gondii. Proceedings of the Royal Society of London, B, 267,* 1591–1594.

Berghöfer, A., Alda, M., Adli, M., Baethge, C., Bauer, M., Bschor, T., et al. (2008). Long-term effectiveness of lithium in bipolar disorder: A multicenter investigation of patients with typical and atypical features. *Journal of Clinical Psychiatry, 69*(12), 1860–1868.

Berkowitz, L. (1990). On the formation and regulation of anger and aggression: A cognitive neo-associationistic analysis. *American Psychologist, 45,* 494–503.

Berkowitz, L., Cochran, S., & Embree, M. (1981). Physical pain and the goal of aversively stimulated aggression. *Journal of Personality and Social Psychology, 40,* 687–700.

Berkowitz, L., & Harmon-Jones, E. (2004). Toward an understanding of the determinants of anger. *Emotion, 4,* 107–130.

Berlin, H. A., Rolls, E. T., & Kischka, U. (2004). Impulsivity, time perception, emotion and reinforcement sensitivity in patients with orbitofrontal cortex lesions. *Brain, 127,* 1108–1126.

Berman, M., Gladue, B., & Taylor, S. (1993). The effects of hormones, Type A behavior pattern, and provocation on aggression in men. *Motivation and Emotion, 17,* 125–138.

Berman, M. E., McCloskey, M. S., Fanning, J. R., Schumacher, J. A., & Coccaro, E. F. (2009). Serotonin augmentation reduces response to attack in aggressive individuals. *Psychological Science, 20,* 714–720.

Bernhardt, P. C. (1997). Influences of serotonin and testosterone in aggression and dominance: Convergence with social psychology. *Current Directions in Psychological Science, 6,* 44–48.

Berntson, G. G., Bechara, A., Damasio, H., Tranel, D., & Cacioppo, J. T. (2007). Amygdala contribution to selective dimensions of emotion. *Social Cognitive & Affective Neuroscience, 2,* 123–129.

Berridge, K. C., & Robinson, T. E. (1995). The mind of an addicted brain: Neural sensitization of wanting versus liking. *Current Directions in Psychological Science, 4,* 71–76.

Berry, J. W., Worthington, E. L., Jr., O'Connor, L. E., Parrott, L., III, & Wade, N. G. (2005). Forgivingness, vengeful rumination, and affective traits. *Journal of Personality, 73*(1), 183–225.

Bersheid, E. (1983). Emotion. In H. H. Kelley, E. Bersheid, A. Christensen, J. H. Harvey, T. L. Huston, G. Levinger, et al., *Close relationships* (pp. 110–168). New York: W. H. Freeman.

Best, M., Williams, J. M., & Coccaro, E. F. (2002). Evidence for a dysfunctional prefrontal circuit in patients with an impulsive aggressive disorder. *Proceedings of the National Academy of Sciences, (USA), 99,* 8448–8453.

Bhattacharyya, M. R., Whitehead, D. L., Rakhit, R., & Steptoe, A. (2008). Depressed mood, positive affect, and heart rate variability in patients with suspected coronary artery disease. *Psychosomatic Medicine, 70*(9), 1020–1027.

Biben, M. (1979). Predation and predatory play behaviour of domestic cats. *Animal Behaviour, 27,* 81–94.

Bierut, L. J., Heath, A. C., Bucholz, K. K., Dinwiddie, S. H., Madden, P. A. F., Statham, D. J., et al. (1999). Major depressive disorder in a community-based twin sample. *Archives of General Psychiatry, 56,* 557–563.

Birbaum, M. H., & Sotoodeh, Y. (1991). Measurement of stress: Scaling the magnitudes of life changes. *Psychological Science, 2,* 236–243.

Birditt, K. S., & Fingerman, K. L. (2003). Age and gender differences in adults' descriptions of emotional reactions to interpersonal problems. *Journal of Gerontology: Psychological Sciences, B, 58,* 237–245.

Birnbaum, M. H. (1999). Testing critical properties of decision making on the Internet. *Psychological Science, 10,* 399–407.

Bishop, S. J., Duncan, J., & Lawrence, A. D. (2004). State anxiety modulation of the amygdala response to unattended threat-related stimuli. *Journal of Neuroscience, 24,* 10364–10368.

Blackford, J. U., & Walden, T. A. (1998). Individual differences in social referencing. *Infant Behavior and Development, 21,* 89–102.

Blair, R. J. R., Mitchell, D. G. V., Peschardt, K. S., Colledge, E., Leonard, R. A., Shine, J. H., et al. (2004). Reduced sensitivity to others' fearful expressions in psychopathic individuals. *Personality and Individual Differences, 37,* 1111–1122.

Blanchard-Fields, F., & Coats, A. H. (2008). The experience of anger and sadness in everyday problems impacts age differences in emotion regulation. *Developmental Psychology, 44,* 1547–1556.

Blascovich, J., & Tomaka, J. (1991). Measures of self-esteem. In J. P. Robinson, R. R. Shaver, & L. S. Wrightsman (Eds.), *Measures of personality and social psychological attitudes* (pp. 115–160). San Diego, CA: Academic Press.

Bless, H., Bohner, G., Schwarz, N., & Strack, F. (1990). Mood and persuasion: A cognitive response analysis. *Personality and Social Psychology Bulletin, 16,* 331–345.

Bless, H., Clore, G. L., Schwarz, N., Golisane, V., Rabe, C., & Wölk, M. (1996). Mood and the use of scripts: Does a happy mood really lead to mindlessness? *Journal of Personality and Social Psychology, 71,* 665–679.

Blood, A. J., & Zatorre, R. J. (2001). Intensely pleasurable responses to music correlate with activity in brain regions implicated in reward and emotion. *Proceedings of the National Academy of Sciences, 98,* 11818–11823.

Bodenhausen, G. V., Kramer, G. P., & Süsser, K. (1994). Happiness and stereotypic thinking in social judgment. *Journal of Personality and Social Psychology, 66,* 621–632.

Bodenhausen, G. V., Sheppard, L. A., & Kramer, G. P. (1994). Negative affect and social judgment: The differential impact of anger and sadness. *European Journal of Social Psychology. Special Issue: Affect in Social Judgments and Cognition, 24* (1), 45–62.

Bodner, G., Ho, A., & Kreek, M. J. (1998). Effect of endogenous cortisol levels on natural killer cell activity in healthy humans. *Brain, Behavior, and Immunity, 12,* 285–296.

Bohns, V. K., & Flynn, F. J. (2010). "Why didn't you just ask?" Underestimating the discomfort of help-seeking. *Journal of Experimental Social Psychology, 46,* 402–409.

Bolles, R. C. (1970). Species-specific defense reactions and avoidance learning. *Psychological Review, 77,* 32–48.

Bolte, A., Goschke, T., & Kuhl, J. (2003). Emotion and intuition: Effects of positive and negative mood on implicit judgments of semantic coherence. *Psychological Science, 14,* 416–421.

Bombar, M. L., & Littig, L. W., Jr. (1996). Babytalk as a communication of intimate attachment: An initial study in adult romances and friendships. *Personal Relationships, 3*(2), 137–158.

Bradley, M. M. (2009). Natural selective attention: Orienting and emotion. *Psychophysiology, 46*(1), 1–11.

Bond, A. J., Bauer, A., & Wingrove, J. (2004). Outcome of aggression affects processing and can legitimise subsequent aggression: Influence of trait aggressiveness. *Aggressive Behavior, 30,* 284–297.

Bond, M. H. (2002). Reclaiming the individual from Hofstede's ecological analysis—A 20-year odyssey: Comment on Oyserman et al. (2002). *Psychological Bulletin, 128,* 73–77.

Boucher, J. D. (1979). Culture and emotion. In A. J. Marsella, R. G. Tharp, & T. V. Ciborowski (Eds.), *Perspectives on cross-cultural psychology* (pp. 159–178). San Diego, CA: Academic Press.

Boucsein, K., Weniger, G., Mursch, K., Steinhoff, B. J., & Irle, E. (2001). Amygdala lesion in temporal lobe epilepsy subjects impairs associative learning of emotional facial expressions. *Neuropsychologia, 39,* 231–236.

Bould, E., Morris, N., & Wink, B. (2008). Recognizing subtle emotional expressions: The role of facial movements. *Cognition and Emotion, 22,* 1569–1587.

Bouton, M. E., Mineka, S., & Barlow, D. H. (2001). A modern learning theory perspective on the etiology of panic disorder. *Psychological Review, 108,* 4–32.

Bower, T. G. R. (1977). *A primer of infant development.* San Francisco: W. H. Freeman.

Bowlby, J. (1969). *Attachment and loss: Vol. 1: Attachment.* New York: Basic Books.

Bowlby, J. (1979). *The making and breaking of affectional bonds.* London: Tavistock Publications.

Bowlby, J. (1980). *Attachment and loss: Vol. 3: Loss: Sadness and depression.* New York: Basic Books.

Boyatzis, C. J., Matillo, G. M., & Nesbitt, K. M. (1995). Effect of the "Mighty Morphin Power Rangers" on children's aggression with peers. *Child Study Journal, 25*(1), 45–55.

Boyle, R. H. (1992, September–October). The joy of cooking insects. *Audubon, 94,* 100–103.

Bracha, H. S. (2006). Human brain evolution and the "neuroevolutionary time-depth principle": Implications for the reclassification of fear-circuitry-related traits in *DSM–V* and for studying resilience to warzone-related posttraumatic stress disorder. *Progress in Neuro-Psychopharmacology and Biological Psychiatry, 30,* 827–853.

Brackett, M. A., Mayer, J. D., & Warner, R. M. (2004). Emotional intelligence and its relation to everyday behaviour. *Personality and Individual Differences, 36,* 1387–1402.

Bradley, M. M. (2009). Natural selective attention: Orienting and emotion. *Psychophysioloigy, 46*(1), 1–11.

Bradley, M. M., Greenwald, M. K., Petry, M. C., & Lang, P. J. (1992). Remembering pictures: Pleasure and arousal in memory. *Journal of Experimental Psychology: Learning, Memory, and Cognition, 18,* 379–390.

Bradley, M. M., & Lang, O. J. (2000). Measuring emotion: Behavior, feeling, and physiology. In R. D. Lane & L. Nadel (Eds.), *Cognitive neuroscience of emotion* (pp. 242–276). New York: Oxford University Press.

Bradshaw, J. W. S., & Cook, S. E. (1996). Patterns of pet cat behaviour at feeding occasions. *Applied Animal Behaviour Science, 47*(1-2), 61–74.

Breiter, H. C., Aharon, I., Kahneman, D., Dale, A., & Shizgal, P. (2001). Functional imaging of neural responses to expectancy and experience of monetary gains and losses. *Neuron, 30,* 619–639.

Breiter, H. C., Etcoff, N. L., Whalen, P. J., Kennedy, W. A., Rauch, S. L., Buckner, R. L., et al. (1996). Response and habituation of the human amygdala during visual processing of facial expression. *Neuron, 17,* 875–887.

Bremner, J. D., Vythilingam, M., Anderson, G., Vermetten, E., McGlashan, T., Heninger, G., et al. (2003). Assessment of the hypothalamic-pituitary-adrenal axis over a 24-hour diurnal period and in response to neuroendocrine challenges in women with and without childhood sexual abuse and posttraumatic stress disorder. *Biological Psychiatry, 54,* 710–718.

Brennan, K. A., Clark, C. L., & Shaver, P. R. (1998). Self-report measurement of adult attachment: An integrative overview. In J. A. Simpson & W. S. Rholes (Eds.), *Attachment theory and close relationships* (pp. 46–76). New York: Guilford.

Brent, D. A., Oquendo, M., Birmaher, B., Greenhill, L., Kolko, D., Stanley, B., et al. (2002). Familial pathways to early onset sicide attempt: Risk for suicidal behavior in offspring of mood-disordered suicide attempters. *Archives of General Psychiatry, 59,* 801–807.

Bretherton, I., Fritz, J., Zahn-Waxler, C., & Ridgeway, D. (1986). Learning to talk about emotions: A functionalist perspective. *Child Development, 57,* 529–548.

Brooks, J. H., & Reddon, J. R. (1996). Serum testosterone in violent and nonviolent young offenders. *Journal of Clinical Psychology, 52,* 475–483.

Brosch, T., Sander, D., Pourtois, G., & Scherer, K. R. (2008). Beyond fear. *Psychological Science, 19,* 362–370.

Brown, G. P., MacLeod, A. K., Tata, P., & Goddard, L. (2002). Worry and the simulation of future outcomes. *Anxiety, Stress and Coping, 15,* 1–17.

Bruce, S. E., Machan, J. T., Dyck, I., & Keller, M. B. (2001). Infrequency of "pure" GAD: Impact of psychiatric comorbidity on clinical course. *Depression and Anxiety, 14,* 219–225.

Buchanan, T. W., Tranel, D., & Adolphs, R. (2009). The human amygdala in social function. In P. J. Whalen & E. A. Phelps (Eds.), *The human amygdala* (pp. 289–318). New York: Guilford Press.

Büchel, C., Morris, J., Dolan, R. J., & Friston, K. J. (1998). Brain systems mediating aversive conditioning: An event-related fMRI study. *Neuron, 20,* 947–957.

Buehler, R., Griffin, D., & Ross, M. (1994). Exploring the "planning fallacy": Why people underestimate their task completion times. *Journal of Personality and Social Psychology, 67,* 366–381.

Bukh, J. D., Bock, C., Vinberg, M., Werge, T., Gether, U., & Kessing, L. V. (2009). Interaction between genetic polymorphisms and stressful life events in first episode depression. *Journal of Affective Disorders, 119* (1-3), 107–115.

Bulbena, A., Gago, J., Martin-Santos, R., Porta, M., Dasquens, J., & Berrios, G. E. (2004). Anxiety disorder & joint laxity: A definitive link. *Neurology, Psychiatry and Brain Research, 11,* 137–140.

Bulbena, A., Gago, J., Sperry, L., & Bergé, D. (2006). The relationship between frequency and intensity of fears and a collagen condition. *Depression and Anxiety, 23,* 412–417.

Burgess, K. B., Marshall, P. J., Rubin, K. H., & Fox, N. A. (2003). Infant attachment and temperament as predictors of subsequent externalizing problems and cardiac physiology. *Journal of Child Psychology and Psychiatry, 44,* 819–831.

Burke, K. C., Burke, J. D., Jr., Regier, D. A., & Rae, D. S. (1990). Age at onset of selected mental disorders in five community populations. *Archives of General Psychiatry, 47,* 511–518.

Burleson, M. H., Poehlmann, K. M., Hawkley, L. C., Ernst, J. M., Berntson, G. G., Malarkey, W. B., et al. (2002). Stress-related immune changes in middle-aged and older women: 1-year consistency of individual differences. *Health Psychology, 21,* 321–331.

Burns, M. O., & Seligman, M. E. P. (1989). Explanatory style across the life span: Evidence for stability over 50 years. *Journal of Personality and Social Psychology, 56,* 471–477.

Burnstein, E., Crandall, C., & Kitayama, S. (1994). Some neo-darwinian decision rules for altruism: Weighing cues for inclusive fitness as a function of the biological importance of the decision. *Journal of Personality and Social Psychology, 67*(5), 773–789.

Burton, C. M., & King, L. A. (2004). The health benefits of writing about intensely positive experiences. *Journal of Research in Personality, 38,* 150–163.

Bushman, B. J., & Anderson, C. A. (2001). Media violence and the American public: Scientific facts versus media misinformation. *American Psychologist, 56,* 477–489.

Bushman, B. J., & Anderson, C. A. (2009). Comfortably numb: Desensitizing effects of violent media on helping others. *Psychological Science, 20,* 273–277.

Buss, D. M. (1989). Sex differences in human mate preferences: Evolutionary hypotheses tested in 37 cultures. *Behavioral and Brain Sciences, 12,* 1–49.

Buss, D. M. (2000). The evolution of happiness. *American Psychologist, 55,* 15–23.

Buss, D. M., Haselton, M. G., Shackelford, T. K., Bleske, A. L., & Wakefield, J. C. (1998). Adaptations, exaptations, and spandrels. *American Psychologist, 53*(5), 533–548.

Butler, E. A., Lee, T. L., & Gross, J. J. (2007). Emotion regulation and culture: Are the social consequences of emotion suppression culture-specific? *Emotion, 7*(1), 30–48.

Butler, E. A., Lee, T. L., & Gross, J. J. (2009). Does expressing your emotions raise or lower your blood pressure?: The answer depends on cultural context. *Journal of Cross-Cultural Psychology, 40*(3), 510–517.

Butler, E. A., Wilhelm, F. H., & Gross, J. J. (2006). Respiratory sinus arrhythmia, emotion, and emotion regulation during social interaction. *Psychophysiology, 43*(6), 612–622.

Buunk, B. P., & Van Yperen, N. W. (1991). Referential comparisons, relational comparisons, and exchange orientation: Their relation to marital satisfaction. *Personality and Social Psychology Bulletin, 17,* 709–717.

Buzi, R. S., Weinman, M. L., & Smith, P. B. (2007). The relationship between adolescent depression and a history of sexual abuse. *Adolescence, 42*(168), 679–688.

Bylsma, L. M., Vingerhoets, A. J. J. M., & Rottenberg, J. (2008). When is crying cathartic? an international study. *Journal of Social & Clinical Psychology, 27*(10), 1165–1187.

Byrne, G. J. A., Raphael, B., & Arnold, E. (1999). Alcohol consumption and psychological distress in recently widowed older men. *Australian and New Zealand Journal of Psychiatry, 33,* 740–747.

Cacioppo, J. T., Berntson, G. G., Larsen, J. T., Pohlmann, K. M., & Ito, T. A. (2000). The psychophysiology of emotion. In M. Lewis & J. M. Haviland-Jones (Eds.), *Handbook of Emotions, Second Edition* (pp. 173–191). New York: Guilford.

Cacioppo, J. T., Gardner, W. L., & Berntson, G. G. (1997). Beyond bipolar conceptualizations and measures: The case of attitudes and evaluative space. *Personality and Social Psychology Review, 1*(1), 3–25.

Cacioppo, J. T., Hawkley, L. C., & Berntson, G. G. (2003). The anatomy of loneliness. *Current Directions in Psychological Science, 12,* 71–74.

Cadoret, R. J., Yates, W. R., Troughton, E., Woodworth, G., & Steward, M. A. (1995). Genetic-environmental interaction in the genesis of aggressivity and conduct disorders. *Archives of General Psychiatry, 52,* 916–924.

Cahill, L., & McGaugh, J. L. (1998). Mechanisms of emotional arousal and lasting declarative memory. *Trends in Neurosciences, 21,* 294–299.

Cahill, L., Prins, B., Weber, M., & McGaugh, J. L. (1994). ß-Adrenergic activation and memory for emotional events. *Nature, 371,* 702–704.

Calder, A. J., Keane, J., Manes, F., Antoun, N., & Young, A. W. (2000). Impaired recognition and experience of disgust following brain injury. *Nature Neuroscience, 3,* 1077–1078.

Calvo, M. G., & Avero, P. (2005). Time course of attentional bias to emotional scenes in anxiety: Gaze direction and duration. *Cognition and Emotion, 19,* 433–451.

Camara, W. J. (1988). Reagan signs ban of polygraph testing for job applicants. *The Industrial-Organizational Psychologist, 26,* 39–41.

Cameron, H. A., & McKay, R. D. G. (1999). Restoring production of hippocampal neurons in old age. *Nature Neuroscience, 2,* 894–897.

Camodeca, M., Goossens, F. A., Schuengel, C., & Terwogt, M. M. (2003). Bullying and victimization among school-age children: Stability and links to proactive and reactive aggression. *Social Development, 11,* 332–345.

Campbell, A. (2002). *A mind of her own: The evolutionary psychology of women.* Oxford, England: Oxford University Press.

Campbell, D. T. (1983). Two distinct routes beyond kin selection to ultrasociality: Implications for the humanities and social sciences. In D. Bridgeman (Ed.), *The Nature of Prosocial Development: Theories and Strategies* (pp. 11–39). New York: Academic Press.

Campos, J. J., Bertenthal, B. I., & Kermoian, R. (1992). Early experience and emotional development: The emergence of wariness of heights. *Psychological Science, 3,* 61–64.

Camras, L. A. (1992). Expressive development and basic emotions. *Cognition and Emotion, 6,* 269–283.

Camras, L. A., Oster, H., Bakeman, R., Meng, Z. L., Ujiie, T., & Campos, J. J. (2007). Do infants show distinct negative facial expressions for fear and anger? Emotional expression in 11-month-old European American, Chinese, and Japanese infants. *Infancy, 11,* 131–155.

Canli, T., Sivers, H., Whitfield, S. L., Gotlib, I. H., & Gabrieli, J. D. E. (2002). Amygdala response to happy faces as a function of extraversion. *Science, 296,* 2191.

Canli, T., Zhao, Z., Brewer, J., Gabrieli, J. D. E., & Cahill, L. (2000). Event-related activation in the human amygdala associates with later memory for individual emotional experience. *The Journal of Neuroscience, 20,* RC99 (1–5).

Canli, T., Zhao, Z., Desmond, J. E., Glover, G., & Gabrieli, J. D. E. (1999). fMRI identifies a network of structures correlated with retention of positive and negative emotional memory. *Psychobiology, 27*(4), 441–452.

Cannon, W. B. (1915). *Bodily changes in pain, hunger, fear and rage: An account of recent researches into the function of emotional excitement.* New York, NY, U.S.: D Appleton & Company.

Cannon, W. B. (1927). The James-Lange theory of emotion. *American Journal of Psychology, 39,* 106–124.

Cannon, P. R., Hayes, A. E., & Tipper, S. P. (2009). An electromyographic investigation of the impact of task relevance on facial mimicry. *Cognition & Emotion, 23,* 918–929.

Carney, D. R., & Harrigan, J. A. (2003). It takes one to know one: Interpersonal sensitivity is related to accurate assessment of others' interpersonal sensitivity. *Emotion, 3,* 194–200.

Carpenter, S., & Halberstadt, A. G. (2000). Mothers' reports of events causing anger differ across family relationships. *Social Development, 9,* 458–477.

Carstensen, L. L. (1992). Social and emotional patterns in adulthood: Support for socioemotional selectivity theory. *Psychology and Aging, 7,* 331–338.

Carstensen, L. L., & Charles, S. T. (1998). Emotion in the second half of life. *Current Directions in Psychological Science, 7,* 144–149.

Carstensen, L. L., Fung, H. H., & Charles, S. T. (2003). Socioemotional selectivity theory and the regulation of emotion in the second half of life. *Motivation and Emotion, 27,* 103–123.

Carstensen, L. L., Gottman, J. M., & Levenson, R. W. (1995). Emotional behavior in long-term marriage. *Psychology and Aging, 10,* 140–149.

Carstensen, L. L., Isaacowitz, D. M., & Charles, S. T. (1999). Taking time seriously: A theory of socioemotional selectivity. *American Psychologist, 54,* 165–181.

Carstensen, L. L., Pasupathi, M., Mayr, U., & Nesselroade, J. R. (2000). Emotional experience in everyday life across the adult life span. *Journal of Personality and Social Psychology, 79,* 644–655.

Carstensen, L. L., & Turk-Charles, S. (1994). The salience of emotion across the life-span. *Psychology and Aging, 9,* 259–264.

Carter, C. S. (1998). Neuroendocrine perspectives on social attachment and love. *Psychoneuroendocrinology, 23,* 779–818.

Carter, J., Lyons, N. J., Cole, H. L., & Goldsmith, A. R. (2008). Subtle cues of predation risk: Starlings respond to a predator's direction of eye-gaze. *Proceedings Biological Sciences/the Royal Society, 275* (1644), 1709–1715.

Carver, C. S., Pozo, C., Harris, S. D., Noriega, V., Scheier, M. F., Robinson, D. S., et al. (1993). How coping mediates the effect of optimism on distress: A study of women with early stage breast cancer. *Journal of Personality and Social Psychology, 65,* 375–390.

Carver, C. S., & Scheier, M. F. (2002). Optimism. In C. R. Snyder & S. J. Lopez (Eds.), *Handbook of positive psychology* (pp. 231–243). New York: Oxford University Press.

Cashdan, E. (1998). Smiles, speech, and body posture: How women and men display sociometric status and power. *Journal of Nonverbal Behavior, 22,* 209–228.

Caspi, A., & Herbener, E. S. (1990). Continuity and change: Assortative marriage and the consistency of personality in adulthood. *Journal of Personality and Social Psychology, 58,* 250–258.

Caspi, A., McClay, J., Moffitt, T. E., Mill, J., Martin, J., Craig, I. W., et al. (2002). Role of genotype in the cycle of violence in maltreated children. *Science, 297,* 851–854.

Cassia, V. M., Turati, C., & Simion, F. (2004). Can a nonspecific bias toward top-heavy patterns explain newborns' face preference? *Psychological Science, 15,* 379–383.

Chaplin, T. M., Cole, P. M., & Zahn-Waxler, C. (2005). Parental socialization of emotion expression: Gender differences and relations to child adjustment. *Emotion, 5,* 80–88.

Chen, D., & Haviland-Jones, J. (2000). Human olfactory communication of emotion. *Perceptual and Motor Skills, 91,* 771–781.

Cheung, F. M., Leung, K., Fan, R. M., Song, W., Zhang, J., & Zhang, J. (1996). Development of the chinese personality assessment inventory. *Journal of Cross-Cultural Psychology, 27*(2), 181–199.

Christie, I. C., & Friedman, B. H. (2003). Autonomic specificity of discrete emotion and dimensions of affective space: A multivariate approach. *International Journal of Psychophysiology, 51,* 143–153.

Chwalisz, K., Diener, E., & Gallagher, D. (1988). Autonomic arousal feedback and emotional experience: Evidence from the spinal cord injured. *Journal of Personality and Social Psychology, 54,* 820–828.

Ciarrochi, J., Chan, A., Caputi, P., & Roberts, R. (2001). Measuring emotional intelligence. In J. Ciarrochi, J. P. Forgas, & J. D. Mayer (Eds.), *Emotional intelligence in everyday life* (pp. 25–45). Philadelphia, PA: Psychology Press.

Ciarrochi, J., Hynes, K., & Crittenden, N. (2005). Can men do better if they try harder: Sex and motivational effects on emotional awareness. *Cognition and Emotion, 19,* 133–141.

Cisler, J. M., & Koster, E. H. W. (2010). Mechanisms of attentional biases towards threat in anxiety disorders: An integrative review. *Clinical Psychology Review, 30*(2), 203–216.

Clark, K. B., Naritoku, D. K., Smith, D. C., Browning, R. A., & Jensen, R. A. (1999). Enhanced recognition memory following vagus nerve stimulation in human subjects. *Nature Neuroscience, 2,* 94–98.

Clark, L., Bechara, A., Damasio, H., Aitken, M. R. F., Sahakian, B. J., & Robbins, T. W. (2008). Differential effects of insular and ventromedial prefrontal cortex lesions on risky decision-making. *Brain: A Journal of Neurology, 131*(5), 1311–1322.

Clark, L., Cools, R., & Robbins, T. W. (2004). The neuropsychology of ventral prefrontal cortex: Decision-making and reversal learning. *Brain and Cognition, 55,* 41–53.

Clohessy, A. B., Posner, M. I., Rothbart, M. K., & Veccra, S. P. (1991). The development of inhibition of return in early infancy. *Journal of Cognitive Neuroscience, 3,* 345–350.

Clore, G. L. (1992). Cognitive phenomenology: Feelings and the construction of judgment. In L. L. Martin & A. Tesser (Eds.), *The construction of social judgments* (pp. 133–163). Hillsdale, NJ: Erlbaum.

Clore, G. L., & Centerbar, D. B. (2004). Analyzing anger: How to make people mad. *Emotion, 4,* 139–144.

Coan, J. A., & Allen, J. J. B. (2004). Frontal EEG asymmetry as a moderator and mediator of emotion. *Biological Psychology, 67,* 7–49.

Coan, J. A., Schaefer, H. S., & Davidson, R. J. (2006). Lending a hand: Social regulation of the neural response to threat. *Psychological Science, 17*(12), 1032–1039.

Cobos, P., Sanchéz, M., Peréz, N., & Vila, J. (2004). Effects of spinal cord injuries on the subjective component of emotions. *Cognition & Emotion, 19,* 281–287.

Cohen, A. B. (2009). Many forms of culture. *American Psychologist, 64*(3), 194–204.

Cohen, A. B., Malka, A., Rozin, P., & Cherfas, L. (2006). Religion and unforgivable offenses. *Journal of Personality, 74,* 85–117.

Cohen, D., & Gunz, A. (2002). As seen by the other…: Perspectives on the self in the memories and emotional perceptions of Easterners and Westerners. *Psychological Science, 13,* 55–59.

Cohen, D., Nisbett, R. E., Bowdle, B. F., & Schwarz, N. (1996). Insult, aggression, and the southern culture of honor: An "experimental ethnography." *Journal of Personality and Social Psychology, 70*(5), 945–960.

Cohen, F., Kearney, K. A., Zegans, L. S., Kemeny, M. E., Neuhaus, J. M., & Stites, D. P. (1999). Differential immune system changes with acute and persistent stress for optimists vs. pessimists. *Brain, Behavior, and Immunity, 13,* 155–174.

Cohen, M., Klein, E., Kuten, A., Fried, G., Zinder, O., & Pollack, S. (2002). Increased emotional distress in daughters of breast cancer patients is associated with decreased natural cytotoxic activity, elevated levels of stress hormones and decreased secretion of Th1 cytokines. *International Journal of Cancer, 100,* 347–354.

Cohen, M. X., Young, J., Baek, J., Kessler, C., & Ranganath, C. (2005). Individual differences in extraversion and dopamine genetics predict neural reward responses. *Cognitive Brain Research, 25*(3), 851–861.

Cohen, S., Frank, E., Doyle, W. J., Skoner, D. P., Rabin, B. S., & Swaltney, J. M., Jr. (1998). Types of stressors that increase susceptibility to the common cold in healthy adults. *Health Psychology, 17,* 214–223.

Cohn, M. A., Fredrickson, B. L., Brown, S. L., Mikels, J. A., & Conway, A. M. (2009). Happiness unpacked: Positive emotions increase life satisfaction by building resilience. *Emotion, 9,* 361–368.

Cole, P. M., Bruschi, C. J., & Tamang, B. L. (2002). Cultural differences in children's emotional reactions to difficult situations. *Child Development, 73,* 983–996.

Cole, P. M., & Tamang, B. L. (1998). Nepali children's ideas about emotional displays in hypothetical challenges. *Developmental Psychology, 34,* 640–646.

Cole, P. M., Teti, L. O., & Zahn-Waxler, C. (2003). Mutual emotion regulation and the stability of conduct problems between preschool and early school age. *Development and Psychopathology, 15,* 1–18.

Collins, N. L., & Miller, L. C. (1994). Self-disclosure and liking: A meta-analytic review. *Psychological Bulletin, 116,* 457–475.

Combs, D. J. Y., Powell, C. A. J., Schurtz, D. R., & Smith, R. H. (2009). Politics, *schadenfreude*, and ingroup identification: The sometimes happy thing about a poor economy and death. *Journal of Experimental Social Psychology, 45*(4), 635–646.

Comings, D. E., Rosenthal, R. J., Lesieur, H. R., Rugle, L. J., Muhleman, D., Chiu, C., et al. (1996). A study of the dopamine D2 receptor gene in pathological gambling. *Pharmacogenetics and Genomics, 6*(3), 223–234.

Conduct Problems Prevention Research Group. (2002). Evaluation of the first 3 years of the Fast Track prevention trial with children at high risk for adolescent conduct problems. *Journal of Abnormal Child Psychology, 30,* 19–35.

Connor, T. J., & Leonard, B. E. (1998). Depression, stress and immunological activation: The role of cytokines in depressive disorders. *Life Sciences, 62,* 583–606.

Connor-Smith, J. K., & Flachsbart, C. (2007). Relations between personality and coping: A meta-analysis. *Journal of Personality and Social Psychology, 93*(6), 1080–1107.

Conroy, M., Hess, R. D., Azuma, H., & Kashiwagi, K. (1980). Maternal strategies for regulating children's behavior: Japanese and American families. *Journal of Cross-Cultural Psychology, 11,* 153–172.

Consedine, N. S., Magai, C., & King, A. R. (2004). Deconstructing positive affect in later life: A differential functionalist analysis of joy and interest. *International Journal of Aging and Human Development, 58,* 49–68.

Conte, J. M. (2005). A review and critique of emotional intelligence measures. *Journal of Organizational Behavior, 26,* 433–440.

Coombs, R. H., & Fawzy, F. I. (1982). The effect of marital status on stress in medical school. *American Journal of Psychiatry, 139,* 1490–1493.

Costa, M., Dinsbach, W., Manstead, A. S. R., & Bitti, P. E. R. (2001). Social presence, embarrassment, and nonverbal behavior. *Journal of Nonverbal Behavior, 25,* 225–240.

Costa, P. T., & McCrae, R. R. (1980). Influence of extraversion and neuroticism on subjective well-being: Happy and unhappy people. *Journal of Personality and Social Psychology, 38,* 668–678.

Covert, M. V., Tangney, J. P., Maddux, J. E., & Heleno, N. M. (2003). Shame-proneness, guilt-proneness, and interpersonal problem solving: A social cognitive analysis. *Journal of Social and Clinical Psychology, 22,* 1–12.

Cox, B. J., McWilliams, L. A., Clara, I. P., & Stein, M. B. (2003). The structure of feared situations in a nationally representative sample. *Journal of Anxiety Disorders, 17,* 89–101.

Craig, A. D., Chen, K., Bandy, D., & Reiman, E. M. (2000). Thermosensory activation of insular cortex. *Nature Neuroscience, 3*(2), 184–190.

Crews, D. J., & Landers, D. M. (1987). A meta-analytic review of aerobic fitness and reactivity to psychological stressors. *Medicine & Science in Sports & Exercise, 19,* S144–S120.

Crews, F. (1996). The verdict on Freud. *Psychological Science, 7,* 63–68.

Crick, N. R., & Dodge, K. A. (1994). A review and reformulation of social information-processing mechanisms in children's social adjustment. *Psychological Bulletin, 115,* 74–101.

Crick, N. R., & Dodge, K. A. (1996). Social information-processing mechanisms in reactive and proactive aggression. *Child Development, 67,* 993–1002.

Critchley, H. D., Mathias, C. J., & Dolan, R. J. (2001). Neuroanatomical basis for first- and second-order representations of bodily states. *Nature Neuroscience, 4,* 207–212.

Critchley, H. D., Wiens, S., Rotshtein, P., Öhman, A., & Dolan, R. J. (2004). Neural systems supporting interoceptive awareness. *Nature Neuroscience, 7,* 189–195.

Crocker, J., & Park, L. E. (2004). The costly pursuit of self-esteem. *Psychological Bulletin, 130,* 392–414.

Crown, C. L., Feldstein, S., Jasnow, M. D., Beebe, B., & Jaffe, J. (2002). The cross-modal coordination of interpersonal timing: Six-weeks-old infants' gaze with adults' vocal behavior. *Journal of Psycholinguistic Research, 31,* 1–23.

Crucian, G. P., Hughes, J. D., Barrett, A. M., Williamson, D. J. G., Bauer, R. M., Bowers, D., et al. (2000). Emotional and physiological responses to false feedback. *Cortex, 36,* 623–647.

Csikszentmihalyi, M. (1999). If we are so rich, why aren't we happy? *American Psychologist, 54,* 821–827.

Cunningham, M. R. (1979). Weather, mood, and helping behavior: Quasi experiments with the sunshine samaritan. *Journal of Personality and Social Psychology, 37,* 1947–1956.

Cunningham, M. R., Roberts, A. R., Barbee, A. P., Druen, P. B., & Wu, C. (1995). "Their ideas of beauty are, on the whole, the same as ours": Consistency and variability in the cross-cultural perception of female physical attractiveness. *Journal of Personality and Social Psychology, 68,* 261–279.

Cunningham, W. A., Van Bavel, J. J., & Johnsen, I. R. (2008). Adaptive flexibility: Evaluative processing goals shape amygdala activity. *Psychological Science, 19,* 152–160.

Cuthbert, B. N., Lang, P. J., Strauss, C., Drobes, D., Patrick, C. J., & Bradley, M. M. (2003). The psychophysiology of anxiety disorder: Fear memory imagery. *Psychophysiology, 40,* 407–422.

Dadds, M. R., Hawes, D. J., Frost, A. D. J., Vassallo, S., Bunn, P., Hunter, K., & Merz, S. (2009). Learning to 'talk the talk': The relationship of psychopathic traits to deficits in empathy across childhood. *Journal of Child Psychology and Psychiatry, 50*(5), 599–606.

Dahlen, E. R., & Deffenbacher, J. L. (2001). Anger management. In W. J. Lyddon & J. V. Jones, Jr. (Eds.), *Empirically supported cognitive therapies* (pp. 163–181). New York: Springer Publishing.

Damasio, A. R. (1994). *Descartes' error: Emotion, reason, and the human brain.* New York: G. P. Putnam.

Damasio, A. R. (1995). On some functions of the human prefrontal cortex. In J. Grafman, K. J. Holyoak & F. Boller (Eds.), *Structure and functions of the human prefrontal cortex.* (pp. 241–251). New York, NY, U.S.: New York Academy of Sciences.

Damasio, A. R. (1999). *The feeling of what happens.* New York: Harcourt Brace.

Damasio, A. R., Grabowski, T. J., Bechara, A., Damasio, H., Ponto, L. L. B., Parvizi, J., et al. (2000). Subcortical and cortical brain activity during the feeling of self-generated emotions. *Nature Neuroscience, 3,* 1049–1056.

Damasio, H. (2002). Impairment of interpersonal social behavior caused by acquired brain damage. In S. G. Post, l. G. Underwood, J. P. Schloss, & W.B. Hurlbut (Eds.), *Altruism & altruistic love* (pp. 272–283). Oxford, England: Oxford University Press.

Damasio, H., Grabowski, T., Frank, R., Galaburda, A. M., & Damasio, A. R. (1994). The return of Phineas Gage: The skull of a famous patient yields clues about the brain. *Science, 264,* 1102–1105.

Danner, D. D., Snowdon, D. A., & Friesen, W. V. (2001). Positive emotions in early life and longevity: Findings from the nun study. *Journal of Personality and Social Psychology, 80,* 804–813.

Darwin, C. (1998). *The expression of the emotions in man and animals.* New York: Oxford University Press. (Original work published 1872.)

Dasgupta, N., McGhee, D. E., Greenwald, A. G., & Banaji, M. (2000). Automatic preference for White Americans: Eliminating the familiarity explanation. *Journal of Experimental Social Psychology, 36,* 316–328.

Daus, C. S., & Ashkanasy, N. M. (2005). The case for the ability-based model of emotional intelligence in organizational behavior. *Journal of Organizational Behavior, 26,* 453–466.

David, C. F., & Kistner, J. A. (2000). Do positive self-perceptions have a "dark side"? Examination of the link between perceptual bias and aggression. *Journal of Abnormal Child Psychology, 28,* 327–337.

Davidson, J. R. T. (2007). A history of the concept of atypical depression. *Journal of Clinical Psychiatry, 68* (Suppl3), 10–15.

Davidson, J. R. T., Hughes, D. C., George, L. K., & Blazer, D. G. (1996). The association of sexual assault and attempted suicide within the community. *Archives of General Psychiatry, 53,* 550–555.

Davidson, K., MacGregor, M. W., Stuhr, J., Dixon, K., & MacLean, D. (2000). Constructive anger verbal behavior predicts blood pressure in a population-based sample. *Health Psychology, 19,* 55–64.

Davidson, R. J. (1984). Hemispheric asymmetry and emotion. In K. Scherer and P. Ekman (Eds.), *Approaches to Emotion* (pp. 39–57). Hillsdale, NJ: Erlbaum.

Davidson, R. J. (2004). What does the prefrontal cortex "do" in affect: Perspectives on frontal EEG asymmetry research. *Biological Psychology, Special Issue: Frontal EEG Asymmetry, Emotion, and Psychopathology, 67*(1-2), 219–233.

Davidson, R. J., & Fox, N. A. (1982). Asymmetrical brain activity discriminates between positive and negative affective stimuli in human infants. *Science, 218,* 1235–1237.

Davidson, R. J., & Harrington, A. (Eds.). (2002). *Visions of compassion: Western scientists and Tibetan Buddhists examine human nature.* New York: Oxford University Press.

Davidson, R. J., & Henriques, J. (2000). Regional brain function in sadness and depression. In J. C. Borod (Ed.), *The neuropsychology of emotion* (pp. 269–297). Series in Affective Science. London: Oxford University Press.

Davidson, R. J., Putnam, K. M., & Larson, C. L. (2000). Dysfunction in the neural circuitry of emotion regulation: A possible prelude to violence. *Science, 289,* 591–594.

Davis, J. L., & Rusbult, C. E. (2001). Attitude alignment in close relationships. *Journal of Personality and Social Psychology, 81,* 65–84.

Daw, N. D., & Shohamy, D. (2008). The cognitive neuroscience of motivation and learning. *Social Cognition, 26,* 593–620.

Dawson, D. A., & Grant, B. F. (1998). Family history of alcoholism and gender: Their combined effects on DSM-IV alcohol dependence and major depression. *Journal of Studies on Alcohol, 59,* 97–106.

Day, A. L., & Carroll, S. A. (2004). Using an ability-based measure of emotional intelligence to predict individual performance, group performance, and group citizenship behaviours. *Personality and Individual Differences, 36,* 1443–1458.

DeCasper, A. J., & Fifer, W. P. (1980). Of human bonding: Newborns prefer their mothers' voices. *Science, 208,* 1174–1177.

Deffenbacher, J. L. (in press). Psychosocial interventions: Anger disorders. In E. F. Coccaro (Ed.), *Aggression: Assessment and treatment.* New York: Marcel Dekker.

de Gelder, B. (2000). Recognizing emotions by ear and by eye. In R. D. Lane & L. Nadel (Eds.), *Cognitive neuroscience of emotion* (pp. 84–105). New York: Oxford University Press.

De Jong, P. J., Peters, M., De Cremer, D., & Vranken, C. (2002). Blushing after a moral transgression in a prisoner's dilemma game: Appeasing or revealing? *European Journal of Social Psychology, 32,* 627–644.

Delplanque, S., Grandjean, D., Chrea, C., Coppin, G., Aymard, L., Cayeux, I., et al. (2009). Sequential unfolding of novelty and pleasantness appraisals of odors: Evidence from facial electromyography and autonomic reactions. *Emotion, 9,* 316–328.

Demaree, H. A., Schmeichel, B. J., Robinson, J. L., & Everhart, D. E. (2004). Behavioural, affective, and physiological effects of negative and positive emotional exaggeration. *Cognition and Emotion, 18*(8), 1079–1097.

Demetriou, H. & Hay, D. F. (2004). Toddlers' reactions to the distress of familiar peers: The importance of context. *Infancy, 6,* 299–318.

DeNeve, K. M. (1999). Happy as an extraverted clam? The role of personality for subjective well-being. *Current Directions in Psychological Science, 8,* 141–144.

DeNeve, K. M., & Cooper, H. (1998). The happy personality: A meta-analysis of 137 personality traits and subjective well-being. *Psychological Bulletin, 124,* 197–229.

Denham, S. A., Workman, E., Cole, P. M., Weissbrod, C., Kendziora, K. T., & Zahn-Waxler, C. (2000). Prediction of externalizing behavior problems from early to middle childhood: The role of parental socialization and emotion expression. *Development and Psychopathology, 12,* 23–45.

Denissen, J. J. A., Butalid, L., Penke, L., & van Aken, M. A. G. (2008). The effects of weather on daily mood. A multilevel approach. *Emotion, 8,* 662–667.

Dennis, P. M. (1998). Chills and thrills: Does radio harm our children? The controversy over program violence in the age of radio. *Journal of the History of the Behavioral Sciences, 34,* 33–50.

Dennis, T. A., Cole, P. M., Zahn-Waxler, C., & Mizuta, I. (2002). Self in context: Autonomy and relatedness in Japanese and U.S. mother-preschooler dyads. *Child Development, 73,* 1803–1817.

Depue, R. A., & Collins, P. (1999). Neurobiology of the structure of personality: Dopamine, facilitation of incentive motivation, and extraversion. *Behavioral and Brain Sciences, 22,* 491–569.

Depue, R. A., & Iacono, W. G. (1989). Neurobehavioral aspects of affective disorders. In M. R. Rosenzweig & L. W. Porter (Eds.), *Annual review of psychology, 40,* 457–492. Palo Alto, CA: Annual Reviews.

Depue, R. A., & Morrone-Strupinsky, J. V. (2005). A neurobehavioral model of affiliative bonding: Implications for conceptualizing a human trait of affiliation. *Behavioral and Brain Sciences, 28,* 313–395.

De Raad, B. (2005). The trait-coverage of emotional intelligence. *Personality and Individual Differences, 38,* 673–687.

Derksen, J., Kramer, I., & Katzko, M. (2002). Does a self-report measure for emotional intelligence assess something different than general intelligence? *Personality and Individual Differences, 32,* 37–48.

DeSteno, D., Valdesolo, P., & Bartlett, M. Y. (2006). Jealousy and the threatened self: Getting to the heart of the green-eyed monster. *Journal of Personality and Social Psychology, 91,* 626–641.

Detillon, C. E., Craft, T. K. S., Glasper, E. R., Prendergast, B. J., & DeVries, A. C. (2004). Social facilitation of wound healing. *Psychoneuroimmunology, 29,* 1004–1011.

Detre, J. A., & Floyd, T. F. (2001). Functional MRI and its applications to the clinical neurosciences. *Neuroscientist, 7,* 64–79.

Detterman, D. K. (1979). Detterman's laws of individual differences research. In R. J. Sternberg & D. K. Detterman (Eds.), *Human intelligence* (pp. 165–175). Norwood, NJ: Ablex.

de Waal, F. B. M. (2000). Primates—A natural heritage of conflict resolution. *Science, 289,* 586–590.

DeWall, C. N., & Baumeister, R. F. (2006). Alone but feeling no pain: Effects of social exclusion on physical pain tolerance and pain threshold, affective forecasting, and interpersonal empathy. *Journal of Personality and Social Psychology, 91,* 1–15.

DeWall, C. N., MacDonald, G., Webster, G. D., Masten, C., Baumeister, R. F., Powell, C., et al. (2010). Tylenol reduces social pain: Behavioral and neural evidence. *Psychological Science, 21*(7).

Diamond, D. M., Bennett, M. C., Fleshner, M., & Rose, G. M. (1992). Inverted-U relationship between the level of peripheral corticosterone and the magnitude of hippocampal primed burst potentiation. *Hippocampus, 2,* 421–430.

Diamond, L. M. (2004). Emerging perspectives on distinctions between romantic love and sexual desire. *Current Directions in Psychological Science, 13,* 116–119.

Diener, E. (2000). Subjective well-being. *American Psychologist, 55,* 34–43.

Diener, E., & Diener, C. (1996). Most people are happy. *Psychologcal Science, 7,* 181–185.

Diener, E., & Seligman, M. E. P. (2002). Very happy people. *Psychological Science, 13,* 81–84.

Diener, E., & Seligman, M. E. P. (2004). Beyond money: Toward an economy of well-being. *Psychological Science in the Public Interest, 5,* 1–31.

Diener, E., Suh, E. M., Lucas, R. E., & Smith, H. L. (1999). Subjective well-being: Three decades of progress. *Psychological Bulletin, 125,* 276–302.

Diener, E., Wolsic, B., & Fujita, F. (1995). Physical attractiveness and subjective well-being. *Journal of Personality and Social Psychology, 69,* 120–129.

Dijk, C., de Jong, P. J., & Peters, M. L. (2009). The remedial value of blushing in the context of transgressions and mishaps. *Emotion, 9,* 287–291.

Dijksterhuis, A., & van Olden, Z. (2006). On the benefits of thinking unconsciously: Unconscious thought can increase post-choice satisfaction. *Journal of Experimental Social Psychology, 42*(5), 627–631.

Dimberg, U., & Thunberg, M. (1998). Rapid facial reactions to emotional facial expressions. *Scandinavian Journal of Psychology, 39,* 39–45.

Dion, K. K., & Dion, K. L. (1993). Individualistic and collectivistic perspectives on gender and the cultural context of love and intimacy. *Journal of Social Issues, 49,* 53–69.

Ditzen, B., Schaer, M., Gabriel, B., Bodenmann, G., Ehlert, U., & Heinrichs, M. (2009). Intranasal oxytocin increases positive communication and reduces cortisol levels during couple conflict. *Biological Psychiatry, 65*(9), 728–731.

Dixon, J. F., & Hokin, L. E. (1998). Lithium acutely inhibits and chronically up-regulates and stabilizes glutamate uptake by presynaptic nerve endings in mouse cerebral cortex. *Proceedings of the National Academy of Sciences, 95*(4), 8363–8368.

Dodd, M. L., Klos, K. J., Bower, J. H., Geda, Y. E., Josephs, K. A., & Ahlskog, J. E. (2005). Pathological gambling caused by drugs used to treat Parkinson's disease. *Archives of Neurology, 62*(9), 1377–1381.

Dodge, K. A., & Coie, J. D. (1987). Social-information-processing factors in reactive and proactive aggression in children's peer groups. *Journal of Personality and Social Psychology, 53,* 1146–1158.

Doi, T. (1973). *The anatomy of dependence* (J. Beste, Trans.). Tokyo: Kodansha International.

Dollard, J., Miller, N. E., Doob, L. W., Mowrer, O. H., & Sears, R. R. (1939). *Frustration and aggression.* New Haven, CT: Yale University Press.

Dondi, M., Messinger, D., Colle, M., Tabasso, A., Simion, F., Dalla Barba, B., & Fogel, A. (2007). A new perspective on neonatal smiling: Differences between the judgments of expert coders and naive observers. *Infancy, 12*(3), 235–255.

Dondi, M. Simion, F., & Caltran, G. (1999). Can newborns discriminate between their own cry and the cry of another newborn infant? *Developmental Psychology, 35,* 418–426.

Donnellan, M. B., Trzesniewski, K. H., Robins, R. W., Moffitt, T. E., & Caspi, A. (2005). Low self-esteem is related to aggression, antisocial behavior, and delinquency. *Psychological Science, 16,* 328–335.

Donohoe, M. L., von Hippel, W., & Brooks, R. C. (2009). Beyond waist–hip ratio: Experimental multivariate evidence that average women's torsos are most attractive. *Behavioral Ecology, 20*(4), 716–721.

Dowden, S. L., & Allen, G. J. (1997). Relationships between anxiety sensitivity, hyperventialation, and emotional reactivity to displays of facial emotion. *Journal of Anxiety Disorders, 11,* 63–75.

Drummond, P. D., Camacho, L., Formentin, N., Heffernan, T. D., Williams, F., & Zekas, T. E. (2003). The impact of verbal feedback about blushing on social discomfort and facial blood flow during embarrassing tasks. *Behaviour Research and Therapy, 41,* 413–425.

Druschel, B. A., & Sherman, M. F. (1999). Disgust sensitivity as a function of the Big Five and gender. *Personality and Individual Differences, 26,* 739–748.

Duclos, S. E., & Laird, J. D. (2001). The deliberate control of emotional experience through control of expressions. *Cognition and Emotion, 15,* 27–65.

Dugas, M. J., Brillon, P., Savard, P., Turcotte, J., Gaudet, A., Ladouceur, R., Leblanc, R., & Gervais, N. J. (2010). A randomized clinical trial of cognitive-behavioral therapy and applied relaxation for adults with generalized anxiety disorder. *Behavior Therapy, 41*(1), 46–58.

Dulewicz, V., Higgs, M., & Slaski, M. (2003). Measuring emotional intelligence: Content, construct and criterion-related validity. *Journal of Managerial Psychology, 18,* 405–420.

Dunn, E. W., Aknin, L. B., & Norton, M. I. (2008). Spending money on others promotes happiness. *Science, 319,* 1687–1688.

Dunn, J., Bretherton, I., & Munn, P. (1987). Conversations about feeling states between mothers and their young children. *Developmental Psychology, 23,* 132–139.

Dunn, J., Brown, J. R., & Maguire, M. (1995). The development of children's moral sensibility: Indvidual differences and emotion understanding. *Developmental Psychology, 31,* 649–659.

Dunning, D., Heath, C., & Suls, J. M. (2005). Flawed self-assessment: Implications for health, education, and the workplace. *Psychological Science in the Public Interest, 5,* 69–106.

Durbin, C. E., Hayden, E. P., Klein, D. N., & Olino, T. M. (2007). Stability of laboratory-assessed temperamental emotionality traits from ages 3 to 7. *Emotion, 7,* 388–399.

Durrett, M. E., Otaki, M., & Richards, P. (1984). Attachment and the mother's perception of support from the father. *International Journal of Behavioral Development, 7,* 167–176.

Dutton, D. G., & Aron, A. P. (1974). Some evidence for heightened sexual attraction under conditions of high anxiety. *Journal of Personality and Social Psychology, 30,* 510–517.

Dyregrov, A., Gjestad, R., & Raundalen, M. (2002). Children exposed to warfare: A longitudinal study. *Journal of Traumatic Stress, 15,* 59–68.

Eaker, E. D., Sullivan, L. M., Kelly-Hayes, M., D'Agostino, R. B., Sr., & Benjamin, E. J. (2004). Anger and hostility predict the development of atrial fibrillation in men in the Framingham Offspring Study. *Circulation, 109,* 1267–1271.

Eatough, V., Smith, J. A., & Shaw, R. (2008). Women, anger, and aggression: An interpretative phenomenological analysis. *Journal of Interpersonal Violence, 23,* 1767–1799.

Ebling, R., & Levenson, R. W. (2003). Who are the marital experts? *Journal of Marriage and the Family, 65,* 130–142.

Ebstein, R. P., Novick, O., Umansky, R., Priel, B., Osher, Y., Blaine, D., et al. (1996). Dopamine D4 receptor (*D4DR*) exon III polymorphism associated with the personality trait of Novelty Seeking. *Nature Genetics, 12,* 78–80.

Edelmann, R. J. (2001). Blushing. In W. R. Crozier & L. E. Alden (Eds.), *International handbook of social anxiety* (pp. 301–323). Chichester, England: John Wiley.

Edelmann, R. J., & McCusker, G. (1986). Introversion, neuroticism, empathy, and embarrassibility. *Personality and Individual Differences, 7,* 133–140.

Edwards, K. (1998). The face of time: Temporal cues in facial expressions of emotion. *Psychological Science, 9,* 270–276.

Edwards, J., Jackson, H. J., & Pattison, P. E. (2002). Emotion recognition via facial expression and affective prosody in schizophrenia: A methodological review. *Clinical Psychology Review, 22,* 789–832.

Egloff, B., Wilhelm, F. H., Neubauer, D. H., Mauss, I. B., & Gross, J. J. (2002). Implicit anxiety measure predicts cardiovacular reactivity to an evaluated speaking task. *Emotion, 2,* 3–11.

Eibl-Eibesfeldt, I. (1973). *Der vorprogrammierte Mensch* [The preprogrammed human]. Vienna: Verlag Fritz Molden.

Eibl-Eibesfeldt, I. (1989). *Human Ethology.* New York: Aldine de Gruyter.

Eich, E. (1995). Searching for mood dependent memory. *Psychological Science, 6,* 67–75.

Eisenberg, N., Fabes, R. A., Miller, P. A., Fultz, J., Shell, R., Mathy, R. M., et al. (1989). Relation of sympathy and personal distress to prosocial behavior: A multimethod study. *Journal of Personality and Social Psychology, 57,* 55–66.

Eisenberg, N., Liew, J., & Pidada, S. U. (2001). The relations of parental emotional expressivity with quality of Indonesian children's social functioning. *Emotion, 1,* 116–136.

Eisenberg, N., Pidada, S., & Liew, J. (2001). The relations of regulation and negative emotionality to Indonesian children's social functioning. *Child Development, 72,* 1747–1763.

Eisenberger, N. I., & Lieberman, M. D. (2004). Why rejection hurts: A common neural alarm system for physical and social pain. *Trends in Cognitive Sciences, 8*(7), 294–300.

Eisenberger, N. I., Lieberman, M. D., & Williams, K. D. (2003). Does rejection hurt? An fMRI study of social exclusion. *Science, 302,* 290–292.

Ek, M., Engblom, D., Saha, S., Blomqvist, A., Jakobsson, P. J., & Ericsson-Dahlstrand, A. (2001). Pathway across the blood-brain barrier. *Nature, 410,* 430–431.

Ekman, P. (1972). Universals and cultural differences in facial expressions of emotion. In J. Cole (Ed.), *Nebraska Symposium on Motivation, 1971* (pp. 207–283). Lincoln: University of Nebraska Press.

Ekman, P. (1992). An argument for basic emotions. *Cognition and Emotion, 6,* 169–200.

Ekman, P. (1994). All emotions are basic. In P. Ekman & R. J. Davidson (Eds.) *The nature of emotion: Fundamental questions* (pp. 15–19). New York: Oxford University Press.

Ekman, P. (2001). *Telling lies* (3rd ed.). New York: Norton.

Ekman, P., & Friesen, W. V. (1975). *Unmasking the face: A guide to recognizing emotions from facial clues.* Oxford, England: Prentice Hall.

Ekman, P., & Friesen, W. V. (1984). *Unmasking the face* (2nd ed.). Palo Alto, CA: Consulting Psychologists Press.

Ekman, P., Friesen, W.V., O'Sullivan, M., Chan, A., Diacoyanni-Tarlatzis, I., Heider, K., et al. (1987). Universals and cultural differences in the judgments of facial expressions of emotion. *Journal of Personality and Social Psychology, 51,* 712–717.

Ekman, P., Levenson, R. W., & Friesen, W. V. (1983). Autonomic nervous system activity distinguishes among emotions. *Science, 221,* 1208–1210.

Ekman, P., & O'Sullivan, M. (1991). Who can catch a liar? *American Psychologist, 46,* 913–920.

Ekman, P., O'Sullivan, M., & Frank, M. G. (1999). A few can catch a liar. *Psychological Science, 10,* 263–266.

Elfenbein, H. A., & Ambady, N. (2002a). On the universality and cultural specificity of emotion recognition: A meta-analysis. *Psychological Bulletin, 128,* 203–235.

Elfenbein, H. A., Beaupré, M., Lévesque, M., & Hess, U. (2007). Toward a dialect theory: Cultural differences in the expression and recognition of posed facial expressions. *Emotion, 7,* 131–146.

Elias, M. J., Hunter, L., & Kress, J. S. (2001). Emotional intelligence and education. In J. Ciarrochi, J. P. Forgas, & J. D. Mayer (Eds.), *Emotional intelligence in everyday life* (pp. 133–149). Philadelphia, PA: Psychology Press.

Ellsworth, P. C. (1994). William James and emotion: Is a century of fame worth a century of misunderstanding? *Psychological Review, 101,* 222–229.

Ellsworth, P. C., & Ross, L. (1983, January). Public opinion and capital punishment: A close examination of the views of abolitionists and retentionists. *Crime and Delinquency, 29,* 116–169.

Ellsworth, P. C., & Tong, E. M. W. (2006). What does it mean to be angry at yourself? Categories, appraisals, and the problem of language. *Emotion, 6,* 572–586.

Emde, R. N., Katz, E. L., & Thorpe, J. K. (1978). Emotional expression in infancy: II. Early deviations in Down's Syndrome. In M. Lewis & L. A. Rosenblum (Eds.), *The development of affect* (pp. 351–360). New York: Plenum.

Emde, R. N., & Koenig, K. (1969). Neonatal smiling and rapid eye movement states. *Journal of American Academic Child Psychiatry, 8,* 57–67.

Emmons, R. A., & McCullough, M. E. (2003). Counting blessings versus burdens: An experimental investigation of gratitude and subjective well-being in daily life. *Journal of Personality and Social Psychology, 84,* 377–389.

Engelberg, E., & Sjöberg, L. (2004). Emotional intelligence, affect intensity, and social adjustment. *Personality and Individual Differences, 37,* 533–542.

Engle, R. W., Conway, A. R. A., Tuholski, S. W., & Shisler, R. J. (1995). A resource account of inhibition. *Psychological Science, 6*(2), 122–125.

Erlenmeyer-Kimling, L., Adamo, U. H., Rock, D., Roberts, S. A., Bassett, A. S., Squires-Wheeler, E., et al. (1997). The New York high-risk project. *Archives of General Psychiatry, 54,* 1096–1102.

Eshel, N., Nelson, E. E., Blair, R. J., Pine, D. S., & Ernst, M. (2007). Neural substrates of choice selection in adults and adolescents: Development of the ventrolateral prefrontal and anterior cingulate cortices. *Neuropsychologia, 45*(6), 1270–1279.

Esslen, M., Pascual-Marqui, R. D., Hell, D., Kochi, K., & Lehmann, D. (2004). Brain areas and time course of emotional processing. *NeuroImage, 21,* 1189–1203.

Esterson, A. (2001). The mythologizing of psychoanalytic history: Deceptions and self-deception in Freud's accounts of the seduction theory episode. *History of Psychology, 12,* 329–352.

Etcoff, N. L., Ekman, P., Magee, J. J., & Frank, M. G. (2000). Lie detection and language comprehension. *Nature, 405,* 139.

Etzel, J. A., Johnsen, E. L., Dickerson, J., Tranel, D., & Adolphs, R. (2006). Cardiovascular and respiratory responses during musical mood induction. *International Journal of Psychophysiology, 61*(1), 57–69.

Eugène, F., Lévesque, J., Mensour, B., Leroux, J-M., Beaudoin, G., Bourgouin, P., et al. (2003). The impact of individual differences on the neural circuitry underlying sadness. *NeuroImage, 19,* 354–364.

Evans, G. W., Bullinger, M., & Hygge, S. (1998). Chronic noise exposure and physiological response: A prospective study of children living under environmental stress. *Psychological Science, 9,* 75–77.

Evans, K., & Brase, G. L. (2007). Assessing sex differences and similarities in mate preferences: Above and beyond demand characteristics. *Journal of Social and Personal Relationships, 24*(5), 781–791.

Even, C., Schröder, C. M., Friedman, S., & Rouillon, F. (2008). Efficacy of light therapy in nonseasonal depression: A systematic review. *Journal of Affective Disorders, 108*(1-2), 11–23.

Fabes, R. A., Eisenberg, N., & Eisenbud, L. (1993). Behavioral and physiological correlates of children's reactions to others in distress. *Developmental Psychology, 29,* 655–663.

Fabes, R. A., Eisenberg, N., Nyman, M., & Michealieu, Q. (1991). Young children's appraisals of others' spontaneous emotional reactions. *Developmental Psychology, 27,* 858–886.

Farmer, E. M. Z., Compton, S. N., Burns, B. J., & Robertson, E. (2002). Review of the evidence base for treatment of childhood psychopathology: Externalizing disorders. *Journal of Consulting and Clinical Psychology, 70,* 1267–1302.

Farris, C., Treat, T. A., Viken, R. J., & McFall, R. M. (2008). Perceptual mechanisms that characterize gender differences in decoding women's sexual intent. *Psychological Science, 19*(4), 348–354.

Fauerbach, J. A., Lawrence, J. W., Haythornthwaite, J. A., & Richter, L. (2002). Coping with the stress of a painful medical procedure. *Behaviour Research and Therapy, 40,* 1003–1015.

Fazio, R. H., & Powell, M. C. (1997). On the value of knowing one's likes and dislikes: Attitude accessibility, stress, and health in college. *Psychological Science, 8,* 430–436.

Feeney, J., Peterson, C., & Noller, P. (1994). Equity and marital satisfaction over the family life cycle. *Personality Relationships, 1,* 83–99.

Fehr, B., & Russell, J. A. (1984). Concept of emotion viewed from a prototype perspective. *Journal of Experimental Psychology: General, 113,* 464–486.

Fehr, B., & Russell, J. A. (1991). The concept of love viewed from a prototype perspective. *Journal of Personality and Social Psychology, 60,* 425–438.

Feinstein, J. S., Adolphs, R., & Tranel, D. (2009). *Probing the experience of fear in patient SM.* Poster at the convention of the Society for Neuroscience.

Feldman, R. (2003). Infant-mother and infant-father synchrony: The coregulation of positive arousal. *Infant Mental Health Journal, 24*(1), 1–23.

Feldman, R. (2007). Parent-infant synchrony: Biological foundations and developmental outcomes. *Current Directions in Psychological Science, 16*(6), 340–345.

Feldman, R. (2009). The development of regulatory functions from birth to 5 years: Insights from premature infants. *Child Development, 80*(2), 544–561.

Feldman, R., & Eidelman, A. I. (2007). Maternal postpartum behavior and the emergence of infant-mother and infant-father synchrony in preterm and full-term infants: The role of neonatal vagal tone. *Developmental Psychobiology, 49*(3), 290–302.

Feldman, R., Greenbaum, C. W., & Yirmiya, N. (1999). Mother-infant affect synchrony as an antecedent of the emergence of self-control. *Developmental Psychology, 35,* 223–231.

Feldman, R., Weller, A., Zagoory-Sharon, O., & Levine, A. (2007). Evidence for a neuroendocrinological foundation of human affiliation: Plasma oxytocin levels across pregnancy and the postpartum period predict mother-infant bonding. *Psychological Science, 18*(11), 965–970.

Fendt, M., Koch, M., & Schnitzler, H. U. (1996). Lesions of the central gray block conditioned fear as measured with the potentiated startle paradigm. *Behavioral Brain Research, 74,* 127–134.

Fessler, D. M. T. (1999). Toward an understanding of the universality of second order emotions. In A. L. Hinton (Ed.), *Biocultural approaches to the emotions* (pp. 75–116). Cambridge, England: Cambridge University Press.

Fiedler, K., Schmid, J., & Stahl, T. (2002). What is the current truth about polygraph lie detection? *Basic and Applied Social Psychology, 24,* 313–324.

Field, T. M., Woodson, R. Greenberg, R., & Cohen, D. (1982). Discrimination and imitation of facial expressions by neonates. *Science, 218,* 179–181.

Fincham, F. D. (2003). Marital conflict: Correlates, structure, and context. *Current Directions in Psychological Science, 12*(1), 23–27.

First, M. B., Spitzer, R. L., Gibbon, M., & Williams, J. B. W. (1997). *Structured Clinical Interview for DSM-IV Axis 1 Disorders.* Arlington, VA: American Psychiatric Press.

Fischer, A. H., Mosquera, P. M. R., van Vianen, A., & Manstead, A. S. R. (2004). Gender and culture differences in emotion. *Emotion, 4,* 87–94.

Fiske, A. P. (2002). Using individualism and collectivism to compare cultures—A critique of the validity and measurement of the constructs: Comment on Oyserman et al. (2002). *Psychological Bulletin, 128,* 78–88.

Fivush, R., Brotman, M. A., Buckner, J. P., & Goodman, S. H. (2000). Gender differences in parent-child emotion narratives. *Sex Roles, 42,* 233–253.

Flack, W. F., Jr., Laird, J. D., & Cavallaro, L. A. (1999). Separate and combined effects of facial expressions and bodily postures on emotional feelings. *European Journal of Social Psychology, 29,* 203–217.

Fleeson, W., & Gallagher, P. (2009). The implications of big five standing for the distribution of trait manifestation in behavior: Fifteen experience-sampling studies and a meta-analysis. *Journal of Personality and Social Psychology, 97*(6), 1097–1114.

Fliessbach, K., Weber, B., Trautner, P., Dohmen, T., Sunde, U., Elger, C. E., et al. (2007). Social comparison affects reward-related brain activity in the human ventral striatum. *Science, 318,* 1305–1308.

Flury, J., & Ickes, W. (2001). Emotional intelligence and empathic accuracy. In J. Ciarrochi, J. P. Forgas, & J. D. Mayer (Eds.), *Emotional intelligence in everyday life* (pp. 113–132.). Philadelphia, PA: Psychology Press.

Folkman, S., & Moskowitz, J. T. (2000). Stress, positive emotion, and coping. *Current Directions in Psychological Science, 9,* 115–118.

Føllesdal, H., & Hagtvet, K. A. (2009). Emotional intelligence: The MSCEIT from the perspective of generalizability theory. *Intelligence, 37*(1), 94–105.

Fontaine, J. R. J., Scherer, K. R., Roesch, E. B., & Ellsworth, P. C. (2007). The world of emotions is not two-dimensional. *Psychological Science, 18,* 1050–1057.

Forbes, E. E., & Dahl, R. E. (2010). Pubertal development and behavior: Hormonal activation of social and emotional tendencies. *Brain and Cognition, 72,* 66–72.

Forgas, J. P. (1995). Mood and judgment: The affect infusion model (AIM). *Psychological Bulletin, 117,* 39–66.

Forgas, J. P. (1998). On being happy and mistaken: Mood effects on the fundamental attribution error. *Journal of Personality and Social Psychology, 75,* 318–331.

Foster, D. J., & Wilson, M. A. (2006). Reverse replay of behavioural sequences in hippocampal place cells during the awake state. *Nature, 440*(7084), 680–683.

Fowler, J. H., & Christakis, N. A. (2008). Dynamic spread of happiness in a large social network: Longitudinal analysis over 20 years in the Framingham Heart Study. *British Medical Journal, 337,* a2338.

Fox, A., & Thomas, T. (2008). Impact of religious affiliation and religiosity on forgiveness. *Australian Psychologist, 43,* 175–185.

Fraiberg, S. (1974). Blind infants and their mothers: An examination of the sign system. In M. Lewis & L. A. Rosenblum (Eds.), *The effect of the infant on its caregiver.* Oxford, England: Wiley-Interscience.

Fraley, R. C., & Shaver, P. R. (1998). Airport separations: A naturalistic study of adult attachments dynamics in separating couples. *Journal of Personality and Social Psychology, 75*(5), 1198–1212.

Fraley, R. C., & Shaver, P. R. (2000). Adult romantic attachment: Theoretical developments, emerging controversies, and unanswered questions. *Review of General Psychology, 4,* 132–154.

Fraley, R. C., & Waller, N. G. (1998). Adult attachment patterns: A test of the typological model. In J. A. Simpson & W. S. Rholed (Eds.), *Attachment theory and close relationships* (pp. 77–114). New York: Guilford.

Frank, M. G., & Stennett, J. (2001). The forced-choice paradigm and the perception of facial expressions of emotion. *Journal of Personality and Social Psychology, 80,* 75–85.

Franken, I. H. A., Kroon, L. Y., Wiers, R. W., & Jansen, A. (2000). Selective cognitive processing of drug cues in heroin dependence. *Journal of Psychopharmacology, 14,* 395–400.

Frankland, P. W., Josselyn, S. A., Bradwejn, J., Vaccarino, F. J., & Yeomans, J. S. (1997). Activation of amygdala cholecystokinin B receptors potentiates the acoustic startle response in the rat. *Journal of Neuroscience, 17,* 1838–1847.

Fredrickson, B. L. (1998). What good are positive emotions? *Review of General Psychology, 2*(3), 300–319.

Fredrickson, B. L. (2000). Cultivating positive emotions to optimize health and well-being. *Prevention & Treatment, 3,* article 0001a. Retrieved October 20, 2004, from http://journals.apa.org/prevention/volume3/pre0030001a.html

Fredrickson, B. L. (2001). The role of positive emotion in psychology: The broaden-and-build theory of positive emotions. *American Psychologist, 56,* 218–226.

Fredrickson, B. L., & Branigan, C. (2005). Positive emotions broaden the scope of attention and thought-action repertoires. *Cognition and Emotion, 19,* 313–332.

Fredrickson, B. L., & Joiner, T. (2002). Positive emotions trigger upward spirals toward emotional well-being. *Psychological Science, 13,* 172–175.

Fredrickson, B. L., & Levenson, R. W. (1998). Positive emotions speed recovery from the cardiovascular sequelae of negative emotions. *Cognition and Emotion, 12,* 191–220.

Fredrickson, B. L., Mancuso, R. A., Branigan, C., & Tugade, M. M. (2000). The undoing effect of positive emotions. *Motivation and Emotion, 24*(4), 237–258.

Freud, S. (1937). Analysis terminable and interminable. *The International Journal of Psychanalysis, 18,* 373–405.

Friedman, M., & Rosenman, R. H. (1974). *Type-A behavior and your heart.* New York: Knopf.

Friedman, S., Smith, L., Fogel, D., Paradis, C., Viswanathan, R., Ackerman, R., et al. (2002). The incidence and influence of early traumatic life events in patients with panic disorder: A comparison with other psychiatric outpatients. *Journal of Anxiety Disorders, 16,* 259–272.

Friesen, W. V. (1972). *Cultural differences in facial expressions in a social situation: An experimental test of display rules.* Unpublished Doctoral Dissertation. San Francisco: University of California.

Frijda, N. H. (1986). *The emotions.* London: Cambridge University Press.

Fry, P. S. (1995). Perfectionism, humor, and optimism as moderators of health outcomes and determinants of coping styles of women executives. *Genetic, Social, and General Psychology Monographs, 121,* 213–245.

Fu, C. H. Y., Williams, S. C. R., Cleare, A. J., Brammer, M. J., Walsh, N. D., Kim, J., et al. (2004). Attenuation of the neural response to sad faces in major depression by antidepressant treatment. *Archives of General Psychiatry, 61,* 877–889.

Fu, Q., Heath, A. C., Bucholz, K. K., Nelson, E., Goldberg, J., Lyons, M. J., et al. (2002). Shared genetic risk of major depression, alcohol dependence, and marijuana dependence. *Archives of General Psychiatry, 59,* 1125–1132.

Fujisawa, K. K., Kutsukake, N., & Hasegawa, T. (2008). Reciprocity of prosocial behavior in Japanese preschool children. *International Journal of Behavioral Development, 32,* 89–97.

Fukuda, S., Morimoto, K., Mure, K., & Maruyama, S. (2000). Effect of the Hanshin-Awaji earthquake on posttraumatic stress, lifestyle changes, and cortisol levels of victims. *Archives of Environmental Health, 55,* 121–125.

Fultz, J., Batson, C. D., Fortenbach, V. A., McCarthy, P. M., & Varney, L. L. (1986). Social evaluation and the empathy-altruism hypothesis. *Journal of Personality and Social Psychology, 50,* 761–769.

Funayama, E. S., Grillon, C., Davis, M., & Phelps, E. A. (2001). A double dissociation in the affective modulation of startle in humans: Effects of unilateral temporal lobectomy. *Journal of Cognitive Neuroscience, 13,* 721–729.

Furman, W., & Burhmester, D. (1992). Age and sex differences in perceptions of networks and social relationships. *Child Development, 63,* 103–115.

Fusar-Poli, P., Placentino, A., Carletti, F., Landi, P., Allen, P., Surguladze, S., et al. (2009). Functional atlas of emotional faces processing: A voxel-based meta-analysis of 105 funcitonal magnetic resonance imaging studies. *Journal of Psychiatry and Neuroscience, 34,* 418–432.

Fuster, J. (2008). *The Prefrontal Cortex* (4th ed.). Boston, MA: Academic Press.

Gable, P. A., & Harmon-Jones, E. (2008). Approach-motivated positive affect reduces breadth of attention. *Psychological Science, 19,* 476–482.

Gable, S. L., Reis, H. T., & Downey, G. (2003). He said, she said: A quasi-signal detection analysis of daily interactions between close relationship partners. *Psychological Science, 14,* 100–105.

Gale, G. D., Anagnostaras, S. G., Godsil, B. P., Mitchell, S., Nozawa, T., Sage, J. R., et al. (2004). Role of the basolateral amygdala in the storage of fear memories across the adult lifetime of rats. *Journal of Neuroscience, 24,* 3810–3815.

Gall, T. L., Evans, D. R., & Bellerose, S. (2000). Transition to first-year university: Patterns of change in adjustment across live domains and time. *Journal of Social and Clinical Psychology, 19,* 544–567.

Gamer, M., & Büchel, C. (2009). Amygdala activation predicts gaze toward fearful eyes. *Journal of Neuroscience, 29,* 9123–9126.

Gannon, N., & Ranzijn, R. (2005). Does emotional intelligence predict unique variance in life satisfaction beyond IQ and personality? *Personality and Individual Differences, 38,* 1353–1364.

Garcia, R., Vouimba, R. M., Baudry, M., & Thompson, R. F. (1999). The amygdala modulates prefrontal cortex activity relative to conditioned fear. *Nature, 402,* 294–296.

Gardner, M., & Steinberg, L. (2005). Peer influence on risk taking, risk preference, and risky decision making in adolescence and adulthood: An experimental study. *Developmental Psychology, 41,* 625–635.

Garfinkel, S. N., & Liberzon, I. (2009). Neurobiology of PTSD: A review of neuroimaging findings. *Psychiatric Annals, 39*(6), 370–372, 376–381.

Garnefski, N., Teerds, J., Kraaij, V., Legerstee, J., & van den Kommer, T. (2004). Cognitive emotion regulation strategies and depressive symptoms: Differences between males and females. *Personality and Individual Differences, 36,* 267–276.

Garnefski, N., van den Kommer, T., Kraaij, V., Teerds, J., Legerstee, J., & Onstein, E. (2002). The relationship between cognitive emotion regulation strategies and emotional problems: Comparison between a clinical and a non-clinical sample. *European Journal of Personality, 16,* 403–420.

Gasper, K., & Clore, G. L. (2002). Attending to the big picture: Mood and global versus local processing of visual information. *Psychological Science, 13,* 34–40.

Geen, R. G. (1978). Effects of attack and uncontrollable noise on aggression. *Journal of Research in Personality, 9,* 270–281.

Geertz, C. (1973). *Interpretation of cultures.* New York: Basic Books.

Gelenberg, A. J., & Chesen, C. L. (2000). How fast are antidepressants? *Journal of Clinical Psychiatry, 61*(10), 712–721.

George, M. S., Ketter, T. A., Parekh, P. I., Horwitz, B., Herscovitch, P., & Post, R. M. (1995). Brain activity during transient sadness and happiness in healthy women. *American Journal of Psychiatry, 152,* 341–351.

Giegling, I., Hartmann, A. M., Moller, H. J., & Rujescu, D. (2006). Anger- and aggression-related traits are associated with polymorphisms in the 5HT-2A gene. *Journal of Affective Behaviors, 96,* 75–81.

Gifkins, A., Greba, Q., & Kokkinidis, L. (2002). Ventral tegmental area dopamine neurons mediate the shock sensitization of acoustic startle: A potential site of action for benzodiazepine anxiolytics. *Behavioral Neuroscience, 116,* 785–794.

Gigerenzer, G. (2004). Dread risk, September 11, and fatal traffic accidents. *Psychological Science, 15,* 286–287.

Gilbert, L. A. & Holahan, C. K. (1982). Conflicts between student/professional, parental, and self-development roles: A comparison of high and low effective copers. *Human Relations, 35*(8), 635–648.

Gilbertson, M. W., Shenton, M. E., Ciszewski, A., Kasai, K., Lasko, N. B., Orr, S. P. et al. (2002). Smaller hippocampal volume predicts pathological vulnerability to psychological trauma. *Nature Neuroscience, 5,* 1242–1247.

Giuliani, D., & Ferrari, F. (1996). Differential behavioral response to dopamine D_2 agonists by sexually naïve, sexually active, and sexually inactive male rats. *Behavioral Neuroscience, 110,* 802–808.

Giuliani, N. R., McRae, K., & Gross, J. J. (2008). The up- and down-regulation of amusement: Experiential, behavioral, and autonomic consequences. *Emotion, 8*(5), 714–719.

Glaser, R., Rice, J., Speicher, C. E., Stout, J. C., & Kiecolt-Glaser, J. K. (1986). Stress depresses interferon production by leukocytes concomitant with a decrease in natural killer cell activity. *Behavioral Neuroscience, 100,* 675–678.

Glass, D. C., Singer, J. E., & Pennebaker, J. W. (1977). Behavioral and physiological effects of uncontrollable environmental events. In D. Stokols (Ed.), *Perspectives on environment and behavior* (pp. 131–151). New York: Plenum.

Glover, D. A., & Poland, R. E. (2002). Urinary cortisol and catecholamines in mothers of child cancer survivors with and without PTSD. *Psychoneuroendocrinology, 27,* 805–819.

Goldberg, L. R. (1990). An alternative "description of personality": The big-five factor structure. *Journal of Personality and Social Psychology, 59*(6), 1216–1229.

Goldin, P. R., McRae, K., Ramel, W., & Gross, J. J. (2008). The neural bases of emotion regulation: Reappraisal and suppression of negative emotion. *Biological Psychiatry, 63*(6), 577–586.

Gonzaga, G. C., Turner, R. A., Keltner, D., Campos, B., & Altemus, M. (2006). Romantic love and sexual desire in close relationships. *Emotion, 6*(2), 163–179.

Gorgulu, Y., & Caliyurt, O. (2009). Rapid antidepressant effects of sleep deprivation therapy correlates with serum BDNF changes in major depression. *Brain Research Bulletin, 80*(3), 158–162.

Gorman, J. M., Kent, J., Martinez, J., Browne, S., Coplan, J., & Papp, L. A. (2001). Physiological changes during carbon dioxide inhalation in patients with panic disorder, major depression, and premenstrual dysphoric disorder. *Archives of General Psychiatry, 58,* 125–131.

Gottman, J. M. (1994). *What predicts divorce?* Hillsdale, NJ: Erlbaum.

Gottman, J. M., Coan, J., Carrere, S., & Swanson, C. (1998). Predicting marital happiness and stability from newlywed interactions. *Journal of Marriage and the Family, 60,* 5–22.

Grammer, K., Kruck, K., Jutte, A., & Fink, B. (2000). Non-verbal behavior as courtship signals: The role of control and choice in selecting partners. *Evolution and Human Behavior, 21,* 371–390.

Grandjean, D., & Scherer, K. R. (2008). Unpacking the cognitive architecture of emotion processes. *Emotion, 8,* 341–351.

Gray, J. A. (1970). The psychophysiological basis of introversion-extraversion. *Behavioural Research Therapy, 8,* 249–266.

Greenberg, M. T., & Marvin, R. S. (1982). Reactions of preschool children to an adult stranger: A behavioral systems approach. *Child Development, 53,* 481–490.

Greene, J. D., Cushman, F. A., Stewart, L. E., Lowenberg, K., Nystrom, L. E., & Cohen, J. D. (2009). Pushing moral buttons: The interaction between personal force and intention in moral judgment. *Cognition, 111*(3), 364–371.

Greene, J. D., Sommerville, R. B., Nystrom, L. E., Darley, J. M., & Cohen, J. D. (2001). An fMRI investigation of emotional engagement in moral judgment. *Science, 293,* 2105–2108.

Griffin, D. W., & Bartholomew, K. (1994). The metaphysics of measurement: The case of adult attachment. In K. Bartholomew & D. Perlman (Eds.), *Advances in personal relationships: Vol. 5. Attachment processes in adulthood* (pp. 17–52). London: Jessica Kingsley.

Grillon, C. (2008). Greater sustained anxiety but not phasic fear in women compared to men. *Emotion, 8,* 410–413.

Griskevicius, V., Shiota, M. N., & Neufeld, S. L. (2010). Influence of Different Positive Emotions on Persuasion Processing: A Functional Evolutionary Approach. *Emotion, 10*(2), 190–206.

Grodnitzky, G. R., & Tafrate, R. C. (2000). Imaginal exposure for anger reduction in adult outpatients: A pilot study. *Journal of Behavior Therapy and Experimental Psychiatry, 31,* 259–279.

Grodzinsky, Y., & Amunts, K. (2006). *Broca's region.* New York, NY, U.S.: Oxford University Press.

Gross, A. E., & Crofton, C. (1977). What is good is beautiful. *Sociometry, 40,* 85–90.

Gross, J. J. (1998). Antecedent- and response-focused emotion regulation: Divergent consequences for experience, expression, and physiology. *Journal of Personality and Social Psychology, 74,* 224–237.

Gross, J. J. (2001). Emotion regulation in adulthood: Timing is everything. *Current Directions in Psychological Science, 10,* 214–219.

Gross, J. J. (2002). Emotion regulation: Affective, cognitive, and social consequences. *Psychophysiology, 39,* 281–291.

Gross, J. J., Carstensen, L. L., Pasupathi, M., Tsai, J., Skorpen, C. G., & Hsu, A. Y. C. (1997). Emotion and aging: Experience, expression, and control. *Psychology and Aging, 12,* 590–599.

Gross, J. J., & John, O. P. (2003). Individual differences in two emotion regulation processes: Implications for affect, relationships, and well-being. *Journal of Personality and Social Psychology, 85,* 348–362.

Gross, J. J., & Levenson, R. W. (1995). Emotion elicitation using films. *Cognition and Emotion, 9*(1), 87–108.

Gross, J. J., & Levenson, R. W. (1997). Hiding feelings: The acute effects of inhibiting positive and negative emotions. *Journal of Abnormal Psychology, 106,* 95–103.

Gross, J. J., Sutton, S. K., & Ketelaar, T. (1998). Relations between affect and personality: Support for the affect-level and affective reactivity views. *Personality and Social Psychology Bulletin, 24*(3), 279–288.

Grossman, K., Grossman, K. E., Spangler, S., Suess, G., & Unzer, L. (1985). Maternal sensitivity and newborn responses as related to quality of attachment in Northern Germany. In I. Bretherton & E. Waters (Eds.), Growing points of attachment theory, *Monographs of the Society for Research in Child Development, 50* (1-2, Serial No. 209).

Gupta, U., & Singh, P. (1982). Exploratory study of love and liking and type of marriages. *Indian Journal of Applied Psychology, 19,* 92–97.

Gyurak, A., & Ayduk, Ö. (2008). Resting respiratory sinus arrhythmia buffers against rejection sensitivity via emotion control. *Emotion, 8*(4), 458–467.

Haas, B. W., Omura, K., Constable, R. T., & Canli, T. (2007). Is automatic emotion regulation associated with agreeableness?: A perspective using a social neuroscience approach. *Psychological Science, 18*(2), 130–132.

Haidt, J. (2001). The emotional dog and its rational tail: A social intuitionist approach to moral judgment. *Psychological Review, 108,* 814–834.

Haidt, J., & Keltner, D. (1999). Culture and facial expression: Open-ended methods find more faces and a gradient of recognition. *Cognition and Emotion, 13,* 225–266.

Haidt, J., McCauley, C., & Rozin, P. (1994). Individual differences in sensitivity to disgust: A scale sampling seven domains of disgust elicitors. *Personality and Individual Differences, 16,* 701–713.

Haidt, J., Rozin, P., McCauley, C. R., & Imada, S. (1997). Body, psyche, and culture: The relationship between disgust and morality. *Psychology and Developing Societies, 9,* 107–131.

Hajcak, G., Castille, C., Olvet, D. M., Dunning, J. P., Roohi, J., & Hatchwell, E. (2009). Genetic variation in brain-derived neurotrophic factor and human fear conditioning. *Genes, Brain and Behavior, 8,* 80–85.

Hajcak, G., & Foti, D. (2008). Errors are aversive: Defensive motivation and the error-related negativity. *Psychological Science, 19*(2), 103–108.

Halberstadt, A. G., Denham, S. A., & Dunsmore, J. C. (2001). Affective social competence. *Social Development, 10,* 79–119.

Hall, J. A. (1978). Gender effects in decoding nonverbal cues. *Psychological Bulletin, 85,* 845–857.

Hall, J. A., & Halberstadt, A. G. (1986). Smiling and gazing. In J. S. Hyde & M. C. Linn (Eds.), *The psychology of gender: Advances through meta-analysis* (pp. 136–158). Baltimore, MD: Johns Hopkins University Press.

Hall, J. A., & Halberstadt, A. G. (1994). "Subordination" and sensitivity to nonverbal cues: A study of married working women. *Sex Roles, 31,* 149–165.

Hall, J. A., & Matsumoto, D. (2004). Gender differences in judgments of multiple emotions from facial expressions. *Emotion, 4,* 201–206.

Hamaguchi, T., Kano, M., Rikimaru, H., Kanazawa, M., Itoh, M., Yanai, K., & Fukudo, S. (2004). Brain activity during distention of the descending colon in humans. *Neurogastroenterology and Motility: The Official Journal of the European Gastrointestinal Motility Society, 16*(3), 299–309.

Hamann, S. B., Ely, T. D., Hoffman, J. M., & Kilts, C. D. (2002). Ecstasy and agony: Activation of the human amygdala in positive and negative emotion. *Psychological Science, 13,* 135–141.

Hanish, L. D., Eisenberg, N., Fabes, R. A., Spinrad, T. L., Ryan, P., & Schmidt, S. (2004). The expression and regulation of negative emotions: Risk factors for young children's peer victimization. *Development and Psychopathology, 16,* 335–353.

Hansson, B., Bensch, S., & Hasselquist, D. (1997). Infanticide in great reed warblers: Secondary females destroy eggs of primary females. *Animal Behaviour, 54,* 297–304.

Hariri, A. R., Mattay, V. S., Tessitore, A., Kolachana, B., Fera, F., Goldman, D., et al. (2002). Serotonin transporter genetic variation and the response of the human amygdala. *Science, 297,* 400–403.

Harker, L. A., & Keltner, D. (2001). Expressions of positive emotion in women's college yearbook pictures and their relationship to personality and life outcomes across adulthood. *Journal of Personality and Social Psychology, 80,* 112–124.

Harmon-Jones, E., & Allen, J. J. B. (1998). Anger and frontal brain activity: EEG asymmetry consistent with approach motivation despite negative affective valence. *Journal of Personality and Social Psychology, 74*(5), 1310–1316.

Harmon-Jones, E., & Peterson, C. K. (2009). Supine body position reduces neural response to anger evocation. *Psychological Science, 20,* 1209–1210.

Harris, C. R., & Pashler, H. (2004). Attention and the processing of emotional words and names. *Psychological Science, 15,* 171–178.

Harris, C. R., & Pashler, H. (2005). Enhanced memory for negatively emotionally changed pictures without rumination. *Emotion, 5,* 191–199.

Harris, R. A., Brodie, M. S., & Dunwiddie, T. V. (1992). Possible substrates of ethanol reinforcement: GABA and dopamine. *Annals of the New York Academy of Sciences, 654,* 61–69.

Harrison, A. O., Wilson, M. N., Pine, C. J., Chan, S. Q., & Buriel, R. (1990). Family ecologies of ethnic minority children. *Child Development, 61,* 347–362.

Harvey, A. G., & Bryant, R. A. (2002). Acute stress disorder: A synthesis and critique. *Psychological Bulletin, 128,* 886–902.

Hatfield, E., & Rapson, R. L. (1993). *Love, sex, and intimacy.* New York: Harper Collins.

Hawton, K., Sutton, L., Haw, C., Sinclair, J., & Harriss, L. (2005). Suicide and attempted suicide in bipolar disorder: A systematic review of risk factors. *Journal of Clinical Psychiatry, 66*(6), 693–704.

Hay, D. F., Nash, A., & Pedersen, J. (1981). Responses of six-month olds to the distress of their peers. *Child Development, 52,* 1071–1075.

Hayman, L. A., Rexer, J. L., Pavol, M. A., Strite, D., & Meyers, C. A. (1998). Klüver-Bucy syndrome after bilateral selective damage of amygdala and its cortical connections. *Journal of Neuropsychiatry, 10,* 354–358.

Hazan, C., & Shaver, P. (1987). Romantic love conceptualized as an attachment process. *Journal of Personality and Social Psychology, 52,* 511–524.

Hazebroek, J. F., Howells, K., & Day, A. (2000). Cognitive appraisals associated with high trait anger. *Personality and Individual Differences, 30,* 31–45.

Heider, E. R. (1972). Universals in color naming and memory. *Journal of Experimental Psychology, 93,* 10–20.

Heine, S. J., Lehman, D. R., Peng, K., & Greenholtz, J. (2002). What's wrong with cross-cultural comparisons of subjective Likert scales? The reference-group effect. *Journal of Personality and Social Psychology, 82,* 903–918.

Hejmadi, A., Davidson, R. J., & Rozin, P. (2000). Exploring Hindu Indian emotion expressions. *Psychological Science, 11,* 183–187.

Heldt, S., Sundin, V., Willott, J. F., & Falls, W. A. (2000). Posttraining lesions of the amygdala interfere with fear-potentiated startle to both visual and auditory conditioned stimuli in C56BL/6J mice. *Behavioral Neuroscience, 114,* 749–759.

Heller, D., Watson, D., & Ilies, R. (2004). The role of person versus situation in life satisfaction: A critical examination. *Psychological Bulletin, 130,* 574–600.

Helweg-Larsen, M., Sadeghian, P., & Webb, M. S. (2002). The stigma of being pessimistically biased. *Journal of Social and Clinical Psychology, 21,* 92–107.

Hemmati, T., Mills, J. F., & Kroner, D. G. (2004). The validity of the Bar-On emotional intelligence quotient in an offender population. *Personality and Individual Differences, 37,* 695–706.

Henderson, J. J. A., & Anglin, J. M. (2003). Facial attractiveness predicts longevity. *Evolution and Human Behavior, 24,* 351–356.

Hendrick, C., & Hendrick, S. S. (1986). A theory and method of love. *Journal of Personality and Social Psychology, 50,* 392–402.

Hendrick, S. S., Hendrick, C., & Adler, N. L. (1988). Romantic relationships: Love, satisfaction, and staying together. *Journal of Personality and Social Psychology, 54,* 980–988.

Hennenlotter, A., Dresel, C., Castrop, F., Baumann, A. O. C., Wohlschlager, A. M., & Haslinger, B. (2009). The link between facial feedback and neural activity within central circuitries of emotion. *Cerebral Cortex, 19,* 537–542.

Henriques, J. B., & Davidson, R. J. (2000). Decreased responsiveness to reward in depression. *Cognition and Emotion, 14,* 711–724.

Herman, B. H., & Panksepp, J. (1978). Effects of morphine and naloxone on separation distress and approach attachment: Evidence for the opiate mediation of social affect. *Pharmacology, Biochemistry, and Behavior, 9,* 213–220.

Hermans, E. J., Ramsey, N. F., & van Honk, J. (2008). Exogenous testosterone enhances responsiveness to social threat in the neural circuitry of social aggression in humans. *Biological Psychiatry, 63,* 263–270.

Hertenstein, M. J., & Campos, J. J. (2004). The retention effects of an adult's emotional displays on infant behavior. *Child Development, 75,* 595–613.

Hertenstein, M. J., Hansel, C. A., Butts, A. M., & Hile, S. N. (2009). Smile intensity in photographs predicts divorce later in life. *Motivation and Emotion, 33,* 99–105.

Heschl, A., & Burkhart, J. (2006). A new mark test for mirror self-recognition in non-human primates. *Primates, 47,* 187–198.

Hess, U., Kappas, A., McHugo, G. J., Lanzetta, J. T., & Kleck, R. E. (1992). The facilitative effect of facial expression on the self-generation of emotion. *International Journal of Psychophysiology, 12,* 251–265.

Heszen-Niejodek, I. (1997). Coping style and its role in coping with stressful encounters. *European Psychologist, 2,* 342–351.

Hettema, J. M., Neale, M. C., & Kendler, K. S. (2001). A review and meta-analysis of the genetic epidemiology of anxiety disorders. *American Journal of Psychiatry, 158,* 1568–1578.

Higley, J. D., Mehlman, P. T., Higley, S. B., Fernald, B., Vickers, J., Lindell, S. G., et al. (1996). Excessive mortality in young free-ranging male nonhuman primates with low cerebrospinal fluid 5-hydroxyindoleacetic acid concentrations. *Archives of General Psychiatry, 53,* 537–543.

Hildebrandt, K. A., & Fitzgerald, H. E. (1979). Facial feature determinants of perceived infant attractiveness. *Infant Behavior and Development, 2*(4), 329–339.

Hitchcock, J. M., & Davis, M. (1991). Efferent pathway of the amygdala involved in conditioned fear as measured with the fear-potentiated startle paradigm. *Behavioral Neuroscience, 105,* 826–842.

Hobson, C. J., & Delunas, L. (2001). National norms and life-event frequencies for the revised social readjustment rating scale. *International Journal of Stress Management, 8,* 299–314.

Hobson, C. J., Kamen, J., Szostek, J., Neithercut, C. M., Tidemann, J. W., & Wojnarowicz, S. (1998). Stressful life events: A revision and update of the social readjustment rating scale. *International Journal of Stress Management, 5,* 1–23.

Hochschild, A. R. (2002). *The managed heart.* Berkeley: University of California Press.

Hodgins, S., Mednick, S. A., Brennan, P. A., Schulsinger, F., & Engberg, M. (1996). Mental disorders and crime. *Archives of General Psychiatry, 53,* 489–496.

Hoehl, S., & Striano, T. (2008). Neural processing of eye gaze and threat-related emotional facial expressions in infancy. *Child Development, 79,* 1752–1760.

Hofstee, W. K. B., Kiers, H. A., de Raad, B., & Goldberg, L. R. (1997). A comparison of big-five structures of personality traits in Dutch, English, and German. *European Journal of Personality, 11*(1), 15–31.

Holahan, C. J., Moos, R. H., Holahan, C. K., Brennan, P. L., & Schutte, K. K. (2005). Stress generation, avoidance coping, and depressive symptoms: A 10-year model. *Journal of Consulting and Clinical Psychology, 73*(4), 658–666.

Hollander, E., Braun, A., & Simeon, D. (2008). Should OCD leave the anxiety disorders in DSM-V? The case for obsessive compulsive-related disorders. *Depression and Anxiety, 25*(4), 317–329.

Holmes, D. S. (1978). Projection as a defense mechanism. *Psychological Bulletin, 85,* 677–688.

Holmes, D. S. (1987). The influence of meditation versus rest on physiological arousal: A second examination. In M. A. West (Ed.), *The psychology of meditation* (pp. 81–103). Oxford, England: Clarendon Press.

Holmes, D. S. (1990). The evidence for repression: An examination of sixty years of research. In J. L. Singer (Ed.), *Repression and dissociation* (pp. 85–102). New York: Wiley.

Holmes, T. H., & Rahe, R. H. (1977). The social readjustment rating scale. *Journal of Psychosomatic Research, 11,* 213–218.

Hong, Y., Morris, M. W., Chiu, C., & Benet-Martinez, V. (2000). Multicultural minds: A dynamic constructivist approach to culture and cognition. *American Psychologist, 55,* 709–720.

Hornstein, S. L., Brown, A. S., & Mulligan, N. W. (2003). Long-term flashbulb memory for learning of Princess Diana's death. *Memory, 11,* 293–206.

Howard, J. W., & Dawes, R. M. (1976). Linear prediction of marital happiness. *Personality and Social Psychology Bulletin, 2,* 478–480.

Howell, S. (1981). Rules not words. In P. Heelas & A. Lock (Eds.), *Indigenous psychologies: The anthropologies of the self* (pp. 133–143). San Diego, CA: Academic Press.

Howell, S., Westergaard, G., Hoos, B., Chavanne, T. J., Shoaf, S. E., Cleveland, A., et al. (2007). Serotonergic influences on life-history outcomes in free-ranging male rhesus macaques. *American Journal of Primatology, 69,* 851–865.

Howells, K., Day, A., Williamson, P., Bubner, S., Jauncey, S., Parker, A., et al. (2005). Brief anger management programs with offenders: Outcomes and predictors of change. *Journal of Forensic Psychiatry & Psychology, 16,* 296–311.

Hudson, J. I., Mangweth, B., Pope, H. G., Jr., De Col, C., Hausmann, A., Gutweniger, S., et al. (2003). Family study of affective spectrum disorder. *Archives of General Psychiatry, 60,* 170–177.

Hugoson, A., Ljungquist, B., & Breivik, T. (2002). The relationship of some negative events and psychological factors to periodontal disease in an adult Swedish population 50 to 80 years of age. *Journal of Clinical Periodontology, 29,* 247–253.

Hull, E. M., Eaton, R. C., Markowski, V. P., Moses, J., Lumley, L. A., & Loucks, J. A. (1992). Opposite influence of medial preoptic D_1 and D_2 receptors on genital reflexes: Implications for copulation. *Life Sciences, 51,* 1705–1713.

Hunt, N., & Evans, D. (2004). Predicting traumatic stress using emotional intelligence. *Behaviour Research and Therapy, 42*(7), 791–798.

Hupka, R. B., Lenton, A. P., & Hutchison, K. A. (1999). Universal development of emotion categories in natural language. *Journal of Personality and Social Psychology, 77,* 247–278.

Huston, T. L., Niehuis, S., & Smith, S. E. (2001). The early marital roots of conjugal distress and divorce. *Current Directions in Psychological Science, 10,* 116–119.

Iacono, W. G., & Patrick, C. J. (1999). Polygraph ("lie detector") testing: The state of the art. In A. K. Hess & I. B. Weiner (Eds.), *Handbook of forensic psychology* (pp. 440–473). New York: Wiley.

Ickes, W., Stinson, L., Bissonnette, V., & Garcia, S. (1990). Naturalistic social cognition: Empathic accuracy in mixed-sex dyads. *Journal of Personality and Social Psychology, 59,* 730–742.

Iidaka, T., Omori, M., Murata, T., Kosaka, H., Yonekura, Y., Okada, T., et al. (2001). Neural interaction of the amygdala with the prefrontal and temporal cortices in the processing of facial expressions as revealed by fMRI. *Journal of Cognitive Neuroscience, 13,* 1035–1047.

Imhoff, R., & Banse, R. (2009). Ongoing victim suffering increases prejudice. *Psychological Science, 20,* 1443–1447.

Inglehart, R., Foa, R., Peterson, C., & Welzel, C. (2008). Development, freedom, and rising happiness. *Perspectives on Psychological Science, 3,* 264–285.

Inoue-Sakurai, C., Maruyama, S., & Morimoto, K. (2000). Posttraumatic stress and lifestyles are associated with natural killer cell activity in victims of the Hanshin-Awaji earthquake in Japan. *Preventive Medicine, 31,* 467–473.

Ireland, J. L. (2004). Anger management therapy with young male offenders: An evaluation of treatment outcome. *Aggressive Behavior, 30,* 174–185.

Iribarren, C., Signey, S., Bild, D. E., Liu, K., Markovitz, J. H., Roseman, J. M., et al. (2000). Association of hostility with coronary artery calcification in young adults. *Journal of the American Medical Association, 283,* 2546–2551.

Irwin, M., Daniels, M., Risch, S. C., Bloom, E., & Weiner, H. (1988). Plasma cortisol and natural killer cell activity during bereavement. *Biological Psychology, 24,* 173–178.

Isaacowitz, D. M., Toner, K., Goren, D., & Wilson, H. R. (2008). Looking while unhappy. *Psychological Science, 19,* 848–853.

Isabella, R. A., & Belsky, J. (1991). Interactional synchrony and the origins of infant-mother attachment. *Child Development, 62,* 373–384.

Isen, A. M., Daubman, K. A., & Nowicki, G. P. (1987). Positive affect facilitates creative problem solving. *Journal of Personality and Social Psychology, 52,* 1122–1131.

Izard, C. E. (1992). Basic emotions, relations among emotions, and emotion-cognition relations. *Psychological Review, 99*(3), 561–555.

Izard, C. E. (1994). Innate and universal facial expressions: Evidence from developmental and cross-cultural research. *Psychological Bulletin, 115,* 288–299.

Izard, C. E. (2001). Emotional intelligence or adaptive emotions? *Emotion, 1,* 249–257.

Izard, C. E., & Abe, J. A. A. (2004). Developmental changes in facial expressions of emotions in the Strange Situation during the second year of life. *Emotion, 4,* 251–265.

Jackson, D. C., Malmstadt, J. R., Larson, C. L., & Davidson, R. J. (2000). Suppression and enhancement of emotional responses to unpleasant pictures. *Psychophysiology, 37,* 515–522.

Jackson, R. W., Treiber, F. A., Turner, J. R., Davis, H., & Strong, W. B. (1999). Effects of race, sex, and socioeconomic status upon cardiovascular stress responsivity and recovery in youth. *International Journal of Psychophysiology, 31,* 111–119.

James, W. (1884). What is an emotion? *Mind, 9,* 188–205.

James, W. (1894). The physical basis of emotion. *Psychological Review, 1,* 516–529.

James, W. (1961). *Psychology: The briefer course.* New York: Harper. (Original work published 1892).

Janis, I. L. (1983). Stress inoculation in health care. In D. Meichenbaum & M. E. Jaremko (Eds.), *Stress reduction and prevention* (pp. 67–99). New York: Plenum.

Jankowiak, W. R., & Fischer, E. F. (1992). A cross-cultural perspective on romantic love. *Ethnology, 31,* 149–155.

Jensen-Campbell, L. A., Knack, J. M., Waldrip, A. M., & Campbell, S. D. (2007). Do big five personality traits associated with self-control influence the regulation of anger and aggression? *Journal of Research in Personality, 41*(2), 403–424.

Jerome, E. M., & Liss, M. (2005). Relationships between sensory processing style, adult attachment, and coping. *Personality and Individual Differences, 38,* 1341–1352.

Johnson, J. G., Cohen, P., Smailes, E. M., Kasen, S., & Brook, J. S. (2002). Television viewing and aggressive behavior during adolescence and adulthood. *Science, 295,* 2468–2471.

Johnson, K. J., & Fredrickson, B. L. (2005). "We all look the same to me": Positive emotions eliminate the own-race bias in face recognition. *Psychological Science, 16*(11), 875–881.

Johnson, M. H., Posner, M. I., & Rothbart, M. K. (1991). Components of visual orienting in early infancy: Contingency learning, anticipatory looking, and disengaging. *Journal of Cognitive Neuroscience, 3,* 335–344.

Joint Committee on Standards. (1999). *Standards for Educational and Psychological Testing.* Washington, D.C.: American Educational Research Association.

Jones, A., & Fitness, J. (2008). Moral hypervigilance: The influence of disgust sensitivity in the moral domain. *Emotion, 8,* 613–627.

Jonsson, C. O., Clinton, D. N., Fahrman, M., Mazzaglia, G., Novak, S., & Sörhus, K. (2001). How do mothers signal share feeling-states to their infants? An investigation of affect attunement and imitation during the first year of life. *Scandinavian Journal of Psychology, 42,* 377–381.

Juslin, P. N., & Laukka, P. (2003). Communication of emotions in vocal expression and music performance: Different channels, same code? *Psychological Bulletin, 129,* 770–814.

Kafetsios, K. (2004). Attachment and emotional intelligence abilities across the life course. *Personality and Individual Differences, 37,* 129–145.

Kagan, J., & Snidman, N. (1991). Infant predictors of inhibited and uninhibited profiles. *Psychological Science, 2,* 40–44.

Kagan, J., Reznick, J. S., & Snidman, N. (1988). Biological bases of childhood shyness. *Science, 240,* 167–171.

Kahneman, D., Krueger, A. B., Schkade, D., Schwarz, N., & Stone, A. A. (2006). Would you be happier if you were richer? A focusing illusion. *Science, 312,* 1908–1910.

Kalick, S. M., Zebrowitz, L. A., Langlois, J. H., & Johnson, R. M. (1998). Does human facial attractiveness honestly advertise health? *Psychological Science, 9,* 8–13.

Kalin, N. H., Shelton, S. E., & Barksdale, C. M. (1988). Opiate modulation of separation-induced distress in non-human primates. *Brain Research, 440,* 285–292.

Kalin, N. H., Shelton, S. E., & Davidson, R. J. (2004). The role of the central nucleus of the amygdala in mediating fear and anxiety in the primate. *Journal of Neuroscience, 24,* 5506–5515.

Kampe, K. K., Frith, C. D., Dolan, R. J., & Frith, U. (2002). Reward value of attractiveness and gaze. *Nature, 413,* 589–590.

Kanwisher, N. (2000). Domain specificity in face perception. *Nature Neuroscience, 3*(8), 759–763.

Karney, B. R., & Bradbury, T. N. (1995). The longitudinal course of marital quality and stability: A review of theory, method, and research. *Psychological Review, 118,* 3–34.

Kassinove, H., Sudholdolsky, D. G., Tsytsarev, S. V., & Solovyova, S. (1997). Self-reported constructions of anger episodes in Russia and America. *Journal of Social Behavior and Personality, 12,* 301–324.

Katkin, E. S. (1985). Blood, sweat, and tears: Individual differences in autonomic self-perception. *Psychophysiology, 22*(2), 125–137.

Katkin, E. S., Wiens, S., & Öhman, A. (2001). Nonconscious fear conditioning, visceral perception, and the development of gut feelings. *Psychological Science, 12,* 366–370.

Kawachi, I., Sparrow, D., Kubzansky, L. D., Spiro, A., Vokonas, P. S., & Weiss, S. T. (1998). Prospective study of a self-report Type A scale and risk of coronary heart disease. *Circulation, 98,* 405–412.

Kawamura, N., Kim, Y., & Asukai, N. (2001). Suppression of cellular immunity in men with a past history of posttraumatic stress disorder. *American Journal of Psychiatry, 158,* 484–486.

Kawasaki, H., Adolphs, R., Kaufman, O., Damasio, H., Damasio, A. R., Granner, M., et al. (2001). Single-neuron responses to emotional visual stimuli recorded in human ventral prefrontal cortex. *Nature Neuroscience, 4,* 15–16.

Keillor, J. M., Barrett, A. M., Crucian, G. P., Kortenkamp, S., & Heilman, K. M. (2002). Emotional experience and perception in the absence of facial feedback. *Journal of the International Neuropsychological Society, 8,* 130–135.

Keith-Lucas, T., & Guttman, N. (1975). Robust single-trial delayed backward conditioning. *Journal of Comparative and Physiological Psychology, 88,* 468–476.

Keller, M. C., Fredrickson, B. L., Ybarra, O., Côté, S., Johnson, K., Mikels, J., et al. (2005). A warm heart and a clear head. *Psychological Science, 16,* 724–731.

Keller, M. C., & Nesse, R. M. (2006). The evolutionary significance of depressive symptoms: Different adverse situations lead to different depressive symptom patterns. *Journal of Personality and Social Psychology, 91*(2), 316–330.

Kelly, K. M., & Jones, W. H. (1997). Assessment of dispositional embarrassibility. *Anxiety, Stress, and Coping, 10,* 307–333.

Keltner, D. (1995). Signs of appeasement: Evidence for the distinct displays of embarrassment, amusement, and shame. *Journal of Personality and Social Psychology, 68,* 441–454.

Keltner, D., & Buswell, B. N. (1997). Embarrassment: Its distinct form and appeasement functions. *Psychological Bulletin, 122,* 250–270.

Keltner, D., Ellsworth, P. C., & Edwards, K. (1993). –Beyond simple pessimism: Effects of sadness and anger on social perception. *Journal of Personality and Social Psychology, 64,* 740–752.

Keltner, D., Gruenfeld, D. H., & Anderson, C. (2003). Power, approach, and inhibition. *Psychological Review, 110,* 265–284.

Keltner, D., & Haidt, J. (1999). Social functions of emotions at four levels of analysis. *Cognition and Emotion, 13,* 505–521.

Keltner, D. Haidt, J., & Shiota, M. N. (2006). Social functionalism and the evolution of emotions. In M. Schaller, J. A. Simpson, & D. T. Kenrick (Eds.), *Evolution and Social Psychology* (pp. 115–142). Madison, CT: Psychosocial Press.

Keltner, D., & Shiota, M. N. (2003). New displays and new emotions: A commentary on Rozin and Cohen (2003). *Emotion, 3,* 86–91.

Keltner, D., Young, R. C., & Buswell, B. N. (1997). Appeasement in human emotion, social practice, and personality. *Aggressive Behavior, Special Issue: Appeasement and Reconciliation, 23*(5), 359–374.

Kendler, K. S., Gardner, C. O., & Prescott, C. A. (1999). Clinical characteristics of major depression that predict risk of depression in relatives. *Archives of General Psychiatry, 56,* 322–327.

Kendler, K. S., Kuhn, J., & Prescott, C. A. (2004). The interrelationship of neuroticism, sex, and stressful life events in the prediction of episodes of major depression. *The American Journal of Psychiatry, 161*(4), 631–636.

Kendler, K. S., Myers, J., & Prescott, C. A. (2002). The etiology of phobias. *Archives of General Psychiaty, 59,* 242–248.

Kendler, K. S., Myers, J., Prescott, C. A., & Neale, M. C. (2001). The genetic epidemiology of irrational fears and phobias in men. *Archives of General Psychiatry, 58,* 257–265.

Kendler, K. S., Walters, E. E., Neale, M. C., Kessler, R. C., Heath, A. C., & Eaves, L. J. (1995). The structure of the genetic and environmental risk factors for six major psychiatric disorders in women. *Archives of General Psychiatry, 52,* 374–383.

Kennedy, D. P., Gläscher, J., Tyszka, J. M., & Adolphs, R. (2009). Personal space regulation by the human amygdala. *Nature Neuroscience, 10,* 1226–1227.

Kennedy, Q., Mather, M., & Carstensen, L. L. (2004). The role of motivation in the age-related positivity effect in autobiographical memory. *Psychological Science, 15*(3), 208–214.

Kensinger, E. A., & Corkin, S. (2003). Memory enhancement for emotional words: Are emotional words more vividly remembered than neutral words? *Memory & Cognition, 31,* 1169–1180.

Keverne, E. B., & Kendrick, K. M. (1992). Oxytocin facilitation of maternal behavior in sheep. *Annals of the New York Academy of Science, 807,* 455–468.

Kiecolt-Glaser, J. K. (1999). Stress, personal relationships, and immune function: Health implications. *Brain, Behavior, and Immunity, 13,* 61–72.

Kiecolt-Glaser, J. K., McGuire, L., Robles, T. F., & Glaser, R. (2002). Psychoneuroimmunology: Psychological influences on immune function and health. *Journal of Consulting and Clinical Psychology, 70,* 537–547.

Kiecolt-Glaser, J. K., & Newton, T. L. (2001). Marriage and health: His and hers. *Psychological Bulletin, 127,* 472–503.

Kiecolt-Glaser, J. K., Robles, T. F., Heffner, K. L., Loving, T. J., & Glaser, R. (2002). Psycho-oncology and cancer: Psychoneuroimmunology and cancer. *Annals of Oncology, 13*(Suppl. 4), 165–169.

Kim, H. S., & Sherman, D. K. (2007). "Express yourself": Culture and the effect of self-expression on choice. *Journal of Personality and Social Psychology, 92*(1), 1–11.

Kim, H. S., Sherman, D. K., & Taylor, S. E. (2008). Culture and social support. *American Psychologist, 63,* 518–526.

Kim, J., & Hatfield, E. (2004). Love types and subjective well-being: A cross cultural study. *Social Behavior and Personality, 32*(2), 173–182.

Kim, S., Healey, M. K., Goldstein, D., Hasher, L., & Wiprzycka, U. J. (2008). Age differences in choice satisfaction. *Psychology and Aging, 23,* 33–38.

King, J. E., & Landau, V. I. (2003). Can chimpanzees (*Pan troglodytes*) happiness be estimated by human raters? *Journal of Research in Personality, 37,* 1–15.

Kirsch, I. (2010). *The emperor's new drugs.* New York: Basic books.

Kirsch, L. G., & Becker, J. V. (2007). Emotional deficits in psychopathy and sexual sadism: Implications for violent and sadistic behavior. *Clinical Psychology Review, 27*(8), 904–922.

Kitayama, S., Markus, H. R., & Kurokawa, M. (2000). Culture, emotion, and well-being: Good feelings in Japan and the United States. *Cognition and Emotion, 14,* 93–124.

Klaus, M. H., & Kennell, J. H. (1976). *Maternal-infant bonding.* St. Louis, MO: Mosby.

Klein, K., & Boals, A. (2001). The relationship of life event stress and working memory capacity. *Applied Cognitive Psychology, 15,* 565–579.

Kleinmuntz, B., & Szucko, J. J. (1984). A field study of the fallibility of polygraphic lie detection. *Nature, 308,* 449–450.

Klineberg, O. (1938). Emotional expression in Chinese literature. *Journal of Abnormal and Social Psychology, 31,* 517–520.

Klinnert, M. D., Emde, R. N., Butterfield, P., & Campos, J. J. (1986). Social referencing: The infant's use of emotional signals from a friendly adult with mother present. *Developmental Psychology, 22,* 427–432.

Klohnen, E. C., & Mendelsohn, G. A. (1998). Partner selection for personality characteristics: A person-centered approach. *Personality and Social Psychology Bulletin, 24,* 268–278.

Kluger, M. J. (1991). Fever: Role of pyrogens and cryogens. *Phsyiological Reviews, 71,* 93–127.

Klüver, H., & Bucy, P. C. (1939). Preliminary analysis of functions of the temporal lobes in monkeys. *Archives of Neurological Psychiatry, 42,* 979–1000.

Kniffin, K. M., & Wilson, D. S. (2004). The effect of nonphysical traits on the perception of physical attractiveness. *Evolution and Human Behavior, 25,* 88–101.

Knight, M., Seymour, T. L., Gaunt, J. T., Baker, C., Nesmith, K., & Mather, M. (2007). Aging and goal-directed emotional attention: Distraction reverses emotional biases. *Emotion, 7,* 705–714.

Knutson, B., Bhanji, J., Cooney, R., Atlas, L., & Gotlib, I. (2008). Neural responses to monetary incentives in major depression. *Biological Psychiatry, 63*(7), 686–692.

Knutson, B., Taylor, J., Kaufman, M., Peterson, R., & Glover, G. (2005). Distributed neural representation of expected value. *Journal of Neuroscience, 25*(19), 4806–4812.

Knyazev, C. G., Slobodskaya, H. R., & Wilson, G. D. (2002). Psychophysiological correlates of behavioural inhibition and activation. *Personality and Individual Differences, 33,* 647–660.

Koehler, N., Simmons, L. W., Rhodes, G., & Peters, M. (2004). The relationship between sexual dimorphism in human faces and fluctuating asymmetry. *Proceedings of the Royal Society of London B, 271* (Biology Letters Suppl. 5), S233–S236.

Koenigs, M., Huey, E. D., Raymont, V., Cheon, B., Solomon, J., Wassermann, E. M., et al. (2008). Focal brain damage protects against post-traumatic stress disorder in combat veterans. *Nature Neuroscience, 11,* 232–237.

Koepp, M. J., Gunn, R. N., Lawrence, A. D., Cunningham, V. J., Dagher, A., Jones, T., et al. (1998). Evidence for striatal dopamine release during a video game. *Nature, 393,* 266–268.

Kohler, C. G., Turner, T. H., Bilker, W. B., Brensinger, C. M., Siegel, S. J., Kanes, S. J., et al. (2003). Facial emotion recognition in schizophrenia: Intensity effects and error pattern. *American Journal of Psychiatry, 160,* 1768–1774.

Kokkinaki, T. (2003). A longitudinal, naturalistic and cross-cultural study on emotions in early infant-parent imitative interactions. *British Journal of Developmental Psychology, 21,* 243–258.

Kontsevich, L. L., & Tyler, C. W. (2004). What makes Mona Lisa smile? *Vision Research, 44,* 1493–1498.

Kornreich, C., Blairy, S., Philippot, P., Hess, U., Noel, X., Streel, E., et al. (2001). Deficits in recognition of emotional facial expression are still present in alcoholics after mid- to long-term abstinence. *Journal of Studies on Alcohol, 62,* 533–542.

Kosfeld, M., Heinrichs, M., Zak, P. J., Fischbacher, U., & Fehr, E. (2005). Oxytocin increases trust in humans. *Nature, 435,* 673–676.

Koster, E. H. W., Crombez, G., Van Damme, S., Verschuere, B., & De Houwer, J. (2004). Does imminent threat capture andhold attention? *Emotion, 4,* 312–317.

Kraaij, V., Pruymboom, E., & Garnefski, N. (2002). Cognitive coping and depressive symptoms in the elderly: A longitudinal study. *Aging & Mental Health, 6,* 275–281.

Kraemer, D. L., & Hastrup, J. L. (1988). Crying in adults: Self-control and autonomic correlates. *Journal of Social and Clinical Psychology, 6,* 53–68.

Kraft, J. B., Slager, S. L., McGrath, P. J., & Hamilton, S. P. (2005). Sequence analysis of the serotonin transporter and associations with antidepressant response. *Biological Psychiatry, 58*(5), 374–381.

Krajbich, I., Adolphs, R., Tranel, D., Denburg, N. L., & Camerer, C. F. (2009). Economic games quantify diminished sense of guilt in patients with damage to the prefrontal cortex. *Journal of Neuroscience, 29,* 2188–2192.

Krauth-Gruber, S., & Ric, F. (2000). Affect and stereotypic thinking: A test of the mood-and-general-knowledge-model. *Personality and Social Psychology Bulletin, 26*(12), 1587–1597.

Krawczyk, D. C. (2002). Contributions of the prefrontal cortex to the neural basis of human decision making. *Neuroscience and Biobehavioral Reviews, 26,* 631–664.

Kring, A. M. (2008). Emotion disturbances as transdiagnostic processes in psychopathology. In M. Lewis, J. M. Haviland-Jones & L. F. Barrett (Eds.), *Handbook of emotions (3rd ed.).* (pp. 691–705). New York, NY, U.S.: Guilford Press.

Kring, A. M., & Neale, J. M. (1996). Do schizophrenic patients show a disjunctive relationship among expressive, experiential, and psychophysiological components of emotion? *Journal of Abnormal Psychology, 105*(2), 249–257.

Kruesi, M. J. P., Hibbs, E. D., Zahn, T. P., Keysor, C. S., Hamburger, S. D., Bartko, J. J., et al. (1992). A 2-year prospective follow-up of children and adolescents with disruptive behavior disorders. *Archives of General Psychiatry, 49,* 429–435.

Kruk, M. R., Halász, J., Meelis, W., & Haller, J. (2004). Fast positive feedback between the adrenocortical stress response and a brain mechanism involved in aggressive behavior. *Behavioral Neuroscience, 118,* 1062–1070.

Kubzansky, L. D., Koenen, K. C., Jones, C., & Eaton, W. W. (2009). A prospective study of posttraumatic stress disorder symptoms and coronary heart disease in women. *Health Psychology, 28*(1), 125–130.

Kübler, A., Kotchoubey, B., Kaiser, J., Wolpaw, J. R., & Birbaumer, N. (2001). Brain-computer communication: Unlocking the locked-in. *Psychological Bulletin, 127,* 358–375.

Kubota, Y., Sato, W., Murai, T., Toichi, M., Ikeda, A., & Sengoku, A. (2000). Emotional cognition without awareness after unilateral temporal lobectomy in humans. *Journal of Neuroscience, 20,* RC97, 1–5.

Kubzhansky, L. D., Martin, L. T., & Buka, S. L. (2004). Early manifestations of personality and adult emotional functioning. *Emotion, 4,* 364–377.

Kuepper, Y., Alexander, N., Osinsky, R., Mueller, E., Schmitz, A., Netter, P., & Hennig, J. (2010). Aggression-Interactions of serotonin and testosterone in healthy men and women. *Behavioural Brain Research, 34*(9), 1294–1303.

Kundera, M. (1980). *The book of laughter and forgetting* (M. H. Heim, Trans.). New York: Knopf. (Original work published 1979).

Kuppens, P. (2005). Interpersonal determinants of trait anger: Low agreeableness, perceived low social esteem, and the amplifying role of the importance attached to social relationships. *Personality and Individual Differences, 38*(1), 13–23.

Kuppens, P., Van Mechelen, I., & Rijmen, F. (2008). Toward disentangling sources of individual differences in appraisal and anger. *Journal of Personality, 76,* 969–1000.

Kuppens, P. P., Van Mechelen, I., Smits, D. J. M., & De Boeck, P. (2003). The appraisal basis of anger: Specificity, necessity, and sufficiency of components. *Emotion, 3,* 254–269.

Kurdek, L. A. (2005). What do we know about gay and lesbian couples? *Current Directions in Psychological Science, 14*(5), 251–254.

Kwon, J. T., & Choi, J.-S. (2009). Cornering the fear engram: Long-term synaptic changes in the lateral nucleus of the amygdala after fear conditioning. *Journal of Neuroscience, 29,* 9700–9703.

LaBar, K. S., Cook, C. A., Torpey, D. C., & Welsh-Bohmer, K. A. (2004). Impact of healthy aging on awareness and fear conditioning. *Behavioral Neuroscience, 118*(5), 905–915.

LaBar, K. S., Gatenby, J. C., Gore, J. C., LeDoux, J. E., & Phelps, E. A. (1998). Human amygdala activation during conditioned fear acquisition and extinction: A mixed trial fMRI study. *Neuron, 20,* 937–945.

LaBar, K. S., & Phelps, E. A. (1998). Arousal-mediated memory consolidation: Role of the medial temporal lobe in humans. *Psychological Science, 9,* 490–493.

Labouvie-Vief, G., Lumley, M. A., Jain, E., & Heinze, H. (2003). Age and gender differences in cardiac reactivity and subjective emotion responses to emotional autobiographical memories. *Emotion, 3,* 115–126.

Lachman, M. E., & Firth, K. M. P. (2004). The adaptive value of feeling in control during midlife. In O. G. Brim, C. D. Ryff, & R. C. Kessler (Eds.), *How healthy are we?* (pp. 320–349). Chicago: University of Chicago Press.

Ladabaum, U., Minoshima, S., Hasler, W. L., Cross, D., Chey, W. D., & Owyang, C. (2001). Gastric distention correlates with activation of multiple cortical and subcortical regions. *Gastroenterology, 120*(2), 369–376.

LaFramboise, T., Coleman, H. L., K., & Gerton, J. (1993). Psychological impact of biculturalism: Evidence and theory. *Psychological Bulletin, 114,* 395–412.

LaFrance, M., Hecht, M. A., & Paluck, E. L. (2003). The contingent smile: A meta-analysis of sex differences in smiling. *Psychological Bulletin, 129,* 305–334.

Laible, D. J., Carlo, G., & Raffaelli, M. (2000). The differential relations of parent and peer attachment to adolescent adjustment. *Journal of Youth and Adolescence, 29,* 45–59.

Lakin, J. L., & Chartrand, T. L. (2003). Using nonconscious behavioral mimicry to create affiliation and rapport. *Psychological Science, 14,* 334–339.

Lang, P. J., Bradley, M. M., & Cuthbert, B. N. (2002). A motivational analysis of emotion: Reflex-cortex connections. In J. T. Cacioppo et al. (Eds.), *Foundations in social neuroscience* (pp. 461–471). Cambridge, MA: MIT Press.

Lange, C. G. (1922). The emotions: A psychological study. (I. A. Haupt, Trans.) In C. G. Lange & W. James, *The emotions* (pp. 33–90). Baltimore, MD: Williams & Wilkins. (Original work published 1885).

Langer, E. J. (1975). The illusion of control. *Journal of Personality and Social Psychology, 32,* 311–328.

Langlois, J. H., & Roggman, L. A. (1990). Attractive faces are only average. *Psychological Science, 1,* 115–121.

Langlois, J. H., Roggman, L. A., & Musselman, L. (1994). What is average and what is not average about average faces? *Psychological Science, 5,* 214–220.

Larkin, G. R. S., Gibbs, S. E. B., Khanna, K., Nielsen, L., Carstensen, L. L., & Knutson, B. (2007). Anticipation of monetary gain but not loss in healthy older adults. *Nature Neuroscience, 10,* 787–791.

Larsen, J. T., Berntson, G. G., Poehlmann, K. M., Ito, T. A., & Cacioppo, J. T. (2008). The psycho-physiology of emotion. In M. Lewis, J. M. Haviland-Jones & L. F. Barrett (Eds.), *Handbook of emotions (3rd ed.).* (pp. 180–195). New York, NY, U.S.: Guilford Press.

Larsen, J. T., McGraw, A. P., & Cacioppo, J. T. (2001). Can people feel happy and sad at the same time? *Journal of Personality and Social Psychology, 81,* 684–696.

Larsen, J. T., McGraw, A. P., Mellers, B. A., & Cacioppo, J. T. (2004). The agony of victory and thrill of defeat. *Psychological Science, 15,* 325–330.

Larsen, R. J., Kasimatis, M., & Frey, K. (1992). Facilitating the furrowed brow—An unobtrusive test of the facial feedback hypothesis applied to unpleasant affect. *Cognition & Emotion, 6,* 321–338.

Larsen, R. J., & Ketelaar, T. (1989). Extraversion, neuroticism, and susceptibility to positive and negative mood induction procedures. *Personality and Individual Differences, 10,* 1221–1228.

Larsson, H., Andershed, H., & Lichtenstein, P. (2006). A genetic factor explains most of the variation in the psychopathic personality. *Journal of Abnormal Psychology, 115*(2), 221–230.

Latta, R. L. (1999). *The Basic Humor Process: A Cognitive-Shift Theory and the Case Against Incongruity.* New York: Mouton de Gruyter.

Laudenslager, M. L., Aasal, R., Adler, L., Berger, C. L., Montgomery, P. T., Sandberg, E., et al. (1998). Elevated cytotoxicity in combat veterans with long-term post-traumatic stress disorder: Preliminary observations. *Brain, Behavior, and Immunity, 12,* 74–79.

Launay, J. M., Del Pino, M., Chironi, G., Callebert, J., Peoc'h, K., Mégnien, J. L., et al. (2009). Smoking induces long-lasting effects through a monoamine-oxidase epigenetic regulation. *PloS One, 4,* e7959.

Laursen, B., Coy, K. C., & Collins, W. A. (1998). Reconsidering changes in parent-child conflict across adolescence: A meta-analysis. *Child Development, 69,* 817–832.

Lavoie, M., Lam, R. W., Bouchard, G., Sasseville, A., Charron, M., Gagné, A., Tremblay, A., Filteau, M., & Hébert, M. (2009). Evidence of a biological effect of light therapy on the retina of patients with seasonal affective disorder. *Biological Psychiatry, 66*(3), 253–258.

Lawton, M. P. (2001). Emotion in later life. *Current Directions in Psychological Science, 10,* 120–123.

Lazarus, R. S. (1977). Cognitive and coping responses in emotion. In A. Monat & R. S. Lazarus (Eds.), *Stress and coping* (pp. 145–158). New York: Columbia University Press.

Lazarus, R. S. (1991). *Emotion and adaptation.* New York: Oxford University Press.

Lazarus, R. S. (2001). Relational meaning and discrete emotions. In K. R. Scherer, A. Schorr, & T. Johnstone (Eds.), *Appraisal processes in emotion* (pp. 37–67). New York: Oxford University Press.

Leach, C. W., Spears, R., Branscombe, N. R., & Doosje, B. (2003). Malicious pleasure: Schadenfreude at the suffering of another group. *Journal of Personality and Social Psychology, 84,* 932–943.

Leary, M. R. (2001). Shyness and the self: Attentional, motivational, and cognitive self-processes in social anxiety and inhibition. In W. R. Crozier & L. E. Alden (Eds.), *International handbook of social anxiety* (pp. 218–234). Chichester, England: John Wiley.

LeDoux, J. (1996). *The emotional brain.* New York: Simon & Schuster.

LeDoux, J. E., Cicchetti, P., Xagoraris, A., & Romanski, L. M. (1990). The lateral amygdaloid nucleus: Sensory interface of the amygdala in fear conditioning. *Journal of Neuroscience, 10,* 1062–1069.

Lee, R. A., Su, J., & Yoshida, E. (2005). Coping with intergenerational family conflict among Asian American college students. *Journal of Counseling Psychology, 52,* 389–399.

Lefcourt, H. M. (2002). Humor. In C. R. Snyder & S. J. Lopez (Eds.), *Handbook of positive psychology* (pp. 619–631). New York: Oxford University Press.

Lefcourt, H. M., Davidson, K., Shepherd, R., Phillips, M., et al. (1995). Perspective-taking humor: Accounting for stress moderation. *Journal of Social and Clinical Psychology, 14*(4), 373–391.

Lehmann, K. A. (1995). New developments in patient-controlled postoperative analgesia. *Annals of Medicine, 27,* 271–282.

Leonard, B. E. (2000). Peripheral markers of depression. *Current Opinion in Psychiatry, 13,* 61–68.

Leppämäki, S., Partonen, T., & Lönnqvist, J. (2002). Bright-light exposure combined with physical exercise elevates mood. *Journal of Affective Disorders, 72,* 139–144.

Leppänen, J. M., & Hietanen, J. K. (2003). Affect and face perception: Odors modulate the recognition advantage of happy faces. *Emotion, 3,* 315–326.

Lerner, J. S., Gonzalez, R. M., Small, D. A., & Fischhoff, B. (2003). Effects of fear and anger on perceived risks of terrorism: A national field experiment. *Psychological Science, 14,* 144–150.

Lerner, J. S., & Keltner, D. (2000). Beyond valence: Toward a model of emotion-specific influences on judgement and choice. *Cognition and Emotion, 14,* 473–493.

Lerner, J. S., Small, D. A., & Loewenstein, G. (2004). Heart strings and purse strings. *Psychological Science, 15,* 337–341.

Leutgeb, V., Schäfer, A., & Schienle, A. (2009). An event-related potential study on exposure therapy for patients suffering from spider phobia. *Biological Psychology, 82*(3), 293–300.

LeVay, S. (1991). A difference in hypothalamic structure between heterosexual and homosexual men. *Science, 253*(5023), 1034–1037.

Levenson, R. W. (1992). Autonomic nervous system differences among emotions. *Psychological Science, 3,* 23–27.

Levenson, R. W. (1999). The intrapersonal functions of emotion. *Cognition & Emotion, 13,* 481–504.

Levenson, R. W., Carstensen, L. L., & Gottman, J. M. (1994). The influence of age and gender on affect, physiology, and their interrelations: A study of long-term marriages. *Journal of Personality and Social Psychology, 67,* 56–68.

Levenson, R. W., Ekman, P., & Friesen, W. V. (1990). Voluntary facial action generates emotion-specific autonomic nervous system activity. *Psychophysiology, 27,* 363–383.

Levenson, R. W., Ekman, P., Heider, K., & Friesen, W. V. (1992). Emotion and autonomic nervous system activity in the Minangkabau of West Sumatra. *Journal of Personality and Social Psychology, 62,* 972–988.

Levenson, R. W., & Gottman, J. M. (1983). Marital interaction: Physiological linkage and affective exchange. *Journal of Personality and Social Psychology, 45,* 587–597.

Levenson, R. W., & Miller, B. L. (2007). Loss of cells-loss of self. *Current Directions in Psychological Science, 16,* 289–294.

Levenson, R. W., & Ruef, A. M. (1992). Empathy: A physiological substrate. *Journal of Personality and Social Psychology, 63,* 234–246.

Levin, J., & Arluke, A. (1982). Embarrassment and helping behavior. *Psychological Reports, 51,* 999–1002.

Levine, G. M., Halberstadt, J. B., & Goldstone, R. L. (1996). Reasoning and the weighting of attributes in attitude judgments. *Journal of Personality and Social Psychology, 70*(2), 230–240.

Levine, L. J., & Pizarro, D. A. (2004). Emotion and memory research: A grumpy overview. *Social Cognition, 22,* 530–554.

Lévy, F., Kendrick, K. M., Keverne, E. B., Piketty, V., & Poindron, P. (1992). Intracerebral oxytocin is important for the onset of maternal behavior in inexperienced ewes delivered under peridural anesthesia. *Behavioral Neuroscience, 106*(2), 427–432.

Levy, R. (1973). *The Tahitians.* Chicago: University of Chicago Press.

Levy, R. I. (1984). The emotions in comparative perspective. In K. R. Scherer & P. Ekman (Eds.), *Approaches to emotion* (pp. 397–412). Hillsdale, NJ: Erlbaum.

Lewandowski, G. W., Jr., Aron, A., & Gee, J. (2007). Personality goes a long way: The malleability of opposite-sex physical attractiveness. *Personal Relationships, 14*(4), 571–585.

Lewicka, M. (1997). Rational or uncommitted? Depression and indecisiveness in interpersonal decision making. *Scandinavian Journal of Psychology, 38,* 227–236.

Lewis, M. (1992). *Shame: The exposed self.* New York: Free Press.

Lewis, M. (1993). The development of anger and rage. In R. A. Glick & S. P. Roose (Eds.), *Rage, power, and aggression* (pp. 148–168). New Haven, CT: Yale University Press.

Lewis, M., & Brooks-Gunn, J. (1979). *Social cognition and the acquisition of self.* New York: Plenum Press.

Lewis, M., Stanger, S., & Sullivan, M. W. (1989). Deception in 3-year-olds. *Developmental Psychology, 25,* 439–443.

Lewis, M., Sullivan, M. W., Stanger, C., & Weiss, M. (1989). Self-development and self-conscious emotions. *Child Development, 60,* 146–156.

Li, N. P., Bailey, J. M., Kenrick, D. T., & Linsenmeier, J. A. W. (2002). The necessities and luxuries of mate preferences: Testing the tradeoffs. *Journal of Personality and Social Psychology, 82*(6), 947–955.

Li, N. P., Griskevicius, V., Durante, K. M., Jonason, P. K., Pasisz, D. J., & Aumer, K. (2009). An evolutionary perspective on humor: Sexual selection or interest induction? *Personality and Social Psychology Bulletin, 35,* 923–936.

Lieberman, D., Tooby, J., & Cosmides, L. (2003). Does morality have a biological basis? An empirical test of the factors governing moral sentiments relating to incest. *Proceedings of the Royal Society B, 270*(1517), 819–826.

Lieberman, D., Tooby, J., & Cosmides, L. (2007). The architecture of human kin detection. *Nature, 445,* 727–731.

Liew, J., Eisenberg, N., & Reiser, M. (2004). Preschoolers' effortful control and negative emotionality, immediate reactions to disappointment, and quality of social functioning. *Journal of Experimental Child Psychology, 89,* 298–319.

Liew, J., McTigue, E. M., Barrois, L., & Hughes, J. N. (2008). Adaptive and effortful control and academic self-efficacy beliefs on achievement: A longitudinal study of 1st through 3rd graders. *Early Childhood Research Quarterly, 23,* 515–526.

Lillberg, K., Verkasalo, P. K., Kaprio, J., Teppo., L., Helenius, H., & Koskenvuo, M. (2003). Stressful life events and risk of breast cancer in 10,808 women: A cohort study. *American Journal of Epidemiology, 157,* 415–423.

Lilly, R., Cummings, J. L., Benson, F., & Frankel, M.. (1983). The human Klüver-Bucy syndrome. *Neurology, 33,* 1141–1145.

Lim, M. M., Wang, Z., Olazábal, D. E., Ren, X., Terwilliger, E. F., & Young, L. J. (2004). Enhanced partner preference in a promiscuous species by manipulating the expression of a single gene. *Nature, 429,* 754–757.

Liu, L. Y., Coe, C. L., Swenson, C. A., Kelly, E. A., Kita, H., & Busse, W. W. (2002). School examinations enhance airway inflammation to antigen challenge. *American Journal of Respiratory and Critical Care Medicine, 165,* 1062–1067.

Locke, E. A. (2005). Why emotional intelligence is an invalid concept. *Journal of Organizational Behavior, 26,* 425–431.

Loewenstein, G. (1987). Anticipation and the valuation of delayed consumption. *The Economic Journal, 97,* 666–684.

Logue, A. W. (1985). Conditioned food aversion learning in humans. *Annals of the New York Academy of Sciences, 443,* 316–329.

Lonsdorf, T. B., Weike, A. I., Nikamo, P., Schalling, M., Hamm, A. O., & Öhman, A. (2009). Genetic gating of human fear learning and extinction. *Psychological Science, 20,* 198–206.

Lopes, P. N., Brackett, M. A., Nezlek, J. B., Schütz, A., Sellin, I., & Salovey, P. (2004). Emotional intelligence and social interaction. *Personality and Social Psychology Bulletin, 30*(8), 1018–1034.

Lorenz, K. (1971). *Studies in animal and human behaviour: II. trans. R. martin.* Oxford, England: Harvard U. Press.

Löw, A., Lang, P. J., Smith, J. C., & Bradley, M. M. (2008). Both predator and prey. *Psychological Science, 19,* 865–873.

Lowe, J., & Carroll, D. (1985). The effects of spinal injury on the intensity of emotional experience. *British Journal of Clinical Psychology, 24,* 135–136.

Lucas, R. E. (2007). Long-term disability is associated with lasting changes in subjective well-being: Evidence from two nationally representative longitudinal studies. *Journal of Personality and Social Psychology, 92,* 717–730.

Lucas, R. E., & Baird, B. M. (2004). Extraversion and emotional reactivity. *Journal of Personality and Social Psychology, 86*(3), 473–485.

Lucas, R. E., Clark, A. E., Georgellis, Y., & Diener, E. (2003). Reexamining adaptation and the set point model of happiness: Reactions to changes in marital status. *Journal of Personality and Social Psychology, 84,* 527–539.

Lucas, R. E., Clark, A. E., Georgellis, Y., & Diener, E. (2004). Unemployment alters the set point for life satisfaction. *Psychological Science, 15,* 8–13.

Lucas, R. E., & Fujita, F. (2000). Factors influencing the relation between extraversion and pleasant affect. *Journal of Personality and Social Psychology, 79*(6), 1039–1056.

Lucas, R. E., & Schimmack, U. (2009). Income and well-being: How big is the gap between the rich and the poor? *Journal of Research in Personality, 43,* 75–78.

Ludwig, D., Goetz, P., Balgemann, D., & Roschke, T. (1972). Language and color perception: A cross-cultural study. *International Journal of Symbology, 3,* 25–29.

Luna, B., Padmanabhan, A., & O'Hearn, K. (2010). What has fMRI told us about the development of cognitive control through adolescence? *Brain and Cognition, 72,* 101–113.

Lutz, C. (1982). The domain of emotion words in Ifaluk. *American Ethnologist, 9,* 113–128.

Lykken, D., & Tellegen, A. (1996). Happiness is a stochastic process. *Psychological Science, 7,* 186–189.

Lyons, M. J., Eisen, S. A., Goldberg, J., True, W., Lin, N., Meyer, J. M., et al. (1998). A registry-based twin study of depression in men. *Archives of General Psychiatry, 55,* 468–472.

Lyons, M. J., True, W. R., Eisen, S. A., Goldberg, J., Meyer, J. M., Faraone, S. V., et al. (1995). Differential heritability of adult and juvenile antisocial traits. *Archives of General Psychiatry, 52,* 906–915.

Lyubomirsky, S., King, L., & Diener, E. (2005). The benefits of frequent positive affect: Does happiness lead to success? *Psychological Bulletin, 131,* 803–855.

Maas, J. W. (1975). Biogenic amines and depression: Biochemical and pharmacological separation of two types of depression. *Archives of General Psychiatry, 32,* 1357–1361.

MacKay, D. G., & Ahmetzanov, M. V. (2005). Emotion, memory, and attention in the taboo Stroop phenomenon. *Psychological Science, 16,* 25–32.

MacLean, P. D. (1985). Brain evolution relating to family, play, and the separation call. *Archives of General Psychiatry, 42*(4), 405–417.

MacLeod, C., Mathews, A., & Tata, P. (1986). Attentional bias in emotional disorders. *Journal of Abnormal Psychology, 95*(1), 15–20.

Mahler, M. S., Pine, F., & Bergman, A. (1975). *The psychological birth of the infant.* New York: Basic Books.

Maier, S. F., & Watkins, L. R. (1998). Cytokines for psychologists: Implications of bidirectional immune-to-brain communication for understanding behavior, mood, and cognition. *Psychological Review, 105,* 83–107.

Makagon, M. M., Funayama, E. S., & Owren, M. J. (2008). An acoustic analysis of laughter produced by congenitally deaf and normally hearing college students. *Journal of the Acoustical Society of America, 124,* 472–483.

Malatesta, C. Z., Grigoryev, P., Lamb, C., Albin, M., & Culver, C. (1986). Emotion socialization and expressive development in preterm and full-term infants. *Child Development, 57,* 316–330.

Malatesta, C. Z., & Haviland, J. M. (1982). Learning display rules: The socialization of emotion expression in infancy. *Child Development, 53,* 991–1003.

Malinosky-Rummell, R., & Hansen, D. J. (1993). Long-term consequences of childhood physical abuse. *Psychological Bulletin, 114,* 68–79.

Malt, B. C., Sloman, S. A., Gennari, S., Shi, M., & Wang, Y. (1999). Knowing versus naming: Similarity and the linguistic categorization of artifacts. *Journal of Memory and Language, 40,* 230–262.

Maltby, J., & Day, L. (2000). The reliability and validity of a susceptibility to embarrassment scale among adults. *Personality and Individual Differences, 29,* 749–756.

Maner, J. K., Kenrick, D. T., Becker, D. V., Robertson, T. E., Hofer, B., Neuberg, S. L., Delton, A. W., Butner, J., & Schaller, M. (2005). Functional projection: How fundamental social motives can bias interpersonal perception. *Journal of Personality and Social Psychology, 88*(1), 63–78.

Mann, J. J., McBride, P. A., Anderson, G. M., & Mieczkowski, T. A. (1992). Platelet and whole-blood serotonin content in depressed inpatients: Correlations with acute and lifetime psycho-pathology. *Biological Psychiatry, 32,* 243–257.

Manor, O., & Eisenbach, Z. (2003). Mortality after spousal loss: Are there socio-demographic differences? *Social Science & Medicine, 56,* 405–413.

Manuck, S. B., Flory, J. D., Ferrell, R. E., Dent, K. M., Mann, J. J., & Muldoon, M. F. (1999). Aggression and anger-related traits associated with a polymorphism of the tryptophan hydroxylase gene. *Biological Psychiatry, 45,* 603–614.

Marchand, A., Roberge, P., Primiano, S., & Germain, V. (2009). A randomized, controlled clinical trial of standard, group and brief cognitive-behavioral therapy for panic disorder with agoraphobia: A two-year follow-up. *Journal of Anxiety Disorders, 23*(8), 1139–1147.

Marcus, D. K., & Miller, R. S. (1999). The perception of "live" embarrassment: A social relations analysis of class presentations. *Cognition and Emotion, 13,* 105–117.

Markus, H. R., & Kitayama, S. (1991). Culture and the self: Implications for cognition, emotion, and motivation. *Psychological Bulletin, 98,* 224–253.

Markus, H. R., Ryff, C. D., Curhan, K. B., & Palmersheim, K. A. (2004). In their own words: Well-being at midlife among high school–educated and college-educated adults. In O. G. Brim,

C. D. Ryff, & R. C. Kessler (Eds.), *How healthy are we?* (pp. 273–319). Chicago: University of Chicago Press.

Marlowe, F., & Wetsman, A. (2001). Preferred waist-to-hip ratio and ecology. *Personality and Individual Differences, 30,* 481–489.

Marsh, E. J. (2007). Retelling is not the same as recalling. *Current Directions in Psychological Science, 16*(1), 16–20.

Marshall, G. D., & Zimbardo, P. G. (1979). Affective consequences of inadequately explained physiological arousal. *Journal of Personality and Social Psychology, 37,* 970–988.

Martin, G. B., & Clark, R. D. (1982). Distress crying in neonates: Species and peer specificity. *Developmental Psychology, 18,* 3–9.

Martin, R., Watson, D., & Wan, C. K. (2000). A three-factor model of trait anger: Dimensions of affect, behavior, and cognition. *Journal of Personality, 68,* 869–897.

Martin, R. A. (2001). Humor, laughter, and physical health: Methodological issues and research findings. *Psychological Bulletin, 127,* 504–519.

Martinez, D., Gil, R., Slifstein, M., Hwang, D., Huang, Y., Perez, A., Kegeles, L., Talbot, P., Evans, S., Krystal, J., Laruelle, M., & Abi-Dargham, A. (2005). Alcohol dependence is associated with blunted dopamine transmission in the ventral striatum. *Biological Psychiatry, 58*(10), 779–786.

Marzillier, S. L., & Davey, G. C. L. (2004). The emotional profiling of disgust-eliciting stimuli: Evidence for primary and complex disgusts. *Cognition and Emotion, 18,* 313–336.

Maslach, C. (1979). Negative emotional biasing of unexplained arousal. *Journal of Personality and Social Psychology, 37,* 953–969.

Maslow, A. H. (1971). *The farther reaches of human nature.* New York: Viking.

Masters, W. H., & Johnson, V. E. (1966). *Human sexual response.* Boston: Little, Brown.

Mastropieri, D., & Turkewitz, G. (1999). Prenatal experience and neonatal responsiveness to vocal expressions of emotion. *Developmental Psychobiology, 35,* 204–214.

Mather, M., Canli, T., English, T., Whitfield, S., Wais, P., Ochsner, K., et al. (2004). Amygdala responses to emotionally valenced stimuli in older and younger adults. *Psychological Science, 15,* 259–263.

Mather, M., & Carstensen, L. L. (2003). Aging and attentional biases for emotional faces. *Psychological Science, 14,* 409–415.

Mathews, A., & Mackintosh, B. (2004). Take a closer look: Emotion modifies the boundary extension effect. *Emotion, 4,* 36–45.

Matsumoto, D. (1990). Cultural similarities and differences in display rules. *Motivation and Emotion, 14,* 195–214.

Matsumoto, D. (1996). *Unmasking Japan: Myths and Realities About the Emotions of the Japanese.* Stanford, CA: Stanford University Press.

Matsumoto, D., Consolacion, T., Yamada, H., Suzuki, R., Franklin, B., Paul, S., et al. (2002). American-Japanese cultural differences in judgements of emotional expressions of different intensities. *Cognition and Emotion, 16,* 721–747.

Matsumoto, D., & Ekman, P. (1989). American-Japanese cultural differences in intensity ratings of facial expressions of emotion. *Motivation and Emotion, 13,* 143–157.

Matsumoto, D., & Willingham, B. (2009). Spontaneous facial expressions of emotion of congenitally and noncongenitally blind individuals. *Journal of Personality and Social Psychology, 96,* 1–10.

Matsumoto, D., Willingham, B., & Olide, A. (2009). Sequential dynamics of culturally moderated facial expressions of emotion. *Psychological Science, 20,* 1269–1274.

Matsumoto, D., Yoo, S. H., Hirayama, S., & Petrova, G. (2005). Development and validation of a measure of display rule knowledge: The display rule assessment inventory. *Emotion, 5,* 23–40.

Matsuyama, Y., Hama., H., Kawamura, Y., & Mine, H. (1978). An analysis of emotional words. *The Japanese Journal of Psychology, 49,* 229–232.

Mauro, R., Sato, K., & Tucker, J. (1992). The role of appraisal in human emotions: A cross-cultural study. *Journal of Personality and Social Psychology, 62,* 301–317.

Mauss, I. B., Levenson, R. W., McCarter, L, Wilhelm, F. W., & Gross, J. J. (2005). The tie that binds?: Coherence among emotion experience, behavior, and physiology. *Emotion, 5,* 175–190.

Mayer, J. D., Caruso, D. R., & Salovey, P. (2000). Emotional intelligence meets traditional standards for an intelligence. *Intelligence, 27,* 267–298.

Mayer, J. D., Perkins, D. M., Caruso, D. R., & Salovey, P. (2001). Emotional intelligence and giftedness. *Roeper Review, 23,* 131–137.

Mayer, J. D., Salovey, P., & Caruso, D. R. (2008). Emotional intelligence: New ability or eclectic traits? *American Psychologist, 63*(6), 503–517.

Mayer, J. D., Salovey, P., Caruso, D. R., & Sitarenios, G. (2001). Emotional intelligence as a standard intelligence. *Emotion, 1,* 232–242.

Mayer, J. D., Salovey, P., Caruso, D. R., & Sitarenios, G. (2003). Measuring emotional intelligence with the MSCEIT V2.0. *Emotion, 3,* 97–105.

Mayne, T. J. (1999). Negative affect and health: The importance of being earnest. *Cognition and Emotion, 13,* 601–635.

McCann, C., Roberts, R. D., Matthews, G., & Zeidner, M. (2004). Consensus scoring and empirical option weighting of performance-based Emotional Intelligence (EI) tests. *Personality and Individual Differences, 36,* 645–662.

McCrae, R. R., & Costa, P. T. (1991). Adding *liebe und arbeit*: The full five-factor model and well-being. *Personality and Social Psychology Bulletin, 17*(2), 227–232.

McCullough, M. E. (2001). Forgiveness: Who does it and how do they do it? *Current Directions in Psychological Science, 10,* 194–197.

McEwen, B. S. (2000). The neurobiology of stress: From serendipity to clinical relevance. *Brain Research, 886,* 172–189.

McGregor, I. S., Hargreaves, G. A., Apfelbach, R., & Hunt, G. E. (2004). Neural correlates of cat odor-induced anxiety in rats: Region-specific effects of the benzodiazepine midazolam. *Journal of Neuroscience, 24,* 4134–4144.

McGue, M., Elkins, I., Walden, B., & Iacono, W. G. (2005). Perceptions of the parent–adolescent relationship: A longitudinal investigation. *Developmental Psychology, 41,* 971–984.

McKendree-Smith, N., & Scogin, F. (2000). Depressive realism: Effects of depression severity and interpretation time. *Journal of Clinical Psychology, 56,* 1601–1608.

McLean, C. P., & Anderson, E. R. (2009). Brave men and timid women? A review of the gender differences in fear and anxiety. *Clinical Psychology Review, 29,* 496–505.

McLean, P. D., & Woody, S. R. (2001). *Anxiety disorders in adults: An evidence-based approach to psychological treatment*. New York, NY, U.S.: Oxford University Press.

McNally, R. J. (2002). Anxiety sensitivity and panic disorder. *Biological Psychiatry, 52,* 938–946.

McNaughton, N., & Corr, P. J. (2004). A two-dimensional neuropsychology of defense: Fear/anxiety and defensive distance. *Neuroscience and Biobehavioral Reviews, 28,* 285–305.

McNiel, J. M., & Fleeson, W. (2006). The causal effects of extraversion on positive affect and neuroticism on negative affect: Manipulating state extraversion and state neuroticism in an experimental approach. *Journal of Research in Personality, 40*(5), 529–550.

Medda, P., Perugi, G., Zanello, S., Ciuffa, M., & Cassano, G. B. (2009). Response to ECT in bipolar I, bipolar II and unipolar depression. *Journal of Affective Disorders, 118*(1-3), 55–59.

Medver, V. H., Madey, S. F., & Gilovich, T. (1995). When less is more: Counterfactual thinking and satisfaction among Olympic athletes. *Journal of Personality and Social Psychology, 69,* 603–610.

Meichenbaum, D. (1985). *Stress inoculation training*. New York: Pergamon.

Meier, B. P., & Robinson, M. D. (2004). Does quick to blame mean quick to anger? The role of agreeableness in dissociating blame and anger. *Personality and Social Psychology Bulletin, 30*(7), 856–867.

Mellers, B. A., & McGraw, A. P. (2001). Anticipated emotions as guides to choice. *Current Directions in Psychological Science, 10,* 210–214.

Meltzoff, A. N., & Moore, M. K. (1977). Imitation of facial and manual gestures by human neonates. *Science, 198,* 75–78.

Meltzoff, A. N., & Moore, M. K. (2002). Imitation, memory, and the representation of persons. *Infant Behavior and Development, 25*(1), 39–61.

Mendes, D. M. L. F., Seidl-de-Moura, M. L., & Siqueira, J. D. (2009). The ontogenesis of smiling and its association with mothers' affective behaviors: A longitudinal study. *Infant Behavior & Development, 32,* 445–453.

Mendl, M. (1999). Performing under pressure: Stress and cognitive function. *Applied Animal Behaviour Science, 65,* 221–244.

Menon, U., & Shweder, R. A. (1994). Kali's tongue: Cultural psychology, cultural consensus and the meaning of "shame" in Orissa, India. In H. Markus & S. Kitayama (Eds.), *Emotion and culture: Empirical studies of mutual influence* (pp. 241–284). Washington, D.C.: American Psychological Association.

Messinger, D. S. (2002). Positive and negative: Infant facial expressions and emotions. *Current Directions in Psychological Science, 11,* 1–6.

Meyer, B., Olivier, L., & Roth, D. A. (2005). Please don't leave me! BIS/BAS, attachment styles, and responses to a relationship threat. *Personality and Individual Differences, 38,* 151–162.

Mikulincer, M., Birnbaum, G., Woddis, D., & Nachmias, O. (2000). Stress and accessibility of proximity-related thoughts: Exploring the normative and intraindividual components of attachment theory. *Journal of Personality and Social Psychology, 78,* 509–523.

Mikulincer, M., Gillath, O., & Shaver, P. (2002). Activation of the attachment system in adulthood: Threat-related primes increase the accessibility of mental representations of attachment figures. *Journal of Personality and Social Psychology, 83,* 881–895.

Milgram, S. (1974). *Obedience to authority*. New York: Harper & Row.

Miller, E. K., & Cohen, J. D. (2001). An integrative theory of prefrontal cortex function. *Annual Review of Neuroscience, 24,* 167–202.

Miller, G. (2007). The mystery of the missing smile. *Science, 316,* 826–827.

Miller, G. E., & Blackwell, E. (2006). Turning up the heat: Inflammation as a mechanism linking chronic stress, depression, and heart disease. *Current Directions in Psychological Science, 15*(6), 269–272.

Miller, R. S. (2001a). Embarrassment and social phobia: Distant cousins or close kin? In S. G. Hofmann & P. M. DiBartolo (Eds.), *From social anxiety to social phobia* (pp. 65–85). Needham Heights, MA: Allyn & Bacon.

Miller, R. S. (2001b). Shyness and embarrassment compared: Siblings in the service of social evaluation. In W. R. Crozier & L. E. Alden (Eds.), *International Handbook of Social Anxiety* (pp. 281–300). Chichester, England: John Wiley.

Mills, D. W., & Ward, R. P. (1986). Attenuation of stress-induced hypertension by exercise independent

of training effects: An animal model. *Journal of Behavioral Medicine, 9,* 599–605.

Miltner, W. H. R., Krieschel, S., Hecht, H., Trippe, R., & Weiss, T. (2004). Eye movements and behavioral responses to threatening and nonthreatening stimuli during visual search in phobic and nonphoic subjects *Emotion, 4,* 323–339.

Mineka, S. (1987). A primate model of phobic fears. In H. Eysenck & I. Martin (Eds.), *Theoretical foundations of behavior therapy* (pp. 81–111). New York: Plenum.

Mineka, S., Davidson, M., Cook, M., & Keir, R. (1984). Observational conditioning of snake fear in rhesus monkeys. *Journal of Abnormal Psychology, 93,* 355–372.

Mirescu, C., Peters, J. D., & Gould, E. (2004). Early life experience alters response of adult neurogenesis to stress. *Nature Neuroscience, 7,* 841–846.

Mitchell, M. (1936). *Gone With the Wind.* New York: Warner.

Miyake, K., Campos, J. J., Kagan, J., & Bradshaw, D. L. (1986). Issues in socioemotional development. In H. Azuma, K. Hakuta, & H. Stevenson (Eds.), *Kodomo: Child development and education in Japan.* San Francisco: W. H. Freeman.

Miyake, K., Chen, S. J., & Campos, J. J. (1985). Infant temperament, mother's mode of interaction, and attachment in Japan: An interim report. In I. Bretherton & E. Waters (Eds.), Growing points of attachment theory and research. *Monographs of the Society for Research in Child Development, 50* (1–2, Serial No. 209).

Mobbs, D., Grecius, M. D., Abdel-Azim, E., Menon, V., & Reiss, A. L. (2003). Humor modulates the mesolimbic reward centers. *Neuron, 40,* 1041–1048.

Modigliani, A. (1968). Embarrassment and embarrassibility. *Sociometry, 31,* 313–326.

Moe, B. K., King, A. R., & Bailly, M. D. (2004). Retrospective accounts of recurrent parental physical abuse as a predictor of adult laboratory-induced aggression. *Aggressive Behavior, 30,* 217–228.

Moles, A., Kieffer, B. L., & D'Amato, F. R. (2004). Deficit in attachment behavior in mice lacking the μ-opioid receptor gene. *Science, 304,* 1983–1986.

Moller, H. J. (1992). Attempted suicide: Efficacy of different aftercare strategies. *International Clinical Psychopharmacology, 6*(Suppl. 6), 58–59.

Montgomery, K. J., Seeherman, K. R., & Haxby, J. V. (2009). The well-tempered social brain. *Psychological Science, 20*(10), 1211–1213.

Moore, M. M. (1985). Nonverbal courtship patterns in women: Context and consequences. *Ethology and Sociobiology, 6,* 237–247.

Moore, T. M., Scarpa, A., & Raine, A. (2002). A meta-analysis of serotonin metabolite 5-HIAA and antisocial behavior. *Aggressive Behavior, 28,* 299–316.

Morling, B., Kitayama, S., & Miyamoto, Y. (2003). American and Japanese women use different coping strategies during normal pregnancy. *Personality and Social Psychology Bulletin, 29,* 1533–1546.

Morris, J. S., deBonis, M., & Dolan, R. J. (2002). Human amygdala responses to fearful eyes. *NeuroImage, 17,* 214–222.

Morrow, J., & Nolen-Hoeksema, S. (1990). Effects of responses to depression on the remediation of depressive affect. *Journal of Personality and Social Psychology, 58,* 518–527.

Morsbach, H., & Tyler, W. J. (1986). A Japanese emotion: Amae. In R. Harre (Ed.), *The social construction of emotions* (pp. 289–307). New York: Blackwell.

Morse, S. J., & Gruzen, J. (1976). The eye of the beholder: A neglected variable in the study of physical attractiveness. *Journal of Psychology, 44,* 209–225.

Moses, L. J., Baldwin, D. A., Rosicky, J. G., & Tidball, G. (2001). Evidence for referential understanding in the emotions domain at twelve and eighteen months. *Child Development, 72,* 718–735.

Moskowitz, J. T., Hult, J. R., Bussolari, C., & Acree, M. (2009). What works in coping with HIV? A meta-analysis with implications for coping with serious illness. *Psychological Bulletin, 135*(1), 121–141.

Mroczek, D. K. (2004). Positive and negative affect at midlife. In O. G. Brim, C. D. Ryff, & R. C. Kessler (Eds.), *How healthy are we?* (pp. 205–226). Chicago: University of Chicago Press.

Mroczek, D. K., & Spiro, A. (2005). Change in life satisfaction during adulthood: Findings from the veterans affairs normative aging study. *Journal of Personality and Social Psychology, 88,* 189–202.

Much, N. C. (1997). A semiotic view of socialization, lifespan development and cultural psychology: With vignettes from the moral culture of traditional Hindu households. *Psychology and Developing Societies, 9,* 65–105.

Mulkens, S., de Jong, P. J., Dobbelaar, A., & Bögels, S. M. (1999). Fear of blushing: Fearful preoccupation irrespective of facial coloration. *Behaviour Research and Therapy, 37,* 1119–1128.

Mulvey, E. P., & Cauffman, E. (2001). The inherent limits of predicting school violence. *American Psychologist, 56,* 797–802.

Mumme, D. L., Fernald, A., & Herrera, C. (1996). Infants' responses to facial and vocal emotional signals in a social referencing paradigm. *Child Development, 67,* 3219–3237.

Munafò, M. R., Clark, T. G., Moore, L. R., Payne, E., Walton, R., & Flint, J. (2003). Genetic polymorphisms and personality in healthy adults: A systematic review and meta-analysis. *Molecular Psychiatry, 8*(5), 471–484.

Munafò, M. R., Clark, T. G., Roberts, K. H., & Johnstone, E. C. (2006). Neuroticism mediates the association of the serotonin transporter gene with lifetime major depression. *Neuropsychobiology, 53*(1), 1–8.

Murberg, T. A., Furze, G., & Bru, E. (2003). Avoidance coping styles predict mortality among patients with congestive heart failure: A 6-year follow-up study. *Personality and Individual Differences, 36*(4), 757–766.

Murphy, F. A. C., Nimmo-Smith, I., & Lawrence, A. D. (2003). Functional neuroanatomy of emotions: A meta-analysis. *Cognitive, Affective, & Behavioral Neuroscience, 3,* 207–233.

Murphy, J. M., Laird, N. M., Monson, R. R., Sobol, A. M., & Leighton, A. H. (2000). A 40-year perspective on the prevalence of depression. *Archives of General Psychiatry, 57,* 209–215.

Murray, J. P. (1998). Studying television violence. A research agenda for the 21st century. In J. K. Asamen & G. L. Berry (Eds.), *Research paradigms, television, and social behavior* (pp. 369–410). Thousand Oaks, CA: Sage.

Murray, S. L., & Holmes, J. G. (1999). The (mental) ties that bind: Cognitive structures that predict relationship resilience. *Journal of Personality and Social Psychology, 77,* 1228–1244.

Murray, S. L., Holmes, J. G., Gellavia, G., Griffin, D. W., & Dolderman, D. (2002). Kindred spirits? The benefits of egocentrism on close relationships. *Journal of Personality and Social Psychology, 82,* 563–581.

Myers, D. G. (2000a). The funds, friends, and faith of happy people. *American Psychologist, 55,* 56–67.

Myers, D. G. (2000b). *The American paradox: Spiritual hunger in an age of plenty.* New Haven, CT: Yale University Press.

Naab, P. J., & Russell, J. A. (2007). Judgments of emotion from spontaneous facial expressions of New Guineans. *Emotion, 7,* 736–744.

Nachson, I., & Zelig, A. (2003). Flashbulb and factual memories: The case of Rabin's assassination. *Applied Cognitive Psychology, 17,* 519–531.

Neimeyer, R. A. (1995). An invitation to constructivist psychotherapies. In R. A. Neimeyer & M. J. Mahoney (Eds.), *Constructivism in psychology* (pp. 1–8). Washington, D.C.: American Psychological Association.

Nelissen, R. M. A., & Zeelenberg, M. (2009). When guilt evokes self-punishment: Evidence for the existence of a *Dobby effect. Emotion, 9,* 118–122.

Nelson, E. E., & Panksepp, J. (1996). Oxytocin mediates acquisition of maternally associated odor preferences in preweaning rat pups. *Behavioral Neuroscience, 110,* 583–592.

Nelson, E. E., & Panksepp, J. (1998). Brain substrates of infant-mother attachment: contributions of opioids, oxytocin, and norepinephrine. *Neuroscience Biobehavioral Review, 22,* 437–452.

Nelson, E. E., Shelton, S. E., & Kalin, N. H. (2003). Individual differences in the responses of naive rhesus monkeys to snakes. *Emotion, 3,* 3–11.

Nelson, L. D., Meyvis, T., & Galak, J. (2009). Enhancing the television-viewing experience through commercial interruptions. *Journal of Consumer Research, 36,* 160–172.

Nelson, R. J., & Trainor, B. C. (2007). Neural mechanisms of aggression. *Nature Reviews Neuroscience, 8,* 536–546.

Nemeroff, C., & Rozin, P. (1989). "You are what you eat": Applying the demand-free "impressions" technique to an unacknowledged belief. *Ethos, 17,* 50–69.

Nestler, E. J., & Carlezon, W. A., Jr. (2006). The mesolimbic dopamine reward circuit in depression. *Biological Psychiatry, 59*(12), 1151–1159.

Neto, F. (1996). Correlates of social blushing. *Personality and Individual Differences, 20,* 365–373.

Neumann, S. A., & Waldstein, S. R. (2001). Similar patterns of cardiovascular response during emotional activation as a function of affective valence and arousal and gender. *Journal of Psychosomatic Research, 50,* 245–253.

Neumeister, A., Nugent, A. C., Waldeck, T., Geraci, M., Schwarz, M., Bonne, O., et al. (2004). Neural and behavioral responses to tryptophan depletion in unmediated patients with remitted major depressive disorder and controls. *Archives of General Psychiatry, 61,* 765–773.

Nezlek, J. B., & Zebrowski, B. D. (2001). Implications of the dimensionality of unrealistic optimism for the study of perceived health risks. *Journal of Social and Clinical Psychology, 20,* 521–537.

Nickerson, C., Schwarz, N., Diener, E., & Kahneman, D. (2003). Zeroing in on the dark side of the American dream: A closer look at the negative consequences of the goal for financial success. *Psychological Science, 14,* 531–536.

Nie, Z., Schweitzer, P., Roberts, A. J., Madamba, S. G., Moore, S. D., & Siggins, G. R. (2004). Ethanol augments GABAergic transmission in the central amygdala via CRF1 receptors. *Science, 303,* 1512–1514.

Niedenthal, P. M., Auxiette, C., Nugier, A., Dalle, N., Bonin, P., & Fayol, M. (2004). A prototype analysis of the French category "émotion." *Cognition and Emotion, 18,* 289–312.

Niedenthal, P. M., Tangney, J. P., & Gavanski, I. (1994). "If only I weren't" versus "If only I hadn't": Distinguishing shame and guilt in conterfactual thinking. *Journal of Personality and Social Psychology, 67,* 585–595.

Nolen-Hoeksema, S. (1991). Responses to depression and their effects on the duration of depressive episodes. *Journal of Abnormal Psychology, 100,* 569–582.

Nolen-Hoeksema, S., Larsen, J., & Grayson, C. (1999). Explaining the gender difference in depressive symptoms. *Journal of Personality and Social Psychology, 77,* 1061–1072.

Nolen-Hoeksema, S., & Morrow, J. (1991). A prospective study of depression and post-traumatic stress symptoms after a natural disaster: The Loma Prieta earthquake. *Journal of Personality and Social Psychology, 61,* 115–121.

Nummenmaa, L., Hyönä, J., & Calvo, M. G. (2006). Eye movement assessment of selective attentional capture by emotional pictures. *Emotion, 6*(2), 257–268.

Nygren, T. E., Isen, A. M., Taylor, P. J., & Dulin, J. (1996). The influence of positive affect on the decision rule in risk situations: Focus on outcome (and especially avoidance of loss) rather than probability. *Organizational Behavior and Human Decision Processes, 66,* 59–72.

Ochsner, K. N., Bunge, S. A., Gross, J. J., & Gabrieli, J. D. E. (2002). Rethinking feelings: An fMRI study of the cognitive regulation of emotion. *Journal of Cognitive Neuroscience, 14,* 1215–1229.

O'Connor, L. E., Berry, J. W., & Weiss, J. (1999). Interpersonal guilt, shame, and psychological problems. *Journal of Social and Clinical Psychology, 18,* 181–203.

O'Connor, R. M., Jr., & Little, I. S. (2003). Revisiting the predictive validity of emotional intelligence: Self-report versus ability-based measures. *Personality and Individual Differences, 35,* 1893–1902.

Ohbuchi, K. O., Tamura, T., Quigley, B. M., Tedeschi, J. T., Madi, N., Bond, M. H., & Mummendey, A. (2004). Anger, blame, and dimensions of perceived norm violations: Culture, gender, and relationships. *Journal of Applied Social Psychology, 34,* 1587–1603.

Öhman, A. (2009). Of snakes and faces: An evolutionary perspective on the psychology of fear. *Scandinavian Journal of Psychology, 50*(6), 543–552.

Öhman, A., Eriksson, A., & Olofsson, C. (1975). One-trial learning and superior resistance to extinction of autonomic responses conditioned to potentially phobic objects. *Journal of Comparative and Physiological Psychology, 88,* 619–627.

Öhman, A., & Mineka, S. (2003). The malicious serpent: Snakes as a prototypical stimulus for an evolved module of fear. *Current Directions in Psychological Science, 12*(1), 5–9.

Olatunji, B. O., Sawchuk, C. N., Arrindell, W. A., & Lohr, J. M. (2005). Disgust sensitivity as a mediator of the sex differences in contamination fears. *Personality and Individual Differences, 38,* 713–722.

Olatunji, B. O., Tolin, D. F., Huppert, J. D., & Lohr, J. M. (2005). The relation between fearfulness, disgust sensitivity and religious obsessions in a non-clinical sample. *Personality and Individual Differences, 38,* 891–902.

Olweus, D. (1995). Bullying or peer abuse at school: Facts and intervention. *Current Directions in Psychological Science, 4,* 196–200.

O'Malley, P. G., Jones, D. L., Feuerstein, I. M., & Taylor, A. J. (2000). Lack of correlation between psychological factors and subclinical coronary artery disease. *New England Journal of Medicine, 343,* 1298–1304.

Ong, A. D., Bergeman, C. S., & Bisconti, T. L. (2005). Unique effects of daily perceived control on anxiety symptomatology during conjugal bereavement. *Personality and Individual Differences, 38,* 1057–1067.

Ortony, A., & Turner, T. J. (1990). What's basic about basic emotions? *Psychological Review, 97,* 315–331.

Orwell, G. (2000). Funny, not vulgar. In S. Orwell & I. Angus (Eds.), *George Orwell: The Collected Essays, Journalism and Letters* (Vol. 3). Boston: Nonpariel. (Reprint of 1968 edition by Harcourt, Brace, & World.)

Oster, H., Hegley, D., & Nagel, L. (1992). Adult judgments and fine-grained analysis of infant facial expressions. *Developmental Psychology, 28,* 1115–1131.

Otto, M. W., Pollack, M. H., Maki, K. M., Gould, R. A., Worthington, J. J., III, Smoller, J. W., et al. (2001). Childhood history of anxiety disorders among adults with social phobia: Rates, correlates, and comparisons with patients with panic disorder. *Depression and Anxiety, 14,* 209–213.

Oveis, C., Cohen, A. B., Gruber, J., Shiota, M. N., Haidt, J., & Keltner, D. (2009). Resting respiratory sinus arrhythmia is associated with tonic positive emotionality. *Emotion, 9*(2), 265–270.

Oxley, D. R., Smith, K. B., Alford, J. R., Hibbing, M. V., Miller, J. L., Scalora, M., et al. (2008). Political attitudes vary with physiological traits. *Science, 321,* 1667–1670.

Oyserman, D., Coon, H. M., & Kemmelmeier, M. (2002). Rethinking individualism and collectivism: Evaluation of theoretical assumptions and meta-analysis. *Psychological Bulletin, 128,* 3–72.

Özgen, E. (2004). Language, learning, and color perception. *Current Directions in Psychological Science, 13,* 95–98.

Papousek, I., Schulter, G., & Lang, B. (2009). Effects of emotionally contagious films on changes in hemisphere-specific cognitive performance. *Emotion, 9*(4), 510–519.

Park, C. L., Moore, P. J., Turner, R. A., & Adler, N. E. (1997). The roles of constructive thinking and optimism in psychological and behavioral adjustment during pregnancy. *Journal of Personality and Social Psychology, 73,* 584–592.

Park, J., & Banaji, M. R. (2000). Mood and heuristics: The influence of happy and sad states on sensitivity and bias in stereotyping. *Journal of Personality and Social Psychology, 78,* 1005–1023.

Parkinson, B. (2007). Getting from situations to emotions: Appraisal and other routes. *Emotion, 7,* 21–25.

Pastor, J. C., Mayo, M., & Shamir, B. (2007). Adding fuel to fire: The impact of followers' arousal on ratings of charisma. *Journal of Applied Psychology, 92,* 1584–1596.

Pavlidis, I., Eberhardt, N. I., & Levine, J. A. (2002). Seeing through the face of deception. *Nature, 415,* 35.

Pavot, W., & Diener, E. (1993). Review of the satisfaction with life scale. *Psychological Assessment, 5,* 164–172.

Payne, J. L. (2003). The role of estrogen in mood disorders in women. *International Review of Psychiatry, 15*(3), 280–290.

Pei, M., Matsuda, K., Sakamoto, H., & Kawata, M. (2006). Intrauterine proximity to male fetuses affects the morphology of the sexually dimorphic nucleus of the preoptic area in the adult rat brain. *European Journal of Neuroscience, 23*(5), 1234–1240.

Pellis, S. M., O'Brien, D. P., Pellis, V. C., Teitelbaum, P., Wolgin, D. L., & Kennedy, S. (1988). Escalation of feline predation along a gradient from avoidance through "play" to killing. *Behavioral Neuroscience, 102,* 760–777.

Peng, K., & Nisbett, R. E. (1999). Culture, dialectics, and reasoning about contradiction. *American Psychologist, 54*(9), 741–754.

Penley, J. A., Tomaka, J., & Wiebe, J. S. (2002). The association of coping to physical and psychological health outcomes: A meta-analytic review. *Journal of Behavioral Medicine, 25*(6), 551–603.

Pennebaker, J. W. (1997). Writing about emotional experiences as a therapeutic process. *Psychological Science, 8,* 162–166.

Pennebaker, J. W., & Graybeal, A. (2001). Patterns of natural language use: Disclosure, personality, and social integration. *Current Directions in Psychological Science, 10,* 90–93.

Persson, M.-L., Wasserman, D., Geijer, T., Frisch, A., Rockah, R., Michaelovsky, E., et al. (2000). Dopamine D$_4$ receptor gene polymorphism and personality traits in healthy volunteers. *European Archives of Psychiatry and Clinical Neuroscience, 250,* 203–206.

Perunovic, W. Q. E., Heller, D., & Rafaeli, E. (2007). Within-person changes in the structure of emotion. *Psychological Science, 18,* 607–613.

Peters, J., & Büchel, C. (2009). Overlapping and distinct neural systems code for subjective value during intertemporal and risky decision making. *The Journal of Neuroscience: The Official Journal of the Society for Neuroscience, 29*(50), 15727–15734.

Peterson, C. (2000). The future of optimism. *American Psychologist, 55,* 44–55.

Peterson, C., Maier, S. F., & Seligman, M. E. P. (1993). *Learned helplessness: A theory for the age of personal control.* New York, NY, U.S.: Oxford University Press.

Peterson, C., & Steen, T. A. (2002). Optimistic explanatory style. In C. R. Snyder & S. J. Lopez (Eds.), *Handbook of positive psychology* (pp. 244–256). New York: Oxford University Press.

Petty, R. E., & Cacioppo, J. T. (1986). *Communication and persuasion: Central and peripheral routes to attitude change.* New York: Springer Verlag.

Pham, K., McEwen, B. S., LeDoux, J. E., & Nader, K. (2005). Fear learning transiently impairs hippocampal cell proliferation. *Neuroscience, 130,* 17–24.

Phan, K. L., Wager, T., Taylor, S. F., & Liberzon, I. (2002). Functional neuroanatomy of emotion: A meta-analysis of emotion activation studies in PET and fMRI. *NeuroImage, 16,* 331–348.

Phelps, E. A. (2004). Human emotion and memory: Interactions of the amygdala and hippocampal complex. *Current Opinion in Neurobiology, 14*(2), 198–202.

Phelps, E. A. (2005). The interaction of emotion and cognition: Insights from studies of the human amygdala. In L. F. Barrett, P. M. Niedenthal & P. Winkielman (Eds.), *Emotion and consciousness.* (pp. 51–66). New York, NY, U.S.: Guilford Press.

Phelps, E. A., O'Connor, K. J., Gatenby, J. C., Gore, J. C., Grillon, C., & Davis, M. (2001). Activation of the left amygdala to a cognitive representation of fear. *Nature Neuroscience, 4,* 437–441.

Phillips, L. H., Bull, R., Adams, E., & Fraser, L. (2002). Positive mood and executive function: Evidence from Stroop and fluency tasks. *Emotion, 2,* 12–22.

Phillips, L. H., Smith, L., & Gilhooly, K. J. (2002). The effects of adult aging and induced positive and negative mood on planning. *Emotion, 2,* 263–272.

Phillips, M. L., Young, A. W., Senior, C., Brammer, M., Andrew, C., Calder, A. J., et al. (1997). A specific neural substrate for perceiving facial expressions of disgust. *Nature, 389,* 495–498.

Phillips, R. G., & LeDoux, J. E. (1992). Differential contribution of amygdala and hippocampus to cued and contextual fear conditioning. *Behavioral Neuroscience, 106,* 274–285.

Piaget, J. (1954). *The construction of reality in the child* (M. Cook, Trans.). New York: Basic books. (Original work published 1937.)

Pine, A., Seymour, B., Roiser, J. P., Bossaerts, P., Friston, K. J., Curran, H. V., & Dolan, R. J. (2009). Encoding of marginal utility across time in the human brain. *The Journal of Neuroscience, 29*(30), 9575–9581.

Pinker, S. (1997). *How the mind works.* New York, NY, U.S.: W. W. Norton & Co.

Pitman, R. K., van der Kolk, B. A., Orr, S. P., & Greenberg, M. S. (1990). Naloxone-reversible analgesic response to combat-related stimuli in posttraumatic stress disorder. *Archives of General Psychiatry, 47,* 541–544.

Plaisant, O., Srivastava, S., Mendelsohn, G. A., Debray, Q., & John, O. P. (2005). Relations entre le *big five inventory* français et le manuel diagnostique des troubles mentaux dans un échantillon clinique français / Relations between the French version of the big five inventory and the DSM classification in a French clinical sample of psychiatric disorders. *Annales Médico-Psychologiques, 163*(2), 161–167.

Plotnik, J. M., de Waal, F. B. M., & Reiss, D. (2006). Self-recognition in an Asian elephant. *Proceedings of the National Academy of Sciences, 103,* 17053–17057.

Plous, S. (1993). *The psychology of judgment and decision making.* Philadelphia, PA: Temple University Press.

Plutchik, R. (1982). A psychoevolutionary theory of emotions. *Social Science Information, 21,* 529–553.

Popenoe, D. (2002). *The top ten myths of divorce.* Unpublished manuscript, National Marriage Project, Rutgers University.

Porges, S. W. (1997). Emotion: An evolutionary by-product of the neural regulation of the autonomic nervous system. In C. S. Carter, I. I. Lederhendler & B. Kirkpatrick (Eds.), *The integrative neurobiology of affiliation.* (pp. 62–77). New York, NY, U.S.: New York Academy of Sciences.

Porter, C. L., Jones, B. L., Evans, C. A., & Robinson, C. C. (2009). A comparative study of arm-restraint methodology: Differential effects of mother and stranger restrainers on infants' distress reactivity at 6 and 9 months of age. *Infancy, 14*(3), 306–324.

Posternak, M. A., & Zimmerman, M. (2002). Partial validation of the atypical features of major depressive disorder. *Archives of General Psychiatry, 59,* 70–76.

Poulin, F., Dishion, T. J., & Burraston, B. (2001). Three-year iatrogenic effects associated with aggregating high-risk adolescents in cognitive-behavioral preventive interventions. *Applied Developmental Science, 5,* 214–224.

Preti, A., Miotto, P., De Coppi, M., Petretto, D., & Carmelo, M. (2002). Psychiatric chrono-epidemiology: Its relevance for the study of aggression. *Aggressive Behavior, 28,* 477–490.

Prichard, Z., Mackinnon, A., Jorm, A. F., & Easteal, S. (2008). No evidence for interaction between MAOA and childhood adversity for antisocial behavior. *American Journal of Medical Genetics Part B—Neuropsychiatric Genetics, B, 147,* 228–232.

Prior, H., Schwarz, A., & Gunturkun, O. (2008). Mirror-induced behavior in the magpie (*Pica pica*): Evidence of self-recognition. *PLoS Biology, 6,* 1642–1650.

Pronin, E., & Jacobs, E. (2008). Thought speed, mood, and the experience of mental motion. *Perspectives on Psychological Science, 3,* 461–485.

Pronin, E., Jacobs, E., & Wegner, D. M. (2008). Psychological effects of thought acceleration. *Emotion, 8,* 597–612.

Provine, R. R. (2000). *Laughter.* New York: Viking.

Provine, R. R., Krosnowski, K. A., & Brocato, N. W. (2009). Tearing: Breakthrough in human emotional signaling. *Evolutionary Psychology, 7,* 52–56.

Quadrel, M. J., Fischhoff, B., & Davis, W. (1993). Adolescent (in)vulnerability. *American Psychologist, 48,* 102–116.

Rachlin, H., Siegel, E., & Cross, D. (1994). Lotteries and the time horizon. *Psychological Science, 5,* 390–393.

Raghunathan, R., & Pham, M. T. (1999). All negative moods are not equal: Motivational influences of anxiety and sadness on decision making. *Organizational Behavior and Human Decision Processes, 79,* 56–77.

Raine, A., Reynolds, C., Venables, P. H., Mednick, S. A., & Farrington, D. P. (1998). Fearlessness, stimulation-seeking, and large body size at age 3 as early predispositions to childhood aggression at age 11 years. *Archives of General Psychiatry, 55,* 745–751.

Raja, M., & Azzoni, A. (2004). Suicide attempts: Differences between unipolar and bipolar patients and among groups with different lethality risk. *Journal of Affective Disorders, 82*(3), 437–442.

Ram, A., Pandey, H. P., Matsumura, H., Kasahara-Orita, K., Nakajima, T., Takahata, R., et al. (1997). CSF levels of prostaglandins, especially the level of prostaglandin D_2 are correlated with increasing propensity towards sleep in rats. *Brain Research, 751,* 81–89.

Ramirez, J. M., Santisteban, C., Fujihara, T., & Van Goozen, S. (2002). Differences between experience of anger and readiness to angry action: A study of Japanese and Spanish students. *Aggressive Behavior, 28,* 429–438.

Rechlin, T., Weis, M., Spitzer, A., & Kaschka, W. P. (1994). Are affective disorders associated with alterations of heart rate variability? *Journal of Affective Disorders, 32*(4), 271–275.

Reddy, P. L., Khanna, S., Subhash, M. N., Channabasavanna, S. M., & Rao, B. S. S. R. (1992). CSF amine metabolites in depression. *Biological Psychiatry, 31,* 112–118.

Reissland, N., & Harris, P. (1991). Children's use of display rules in pride-eliciting situations. *British Journal of Developmental Psychology, 9,* 431–435.

Reijntjes, A., Stegge, H., Terwogt, M. M., Kamphuis, J. H., & Telch, M. J. (2006). Emotion regulation and its effects on mood improvement in response to an in vivo peer rejection challenge. *Emotion, 6*(4), 543–552.

Remington, N. A., Fabrigar, L. R., & Visser, P. S. (2000). Reexamining the circumplex model of affect. *Journal of Personality and Social Psychology, 79,* 286–300.

Reuter-Lorenz, P., & Davidson, R. J. (1981). Differential contributions of the two cerebral hemispheres to the perception of happy and sad faces. *Neuropsychologia, 19,* 609–613.

Reyna, V. F., & Farley, F. (2006). Risk and rationality in adolescent decision making: Implications for theory, practice, and public policy. *Psychological Science in the Public Interest, 7,* 1–44.

Rhee, S. H., & Waldman, I. D. (2002). Genetic and environmental influences on antisocial behavior: A meta-analysis of twin and adoption studies. *Psychological Bulletin, 128,* 490–529.

Richards, A., French, C. C., Calder, A. J., Webb, B., Fox, R., & Young, A. W. (2002). Anxiety-related bias in the classification of emotionally ambiguous facial expressions. *Emotion, 2,* 273–287.

Richards, J. M., Butler, E. A., & Gross, J. J. (2003). Emotion regulation in romantic relationships: The cognitive consequences of concealing feelings. *Journal of Social and Personal Relationships, 20,* 599–620.

Richards, J. M., & Gross, J. J. (1999). Composure at any cost? The cognitive consequences of emotion suppression. *Personality and Social Psychology Bulletin, 25,* 1033–1044.

Riesman, P. (1977). *Freedom in Fulani social life: An introspective ethnography* (M. Fuller, Trans.). Chicago: University of Chicago Press.

Rihmer, Z. (2009). Suicide and bipolar disorder. In C. A. Zarate Jr., & H. K. Manji (Eds.), *Bipolar depression: Molecular neurobiology, clinical diagnosis and pharmacotherapy.* (pp. 47–56). Cambridge, MA, U.S.: Birkhäuser.

Rind, B., Tromovitch, B., & Bauserman, R. (1998). A meta-analytic examination of assumed properties of child sexual abuse using college samples. *Psychological Bulletin, 124,* 22–53.

Riolo, S. A., Nguyen, T. A., Greden, J. F., & King, C. A. (2005). Prevalence of depression by Race/Ethnicity: Findings from the national health and nutrition examination survey III. *American Journal of Public Health, 95*(6), 998–1000.

Ritter, D., & Eslea, M. (2005). Hot sauce, toy guns, and graffiti: A critical account of current laboratory aggression paradigms. *Aggressive Behavior, 31,* 407–419.

Rivkin, I. D., & Taylor, S. E. (1999). The effects of mental stimulation on coping with controllable stressful events. *Personality and Social Psychology Bulletin, 25,* 1451–1462.

Roberson, D., Davies, I., & Davidoff, J. (2000). Color categories are not universal: Replications and new evidence from a Stone-Age culture. *Journal of Experimental Psychology: General, 129,* 369–398.

Roberts, R. D., Schulze, R., O'Brien, K., MacCann, C., Reid, J., & Maul, A. (2006). Exploring the validity of the Mayer-Salovey-Caruso Emotional Intelligence Test (MSCEIT) with established emotions measures. *Emotion, 6,* 663–669.

Roberts, R. D., Zeidner, M., & Matthews, G. (2001). Does emotional intelligence meet traditional standards for an intelligence? Some new data and conclusions. *Emotion, 1,* 196–231.

Robinson, M. D., & Clore, G. L. (2002). Belief and feeling: Evidence for an accessibility model of emotional self-report. *Psychological Bulletin, 128,* 934–960.

Robinson, M. D., Vargas, P. T., Tamir, M., & Solberg, E. C. (2004). Using and being used by categories. *Psychological Science, 15,* 521–526.

Rogers, S. J., & Puchalski, C. B. (1986). Social smiles of visually impaired infants. *Journal of Visual Impairment & Blindness, 80,* 863–865.

Rosaldo, M. Z. (1980). *Knowledge and passion: Ilongot notions of self and social life.* Cambridge, England: Cambridge University Press.

Roselli, C. E., Larkin, K., Resko, J. A., Stellflug, J. N., & Stormshak, F. (2004). The volume of a sexually dimorphic nucleus in the ovine medial preoptic area/anterior hypothalamus varies with sexual partner preference. *Endocrinology, 145*(2), 478–483.

Rosen, H. J., Perry, R. J., Murphy, J., Kramer, J. H., Mychack, P., Schuff, N., et al. (2002). Emotion comprehension in the temporal variant of frontotemporal dementia. *Brain, 125,* 2286–2295.

Rosen, J. B., & Schulkin, J. (1998). From normal fear to pathological anxiety. *Psychological Review, 105,* 325–350.

Rosen, J. B., & Schulkin, J. (2004). Adaptive fear, allostasis, and the pathology of anxiety and depression. In J. Schulkin (Ed.), *Allostasis, homeostasis, and the costs of physiological adaptation* (pp. 164–227). Cambridge, England: Cambridge University Press.

Rosenberg, E. L., Ekman, P., Jiang, W., Babyak, M., Coleman, R. E., Hanson, M., et al. (2001). Linkages between facial expressions of anger and transient myocardial ischemia in men with coronary artery disease. *Emotion, 1,* 107–115.

Rossen, E., & Kranzler, J. H. (2009). Incremental validity of the mayer-salovey-caruso emotional intelligence test version 2.0 (MSCEIT) after controlling for personality and intelligence. *Journal of Research in Personality, 43*(1), 60–65.

Rosvold, H. E., Mirsky, A. F., & Pribram, K. H. (1954). Influence of amygdalectomy on social behavior in monkeys. *Journal of Comparative and Physiological Psychology, 47,* 173–178.

Rothbaum, F., Weisz, J., Pott, M., Miyake, K., & Morelli, G. (2000). Attachment and culture: Security in the United States and Japan. *American Psychologist, 55,* 1093–1104.

Rottenberg, J., Gross, J. J., Wilhelm, F. H., Najmi, S., & Gotlib, I. H. (2002). Crying threshold and intensity in major depressive disorder. *Journal of Abnormal Psychology, 111,* 302–312.

Rottenberg, J., Kasch, K. L., Gross, J. J., & Gotlib, I. H. (2002). Sadness and amusement reactivity differentially predict concurrent and prospective functioning in major depressive disorder. *Emotion, 2,* 135–146.

Roy, A., DeJong, J., & Linnoila, M. (1989). Cerebrospinal fluid monoamine metabolites and suicidal behavior in depressed patients. *Archives of General Psychiatry, 46,* 609–612.

Røysamb, E., Harris, J. R., Magnus, P., Vittersø, J., & Tambs, K. (2002). Subjective well-being: Sex-specific effects of genetic and environmental factors. *Personality and Individual Differences, 32,* 211–223.

Royzman, E. B., & Sabini, J. (2001). Something it takes to be an emotion: The interesting case of disgust. *Journal for the Theory of Social Behavior, 31,* 29–59.

Rozenblit, L., & Keil, F. (2002). The misunderstood limits of folk science: An illusion of explanatory depth. *Cognitive Science, 26,* 521–562.

Rozin, P., & Cohen, A. B. (2003). High frequency of facial expressions corresponding to confusion, concentration, and worry in an analysis of naturally occurring facial expressions of Americans. *Emotion, 3,* 68–75.

Rozin, P., & Fallon, A. (1987). A perspective on disgust. *Psychological Review, 94,* 23–41.

Rozin, P., Fallon, A., & Augustoni-Ziskind, M. L. (1985). The child's conception of food: The development of contamination sensitivity to "disgusting" substances. *Developmental Psychology, 21,* 1075–1079.

Rozin, P., Hammer, L., Oster, H., Horowitz, T., & Marmora, V. (1986). The child's conception of food: Differentiation of categories of rejected substances in the 16 months to 5 year age range. *Appetite, 7,* 141–151.

Rozin, P., & Kalat, J. W. (1971). Specific hungers and poison avoidance as adaptive specializations of learning. *Psychological Review, 78,* 459–486.

Rozin, P., Lowery, L., Imada, S., & Haidt, J. (1999). The CAD triad hypothesis: A mapping between three moral emotions (contempt, anger, disgust) and three moral codes (community, autonomy, divinity). *Journal of Personality and Social Psychology, 76,* 574–586.

Rozin, P., Millman, L., & Nemeroff, C. (1986). Operation of the laws of sympathetic magic in disgust and other domains. *Journal of Personality and SocialPsychology, 50,* 703–712.

Rozin, P., Taylor, C., Ross, L., Bennett, G., & Hejmadi, A. (2005). General and specific abilities to recognise negative emotions, especially disgust, as portrayed in the face and the body. *Cognition and Emotion, 19,* 397–412.

Rubin, K. H., Dwyer, K. M., Booth-LaForce, C., Kim, A. H., Burgess, K. B., & Rose-Krasnor, L. (2004). Attachment, friendship, and psychosocial functioning in early adolescence. *Journal of Early Adolescence, 24,* 326–356.

Rubin, Z. (1970). Measurement of romantic love. *Journal of Personality and Social Psychology, 16,* 265–273.

Rubin, Z., Peplau, L. A., & Hill, C. T. (1981). Loving and leaving: Sex differences in romantic attachments. *Sex Roles, 7,* 821–835.

Rujescu, D., Giegling, I., Bondy, B., Gieti, A., Zill, P., & Möller, H.-J. (2002). Association of anger-related traits with SNPs in the TPH gene. *Molecular Psychiatry, 7,* 1023–1029.

Rushton, D. H. (2002). Nutritional factors and hair loss. *Clinical and experimental dermatology, 27,* 396–404.

Russell, J. A. (1980). A circumplex model of affect. *Journal of Personality and Social Psychology, 39,* 1161–1178.

Russell, J. A. (1991). Culture and the categorization of emotions. *Psychological Bulletin, 110,* 426–450.

Russell, J. A. (1994). Is there a universal recognition of emotion from facial expression? A review of the cross-cultural studies. *Psychological Bulletin, 115,* 102–141.

Russell, J. A. (2003). Core affect and the psychological construction of emotion. *Psychological Review, 110,* 145–172.

Rutledge, T., & Hogan, B. E. (2002). A quantitative review of prospective evidence linking psychological factors with hypertension development. *Psychosomatic Medicine, 64,* 758–766.

Ruys, K. I., & Stapel, D. A. (2008). The secret life of emotions. *Psychological Science, 19,* 385–391.

Ryff, C. D., & Singer, B. (2003). Thriving in the face of challenge. In F. Kessel, P. L. Rosenfield, & N. B. Anderson (Eds.), *Expanding the boundaries of health and social science* (pp. 181–205). Oxford, England: Oxford University Press.

Sabini, J., Siepmann, M., Stein, J., & Meyerowitz, M. (2000). Who is embarrassed by what? *Cognition and Emotion, 14,* 213–240.

Sacco, D. F., & Hugenberg, K. (2009). The look of fear and anger: Facial maturity modulates recognition of fearful and angry expressions. *Emotion, 9,* 39–49.

Sacks, O. (1985). *The Man Who Mistook His Wife for a Hat and Other Clinical Tales.* New York: Summit.

Salemink, E., van den Hout, M. A., & Kindt, M. (2007). Selective attention and threat: Quick orienting versus slow disengagement and two versions of the dot probe task. *Behaviour Research and Therapy, 45*(3), 607–615.

Salmivalli, C., & Kaukiainen, A. (2004). "Female aggression" revisited: Variable and person-centered approaches to studying gender differences in different types of aggression. *Aggressive Behavior, 30,* 158–163.

Salmon, P. (2001). Effects of physical exercise on anxiety, depression, and sensitivity to stress: A unifying theory. *Clinical Psychology Review, 21,* 33–61.

Salomons, T. V., Johnstone, T., Backonja, M.-M., & Davidson, R. J. (2004). Perceived controllability modulates the neural response to pain. *Journal of Neuroscience, 24,* 7199–7203.

Salovey, P., & Birnbaum, D. (1989). Influence of mood on health-relevant cognitions. *Journal of Personality and Social Psychology, 57,* 539–551.

Sanderson, C. A., & Cantor, N. (2001). The association of intimacy goals and marital satisfaction: A test of four mediational hypotheses. *Personality and Social Psychology Bulletin, 27,* 1567–1577.

Sanefuji, W. (2008). "Like me" detection in infancy: Toward understanding other's mental states. *Psychologia, 51,* 46–60.

Sanna, L. J. (2000). Mental simulation, affect, and personality: A conceptual framework. *Current Directions in Psychological Science, 9,* 168–173.

Sapir, E. (1921). *Language: An introduction to the study of speech.* New York: Harcourt, Brace.

Sapolsky, R. M. (1992). *Stress, the aging brain, and the mechanisms of neuron death.* Cambridge, MA: MIT Press.

Sapolsky, R. M. (1998). *Why zebras don't get ulcers.* New York: W. H. Freeman.

Sarason, I. G., Johnson, J. H., & Siegel, J. M. (1979). Assessing the impact of life changes: Development of the life experiences survey. *Journal of Consulting and Clinical Psychlogy, 46,* 932–946.

Sarlo, M., Palomba, D., Angrilli, A., & Stegagno, L. (2002). Blood phobia and spider phobia: Two specific phobias with different autonomic cardiac modulations. *Biological Psychology, 60,* 91–108.

Sato, W., Yoshikawa, S., Kochiyama, T., & Matsumura, M. (2004). The amygdala processes the emotional significance of facial expressions: An fMRI investigation using the interaction between expression and face direction. *NeuroImage, 22,* 1006–1013.

Saudou, F., Amara, D. A., Dierich, A., LeMeur, M., Ramboz, S., Segu, L., et al. (1994). Enhanced aggressive behavior in mice lacking 5-HT$_{1B}$ receptor. *Science, 265,* 1875–1878.

Saxe, L., & Ben-Shakhar, G. (1999). Admissibility of polygraph tests: The applicability of scientific standards post-Daubert. *Psychology, Public Policy and Law, 5,* 203–223.

Schachter, S., & Singer, J. (1962). Cognitive, social, and physiological determinants of emotional state. *Psychological Review, 69,* 379–399.

Schafe, G. E., Atkins, C. M., Swank, M. W., Bauer, E. P., Sweatt, J. D., & LeDoux, J. E. (2000). Activation of ERK/MAP kinase in the amygdala is required for memory consolidation of Pavlovian fear conditioning. *Journal of Neuroscience, 20,* 8177–8187.

Schaffer, H. R. (1971). *The growth of sociability.* Baltimore, MD: Penguin.

Scheier, M. F., Carver, C. S., & Bridges, M. W. (1994). Distinguishing optimism from neuroticism (and trait anxiety, self-mastery, and self-esteem): A reevaluation of the Life Orientation Test. *Journal of Personality and Social Psychology, 67,* 1063–1078.

Scheier, M. F., Matthews, K. A., Owens, J. F., Magovern, G. J., Sr., Lefebvre, R. C., Abbott, R. A., et al. (1989). Dispositional optimism and recovery from coronary artery bypass surgery: The beneficial effects on physical and psychological well-being. *Journal of Personality and Social Psychology, 57,* 1024–1040.

Scherer, K. R. (1992). What does facial expression express? In K. T. Strongman (Ed.), *International review of studies on emotion* (Vol. 2, pp. 139–165). Chichester, England: Wiley.

Scherer, K. R. (1997). The role of culture in emotion-antecedent appraisal. *Journal of Personality and Social Psychology, 73*(5), 902–922.

Scherer, K. R., & Brosch, T. (2009). Culture-specific appraisal biases contributed to emotion dispositions. *European Journal of Personality, Special Issue: Personality and Culture, 23*(3), 265–288.

Scherer, K. R., & Ellgring, H. (2007). Multimodal expression of emotion: Affect programs or componential appraisal patterns? *Emotion, 7,* 158–171.

Scherer, K. R., & Wallbott, H. G. (1994). Evidence for universality and cultural variation of differential emotion response patterning. *Journal of Personality and Social Psychology, 66,* 310–328.

Scherer, K. R., & Zentner, M. R. (2001). Emotional effects of music: Production rules. In J. A. Sloboda & P. W. Juslin (Eds.), *Music and emotion: Theory and research* (pp. 361–392). London: Oxford University Press.

Scherer, K. R., Zentner, M. R., & Stern, D. (2004). Beyond surprise: The puzzle of infants' expressive reactions to expectancy violation. *Emotion, 4,* 389–402.

Schienle, A., Schäfer, A., Hermann, A., Rohrmann, S., & Vaitl, D. (2007). Symptom provocation and reduction in patients suffering from spider phobia: An fMRI study on exposure therapy. *European Archives of Psychiatry and Clinical Neuroscience, 257*(8), 486–493.

Schienle, A., Stark, R., Walter, B., Blecker, C., Ott, U., Kirsch, P., et al. (2002). The insula is not specifically involved in disgust processing: An fMRI study. *NeuroReport, 13,* 2023–2026.

Schkade, D. A., & Kahneman, D. (1998). Does living in California make people happy? *Psychological Science, 9,* 340–346.

Schmidt, S. R. (2002). Outstanding memories: The positive and negative effects of nudes on memory. *Journal of Experimental Psychology: Learning Memory and Cognition, 28,* 353–361.

Schreckenberger, M., Siessmeier, T., Viertmann, A., Landvogt, C., Buchholz, H.., Rolke, R., Treede, R., Bartenstein, P., & Birklein, F. (2005). The unpleasantness of tonic pain is encoded by the insular cortex. *Neurology, 64*(7), 1175–1183.

Schulman, P., Keith, D., & Seligman, M. E. P. (1993). Is optimism heritable? A study of twins. *Behaviour Research and Therapy, 31,* 569–574.

Schupp, H. T., Öhman, A., Junghöfer, M., Weike, A. I., Stockburger, J., & Hamm, A. O. (2004). The facilitated processing of threatening faces; An ERP analysis. *Emotion, 4,* 189–200.

Schutte, N. S., Malouff, J. M., Simunek, M., McKenley, J., & Hollander, S. (2002). Characteristic emotional intelligence and emotional well-being. *Cognition and Emotion, 16,* 769–785.

Schwartz, C. E., Wright, C. I., Shin, L. M., Kagan, J., & Rauch, S. L. (2003). Inhibited and uninhibited infants "grown up": Adult amygdalar response to novelty. *Science, 300,* 1952–1953.

Schwartz, D., Dodge, K. A., Pettit, G. S., & Bates, J. E. (2000). Friendship as a moderating factor in the pathway between early harsh home environment and later victimization in the peer group. *Developmental Psychology, 36,* 646–662.

Schwarz, N., & Clore, G. L. (1983). Mood, misattribution, and judgments of well-being: Informative and directive functions of affective states. *Journal of Personality and Social Psychology, 45,* 513–523.

Scollon, C. N., Diener, E., Oishi, S., & Biswas-Diener, R. (2004). Emotions across cultures and methods. *Journal of Cross-Cultural Psychology, 35*(3), 304–326.

Scott, S. K., Young, A. W., Calder, A. J., Hellawell, D. J., Aggleton, J. P., & Johnson, M. (1997). Impaired auditory recognition of fear and anger following bilateral amygdala lesions. *Nature, 385,* 254–257.

Segerstrom, S. C., & Miller, G. E. (2004). Psychological stress and the human immune system: A meta-analytic study of 30 years of inquiry. *Psychological Bulletin, 130,* 601–630.

Seidman, S. N., Orr, G., Raviv, G., Levi, R., Roose, S. R., Kravitz, E., Amiaz, R., & Weiser, M. (2009).

Effects of testosterone replacement in middle-aged men with dysthymia: A randomized, placebo-controlled clinical trial. *Journal of Clinical Psychopharmacology, 29*(3), 216–221.

Seidner, L. B., Stipek, D. J., & Feshbach, N. D. (1988). A developmental analysis of elementary school-aged children's concepts of pride and embarrassment. *Child Development, 59,* 367–377.

Seligman, M. E. P. (1971). Phobias and preparedness. *Behavior Therapy, 2,* 307–320.

Seligman, M. E. P., & Maier, S. F. (1967). Failure to escape traumatic shock. *Journal of Experimental Psychology, 74*(1), 1–9.

Seligman, M. E. P., Schulman, P., DeRubeis, R. J., & Hollon, S. D. (1999). The prevention of depression and anxiety. *Prevention and Treatment, 2,* article 8.

Semin, G. R., & Manstead, A. S. (1982). The social implications of embarrassment displays and restitution behavior. *European Journal of Social Psychology, 12,* 367–377.

Semin, G. R., & Papadopoulou, K. (1990). The acquisitioin of reflexive social emotions: The transmission and reproduction of social control through joint action. In G. Duveen & B. Lloyd (Eds.), *Social representations and the development of knowledge* (pp. 107–125). New York: Cambridge University Press.

Shackelford, T. K., & Larsen, R. J. (1999). Facial attractiveness and physical health. *Evolution and Human Behavior, 20,* 71–76.

Shackelford, T. K., Schmitt, D. P., & Buss, D. M. (2005). Universal dimensions of human mate preferences. *Personality and Individual Differences, 39* (2), 447–458.

Shair, H. N., Brunelli, S. A., Masmela, J. R., Boone, E., & Hofer, M. A. (2003). Social, thermal, and temporal influences on isolation-induced and maternally potentiated ultrasonic vocalizations of rat pups. *Developmental Psychobiology, 42,* 206–222.

Shalev, A. Y., Peri, T., Brandes, D., Freedman, S., Orr, S. P., & Pitman, R. K. (2000). Auditory startle response in trauma survivors with posttraumatic stress disorder: A prospective study. *American Journal of Psychiatry, 157,* 255–261.

Shamay-Tsoory, S. G., Tomer, R., Goldsher, D., Berger, B. D., & Aharon-Peretz, J. (2004). Impairment in cognitive and affective empathy in patients with brain lesions: Anatomical and cognitive correlates. *Journal of Clinical and Experimental Neuropsychology, 26,* 1113–1127.

Shapiro, D. H., Jr., Schwartz, E. D., & Astin, J. A. (1996). Controlling ourselves, controlling our world. *American Psychologist, 51,* 1213–1230.

Shariff, A. F., & Tracy, J. L. (2009). Knowing who's boss: Implicit perceptions of status from the nonverbal expression of pride. *Emotion, 9*(5), 631–639.

Sharot, T., Delgado, M. R., & Phelps, E. A. (2004). How emotion enhances the feeling of remembering. *Nature Neuroscience, 7,* 1376–1380.

Shaver, P. R., Morgan, H. J., & Wu, S. (1996). Is love a "basic" emotion? *Personal Relationships, 3,* 81–96.

Shaver, P., Schwartz, J., Kirson, D., & O'Connor, C. (1987). Emotion knowledge: Further exploration of a prototype approach. *Journal of Personality and Social Psychology, 52,* 1061–1086.

Shearn, D., Spellman, L., Straley, B., Meirick, J., & Stryker, K. (1999). Empathic blushing in friends and strangers. *Motivation and Emotion, 23,* 307–316.

Sheldon, K. M., & Lyubomirsky, S. (2006). Achieving sustainable gains in happiness: Change your actions, not your circumstances. *Journal of Happiness Studies, 7,* 55–86.

Shen, B. J., Stroud, L. R., & Niaura, R. (2004). Ethnic differences in cardiovascular responses to laboratory stress: A comparison between Asian and white Americans. *International Journal of Behavioral Medicine, 11,* 181–186.

Shepher, J. (1971). Mate selection among second generation kibbutz adolescents and adults: Incest avoidance and negative imprinting. *Archives of Sexual Behavior, 1*(4), 293–307.

Sheppard, W. D., II, Staggers, F. J., Jr., & John, L. (1997). The effects of a stress management program in a high security government agency. *Anxiety, Stress, and Coping, 10,* 341–350.

Sherrod, D. R., Hage, J. N., Halpern, P. L., & Moore, B. S. (1977). Effects of personal causation and perceived control on responses to an aversive environment: The more control, the better. *Journal of Experimental Social Psychology, 13,* 14–27.

Shifren, J. L., Braunstein, G. D., Simon, J. A., Casson, P. R., Buster, J. E., Redmond, G. P., et al.

(2000). Transdermal testosterone treatment in women with impaired sexual function after oophorectomy. *The New England Journal of Medicine, 343*(10), 682–688.

Shiota, M. N., Campos, B., Gonzaga, G. C., Keltner, D., & Peng, K. (2010). I love you but...: Cultural differences in emotional complexity during interaction with a romantic partner. *Cognition and Emotion, 24(5),* 786–799.

Shiota, M. N., Campos, B., & Keltner, D. (2003). The faces of positive emotion: prototype displays of awe, amusement, and pride. *Annals of the New York Academy of Sciences, 1000,* 296–299.

Shiota, M. N., Campos, B., Keltner, D., & Hertenstein, M. J. (2004). Positive emotion and the regulation of interpersonal relationships. In P. Philippot & R. S. Feldman (Eds.), *The regulation of emotion.* Mahwah, NJ: Erlbaum.

Shiota, M. N., Keltner, D., & John, O. P. (2006). Positive emotion dispositions differentially associated with Big Five personality and attachment style. *Journal of Positive Psychology, 1*(2), 61–71.

Shiota, M. N., & Levenson, R. W. (2007). Birds of a feather don't always fly farthest: Similarity in big five personality predicts more negative marital satisfaction trajectories in long-term marriages. *Psychology and Aging, 22*(4), 666–675.

Shiota, M. N., & Levenson, R. W. (2009). Effects of aging on experimentally instructed detached reappraisal, positive reappraisal, and emotional behavior suppression. *Psychology and Aging, 24*(4), 890–900.

Shrauger, J. S., Mariano, E., & Walter, T. J. (1988). Depressive symptoms and accuracy in the prediction of future events. *Personality and Social Psychology Bulletin, 24,* 880–892.

Shweder, R. A. (1993). The cultural psychology of the emotions. In M. Lewis & J. A. Haviland (Eds.), *Handbook of emotions* (pp. 417–434). New York: Guilford.

Siebert, M., Markowitsch, H. J., & Bartel, P. (2003). Amygdala, affect and cognition: Evidence from 10 patients with Urbach-Wiethe disease. *Brain, 126,* 2627–2637.

Siegel, J. M. (1986). The multidimensional anger inventory. *Journal of Personality and Social Psychology, 51,* 191–200.

Simpson, J. A., Ickes, W., & Blackstone, T. (1995). When the head protects the heart: Empathic accuracy in dating relationships. *Journal of Personality and Social Psychology, 69,* 629–641.

Simpson, J. A., Oriña, M. M., & Ickes, W. (2003). When accuracy hurts, and when it helps: A test of the empathic accuracy model in marital interactions. *Journal of Personality and Social Psychology, 85,* 881–893.

Sinaceur, M., Heath, C., & Cole, S. (2005). Emotional and deliberative reactions to a public crisis: Mad cow disease in France. *Psychological Science, 16,* 247–254.

Singh, D. (1993). Adaptive significance of female physical attractiveness: Role of waist to hip ratio. *Journal of Personality and Social Psychology, 65,* 293–307.

Sivak, M., & Flannagan, M. J. (2003, January-February). Flying and driving after the September 11 attacks. *American Scientist, 91*(1), 6–8.

Skinner, E. A., Edge, K., Altman, J., & Sherwood, H. (2003). Searching for the structure of coping: A review and critique of category systems for classifying ways of coping. *Psychological Bulletin, 129,* 216–269.

Skolnick, A. (1978). *The intimate environment: Exploring marriage and the family* (2nd ed.). Boston: Little, Brown.

Skre, I., Onstad, S., Torgerson, S., Lygren, S., & Kringlen, E. (2000). The heritability of common phobic fear: A twin study of a clinical sample. *Journal of Anxiety Disorders, 14,* 549–562.

Sloan, D. M., Strauss, M. E., & Wisner, K. L. (2001). Diminished response to pleasant stimuli by depressed women. *Journal of Abnormal Psychology, 110,* 488–493.

Small, D. M., Zatorre, R. J., Dagher, A., Evans, A. C., & Jones-Gotman, M. (2001). Changes in brain activity related to eating chocolate: From pleasure to aversion. *Brain, 124,* 1720–1733.

Smith, C. A., & Ellsworth, P. C. (1985). Patterns of cognitive appraisal in emotion. *Journal of Personality and Social Psychology, 48*(4), 813–838.

Smith, C. A., & Kirby, L. D. (2004). Appraisal as a pervasive determinant of anger. *Emotion, 4,* 133–138.

Smith, D. M., Langa, K. M., Kabeto, M. U., & Ubel, P. A. (2005). Health, wealth, and happiness. *Psychological Science, 16,* 663–666.

Smith, P., & Waterman, M. (2004). Role of experience in processing bias for aggressive words in forensic and non-forensic populations. *Aggressive Behavior, 30,* 105–122.

Smith, R. H., & Kim, S. H. (2007). Comprehending envy. *Psychological Bulletin, 133,* 46–64.

Smith, T. W. (2006). The national spiritual transformation study. *Journal for the Scientific Study of Religion, 45*(2), 283–296.

Snyder, C. R., Sympson, S. C., Michael, S. T., & Cheavens, J. (2001). Optimism and hope constructs: Variants on a ositive expectancy theme. In E. C. Chang (Ed.), *Optimism & pessimism: Implications for theory, research, and practice* (pp. 101–125). Washington: American Psychological Association.

Solomon, M. R. (2001). Eating as both coping and stressor in overweight control. *Journal of Advanced Nursing, 36,* 563–572.

Sorce, J. F., Emde, R. N., Campos, J. J., & Klinnert, M. D. (1985). Maternal emotional signaling: Its effect on the visual cliff behavior of 1-year-olds. *Developmental Psychology, 21,* 195–200.

Soussignan, R. (2002). Duchenne smile, emotional experience, and autonomic reactivity. A test of the facial feedback hypothesis. *Emotion, 2,* 52–74.

Sowell, E. R., Thompson, P. M., Holmes, C. J., Jernigan, T. L., & Toga, A. W. (1999). In vivo evidence for post-adolescent brain maturation in frontal and striatal regions. *Nature Neuroscience, 2,* 859–861.

Sowell, E. R., Thompson, P. M., Tessner, K. D., & Toga, A. W. (2001). Mapping continued brain growth and gray matter density reduction in dorsal frontal cortex: Inverse relationships during postadolescent brain maturation. *Journal of Neuroscience, 21,* 8819–8829.

Soyka, M., Preuss, U. W., Koller, G., Zill, P., & Bondy, B. (2002). Dopamine D_4 receptor gene polymorphism and extraversion revisited: Results from the Munich gene bank project for alcoholism. *Journal of Psychiatric Research, 36,* 429–435.

Spangler, D. L., & Burns, D. D. (1999). Are dysfunctional attitudes and attributional style the same or different? *Behavior Therapy, 30,* 239–252.

Spear, L. P. (2000). Neurobehavioral changes in adolescence. *Current Directions in Psychological Science, 9,* 111–114.

Spence, G., Oades, L. G., & Caputi, P. (2004). Trait emotional intelligence and goal self-integration: Important predictors of emotional well-being? *Personality and Individual Differences, 37,* 449–461.

Spielberger, C. D. (1991). *State-trait anger expression inventory revised research edition, professional manual.* Odessa, FL: Psychological Assessment Resources.

Spielberger, C. D., Jacobs, G., Russell, S., & Crane, R. S. (1983). Assessment of anger: The state-trait scale. *Advances in Personality Assessment, 2,* 161–189.

Spitz, R. (1965). *The first year of life.* New York: International Universities Press.

Spivak, B., Shohat, B., Mester, R., Avraham, S., Gil-Ad, I., Bleich, A.V. et al. (1997). *Biological Psychiatry, 42,* 345–348.

Spreux-Varoquaux, O., Alvarez, J. C., Berlin, I., Batista, G., Despierre, P.-G., Gilton, A., et al. (2001). Differential abnormalities in plasma 5-HIAA and platelet serotonin concentrations in violent suicide attempters. Relationships with impulsivity and depression. *Life Science, 69,* 647–657.

Sprecher, S., & Regan, P. C. (2002). Liking some things (in some people) more than others: Partner preferences in romantic relationships and friendships. *Journal of Social and Personal Relationships, 19*(4), 463–481.

Srivastava, S., Angelo, K. M., & Vallereux, S. R. (2008). Extraversion and positive affect: A day reconstruction study of person–environment transactions. *Journal of Research in Personality, 42*(6), 1613–1618.

Srivastava, S., Tamir, M., McGonigal, K. M., John, O. P., & Gross, J. J. (2009). The social costs of emotional suppression: A prospective study of the transition to college. *Journal of Personality and Social Psychology, 96*(4), 883–897.

Sroufe, L. A. (1977). Wariness of strangers and the study of infant development. *Child Development, 48,* 1184–1199.

Sroufe, L. A. (1996). *Emotional development: The organization of emotional life in the early years.* Cambridge, England: Cambridge University Press.

Stekelenburg, J. J., & van Boxtel, A. (2002). Pericranial muscular, respiratory, and heart rate components of the orienting response. *Psychophysiology, 39,* 707–722.

Stein, M. B., Goldin, P. R., Sareen, J., Zorrilla, L. T. E., & Brown, G. G. (2002). Increased amygdala activation to angry and contemptuous faces in generalized socialized phobia. *Archives of General Psychiatry, 59,* 1027–1034.

Stein, M. B., Hanna, C., Koverola, C., Torchia, M., & McClarty, B. (1997). Structural brain changes in PTSD. *Annals of the New York Academy of Sciences, 821,* 76–82.

Steinberg, L., Cauffman, E., Woolard, J., Graham, S., & Banich, M. (2009). Are adolescents less mature than adults? *American Psychologist, 64,* 583–594.

Stemmler, G., Aue, T., & Wacker, J. (2007). Anger and fear: Separable effects of emotion and motivational direction on somatovisceral responses. *International Journal of Psychophysiology, 66*(2), 141–153.

Sternberg, C. R., & Campos, J. J. (1990). The development of anger expressions in infancy. In N. L. Stein, B. Leventhal, & T. Trabasso (Eds.), *Psychological and biological approaches to emotion* (pp. 297–310). Hillsdale, NJ: Erlbaum.

Sternberg, C. R., Campos, J. J., & Emde, R. N. (1983). The facial expression of anger in seven-month infants. *Child Development, 54,* 178–184.

Steuer, F. B., Applefield, J. M., & Smith, R. (1971). Televised aggression and the interpersonal aggression of preschool children. *Journal of Experimental Child Psychology, 11,* 442–447.

Stipek, D. (1998). Differences between Americans and Chinese in the circumstances evoking pride, shame, and guilt. *Journal of Cross-Cultural Psychology, 29,* 616–629.

Stone, E. R., Dodrill, C. L., & Johnson, N. (2001). Depressive cognition: A test of depressive realism versus negativity using general knowledge items. *Journal of Psychology, 135,* 583–602.

Strack, F., Martin, L. L., & Stepper, S. (1988). Inhibiting and facilitating conditions of the human smile: A nonobtrusive test of the facial feedback hypothesis. *Journal of Personality and Social Psychology, 54,* 768–777.

Streeter, S. A., & McBurney, D. H. (2003). Waist-hip ratio and attractiveness: New evidence and critique of "a critical test." *Evolution and Human Behavior, 24,* 88–98.

Striano, T., & Bertin, E. (2005). Coordinated affect with mothers and strangers: A longitudinal analysis of joint engagement between 5 and 9 months of age. *Cognition & Emotion, 19,* 781–790.

Struthers, C. W., Easton, J.. Shirvani, N., Georghiou, M., & Edell, E. (2008). The effect of preemptive forgiveness and a transgressor's responsibility on shame, motivation to reconcile, and repentance. *Basic and Applied Social Psychology, 30,* 130–141.

Strzelczuk, M., & Romaniuk, A. (1996). Fear induced by the blockade of $GABA_A$-ergic transmission in the hypothalamus of the cat: Behavioral and neurochemical study. *Behavioural Brain Research, 72,* 63–71.

Sturm, V. E., Ascher, E. A., Miller, B. L., & Levenson, R. W. (2008). Diminished self-conscious emotional responding in frontotemporal lobar degeneration patients. *Emotion, 8,* 861–869.

Sturm, V. E., Rosen, H. J., Allison, S., Miller, B. L., & Levenson, R. W. (2006). Self-conscious emotion deficits in frontotemporal lobar degeneration. *Brain: A Journal of Neurology, 129*(9), 2508–2516.

Susskind, J. M., Lee, D. H., Cusi, A., Feiman, R., Grabski, W., & Anderson, A. K. (2008). Expressing fear enhances sensory acquisition. *Nature Neuroscience, 11,* 843–850.

Sutton, S. K., & Davidson, R. J. (1997). Prefrontal brain asymmetry: A biological substrate of the behavioral approach and inhibition systems. *Psychological Science, 8*(3), 204–210.

Swaab, D. F., & Fliers, E. (1985). A sexually dimorphic nucleus in the human brain. *Science, 228*(4703), 1112–1115.

Swaddle, J. P., & Reierson, G. W. (2002). Testosterone increases perceived dominance but not attractiveness in human males. *Proceedings Biological Sciences/the Royal Society, 269*(1507), 2285–2289.

Swann, W. B., Jr., & Gill, M. J. (1997). Confidence and accuracy in person perception: Do we know what we think we know about our relationship partners? *Journal of Personality and Social Psychology, 73,* 747–757.

Swidler, A. (2001). *Talk of love: How culture matters.* Chicago: University of Chicago Press.

Sykes, D. H., Arveiler, D., Salters, C. P., Ferrieres, J., McCrum, E., Amouyel, P., et al. (2002). Psychosocial risk factors for heart disease in France and Northern Ireland: The Prospective Epidemiological Study of Myocardial Infarction

(PRIME). *International Journal of Epidemiology, 31,* 1227–1234.

Tafrate, R. C., Kassinove, H., & Dundin, L. (2002). Anger episodes in high- and low-trait anger community adults. *Journal of Clinical Psychology, 58,* 1573–1590.

Takahashi, H., Yahata, N., Koeda, M., Matsuda, T., Asai, K., & Okubo, Y. (2004). Brain activation associated with evaluative processes of guilt and embarrassment: An fMRI study. *NeuroImage, 23,* 967–974.

Takano, Y., & Osaka, E. (1999). An unsupported common view: Comparing Japan and the U.S. on individualism/collectivism. *Asian Journal of Social Psychology, 2,* 311–341.

Takeuchi, M. S., Miyaoka, H., Tomoda, A., Suzuki, M., Liu, Q., Kitamura, T., et al. (2010). The effect of interpersonal touch during childhood on adult attachment and depression: A neglected area of family and developmental psychology? *Journal of Child and Family Studies, 19,* 109–117.

Talarico, J. M., & Rubin, D. C. (2003). Confidence, not consistency, characterizes flashbulb memories. *Psychological Science, 14,* 455–461.

Tamir, M., Mitchell, C., & Gross, J. J. (2008). Hedonic and instrumental motives in anger regulation. *Psychological Science, 19,* 324–328.

Tandon, R., & Jibson, M. D. (2002). Extrapyramidal side effects of antipsychotic treatment: Scope of problem and impact of outcome. *Annals of Clinical Psychiatry, 14*(2), 123–129.

Tangney, J. P. (1996). Conceptual and methodological issues in the assessment of shame and guilt. *Behaviour Research and Therapy, 34,* 741–754.

Tangney, J. P., Burggraf, S. A., & Wagner, P. E. (1995). Shame-proneness, guilt-pronness, and psychological symptoms. In J. P. Tangney & K. W. Fischer (Eds.), *Self-conscious emotions: The psychology of shame, guilt, embarrassment, and pride* (pp. 343–367), New York: Guilford Press.

Tangney, J. P., Miller, R. S., Flicker, L., & Barlow, D. H. (1996). Are shame, guilt, and embarrassment distinct emotions? *Journal of Personality and Social Psychology, 70,* 1256–1264.

Tangney, J. P., Wagner, P. E., Hill-Barlow, D., Marschall, D. E., & Gramzow, R. (1996). Relation of shame and guilt to constructive versus destructive responses to anger across the lifespan. *Journal of Personality and Social Psychology, 70,* 797–809.

Tanner, R. J., & Carlson, K. A. (2008). Unrealistically optimistic consumers: A selective hypothesis testing account for optimism in predictions of future behavior. *Journal of Consumer Research, 35,* 810–822.

Tassinary, L. G., & Hansen, K. A. (1998). A critical test of the waist-to-hip ratio hypothesis of female attractiveness. *Psychological Science, 9,* 150–155.

Taylor, S. E., & Brown, J. D. (1988). Illusion and well-being: A social psychological perspective on mental health. *Psychological Bulletin, 103,* 193–210.

Taylor, S. E., Kemeny, M. E., Reed, G. M., Bower, J. E., & Gruenwald, T. L. (2000). Psychological resources, positive illusions, and health. *American Psychologist, 55,* 99–109.

Taylor, S. E., Pham, L. B., Rivkin, I. D., & Armor, D. A. (1998). Harnessing the imagination: Mental simulation, self-regulation, and coping. *American Psychologist, 53,* 429–439.

Taylor, S. E., Seeman, T. E., Eisenberger, N. I., Kozanian, T. A., Moore, A. N., & Moons, W. G. (2010). Effects of a supportive or an unsupportive audience on biological and psychological responses to stress. *Journal of Personality and Social Psychology, 98*(1), 47–56.

Teigen, K.-H. (1994). Yerkes-Dodson: A law for all seasons. *Theory and Psychology, 4,* 525–547.

Tellegen, A., Watson, D., & Clark, L. A. (1999). On the dimensional and hierarchical structure of affect. *Psychological Science, 10,* 297–303.

Tennant, C. (2002). Life events, stress and depression: A review of the findings. *Australian and New Zealand Journal of Psychiatry, 36*(2), 173–182.

Theodoridou, A., Rowe, A. C., Penton-Voak, I. S., & Rogers, P. J. (2009). Oxytocin and social perception: Oxytocin increases perceived facial trustworthiness and attractiveness. *Hormones and Behavior, 56*(1), 128–132.

Thompson, W. F., Schellenberg, E. G., & Husain, G. (2004). Decoding speech prosody: Do music lessons help? *Emotion, 4,* 46–64.

Thoren, P., Floras, J. S., Hoffman, P., & Seals, D. R. (1990). Endorphins and exercise: Physiological mechanisms and clinical implications. *Medicine and Science in Sports and Exercise, 22,* 417–428.

Thorndike, E. (1918). The nature, purposes, and general methods of measurements of educational products. In E. J. Ashbaugh, W. A. Averill, L. P. Ayres,

F. W. Ballou, E. Bryner, B. R. Buckingham, et al. (Eds.), *The seventeenth yearbook of the National Society for the Study of Education, Part II: The measurement of educational products* (pp. 16–24). Bloomington, IN: Public School Publishing.

Thornton, B. (1977). Toward a linear prediction model of marital happiness. *Personality and Social Psychology Bulletin, 3,* 674–676.

Tiedens, L. Z. (2001). Anger and advancement versus sadness and subjugation: The effect of negative emotion expressions on social status conferral. *Journal of Personality and Social Psychology, 80,* 86–94.

Tiedens, L. Z., Ellsworth, P. C., & Mesquita, B. (2000). Stereotypes about sentiments and status: Emotional expectations for high- and low-status group members. *Personality and Social Psychology Bulletin, 26,* 560–574.

Tiedens, L. Z., & Linton, S. (2001). Judgment under emotional certainty and uncertainty: The effects of specific emotions on information processing. *Journal of Personality and Social Psychology, 81,* 973–988.

Tisserand, D. J., van Boxtel, M. P. J., Pruessner, J. C., Hofman, P., Evans, A. C., & Jolles, J. (2004). A voxel-based morphometric study to determine individual differences in gray matter density associated with age and cognitive change over time. *Cerebral Cortex, 14*(9), 966–973.

Tom, S. M., Fox, C. R., Trepel, C., & Poldrack, R. A. (2007). The neural basis of loss aversion in decision-making under risk. *Science, 315*(5811), 515–518.

Tomaka, J., Blascovich, J., Kibler, J, & Ernst, J. M. (1997). Cognitive and physiological antecedents of threat and challenge appraisal. *Journal of Personality and Social Psychology, 73,* 63–72.

Tomarken, A. J., Davidson, R. J., Wheeler, R. E., & Doss, R. C. (1992). Individual differences in anterior brain asymmetry and fundamental dimensions of emotion. *Journal of Personality and Social Psychology, 62*(4), 676–687.

Tooby, J., & Cosmides, L. (1990). The past explains the present: Emotional adaptations and the structure of ancestral environments. *Ethology & Sociobiology, 11*(4-5), 375–424.

Tooby, J., & Cosmides, L. (2006). The evolved architecture of hazard management: Risk detection reasoning and the motivational computation of threat magnitudes. *Behavioral and Brain Sciences, 29*(6), 631–633.

Tooby, J., & Cosmides, L. (2008). The evolutionary psychology of the emotions and their relationship to internal regulatory variables. In M. Lewis, J. M. Haviland-Jones & L. F. Barrett (Eds.), *Handbook of emotions (3rd ed.).* (pp. 114–137). New York, NY, U.S.: Guilford Press.

Toufexis, D. (2007). Region- and sex-specific modulation of anxiety behavours in the rat. *Journal of Neuroendocrinology, 19,* 461–473.

Townshend, J. M., & Duka, T. (2003). Mixed emotions: Alcoholics' impairments in the recognition of specific emotional facial expressions. *Neuropsychologia, 41,* 773–782.

Tracy, J. L., & Robins, R. W. (2004). Show your pride: Evidence for a discrete emotion expression. *Psychological Science, 15,* 194–197.

Tracy, J. L., & Robins, R. W. (2008). The automaticity of emotion recognition. *Emotion, 8,* 81–95.

Trentacosta, C. J., & Shaw, D. S. (2009). Emotional self-regulation, peer rejection, and antisocial behavior: Developmental associations from early childhood to early adolescence. *Journal of Applied Developmental Psychology, 30,* 356–365.

Trevarthen, C., & Hubley, P. (1978). Secondary intersubjectivity: Confidence, confiders, and acts of meaning in the first year of life. In A. Lock (Ed.), *Action, gesture, and symbol: The emergence of language* (pp. 183–229). New York: Academic Press.

Triandis, H., McCusker, C., & Hui, C. (1990). Multimethod probes of individualism and collectivism. *Journal of Personality and Social Psychology, 59,* 1006–1020.

Trimmer, C. G., & Cuddy, L. L. (2008). Emotional intelligence, not music training, predicts recognition of emotional speech prosody. *Emotion, 8*(6), 838–849.

Trull, T. J., & Geary, D. C. (1997). Comparison of the big-five factor structure across samples of chinese and american adults. *Journal of Personality Assessment, 69*(2), 324–341.

Tsai, J. L. (2007). Ideal affect: Cultural causes and behavioral consequences. *Perspectives on Psychological Science, 2,* 242–259.

Tsai, J. L., & Chentsova-Dutton, Y. (2003). Variation among European Americans in emotional facial expression. *Journal of Cross-Cultural Psychology, 34,* 650–657.

Tsai, J. L., Chentsova-Dutton, Y., Freire-Bebeau, L., & Przymus, D. E. (2002). Emotional expression and physiology in European Americans and Hmong Americans. *Emotion, 2,* 380–397.

Tsai, J. L., Simeonova, D. I., & Watanabe, J. T. (2004). Somatic and social: Chinese Americans talk about emotion. *Personality and Social Psychology Bulletin, 30,* 1226–1238.

Tsankova, N., Renthal, W., Kumar, A., & Nestler, E. J. (2007). Epigenetic regulation in psychiatric disorders. *Nature Reviews Neuroscience, 8,* 355–367.

Tugade, M. M., & Fredrickson, B. L. (2004). Resilient individuals use positive emotions to bounce back from negative emotional experiences. *Journal of Personality and Social Psychology, 86,* 320–333.

Twenge, J. M. (2002). Birth cohort, social change, and personality. In D. Cervone & W. Mischel (Eds.), *Advances in personality science* (pp. 196–218). NewYork: Guilford.

Tzeng, M. (1992). The effects of socioeconomic heterogamy and changes on marital dissolution for first marriages. *Journal of Marriage and the Family, 54,* 609–619.

Uchida, Y., & Kitayama, S. (2009). Happiness and unhappiness in East and West: Themes and variations. *Emotion, 9,* 441–456.

Uchida, Y., Norasakkunkit, V., & Kitayama, S. (2004). Cultural constructions of happiness: Theory and empirical evidence. *Journal of Happiness Studies, 5,* 223–239.

Unsworth, G., Devilly, G. J., & Ward, T. (2007). The effect of playing violent video games on adolescents: Should parents be quaking in their boots? *Psychology, Crime and Law, 13,* 383–394.

Urry, H. L., Nitschke, J. B., Dolski, I., Jackson, D. C., Dalton, K. M., Mueller, C. J., et al. (2004). Making a life worth living: Neural correlates of well-being. *Psychological Science, 15,* 367–372.

Uwano, T., Nishijo, H., Ono, T., & Tamura, R. (1995). Neuronal responsiveness to various sensory stimuli, and associative learning in the rat amygdala. *Neuroscience, 68,* 339–361.

Vaillant, G. E. (1977). *Adaptation to Life: How the Best and Brightest Came of Age.* Boston, MA: Little, Brown & Company.

Vaish, A., Grossman, T., & Woodward, A. (2008). Not all emotions are created equal: The negativity bias in social-emotional development. *Psychological Bulletin, 134,* 383–403.

Valiente, C., Eisenberg, N., Shepard, S. A., Fabes, R. A., Cumberland, A. J., Losoya, S. H., et al. (2004). The relations of mothers' negative expressivity to children's experience and expression of negative emotion. *Applied Devlopmental Psychology, 25,* 215–235.

Vallotton, C. D. (2008). Signs of emotion: What can preverbal children "say" about internal states? *Infant Mental Health Journal, 29,* 234–258.

Valzelli, L. (1973). The "isolation syndrome" in mice. *Psychopharmacologia, 31,* 305–320.

Valzelli, L. (1979). Effect of sedatives and anxiolytics on aggressivity. *Modern Problems in Pharmacopsychiatry, 14,* 143–156.

Valzelli, L., & Bernasconi, S. (1979). Aggressiveness by isolation and brain serotonin turnover changes in different strains of mice. *Neuropsychobiology, 5,* 129–135.

van Baardewijk, Y., Stegge, H., Bushman, B. J., & Vermeiren, R. (2009). Psychopathic traits, victim distress and aggression in children. *Journal of Child Psychology and Psychiatry, 50*(6), 718–725.

van de Ven, N., Zeelenberg, M., & Pieters, R. (2009). Leveling up and down: The experiences of benign and malicious envy. *Emotion, 9,* 419–429.

Van den Stock, J., Righart, R., & de Gelder, B. (2007). Body expressions influence recognition of emotions in the face and voice. *Emotion, 7,* 487–494.

Van der Does, A. J. W. (2001). The effects of tryptophan depletion on mood and psychiatric symptoms. *Journal of Affective Disorders, 64,* 107–119.

van der Vegt, B. J., Lieuwes, N., van de Wall, E. H. E. M., Kato, K., Moya-Albiol, L., Martínez-Sanchez, S., et al. (2003). Activation of serotonergic neurotransmission during the performance of aggressive behavior in rats. *Behavioral Neuroscience, 117,* 667–674.

van der Zee, K. I., Huet, R. C. G., Cazemier, C., & Evers, K. (2002). The influence of the premedication consult and preparatory information about anesthesia on anxiety among patients undergoing cardiac surgery. *Anxiety, Stress, and Coping, 15,* 123–133.

van Honk, J., & Schutter, D. J. L. G. (2007). Testosterone reduces conscious detection of signals serving social correction. *Psychological Science, 18,* 663–667.

Van Kleef, G. A., De Dreu, C. K. W., & Manstead, A. S. R. (2004). The interpersonal effects of anger and happiness in negotiations. *Journal of Personality and Social Psychology, 86,* 57–76.

Van Rooy, D. L., Alonso, A., & Viswesvaran, C. (2005). Group differences in emotional intelligence scores: Theoretical and practical implications. *Personality and Individual Differences, 38,* 689–700.

Van Yperen, N. W., & Buunk,. B. P. (1990). A longitudinal study of equity and satisfaction in intimate relationships. *European Journal of Social Psychology, 20,* 287–309.

Vasilev, C. A., Crowell, S. E., Beauchaine, T. P., Mead, H. K., & Gatzke-Kopp, L. M. (2009). Correspondence between physiological and self-report measures of emotion dysregulation: A longitudinal investigation of youth with and without psychopathology. *Journal of Child Psychology and Psychiatry, 50*(11), 1357–1364.

Vedhara, K., Cox, N. K. M., Wilcock, G. K., Perks, P., Hunt, M., Anderson, S., et al. (1999). Chronic stress in elderly carers of dementia patients and antibody response to influenza vaccination. *Lancet, 353,* 627–631.

Vella, E. J., & Friedman, B. H. (2009). Hostility and anger in: Cardiovascular reactivity and recovery to mental arithmetic stress. *International Journal of Psychophysiology, 72*(3), 253–259.

Verheyden, S. L., Henry, J. A., & Curran, H. V. (2003). Acute, sub-acute and long-term subjective consequences of 'ecstasy' (MDMA) consumption in 430 regular users. *Human Psychopharmacology: Clinical and Experimental, 18*(7), 507–517.

Virkkunen, M., DeJong, J., Bartko, J., Goodwin, F. K., & Linnoila, M. (1989). Relationship of psychobiological variables to recidivism in violent offenders and impulsive fire setters. *Archives of General Psychiatry, 46,* 600–603.

Virkkunen, M., Eggert, M., Rawlings, R., & Linnoila, M. (1996). A prospective follow-up study of alcoholic violent offenders and fire setters. *Archives of General Psychiatry, 53,* 523–529.

Virkkunen, M., Nuutila, A., Goodwin, F. K., & Linnoila, M. (1987). Cerebrospinal fluid monoamine metabolite levels in male arsonists. *Archives of General Psychiatry, 44,* 241–247.

Volkow, N. D., Fowler, J. S., Wang, G., Swanson, J. M., & Telang, F. (2007). Dopamine in drug abuse and addiction: Results of imaging studies and treatment implications. *Archives of Neurology, 64*(11), 1575–1579.

Vuilleumier, P. (2005). Cognitive science: Staring fear in the face. *Nature, 433,* 22–23.

Vuilleumier, P., Armony, J. L., Driver, J., & Dolan, R. J. (2001). Effects of attention and emotion on face processing in the human brain: An event-related fMRI study. *Neuron, 30,* 829–841.

Wagner, G., Rabkin, J., & Rabkin, R. (1997). Effects of testosterone replacement therapy on sexual interest, function and behavior in HIV+ men. *Journal of Sex Research, 34*(1), 27–33.

Wakely, A., Rivera, S., & Langer, J. (2000). Can young infants add and subtract? *Child Development, 71,* 1525–1534.

Walden, T. A., & Baxter, A. (1989). The effect of context and age on social referencing. *Child Development, 60,* 1511–1518.

Walf, A. A., & Frye, C. A. (2006). A review and update of mechanisms of estrogen in the hippocampus and amygdala for anxiety and depression behavior. *Neuropsychopharmacology, 31*(6), 1097–1111.

Wallace, A. F. C., & Carson, M. T. (1973). Sharing and diversity in emotion terminology. *Ethos, 1,* 1–29.

Wallace, H. M., Exline, J. J., & Baumeister, R. F. (2008). Interpersonal consequences of forgiveness: Does forgiveness deter or encourage repeat offenses? *Journal of Experimental Social Psychology, 44,* 453–460.

Walum, H., Westberg, L., Henningsson, S., Neiderhiser, J. M., Reiss, D., Igl, W., Ganiban, J. M., Spotts, E. L., Pedersen, N. L., Eriksson, E., & Lichtenstein, P. (2008). Genetic variation in the vasopressin receptor 1a gene (*AVPR1A*) associates with pair-bonding behavior in humans. *Proceedings of the National Academy of Sciences, 105*(37), 14153–14156.

Wang, L., McCarthy, G., Song, A. W., & LaBar, K. S. (2005). Amygdala activation to sad pictures during high-field (4 Tesla) functional magnetic resonance imaging. *Emotion, 5,* 12–22.

Wang, L., Shi, Z., & Li, H. (2009). Neuroticism, extraversion, emotion regulation, negative affect and positive affect: The mediating roles of reappraisal and suppression. *Social Behavior and Personality, 37*(2), 193–194.

Warwick, J., & Nettelbeck, T. (2004). Emotional intelligence is...? *Personality and Individual Differences, 37,* 1091–1100.

Waters, A., Hill, A., & Waller, G. (2001). Bulimics' responses to food cravings: Is binge-eating a product of hunger or emotional state? *Behaviour Research and Therapy, 39,* 877–886.

Watson, D. (2002). Positive affectivity. In C. R. Snyder & S. J. Lopez (Eds.), *Handbook of positive psychology* (pp. 106–119). New York: Oxford University Press.

Watson, D., Clark, L. A., & Tellegen, A. (1984). Cross-cultural convergence in the structure of mood: A Japanese replication and a comparison with U.S. findings. *Journal of Personality and Social Psychology, 47,* 127–144.

Watson, D., Clark, L. A., & Tellegen, A. (1988). Development and validation of brief measures of positive and negative affect: The PANAS scales. *Journal of Personality and Social Psychology, 54,* 1063–1070.

Watson, D., & Tellegen, A. (1985). Toward a consensual structure of mood. *Psychological Bulletin, 98,* 219–235.

Watson, J. B., & Rayner, R. (1920). Conditioned emotional reactions. *Journal of Experimental Psychology, 3,* 1–14.

Weaver, C. A., III (1993). Do you need a "flash" to form a flashbulb memory? *Journal of Experimental Psychology: General, 122,* 39–46.

Weber, H., & Wiedig-Allison, M. (2007). Sex differences in anger-related behaviour: Comparing expectancies to actual behaviour. *Cognition & Emotion, 21,* 1669–1698.

Weeden, J., & Sabini, J. (2005). Physical attractiveness and health in western societies: A review. *Psychological Bulletin, 131*(5), 635–653.

Wegner, D. M., Schneider, D. J., Carter, S. R., III, & White, T. L. (1987). Paradoxical effects of thought suppression. *Journal of Personality and Social Psychology, 53,* 5–13.

Wehr, T. A., Turner, E. H., Shimada, J. M., Lowe, C. H., Barker, C., & Leinbenluft, E. (1998). Treatment of a rapidly cycling bipolar patient by using extended bed rest and darkness to stabilize the timing and duration of sleep. *Biological Psychiatry, 43,* 822–828.

Weiss, A., Bates, T. C., & Luciano, M. (2008). Happiness is a personal(ity) thing. *Psychological Science, 19,* 205–210.

Weissman, M. M., Bland, R. C., Canino, G. J., Faravelli, C., Greenwald, S., Hwu, H.-G., et al. (1997). The cross-national epidemiology of panic disorder. *Archives of General Psychiatry, 54,* 305–309.

Wells, G. L., Olson, E. A., & Charman, S. D. (2002). The confidence of eyewitnesses in their identifications from lineups. *Current Directions in Psychological Science, 11,* 151–154.

Wender, P. H., Kety, S. S., Rosenthal, D., Schulsinger, F., Ortmann, J., & Lunde, I. (1986). Psychiatric disorders in the biological and adoptive families of adopted individuals with affective disorders. *Archives of General Psychiatry, 43,* 923–929.

Westergaard, G. C., Cleveland, A., Trenkle, M. K., Lussier, I. D., & Higley, J. D. (2003). CSF 5-HIAA concentration as an early screening tool for predicting significant life history outcomes in female specific-pathogen-free (SPF) rhesus macaques (*Macaca mulatta*) maintained in captive breeding groups. *Journal of Medical Primatology, 32,* 95–104.

Westermarck, E. (1893/1922). *The History of Human Marriage,* Vol. 2. New York: Allerton.

Wheeler, R. E., Davidson, R. J., & Tomarken, A. J. (1993). Frontal brain asymmetry and emotional reactivity: A biological substrate of affective style. *Psychophysiology, 30*(1), 82–89.

White, M. P., & Dolan, P. (2009). Accounting for the richness of daily activities. *Psychological Science, 20,* 1000–1008.

Whorf, B. L. (1956). *Language, thought, and reality.* Cambridge, MA: Technology Press of the Massachusetts Institute of Technology.

Wicker, B., Keysers, C., Plailly, J., Royet, J.-P., Gallese, V., & Rizzolatti, G. (2003). Both of us disgusted in *my* insula: The common neural basis of seeing and feeling disgust. *Neuron, 40,* 655–664.

Widen, S. C., & Russell, J. A. (2008). Children acquire emotion categories gradually. *Cognitive Development, 23,* 291–312.

Widom, C. S. (1989). Does violence beget violence? A critical examination of the literature. *Psychological Bulletin, 106,* 3–28.

Wieselquist, J., Rusbult, C. E., Foster, C. A., & Agnew, C. R. (1999). Commitment, pro-relationship behavior, and trust in close relationships. *Journal of Personality and Social Psychology, 77,* 942–966.

Wiggins, J. S. (1979). A psychological taxonomy of trait-descriptive terms: The interpersonal domain. *Journal of Personality and Social Psychology, 37*(3), 395–412.

Wilde, J. (2001). Interventions for children with anger problems. *Journal of Rational-Emotive & Cognitive-Behavior Therapy, 19,* 191–197.

Wilensky, A. E., Schafe, G. E., Kristensen, M. P., & LeDoux, J. E. (2006). Rethinking the fear circuit. *Journal of Neuroscience, 26,* 12387–12396.

Williams, J. E., Paton, C. C., Siegler, I. C., Eigenbrodt, M. L., Nieto, F. J., & Tyroler, H. A. (2000). Anger proneness predicts coronary heart disease risk. *Circulation, 101,* 2034–2039.

Williams, J. R., Insel, T. R., Harbaugh, C. R., & Carter, C. S. (1994). Oxytocin centrally administered facilitates formation of a partner preference in female prairie voles. *Journal of Neuroendocrinology, 6,* 247–250.

Williams, L. A., & DeSteno, D. (2009). Pride: Adaptive social emotion or seventh sin? *Psychological Science, 20,* 284–288.

Wilson, G. S., Raglin, J. S., & Pritchard, M. E. (2002). Optimism, pessimism, and precompetition anxiety in college athletes. *Personality and Individual Differences, 32,* 893–902.

Wilson, K. A., & Hayward, C. (2005). A prospective evaluation of agoraphobia and depression symptoms following panic attacks in a community of adolescents. *Journal of Anxiety Disorders, 19,* 87–103.

Wilson, T. D., Lisle, D. J., Schooler, J. W., & Hodges, S. D. (1993). Introspecting about reasons can reduce post-choice satisfaction. *Personality and Social Psychology Bulletin, 19*(3), 331–339.

Wirtz, D., Kruger, J., Scollon, C. N., & Diener, E. (2003). What to do on spring break? The role of predicted, on-line, and remembered experience in future choice. *Psychological Science, 14,* 520–524.

Wiseman, R. (1995). The megalab truth test. *Nature, 373,* 391.

Witherington, D. C., Campos, J. J., & Hertenstein, M. J. (2001). Principles of emotion and its development in infancy. In G. Bremner & A. Fogel (Eds.), *Blackwell handbook of infant development. Handbooks of developmental psychology* (pp. 427–464). Malden, MA: Blackwell.

Wittchen, H.-U., Reed, V., & Kessler, R. C. (1998). The relationship of agoraphobia and panic in a community sample of adolescents and young adults. *Archives of General Psychiatry, 55,* 1017–1024.

Wittchen, H.-U., Zhao, S., Kessler, R. C., & Eaton, W. W. (1994). *DSM-III-R* generalized anxiety disorder in the National Comorbidity Survey. *Archives of General Psychiatry, 51,* 355–364.

Witvliet, C. V. O., Ludwig, T. E., & Vander Laan, K. L. (2001). Granting forgiveness or harboring grudges: Implications for emotion, physiology, and health. *Psychological Science, 12,* 117–123.

Wolf, A., & Durham, W. (2005). *Inbreeding, Incest, and the Incest Taboo: The State of Knowledge at the Turn of the Century.* Stanford, CA: Stanford University Press.

Wolf, E. J., & Mori, D. L. (2009). Avoidant coping as a predictor of mortality in veterans with end-stage renal disease. *Health Psychology, 28*(3), 330–337.

Wolf, S. (1995). Dogmas that have hindered understanding. *Integrative Physiological and Behavioral Science, 30,* 3–4.

Wolff, P. H. (1987). *The development of behavioral states and the expression of emotions in early infancy.* Chicago: University of Chicago Press.

Woody, S. R., & Teachman, B. A. (2000). Intersection of disgust and fear: Normative and pathological views. *Clinical Psychology: Science and Practice, 7,* 291–311.

Wray, N. R., James, M. R., Gordon, S. D., Dumenil, T., Ryan, L., Coventry, W. L., et al. (2009). Accurate, large-scale genotyping of 5HTTLPR and flanking single nucleotide polymorphisms in an association study of depression, anxiety, and personality measures. *Biological Psychiatry, 66,* 468–476.

Wundt, W. M. (1977). *Lectures on human and animal psychology.* Washington, D.C.: University Publications of America. (Original work published in German in 1907).

Wynn, K., & Chiang, W.-C. (1998). Limits to infants' knowledge of objects: The case of magical appearance. *Psychological Science, 9,* 448–455.

Xie, H., Cairns, R. B., & Cairns, B. D. (2002). The development of social aggression and physical aggression: A narrative analysis of interpersonal conflicts. *Aggressive Behavior, 28,* 341–355.

Xu, X., & Whyte, M. (1990). Love matches and arranged marriages: A Chinese replication. *Journal of Marriage and the Family, 52,* 709–722.

Yan, L. L., Liu, K., Matthews, K. A., Daviglus, M. L., Ferguson, T. F., & Kiefe, C. I. (2003). Psychosocial factors and risk of hypertension. *Journal of the American Medical Association, 290,* 2138–2148.

Yehuda, R. (1997). Sensitization of the hypothalamic-pituitary-adrenal axis in posttraumatic stress disorder. *Annals of the New York Academy of Sciences, 821,* 57–75.

Yeomans, J. S., & Frankland, P. W. (1996). The acoustic startle reflex: Neurons and connections. *Brain Research Reviews, 21,* 301–314.

Yerkes, R. M., & Dodson, J. D. (1908). The relation of strength of stimulus to rapidity of habit formation. *Journal of Comparative Neurology and Psychology, 18,* 459–482.

Yik, M. S. M., & Russell, J. A. (2003). Chinese affect circumplex: I. Structure of recalled momentary affect. *Asian Journal of Social Psychology, 6,* 185–200.

Young, L. J. (2002). The neurobiology of social recognition, approach, and avoidance. *Biological Psychiatry, 51,* 18–26.

Young, S. (2005). Coping strategies used by adults with ADHD. *Personality and Individual Differences, 38,* 809–816.

Yu, D. W., & Shepard, G. H., Jr. (1998). Is beauty in the eye of the beholder? *Nature, 396,* 321–322.

Zajonc, R. B., & McIntosh, D. N. (1992). Emotions research: Some promising questions and some questionable promises. *Psychological Science, 3*(1), 70–74.

Zangara, A., Blair, R. J. R., & Curran, H. V. (2002). A comparison of the effects of a β-adrenergic blocker and a benzodiazepine upon the recognition of human facial expressions. *Psychopharmacology, 163,* 36–41.

Zarinpoush, F., Cooper, M., & Moylan, S. (2000). The effects of happiness and sadness on moral reasoning. *Journal of Moral Education, 29,* 397–412.

Zeelenberg, M., & Breugelmans, S. M. (2008). The role of interpersonal harm in distinguishing regret from guilt. *Emotion, 8,* 589–596.

Zeidner, M., Matthews, G., & Roberts, R. D. (2001). Slow down, you move too fast: Emotional intelligence remains an "elusive" intelligence. *Emotion, 1,* 265–275.

Zemborain, M. R., & Johar, G. V. (2007). Attitudinal ambivalence and openness to persuasion: A framework for interpersonal influence. *Journal of Consumer Research, 33*(4), 506–514.

Zentner, M., Grandjean, D., & Scherer, K. R. (2008). Emotions evoked by the sound of music: Characterization, classification, and measurement. *Emotion, 8,* 494–521.

Zhou, W., & Chen, D. (2009). Fear-related chemosignals modulate recognition of fear in ambiguous facial expressions. *Psychological Science, 20,* 177–183.

Zillmann, D., Baron, R. A., & Tamborini, R. (1981). Social costs of smoking: Effects of tobacco smoke on hostile behavior. *Journal of Applied Social Psychology, 11,* 548–561.

Zorrilla, E. P., Luborsky, L., McKay, J. R., Rosenthal, R., Houldin, A., Tax, A., et al. (2001). The relationship of depression and stressors to immunological assays: A meta-analytic review. *Brain, Behavior, and Immunity, 15,* 199–226.

Zubieta, J.-K., Ketter, T. A., Bueller, J. A., Xu, Y., Kilbourn, M. R., Young, E. A., et al. (2003). Regulation of human affective responses by anterior cingulate and limbic μ-opioid neurotransmission. *Archives of General Psychiatry, 60,* 1145–1153.

Photo Credits

This page constitutes an extension of the copyright page. We have made every effort to trace the ownership of all copyrighted material and to secure permission from copyright holders. In the event of any question arising as to the use of any material, we will be pleased to make the necessary corrections in future printings. Thanks are due to the following authors, publishers, and agents for permission to use the material indicated.

Inside front cover, bottom: Pavlidis, I., Eberhardt, N. L., and Levine, J. A., Seeing through the face of deception. *Nature*, 415, 35. Reproduced with permission of Nature Publishing Group.

Chapter 1. Page 9: top right, Adam Pretty/Getty Images. **Page 9:** top left, AP Photo/Greg Baker. **Page 11:** top left, Lester Lefkowitz/Corbis. **Page 11:** bottom right, WDCN/Univ. College London/Photo Researchers, Inc. **Page 12:** top right, Michelle Shiota. **Page 13:** top right, FPG/Hulton Archive/Getty Images. **Page 21:** bottom left, AP Images/Michael Tweed. **Page 21:** bottom right, AP Photo/Nick Ut. **Page 22:** top left, Kathleen Olson, **Page 22:** top right, Kathleen Olson. **Page 24:** top left, Cut and Deal Ltd/Alamy. **Page 24:** top right, Philippe Marchand/Photonica/Getty Images.

Chapter 2. Page 34: top left, Spencer Arnold/Getty Images. **Page 39:** top left, HannamariaH/istockphoto. com. **Page 39:** center left, Simone van den Berg/istock photo.com. **Page 39:** bottom left, Mary Morgan/istock photo. **Page 44:** bottom left, Joseph Van Os/The Image Bank/Getty Images. **Page 44:** bottom center, Tom McHugh/Photo Researchers, Inc. **Page 44:** bottom right, Stuart Westmorland/Corbis. **Page 45:** bottom right, Eibl-Eibesfeldt. **Page 46:** bottom right, from: P. Ekman & W. Friesen, *Unmasking the Face*, 2nd edition 1984.

Used by permission of P. Ekman. **Page 48:** bottom, from: Aviezer, H., Hassin, R. R., Ryan, J., Grady, C., Susskind, J., Anderson, A., et al. (2008). Angry, disgusted, or afraid? *Psychological Science*, 19, 724–732. Reprinted by permission of SAGE Publications. **Page 49:** bottom left, Image copyright absolut. Used under license from Shutterstock. com **Page 49:** bottom right, from: Adams, R. B., & Kleck, R. E. (2003). Perceived gaze direction and the processing of facial displays of emotion. *Psychological Science*, 14, 644–647. Reprinted by permission of SAGE Publications. **Page 54:** bottom, from: Levenson, R.W., Ekman, P., Heider, K., Friesen, W.V., 1992. Emotion and autonomic nervous system activity in the Minangkabau of West Sumatra. *Journal of Personality and Social Psychology* 62, 972–988.

Chapter 3. Page 62: top left, Walt Disney/Everett Collection. **Page 62:** bottom left, Warner Bros./Everett Collection. **Page 68:** top left, Mark Richards/PhotoEdit. **Page 68:** bottom left: Antoine Gyori/AGP/Corbis. **Page 71:** bottom left, Photo courtesy of Dr. David Matsumoto.

Chapter 4. Page 85: bottom right, Leslie Keating/istock-photo.com. **Page 86:** bottom right, Jesse Karjalainen/ istockphoto.com. **Page 91:** top, Michelle Shiota. **Page 100:** top, John Olson/Time & Life Pictures/Getty Images.

Chapter 5. Page 113: top, Image copyright Julie Lutcht. Used under license by Shutterstock.com.

Name Index

A

Abbar, M., 189
Abbey, A., 211
Abdel-Azim, E., 129, 246
Abe, J. A. A., 284
Abercrombie, H. C, 316
Abramov, I., 278
Abramson, L. Y., 324
Abu-Lughod, L., 74, 82
Ackerman, J. M., 314
Ackermann, R., 324
Acree, M., 147
Adamec, R. E., 180
Adams, E., 322
Adams, R. B., 49
Adler, A., 237
Adler, N. E., 248
Adli, M., 345
Admon, R., 170
Adolph, K. E., 275
Adolphs, R., 98, 118, 120, 121, 169,
170, 263, 305, 314
Aharon, I., 246
Ahlskog, J. E., 131
Ahmetzanov, M. V., 318
Ainsworth, M. D. S., 206, 212, 220
Aitken, M. R. F., 112
Akirav, I., 316
Akiskal, H. S., 345
Aknin, L. B., 240
Albin, M., 285

Alda, M., 345
Aleman, A., 172
Alexander, N., 88
Allen, G. J., 305
Allen, J. J. B., 244, 300
Allison, S., 258
Alloy, L. B., 140, 324, 341
Alonso, A., 304
Altemus, M., 213
Altman, J., 152
Amaral, D. G., 119
Amatea, E. S., 208, 209
Ambadar, Z., 48
Ambady, N., 47, 70
American Psychiatric Association, 337
Amodio, D. M., 263
Amunts, K., 300
Andershed, H., 351
Anderson, A. K., 121
Anderson, C., 160, 179, 219
Anderson, C. A., 192, 193
Anderson, E. R., 171
Anderson, G. M., 343
Anderson, S. W., 127
Anglin, J. M., 210
Angrilli, A., 120, 347
Antoniadis, E. A., 119
Antoun, N., 199
Apfelbach, R., 118
Applefield, J. M., 193
Arana, G. W., 131

Archer, J., 190
Arluke, A., 257
Armony, J. L., 18, 120
Armor, D. A., 141, 248
Arnold, E., 151
Arnold, M. B., 138
Arnold, M. J., 230
Arnow, B. A., 342
Aron, A. P., 17, 210, 218,
219, 220, 225
Aron, E. N., 218, 220
Arslan, C., 188
Ascher, E. A., 259
Ashkanasy, N. M., 307
Ashton-Jones, C. E., 242
Astin, J. A., 141
Astington, J. W., 279
Asukai, N., 106
Atkins, C. M., 119
Atlas, L., 340
Aue, T., 98
Augustine, 3
Augustoni-Ziskind, M. L., 200
Aumer, K., 210
Austin, E. J., 303
Averill, J. R., 190
Avero, P., 164, 311
Aviezer, H., 48
Ayduk, Ö., 107, 143, 146, 195
Azuma, H., 287
Azzoni, A., 345

Subject Index

A

ability tests, 302–303
abuse
  childhood, 191–192
  sexual, 192, 339, 347
  substance, 187, 188, 191
ACTH (adrenocorticotropic hormone), 105
action tendencies
  Cannon-Bard theory of, 14–15
  defining emotion in terms of, 4–5
  James-Lange theory of, 13–14
  physiological measurements of, 9–12
  usefulness of, 4–5
adaptation, 36
addiction, 131
adolescents
  embarrassment and, 261
  friendship and, 224
adoption, violence and, 192
adrenal glands
  aggression and, 187
  memory and, 316
  stress and, 105
adrenaline, as stress hormone, 88
adrenocorticotropic hormone (ACTH), 105
adult attachments
  attraction and, 220

defined, 220
oxytocin and, 220
in romantic relationships, 220–223
adulthood, emotional development in, 288–291
Affect Infusion Model, 326
affectional bonds, 205–212
Africans
  bodily signs of stress in, 67
  negative emotions and, 66
  role of morality in appraisal of emotional events and, 50–53
aging
  emotion regulation and, 290–291
  emotional intelligence and, 301
  emotional salience and, 290
  happiness and, 238, 248
  as predictor of susceptibility to embarrassment, 261
  trends in emotional intensity, 288–290
aggression
  alarm stage and, 101
  behaviors of, 184
  biology of, 185–187
  envy and, 266
  family environment and, 191–192
  frustration-aggression hypothesis, 178
  genetics and, 189–190

hostile, 184
implicit measures of anger and, 184–185
instrumental, 184
jealousy and, 266
laboratory studies of, 184
neuroanatomy of, 185–186
serotonin and, 132, 186
sex differences and, 190–191
substance abuse and, 187, 188
agoraphobia, 346
agreeableness
  defined, 295
  research studies on, 297–298
alarm stage, 101
alcohol
  dopamine and, 130–131
  as emotional escape strategy, 151
alprazolam, 171, 349
amae
  attachment and, 207
  defined, 207
  overview of, 63–64
American Enterprise, 224
American Psychological Association (APA), 287
Americans
  attachment behaviors of children and, 286–287
  concepts of romantic love and, 61–62